SEVENTH EDITION

SCHOOL LAW
Cases and Concepts

MICHAEL W. LA MORTE

ALLYN AND BACON
Boston   London   Toronto   Sydney   Tokyo   Singapore

Series Editor: Arnis E. Burvikovs
Editorial Assistant: Matthew Forster
Production Coordinator: Susan Brown
Marketing Manager: Kathleen Morgan
Editorial-Production Service: Matrix Productions
Cover Administrator: Kristina Mose-Libon
Composition Buyer: Linda Cox
Manufacturing Buyer: Julie McNeill

Copyright © 2002, 1999, 1996, 1993, 1990, 1987, 1982 by Allyn & Bacon
A Pearson Education Company
75 Arlington Street
Boston, MA 02116
www.ablongman.com

Library of Congress Cataloging-in-Publication Data

La Morte, Michael W.
    School law : cases and concepts / Michael W. La Morte.—7th ed.
        p.   cm.
    Includes index.
    ISBN 0-205-34284-1
    1. Educational law and legislation—United States—Cases. I. Title.

    KF4118 L25 2001
    344.73′07—dc21   2001018205

Printed in the United States of America
10 9 8 7 5 4 3 2 1   05   04   03   02   01

ISBN 0-205-34284-1

Dedication

This book is dedicated to my grandfather, Heinrich Schroeder, the only truly politically brave person I have ever known personally. As a young boy living in Nazi Germany in the 1930s, I saw him constantly standing up to the Nazi regime by engaging in conduct that was not allowed by the authorities. This included clandestinely listening to the shortwave radio, publicly speaking up against Adolf Hitler and the Nazi regime, and refusing to salute the swastika or greet people with the mandatory "heil Hitler." It should be remembered that this defiance took place during a period when Jewish or politically suspect neighbors disappeared and no one would dare inquire about their disappearance and when a young boy like me was questioned by the gestapo about his grandfather's activities.

My grandfather refused to conform to the demands of a despotic totalitarian regime and, as a result, although he was not a Jew, he was sent to a concentration camp. This incarceration was a high price to pay for standing up for his political beliefs.

His example instilled a lifelong respect in me for the importance of living under the rule of law. Instilling students with this notion should be every educator's goal. It is my hope that the information contained in this book will assist educators in that pursuit.

Contents

2 *Schools and the State*   *19*

4 *Teachers and the Law*   *176*

Table of Cases*

Note: Edited cases are indicated by boldface.

Preface

Public school educators are aware that courts play a significant role in establishing educational policy. Decisions, especially by the federal judiciary over the last fifty years, in such areas as school desegregation, separation of church and state, freedom of expression, student rights, individuals with disabilities, and personnel issues attest to the extent and magnitude of judicial influence. Foremost among the many reasons for the increased court involvement during these years has been the perception, especially by those who perceive they are being treated unfairly by governmental action, that the judiciary was a receptive and efficacious branch of government.

Judicial activity has produced a sizable body of school law with which educators should be familiar if they wish to conduct themselves in a legally defensive manner. Those educators who fly by the seat of their pants or who act on the basis of what they think the law "should be" may be in difficulty if sufficient thought is not given to the legal implications and ramifications of their policies or conduct. Consequently, this text provides introductory material for those educators and laypersons interested in K–12 educational issues, who have little or no knowledge of, or background in, school law. This group would include teachers, school administrators, school board members, preservice teachers, and public school students and their families.

It would be difficult for a one-volume work to cover all of the significant topics in school law. Therefore, this text attempts to emphasize school law issues having direct impact at the school-building level. When appropriate, a historical perspective is provided in addition to case and statutory law.

Chapter 1 offers sufficient background to facilitate comprehension of succeeding chapters. Included in this chapter is a discussion of topics of underlying importance with which educators may be unfamiliar: the legal significance of the sources of law under which educators operate, federal and state constitutions, federal and state statutes, state school board policy, attorney general opinions, local school board policy and local school policy, the significance of the Fourteenth Amendment's Due Process and Equal Protection provisions as a basis for many school lawsuits, the importance of case law in establishing educational policy, and the organization of the American dual court system.

Chapter 2 examines the extent of the state's and local school system's authority when patrons disagree with educational policy. A reading of the court decisions in this chapter reveals the judiciary's attempt to establish a balance between the legitimate demands or objections of individuals toward education policy and school authorities' perception of their responsibility to the greater population. School law issues selected to illuminate this area include compulsory school attendance, religion in the schools, use of school facilities, aid to nonpublic schools, school fees, and health services.

This writer has found that issues pertaining to students and teachers are of particular interest to school law students; therefore, Chapters 3 and 4, which address these topics, comprise a major portion of the text. Chapter 3 presents material pertinent to student interests, such as freedom of expression; suspension, disciplinary transfer, and expulsion; corporal punishment; search of students; student appearance; pregnancy, parenthood, and marriage; participation in extracurricular activities; and school punishment for out-of-school offenses. Chapter 4 examines such teacher-related issues as nonrenewal and dismissal; freedom of expression; academic freedom; drug testing; dress; the teacher as an exemplar; employment discrimination based on race, sex, pregnancy, religion, and age; teacher bargaining; and political activities of teachers.

Chapter 5 provides a historical legal perspective to the issues of school desegregation. Early desegregation efforts in the South and more recent desegregation endeavors in non-Southern states are examined. Such current issues as the release from desegregation court orders and the race-related placement of students are also reviewed.

Chapter 6, written by Professor John Dayton, addresses the legal status of individuals with disabilities. Historical perspective is provided for this important area of school law in addition to an in-depth examination of major legislation and court decisions. Emphasis is given to the Individuals with Disabilities Education Act, the 1997 Amendments, and the 1999 regulations.

Chapter 7 provides a historical perspective to the legal attacks on the financing and adequacy of state school finance plans. These legal issues emerged in the early 1970s and continue to be litigated in many states. Also discussed is the school reform measure known as school choice. Legal decisions addressing such school choice issues as voucher programs, tuition reimbursement policies, and charter schools are presented. A knowledge of the complexities of school finance is not necessary for an understanding of the material in this chapter.

Chapter 8 addresses the extent, if any, of educator and school district liability for damages as a result of their official action or inaction. Because the law in this area varies considerably among the states, emphasis is given to such general concepts as duty and standard of care, school district immunity, duties of supervision, and malpractice. Liability for damages under Title IX pertaining to teacher-to-student and student-to-student harassment is also presented. Tort law is a highly specialized branch of law that is exceedingly complicated; therefore, this chapter makes the reader aware of the potential of liability for damages resulting from improper behavior.

Appendices provide additional information enabling the reader to gain a broader perspective. Appendices A and B are designed to be primers for the reader who wishes to become more adept at analyzing court decisions or engaging in school-related legal research. Appendix B is designed to provide rudimentary legal-research methodology and information on primary and secondary legal resources available to those interested in legal research. Computer-minded readers may be interested in the brief section discussing legal material available on the Internet. Appendix C contains sections of the U.S. Constitution and amendments that are most relevant for educators. Appendix D contains edited federal statutes having significance for educators. A glossary of often-used legal terminology is included for the reader's convenience in better understanding the edited court decisions. An index lists many school law topics for facilitating their reference.

Edited, reported, verbatim decisions constitute a substantial portion of this book. Such decisions provide a rich source of information, enabling a reader to gain insight and an understanding of school law that cannot be obtained through secondary analysis. The reading of a judge's or justice's written opinion—majority, concurring, or dissenting— provides valuable philosophical underpinnings for a thorough understanding of judicial rationale. It also enables the reader to relate a court's legal rationale to a specific factual context. Emphasis is on substantive school law issues. Deleted from the edited cases is material not related to the issue being examined, material pertaining to technical legal matters, and procedural legal issues that are of primary interest to attorneys. Students of school law are encouraged to read entire unedited court opinions in those areas of school law in which they have a particular interest. Case citations are provided to facilitate this endeavor.

Inclusion in this text of a particular decision was based on several factors, which included selecting the case decided by the highest-level court that had addressed the specific school law issue under consideration, thereby providing the widest applicability; the case that best represented the majority of cases in areas where the law was not well settled; or the case that best illustrated the historic evolvement of the case law under consideration.

Notes and questions follow many of the edited decisions. The notes are designed to provide helpful information such as background material, additional citations for those interested in pursuing further the issue under consideration, the extent to which the law is well settled, or other views if the law is not well settled. Provocative questions are included to illuminate the topic and foster discussion.

This book has not been written with the intention of expressing opinions for or against views espoused by school administrators, teachers, or students, nor to contend that the judiciary is a meddlesome institution thwarting the efforts of educators. Rather, the book's purpose is to provide those who are involved in public education with a rudimentary knowledge base for making educationally sound decisions within the legal framework. Having such knowledge may reduce the tendency to act on the basis of what the law should be rather than what it is. In that sense, this book stresses the descriptive, not the prescriptive.

The author assumes that public school students learn best about law and order through its observance by knowledgeable teachers, school administrators, and school board members. And because an important aspect of public school education is the inculcation in students of the notion that we are a "nation of laws and not of men," educators must be familiar with school law to abide by the law. This is of considerable concern to the author because of his experience as a youth under Adolf Hitler in Nazi Germany. It was observed that one strategy a dictator such as Hitler used to strengthen and solidify his power was the systematic breakdown of law in Germany. As the law was increasingly disregarded, the power of the Nazis increased, and the country became a "nation of men and not of laws."

Students in my school law classes over the years deserve a special word of thanks, not only for their scintillating and penetrating questions but also for sharing with me those school law topics they deemed important as they carried out their school-related responsibilities. Over the years, several students—Robert Meadows, Betty Hull, Jeffrey Williams, Pat McCollum, and Neil McIntyre—have made valuable contributions, and they have my gratitude. A special thank-you is due Professor John Dayton, Department of Leadership, College of Education, at the University of Georgia. His chapter, entitled "Individuals with Disabilities and the Law," is a welcome addition to this seventh edition. He is a delightful colleague who continues to share his valuable insights and suggestions. Additionally, over the years, Dr. Joe Falzon, Professional Associate with the National Education Association, has been generous in providing me with statistical data. Dan Long, Technical Assistant to the Reporter of Decisions at the United States Supreme Court, has been most helpful in providing me with the most current Court citations. Of course, any failure of omission or commission in this book is the sole responsibility of the author.

This book does not serve as a substitute for competent legal advice should it be needed. However, in addition to a knowledge of school law, an understanding of the material in this book should help to foster a more fruitful exchange with an attorney when that is necessary.

Finally, it was a delight to have the opportunity of again revising this text, as the examination of school law issues continues to be, for me, an exciting and rewarding enterprise.

A Note to Users of This Text

This textbook borrows from the teaching traditions of the legal community. It is a "casebook" not unlike those routinely used in the preparation of lawyers in law schools. Such texts are collections of actual court opinions, in which instructional material and exposition are minimized, and through which students are expected on their own to induce legal principles. Casebook authors—who must also be considered to be editors if one is to understand the essence of a casebook—select, edit, and arrange judicial opinions to facilitate extracting what the author considers to be important points of law. Brief written comments and questions assist in this process. Accordingly, this author intends the presentation of cases herein not as supplementary illustrations of the textual material but rather as the book's primary raw material.

A major advantage ascribed to discovering the law from casebooks is the opportunity to learn both legal rationale and reasoning. To this end, students encounter noteworthy examples of judicial decision making and engage, themselves, in such reasoning. Although a knowledge of specific information is essential, understanding legal rationale and learning to engage in legal reasoning are more important, in this author's view, than acquiring an encyclopedic knowledge of specific laws. The author submits that educators must be able to do more than merely recite laws affecting schools, and readers looking for a comprehensive treatment of school law in this text will be frustrated. Few factual patterns encountered by the practicing educator will match perfectly an explicit legal rule. Having a broad understanding of legal precedent combined with staying abreast of school law developments will provide the educator on the firing line with a background to deal with the host of novel situations that may be faced.

This text may be used with a Socratic method of teaching. When employing this teaching strategy, the instructor assigns a group of cases to be read and analyzed, and in class he or she calls individually on students orally to "brief" the cases (see Analyzing a Court Decision—Appendix A). The instructor attempts through questioning to draw from students relevant legal principles; in this process, students are challenged to the limits of their abilities to make increasingly fine observations and distinctions; and criticism of the student's recitation is provided. Initially, this individual questioning may not always be pleasant for students, but they soon learn that casual readings of cases for their main ideas are insufficient;

instead, cases must be read slowly, deliberately, and repeatedly. The technique demands thorough preparation from both instructor and student. This method prepares students well for written examinations consisting of complex, hypothetical fact patterns, which students are required to analyze in accordance with applicable law.

This author successfully employed this demanding method in his school law classes. He has found that analyzing case law does indeed cause students to restructure their thinking on the law. Additionally, the promise of reciting in class motivates most students to superb performance, which unquestionably enhances learning. Inducing students to think on their feet and to perform under pressure seems to be highly appropriate in the preparation of educational leaders. Whether or not other instructors choose to complement this casebook with the Socratic method, it is hoped that the cases speak to at least the rudiments of an enormous, diffuse body of law and that the book will challenge readers to further study.

Finally, for those instructors who have access to a law library, a class visit is highly recommended. Such a visit has a number of advantages. It not only provides an opportunity to discuss and locate legal material (see An Introduction to Research in School Law—Appendix B), but it also lessens the common perception that a law library is a forbidding place where only lawyers are welcome. Introducing students in this manner to the various reporter systems, *Index to Legal Periodicals*, law reviews, state materials, *Shepard's Citations*, "slip" opinions, *United States Law Week*, and *Martindale–Hubbell Law Directory* (a listing and rating of attorneys and law firms by state) has always been a well-received class activity.

CHAPTER ONE

Educational Governance: Sources of Law and the Courts

Governance in America is based on the notion that we are "a nation of laws and not of men." Consequently, those involved in making and enforcing public school policy should ensure that their actions are lawful. Educational policy may not be enforced arbitrarily or capriciously but must be based on such appropriate legal authority as federal or state constitutional or statutory provisions, state board of education or state department of education regulations, case law, or local school board policy.

Several forces operate, however, that at times make it difficult for those who administer public schools to function in a lawful manner. These forces include a federal system of government composed of several levels and corresponding branches that bear on the educational enterprise, changing and sometimes conflicting laws or policies emanating from these levels and branches, and a climate of legal uncertainty surrounding certain controversial educational issues that become highly politicized.

Under the federal system, the three levels of government—federal, state, and local—all have a voice in educational matters, although not necessarily in unison. Difficulties may develop when areas of educational governance overlap considerably in responsibility among the three levels of government and their corresponding branches—executive, legislative, and judicial. These difficulties are exacerbated not only by the unclear delineation of authority but also in determining with certainty which authority is supreme when irreconcilable conflicts exist.

Although education is not specifically mentioned in the federal Constitution, the federal government has had a historic involvement in it. In fact, programs under various federal laws pertaining to K–12 education in recent years have made up nearly 7 percent of the total amount of money expended for public elementary and secondary education. Perhaps of greater importance has been the pervasive and significant force of the

1

federal judiciary in influencing educational policy. Controversial education issues such as racial segregation in schools, financing of schools, due process for both students and teachers, the role of religion in the schools, search of students and teachers, and the extent to which students and teachers may engage in freedom of expression have all been addressed by the federal judiciary.

State government has plenary power* over public education, and this power is carried out by constitutional and statutory provisions, executive acts, state board of education policies, and actions of chief state school officers. The roles of governmental participants vary among the state governments. The extent of state authority over local school systems is also not uniform; however, it is generally considered to be directly proportional to the state's financial contribution to public education.

The degree of authority that local school systems have over educational matters depends on a state's constitutional and statutory provisions. These local powers may be delegated or implied. Although it is the prevailing belief that public schools are controlled locally, many students of educational governance suggest that a so-called myth of local control may be operating. They argue that in many instances, especially when the state is heavily involved in financing education, the state has more meaningful power over education policy than the local school system does.

Because each level of government is inextricably intertwined in public educational governance, problems have often arisen for building-level educators, for instance, when one level or branch of government does not agree with policies or decisions made by another level or branch. Misunderstanding on the part of educators may also exist regarding the legitimate role of each of the levels of governance. Examples of these conflicts abound: a local school system not wishing to allow after-hours use of its schools to certain types of groups but forced to do so by a federal court order; "wealthy" local school systems barred, as a result of a state supreme court decision, from appreciably supplementing the state-financed program; and local school systems having to accept an amount of disruption by students wishing to express themselves on political, social, or economic matters, protected by a United States Supreme Court decision.

The difficulty of attempting to administer schools in a lawful manner is compounded when educators, unfamiliar with the nuances of the legal system, perceive that there are seeming inconsistencies and occasionally acrimonious disagreement among judges in certain court decisions. Such a situation occurs when a decision is changed one or more times as an educational issue winds its way through the appellate process. Occasionally, this process reveals sharp philosophical differences among judges. The lack of consistency in court decisions regarding certain issues is also trou-

---

*This plenary power is diminished, of course, when the state accepts federal education funds, which requires compliance with federal mandates.

bling to some educators. They often find it difficult to understand why an educational practice has court approval in one state or area of federal jurisdiction and not in another. The legitimacy of a federal court overruling a state court's decision is also not always completely understood, especially when such a ruling increases the difficulty of administering schools because of strong local, state, or regional disagreement with such a ruling.

School administrators often view themselves as working in a climate of uncertainty as to the legality of their administrative decisions. This may be due to an insufficient knowledge of constitutional law as it pertains to educational matters or an inadequate knowledge of recent court decisions. Relying on what is perceived as sound educational practice in making administrative decisions is helpful, but it is not always a guarantee that the practice will avoid conflict with case law.

One remedy for ensuring lawful administrative conduct and reducing conflict and misunderstanding among educators is a systematic study of the sources of law under which educators operate. Such a study follows and is designed to illuminate the legitimate role of the various levels of government and their component branches. Although sources of law may be examined in various ways, a particularly fruitful method is to analyze those sources that spring from each level of government.

I. SOURCES OF LAW

A. Federal Level

At the federal level, the Constitution and its amendments, statutes, rules and regulations of administrative agencies, case law, presidential executive orders, and attorney general opinions all constitute sources of law under which educators operate.

1. Constitution and Amendments

Although the federal Constitution does not contain the word *education*, constitutional interpretation by the judiciary has had unquestionable impact on educational policymaking. Particularly significant is the judiciary's interpretation of the Fourteenth Amendment to the Constitution. A brief examination of this amendment may be helpful, on the basis both of its historical origins and of its requirements for due process and equal protection of the law as they pertain to educational matters.

a. Historical Perspective. Prior to the adoption of the Fourteenth Amendment in 1868, Americans, under the federal system of government, had a particular kind of dual relationship with state and national governments regarding their civil rights. This came about largely as a result of skepticism, if not an outright distrust, of central government that existed after the Revolutionary War as a consequence of experiences under British rule. To ensure that a central government would not again run roughshod over an individual's civil rights, a Bill of Rights was added to the Constitution shortly after that document was ratified. Protections afforded those early Americans under the Bill of Rights included freedoms regarding religion, speech, press, peaceable assembly, and petitioning for a redress of grievances; a right to bear arms; protection against unreasonable searches and seizures; guarantee of a grand jury indictment in capital offenses; protection against being subject to double jeopardy or self-incrimination; the right of due process; the right to own property; the right to have a speedy trial by an impartial jury; and protection against excessive bail and cruel and unusual punishments. These protections, however, were those that Americans had against their *central* government. They did not automatically have these rights against their state government as a result of the inclusion of the rights in the federal Constitution.

Protection of civil rights against state action was provided by state constitutions, and every state, as it was accepted into the Union, provided for a Bill of Rights similar to that found in the federal Constitution. It should be noted, however, that prior to the adoption of the Fourteenth Amendment, if a state's constitution did not contain a provision for guaranteeing, for instance, freedom of speech or religion, an American did not necessarily have those protections against his or her state. Although state constitutions may have contained language that afforded individuals their civil rights, as a practical matter, state-guaranteed civil rights protections were not always uniformly applied.

In the years preceding the Civil War, another factor influenced the dual relationship Americans had with their state and federal governments. For the most part, Americans, during that time, thought of themselves primarily as citizens of the state within which they resided and citizens of the United States secondarily. An individual considered himself a Virginian or New Yorker first, for instance, and an American citizen second.

This dual relationship with state and central governments and the historic primary allegiance to one's state was significantly altered by the adoption of the Fourteenth Amendment to the Constitution in 1868. This amendment provided, in part, that:

> All persons born or naturalized in the United States and subject to the jurisdiction thereof, are citizens of the United States and of the State wherein they reside. No state shall make or enforce any law which shall abridge the privileges or immunities of citizens of the United States. Nor shall any State deprive any person of life, liberty, or property, without due process of law, nor deny to any person within its jurisdiction the equal protection of the laws.

From a constitutional standpoint, the juxtaposition of the phrases *"citizens of the United States* and *of the State wherein they reside"* is most revealing, because the United States is mentioned first. The legal significance of this juxtaposition and subsequent language of the amendment have been interpreted as establishing national citizenship as being primary where certain questions dealing with individual rights are concerned.

This amendment, which was intended initially to guarantee rights to newly freed slaves, has also provided protection for the individual from various forms of arbitrary or capricious state action. Because the amendment affords national citizenship primacy regarding constitutional rights, an individual is shielded against state action that may run counter to guarantees he or she has as a citizen of the United States. Under this concept, a state cannot deprive a person of rights he or she has as an American. As a result of federal court action, for instance, teachers may not arbitrarily be dismissed without due process. Neither may students be deprived of their freedoms pertaining to religion by school board policy that allows Bible reading or school-sponsored prayers during normal school hours. These are the kinds of rights individuals have as United States citizens, and no state action, local administrative conduct, or local school board policy may violate them.

Under the Fourteenth Amendment, a state and those operating under its auspices (such as local school systems) must honor those rights, guaranteed by the Constitution, federal statutes, and case law, that a person has as a result of being an American. From a constitutional standpoint, these rights must be observed by the state and those operating under the color of the state, and they may not be infringed upon as a result of a state or local election, state or local administrative action, or state court action.

It should be noted that not all constitutional scholars agree with this type of interpretation of the Fourteenth Amendment. Proponents of a "states' rights theory" for American government have reluctantly accepted certain court decisions based on the Fourteenth Amendment and have adamantly refused to abide by others. Objection to the amendment by such groups is often based on the method used to gain its ratification. Ratification of the amendment was a required step for readmittance to the Union after the Civil War. Additionally, it is argued that courts should follow the jurisprudence of original intention. Under this doctrine, courts should be guided solely by the literal text of the Constitution and the specific, ascertainable intentions of the framers and not the ruminations of latter-day judges.

b. Due Process and Equal Protection.   In addition to establishing the primacy of national citizenship with the protection of certain individual rights, the Fourteenth Amendment also provides for due process and equal protection of the law. These two concepts stem from an ideal of fairness in applying the law, and they are not necessarily mutually exclusive. In cases dealing with educational matters where the Fourteenth Amendment is cited, it is generally alleged that either (or both) due process or equal protection of the law has been denied. Although extremely complex in a legal sense, these concepts may best be understood by keeping in mind that they require government officials, which of course includes educators, to be fair as they conduct governmental business. This necessitates reasonable and noncapricious action, in addition to abiding by statute and case law, on the part of public school officials when dealing with clients or personnel.

[1] Due Process.   In the broadest sense, a person has received due process of law under the Fourteenth Amendment when he or she has been treated essentially the same by state action or local government action as another person has under similar circumstances when he or she is subject to deprivation of life, liberty, or property. Under this concept, governmental action may not be unreasonable or capricious, and when clients are not treated alike there must be a sound basis for dissimilar treatment.

Although the line between substance and procedure is often quite hazy, some have drawn a distinction between so-called procedural and substantive due process of law. According to this view, procedural due process, in the larger sense, deals with the question of whether or not a person has been accorded fair and proper treatment or procedure when apprehended or tried in a court. Accused persons must be given twelve jurors, for instance, if everyone else in their circumstances is given twelve jurors. Evidence to be presented against them must have been obtained properly, and their trials must be conducted according to established procedures. Questions dealing with procedural due process in the educational arena have received much attention, particularly in the area of suspension and expulsion from school. Substantive due process essentially deals with the question of fair treatment of persons by those acting under the color of the state and also with the question of the fairness and reasonableness of laws, regulations, and policies in the light of our constitutional heritage. The Fifth Amendment also contains a due process clause, and although there are similarities with the Fourteenth Amendment provision, the Fifth Amendment is considered exclusively to be protection against the federal government.

As is the case with many concepts, due process resists definition in the dictionary sense. It is a dynamic rather than a static concept. The definition in each instance depends largely on a combination of the specific facts in a situation, the law governing the situation, the particular time in history in which judgment is being rendered, and the predilections of the individual judge(s) rendering the decision. The Supreme Court, for instance, has never unanimously agreed on a standard for due process. Yet, it is the body that renders the ultimate and final decision regarding whether or not due process has been denied. This point, in addition to a discussion of the question of due process, was asserted by Justice Frankfurter in *Sweezy v. New Hampshire*, 354 U.S. 234 (1957):

> To be sure, this is a conclusion based on a judicial judgment in balancing two contending principles—the right of the citizen to political privacy, as

protected by the Fourteenth Amendment, and the right of the State to self-protection. And striking the balance implies the exercise of judgment. This is the inescapable judicial task in giving substantive content, legally enforced, to the Due Process Clause, and it is a task ultimately committed to this Court. It must not be an exercise of whim or will. It must be an overriding judgment founded on something much deeper and more justifiable than personal preference. As far as it lies within human limitations, it must be an impersonal judgment. It must rest on fundamental presuppositions rooted in history to which widespread acceptance may be fairly attributed. Such a judgment must be arrived at in a spirit of humility when it counters the judgment of the State's highest court. But, in the end, judgment cannot be escaped—the judgment of this Court. (pp. 266–67)

A basic issue—the balance between an individual's rights and the necessity to protect the larger society—is addressed by courts when deprivation of due process is alleged. Courts must determine whether or not a regulation, policy, law, lower-court decision, or action on the part of someone who had a duty to perform was warranted in either limiting or condoning a person's actions. A review of decisions involving educational matters reveals that courts consider many factors when examining alleged deprivation of due process by school officials. Foremost among these factors is whether, overall, the school official's judgment was educationally sound. Additionally, courts examine whether an official's actions were guided primarily by administrative convenience or represented the spirit of a conformity-minded, arrogant majority when there should have been a willingness on the part of the majority to accept a degree of nondisruptive deviance.

A brief discussion of social contract theory may amplify the genesis of the due process idea. Although the theory was discussed as early as Plato, its more familiar philosophical underpinnings were advanced by political philosophers several centuries ago, notably, Thomas Hobbes (*Leviathan*), John Locke (*Two Treatises of Government*), and Jean Jacques Rousseau (*The Social Contract*). Locke, whose social contract theory is probably the one most familiar in the English-speaking world, attacked the divine right of kings theory. He contended that societies were organized and ruled by the consent of the governed and not by one who had potential for becoming autocratic. Furthermore, he asserted that individuals by their nature had certain rights, which included life, liberty, and property. When by their own volition individuals left the primitive state of nature and agreed to be governed, they made a social contract with government that protected these natural rights. The justification for the state's existence, according to Locke, was based on its ability to protect these rights better than individuals could on their own. The price individuals paid for governmental protection was a diminution of the freedom they had in the state of nature. This freedom was extremely limited, however, because it existed in an environment where there was greater potential for the "law of the jungle" and "might makes right" to prevail.

Many modern-day political theorists agree that the original thoughts of Locke and others regarding the social contract have come to stand for several propositions concerning the individual's relationship to government. These propositions include the notion that government rests on the consent of the governed; persons willingly yielded the freedom they had in the state of nature because they thought the state could offer them certain protections they could not provide for themselves; and although persons relinquished the freedom they had in the state of nature, their entering into a social contract with government included the government's guarantee against an arbitrary, capricious, and unreasonable denial of their rights of life, liberty, and property when they and the government interacted.

These propositions have considerable implications for educators. In accordance with social contract theory, school authorities not only have a legitimate but a mandatory role to play in protecting health and safety and in maintaining order. Students violating legitimate school rules may be subject to appropriate punitive action. Yet, school authorities may not act arbitrarily, capriciously, or unreasonably toward individuals when protecting the majority, and due process must be provided when a liberty or property interest is involved.

[2] *Equal Protection.*   Constitutional authorities contend that the Equal Protection Clause was inserted in the Fourteenth Amendment to ensure that former slaves would be provided the same civil protections as white Americans. Under this notion, blacks (referred to as Negroes at the time of the clause's adoption) would not only have their civil rights protected, but they would also have the benefit of applicable laws. Although originally intended to ameliorate the transition from slavery to free status, the equal protection provision has had a dramatic effect in influencing policy in American public education.

From an educational standpoint, the Equal Protection Clause represents the legal basis for prohibiting unreasonable classifications. Although some type of classification is often necessary in laws, rules, or policies, arbitrariness may not play a part. Methods of classifying students in public schools have often been based on such factors as sex, age, intelligence, marital status, parents' residence, race, pregnancy or motherhood, conduct, test scores, and wealth of their community. For these methods of classification to conform with equal protection guarantees, a reasonable relationship must exist between the objective to be accomplished and the type of classification employed. Also, if the state renders a benefit to one person within a class, all within that class must receive the benefit equally; and if one person within a class is deprived of a benefit by the state, all within that class must be deprived equally. This concept was expressed many years ago by the United States Supreme Court in *Barbier* v. *Connolly*, 113 U.S. 27 (1885), when it stated:

Class legislation, discriminating against some and favoring others, is prohibited, but legislation which, in carrying out a public purpose, is limited in its application, if within the sphere of its operation it affects alike all persons similarly situated, is not within the amendment. (p. 32)

The principal idea inherent in equal protection, as in due process, is the concept of fairness. And as is the case with due process, whether or not equal protection has been granted or denied depends on a balancing of several elements. These include sociological and psychological factors, sound educational policy, the benefit of a larger good to society as a result of the classification, contemporary customs and mores, and the protection of the individual's rights in the light of these considerations.

Courts have often employed a two-level test for measuring classifications against the Equal Protection Clause. One is a "rational basis" test, which is employed when a "fundamental interest" is not involved. Under this test, there must be a sound reason for the classification, and all those classified alike must be treated as uniformly as possible. Additionally, the burden of proof is on the complainant to demonstrate that a challenged law or policy has no rational basis to achieve a legitimate state objective. By using this test, the United States Supreme Court has commonly exercised restraint in holding legislation in violation of the equal protection provision of the Fourteenth Amendment.

A strict-scrutiny test is applied when a "fundamental interest" or "suspect classification" is involved. A presumption of constitutional validity disappears when a classification is "suspect." Examples of such classification include race, national origin, alienage, indigency, and illegitimacy. To date, one's sex has not been considered a suspect classification. The strict scrutiny test was discussed by the United States Supreme Court in *Plyler* v. *Doe*, 457 U.S. 202 (1982). The Court explained that some classifications are more likely than others to reflect deep-seated prejudice rather than legislative rationality in pursuit of some legitimate objective. It also stated that certain groups have historically experienced "political powerlessness" and thus have needed special protection from the majority. In situations where a suspect class or fundamental right is involved, the Court indicated that it is appropriate to enforce the mandate of equal protection by requiring the state to demonstrate that its classification has been precisely tailored to serve a compelling governmental interest. Although the complainant has the burden of proof when the rational basis test is used, under the strict-scrutiny test the burden of proof is placed upon the state to show that the law or policy in question is necessary to accomplish a compelling state interest.

2. Statutes

Congress has enacted many statutes that provide educators with sources of law. The legal basis for this congressional involvement derives from the so-called General Welfare Clause in Article I of the United States

Constitution. Some of the areas the national legislature has dealt with over the years include vocational education (Vocational Education Act of 1963); defense (National Defense Education Act of 1958); elementary and secondary education (Elementary and Secondary Education Act of 1965); civil rights (Civil Rights Act of 1964*); protecting information concerning students (Family Educational Rights and Privacy Act of 1974*); sex discrimination (Title IX of the Education Amendments of 1972*); with disabilities children (Section 504 of the Rehabilitation Act of 1973,* the Education for all Handicapped Children Act of 1975, renamed the Individuals with Disabilities Act of 1990, the Individuals with Disabilities Education Act of 1990, and the Individuals with Disabilities Education Act of 1997); bilingual education (Bilingual Education Act of 1968 and Title VII of the Elementary and Secondary Education Act of 1965); and pregnancy bias (Pregnancy Discrimination Act of 1978*).

Although local and federal educational agencies may occasionally disagree over the purpose and administration of federal statutes, compliance at the local level with controversial federal legislation has often been attained by the threat of a lawsuit, the lure of federal money, or a threat of a cutoff of federal funds already being received.

3. Case Law

Case law refers to principles of law established by courts. It is largely based on legal precedents declared in earlier court decisions in which there were similar factual situations. It is believed that following precedent affords a greater likelihood that citizens will be treated equally, and it has the added advantage of allowing a degree of predictability in future disputes. Under the doctrine of *stare decisis*, for instance, a court may stand by precedent and thereby not disturb a settled point of law. Although generally guided by precedent, courts are not bound by it in reaching a decision. A court may decide that the factual situation in the case being decided is not sufficiently similar to the one offering precedent or that the legal or philosophical rationale in the precedent-setting case no longer applies.

Federal courts, especially in the last several decades, have established a sizable body of case law. As a result, federal case law has been an influential, if not significant, force in educational policymaking over the last half century. Federal courts have addressed such issues as racial segregation, questions of equity in state methods for financing education, separation of church and state, due process and equal protection considerations involving both students and teachers, the extent of freedom of expression for students and teachers, and dress and grooming standards for students and teachers. Precedent established by the federal judiciary in these areas provides educators with a significant source of law. Unfortunately, the case

---

*See Appendix D for material pertaining to this legislation.

law is not always well settled, and conflicting opinions may occur among the federal district courts and courts of appeals. In this event, educators must follow the case law established for their particular jurisdiction; however, vigilance must be exercised to ascertain appellate or Supreme Court actions that may reverse or modify existing case law. Therefore, it is vital that educators have a thorough understanding of well-settled case law and also be familiar with those relating to areas of the law where it is not.

Although not always clearly understood by educators, a decision of the United States Supreme Court has the full force of law and may be altered or modified only by another High Court decision or an amendment to the Constitution.* Unfortunately, High Court decisions have not always been observed by local school systems. Desegregation decisions and those dealing with Bible reading and recitation of sectarian prayers during school hours are prime examples. Because the Court does not have an enforcement arm, compliance with a decision must often be gained by continued court action, which may include requesting writs of injunction or mandamus.

4. Executive Orders and Attorney General Opinions

The president of the United States may issue an executive order that applies to education. Once issued, it would be a source of law for educators.

The attorney general of the United States may be asked to provide an official opinion pertaining to a constitutional or statutory educational provision or a controversial educational practice. Such an opinion may be thought of as advisory and does not represent as compelling a source of law as case law.

B. State Level

Major state-level sources of law include the state's constitution, statutes, case law, state board of education policy, state department of education directives, rules and regulations of administrative agencies, executive orders, and attorney general opinions. As discussed previously, these state-level sources of law may not deprive individuals of the due process or equal protection of the laws they have as persons under the Fourteenth Amendment.

1. State Constitutions

All state constitutions contain language committing the state to a responsibility for providing education. Although the constitutional terminology varies, it often takes the form of requiring that the legislature

---

*Article III of the Constitution provides that the Supreme Court has appellate jurisdiction "with such exceptions, and under such regulations as the Congress shall make." Therefore, congressional action could conceivably restrict the Court's jurisdiction.

ensure the establishment and maintenance of a thorough and uniform or efficient system of schools. Such broad language is recognized as the ultimate authority within a state for furnishing education. Constitutional provisions may designate constitutional offices for education officials, such as state superintendent of schools and state board members. Constitutional provisions may also specify the creation of local school systems, method of selection and number of members for local school boards, qualifications and selection of local school superintendents, and authority and possibly limitations for local taxation for school purposes. A review of constitutional provisions pertaining to educational matters among the states reveals a wide range of format, from a few general designations in some states to a large number that are rather specific in other states.

Many states also have due process and/or equal protection of the law requirements similar to those found in the amendments to the federal Constitution. Consequently, state courts are often asked to interpret these in an educational context.

2. State Statutes

State statutes represent a significant source of law for educators. They are often more explicit than state constitutional provisions, and their purpose is to bring a more specific outline to broad constitutional directives or to codify case law. Statutes may regulate governmental functions such as the method of selection, terms, and responsibilities of state-level education officials. They may also stipulate the type of local or regional school systems; the method of selection, responsibilities, and terms of local school officials; and the powers of local education units.

State statutes often deal with financing of the public schools, tax instruments, and the degree to which these instruments may be employed to raise local revenue. Often teacher-pupil ratios are specified, as are the teaching of certain subjects, minimum and maximum ages for subjection to compulsory education laws, length of school day and year, and rules regarding suspension and expulsion of students.

State statutes may also address areas dealing with personnel, such as tenure, retirement, collective bargaining or professional negotiation, meet-and-confer provisions, and fair dismissal procedures. Details pertaining to teaching certificates may be written into law, although this area is usually covered by state board of education policies.

3. Case Law

State court decisions can greatly aid educators in sensitive areas where there is no policy direction from statute law, the constitution, the state board of education, or local rules and regulations. A decision by one state's highest court does not serve as binding precedent in another state. However, such an opinion does provide educators with the rationale or philosophy of another state's highest legal body regarding an area of conflict. There is no appeal of a decision of a state's highest court unless a federal issue is involved.

There are notable exceptions, but in general, state courts historically have been reluctant to overturn existing school policies in the absence of clearly unreasonable, capricious, or arbitrary conduct on the part of school officials. Consequently, plaintiffs, when possible, have often opted to have their day in federal court instead of a state court.

4. State Board of Education, Chief State School Officer, and State Department of Education

The specific roles of the state board of education, the chief state school officer, and the state department of education vary considerably among the states; yet, these offices collectively and individually provide an important source of law for educators. Functional diversity among these offices in the various states often stems from different constitutional or statutory provisions and the political dynamism of the individuals associated with these offices. The formal relationship among the state board of education, the chief state school officer, and the state department of education is rarely detailed in state legislation. Therefore, in practice, the relationship often depends on the individuals involved. Occasionally, educators at the local level are not sufficiently familiar with the differences in authority among the three divisions. Consequently, pronouncements from one of these authorities may be viewed mistakenly as agreed-upon policy emanating from the state level.

Although the duties and responsibilities of state boards of education also vary, their primary function is to adopt the necessary policies, rules, and regulations to implement legislation and constitutional requirements. When not in conflict with constitutional decrees, these policies, rules, and regulations have the force of law.

The chief state school officer's role does not have uniformity among the states. This person administers the state department of education, the agency that deals directly with the local school systems. The department is the bureaucratic mechanism through which state policy is transmitted to local systems.

5. Attorney General Opinions

As the state's legal counsel, the attorney general may be asked for an opinion regarding an educational question when a constitutional or statutory provision is not clear or when case law does not serve as a distinct precedent. Such attorney general opinions serve as useful guides for the educator, but they do not represent the same degree of authority as a decision by a state's courts or by a federal court in whose jurisdiction the state lies.

C. Local Level

Sources of law with which educators in a local school system are most familiar are the local school board policies, rules, or regulations and their individual school's rules or regulations. Such local sources of law, among school systems, are widely dissimilar in regard to their length, comprehensiveness, and compliance with federal and/or state constitutional or statutory provisions. In many instances, building-level administrators rely on this authority in dealing with such issues as administering corporal punishment, suspending a student, searching a student, censorship of the school newspaper or yearbook, student or teacher refusal to participate in patriotic exercises, use of a school building by members of the community, and dress and grooming standards for both students and teachers.

II. THE AMERICAN JUDICIAL SYSTEM

A dual judicial system composed of state and federal courts exists in the United States. The federal court system has its basis in the United States Constitution, which may be limited by acts of Congress or rulings of the United States Supreme Court. State court systems have their basis in state constitutional provisions or statutory enactments.

In some instances, state and federal courts have concurrent jurisdiction, which presents a unique interplay between the two legal systems. Having concurrent jurisdiction provides a prospective litigant with a choice in selecting the judicial system in which he or she wishes to initiate court action. Federal courts may be used, however, only if it can be shown that a federal question exists, and they may not interfere with state court proceedings unless a federal question is present, such as an alleged abridgement of a constitutional right.

When concurrent jurisdiction exists, plaintiffs will naturally select the court system perceived to be more sympathetic to their cause of action. From the mid-1950s through the mid-1980s, plaintiffs viewed the federal judiciary in this light due to the activist reputation of the Supreme Court. During that time, many cases were brought to the federal courts that historically would have been brought to state courts. That impetus no longer exists, however, because the Court can no longer be considered to be an activist one.

Prior to instituting court action, with few exceptions, one must exhaust all local and state administrative remedies before seeking a redress of grievances through court litigation. Failure to exhaust these administrative remedies by the plaintiff may result in a court's refusal to grant standing required for a hearing before the court.

Proceedings in school law often involve suits dealing with questions of due process and equal protection of the law brought in a branch of civil law termed *equity law*. The regular court system usually administers equity law, as separate courts do not normally exist to deal with it. However, in this type of action there is generally no jury, and the judge(s) is the sole determiner of what constitutes due process or equal protection, subject only to review by a higher court. Equity judgments regarding due process and equal protection are generally made on the basis of many variables, such as a close examination of the particular facts of a case, decisions in previous cases, and possibly the introduction of social science findings. If arbitrary or capricious conduct on the part of a governmental official can be demonstrated, the likelihood increases that either due process or equal protection has been denied. On the other hand, if educationally sound reasons are offered by the educator in attempting to explain the actions or conduct in dispute, the likelihood increases that due process or equal protection has been afforded. Ultimately, however, the judge(s) must determine—given a particular factual situation, present societal mores, actual or possible inconvenience or danger to society, precedent, and constitutional and other rights—where the balance lies between providing an individual with his or her constitutional rights and the legitimate demands of the larger society.

A. State Court Systems

Each state has the responsibility of establishing its own judicial system. Although this has resulted in the creation of fifty independent state court systems, certain basic similarities exist among them. Common to most states' judicial systems is a court of original jurisdiction and some sort of appellate structure.

In most instances, cases dealing with educational matters are initiated in the state's appropriate court of original jurisdiction. These courts are called circuit courts, district courts, courts of common pleas, or supreme courts (New York only), but in many states they are referred to as superior courts. Most litigation is settled in these courts, and they serve as the sole determiner of the facts in most cases.

Intermediate appellate courts constitute a second level of many state court systems. Approximately half of the states have established intermediate appellate courts, and they are called courts of appeals, appellate divisions or departments of the superior courts, appellate divisions of the supreme court (New York only), or appeals courts. Where present, these appellate-level courts provide a tribunal between the trial court and the state's highest court of last resort. Unlike courts of original jurisdiction, state appellate courts do not engage in factual inquiries; rather, these courts determine questions of law. Opinions are based on a written record provided by the court of original jurisdiction.

A state's highest-level court is generally called the supreme court; however, it may be called the court of appeals, supreme judicial court, or the supreme court of appeals. Most state supreme courts rarely have original jurisdiction except under specific conditions mandated by state law. Their basic function is to review lower-court decisions on appeal. Purely state matters may not be appealed beyond a state's supreme court; however, if a federal question is involved an appeal may be made to the federal courts or the United States Supreme Court if the state is a party.

B. Federal Court System

By constitutional design, the federal judiciary was established as a separate and independent branch of the United States government. Subsequent federal legislation has provided for a federal judicial system, which presently includes district courts, courts of appeals, and the United States Supreme Court. A litigant must raise a federal question to have standing in a federal court. When dealing with educational issues, this may be accomplished by alleging violation of a federal statute, such as 42 U.S.C. § 1983, or of amendments to the Constitution, such as the First, Fourth, Fifth or Fourteenth.

1. District Courts
The district court, of which there are more than ninety, is the court of original jurisdiction in the federal judicial system. Each state has at least one district court, and many states have between two and four districts. A district may be divided into divisions, and cases may be heard in different locations within those divisions.

2. Courts of Appeals
Courts of appeals represent the intermediate appellate level of the federal court system. Their primary function is to review appeals from district courts within the circuit, and decisions by a court of appeals are binding on the lower federal courts in the circuit. A decision by one court of appeals may stand as a persuasive decision for other courts of appeals, but it does not stand as binding authority. Courts of appeals base their decisions on the trial court's proceedings and any briefs filed by concerned parties. A case may be remanded to a lower court for further proceedings when the appellate court finds that the facts presented in the written record are insufficient to render a decision. The nation is divided into thirteen federal judicial circuits, comprising eleven geographic regions and the District of Columbia Circuit and Federal Circuit (see Figure 1–1).

3. Supreme Court
The Supreme Court is the highest-level court in the federal judicial system, and there is no appeal from a decision rendered by this court. When ruling on the constitutionality of a federal statute or practices within

a state or local subdivision, such a ruling can be overturned only by an amendment to the Constitution or by a subsequent ruling by the Court. Nine justices including one chief justice make up the Court. As with other federal judges, their appointment is for life, and their compensation cannot be reduced during their tenure.

Most cases reach the Supreme Court by means of a writ of certiorari. Under this method, an unsuccessful litigant in a lower-court decision petitions the Court to review the case, setting forth reasons why the case should be granted a writ. A case is accepted for review only if four justices vote to grant certiorari. Acceptance for review under this "rule of four" indicates that at least four members of the Court consider the case to have sufficient merit to be considered by the entire Court. Denial of certiorari leaves the decision of the lower court undisturbed and applicable only in the lower court's jurisdiction. Such a denial does not have the force of a written decision, which directly addresses the merits of a case.

The Court's term begins on the first Monday in October and usually lasts for nine months. The number of cases docketed during a term has increased significantly. More than 6,000 cases have been docketed in recent years, whereas 2,313 cases were docketed in 1960 and 1,460 in 1945. Although the Court decides between 200 and 250 cases in a term, formal written opinions are rendered in approximately half of these decisions.

Court decisions dealing with educational matters have had a significant impact on educational policy in the last several decades. Many difficult social-policy decisions have been made by the Court because other branches or levels of government were unable to agree or were unwilling to make them. This has prompted some observers to suggest that the United States Supreme Court may have become the modern-day American oracle. However, a different judicial philosophy, as a result of appointments made between 1969 and 1991, has made the Court less inclined to effect social change in recent years, thereby somewhat diminishing this perceived role.

Some educators have doubts about the authority under which the Supreme Court determines questions of constitutionality. Although this right of judicial review is not explicitly provided for in the United States Constitution, many scholars agree that the framers of the Constitution expected the Court to assume this function. This notion was addressed by Alexander Hamilton in *The Federalist*, No. 78, in which he asserted:

> . . . the courts were designed to be an intermediate body between the people and the legislature . . . to keep the latter within the limits assigned to their authority. The interpretation of the laws is the proper and peculiar province of the courts. . . . It therefore belongs to them to ascertain its meaning, as well as the meaning of any particular act proceeding from the legislative body. . . .

The Court's role as the final authority on interpreting the Constitution was established in its landmark decision, *Marbury v. Madison*, 1 Cranch 137 (1803), and it has continued to engage in judicial review since that time.

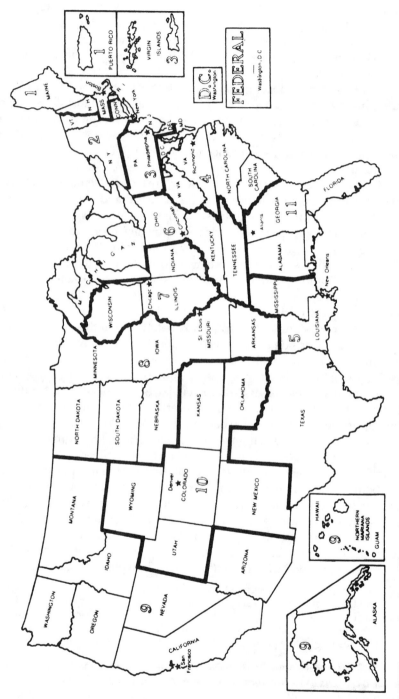

FIGURE 1-1 The Thirteen Federal Judicial Circuits (see 28 U.S.C.A. § 41)

18

CHAPTER TWO

Schools and the State

Public education is a governmental enterprise that receives enormous resources from the citizenry and with which most persons have direct contact for fairly extended periods of time. Consequently, because we live in a democratic society that allows for the close scrutiny of such public institutions, honest differences often arise between school clients and those running them about public school policies. This chapter's purpose is to examine the extent of state and local authority when individuals disagree with educational policy involving such issues as compulsory attendance, religion in the schools, before- and after-school use of facilities, aid to nonpublic schools, school fees, and health services. The thread woven throughout many of the court decisions dealing with these issues is the attempt by the courts to establish a balance between the legitimate demands or objections of individuals toward educational policy and school authorities' perception of their responsibility to the greater population.

I. COMPULSORY ATTENDANCE

A. Satisfied by Parochial, Private, or Home School Attendance

Every state has some form of compulsory education law. These laws generally provide that children between certain ages must attend public, private, or home school, and failure to comply may be a criminal violation. Central to the legal disputes pertaining to compulsory attendance laws is the balancing of the state's interest in ensuring that students receive an appropriate education and the rights of parents to decide when and where their child attends school.

    Pierce v. *Society of Sisters*, a landmark United States Supreme Court decision, affirmed the doctrine of compulsory school attendance. It also established the role of parochial and private schools in satisfying the state's demand that children receive schooling.

PIERCE v. SOCIETY OF SISTERS
Supreme Court of the United States, 1925
268 U.S. 510

MR. JUSTICE McREYNOLDS delivered the opinion of the Court.

These appeals are from decrees, based upon undenied allegations, which granted preliminary orders restraining appellants from threatening or attempting to enforce the Compulsory Education Act adopted November 7, 1922, under the initiative provision of her Constitution by the voters of Oregon. * * *

The challenged Act, effective September 1, 1926, requires every parent, guardian or other person having control or charge or custody of a child between eight and sixteen years to send him "to a public school for the period of time a public school shall be held during the current year" in the district where the child resides; and failure to do so is declared a misdemeanor. * * * The manifest purpose is to compel general attendance at public schools by normal children, between eight and sixteen, who have not completed the eighth grade. And without doubt enforcement of the statute would seriously impair, perhaps destroy, the profitable features of appellees' business and greatly diminish the value of their property.

Appellee, the Society of Sisters, is an Oregon corporation, organized in 1880, with power to care for orphans, educate and instruct the youth, establish and maintain academies or schools, and acquire necessary real and personal property. It has long devoted its property and effort to the secular and religious education and care of children, and has acquired the valuable good will of many parents and guardians. It conducts interdependent primary and high schools and junior colleges, and maintains orphanages for the custody and control of children between eight and sixteen. In its primary schools many children between those ages are taught the subjects usually pursued in Oregon public schools during the first eight years. Systematic religious instruction and moral training according to the tenets of the Roman Catholic Church are also regularly provided. All courses of study, both temporal and religious, contemplate continuity of training under the appellee's charge; the primary schools are essential to the system and the most profitable. It owns valuable buildings, especially constructed and equipped for school purposes. The business is remunerative—the annual income from primary schools exceeds thirty thousand dollars—and the successful conduct of this requires long-time contracts with teachers and parents. The Compulsory Education Act of 1922 has already caused the withdrawal from its schools of children who would otherwise continue, and their income has steadily declined. The appellants, public officers, have proclaimed their purpose strictly to enforce the statute.

After setting out the above facts the Society's bill alleges that the enactment conflicts with the right of parents to choose schools where their children will receive appropriate mental and religious training, the right of the child to influence the parents' choice of a school, the right of schools and teachers therein to engage in a useful business or profession, and is accordingly repugnant to the Constitution and void. And, further, that unless enforcement of the measure is enjoined, the corporation's business and property will suffer irreparable injury.

Appellee, Hill Military Academy, is a private corporation organized in 1908 under the laws of Oregon, engaged in owning, operating and conducting for profit an elementary, college preparatory and military training school for boys between the ages of five and twenty-one years. * * * It owns considerable real and personal property, some useful only for school purposes. The business and incident good will are very valuable. In order to conduct its affairs long time contracts must be made for supplies, equipment, teachers and pupils. Appellants, law officers of the State and County, have publicly announced that the Act of November 7, 1922, is valid and have declared their intention to enforce it. By reason of the statute and threat of enforcement appellee's business is being destroyed and its property depreciated; parents and guardians are refusing to make contracts for the future instruction of their sons, and some are being withdrawn.

The Academy's bill states the foregoing facts and then alleges that the challenged Act contravenes the corporation's rights guaranteed by the Fourteenth Amendment and that unless appellants are restrained from proclaiming its validity and threatening to enforce it irreparable injury will result. The prayer is for an appropriate injunction.

No answer was interposed in either cause, and after proper notices they were heard by three judges * * * on motions for preliminary injunctions upon the specifically alleged facts. The court ruled that the Fourteenth Amendment guaranteed appellees against the deprivation of their property without due process of law consequent upon the unlawful interference by appellants with the free choice of patrons, present and prospective. It declared the right to conduct schools was property and that parents and guardians, as part of their liberty, might direct the education of children by selecting reputable teachers and places. Also, that these schools were not unfit or harmful to the public, and that enforcement of the challenged statute would unlawfully deprive them of patronage and thereby destroy their owners' business and property. Finally, that the threats to enforce the Act would continue to cause irreparable injury; and the suits were not premature.

No question is raised concerning the power of the State reasonably to regulate all schools, to inspect, supervise and examine them, their teachers and pupils; to require that all children of proper age attend some school, that teachers shall be of good moral character and patriotic disposition, that certain studies plainly essential to good citizenship must be taught, and that nothing be taught which is manifestly inimical to the public welfare.

The inevitable practical result of enforcing the Act under consideration would be destruction of appellees' primary schools, and perhaps all other private primary schools for normal children within the State of Oregon. These parties are engaged in a kind of undertaking not inherently harmful, but long regarded as useful and meritorious. Certainly there is nothing in the present records to indicate that they have failed to discharge their obligations to patrons, students or the State. * * *

* * * [We] think it entirely plain that the Act of 1922 unreasonably interferes with the liberty of parents and guardians to direct the upbringing and education of children under their control. As often heretofore pointed out, rights guaranteed by the Constitution may not be abridged by legislation which has no reasonable relation to some purpose within the competency of the State. The fundamental theory of liberty upon which all governments in this Union repose excludes any general power of the State to standardize its children by forcing them to accept instruction from public teachers only. The child is not the mere creature of the State; those who nurture him and direct his destiny have the right, coupled with the high duty, to recognize and prepare him for additional obligations.

* * *

Generally it is entirely true, as urged by counsel, that no person in any business has such an interest in possible customers as to enable him to restrain exercise of proper power of the State upon the ground that he will be deprived of patronage. But the injunctions here sought are not against the exercise of any *proper* power. Plaintiffs asked protection against arbitrary, unreasonable and unlawful interference with their patrons and the consequent distribution of their business and property. Their interest is clear and immediate. * * *

The suits were not premature. The injury to appellees was present and very real, not a mere possibility in the remote future. If no relief had been possible prior to the effective date of the Act, the injury would have become irreparable. Prevention of impending injury by unlawful action is a well-recognized function of courts of equity.

The decrees below are

Affirmed.

Notes and Questions

Pierce, one of the original defendants in this case, was the governor of Oregon.

Does the Court's decision in *Pierce* reveal a bias in favor of the individual parent to have access to a pluralistic educational system by not allowing the state to have a monopoly over education?

The challenged Oregon law in *Pierce* had been promoted primarily by members of the Ku Klux Klan and Oregon's Scottish Rite Masons. Their actions were evidence of a xenophobic response on the part of some Americans after World War I to ensure that children would be properly socialized in the tenets of Americanism. The strong feelings against many foreigners and Catholics in particular at that time prompted a leading klansman to state: "Somehow these mongrel hordes must be Americanized; failing that, deportation is the only remedy." An attempt was made to picture Catholics as members of an organization that conducted its worship services in a foreign language, was controlled by a foreigner called a Pope, and practiced secret rituals.

The Supreme Court decision in *Pierce* had immediate applicability only to the contested Oregon Compulsory Education Act and the issues arising from its attempted implementation. It did not automatically affect similar laws in other states. Individual state legislative action would be necessary to revoke similar laws in those states, and the absence of such legislative action would require a lawsuit to gain compliance with the *Pierce* rationale. Given the *Pierce* precedent, such a suit would undoubtedly be successful.

An Amish group contested Wisconsin's compulsory attendance law, which required attendance at a public or private school until age sixteen. The Amish did not want their children to attend either a public or private high school after the eighth grade, because they considered such schools to be "worldly." A Supreme Court decision upheld the Amish position on several grounds. The Court contended that enforcing the state law would gravely endanger, if not destroy, the free exercise of Amish religious beliefs. Additionally, the Court's decision was influenced not only by the group's nearly three hundred years of existence but also by the perception that, although perhaps unconventional, the Amish had evidenced a highly successful social unit characterized by members who were productive, law abiding, and unwilling to accept welfare in any of its usual modern forms. See *Wisconsin* v. *Yoder*, 406 U.S. 205 (1972). Would the Court's rationale prevail if the group contesting a compulsory attendance law were the Ku Klux Klan rather than the Amish? Should students have a voice in this issue? Justice Douglas's opinion in *Yoder*, in which he dissents in part, suggests that students should have such a voice.

A Pentecostal parent who objected to sending his children to public schools was not upheld. The court ruled that the state's interest in compulsory attendance overrides the parent's interest in avoiding exposure to the unisex movement, secular humanism, and medical care. See *Duro* v. *District Attorney, Second Judicial District of North Carolina*, 712 F.2d 96 (4th

Cir. 1983), *cert. denied,* 465 U.S. 1006 (1984). Parents were also not upheld when they refused to send their children to public school because those schools did not teach Indian heritage and culture. See *Matter of McMillan,* 30 N.C.App. 235, 226 S.E.2d 693 (1976).

What are the provisions of the compulsory attendance law in your state?

B. Regulation of Nonpublic Schools

Once *Pierce* established the doctrine that private school attendance could satisfy a state's compulsory attendance requirements, the question arose as to the extent to which a state could regulate the private schools within its jurisdiction. The United States Supreme Court addressed this issue, one year after its *Pierce* decision, in *Farrington v. Tokushige,* 273 U.S. 284 (1926).

Farrington resulted from a state attempt to Americanize students: in this case Hawaii's attempt to regulate the predominantly Japanese foreign language schools on the islands. The contested regulations required teachers in these schools to possess "ideals of democracy," knowledge of American history, and fluency in English. Additionally, they restricted hours of operation, established entrance requirements, and prescribed textbooks. These regulations, the Court held, served no demonstrable public interest, but instead amounted to a deliberate plan of strict governmental control, infringing on the rights of both parents and school owners.

Both *Pierce* and *Farrington* reflect a philosophy that parents should have freedom of choice in the education of their children. Moreover, in sanctioning what many people at the time feared was subversive, these decisions affirm a faith in the sustaining power of American tolerance for diversity among its citizenry.

Regulation of private schools varies among the states. Some states require that the quality of education provided by the private school be essentially equivalent to that provided in the public schools. This may include a requirement for certified teachers and certain course offerings. Other states merely have regulations dealing primarily with health, safety, and sanitation. Because attendance at a private school satisfies a state's compulsory attendance law, it is a legitimate state function to require attendance information from private schools.

State regulation of religious private schools has received increased court attention in recent years. In these suits, private schools frequently allege that their First Amendment religious freedom is being restricted. Courts have tended to reject these challenges to minimal instructional programs and requirements that teachers have baccalaureate degrees. See *Nebraska v. Faith Baptist Church,* 301 N.W.2d 571 (Neb. 1981), *appeal dismissed,* 454 U.S. 803 (1981), *Bangor Baptist Church v. Maine,* 549 F.Supp. 1208 (Me.

1982), *North Dakota* v. *Shaver*, 294 N.W.2d 883 (N.D. 1981), and *North Dakota* v. *Rivinius*, 328 N.W.2d 220 (N.D. 1982), *cert. denied*, 460 U.S. 1070 (1983). Also see *New Life Baptist Church Academy* v. *Town of East Long Meadow*, 885 F. 2d 940 (1st Cir. 1989), *cert. denied*, 494 U.S.1066 (1990), in which the court interpreted a Massachusetts law requiring a local school committee to "approve" a private school in order for attendance at the private school to satisfy that state's compulsory attendance law. Although the private school believed it was a sin to submit its educational enterprise to a secular authority for approval, the court upheld school committee procedures such as gathering written information, reviewing the academic credentials of teachers, and visiting the school to observe the quality of the teaching. The private school preferred voluntary standardized pupil testing. The court contended that the state's interest in making certain that its children receive an adequate secular education was "compelling" and did not violate the Free Exercise or Establishment Clauses of the First Amendment.

What is the status of private school regulation in your state? In addition to reviewing court decisions, you may wish to consult your state constitution, statutes, state school board policies, and attorney general opinions.

C. Home Instruction

Parents dissatisfied with both public and private schools have increasingly chosen to instruct their children at home. This has resulted in a dramatic increase in the number of students home-schooled, which is presently estimated at over a million and a half students and growing at approximately 12 percent per year. Although the practice is authorized in every state, statutory provisions vary greatly among the states. Those states having regulatory home-schooling statutes may require: the home program to be essentially "equivalent" to that offered in the public schools; student participation, and possible minimum requirements, in standardized testing or other forms of evaluation; a minimum number of yearly hours for instruction, submission of lesson plans, adherence to a minimum curriculum; and minimum academic requirements for parents. When challenged by local school authorities and law enforcement officials, parents engaged in home instruction are generally brought to trial in a criminal action for failure to comply with a state's compulsory education law.

Earliest cases challenging home instruction alleged that home schooling was not "equivalent" to that offered in the public schools. In one of the earliest decisions, *New Jersey* v. *Massa*, 231 A.2d 252 (N.J. Super. Ct. 1967), the court held that equivalent education elsewhere than at school requires only a showing of academic equivalence and that the absence of social contact does not vitiate a home-instruction program.

Overall, courts have overwhelmingly upheld the constitutionality of restrictions on home instruction, including the requirement of teacher certification. A Virginia court upheld the state's compulsory attendance law, which required home school instructors to be "tutors or teachers" but did not require similar qualifications for private school instructors. See *Grigg v. Virginia*, 297 S.E.2d 799 (Va. 1982). A Michigan law requiring home schools to comply with teacher-certification requirements was similarly upheld. See *People v. Bennett*, 501 N.W.2d 106 (Mich. 1993) and *Clonlara Inc. v. State Board of Education*, 501 N.W.2d 88 (Mich. 1993). However, the Michigan Supreme Court did not uphold the requirement for having a teaching certificate for home-school parents who had objected to the requirement on religious grounds. See *People v. DeJonge*, 501 N.W.2d 127 (Mich. 1993).

A federal district court, in *Null v. Board of Education*, 815 F. Supp. 937 (W. Va. 1993), upheld a statute that made children ineligible for home schooling if their standardized test scores fell below the 40th percentile and did not improve above that level after remedial home instruction. Such legislation, the court contended, had a rational basis and did not violate parents' general liberty interests nor their equal protection rights. Massachusetts's highest court, in *Brunelle v. Lynn Public Schools*, 702 N.E.2d 1182 (Mass. 1998), held that approval of a home-education program conditioned on a requirement of home visits by the local school superintendent was invalid. The court reasoned that home visits were not essential to the state's interest in education and could not be imposed as a condition of approval of parents' home-education plans. In its decision, the court noted that school officials had examined the home-education proposals, and were satisfied with the qualifications of the parents as teachers, the contents of the curricula and instructional materials to be used, the amount of time to be devoted to instruction, and the student evaluation plans.

Objections on religious grounds to verifying compliance with attendance laws were not upheld in *Mazanec v. North Judson–San Pierre School Corporation*, 798 F.2d 230 (7th Cir. 1987). State home-schooling reporting requirements were also upheld in *State v. Rivera*, 497 N.W.2d 878 (Iowa 1993). The requirements, which were challenged on free exercise grounds, included course outlines, weekly lesson plans, and providing the amount of time spent on areas of instruction. A Maryland law regarding the state's monitoring of home education was also upheld, although a parent complained that the required curriculum promoted atheism, paganism, and evolutionism, and diminished the importance of Christian holidays by introducing secular figures such as the Easter Bunny and Santa Claus. The court reasoned that the law did not violate free exercise rights as it applied to all children and did not require the parent to alter her religious beliefs.

See *Battles* v. *Anne Arundel County Board of Education*, 904 F. Supp. 471 (Md. 1995), *aff'd*, 95 F.3d 41 (4th Cir. 1996).

Initially, home instruction was the province of conservative Christian families who were concerned about their children's moral education, in addition to the 3 Rs. Increasingly, over the years, home instruction has also been embraced by those dissatisfied with the effectiveness of the public schools.

Some less ideologically motivated parents, in recent years, have attempted to take advantage of public school services they deem beneficial to their children's success. These parents would like their children to take advanced mathematics and science courses, foreign language, band, or art, for instance. Others would like their children to participate in extracurricular activities such as athletics or other after-school activities. To date, courts have not been sympathetic to the notion of home-schooled students participating in extracurricular activities or taking courses. See *Swanson* v. *Guthrie Independent School District No. I-1*, 135 F.3d 694 (10th Cir. 1998), upholding a school district's full-time attendance policy, which did not allow a home-schooled student to attend public school on a part-time basis. The court disagreed that the policy had an incidental impact on the family's religious beliefs or practices and declared "The policy does not prohibit [the Swansons] from home-schooling Annie in accordance with their religious beliefs, and does not force them to do anything that is contrary to those beliefs." Because part-time students did not qualify for state financial aid, the school board feared that the student's attendance "could set a precedent allowing other home-schooled children as well as private-school students to use the public school's facilities on an as-wanted basis, without a corresponding increase in state financial aid."

Since their lack of success in the courts, home-schooling proponents focused their attention on state legislatures. As a result, several states including Oregon, Florida, and Idaho have passed statutes that create a qualified right for home-schooled students to participate in public school activities. Although the statutes differ in several respects, participation is generally conditioned on students' attaining a minimum score on a standardized test, complying with requirements of regularly enrolled students, and conforming to standards of behavior and performance of other students participating in the activity. Some other states, such as Maine, have enacted statutes that allow participation upon the approval of the local school system.

Does your state or local system have any provisions concerning home instruction for those unwilling to attend either public or private schools? May home-schooled students spend part of the day taking courses or engaging in extracurricular activities?

D. Admission Issues

Compulsory attendance laws often state a minimum age at which formal education must begin. Disputes may arise when a child's birthday is a few days or perhaps weeks after a designated date or when parents believe their child is emotionally and intellectually ready to begin school at an earlier age.

This issue was addressed by the West Virginia Supreme Court of Appeals. Although a state statute required, as a prerequisite to school admittance, that students attain the age of five on or before September 1, the court found that an intellectually mature child whose birthday fell on September 3 should have been admitted to school. The court reasoned that it was the state legislature's intent that school boards adopt flexible policies—consistent with resources at their disposal—to ease the burden of such unfortunate situations. See *Blessing* v. *Mason County Board of Education*, 341 S.E.2d 407 (W. Va. 1985). In the absence of state statutes or constitutional provisions establishing the age for entrance to school, local school boards of education have an implied authority to establish them. See *Zweifel* v. *Joint District No. 1*, 251 N.W.2d 822 (Wis. 1977).

The United State Supreme Court addressed the issue of public school admission of illegal aliens in *Plyler* v. *Doe*, 457 U.S. 202 (1982). The Court, in a five-to-four decision, held that funding for the education of these children could not be withheld from local school districts, nor could local school districts deny enrollment to children not legally admitted to the country. This decision emphasized both the importance of public education in maintaining basic civic institutions and the lasting impact of educational deprivation on the life of a child. Provisions of a 1994 California initiative (Proposition 187) that sought to exclude illegal aliens and children who were citizens, but whose parents were illegal aliens, from public elementary and secondary schools was struck down as being in conflict with *Plyler* and other Supreme Court decisions. Another provision of the initiative requiring school districts to verify the immigration status of prospective and current students and their parents and to notify them of their suspected status, and to report this information to state and federal officials was also struck down as violative of federal law. See *League of United Latin American Citizens* v. *Wilson*, 908 F. Supp. 755 (Cal. 1995) and 997 F. Supp. 1244 (Cal. 1997). In addition to agreeing with the 1995 decision, the latter decision held Proposition 187 invalid under the congressionally enacted Personal Responsibility and Work Opportunity Reconciliation Act (PRA) of 1996, which restricted alien access to substantially all public benefits and declared the state powerless to legislate in the area of public benefits for aliens. However, the PRA did not deny public elementary and secondary education benefits to aliens.

Does your state or local school system have any provisions concerning a minimum age for school entry? If so, is there a provision for early admission or transfer from other states?

II. RELIGION IN THE SCHOOLS

Although the United States Supreme Court and lower federal court decisions have been consistent in declaring Bible reading for sectarian purposes and school-sponsored prayer during normal school hours to be unconstitutional, this issue and others dealing with religious activities at public schools remain highly charged and emotional ones. Consequently, these issues have provided a persistent stream of litigation focusing on church–state relations.

In an effort to ensure a separation of church and state, the framers of the Constitution included the following language in the First Amendment: "Congress shall make no law respecting an *establishment of religion*, or prohibiting the *free exercise thereof.*" (Emphasis added). On the basis of these words, courts must determine the constitutionality of such questions as allowing prayer and Bible reading in the public schools during normal school hours, prayer at graduation exercises or football games, conducting baccalaureate services, permitting Bible study or other religious clubs, disseminating Gideon Bibles or other religious tracts, or observing religious holidays.

Courts have not erected an unassailably high wall between the church and the state that would absolutely restrict governmental involvement with religion. Rather, a review of court decisions dealing with these issues reveals that the thread woven throughout the decisions is the attempt by courts to determine the proper height of the wall separating church and state, given a particular factual situation.

A. School-Sponsored Prayer and Bible Reading

Two United States Supreme Court decisions in the early 1960s dramatically established the case law pertaining to prayer and Bible reading in the public schools. In *Engel v. Vitale*, the Court, with one dissent, held that recitation of a prayer composed by the New York State Board of Regents, which was to be said in the presence of a teacher at the beginning of school each day, was unconstitutional and in violation of the Establishment Clause.

In *School District of Abington Township v. Schempp*, a lengthy decision of 117 pages, which included a majority opinion, three concurring opinions, and one dissent, the Court held that reading the Bible for sectarian purposes and reciting the Lord's Prayer in public schools during normal hours were unconstitutional. However, the Court asserted that the Bible could be read as literature in an appropriate class and that the history of religion or comparative religion could be taught.

1. Recitation of a State Prayer

ENGEL v. VITALE
Supreme Court of the United States, 1962
370 U.S. 421

MR. JUSTICE BLACK delivered the opinion of the Court.

The respondent Board of Education of Union Free School District No. 9, New Hyde Park, New York, acting in its official capacity under state law, directed the School District's principal to cause the following prayer to be said aloud by each class in the presence of a teacher at the beginning of each school day:

> "Almighty God, we acknowledge our dependence upon Thee, and we beg Thy blessings upon us, our parents, our teachers and our Country."

This daily procedure was adopted on the recommendation of the State Board of Regents, a governmental agency created by the State Constitution to which the New York Legislature has granted broad supervisory, executive, and legislative powers over the State's public school system. These state officials composed the prayer which they recommended and published as part of their "Statement on Moral and Spiritual Training in the Schools," saying: "We believe that this Statement will be subscribed to by all men and women of good will, and we call upon all of them to aid in giving life to our program."

Shortly after the practice of reciting the Regents' prayer was adopted by the School District, the parents of ten pupils brought this action in a New York State Court insisting that use of this official prayer in the public schools was contrary to the beliefs, religions, or religious practices of both themselves and their children. Among other things, these parents challenged the constitutionality of both the state law authorizing the School District to direct the use of prayer in public schools and the School District's regulation ordering the recitation of this particular prayer on the ground that these actions of official governmental agencies violate that part of the First Amendment of the Federal Constitution which commands that "Congress shall make no law respecting an establishment of religion"—a command which was "made applicable to the State of New York by the Fourteenth Amendment of the said Constitution." The New York Court of Appeals * * * sustained an order of the lower state courts which had upheld the power of New York to use the Regents' prayer as a part of the daily procedures of its public schools so long as the schools did not compel any pupil to join in the prayer over his or her parents' objection. We granted certiorari to review this important decision involving the rights protected by the First and Fourteenth Amendments.

We think that by using its public school system to encourage recitation of the Regents' prayer, the State of New York has adopted a practice wholly inconsistent with the Establishment Clause. There can, of course, be no doubt that New York's program of daily classroom invocation of God's blessings as prescribed in the Regents' prayer is a religious activity. It is a solemn avowal of divine faith and supplication for the blessings of the Almighty. The nature of such a prayer has always been religious, none of the respondents has denied this and the trial court expressly so found. * * *

The petitioners contend among other things that the state laws requiring or permitting use of the Regents' prayer must be struck down as a violation of the Establishment Clause because that prayer was composed by government officials as a part of a governmental program to further religious beliefs. For this reason, petitioners argue, the State's use of the Regents' prayer in its public school system breaches the constitutional wall of separation between Church and State. We agree with that contention since we think that the constitutional prohibition against laws respecting an establishment of religion must at least mean that in this country it is no part of the business of government to compose official prayers for any group of the American people to recite as a part of a religious program carried on by government.

It is a matter of history that this very practice of establishing governmentally composed prayers for religious services was one of the reasons which caused many of our early colonists to leave England and seek religious freedom in America. The Book of Common Prayer, which was created under governmental direction and which was approved by Acts of Parliament in 1548 and 1549, set out in minute detail the accepted form and content of prayer and other religious ceremonies to be used in the established, tax-supported Church of England. The controversies over the Book and what should be its content repeatedly threatened to disrupt the peace of that country as the accepted forms of prayer in the established church changed with the views of the particular ruler that happened to be in control at the time. Powerful groups representing some of the varying religious views of the people struggled among themselves to impress their particular views upon the Government and obtain amendments of the Book more suitable to their respective notions of how religious services should be conducted in order that the official religious establishment would advance their particular beliefs. Other groups, lacking the necessary political power to influence the Government on the matter, decided to leave England and its established church and seek freedom in America from England's governmentally ordained and supported religion.

It is an unfortunate fact of history that when some of the very groups which had most strenuously opposed the established Church of England found themselves sufficiently in control of colonial governments in this country to write their own prayers into law, they passed laws making their own religion the official religion of their respective colonies. Indeed, as late as the time of the Revolutionary War, there were established churches in at least eight of the thirteen former colonies and established religions in at least four of the other five. But the successful Revolution against English political domination was shortly followed by intense opposition to the practice of establishing religion by law. * * *

By the time of the adoption of the Constitution, our history shows that there was a widespread awareness among many Americans of the dangers of a union of Church and State. These people knew, some of them from bitter personal experience, that one of the greatest dangers to the freedom of the individual to worship in his own way lay in the Government's placing its official stamp of approval upon one particular kind of prayer or one particular form of religious services. They knew the anguish, hardship and bitter strife that could come when zealous religious groups struggled with one another to obtain the Government's stamp of approval from each King, Queen, or Protector that came to temporary power. The Constitution was intended to avert a part of this danger by leaving the government of this country in the hands of the people rather than in the hands of any monarch. But this safeguard was not enough. Our Founders were no more willing to let the content of their prayers and their privilege of praying whenever they pleased be influenced by the ballot box than they were to let these vital matters of personal conscience depend upon the succession of monarchs. The First Amendment was added to the Constitution to stand as a guarantee that neither the power nor the prestige of the Federal Government would be used to control, support or influence the kinds of prayer the American people can say—that the people's religions must not be subjected to the pressures of government for change each time a new political administration is elected to office. Under that Amendment's prohibition against governmental establishment of religion, as reinforced by the provisions of the Fourteenth Amendment, government in this country, be it state or federal, is without power to prescribe by law any particular form of prayer which is to be used as an official prayer in carrying on any program of governmentally sponsored religious activity.

There can be no doubt that New York's state prayer program officially establishes the religious beliefs embodied in the Regents' prayer. The respondents' argument to the contrary, which is largely based upon the contention that the Regents' prayer is "non-denominational" and the fact that the program, as modified and approved by state courts, does not require all pupils to recite the prayer but permits those who wish to do so to remain silent or be excused from the room, ignores the essential nature of the program's constitutional defects. Neither the fact that the prayer may be denominationally neutral nor the fact that its observance on the part of the students is voluntary can serve to free it from the limitations of the Establishment Clause, as it might from the Free Exercise Clause, of the First Amendment, both of which are operative against the States by virtue of the Fourteenth Amendment. Although these two clauses may in certain instances overlap, they forbid two quite different kinds of governmental encroachment upon religious freedom. The Establishment Clause, unlike the Free Exercise Clause, does not depend upon any showing of direct governmental compulsion and is violated by the enactment of laws which establish an official religion whether those laws operate directly to coerce nonobserving individuals or not. This is not to say, of course, that laws officially prescribing a particular form of religious worship do not involve coercion of such individuals. When the power, prestige and financial support of the government is placed behind a particular religious belief, the indirect coercive pressure upon religious minorities to conform to the prevailing officially approved religion is plain. But the purposes underlying the Establishment Clause go much further than that. Its first and most immediate purpose rested on the belief that a union of government and religion tends to destroy government and degrade religion. The history of governmentally established religion, both in England and in this country, showed that whenever government had allied itself with one particular form of religion, the inevitable result had been that it had incurred the hatred, disrespect and even contempt of those who held contrary beliefs. That same history showed that many people had lost their respect for any religion that had relied upon the support of government to spread its faith. The Establishment Clause thus stands as an expression of principle on the part of the Founders of our Constitution that religion is too personal, too sacred, too holy, to permit its "unhallowed perversion" by a civil magistrate. Another purpose of the Establishment Clause rested upon an awareness of the historical fact that governmentally established religions and religious persecutions go hand in hand. The Founders knew that only a few years after the Book of Common Prayer became the only accepted form of religious services in the established Church of England, an Act of Uniformity was passed to compel all the Englishmen to attend those services and to make it a criminal offense to conduct or attend religious gatherings of any kind—a law which was consistently flouted by dissenting religious groups in England and which contributed to widespread persecutions of people like John Bunyan who persisted in holding "unlawful [religious] meetings . . . to the great disturbance and distraction of the good subjects of this kingdom. . . ." And they knew that similar persecutions had received the sanction of law in several of the colonies in this country soon after the establishment of official religions in those colonies. It was in large part to get completely away from this sort of systematic religious persecution that the Founders brought into being our Nation, our Constitution, and our Bill of Rights with its prohibition against any governmental establishment of religion. The New York laws officially prescribing the Regents' prayer are inconsistent both with the purposes of the Establishment Clause and with the Establishment Clause itself.

It has been argued that to apply the Constitution in such a way as to prohibit state laws respecting an establishment of religious services in public schools is to indicate a hostility toward religion or toward prayer. Nothing, of course, could be more wrong. The history of man is inseparable from the history of religion. And perhaps it is not too much to say that since the beginning of that history many people have devoutly believed that "More things are wrought with prayer than this world dreams of." It was doubtless largely due to men who believed this that there grew up a sentiment that caused men to leave the crosscurrents of officially established state religions and religious persecution in Europe and come to this country filled with the hope that they could find a place in which they could pray when they pleased to the God of their faith in the language they chose. And there were men of this same faith in the power of prayer who led the fight for adoption of our Constitution and also for our Bill of Rights with the very guarantees of religious freedom that forbid the sort of governmental activity which New York has attempted here. These men knew that the First Amendment, which tried to put an end to governmental control of religion and prayer, was not written to destroy either. They knew rather that it was written to quiet well-justified fears which nearly all of them felt arising out of an awareness that governments of the past had shackled men's tongues to make them speak only the religious thoughts that government wanted them to speak and to pray only to the God that government wanted them to pray to. It is neither sacrilegious nor antireligious to say that each separate government in this country should stay out of the business of writing or sanctioning official prayers and leave that purely religious function to the people themselves and to those the people choose to look to for religious guidance.

It is true that New York's establishment of its Regents' prayer as an officially approved religious doctrine of that State does not amount to a total establishment of one particular religious sect to the exclusion of all others—that, indeed, the government endorsement of that prayer seems relatively insignificant when compared to the governmental encroachments upon religion which were commonplace 200 years ago. To those who may subscribe to the view that because the Regents' official prayer is so brief and general there can be no danger to religious freedom in its governmental establishment, however, it may be appropriate to say in the words of James Madison, the author of the First Amendment:

> "[I]t is proper to take alarm at the first experiment on our liberties. . . . Who does not see that the same authority which can establish Christianity, in exclusion of all other Religions, may establish with the same ease any particular sect of Christians, in exclusion of all other Sects? That the same authority which can force a citizen to contribute three pence only of his property for the support of any one establishment, may force him to conform to any other establishment in all cases whatsoever?"

The judgment of the Court of Appeals of New York is reversed and the cause remanded for further proceedings not inconsistent with this opinion.

Reversed and remanded.

2. Prayer and Bible Reading

SCHOOL DISTRICT OF ABINGTON TOWNSHIP v. SCHEMPP
MURRAY v. CURLETT

Supreme Court of the United States, 1963
374 U.S. 203

MR. JUSTICE CLARK delivered the opinion of the Court.

* * * These companion cases present the issues in the context of state action requiring that schools begin each day with readings from the Bible. While raising the basic questions under slightly different factual situations, the cases permit joint treatment. In light of the history of the First Amendment and of our cases interpreting and applying its requirements, we hold that the practices at issue and the laws requiring them are unconstitutional under the Establishment Clause, as applied to the States through the Fourteenth Amendment.

* * * The Commonwealth of Pennsylvania by law * * * requires that "At least ten verses from the Holy Bible shall be read, without comment, at the opening of each public school on each school day. Any child shall be excluded from such Bible reading, or attending such Bible reading, upon the written request of his parent or guardian." The Schempp family, husband and wife and two of their three children, brought suit to enjoin enforcement of the statute * * * . A three-judge statutory District Court for the Eastern District of Pennsylvania held that the statute is violative of the Establishment Clause of the First Amendment as applied to the States by the Due Process Clause of the Fourteenth Amendment and directed that appropriate injunctive relief issue. * * *

The appellees Edward Lewis Schempp, his wife Sidney, and their children, Roger and Donna, are of the Unitarian faith and are members of the Unitarian Church in Germantown, Philadelphia, Pennsylvania, where they * * * regularly attend religious services. * * *

On each school day at the Abington Senior High School between 8:15 and 8:30 a.m., while the pupils are attending their home rooms or advisory sections, opening exercises are conducted pursuant to the statute. The exercises are broadcast into each room in the school building through an intercommunications system and are conducted under the supervision of a teacher by students attending the school's radio and television workshop.

Selected students from this course gather each morning in the school's work-shop studio for the exercises, which include readings by one of the students of 10 verses of the Holy Bible, broadcast to each room in the building. This is followed by the recitation of the Lord's Prayer, likewise over the intercommunications system, but also by the students in the various classrooms, who are asked to stand and join in repeating the prayer in unison. The exercises are closed with the flag salute and such pertinent announcements as are of interest to the students. Participation in the opening exercises, as directed by the statute, is voluntary. The student reading the verses from the Bible may select the passages and read from any version he chooses, although the only copies furnished by the school are the King James version, copies of which are circulated to each teacher by the school district. During the period in which the exercises have been conducted the King James, the Douay and the Revised Standard versions of the Bible have been used, as well as the Jewish Holy Scriptures. There are no prefatory statements, no questions asked or solicited, no comments or explanations made and no interpretations given at or during the exercises. The students and parents are advised that the student may absent himself from the classroom or, should he elect to remain, not participate in the exercises.

* * *

At the first trial Edward Schempp and the children testified as to specific religious doctrines purveyed by a literal reading of the Bible "which are contrary to the religious beliefs which they held and to their familial teaching." * * * The children testified that all of the doctrines to which they referred were read to them at various times as part of the exercises. Edward Schempp testified at the second trial that he had considered having Roger and Donna excused from attendance at the exercise but decided against it for several reasons, including his belief that the children's relationships with their teachers and classmates would be adversely affected.

* * *

In 1905 the Board of School Commissioners of Baltimore City adopted a rule * * * . The rule provided for the holding of opening exercises in the schools of the city, consisting primarily of the "reading, without comment, of a chapter in the Holy Bible and/or the use of the Lord's Prayer." The petitioners, Mrs. Madalyn Murray and her son, William J. Murray III, are both professed atheists. Following unsuccessful attempts to have the respondent school board rescind the rule, this suit was filed for mandamus to compel its recision and cancellation. It was alleged that William was a student in a public school of the city and Mrs. Murray, his mother, was a taxpayer therein; that it was the practice under the rule to have a reading on each school morning from the King James version of the Bible; that at petitioners' insistence the rule was amended to permit children to be excused from the exercise on request of the parent and that William had been excused pursuant thereto; that nevertheless the rule as amended was in violation of the petitioners' rights to "freedom of religion under the First and Fourteenth Amendments" and in violation of "the principle of separation between church and state, contained therein. . . ." The petition particularized the petitioners' atheistic beliefs and stated that the rule, as practiced, violated their rights:

> "in that it threatens their religious liberty by placing a premium on belief as against non-belief and subjects their freedom of conscience to the rule of the majority; it pronounces belief in God as the source of all moral and spiritual values, equating these values with religious values, and thereby renders sinister, alien and suspect the beliefs and ideals of your Petitioners, promoting doubt and question of their morality, good citizenship and good faith."

* * * The Maryland Court of Appeals affirmed, the majority of four justices holding the exercise not in violation of the First and Fourteenth Amendments, with three justices dissenting. * * *

* * *

The wholesome "neutrality" of which this Court's cases speak * * * stems from a recognition of the teachings of history that powerful sects or groups might bring about a fusion of governmental and religious functions or a concert of dependency of one upon the other to the end that official support of the State or Federal Government would be placed behind the tenets of one or of all orthodoxies. This the Establishment Clause prohibits. And a further reason for neutrality is found in the Free Exercise Clause, which recognizes the value of religious training, teaching and observance and, more particularly, the right of every person to freely choose his own course with reference thereto, free of any compulsion from the state. This the Free Exercise Clause guarantees. Thus, as we have seen, the two clauses may overlap. As we have indicated, the Establishment Clause has been directly considered by this Court eight times in the past score of years and, with only one Justice dissenting on the point, it has consistently held that the clause withdrew all legislative power respecting religious belief or the expression thereof. The test may be stated as follows: what are the purpose and the primary effect of the enactment? If either is the advancement or inhibition of religion, then the enactment exceeds the scope of legislative power as circumscribed by the Constitution. That is to say that to withstand the strictures of the Establishment Clause there must be a secular legislative purpose and a primary effect that neither advances nor inhibits religion.

Applying the Establishment Clause principles to the cases at bar we find that the States are requiring the selection and reading at the opening of the school day of verses from the Holy Bible and the recitation of the Lord's Prayer by the students in unison. These exercises are prescribed as part of the curricular activities of students who are required by law to attend school. They are held in the school buildings under the supervision and with the participation of teachers employed in those schools. * * * The trial court * * * has found that such an opening exercise is a religious ceremony and was intended by the State to be so. We agree with the trial court's finding as to the religious character of the exercises. Given that finding, the exercises and the law requiring them are in violation of the Establishment Clause.

* * *

It is insisted that unless these religious exercises are permitted a "religion of secularism" is established in the schools. We agree of course that the State may not establish a "religion of secularism" in the sense of affirmatively opposing or showing hostility to religion, thus "preferring those who believe in no religion over those who do believe." * * * We do not agree, however, that this decision in any sense has that effect. In addition, it might well be said that one's education is not complete without a study of comparative religion or the history of religion and its relationship to the advancement of civilization. It certainly may be said that the Bible is worthy of study for its literary and historic qualities. Nothing we have said here indicates that such study of the Bible or of religion, when presented objectively as part of a secular program of education, may not be effected consistently with the First Amendment. But the exercises here do not fall into those categories. They are religious exercises, required by the States in violation of the command of the First Amendment that the Government maintain strict neutrality, neither aiding nor opposing religion.

* * *

The place of religion in our society is an exalted one, achieved through a long tradition of reliance on the home, the church and the inviolable citadel of the individual heart and mind. We have come to recognize through bitter experience that it is not within the power of government to invade that citadel, whether its purpose of effect be to aid or oppose, to advance or retard. In the relationship between man and religion, the State is firmly committed to a position of neutrality. Though the application of that rule requires interpretation of a delicate sort, the rule itself is clearly and concisely stated in the words of the First Amendment. * * *

Notes and Questions

Suppose that every child in a public school classroom voted to begin each class with a prayer and Bible reading. Would this lift any constitutional infirmity? Is there a difference if a local school board or state statute authorizes such practices?

American notions regarding the separation of church and state are not shared in many other countries. Religion is still only grudgingly tolerated in countries such as Russia. There is a Church of England and that country's monarch is also the church's head; many Latin countries' laws are based on Catholic Church dogma; and teachings from the Koran not only underpin governmental policy in Islamic countries, but religious leaders often exert enormous political and societal influence. Germany has a voluntary national church tax of 9 percent imposed on income derived from wages and salaries. In recent years, daily, state-sanctioned prayer periods have been allowed in the public schools of Colombia, Finland, Britain, Greece, Libya, Nepal, Pakistan, Romania, Saudi Arabia, Sweden, Thailand, and the two Canadian provinces of Newfoundland and Saskatchewan.

At the time they were rendered, the decisions in *Engel* and *Schempp* were considered to be highly controversial and were widely discussed. Many citizens berated the Court for being Godless, while others applauded the Court's actions. Over the years, the decisions were flouted, often openly, by many public school teachers, administrators, and board members. Opponents of the decisions stimulated debate at the local, state, and national levels of government and attempted to introduce a constitutional amendment that would allow school prayer. To date, these political efforts have not been successful in allowing prayer in the public schools.

Although litigation involving school prayer has continued uninterrupted in the lower courts since *Engel* and *Schempp*, the United States Supreme Court did not directly address the issue again until *Wallace* v. *Jaffree*, 472 U.S. 38 (1985). This six-to-three decision held that the setting aside of classroom time for school-sponsored silent prayer, which was authorized in sixteen states at the time of the decision, was unconstitutional. A careful reading of the decision suggests that allowing for a moment of silence, which was authorized in nine states, may be constitutional. According to Justice O'Connor, who wrote a concurring opinion, the crucial question regarding a moment of silence is "whether the state has conveyed or *attempted* to convey the message that children should use the moment of silence for prayer." The United States Supreme Court again addressed a school prayer issue in *Lee* v. *Weisman* in 1992, in which the Court held that prayers organized by school officials at graduation exercises were unconstitutional and in *Santa Fe Independent School District* v. *Doe* in 2000, which held that student-led, student-initiated prayer at football games violated the Establishment Clause.

A number of forces contribute to the continuing acrimony and hostility surrounding prayer and other religious observances in public schools. One of these forces is the lack of understanding, or the refusal to accept, by some otherwise law-abiding citizens that a Supreme Court decision is the law of the land. Many proponents of school prayer do not accept that a Supreme Court decision must be obeyed until it is changed through specific means such as the passage of an appropriate law by Congress, the Court's overturning its decision, or an amendment to the Constitution. This unwillingness to obey Supreme Court case law is often particularly evident when a significant majority in a homogeneous Christian community (with few Jews or Muslims and perhaps even Catholics), strongly disagree with a decision dealing with separation of church and state. Such majorities at the local or state level often attempt to make permissible, by exerting political pressure, what the Supreme Court has ruled impermissible.

Proponents of prayer in the public schools also have difficulty in understanding what appears to them to be seemingly blatant inconsistencies in public policy and the utterances of some government officials. Such proponents do not understand why "government" does not allow school prayer yet allows legislatures to begin sessions with prayers, the term "God" in the Pledge of Allegiance and on legal tender, taking an oath on a Bible in a court of law, employing chaplains in the military, and allowing churches and church services on military bases. Many proponents also do not understand why prayer is banned in the schools when some high government officials lambast Court prayer decisions and reveal their strong endorsement of school prayer. Unfortunately, such statements by local, state, and federal officials often cause confusion among the public. In fact, such rhetoric may even encourage inadvertent lawlessness at the local level by boards of education, school administrators, teachers, or parents who do not feel compelled to obey a controversial decision, in spirit or in fact, because of such statements.

Also contributing to the confusion over school prayer and related religious issues has been the lack of a clear message from the judiciary regarding the height of the wall that separates church and state. This may be seen in United States Supreme Court split decisions that are rife with strident and often acrimonious dissenting opinions. Conflicting rulings by federal appellate courts also tend to erode confidence in the judiciary as a dependable government authority. For instance, laypersons have had enormous difficulty in understanding why high school seniors were allowed to select fellow students to deliver nonsectarian invocations at their graduation in some parts of the country, but not in others, until the issue was resolved by the Supreme Court's 2000 decision in *Santa Fe Independent School District* v. *Doe*. At the lower court level, clearly unconstitutional prayer and other religious activities in the public schools are occasionally upheld by plaintiffs carefully selecting trial judges; yet, these decisions are often touted by "true believers" as being "the law" during the appellate process and even after these decisions have been reversed.

A large picture of Jesus Christ, which had hung in the hallway of a high school, was found to endorse religion and violate the First Amendment. The court contended that the picture's prominence in the hallway, that it was not part of a larger display, and that it was not incorporated into a class lecture or other context had the effect of endorsing religion in general and Christianity in particular. See *Washegesic* v. *Bloomingdale Public Schools*, 813 F.Supp. 559 (Mich. 1993), *aff'd*, 33 F.3d 679 (6th Cir. 1994). North Dakota's Ten Commandments Law, which required the display of a placard containing the Ten Commandments of the Christian and Jewish religions in a conspicuous place in every classroom, was also held to violate the Establishment Clause of the First Amendment. See *Ring* v. *Grand Forks School District No. 1*, 483 F.Supp. 272 (N.D. 1980). Although a state law that required the posting of the Ten Commandments in public classrooms was upheld by a tie vote of the Kentucky Supreme Court, *Stone* v. *Graham*, 599 S.W.2d 157 (Ky. 1980), this provision was struck down by a five-to-four decision of the United States Supreme Court in 449 U.S. 1104 (1981).

Some proponents of prayer in the public schools contend that Halloween is a pagan festival that has no place in the public schools. This issue was addressed in *Guyer* v. *School Board of Alachua County*, 634 So.2d 806 (Fla. App. 1994), *cert. denied*, 513 U.S. 1044 (1994), where it was alleged that the depiction of witches, cauldrons, and brooms, and the wearing of related costumes was a celebration of the Wiccan religion. The court held that the use of these symbols did not constitute an establishment of religion and that Halloween signified nothing more than the secular celebration of a traditional cultural event.

In another case, Roman Catholic parents objected to the so-called Bedford Program which included such activities as allowing students to play a card game called "Magic: The Gathering," which contained cards containing unrealistic fantasy representations that permitted a player to cast a spell; a teacher's reading a story about Lord Ganesha, a Hindu God; yoga exercises conducted by a presenter in a turban who wore the beard of a Sikh minister; a member of mineralogical society, while discussing rocks, minerals, and fossils, told the students that some people believe crystals (rocks) have supernatural powers; a teacher reading the students an account of the life of Buddha; and having students write poems entitled "How God Messed Up." Aggrieved parents alleged that these activities promoted Satanism, occultism, pagan religions, and New Age Spirituality. In its opinion, the court in *Altman* v. *Bedford Central School District*, 45 F.Supp.2d 368 (N. Y. 1999), held that although these alleged activities may have been offensive to Roman Catholics, these activities did not violate the First Amendment. However, the court did enjoin the school district from having students pray to Mother Earth and engage in the Earth Day Liturgy; promoting Worry Dolls by selling them in the school store or encouraging students to make them in class and use them for relief from worry; and allowing students to make a likeness of a graven image of a god or religious symbol such as Lord Ganesha with his elephant head.

May the singing of Christmas carols with religious significance be prohibited as part of a school program? See *Muka* v. *Sturgis*, 53 App. Div.2d, 383 N.Y.S.2d 933 (App. Div. 1976), which upheld such a prohibition. But see *Citizens Concerned for Separation of Church and State* v. *City and County of Denver*, 508 F.Supp. 823 (Col. 1981), upholding a city's observance of a holiday with religious music, and *Florey* v. *Sioux Falls School*

District 49-5, 619 F.2d 1311 (8th Cir. 1980), *cert. denied*, 449 U.S. 987 (1980), which upheld the presentation of holiday assemblies that contained religious art, literature, and music, as long as such materials were not presented in an attempt to advance or inhibit religion. The decision held that

> Only holidays with both religious and secular bases may be observed; music, art, literature and drama may be included in the curriculum only if presented in a prudent and objective manner and only as part of the cultural and religious heritage of the holiday; and religious symbols may be used only as a teaching aid or resource and only if they are displayed as part of the cultural and religious heritage of the holiday and are temporary in nature. Since all programs and materials authorized by the rules must deal with the secular or cultural basis or heritage of the holidays and since the materials must be presented in a prudent and objective manner and symbols used as a teaching aid, the advancement of a "secular program of education," and not of religion, is the primary effect of the rules. (p. 1317)

However, this court stated that a kindergarten program that was primarily religious in content was unconstitutional.

Prayer issues dealing with governmental agencies other than public schools have also appeared before the judiciary. See *Marsh* v. *Chambers*, 463 U.S. 783 (1983), which upheld the Nebraska legislative practice of opening the day with prayer. Many persons do not understand why this and similar practices by other levels and branches of government are allowed by the Supreme Court, while school prayers are not allowed.

Holiday displays have been the subject of several United States Supreme Court opinions. In *Allegheny County* v. *American Civil Liberties Union*, 492 U.S. 573 (1989), the Court ruled, in a five-to-four vote, that a crèche depicting the Christian nativity scene placed in a county courthouse violated the Establishment Clause of the First Amendment. However, in the same decision, the Court, by a six-to-three margin, upheld a holiday display featuring an 18-foot Chanukah menorah, which was placed just outside a city–county building next to the city's 45-foot decorated Christmas tree and a sign saluting liberty. The combined display, the Court reasoned, was a recognition that both Christmas and Chanukah are part of the same winter-holiday season. Five years earlier, a forty-year practice of having a city-erected Christmas display in a park owned by a nonprofit organization was upheld by the Court. The display included a Santa Claus house, a Christmas tree, a banner that read "Seasons Greetings," and a nativity scene. In its five-to-four decision, the Court contended that, in context, the display did not endorse religion. See *Lynch* v. *Donnelly*, 465 U.S. 668 (1984). In 1995, the Court, in a seven-to-two decision, upheld the right of the Ku Klux Klan to place an unattended cross in a government plaza during the Christmas season. The Court stated that this action on the Klan's part represented private expression and reiterated that private religious speech is as fully protected as secular private expression. The Court ruled that a public forum had been created because the square had been used for over a century for public speeches, gatherings, and festivals advocating and celebrating a variety of causes, both secular and religious. Finally, the Court held that religious expression does not violate the Establishment Clause when it is (1) purely private and (2) occurs in a traditional or designated public forum, publicly announced and open to all on equal terms. See *Capitol Square Review and Advisory Board* v. *Pinette*, 515 U.S. 753 (1995). These seemingly contradictory decisions and the often acrimonious language in the individual opinions reveal a wide divergence among several of the justices regarding separation of church and state issues.

In response to the United States Supreme Court's decision in *Employment Division, Department of Human Resources of Oregon* v. *Smith*, 494 U.S. 872 (1990), which held that a state did not violate a Native American's free exercise rights by refusing him employment benefits for smoking peyote as part of his religious observances, Congress passed the Religious Freedom Restoration Act (RFRA) in 1993. This law was designed to make it more difficult for state and local governments to limit an individual's free exercise of religion. However, the RFRA was held to be unconstitutional in *City of Boerne* v. *Flores*, 521 U.S. 507 (1997). The Court held that Congress overstepped its authority by improperly expanding the scope of the First Amendment's guarantee of the free exercise of religion. The Court contended that the law's sweeping coverage ensured its intrusion at every level of government and made almost any governmental action or law subject to challenge by any individual who alleged a substantial burden on his or her free exercise of religion. Additionally, the Court emphasized that Congress cannot change the meaning of the Constitution by merely passing an ordinary statute or by doing so telling the judiciary how to decide cases.

Many court decisions that forced school officials to allow religious practices with which they were in disagreement were rendered by applying the Religious Freedom Restoration Act before it was held to be unconstitutional. In one of these decisions, *Cheema* v. *Thompson*, 67 F.3d 883 (9th Cir. 1995), the court allowed male Sikh students to wear a kirpan, a 6½–7-inch curved, dull-edged ceremonial dagger worn in a sheath, which hangs around the neck and under clothing, even though the school had a no-weapons policy.

The RFRA also created many problems in nonschool settings such as prisons. Under their interpretation of the RFRA, some prisoners demanded to be able to have sex because their reading of the scriptures told them to procreate. Others wanted certain dietary food, in one instance steak and lobster, based on their religion. These and similar, often bizarre, requests permeated every level of government before the law was held to be unconstitutional.

Court decisions have not banned Bible reading for nonsectarian reasons, such as the teaching of the history of religions and the study of comparative religions. Yet, many parents have contended that fear of lawsuits has been responsible for public school educators seemingly excluding religion from the curriculum, thereby providing the perception that schools exhibit a hostility toward religion. In an effort to counter such perceptions, several states have launched efforts to adopt books that promote teaching about religion or have endorsed plans to teach more about religion. Some observers have referred to this as a return to the "Fourth R." Proponents contend that such programs, in addition to imparting useful knowledge, will also promote understanding and heightened sensitivity toward all religions. Opponents view such programs as being fraught with potential controversies such as the fear that the dominant local religions will receive preferential treatment and whether teachers will be able to provide "religiously correct" answers to such potentially difficult student questions as Did Jews kill Jesus? Did God really part the Red Sea? Do non-Christians go to hell? Why have people killed each other in the name of religion? Do all religions condemn homosexuality, divorce, or unmarried couples living together?

Does your state or local school system have provisions for school-sponsored teaching about religion, Bible reading or prayer, Bible study, silent prayer, meditation, voluntary prayer, or observance of religious holidays? Will noncompliance with statutory provisions prohibiting Bible reading or prayer result in any penalties in your state?

3. Prayers at Graduation Exercises and other Public School-Sponsored Activities

Many courts have been asked to rule on the constitutionality of invocations and benedictions at graduation exercises and prayer at other school-sponsored activities outside the classroom such as football games, school assemblies, team prayers at the end of games and practices and prior to band concerts and practices. In a dramatic five-to-four decision, which revealed a deep split among the justices, the United States Supreme Court in *Lee v. Weisman* ruled that prayers mandated or organized by school officials at graduation exercises were unconstitutional.

a. Prayer at Graduation Exercises

LEE v. WEISMAN
Supreme Court of the United States, 1992
505 U. S. 577

JUSTICE KENNEDY delivered the opinion of the Court.

School principals in the public school system of the city of Providence, Rhode Island, are permitted to invite members of the clergy to offer invocation and benediction prayers as part of the formal graduation ceremonies for middle schools and for high schools. The question before us is whether including clerical members who offer prayers as part of the official school graduation ceremony is consistent with the Religion Clauses of the First Amendment, provisions the Fourteenth Amendment makes applicable with full force to the States and their school districts.

Deborah Weisman graduated from Nathan Bishop Middle School, a public school in Providence, at a formal ceremony in June 1989. She was about 14 years old. For many years it has been the policy of the Providence School Committee and the Superintendent of Schools to permit principals to invite members of the clergy to give invocations and benedictions at middle school and high school graduations. Many, but not all, of the principals elected to include prayers as part of the graduation ceremonies. Acting for himself and his daughter, Deborah's father, Daniel Weisman, objected to any prayers at Deborah's middle school graduation, but to no avail. The school principal, petitioner Robert E. Lee, invited a rabbi to deliver prayers at the graduation exercises for Deborah's class. Rabbi Leslie Gutterman, of the Temple Beth El in Providence, accepted.

It has been the custom of Providence school officials to provide invited clergy with a pamphlet entitled "Guidelines for Civic Occasions," prepared by the National Conference of Christians and Jews. The Guidelines recommend that public prayers of nonsectarian civic ceremonies be composed with "inclusiveness and sensitivity," though they acknowledge that "[p]rayer of any kind may be inappropriate on some civic occasions." The principal gave Rabbi Gutterman the pamphlet before the graduation and advised him the invocation and benediction should be nonsectarian.

Rabbi Gutterman's prayers were as follows:

"INVOCATION

"God of the Free, Hope of the Brave:

"For the legacy of America where diversity is celebrated and the rights of minorities are protected, we thank You. May these young men and women grow up to enrich it.

"For the liberty of America, we thank You. May these new graduates grow up to guard it.

"For the political process of America in which all its citizens may participate, for its court system where all may seek justice we thank You. May those we honor this morning always turn to it in trust.

"For the destiny of America we thank You. May the graduates of Nathan Bishop Middle School so live that they might help to share it.

"May our aspirations for our country and for these young people, who are our hope for the future, be richly fulfilled.

"AMEN"

"BENEDICTION

"O God, we are grateful to You for having endowed us with the capacity for learning which we have celebrated on this joyous commencement.

"Happy families give thanks for seeing their children achieve an important milestone. Send Your blessings upon the teachers and administrators who helped prepare them.

"The graduates now need strength and guidance for the future, help them to understand that we are not complete with academic knowledge alone. We must each strive to fulfill what You require of us all: To do justly, to love mercy, to walk humbly.

"We give thanks to You, Lord, for keeping us alive, sustaining us and allowing us to reach this special, happy occasion.

"AMEN"

* * *

The case was submitted on stipulated facts. The District Court held that petitioners' practice of including invocations and benedictions in public school graduations violated the Establishment Clause of the First Amendment, and it enjoined petitioners from continuing the practice. The court applied the three-part Establishment Clause test set forth in *Lemon* v. *Kurtzman*. Under that test as described in our past cases, to satisfy the Establishment Clause a governmental practice must (1) reflect a clearly secular purpose; (2) have a primary effect that neither advances nor inhibits religion; and (3) avoid excessive government entanglement with religion. * * * The District Court held that petitioners' actions violated the second part of the test, and so did not address either the first or the third. The court decided, based on its reading of our precedents, that the effects test of *Lemon* is violated whenever government action "creates an identification of the state with a religion, or with religion in general," or when "the effect of the governmental action is to endorse one religion over another, or to endorse religion in general." The court determined that the practice of including invocations and benedictions, even so-called nonsectarian ones, in public school graduations creates an identification of governmental power with religious practice, endorses religion, and violates the Establishment Clause. * * *

* * *

These dominant facts mark and control the confines of our decision: State officials direct the performance of a formal religious exercise at promotional and graduation ceremonies for secondary schools. Even for those students who object to the religious exercise, their attendance and participation in the state-sponsored religious activity are in a fair and real sense obligatory, though the school district does not require attendance as a condition for receipt of the diploma.

This case does not require us to revisit the difficult questions dividing us in recent cases, questions of the definition and full scope of the principles governing the extent of permitted accommodation by the State for the religious beliefs and practices of many of its citizens. See *Allegheny County* v. *Greater Pittsburgh ACLU*; *Wallace* v. *Jaffree*; *Lynch* v. *Donnelly*. For without reference to those principles in other contexts, the controlling precedents as they relate to prayer and religious exercise in primary and secondary public schools compel the holding here that the policy of the city of Providence is an unconstitutional one. We can decide the case without reconsidering the general constitutional framework by which public schools' efforts to accommodate religion are measured. Thus we do not accept the invitation of petitioners and *amicus* the United States to reconsider our decision in *Lemon v. Kurtzman, supra*. The government involvement with religious activity in this case is pervasive, to the point of creating a state-sponsored and state-directed religious exercise in a public school. Conducting this formal religious observance conflicts with settled rules pertaining to prayer exercises for students, and that suffices to determine the question before us.

The principle that government may accommodate the free exercise of religion does not supersede that fundamental limitations imposed by the Establishment Clause. It is beyond dispute that, at a minimum, the Constitution guarantees that government may not coerce anyone to support or participate in religion or its exercise, or otherwise act in a way which "establishes a [state] religion or religious faith, or tends to do so." * * *

* * *

We are asked to recognize the existence of a practice of nonsectarian prayer, prayer within the embrace of what is known as the Judeo-Christian tradition, prayer which is more acceptable than one which, for example, makes explicit references to the God of Israel, or to Jesus Christ, or to a patron saint. There may be some support, as an empirical observation, to the statement of the Court of Appeals for the Sixth Circuit, picked up by Judge Campbell's dissent in the Court of Appeals in this case, that there has emerged in this country a civic religion, one which is tolerated when sectarian exercises are not. * * *

The First Amendment's Religion Clauses mean that religious beliefs and religious expression are too precious to be either proscribed or prescribed by the State. The design of the Constitution is that preservation and transmission of religious beliefs and worship is a responsibility and a choice committed to the private sphere, which itself is promised freedom to pursue that mission. It must not be forgotten then, that while concern must be given to define the protection granted to an objector or a dissenting nonbeliever, these same Clauses exist to protect religion from government interferences. * * *

* * *

The lessons of the First Amendment are as urgent in the modern world as in the 18th Century when it was written. One timeless lesson is that if citizens are subjected to state-sponsored religious exercises, the State disavows its own duty to guard and respect that sphere of inviolable conscience and belief which is the mark of a free people. To compromise that principle today would be to deny our own tradition and forfeit our standing to urge others to secure the protections of that tradition for themselves.

As we have observed before, there are heightened concerns with protecting freedom of conscience from subtle coercive pressure in the elementary and secondary public schools. * * * Our decisions in *Engel* v. *Vitale* and

Abington School District, supra, recognize, among other things, that prayer exercises in public schools carry a particular risk of indirect coercion. * * * See *Allegheny County* v. *Greater Pittsburgh ACLU.* What to most believers may seem nothing more than a reasonable request that the nonbeliever respect their religious practices, in a school context may appear to the nonbeliever or dissenter to be an attempt to employ the machinery of the State to enforce a religious orthodoxy.

We need not look beyond the circumstances of this case to see the phenomenon at work. The undeniable fact is that the school district's supervision and control of a high school graduation ceremony places public pressure, as well as peer pressure, on attending students to stand as a group or, at least, maintain respectful silence during the Invocation and Benediction. This pressure, though subtle, and indirect, can be as real as any overt compulsion. * * * There can be no doubt that for many, if not most, of the students at the graduation, the act of standing or remaining silent was an expression of participation in the Rabbi's prayer. That was the very point of the religious exercise. It is of little comfort to a dissenter, then, to be told that for her the act of standing or remaining in silence signifies mere respect, rather than participation. What matters is that, given our social conventions, a reasonable dissenter in this milieu could believe that the group exercise signified her own participation or approval of it.

Finding no violation under these circumstances would place objectors in the dilemma of participating, with all that implies, or protesting. We do not address whether that choice is acceptable if the affected citizens are mature adults, but we think the State may not, consistent with the Establishment Clause, place primary and secondary school children in this position. Research in psychology supports the common assumption that adolescents are often susceptible to pressure from their peers towards conformity, and that the influence is strongest in matters of social convention. * * * To recognize that the choice imposed by the State constitutes an unacceptable constraint only acknowledges that the government may no more use social pressure to enforce orthodoxy than it may use more direct means.

The injury caused by the government's action, and the reason why Daniel and Deborah Weisman object to it, is that the State, in a school setting, in effect required participation in a religious exercise. It is, we concede, a brief exercise during which the individual can concentrate on joining its message, meditate on her own religion, or let her mind wander. But the embarrassment and the intrusion of the religious exercise cannot be refuted by arguing that these prayers, and similar ones to be said in the future, are of a *de minimis* character. To do so would be an affront to the Rabbi who offered them and to all those for whom the prayers were an essential and profound recognition of divine authority. And for the same reason, we think that the intrusion is greater than the two minutes or so of time consumed for prayers like these. * * *

* * *

True, Deborah could elect not to attend commencement without renouncing her diploma; but we shall not allow the case to turn on this point. Everyone knows that in our society and in our culture high school graduation is one of life's most significant occasions. A school rule which excuses attendance is beside the point. Attendance may not be required by official decree, yet it is apparent that a student is not free to absent herself from the graduation exercise in any real sense of the term "voluntary," for absence would require forfeiture of those intangible benefits which have motivated the student through youth and all her high school years. Graduation is a time for family and those closest to the student to celebrate success and express mutual wishes of gratitude and respect, all to the end of impressing upon the young person the role that it is his or her right and duty to assume in the community and all of its diverse parts.

The importance of the event is the point the school district and the United States rely upon to argue that a formal prayer ought to be permitted, but it becomes one of the principal reasons why their argument must fail. Their contention, one of considerable force were it not for the constitutional constraints applied to state action, is that the prayers are an essential part of these ceremonies because for many persons an occasion of this significance lacks meaning if there is no recognition, however brief, that human achievements cannot be understood apart from their spiritual essence. We think the Government's position that this interest suffices to force students to choose between compliance or forfeiture demonstrates fundamental inconsistency in its argumentation. It fails to acknowledge that what for many of Deborah's classmates and their parents was a spiritual imperative was for Daniel and Deborah Weisman religious conformance compelled by the State. While in some societies the wishes of the majority might prevail, the Establishment Clause of the First Amendment is addressed to this contingency and rejects the balance urged upon us. The Constitution forbids the State to exact religious conformity from a student as the price of attending her own high school graduation. This is the calculus the Constitution commands.

The Government's argument gives insufficient recognition to the real conflict of conscience faced by the young student. The essence of the Government's position is that with regard to a civic, social occasion of this importance it is the objector, not the majority, who must take unilateral and private action to avoid compromising religious scruples, here by electing to miss the graduation exercise. This turns conventional First Amendment analysis on its head. It is a tenet of the First Amendment that the State cannot require one of its citizens to forfeit his or her rights and benefits as the price of resisting conformance to state-sponsored religious practice. To say that a student must remain apart from the ceremony at the opening invocation and closing benediction is to risk compelling conformity in an environment analogous to the classroom setting, where, we have said the risk of compulsion is especially high. * * *

Inherent differences between the public school system and a session of a State Legislature distinguish this case from *Marsh* v. *Chambers*. The considerations we have raised in objection to the invocation and benediction are in many respects similar to the arguments we considered in *Marsh*. But there are also obvious differences. The atmosphere at the opening of a session of a state legislature where adults are free to enter and leave with little comment and for any number of reasons cannot compare with the constraining potential of the one school event most important to the student to attend. The influence and force of a formal exercise in a school graduation are far greater than the prayer exercise we condoned in *Marsh*. At a high school graduation, teachers and principals must and do retain a high degree of control over the precise contents of the program, the speeches, the timing, the movements, the dress, and the decorum of the students. * * * In this atmosphere the state-imposed character of an invocation and benediction by clergy selected by the school combine to make the prayer a state-sanctioned religious exercise in which the student was left with no alternative but to submit. This is different from *Marsh* and suffices to make the religious exercise a First Amendment violation. * * *

We do not hold that every state action implicating religion is invalid if one or a few citizens find it offensive. People may take offense at all manner of religious as well as nonreligious messages, but offense alone does not in every case show a violation. We know too that sometimes to endure social isolation or even anger may be the price of conscience or nonconformity. But, by any reading of our cases, the conformity required of the student in this case was too high an exaction to withstand the test of the Establishment Clause. The prayer exercises in this case are especially improper because the State has in every practical sense compelled attendance and participation in an explicit religious exercise at an event of singular importance to every student, one the objecting student had no real alternative to avoid.

* * *

Our society would be less than true to its heritage if it lacked abiding concern for the values of its young people, and we acknowledge the profound belief of adherents to many faiths that there must be a place in the student's life for precepts of a morality higher even than the law we today enforce. We express no hostility to those aspirations, nor would our oath permit us to do so. A relentless and all-pervasive attempt to exclude religion from every aspect of public life could itself become inconsistent with the Constitution. * * * We recognize that, at graduation time and throughout the course of the educational process, there will be instances when religious values, religious practices, and religious persons will have some interaction with the public schools and their students. * * * But these matters, often questions of accommodation of religion, are not before us. The sole question presented is whether a religious exercise may be conducted at a graduation ceremony in circumstances where, as we have found, young graduates who object are induced to conform. No holding by this Court suggests that a school can persuade or compel a student to participate in a religious exercise. That is being done here, and it is forbidden by the Establishment Clause of the First Amendment.

For the reasons we have stated, the judgment of the Court of Appeals is

Affirmed.

JUSTICE SCALIA, with whom THE CHIEF JUSTICE, JUSTICE WHITE, and JUSTICE THOMAS join, dissenting.

Three Terms ago, I joined an opinion recognizing that the Establishment Clause must be construed in light of the "[g]overnment policies of accommodation, acknowledgment, and support for religion [that] are an accepted part of our political and cultural heritage." That opinion affirmed that "the meaning of the Clause is to be determined by reference to historical practices and understandings." It said that "[a] test for implementing the protections of the Establishment Clause that, if applied with consistency, would invalidate longstanding traditions cannot be a proper reading of the Clause." *Allegheny County* v. *Greater Pittsburgh ACLU.*

These views of course prevent me from joining today's opinion, which is conspicuously bereft of any reference to history. In holding that the Establishment Clause prohibits invocations and benedictions at public-school graduation ceremonies, the Court—with nary a mention that it is doing so—lays waste a tradition that is as old as public-school graduation ceremonies themselves, and that is a component of an even more longstanding American tradition of nonsectarian prayer to God at public celebrations generally. As its instrument of destruction, the bulldozer of its social engineering, the Court invents a boundless, and boundlessly manipulable, test of psychological coercion, * * * Today's opinion shows more forcefully than volumes of argumentation why our Nation's protection, that fortress which is our Constitution, cannot possibly rest upon the changeable philosophical predilections of the Justices of this Court, but must have deep foundations in the historic practices of our people.

* * *

The history and tradition of our nation are replete with public ceremonies featuring prayers of thanksgiving and petition. * * *

From our Nation's origin, prayer has been a prominent part of governmental ceremonies and proclamations. * * *

* * *

The other two branches of the Federal Government also have a long-established practice of prayer at public events. As we detailed in *Marsh,* Congressional sessions have opened with a chaplain's prayer ever since the First Congress. And this Court's own sessions have opened with the invocation "God save the United States and this Honorable Court" since the days of Chief Justice Marshall. * * *

In addition to this general tradition of prayer at public ceremonies, there exists a more specific tradition of invocations and benedictions at public-school graduation exercises. * * * As the Court obliquely acknowledges in describing the "customary features" of high school graduations, and as respondents do not contest, the invocation and benediction have long been recognized to be "as traditional as any other parts of the [school] graduation program and are widely established." * * *

The Court presumably would separate graduation invocations and benedictions from other instances of public "preservation and transmission of religious beliefs" on the ground that they involve "psychological coercion." I find it a sufficient embarrassment that our Establishment Clause jurisprudence regarding holiday displays, see *Allegheny County* v. *Greater Pittsburgh ACLU*, has come to "requir[e] scrutiny more commonly associated with interior decorators than with the judiciary." * * * But interior decorating is a rock-hard science compared to psychology practiced by amateurs. A few citations of "[r]esearch in psychology" that have no particular bearing upon the precise issue here, cannot disguise the fact that the Court has gone beyond the realm where judges know what they are doing. The Court's argument that state officials have "coerced" students to take part in the invocation and benediction at graduation ceremonies is, not to put too fine a point on it, incoherent.

* * *

The Court declares that students' "attendance and participation in the [invocation and benediction] are in a fair and real sense obligatory." But what exactly is this "fair and real sense"? According to the Court, students at graduation who want "to avoid the fact or appearance of participation," in the invocation and benediction are *psychologically* obligated by "public pressure, as well as peer pressure, . . . to stand as a group or, at least, maintain respectful silence" during those prayers. This assertion—*the very linchpin of the Court's opinion*—is almost as intriguing for what it does not say as for what it says. It does not say, for example, that students are psychologically coerced to bow their heads, place their hands in a Dürer-like prayer position, pay attention to the prayers, utter "Amen," or in fact pray. (Perhaps further intensive psychological research remains to be done on these matters.) It claims only that students are psychologically coerced "to stand . . . or, at least, maintain respectful silence." * * *

* * *

The opinion manifests that the Court itself has not given careful consideration to its test of psychological coercion. For if it had, how could it observe, with no hint of concern or disapproval, that students stood for the Pledge of Allegiance, which immediately preceded Rabbi Gutterman's invocation? The government can, of course, no more coerce political orthodoxy than religious orthodoxy. *West Virginia Board of Education* v. *Barnette*. Moreover, since the Pledge of Allegiance has been revised since *Barnette* to include the phrase "under God," recital of the Pledge would appear to raise the same Establishment Cause issue as the invocation and benediction. If students were psychologically coerced to remain standing during the invocation, they must also have been psychologically coerced, moments before, to stand for (and thereby, in the Court's view, take part in or appear to take part in) the Pledge.

* * *

The other "dominant fac[t]" identified by the Court is that "[s]tate officials direct the performance of a formal religious exercise" at school graduation ceremonies. * * * All the record shows is that principals of the Providence public schools, acting within their delegated authority, have invited clergy to deliver invocations and benedictions at graduations; and that Principal Lee invited Rabbi Gutterman, provided him a two-page flyer, prepared by the National Conference of Christians and Jews, giving general advice on inclusive prayer for civic occasions, and advised him that his prayers at graduation should be nonsectarian. How these facts can fairly be transformed into the charges that Principal Lee "directed and controlled the content of [Rabbi Gutterman's] prayer," that school officials "monitor prayer," and attempted to " 'compose official prayers,' " and that the "government involvement with religious activity in this case is pervasive," is difficult to fathom.

* * *

The deeper flaw in the Court's opinion does not lie in its wrong answer to the question whether there was state-induced "peer-pressure" coercion; it lies, rather, in the Court's making violation of the Establishment Clause hinge on such a precious question. The coercion that was a hallmark of historical establishments of religion was coercion of religious orthodoxy and of financial support by *force of law and threat of penalty*. Typically, attendance at the state church was required; only clergy of the official church could lawfully perform sacraments; and dissenters, if tolerated, faced an array of civil disabilities. * * *

The Establishment Clause was adopted to prohibit such an establishment of religion at the federal level (and to protect state establishments of religion from federal interference). * * *

Thus, while I have no quarrel with the Court's general proposition that the Establishment Clause "guarantees that government may not coerce anyone to support or participate in religion or its exercise," I see no warrant for expanding the concept of coercion beyond acts backed by threat of penalty—a brand of coercion that, happily, is readily discernible to those of us who have made a career of reading the disciples of Blackstone rather than of Freud. * * *

* * *

Our religion-clause jurisprudence has become bedeviled (so to speak) by reliance on formulaic abstractions that are not derived from, but positively conflict with, our long-accepted constitutional traditions. Foremost among these has been the so-called *Lemon* test, see *Lemon* v. *Kurtzman*, which has received well-earned criticism from many members of this Court. * * * The Court today demonstrates the irrelevance of *Lemon* by essentially ignoring it, and the interment of that case may be the one happy byproduct of the Court's otherwise lamentable decision. Unfortunately, however, the Court has replaced *Lemon* with its psycho-coercion test, which suffers the double disability of having no roots whatever in our people's historic practice, and being as infinitely expandable as the reasons for psychotherapy itself.

Another happy aspect of the case is that it is only a jurisprudential disaster and not a practical one. Given the odd basis for the Court's decision, invocations and benedictions will be able to be given at public-school graduations next June, as they have for the past century and a half, so long as school authorities make clear that anyone who abstains from screaming in protest does not necessarily participate in the prayers. All that is seemingly needed is an announcement, or perhaps a written insertion at the beginning of the graduation Program, to the effect that, while all are asked to rise for the invocation and benediction, none is compelled to join in them, nor will be assumed, by rising, to have done so. That obvious fact recited, the graduates and their parents may proceed to thank God, as Americans have always done, for the blessings He has generously bestowed on them and on their country.

* * *

Notes and Questions

Many observers thought that due to several personnel changes on the Court, this decision would become a vehicle for changing the legal rules regarding prayer in public schools. Rather, in addition to clearly revealing the basic philosophic differences regarding this issue, the majority, concurring, and dissenting opinions also expose the high degree of acrimony among the justices. Although seeming not to be abandoning the *Lemon* test, does the decision tacitly usher in a coercion test? Under the *Lemon* test, to satisfy the Establishment Clause, a governmental practice must (1) reflect a clearly secular purpose; (2) have a primary effect that neither advances nor inhibits religion; and (3) avoid excessive entanglement with religion.

Justice Anthony Kennedy, who wrote the majority opinion in *Lee*, had been in private practice and a member of the United States Court of Appeals for the Ninth Circuit before being appointed to the Supreme Court by President Ronald Reagan in 1987. Joining Justice Kennedy in the decision were Justices Blackmun, Stevens, O'Connor, and Souter. Justice Blackmun was appointed to the Court by President Richard Nixon in 1970 and retired in 1994. He was replaced in 1994 by Stephen Breyer, who had been chief judge of the United States Court of Appeals for the First Circuit. Justice Stevens had been in private practice and a member of the United States Court of Appeals for the Seventh Circuit before being appointed to the Supreme Court by President Gerald Ford in 1975. Sandra Day O'Connor is the first woman to be appointed a Supreme Court justice. Before her appointment by President Reagan in 1981, she was an assistant attorney general, a state appellate court judge, and a legislator in Arizona. Justice David Souter was appointed to the Court by President Bush in 1990. He had been state attorney general and a member of the New Hampshire Supreme Court.

Justice Antonin Scalia, who wrote the dissenting opinion in *Lee*, was joined by Chief Justice Rehnquist and Justices White and Thomas. Justice Scalia was appointed by President Reagan in 1986 to replace Justice Rehnquist, who was elevated to the Chief Justiceship. Justice Scalia came to the High Court from the United States Court of Appeals for the District of Columbia. He had been a practicing attorney, law school professor, and an assistant attorney general in the Justice Department. Chief Justice William H. Rehnquist was appointed by President Reagan in 1986 to become the sixteenth Chief Justice of the Supreme Court, replacing Chief Justice Warren Burger. Rehnquist had been an associate justice since 1972. Before his tenure on the Court, he had been a law clerk for Justice Robert Jackson, in private practice, and an assistant attorney general in the Justice Department. Justice Byron "Whizzer" White brought a unique background to the Supreme Court. Justice White was a Phi Beta Kappa, Rhodes scholar, all-American football star at the University of Colorado, professional football player (leading ground gainer in the National Football League in 1938), member of the Football Hall of Fame, decorated naval officer, Supreme Court clerk, lawyer, and a deputy attorney general in the Justice Department. He was the leader of the Citizens for Kennedy in Colorado, and he was appointed to the Court by President Kennedy in 1962. Justice White left the Court in 1993. Justice Clarence Thomas was appointed to the Court by President Bush in 1991. He had been an assistant attorney general in Missouri, Chairman of the Equal Employment Opportunity Commission, and a judge on the United States Court of Appeals for the District of Columbia. His nomination drew intense scrutiny during confirmation hearings related to allegations of sexual harassment, unfitness, and being a right-wing ideologue. Justice Ruth Bader Ginsburg, who replaced Justice White, is the second female on the Court. She has been a law school professor and spent thirteen years on the United States Court of Appeals for the District of Columbia prior to her appointment.

Justice Scalia's dissent contains several remarkable statements whose discussion should enliven class debate. He states that the majority opinion "...lays waste [to a] longstanding American tradition of nonsectarian prayer to God at public celebrations generally." Could not the same argument have been made regarding a long-standing tradition when the Court struck down segregation in the public schools in 1954? He asserts that the Court's decision has replaced the *Lemon* test, yet the majority opinion states ". . . we do not accept the invitation . . . to reconsider *Lemon* . . . ," and affirmed the lower courts' use of the test. Does Justice Scalia suggest that states may establish an official state religion when he asserts "The Establishment Clause was adopted to prohibit such an establishment of religion at the federal level *and to protect state establishments of religion from federal interference*" (emphasis added)? Does Justice Scalia undermine the spirit of the majority decision when he offers a suggestion for circumventing the *Lee* decision whereby school officials could merely insert a disclaimer in the graduation announcement? Does his dissent accurately reflect the view of the majority of Americans on the prayer issue?

b. Prayer at other Public School Activities

In *Santa Fe Independent School District* v. *Doe*, 530 U.S. 290 (2000), the United States Supreme Court, in a six-to-three decision, extended a line of rulings since 1962 barring state-sponsored school prayer by holding that student-led, student-initiated prayer at football games violated the Establishment Clause. In this case, a school policy was challenged that authorized two student elections, the first to determine whether invocations should be delivered at games, and the second to select the spokesperson to deliver them. In its decision, the Court reiterated its language regarding coercion in *Lee* v. *Weisman* that, "at a minimum, the Constitution guarantees that government may not coerce anyone to support or participate in religion or its exercise, or otherwise act in a way that establishes a state religion or religious faith, or tends to do so." Additionally, the Court addressed (1) whether or not the disputed practice was private speech, (2) the district's attempt to introduce prayer at football games by having a student election sanction it, (3) the school districts's attempt to ferret out the plaintiffs' identities, and (4) the district's policy being a sham.

The Court asserted that coercion in this case manifested itself in several ways. Having student elections did not absolve the district from impermissible coercion as it was the district's decision to hold the "constitutionally problematic election." The Court also held that the district's assertion that attendance at a football game was voluntary, unlike graduation, was also unpersuasive, because several groups of students such as cheerleaders, band members (sometimes for class credit) and football players would have to attend games. Also not to be overlooked, the Court maintained, was the genuine desire and immense social pressure to attend "the extracurricular event that is American football." And the Court stated that "The Constitution demands that schools not force on students the difficult choice between whether to attend these games or to risk facing a personally offensive religious ritual."

Giving the invocation at games was not private speech, as the district argued. The Court determined that the invocation was given on school property, at a school-sponsored event, using the school's public address system, by a speaker representing the student body, under the supervision of the faculty, and pursuant to a school policy that explicitly and implicitly encouraged school prayer. The pregame ceremony could not be considered an open forum, the Court reasoned, because the ceremony was not open to indiscriminate use by the student body.

Establishing a student electoral mechanism, the Court held, turned the school into a forum for religious debate and empowered the student majority with the authority to subject students of minority views to constitutionally improper messages. Such a system, the Court stated, undermines the essential protection of minority viewpoints and ". . . encourages divisiveness along religious lines and threatens the imposition of coercion upon these students not desiring to participate in a religious exercise."

The Court also expressed its concern that the plaintiffs, Mormon and Catholic families, needed protection from intimidation and harassment resulting in the district court allowing them to litigate anonymously as "Does" and issuing an order that provided, in part:

> [A]ny further attempt on the part of the District or school administration, officials, counselors, teachers, employees or servants of the School District, parents, students or anyone else, overtly or covertly to ferret out the identities of the Plaintiffs in this cause, by means of bogus petitions, questionnaires, individual interrogation, or downright 'snooping' will cease immediately. ANYONE TAKING ANY ACTION ON SCHOOL PROPERTY, DURING SCHOOL HOURS, OR WITH SCHOOL RESOURCES OR APPROVAL FOR PURPOSES OF ATTEMPTING TO ELICIT THE NAMES OR IDENTITIES OF THE PLAINTIFFS IN THIS CAUSE OF ACTION, BY OR ON BEHALF OF ANY OF THESE INDIVIDUALS, WILL FACE THE HARSHEST POSSIBLE CONTEMPT SANCTIONS FROM THIS COURT, AND MAY ADDITIONALLY FACE CRIMINAL LIABILITY. . . . (pp. 294–95, n. 1)

The strongly worded majority opinion in *Santa Fe* revealed the Court's attitude toward the school district's impermissible attempt to introduce prayer at football games. The Court referred to the policy's sham secular purpose and announced that the district ". . . asks us to pretend that we do not recognize what every Santa Fe High School student understands clearly—that this policy is about prayer. The District further asks us to accept what is obviously untrue: that these messages are necessary to 'solemnize' a football game and that this single-student, year-long position is essential to the protection of student speech."

In this case, the school district obviously reflected the community's values regarding prayer at football games by instituting the policy under which prayers would be given and, when that was challenged, engaged in litigation all the way to the United States Supreme Court. The district clearly revealed that it would fight with all its might to preserve values it considered important. Would you consider the district to be a role model to students by its conduct in this case? To show their displeasure with the *Santa Fe* decision, prayer continued to be offered before 2000 football games in several southern states. Although not student led, the effort was often promoted by local clergy.

Prior to *Santa Fe*, but after *Lee*, two federal appellate courts—the U.S. Court of Appeals for the Fifth and Eleventh Circuits—had upheld the practice of prayers at graduation exercises being initiated by students who had been elected by their classmates. Although prayer at football games was the issue in *Santa Fe*, does the language of the Court suggest that the practice of allowing prayer at graduation is unconstitutional? Prayer at other school-sponsored activities outside the classroom such as school assemblies, team prayers before or at the end of games or practices, and prior to band concerts and practices are also not directly addressed in *Santa Fe*. Does the language in the decision provide sufficient guidance for the permissibility of prayer at such activities?

What has been your school system's policy regarding prayer at graduation or other school-sponsored activities?

B. Equal Access

Many public schools have Bible or other religious study groups that meet on school grounds before, during, or after school. In some instances, they have been recognized as official student-body organizations and have often advertised their activities on bulletin boards or through the school newspaper. Occasionally, such groups meet during an "activity period."

Fearful that official recognition of religious groups would raise separation of church and state issues, some school administrators were reluctant to grant them student-body status. Refusal to grant official recognition often resulted in litigation, and in an attempt to address the issue, Congress in 1984 passed the Equal Access Act.* Under this act, it is unlawful for a public secondary school that receives federal financial assistance and has created a limited open forum to deny recognition of student-initiated groups on the basis of the religious, political, or philosophical content of the speech at meetings. Although faculty members may be present, they may not participate, and outsiders may not control or regularly attend group meetings. The law declares that a limited open forum has been created when one or more noncurricular student groups are allowed to meet on school premises during noninstructional time. A limited open forum is not created when the clubs are curriculum oriented.

Passage of the Equal Access Act did not eliminate controversies surrounding the recognition of religion-oriented clubs by public schools, and

---

*See Appendix D for a partial text of this act.

the issue was addressed by nearly half of the federal appellate courts. In its decision in *Board of Education of the Westside Community Schools* v. *Mergens*, 496 U.S. 226 (1990), the United States Supreme Court in an eight-to-one ruling upheld the constitutionality of the Equal Access Act.

In defining "a limited open forum," the Court stated that such a forum exists when the school "grants an offering to or opportunity for one or more non-curriculum related student groups to meet on school premises during noninstructional time." Under the Equal Access Act, a fair opportunity has been given students who wish to conduct a meeting within its limited forum

> . . . if the school uniformly provides that the meetings are voluntary and student-initiated; are not sponsored by the school, the government, or its agents or employees; do not materially and substantially interfere with the orderly conduct of educational activities within the school; and are not directed, controlled, conducted, or regularly attended by nonschool persons. (p. 236)

A curriculum-related group, the Court revealed, is one that has more than just a tangential or attenuated relationship to courses offered by the school. Such a group directly relates to the school's curriculum if the subject matter of the group is actually taught, or will be taught, in a regularly offered course; if the subject matter of the group concerns the body of courses as a whole; if participation in the group is required for a particular course; or if participation in the group results in academic credit. Examples of such groups might include French club, student government, or band. Normally, groups such as a chess club, stamp collecting club, or a community service club would be considered to be "non-curriculum related student groups."

There is little doubt that the primary intent of the Equal Access Act was to ensure official school recognition for religious student groups; consequently, the Court's decision may be viewed as lowering the so-called wall of separation of church and state by allowing an accommodation to religiously oriented groups. Perhaps not fully recognized at the time of its passage, however, was that the language of the act also protected religious and political groups that may have little local community support, such as Satanists, Skinheads, Homosexuals for Christ, Hemlock Society members, and various nonviolent "gangs." Official school recognition of such politically or religiously oriented student clubs entitles them to be a part of the student activities program. This carries with it access to the school newspaper, bulletin boards, the public address system, and school fairs. Under provisions of the Equal Access Act, the only way these groups may be denied official recognition is by sanctioning only curriculum-related groups or by declining federal funding.

Disputes involving the Equal Access Act have continued since it was passed and upheld in *Mergens*. In one case, a Gay–Straight Alliance club was denied equal access to school facilities. In its ruling in *Colin ex. rel. Colin* v. *Orange Unified School District*, 83 F.Supp.2d 1135 (Cal. 2000) the court ruled that the group could meet on campus. The court reasoned that by recognizing such noncurriculum groups as the Asian Club and Christian Club, the board had established a limited open forum. The court also held that the proposed club was noncurriculum related, nonschool persons did not direct or control the club, the possibility for students to meet informally did not satisfy requirements of the Equal Access Act, and conditioning of recognition upon changes to the club's name and mission statement violated the Act.

In another case, a religious club was not allowed to meet during the lunch period although other clubs could. In addressing this issue, the court, in *Ceniceros* v. *Board of Trustees of the San Diego Unified School District*, 106 F.3d 878 (9th Cir. 1997), reasoned that because no classes were held during the lunch period it was "noninstructional time" within the meaning of the Act and because other clubs met at that time, meetings at lunchtime did not violate the Establishment Clause. In *Hsu* v. *Roslyn Union Free School District No. 3*, 85 F.3d 838 (2nd Cir. 1996), *cert. denied*, 519 U.S. 1040 (1996), the court ruled that a school system should allow the formation of the "Walking on Water" student Bible club although certain club officers had to be Christians who had accepted Jesus Christ as their savior.

The Equal Access Act has been challenged on the grounds that student religiously oriented meetings could be restricted under the Washington state constitution, which barred school officials from permitting religious organizations to meet on school property. A federal appellate court did not agree with this contention and held that states cannot abridge rights granted by a federal law such as the Equal Access Act. See *Garnett* v. *Renton School District No. 403*, 987 F.2d 641 (9th Cir. 1993), *cert. denied*, 510 U.S. 819 (1993).

A set of religious liberty guidelines, addressing the Equal Access Act, was issued by the Department of Education in 1998 included the following:

> The Equal Access Act is designed to ensure that, consistent with the First Amendment, student religious activities are accorded the same access to public school facilities as are student secular activities. Based on decisions of the Federal courts, as well as its interpretations of the Act, the Department of Justice has advised that the Act should be interpreted as providing, among other things, that:
>
> *General provisions*
> Student religious groups at public secondary schools have the same right of access to school facilities as is enjoyed by other comparable student groups. Under the Equal Access Act, a school receiving Federal funds that allows one or more student noncurriculum-related clubs to meet on its premises during noninstructonal time may not refuse access to student religious groups.
>
> *Prayer services and worship exercises covered*
> A meeting, as defined and protected by the Equal Access Act, may include a prayer service, Bible reading, or other worship exercise.

Equal access to means of publicizing meetings
A school receiving Federal funds must allow student groups meeting under the Act to use the school media—including the public address system, the school newspaper, and the school bulletin board—to announce their meetings on the same terms as other noncurriculum-related student groups are allowed to use the school media. Any policy concerning the use of school media must be applied to all noncurriculum-related student groups in a nondiscriminatory manner. Schools, however, may inform students that certain groups are not school sponsored.

Lunchtime and recess covered
A school creates a limited open forum under the Equal Access Act, triggering equal access rights for religious groups, when it allows students to meet during their lunch periods or other noninstructional time during the school day, as well as when it allows students to meet before and after the school day.

Does a potential for faculty conflict present itself if a faculty member, who is merely asked to be present at a group's meeting for maintaining order or for tort liability reasons and who does not participate, objects to such an assignment because of religious or political disagreements with the group's views?

C. The Teaching of Evolution

The famous "Scopes monkey trial" in 1925 focused the nation's attention on the teaching of evolution in the public schools. Although John Scopes was found guilty of teaching evolution, his conviction was overturned on a technicality, and the issue remained relatively dormant until the 1970s. At that time, forces opposed to the teaching of evolution developed a new strategy, which sought to establish that the biblical account of creation is a respectable scientific theory and thus deserves public classroom time for its teaching. Although debated in several legislatures, creationism, as this theory became known, was enacted into law in Arkansas and Louisiana. These statutes were quickly challenged on the basis of their constitutionality. In *Edwards* v. *Aguillard*, a seven-to-two decision, the United States Supreme Court declared the practice as violative of the First Amendment's prohibition against establishment of religion.

EDWARDS v. AGUILLARD
Supreme Court of the United States, 1987
482 U.S. 578

JUSTICE BRENNAN delivered the opinion of the Court.
The question for decision is whether Louisiana's "Balanced Treatment for Creation-Science and Evolution-Science in Public School Instruction" Act (Creationism Act), La. Rev. Stat. Ann. §§ 17:286.1-17:286.7 is facially invalid as violative of the Establishment Clause of the First Amendment.

The Creationism Act forbids the teaching of the theory of evolution in public schools unless accompanied by instruction in "creation science." No school is required to teach evolution or creation science. If either is taught, however, the other must also be taught. The theories of evolution and creation science are statutorily defined as "the scientific evidences for [creation or evolution] and inferences from those scientific evidences."

* * *

It is clear from the legislative history that the purpose of the legislative sponsor, Senator Bill Keith, was to narrow the science curriculum. During the legislative hearings, Senator Keith stated: "My preference would be that neither [creationism nor evolution] be taught." Such a ban on teaching does not promote—indeed, it undermines—the provision of a comprehensive scientific education.

It is equally clear that requiring schools to teach creation science with evolution does not advance academic freedom. The Act does not grant teachers a flexibility that they did not already possess to supplant the present science curriculum with the presentation of theories, besides evolution, about the origin of life. Indeed, the Court of Appeals found that no law prohibited Louisiana public schoolteachers from teaching any scientific theory. * * * As the president of the Louisiana Science Teachers Association testified, "[a]ny scientific concept that's based on established fact can be included in our curriculum already, and no legislation allowing this is necessary." The Act provides Louisiana schoolteachers with no new authority. Thus the stated purpose is not furthered by it.

* * *

Furthermore, the goal of basic "fairness" is hardly furthered by the Act's discriminatory preference for the teaching of creation science and against the teaching of evolution. While requiring that curriculum guides be developed for creation science, the Act says nothing of comparable guides for evolution. * * * Similarly, research services are supplied for creation science but not for evolution. Only "creation scientists" can serve on the panel that supplies the resource services. The Act forbids school boards to discriminate against anyone who "chooses to be a creation scientist" or to teach "creationism," but fails to protect those who choose to teach evolution or any other non-creation science theory, or who refuse to teach creation science.

If the Louisiana legislature's purpose was solely to maximize the comprehensiveness and effectiveness of science instruction, it would have encouraged the teaching of all scientific theories about the origins of humankind. But under the Act's requirements, teachers who were once free to teach any and all facets of this subject are now unable to do so. Moreover, the Act fails even to ensure that creation science will be taught, but instead requires the teaching of this theory only when the theory of evolution is taught. Thus we agree with the Court of Appeals' conclusion that the Act does not serve to protect academic freedom, but has the distinctly different purpose of discrediting "evolution by counterbalancing its teaching at every turn with the teaching of creation science. . . ."

* * *

As in *Stone* and *Abington*, we need not be blind in this case to the legislature's preeminent religious purpose in enacting this statute. There is a historic and contemporaneous link between the teachings of certain religious denominations and the teaching of evolution. It was this link that concerned the Court in *Epperson* v. *Arkansas*, which also involved a facial challenge in a statute regulating the teaching of evolution. In that case, the Court reviewed an Arkansas statute that made it unlawful for an instructor to teach evolution or to use a textbook that referred to this scientific theory. Although the Arkansas antievolution law did not explicitly state its predominant religious purpose, the Court could not ignore that "[t]he statute was a product of the upsurge of 'fundamentalist' religious fervor" that has long viewed this particular scientific theory as contradicting the literal interpretation of the Bible. After reviewing the history of antievolution statutes, the Court determined that "there can be no doubt that the motivation for the [Arkansas] law was the same [as other antievolution statutes]: to suppress the teaching of a theory which, it was thought, 'denied' the divine creation of man." The Court found that there can be no legitimate state interest in protecting particular religions from scientific views "distasteful to them," and concluded "that the First Amendment does not permit the State to require that teaching and learning must be tailored to the principles or prohibitions of any religious sect or dogma." * * *

These same historic and contemporaneous antagonisms between the teachings of certain religious denominations and the teaching of evolution are present in this case. The preeminent purpose of the Louisiana legislature was clearly to advance the religious viewpoint that a supernatural being created humankind. The term "creation science" was defined as embracing this particular religious doctrine by those responsible for the passage of the Creationism Act. Senator Keith's leading expert on creation science, Edward Boudreaux, testified at the legislative hearings that the theory of creation science included belief in the existence of a supernatural creator. * * * Senator Keith also cited testimony from other experts to support the creation science view that "a creator [was] responsible for the universe and everything in it." The legislative history therefore reveals that the term "creation science," as contemplated by the legislature that adopted this Act, embodies the religious belief that a supernatural creator was responsible for the creation of mankind.

Furthermore, it is not happenstance that the legislature required the teaching of a theory that coincided with this religious view. The legislative history documents that the Act's primary purpose was to change the science curriculum of public schools in order to provide persuasive advantage to a particular religious doctrine that rejects the factual basis of evolution in its entirety. The sponsor of the Creationism Act, Senator Keith, explained during the legislative hearings that his disdain for the theory of evolution resulted from the support that evolution supplied to views contrary to his own religious beliefs. According to Senator Keith, the theory of evolution was consonant with the "cardinal principle[s] of religious humanism, secular humanism, theological liberalism, aetheistism *[sic]*." * * * The state senator repeatedly stated that scientific evidence supporting his religious views should be included in the public school curriculum to redress the fact that the theory of evolution incidentally coincided with what he characterized as religious beliefs antithetical to his own. The legislation therefore sought to alter the science curriculum to reflect endorsement of a religious view that is antagonistic to the theory of evolution.

In this case, the purpose of the Creationism Act was to restructure the science curriculum to conform with a particular religious viewpoint. Out of many possible science subjects taught in the public schools, the legislature chose to affect the teaching of the one scientific theory that historically has been opposed by certain religious sects.

* * *

We do not imply that a legislature could never require that scientific critiques of prevailing scientific theories be taught. Indeed, the Court acknowledged in *Stone* that its decision forbidding the posting of the Ten Commandments did not mean that no use could ever be made of the Ten Commandments, or that the Ten Commandments played an exclusively religious role in the history of Western Civilization. In a similar way, teaching a variety of scientific theories about the origins of humankind to schoolchildren might be validly done with the clear secular intent of enhancing the effectiveness of science instruction. But because the primary purpose of the Creationism Act is to endorse a particular religious doctrine, the Act furthers religion in violation of the Establishment Clause.

* * *

The Louisiana Creationism Act advances a religious doctrine by requiring either the banishment of the theory of evolution from public school classrooms or the presentation of a religious viewpoint that rejects evolution in its entirety. The Act violates the Establishment Clause of the First Amendment because it seeks to employ the symbolic and financial support of government to achieve a religious purpose. The judgment of the Court of Appeals therefore is

Affirmed.

* * *

JUSTICE SCALIA, with whom THE CHIEF JUSTICE joins, dissenting.

Even if I agreed with the questionable premise that legislation can be invalidated under the Establishment Clause on the basis of its motivation alone, without regard to its effects, I would still find no justification for today's decision. The Louisiana legislators who passed the "Balanced Treatment for Creation-Science and Evolution-Science Act," * * * each of whom had sworn to support the Constitution, were well aware of the potential Establishment Clause problems and considered that aspect of the legislation with great care. After seven hearings and several months of study, resulting in substantial revision of the original proposal, they approved the Act overwhelmingly and specifically articulated the secular purpose they meant it to serve. Although the record contains abundant evidence of the sincerity of that purpose (the only issue pertinent to this case), the Court today holds, essentially on the basis of "its visceral knowledge regarding what *must* have moved the legislators," * * * that the members of the Louisiana Legislature knowingly violated their oaths and then lied about it. I dissent. Had requirements of the Balanced Treatment Act that are not apparent on its face been clarified by an interpretation of the Louisiana Supreme Court, or by the manner of its implementation, the Act might well be found unconstitutional; but the question of its constitutionality cannot rightly be disposed of on the gallop, by impugning the motives of its supporters.

* * *

* * * Even if one concedes, for the sake of argument, that a majority of the Louisiana Legislature voted for the Balanced Treatment Act partly in order to foster (rather than merely eliminate discrimination against) Christian fundamentalist beliefs, our cases establish that that alone would not suffice to invalidate the Act, so long as there was a genuine secular purpose as well.

* * *

The people of Louisiana, including those who are Christian fundamentalists, are quite entitled, as a secular matter, to have whatever scientific evidence there may be against evolution presented in their schools, just as Mr. Scopes was entitled to present whatever scientific evidence there was for it. Perhaps what the Louisiana Legislature has done is unconstitutional because there *is* no such evidence, and the scheme they have established will amount to no more than a presentation of the Book of Genesis.

* * *

Because I believe that the Balanced Treatment Act had a secular purpose, which is all the first component of the *Lemon* test requires, I would reverse the judgment of the Court of Appeals and remand for further consideration.

* * *

Notes

In an earlier decision, the Court held that an Arkansas "anti-evolution" statute violated the Establishment Clause. See *Epperson* v. *Arkansas*, 393 U.S. 97 (1968).

Justice William Brennan, who wrote the majority opinion in *Aguillard*, was appointed to the Court by President Dwight D. Eisenhower in

1956. He had been an associate justice of the New Jersey Supreme Court. Justice Brennan retired from the Court in 1990 and was replaced by Justice David Souter. Both Justice Scalia and Chief Justice Rehnquist, as their dissent in *Aguillard* and other decisions reveals, have shown strong dissatisfaction with prevailing legal rationale used to decide certain issues.

Although opponents of the teaching of evolution have not prevailed in the courts, controversy surrounding the issue continues; and the teaching of evolution continues to be challenged at the state and local levels in some states. In several states, science books carry a disclaimer regarding evolution's scientific status or a similar disclaimer is read to the students. A disclaimer, which was to be read immediately before the teaching of evolution, in all elementary and secondary classes was challenged in *Freiler* v. *Tangipahoa Parish Board of Education*, 185 F.3d 337 (5th Cir 1999), *cert. denied* 530 U.S. 1251 (2000). The disclaimer contained such statements as: evolution is presented "to inform students of the scientific concept and not intended to influence or dissuade the Biblical version of Creation or any other concept," and "Students are urged to exercise critical thinking and gather all information possible and closely examine each alternative toward forming an opinion." In declaring the disclaimer unconstitutional, the appellate court stated that the primary effect of the disclaimer was to "protect and maintain a particular religious viewpoint, namely belief in the Biblical version of creation." This had the effect, the court concluded, of "impermissibly advancing religion, thereby violating the second prong of the *Lemon* test as well as the endorsement test."

A teacher's First Amendment rights were not violated when he was prohibited from teaching a nonevolutionary theory of creation. The court did not accept the teacher's contention that he was developing an open mind in his students and encouraging students to explore alternative viewpoints. See *Webster* v. *New Lenox School District*, 917 F.2d 1004 (7th Cir. 1990). For a similar holding see *Peloza* v. *Capistrano Unified School District*, 37 F.3d 517 (9th Cir. 1994).

In another instance, a state supreme court upheld the nonrenewal of the contract of a teacher who devoted excessive time to creationism and religion in his biology class and who failed to cover basic biology principles. The school board had established guidelines that allowed the teacher a specified amount of time to teach the theories of evolution or creation. See *Dale* v. *Board of Education, Lemmon Independent School District*, 316 N.W.2d 108 (N.D. 1982).

D. Textbooks

Parents may object to the use of certain textbooks on the grounds that the books advance secular humanism and inhibit theistic religion. In one instance, parents charged that history, social studies, and home economics books promoted secular humanism by excluding facts about religion and by failing to present a Biblically-based or divine framework for decision making. The U.S. Court of Appeals for the Eleventh Circuit did not uphold the parents' contentions and declared:

> Examination of the contents of these textbooks, including the passages pointed out by Appellees as particularly offensive, in the context of the books as a whole and the undisputedly nonreligious purpose sought to be achieved by their use, reveals that the message conveyed is not one of endorsement of secular humanism or any religion. Rather, the message conveyed is one of a governmental attempt to instill in Alabama public school children such values as independent thought, tolerance of diverse views, self-respect, maturity, self-reliance and logical decision-making. This is an entirely appropriate secular effect. Indeed, one of the major objectives of public education is the "inculcat[ion of] fundamental values necessary to the maintenance of a democratic political system." *** Nor do these textbooks evidence an attitude antagonistic to theistic belief. The message conveyed by these textbooks with regard to theistic religion is one of neutrality: the textbooks neither endorse theistic religion as a system of belief, nor discredit it. Indeed, many of the books specifically acknowledge that religion is one source of moral values and none preclude that possibility. (p. 692)

See *Smith* v. *Board of School Commissioners of Mobile County*, 827 F.2d 684 (11th Cir. 1987).

In another instance, a parent objected to the use of the Holt, Rinehart and Winston basic reading series and specifically to a story about mental telepathy. The parent wanted an alternative reading program. In rejecting this petition, the U.S. Circuit Court of Appeals for the Sixth Circuit stated:

> The divisiveness and disruption caused by the opt-out remedy would be magnified if the schools had to grant other exemptions. Although the District Court found that no other objections to the Hawkins County public school curriculum have been raised and that Hawkins County is homogeneous from a religious perspective, this case would create a precedent for persons from other religions to request exemptions from core subjects because of religious objections. If the school district were required to accommodate exceptions and permit other students to opt-out of the reading program and other core courses with materials others found objectionable, this would result in a public school system impossible to administer. (pp. 1072–73)

See *Mozert* v. *Hawkins County Board of Education*, 827 F.2d 1058 (6th Cir. 1987), *cert. denied*, 484 U.S. 1066 (1988).

In a case dealing with an elementary teacher, a federal court of appeals held that school officials could not require removal of the Bible from the school's library but could require the removal of religiously oriented books from the classroom library and require the teacher to keep his Bible out of sight and refrain from silently reading it during classroom hours. See *Roberts* v. *Madigan*, 921 F.2d. 1047, *cert. denied*, 505 U.S. 1218 (1992).

E. Distribution of Religious Literature

Distribution in the public schools of Bibles and other religious literature has been a much litigated issue over the years. In one of the earliest decisions, *Tudor v. Board of Education of Borough of Rutherford*, 100 A.2d 857 (N.J. 1953), allowing Gideons to distribute Bibles to public school students was held to violate the Establishment Clause. In a decision nearly a half-century later addressing the issue of distributing religious or other non-school materials, the court in *Muller v. Jefferson Lighthouse School*, 98 F.3d 1530 (7th Cir. 1996), *cert. denied*, 520 U.S. 1156 (1997), held that such distribution may take place, but because a public elementary school is a "nonpublic forum" certain restrictions may be imposed. These include prior approval and screening for offensive messages, time and place requirements, and a disclaimer that the materials were not endorsed by the school. It should be noted that allowing one religious group to distribute its literature opens a forum for such distribution that cannot be closed to groups that are often objects of community opprobrium, such as Satanists or atheists.

Limited and passive distribution of Bibles and other religious material during school hours was upheld in *Peck v. Upshur County Board of Education*, 155 F.3d 274 (4th Cir. 1998). The court cited the well established, historical practice of the school board allowing private groups such as Little League, Boy Scouts, Girl Scouts, and the Women's Christian Temperance Union to distribute literature. The court considered the "age appropriate" (the ability to distinguish between private and government speech) distribution policy to be a neutral one that did not advance religion, but had a secular purpose of keeping a forum open that was already open to other private materials. Restrictions on the manner in which the Bibles could be made available included:

1. The private groups making the Bibles available were to be responsible for setting up the tables on which the Bibles would be displayed.
2. Bibles not picked up by students during the day were to be removed at the end of that day by the groups responsible for the display.
3. No teacher or other school employee was to participate in these or any other custodial activity relating to the Bible displays.
4. The tables were to be placed in a location in each school . . . that was accessible to students . . . "where students normally congregate and would not feel they were being watched or pressured into taking a Bible."
5. There was to be a sign on each table that read "Please feel free to take one . . ."
6. The source of the Bible was not to be identified.
7. No one was allowed to stand at the table to encourage or pressure students to take Bibles.

8. No one was to be allowed to enter classrooms to discuss the Bibles' availability.
9. The schools were not to announce that Bibles were available or hold any school assembly in connection with the availability of the Bibles. (p. 277)

A school district's policy of barring distribution of any materials on the sidewalk in front of the high school violated the First Amendment rights of individuals wishing to distribute Gideon Bibles. The court contended that the sidewalk was a public forum by virtue of its unrestricted use by the public, and the school's policy could not be justified to ensure student safety or prevent the distribution of drugs. See *Bacon* v. *Bradley-Bourbonnais High School District*, 707 F. Supp. 1005 (Ill. 1989).

F. Released and Shared Time and Religious Instruction

Two significant early United States Supreme Court decisions have addressed the questions of releasing public school students during normal school hours and thereby enabling them to receive religious instruction. In one of the decisions, *McCollum* v. *Board of Education of School District No. 71*, 333 U.S. 203 (1948), the Court invalidated a plan under which separate Protestant, Catholic, and Jewish religious classes were taught in the public school buildings. The Court contended that the use of tax-supported property for religious instruction, the close cooperation between school authorities and religious officials, and the use of the state's compulsory-education system all tended to promote religious education, and, therefore, violated the First Amendment. In another decision, *Zorach* v. *Clauson*, 343 U.S. 306 (1952), the Court upheld a plan whereby students were released during public school hours to attend religious instruction classes off the school premises. The Court stated:

> The government must be neutral when it comes to competition between sects. It may not thrust any sect on any person. It may not make a religious observance compulsory. It may not coerce anyone to attend church, to observe a religious holiday, or to take religious instruction. But it can close its doors or suspend its operations as to those who want to repair to their religious sanctuary for worship or instruction. No more than that is undertaken here. (p. 314)

A federal district court, in *Lanner* v. *Wimmer*, 463 F. Supp. 867 (Utah 1978), held that academic credit could not be given in a released-time seminary program for courses in the Old Testament and New Testament; however, the U.S. Court of Appeals for the Tenth Circuit modified this decision in 662 F.2d 1349 (10th Cir. 1981). The appellate court ruled that the process of gathering attendance slips and the necessity of judging whether the courses were mainly denominational violated the First Amendment. Additionally, the court held that neither the released-time program itself nor the granting of credit toward participation in extracurricular activities offended the Establishment and Free Exercise Clauses.

Several cases have addressed the issue of shared time. In one case, a public school would not enroll a parochial school student in a band course at the public school. The public school had a policy of allowing attendance in its schools only by full-time students. See *Snyder* v. *Charlotte Public School District*, 365 N.W.2d 151 (Mich. 1984), in which the Michigan Supreme Court ruled that public schools must open "nonessential elective courses" such as band, art, and advanced mathematics to private school students.

Is it permissible for a public school system to offer Bible study courses? See *Wiley* v. *Franklin*, 474 F. Supp. 525 (Tenn. 1979), which held that such courses could not be offered unless they were (1) secular in nature, intent, and purpose; (2) neither advancing nor inhibiting religion; and (3) offered in a manner that avoided excessive entanglement between government and religion. See *Crockett* v. *Sorenson*, 568 F. Supp. 1422 (Va. 1983) for a similar view. A course entitled Science of Creative Intelligence—Transcendental Meditation, which involved religious activity, was held to constitute establishment of religion proscribed by the First Amendment. See *Malnak* v. *Yogi*, 592 F.2d 197 (3rd Cir. 1979)

G. Religious Holidays

Given the many court decisions requiring school systems not to favor one religion, closing schools on Christian holidays such as Christmas, Easter, and Good Friday has received much attention. Christmas has generally been acknowledged to have sufficient secular connotations to warrant closing the schools during that holiday, but Easter and Good Friday have not been similarly viewed. Consequently, many school systems wishing to continue having a break in the spring have renamed their Easter break "spring break."

An Illinois statute designating Good Friday as one of twelve state-mandated school holidays was held to be in violation of the Establishment Clause. The court declared that unlike Christmas or Thanksgiving, and to some extent Easter, which have both secular and religious connotations, Good Friday has no secular aspect. Such a statute, the court contended, conveyed the impermissible message that Christianity was the favored religion in the state of Illinois. The court asserted that "The state has accorded special recognition to Christianity beyond anything that has been shown to be necessary to accommodate the religious needs of the Christian majority." This suit was brought by a public school teacher who objected to tax dollars being paid to teachers on the Good Friday holiday. See *Metzl v. Leininger*, 57 F.3d 618 (7th Cir. 1995). However, for an opposite opinion see *Koenick v. Felton*, 190 F.3d 259 (4th Cir 1999), *cert. denied*, 528 U.S. 1118 (2000), which held that a Maryland statute creating a public school holiday from Friday before Easter through the Monday after Easter did not violate the Establishment Clause. The court reasoned that the statute passed the three-pronged *Lemon* test. In its decision, the court argued that the law provided a four-day holiday for all students and teachers and did not express a preference for one religion; the statutory holiday around Easter had been part of the school calendar for 130 years and had become part of the community's expectations and plans; and the board had satisfactorily solved the problem of some Christian religions observing Easter on different days by consulting commercially printed calendars to determine the date of Easter each year.

H. Suggested Guidelines Regarding Religion in the Public Schools

Controversies surrounding separation of church and state issues over the years have resulted in some school officials, teachers, and parents assuming that religious expression of any type is either inappropriate or forbidden altogether in public schools. In some instances, this assumption has resulted in implementation of school policies that appeared to be hostile toward religious expression. In an effort to remedy this situation, guidelines regarding religion in the public schools were suggested in 1995 both by President Bill Clinton and in a document titled "Religion in the Public Schools: A Joint Statement of Current Law" drafted by a broad-based religious coalition that also included the American Civil Liberties Union and other public policy groups. Updated guidelines, entitled "Religious Expression in Public Schools," were revised by religious and educational groups from across the political and religious spectrum and distributed by the Department of Education in 1998. The revised guidelines include the following:

> *Student prayer and religious discussion*
> The Establishment Clause of the First Amendment does not prohibit purely private religious speech, by students. Students therefore have the same right to engage in individual or group prayer and religious discussion during the school day as they do to engage in other comparable activity. For example, students may read their Bibles or other scriptures, say grace before meals, and pray before tests to the same extent they may engage in comparable nondisruptive activities. Local school authorities possess substantial discretion to impose rules of order and other pedagogical restrictions on student

activities, but they may not structure or administer such rules to discriminate against religious activity or speech.

Generally, students may pray in a nondisruptive manner when not engaged in school activities or instruction, and subject to the rules of that normally pertain in the applicable setting. Specifically, students in informal settings, such as cafeterias and hallways, may pray and discuss their religious views with each other, subject to the same rules of order as apply to other student activities and speech. Students may also speak to, and attempt to persuade, their peers about religious topics just as they do with regard to political topics. School officials, however, should intercede to stop student speech that constitutes harassment aimed at a student or a group of students.

Students may also participate in before- or after-school events with religious content, such as "see you at the flag pole" gatherings, on the same terms as they may participate in other noncurriculum activities on school premises. School officials may neither discourage nor encourage participation in such an event.

The right to engage in voluntary prayer or religious discussion free from discrimination does not include the right to have a captive audience listen, or to compel other students to participate. Teachers and school administrators should ensure that no student is in any way coerced to participate in religious activity.

Graduation prayer and baccalaureates
Under current Supreme Court decisions, school officials may not mandate or organize prayer at graduation, nor organize religious baccalaureate ceremonies. If a school generally opens its facilities to private groups, it must make its facilities available on the same terms to organizers of privately sponsored religious baccalaureate services. A school may not extend preferential treatment to baccalaureate ceremonies and may in some instances be obliged to disclaim official endorsement of such ceremonies.

Official neutrality regarding religious activity
Teachers and school administrators, when acting in those capacities, are representatives of the state and are prohibited by the establishment clause from soliciting or encouraging religious activity, and from participating in such activity with students. Teachers and administrators also are prohibited from discouraging activity because of its religious content, and from soliciting or encouraging antireligious activity.

Teaching about religion
Public schools may not provide religious instruction, but they may teach about religion, including the Bible or other scripture; the history of religion, comparative religion, the Bible (or other scripture) -as-literature, and the role of religion in the history of the United States and other countries all are permissible public school subjects. Similarly, it is permissible to consider religious influences on art, music, literature, and social studies. Although public schools may teach about religious holidays, including their religious aspects, and may celebrate the secular aspects of holidays, schools may not observe holidays as religious events or promote such observance by students.

Student assignments
Students may express their beliefs about religion in the form of homework, artwork, and other written and oral assignments free of discrimination

based on the religious content of their submissions. Such home and class-room work should be judged by ordinary academic standards of substance and relevance, and against other legitimate pedagogical concerns identified by the school.

Religious literature
Students have a right to distribute religious literature to their schoolmates on the same terms as they are permitted to distribute other literature that is unrelated to school curriculum or activities. Schools may impose the same reasonable time, place, and manner or other constitutional restrictions on distribution of religious literature as they do on nonschool literature generally, but they may not single out religious literature for special regulation.

Religious excusals
Subject to applicable State laws, schools enjoy substantial discretion to excuse individual students from lessons that are objectionable to the student or the students' parents on religious or other conscientious grounds. However, students generally do not have a Federal right to be excused from lessons that may be inconsistent with their religious beliefs or practices. School officials may neither encourage nor discourage students from availing themselves of an excusal option.

Released time
Subject to applicable State laws, schools have the discretion to dismiss students to off-premises religious instruction, provided that schools do not encourage or discourage participation or penalize those who do not attend. Schools may not allow religious instruction by outsiders on school premises during the school day.

Teaching values
Though schools must be neutral with respect to religion, they may play an active role with respect to teaching civic values and virtue, and the moral code that holds us together as a community. The fact that some of these values are held also by religions does not make it unlawful to teach them in school.

Student garb
Schools enjoy substantial discretion in adopting policies relating to student dress and school uniforms. Students generally have no Federal right to be exempted from religiously neutral and generally applicable school dress rules based on their religious beliefs or practices; however, schools may not single out religious attire in general, or attire of a particular religion, for prohibition or regulation. Students may display religious messages on items of clothing to the same extent that they are permitted to display other comparable messages. Religious messages may not be singled out for suppression, but rather are subject to the same rules as generally apply to comparable messages.

The guidelines state that generally there is no federal right "to be excused from lessons that may be inconsistent with their religious beliefs or practices" and "to be exempted from religiously neutral and generally applicable school dress rules based on their religious beliefs or practices"; however, students may have such protection under state constitutional free exercise provisions.

III. USE OF FACILITIES

Another issue that often arises at the local school level concerns the extent, if any, that school buildings may be used by the public during noninstructional hours. In most instances, the local school board has either implied or specific authority to promulgate reasonable rules for the use of school buildings when they are not being used for school purposes or when their use does not interfere with normal school operations. Controversies often arise when the use of school facilities is requested by a group whose purpose or speaker may be offensive to some in the community, that represents certain religious organizations, or that is primarily interested in using the facility for commercial gain.

A general rule that has evolved concerning the use of school facilities suggests, that if facilities are to be leased to one type of group, they must be available to all within the group. However, such use may be denied if (1) the user fails or refuses to abide by reasonable rules and regulations pertaining to the use, (2) there is a demonstrated danger of violence or disruption associated with meetings of this particular group, or (3) the meeting violates a local ordinance or either state or federal constitutional provisions or law. It should be noted that in the absence of a state statute mandating their use, local systems are not obligated to make school buildings available for public activities.

Those denied use of a school facility often allege that their right of freedom of expression has been denied. The United States Supreme Court addressed this notion in *Police Department of the City of Chicago* v. *Mosley*, 408 U.S. 92 (1972), when it stated:

> Necessarily, then, under the Equal Protection Clause, not to mention the First Amendment itself, government may not grant the use of a forum to people whose views it finds acceptable, but deny use to those wishing to express less favored or more controversial views. And it may not select which issues are worth discussing or debating in public facilities. There is an "equality of status in the field of ideas," and government must afford all points of view an equal opportunity to be heard. Once a forum is opened up to assembly or speaking by some groups, government may not prohibit others from assembling or speaking on the basis of what they intend to say. Selective exclusions from a public forum may not be based on content alone, and may not be justified by reference to content alone. (p. 96)

Although allowing buildings to be used for social, civic, and recreational meetings outside of school hours, many school systems fearing lawsuits, have not allowed their buildings to be used for religious purposes. Such restrictions resulted in many lawsuits brought by churches and religious organizations, over the years, claiming unfair treatment. Although not specifically addressing the issue of after-hours church use, a unanimous Supreme Court decision in **Lamb's Chapel v. Center Moriches Union Free School District** ruled that a church should be allowed to show, after normal school hours on school premises, a family-oriented movie that presented views about family issues and child-rearing from a Christian perspective.

LAMB'S CHAPEL v. *CENTER MORICHES UNION FREE SCHOOL DISTRICT*
Supreme Court of the United States, 1993
508 U.S. 384

JUSTICE WHITE delivered the opinion of the Court.

Section 414 of the New York Education Law (McKinney 1988 and Supp. 1993), authorizes local school boards to adopt reasonable regulations for the use of school property for 10 specified purposes when the property is not in use for school purposes. Among the permitted uses is the holding of "social, civic and recreational meetings and entertainments, and other uses pertaining to the welfare of the community; but such meetings, entertainment and uses shall be non-exclusive and open to the general public." The list of permitted uses does not include meetings for religious purposes. * * *

Pursuant to §414's empowerment of local school districts, the Board of Center Moriches Union Free School District (District) has issued rules and regulations with respect to the use of school property when not in use for school purposes. The rules allow only 2 of the 10 purposes authorized by §414: social, civic, or recreational uses (Rule 10) and use by political organizations if secured in compliance with §414 (Rule 8). Rule 7, however, consistent with the judicial interpretation of state law, provides that "[t]he school premises shall not be used by any group for religious purposes."

The issue in this case is whether, against this background of state law, it violates the Free Speech Clause of the First Amendment, made applicable to the States by the Fourteenth Amendment, to deny a church access to school premises to exhibit for public viewing and assertedly religious purposes, a film dealing with family and child-rearing issues faced by parents today.

Petitioners (Church) are Lamb's Chapel, an evangelical church in the community of Center Moriches, and its pastor John Steigerwald. Twice the Church applied to the District for permission to use school facilities to show a six-part film series containing lectures by Doctor James Dobson. A brochure provided on request of the District identified Dr. Dobson as a licensed psychologist, former associate clinical professor of pediatrics at the University of Southern California, best-selling author, and radio commentator. The brochure stated that the film series would discuss Dr. Dobson's views on the undermining influences of the media that could only be counterbalanced by returning to traditional, Christian family values instilled at an early stage. The brochure went on to describe the contents of each of the six parts of the series. The District denied the first application, saying that "[t]his film does appear to be church related and therefore your request must be refused." The second application for permission to use school premises for showing the film, which described it as a "Family oriented movie—from the Christian perspective," was denied using identical language.

The Church brought suit in District Court, challenging the denial as a violation of the Freedom of Speech and Assembly Clauses, the Free Exercise Clause, and the Establishment Clause of the First Amendment, as well as the Equal Protection Clause of the Fourteenth Amendment. As to each cause of action, the Church alleged that the actions were undertaken under color of state law, in violation of 42 U.S.C. §1983. The District Court granted summary judgment for respondents, rejecting all of the Church's claims. * * * Noting that the District had not opened its facilities to organizations similar to Lamb's Chapel for religious purposes, the District Court held that the denial in this case was viewpoint neutral and, hence, not a violation of the Freedom of Speech Clause. The District Court also rejected the assertion by the Church that denying its application demonstrated a hostility to religion and advancement of nonreligion not justified under the Establishment of Religion Clause of the First Amendment.

The Court of Appeals affirmed the judgment of the District Court "in all respects." It held that the school property, when not in use for school purposes, was neither a traditional nor a designated public forum; rather, it was a limited public forum open only for designated purposes, a classification that "allows it to remain non-public except as to specified uses." The court observed that exclusions in such a forum need only be reasonable and viewpoint neutral, and ruled that denying access to the Church for the purpose of showing its film did not violate this standard. Because the holding below was questionable under our decisions, we granted the petition for certiorari, which in principal part challenged the holding below as contrary to the Free Speech Clause of the First Amendment.

There is no question that the District, like the private owner of property, may legally preserve the property under its control for the use to which it is dedicated. * * * It is also common ground that the District need not have permitted after-hours use of its property for any of the uses permitted by §414 of the state education law. The District, however, did open its property for 2 of the 10 uses permitted by §414. The Church argued below that because under Rule 10 of the rules issued by the District, school property could be used for "social, civic, and recreational" purposes, the District had opened its property for such a wide variety of communicative purposes that restrictions on communicative uses of the property were subject to the same constitutional limitations as restrictions in traditional public fora such as parks and sidewalks. Hence, its view was that subject-matter or speaker exclusions on District property were required to be justified by a compelling state interest and to be narrowly drawn to achieve that end. Both the District Court and the Court of Appeals rejected this submission, which is also presented to this Court. The argument has considerable force, for the District's property is heavily used by a wide variety of private organizations, including some that presented a "close question," which the Court of Appeals resolved in the District's favor, as to whether the District had in fact already opened its property for religious uses. We need not rule on this issue, however, for even if the courts below were correct in this respect—and we shall assume for present purposes that they were—the judgment below must be reversed.

With respect to public property that is not a designated public forum open for indiscriminate public use for communicative purposes, we have said that "[c]ontrol over access to a nonpublic forum can be based on subject matter and speaker identity so long as the distinctions drawn are reasonable in light of the purpose served by the forum and are viewpoint neutral." The Court of Appeals appeared to recognize that the total ban on using District property for religious purposes could survive First Amendment challenge only if excluding this category of speech was reasonable and viewpoint neutral. The court's conclusion in this case was that Rule 7 met this test. We cannot agree with this holding, for Rule 7 was unconstitutionally applied in this case.

The Court of Appeals thought that the application of Rule 7 in this case was viewpoint neutral because it had been and would be applied in the same way to all uses of school property for religious purposes. That all religions and all uses for religious purposes are treated alike under Rule 7, however, does not answer the critical question whether it discriminates on the basis of viewpoint to permit school property to be used for the presentation of all views about family issues and child-rearing except those dealing with the subject matter from a religious standpoint.

There is no suggestion from the courts below or from the District or the State that a lecture or film about child-rearing and family values would not be a use for social or civic purposes otherwise permitted by Rule 10. That subject matter is not one that the District has placed off limits to any and all speakers. Nor is there any indication in the record before us that the application to exhibit the particular film involved here was or would have been denied for any reason other than the fact that the presentation would have been from a religious perspective. * * * The film involved here no doubt dealt with a subject otherwise permissible under Rule 10, and its exhibition was denied solely because the film dealt with the subject from a religious standpoint. The principle that has emerged from our cases "is that the First Amendment forbids the government to regulate speech in ways that favor some viewpoints or ideas at the expense of others." * * *

The District, as a respondent, would save its judgment below on the ground that to permit its property to be used for religious purposes would be an establishment of religion forbidden by the First Amendment. This Court suggested in *Widmar* v. *Vincent,* that the interest of the State in avoiding an Establishment Clause violation "may be [a] compelling" one justifying an abridgment of free speech otherwise protected by the First Amendment; but the Court went on to hold that permitting use of University property for religious purposes under the open access policy involved there would not be incompatible with the Court's Establishment Clause cases.

We have no more trouble than did the *Widmar* Court in disposing of the claimed defense on the ground that the posited fears of an Establishment Clause violation are unfounded. The showing of this film would not have been during school hours, would not have been sponsored by the school, and would have been open to the public, not just to church members. The District property had repeatedly been used by a wide variety of private organizations. Under these circumstances, as in *Widmar*, there would have been no realistic danger that the community would think that the District was endorsing religion or any particular creed, and any benefit to religion or to the Church would have been no more than incidental. As in *Widmar*, permitting District property to be used to exhibit the film involved in this case would not have been an establishment of religion under the three-part test articulated in *Lemon v. Kurtzman*: The challenged governmental action has a secular purpose, does not have the principal or primary effect of advancing or inhibiting religion, and does not foster an excessive entanglement with religion.

The District also submits that it justifiably denied use of its property to a "radical" church for the purpose of proselytizing, since to do so would lead to threats of public unrest and even violence. There is nothing in the record to support such a justification, which in any event would be difficult to defend as a reason to deny the presentation of a religious point of view about a subject the District otherwise makes open to discussion on District property.

* * *

For the reasons stated in this opinion, the judgment of the Court of Appeals is

Reversed.

JUSTICE SCALIA, with whom JUSTICE THOMAS joins, concurring in the judgment.

I join the Court's conclusion that the District's refusal to allow use of school facilities for petitioners' film viewing, while generally opening the schools for community activities, violates petitioners' First Amendment free-speech rights. I also agree with the Court that allowing Lamb's Chapel to use school facilities poses "no realistic danger" of a violation of the Establishment Clause, but I cannot accept most of its reasoning in this regard. The Court explains that the showing of petitioners' film on school property after school hours would not cause the community to "think that the District was endorsing religion or any particular creed," and further notes that access to school property would not violate the three-part test articulated in *Lemon v. Kurtzman*.

As to the Court's invocation of the *Lemon* test: Like some ghoul in a late-night horror movie that repeatedly sits up in its grave and shuffles abroad, after being repeatedly killed and buried, *Lemon* stalks our Establishment Clause jurisprudence once again, frightening the little children and school attorneys of Center Moriches Union Free School District. Its most recent burial, only last Term, was, to be sure, not fully six-feet under: our decision in *Lee* v. *Weisman*, conspicuously avoided using the supposed "test" but also declined the invitation to repudiate it. Over the years, however, no fewer than five of the currently sitting Justices have, in their own opinions, personally driven pencils through the creature's heart (the author of today's opinion repeatedly), and a sixth has joined an opinion doing so. * * *

The secret of the *Lemon* test's survival, I think, is that it is so easy to kill. It is there to scare us (and our audience) when we wish it to do so, but we can command it to return to the tomb at will. See, *e.g.*, *Lynch* v. *Donnelly* (noting instances in which Court has not applied *Lemon* test). When we wish to strike down a practice it forbids, we invoke it, see, *e.g.*, *Aguilar* v. *Felton* (striking down state remedial education program administered in part in parochial schools); when we wish to uphold a practice it forbids, we ignore it entirely, see *Marsh* v. *Chambers* (upholding state legislative chaplains). Sometimes, we take a middle course, calling its three prongs "no more than helpful signposts." Such a docile and useful monster is worth keeping around, at least in a somnolent state; one never knows when one might need him.

For my part, I agree with the long list of constitutional scholars who have criticized *Lemon* and bemoaned the strange Establishment Clause geometry of crooked lines and wavering shapes its intermittent use has produced. * * *

* * *

Notes and Questions

Given the wording in **Lamb's Chapel**, does the decision imply that the Court would uphold after-hours church use if other organizations were allowed to use school buildings? Relying on **Lamb's Chapel**, a federal district court held that refusing to rent a high school gymnasium to a private parents' group to hold a baccalaureate ceremony for graduating seniors violated the First Amendment. The court declared that the baccalaureate ceremony was privately sponsored, open to the public, unrelated to any school or state activity, and participation in the ceremony was completely voluntary. See *Shumway* v. *Albany County School District No. 1 Board of Education*, 826 F. Supp. 1320 (Wyo. 1993).

Citing the **Lamb's Chapel** decision, a court held that a policy that did not allow a community-based, nonaffiliated group that sought to foster the moral development of junior high students from a Christian perspective to hold meetings immediately after school was unconstitutional. The court reasoned that allowing other secular groups concerned with the moral development of young people such as Scouts (Girl, Boy, Cub, Tiger Cub, and Brownies) to meet immediately after school resulted in viewpoint discrimination that did not serve a compelling governmental interest. See *Good News/Good Sports Club* v. *School District of the City of Ladue*, 28 F.3d 1501 (8th Cir. 1994). For similar rulings see *Local Organizing Committee, Million Man March* v. *Cook*, 922 Fed. Supp. 1494 (Co. 1996) and *Trinity United Methodist Parish* v. *Board of Education of the City School District of Newburgh*, 907 F. Supp. 707 (N.Y. 1995).

A school district's Community Use Policy, under which a nondenominational children's club was denied use of a school cafeteria, was challenged in *Good News Club* v. *Milford Central School*, 202 F.3d 502 (2nd Cir. 2000), cert. granted 531 U.S. 923 (2000). The policy provided that facilities could be used for "holding social, civic and recreational meetings and entertainment events and other uses pertaining to the welfare of the community, provided that such uses shall be nonexclusive and shall be open to the general public" and that such use must be for nonreligious purposes. Although allowing the Boy Scouts and 4-H to use its facilities, the school district denied use to a community-based Christian youth organization that argued its activities were secular and similar to organizations that were allowed to use school facilities. In upholding the school system, a federal court held that the subject matter of the club was religious in nature and not merely a discussion of secular matters such as the "moral development of young people." The court noted that meetings included prayer, singing of Christian songs, memorization and recitation of Biblical verses and scripture, and the use of teaching materials and lessons that were designed to inspire a personal relationship with Christ. Because this was a limited public forum, the court held the school district could impose a blanket exclusion on certain types of speech. However, once the district allowed expressive activities of a certain genre, it could not selectively deny access to that genre. In its holding, the court recognized that the school district had not allowed organizations with similar strongly based sectarian programs to use school facilities.

Gregoire v. *Centennial School District*, 907 F.2d 1366 (3rd Cir. 1990), *cert. denied*, 498 U.S. 899 (1990) focuses on the legal characteristics of the forum in which disputed activity takes place. The court's description of a traditional public forum, a designated open public forum that is sometimes referred to as a limited public forum, and a nonpublic forum should be useful to the school law student.

After-hours use of school facilities for religious services was addressed in *Bronx Household of Faith* v. *Community School District No. 10*, 127 F. 3rd 207 (2nd Cir. 1997), *cert. denied*, 523 U.S. 1074 (1998), where a district policy was challenged which stated:

No outside organization or group may be allowed to conduct religious services or religious instruction on school premises after school. However, the use of school premises by outside organizations or groups after school for the purposes of discussing religious material or material which contains a religious viewpoint or for distributing such material is permissible. (p. 210)

In its decision upholding the policy, the court identified the policy as creating a limited public forum. Therefore, prohibiting use for religious services, but permitting speech from a religious viewpoint, was held to be reasonable and viewpoint neutral and did not violate the First Amendment's free speech provisions.

A rental regulation was not upheld under which a church paid a noncommercial rate (based on actual cost) for the first five years but, thereafter, required the church to pay a rate that escalated to the commercial rate over the next four years. The commercial rate was five times the noncommercial rate and was intended to reflect market rental rates. The federal appellate court reasoned that this policy, under which rates escalated, discriminated against religious speech in violation of the Free Speech and Free Exercise Clauses. See *Fairfax Covenant Church* v. *Fairfax City School Board*, 17 F.3d 703 (4th Cir. 1994) *cert. denied*, 511 U.S. 1143 (1994). However, a school district's policy of renting its elementary school buildings for use immediately before and after regular school hours was held to be unconstitutional. In its holding, a federal district court contended that such a practice creates an appearance of official support for religious instruction and that it benefits from students' compliance with compulsory attendance law. See *Ford* v. *Manuel*, 629 F. Supp. 771 (Ohio 1985).

In addressing the issue of conditioning the off-time use of public school facilities on the political or ideological views of the applicant, on its membership policies, or on its attendance restrictions, a federal appellate court declared that the school system was not responsible for the views expressed or for the composition of the group that expressed them. The court also stated that "merely permitting the occasional and temporary use of state facilities by racially discriminatory groups along with all others does not constitute significant state involvement in their practices." See *Knights of the Ku Klux Klan* v. *East Baton Rouge Parish School Board*, 578 F.2d 1122 (5th Cir. 1978). Also see *National Socialist White People's Party* v. *Ringers*, 473 F.2d 1010 (4th Cir. 1973).

Local business people are often concerned that allowing the use of school facilities, which have been constructed at public expense, is a form of competition against them. This view was not upheld in *Hall* v. *Shelby County Board of Education*, 472 S.E.2d 489 (Ky. 1971), where a local civic group organized and charged admission to musical programs. All profits were used for civic activities.

Assume that a local school board had a policy of allowing school facilities to be used by local groups. Would the school board be on sound constitutional footing if it barred any of the following local groups: the Gay Liberation League? Committee to Legalize the Use of Marijuana, Cocaine, and Heroin? American Nazis? Suicide Advocates? Abortion Advocates? Committee to Recall Local School Board Members? Devil worshipers? Nudists? What is the basis for your response in each of these instances?

Does your state have legislation pertaining to the use of public school facilities when they are not being used by the school system? Does your public school system have policies regulating the use of facilities?

IV. AID TO NONPUBLIC SCHOOLS

Approximately 12 percent of American students attend nonpublic schools. Nearly two-thirds of those students are enrolled in Catholic schools, and approximately 15 percent of nonpublic school students attend non-church-related schools. Legislatures in several states having large numbers of nonpublic school students have passed measures that have attempted to financially assist the nonpublic school sector. Because these measures have raised serious questions pertaining to the proper separation of church and state under the First Amendment, their constitutionality has been examined by the United States Supreme Court.

In *Lemon* v. *Kurtzman*, 403 U.S. 602 (1971) the Court struck down both an attempt by the Rhode Island legislature to provide a 15 percent salary supplement to be paid to those teachers dealing with secular subjects in nonpublic schools and a Pennsylvania statute that provided financial support to nonpublic elementary and secondary schools by way of reimbursement for the cost of teachers' salaries, textbooks, and instructional materials in specified secular subjects. The Court held that the "cumulative impact of the entire relationship arising under the statutes in each state involves excessive entanglement between government and religion." Furthermore, the Court reasoned that these state programs had a divisive political potential that would be a threat to the normal political process. Because candidates would be forced to declare their position on amounts of money to be expended in such programs, political division along religious lines would develop. The Court contended that this was a principal evil that the First Amendment was intended to protect against.

A New York statute was struck down by the Court in *Levitt* v. *Committee for Public Education and Religion Liberty*, 413 U.S. 472 (1973). Under this statute, nonpublic schools would have been reimbursed for expenses incurred in administering, grading, compiling, and reporting test results; maintaining pupil attendance and health records; recording qualifications and characteristics of personnel; and preparing and submitting various reports to the state. The Court ruled that such aid would have the primary purpose or effect of advancing religion or religious education and that it would lead to excessive entanglement between church and state. However, in *Committee for Public Education and Religious Liberty* v. *Regan*, 442 U.S. 928 (1980), a five-to-four opinion, the Court upheld a revised version of the law that had been declared unconstitutional in *Levitt*. The revised law allowed the state to reimburse private schools, including sectarian schools, for the expenses connected with keeping official attendance and other records, for administering three state tests, and for grading two of the tests.

Another New York law was invalidated, in *Committee for Public Education and Religious Liberty* v. *Nyquist*, 413 U.S. 756 (1973), which provided for the maintenance and repair of nonpublic school facilities, tuition reimbursement for parents of nonpublic school students, and tax relief for those not qualifying for tuition reimbursement. And a Pennsylvania law providing for parent reimbursement for nonpublic school students was also invalidated in *Sloan* v. *Lemon*, 413 U.S. 825 (1973). The majority opinion declared that there was no constitutionally significant difference between Pennsylvania's tuition-grant scheme and New York's tuition-reimbursement program, which was held violative of the Establishment Clause in *Nyquist*.

In *Meek* v. *Pittenger*, 421 U.S. 349 (1975), the Court was asked to rule on a Pennsylvania statute that provided for auxiliary services for exceptional, remedial, or educationally disadvantaged nonpublic school students; for lending instructional materials and equipment to nonpublic schools; and for lending textbooks to nonpublic school students. The Court invalidated all but the textbook-loan provision of the Pennsylvania law. It held that the act had the unconstitutional primary effect of advancing religion because of the predominantly religious character of the benefiting schools. Additionally, the Court stated that the act provided excessive opportunities for political fragmentation and division along religious lines. Expanding on this theme, the Court declared:

> This potential for political entanglement, together with the administrative entanglement which would be necessary to ensure that auxiliary-services personnel remain strictly neutral and nonideological when functioning in church-related schools . . . violates the constitutional prohibition against laws "respecting an establishment of religion." (p. 372)

In another decision, *Wolman* v. *Walter*, 433 U.S. 229 (1977), the Court addressed the constitutionality of an Ohio statute that had attempted to conform to the *Meek* ruling. The decision, which revealed wide disagreement among the justices, held that the provisions providing nonpublic school students with books, standardized testing and scoring, diagnostic services, and therapeutic and remedial services were constitutional. However, provisions relating to instructional materials and equipment and field-trip services were held to be unconstitutional.

Initially, the major impetus for obtaining government financial assistance for nonpublic schools came from Catholic parochial school supporters who were largely responsible for bringing the cases discussed above. These supporters thought it only fair to receive such assistance because, although they were paying taxes for the public schools, they were not using them. Opponents, some of whom were accused of having an anti-Catholic bias, argued that tax money should not be expended for schools that had a religious orientation. In time, supporters of assistance to nonpublic schools were joined by those who were interested in government aid to private schools in general and those who thought if nonpublic schools received aid, religiously oriented schools should not be discriminated against. Two United States Supreme Court decisions, *Agostini* v. *Felton* (1997) and *Mitchell* v. *Helms* (2000), reflected a shift in the Court's thinking regarding financial aid to nonpublic religious schools.

Using federal education funds under Chapter I (formerly Title I of the Elementary and Secondary Education Act) to pay public school teachers who taught in programs aimed at helping low-income, educationally deprived students within parochial schools was allowed in *Agostini* v. *Felton*, 521 U.S. 203 (1997). This five-to-four decision overruled both *Aguilar* v. *Felton*, 473 U.S. 402 (1985) and *Grand Rapids School District* v. *Ball*, 473 U.S. 373 (1985), which had not allowed the practice. In *Agostini*, the Court abandoned its previous assumption that public school teachers within parochial schools would inevitably inculcate religion to their students or that their presence constituted a symbolic union between government and religion. The Court established the following criteria for determining whether or not school-aid programs have an impermissible effect: (1) whether the aid results in governmental indoctrination, (2) whether the program defines its recipients by reference to religion, and (3) whether the aid creates an excessive entanglement between government and religion. The United States Supreme Court rarely overrules previous decisions. It does so when a majority on the Court prevails on a doctrinal position, such as in this case, of where to place the proverbial "line in the sand" on the issue of separation of church and state.

A federal program involving Chapter 2 (technically Subchapter VI of Chapter 70 of 20 U.S.C.) that loaned computers, software, and library books to religious schools was upheld in a six-to-three decision in *Mitchell* v. *Helms*, 530 U.S. 793 (2000). The plurality opinion held that the aid was allocated on the basis of neutral, secular criteria that neither favored nor disfavored religion, and was made available to both religious and secular beneficiaries on a nondiscriminatory basis. However, the concurring opinion states:

> The plurality announces a rule of unprecedented breadth for the evaluation of Establishment Clause challenges to government school-aid programs. That rule is particularly troubling because, first, its treatment of neutrality

comes close to assigning that factor singular importance . . . . Second, the plurality's approval of actual diversion of government aid to religious indoctrination is in tension with this Court's precedents. Because *Agostini* represents the Court's most recent attempt to devise a general framework [its] criteria should control here.

Mitchell overruled key holdings in *Meek* v. *Pittenger* and *Wolman* v. *Walter* that had barred the government from providing maps, charts, overhead projectors, and other instructional materials to religious schools.

In a five-to-four decision, *Mueller* v *Allen.*, 463 U.S. 388 (1983), the Court upheld a Minnesota law permitting taxpayers to claim a deduction from gross income on their state income tax returns for expenses incurred for "tuition, textbooks and transportation" not exceeding $500 for dependents in grades K–6 and $700 for dependents in grades 7–12. A distinction between this decision and the Court's 1973 *Nyquist* ruling appears to be that *Nyquist* rejected a tax credit for parents whose children attended nonpublic school, whereas *Mueller* allowed a tax deduction for all parents, including those whose children attended public schools. The tax deduction, the *Mueller* majority reasoned, was simply part of the state's tax law permitting deductions for a number of things. The dissenters argued that the difference between a tax credit and a deduction was "a distinction without a difference," and that 90 percent of private school students were in sectarian schools. However, a New Jersey statute that provided taxpayers with a $1,000 tax deduction for each child attending nonpublic schools was held to be unconstitutional. See *Public Funds for Public Schools of New Jersey* v. *Byrne*, 590 F.2d 514 (3rd Cir. 1979), *aff'd*, 442 U.S. 907 (1979).

The United States Supreme Court, in a five-to-four decision, upheld the constitutionality of providing transportation to parochial school students in *Everson* v. *Board of Education of Township of Ewing*, 330 U.S. 1 (1947). Over thirty years later, a Rhode Island statute providing for the busing of students to nonpublic schools was held not to violate state or federal constitutional provisions. See *Members of the Jamestown School Committee* v. *Schmidt*, 405 A.2d 16 (R.I. 1979). The Connecticut Supreme Court was asked to determine whether a state statute authorizing transportation for private and parochial students required transportation by a school district on days that public schools were not in session. In determining that such transportation was required, the court held that the intent of the statute was to provide private school students with the same quality of transportation public school students received, regardless of schools' schedules. See *Board of Education of the Town of Stafford* v. *State Board of Education*, 243 Conn. 772 (1998).

Under the Internal Revenue Code, tax exemptions may be granted to "corporations . . . organized and operated exclusively for religious, charitable . . . or educational purposes." A private religious university was devoted to the teaching and propagation of fundamentalist religious beliefs, which included that God intended segregation of the races and that scripture forbids interracial dating and marriage. Students were expelled if they did not follow these prohibitions. The Internal Revenue Service, upheld by the Supreme Court, withdrew the college's tax exempt status, having determined that the racial policy was not "charitable" as required by the Code. See *Bob Jones University* v. *United States*, 461 U.S. 574 (1983).

Does your state have any provisions for aid to nonpublic schools?

V. SCHOOL FEES

Disputes often arise in regard to the charging of fees by public school systems for supplies, materials, extracurricular activities, transportation to school, and texts. Whether or not fees may be charged legitimately depends on statutory provisions or the interpretation of a state's constitution. Although decisions in several states have denied the charging of fees for textbooks and/or supplies, decisions in other states have taken an opposite view.

The California Supreme Court considered the issue of charging fees for extracurricular activities in *Hartzell* v. *Connell.*

HARTZELL v. *CONNELL*
Supreme Court of California, 1984
679 P.2d 35

BIRD, Chief Justice.

May a public high school district charge fees for educational programs simply because they have been denominated "extracurricular"?

The Santa Barbara High School District (District) offers a wide variety of extracurricular activities, ranging from cheerleading to madrigal singing, and from archery to football. Many of these activities are of relatively recent origin. For example, in 1956, Santa Barbara High School fielded six athletic teams while today there are thirty-eight.

Prior to the 1980–1981 school year, any student could participate in these activities free of charge. The programs were financed by a combination of District contributions (mostly state aid and local tax revenues), ticket sales, and fundraising activities conducted by the constituent high schools.

In the spring of 1980, the District school board (Board) decided to cut its budget by $1.1 million. This decision reflected a drop in revenues due to the combined effects of inflation, declining enrollment, and the adoption of Proposition 13. Among the items to be reduced was the District's contribution to the high school extracurricular programs.

The Board considered two plans for adapting the programs to fit its reduced budget. The first plan called for a major cut in interscholastic athletic competition, including the reduction of the high school program from over 30 teams to only 8 and the elimination of interscholastic competition at the ninth grade level. Under this plan, the surviving programs were to remain open to all students free of charge.

The second plan provided for a less extensive cut in athletic competition—elimination of the ninth grade program only. To make up the difference, it proposed to raise money by charging students fees for participation in dramatic productions, musical performances, and athletic competition.

The Board chose the second option. Under the plan finally adopted, students are required to pay $25 for *each* athletic team in which they wish to participate, and $25 per category for any or all activities in *each* of the following four categories: (1) dramatic productions (e.g., plays, dance performances and musicals); (2) vocal music groups (e.g., choir and madrigal groups); (3) instrumental groups (e.g., orchestra, marching band, and related groups such as the drill team and flag twirlers); and (4) cheerleading groups.

* * *

In an attempt to ensure that the fees would not prevent any students from participating, the District has implemented a fee waiver program. Upon showing a financial need, a student may obtain a "scholarship" to participate without paying the fee. The standard of need is similar to that of the free lunch program.

The fee-waiver policy has been supplemented with an outreach program. Teachers and coaches are asked to inform their principals of any students who, though expected to participate in an activity, do not do so. These students are then interviewed by the principal to determine whether the fee prevented them from participating.

* * *

The trial court rejected all of the plaintiffs' claims, primarily on the ground that none of the activities covered by the fee program are "integral" to credit courses.

The California Constitution requires the Legislature to "provide for a system of common schools by which a *free school* shall be kept up and supported in each district. . . ." (Cal. Const., art. IX, § 5, emphasis added.) This provision entitles "the youth of the State . . . to be educated at the public expense." * * *

Plaintiffs assert that the imposition of fees for educational extracurricular activities violates the free school guarantee. They are correct.

* * *

Accordingly, this court holds that all educational activities—curricular or "extracurricular"—offered to students by school districts fall within the free school guarantee of article IX, section 5. Since it is not disputed that the programs involved in this case are "educational" in character, they fall within that guarantee.

Defendants argue, however, that the fee waiver policy for needy students satisfies the requirement of the free school guarantee. They suggest that the right "to be educated at the public expense" ∗ ∗ ∗ amounts merely to a right *not to be financially prevented* from enjoying educational opportunities. This argument contradicts the plain language of the Constitution.

In guaranteeing "free" public schools, article IX, section 5 fixes the precise extent of the financial burden which may be imposed on the right to an education—none. ∗ ∗ ∗ A school which conditions a student's participation in educational activities upon the payment of a fee clearly is *not* a "free school."

The free school guarantee reflects the people's judgment that a child's public education is too important to be left to the budgetary circumstances and decisions of individual families. It makes no distinction between needy and nonneedy families. Individual families, needy or not, may value education more or less depending upon conflicting budget priorities. ∗ ∗ ∗

The free school guarantee lifts budgetary decisions concerning public education out of the individual family setting and requires that such decisions be made by the community as a whole. Once the community has decided that a particular educational program is important enough to be offered by its public schools, a student's participation in that program cannot be made to depend upon his or her family's decision to pay a fee or buy a toaster.

Nor may a student's participation be conditioned upon application for a special waiver. The stigma that results from recording some students as needy was recognized early in the struggle for free schools. ∗ ∗ ∗

Finally, defendants warn that, if the fees are invalidated, many school districts may be forced to drop some extracurricular activities. They argue that invalidation would—in the name of the free school guarantee—produce the anomalous result of reducing the number of educational opportunities available to students.

This court recognizes that, due to legal limitations on taxation and spending ∗ ∗ ∗, school districts do indeed operate under difficult financial constraints. However, financial hardship is not defense to a violation of the free school guarantee. ∗ ∗ ∗

Perhaps, in the view of some, public education could be more efficiently financed by peddling it on the open market. Under the California Constitution, however, access to public education is a right enjoyed by all— not a commodity for sale. Educational opportunities must be provided to all students without regard to their families' ability or willingness to pay fees or request special waivers. This fundamental feature of public education is not contingent upon the inevitably fluctuating financial health of local school districts. A solution to those financial difficulties must be found elsewhere— for example, through the political process.

In conclusion, this court holds that the imposition of fees for educational activities offered by public high school districts violates the free school guarantee. The constitutional defect in such fees can neither be corrected by providing waivers to indigent students, nor justified by pleading financial hardship.

Plaintiffs also argue that the fee requirement violates title 5, section 350 of the California Administrative Code (hereafter title 5, section 350). That section provides: "A pupil enrolled in a school shall not be required to pay *any* fee, deposit, or other charge not specifically authorized by law." * * *

* * *

In conclusion, the imposition of fees as a precondition for participation in educational programs offered by public high schools on a non-credit basis violates the free school guarantee of the California Constitution and the prohibition against school fees contained in title 5, section 350 of the California Administrative Code.

The judgment is reversed.

* * *

Notes and Questions

A brief survey of states' constitutional provisions and case law concerning the issue of school fees is discussed in *Cardiff* v. *Bismarck Public School District*, 263 N.W.2d 105 (N.D. 1978). May a student's transcript be withheld for failure to pay school fees? See *Paulson* v. *Minidoka County School District No. 331*, 463 P.2d 935 (Idaho 1970), where the court stated that "free common schools" were not being provided when access to official reports of students' records depended upon payment of a $25 unconstitutional school fee. May a transcript of grades be withheld for failure to pay a legitimate fee?

Incidental fees for attendance at athletic or literary events and the use of the library have generally been upheld even when there is a constitutional requirement for providing free public schools. What determines whether or not a school may charge an "incidental" fee but not other fees?

A United States Supreme Court decision upheld a North Dakota statute that allowed local school boards to assess fees for transporting pupils to school. Inasmuch as the policy caused education to be more expensive for some citizens than for others, plaintiffs contended that the statute offended the Equal Protection Clause of the United States Constitution. In rejecting that contention, the Court declined on two counts to subject the statute to "strict scrutiny." First, it reaffirmed its position that education is not a "fundamental" constitutional right. Second, it held that laws impacting disproportionately on the poor do not, on that account, invoke such scrutiny. Moreover, the Court declared, a state's choosing to offer a service does not impose upon the state a constitutional obligation to offer it free of charge. See *Kadrmas* v. *Dickinson Public Schools*, 487 U.S. 450 (1988).

A California statute allowing school districts to assess fees for children who ride school buses was held to be violative of the state constitution's equal protection clause. The California court held that such a law was counter to the guarantee of free schools, and it failed to meet the state's strict-scrutiny test. See *Salazer* v. *Honig*, 246 Cal. Rptr. 837 (Cal. Ct. App. 1988).

Does your state constitution or statutory law address the issue of school fees? What is the practice or policy regarding fees in your school system?

VI. HEALTH SERVICES

Over the years, school systems have attempted to impose health services on students with which some parents disapproved. The most notable and heavily litigated issue has dealt with immunization. In recent years many parents have objected to the distribution of condoms, although the rationale for the distribution was based on its being a health service for the prevention of disease.

A. Immunization

State statutes authorizing or requiring vaccination or immunization as a condition of school attendance have been upheld in every instance where they have been challenged. Such statutes often contain an exemption for those who are members of religious organizations that do not permit inoculation or that rely on spiritual means or prayer for healing.

BERG v. *GLEN COVE CITY SCHOOL DISTRICT*
United States District Court, Eastern District of
New York, 1994
853 F. Supp. 651

WEXLER, District Judge

* * *

The facts as alleged in the complaint, and as adduced at the hearing, are summarized as follows: In or before April 1993, Kathryn and David Berg sought to enroll their five-year-old twin daughters, Emily and Sasha, in the Glen Cove City School District, and requested exemption from the immunization requirement of New York Public Health Law § 2164. This section requires that all children be immunized against certain communicable diseases before they enter school. * * *

By letters dated April 28, 1993 and July 22, 1993, defendant, through Assistant Superintendent Michael S. Perricone ("Perricone"), sought information from plaintiffs to determine whether the requirements for exemption were satisfied. In particular, Perricone asked plaintiffs to identify the religion to which they claimed to belong and the tenets of that religion that would be violated by permitting immunization.

Plaintiffs responded to Perricone's request by summarizing their purported religious beliefs in a letter dated July 29, 1993. As alleged in paragraph 17 of the Complaint, the July 29 letter described plaintiffs' religious beliefs as follows:

> While we feel we are members of the Jewish Faith and we believe in God, we adhere to certain personal and sacred religious beliefs. Our beliefs are partly based on Torah and what we believe that God commands of us. We believe that God has endowed us with the energy of life. We believe that this special energy, directed by God, has constructed our cells, our tissues, and our organs with infinite intelligence and these interconnected systems function in perfect harmony when we follow nature's laws which are the Laws of God. We believe a lifestyle that is in accordance with the Laws of God creates healthy bodies and healthy minds. God is pure and we must strive to live our lives as purely as possible. Eating unpure substances or injecting substances unnaturally into our bloodstreams is in our opinion a violation of these laws. * * *

Plaintiffs thereafter filed their complaint in this action on November 9, 1993, ultimately seeking: (1) a declaratory judgment, that they are entitled to the exemption from immunizations provided in § 2164(9); (2) a permanent injunction preventing defendant from violating plaintiffs' constitutional rights; and (3) damages in the amount of $1 million for violation of their constitutional rights, together with costs and disbursements of this action, including reasonable attorney's fees pursuant to 42 U.S.C. § 1988. * * *

Before a discussion of the merits, the Court notes that in *Sherr v. Northport–East Northport Union Free School Dist.*, 672 F. Supp. 81 (E.D.E.Y. 1987), this Court declared that the predecessor of § 2164(9) violated both the establishment and free exercise clauses of the First Amendment. The earlier version of § 2164(9) required that the parent or guardian seeking the exception be a "bona fide member of a recognized religious organization" whose doctrines oppose such immunizations. In response to this Court's *Sherr* decision, the New York legislature amended § 2164(9) to require that the parent or guardian "hold genuine and sincere religious beliefs which are contrary to the practices herein required." Because the statutory exception is for persons whose opposition to immunizations stems from *religious* beliefs, it does not extend to persons whose views are founded upon, for instance, "medical or purely moral considerations," *Sherr*, 672 F. Supp. at 92, "scientific and secular theories," or "philosophical and personal" beliefs. *Mason v. General Brown Cent. School Dist.*, 851 F.2d 47, 51–52 (2d Cir. 1988). Thus, this Court must first determine whether plaintiffs' purported beliefs are "religious." Only if they are, then this Court must determine whether those beliefs are genuinely and sincerely held. Moreover, the Court is mindful that attempts to ascertain the sincerity of claims of religious beliefs must be undertaken with extreme caution. * * *

As for plaintiffs' beliefs, both Kathryn and David Berg testified that they consider themselves "Jewish," but that they do not fit within any recognized classification of Judaism; rather, they adhere to their own concept of being Jewish. Although defendant offered testimony from an expert in Jewish religion that there is nothing in the teachings of the Jewish religion that would proscribe immunization for children, plaintiffs maintained, nevertheless, that the basis for their opposition to immunization was their *own* interpretation of passages from certain Hebrew scripture, and claimed to adhere strongly to those passages, as they interpreted them, for at least the past six years.

Based on this testimony and plaintiffs statement of their beliefs in the complaint, it appears that plaintiffs' will likely succeed on their claim that the beliefs they hold opposing immunization qualify as "religious."

As for plaintiffs' claim that their beliefs are genuinely and sincerely held, this Court's examination of certain medical and dental records substantiates plaintiffs' claim that for at least six years they have practiced those beliefs they contend are opposed to immunization in contexts other than immunization, for instance, in the receipt of prenatal, pediatric and dental care. Although it may seem odd that plaintiffs interpret certain tenets of the Jewish religion to prohibit immunization, while Jewish teaching, according to defendant's expert, imposes no such prohibition, and although these facts bear on determining whether plaintiffs' beliefs are genuine and sincere, plaintiffs have thus far sufficiently shown that they hold *their* beliefs genuinely and sincerely.

Based on the record presented thus far, this Court finds that plaintiffs have established a likelihood of success on the merits of their claim that their opposition to the required immunizations is based on beliefs which qualify as "religious," and that they hold these beliefs both "genuinely" and "sincerely." * * *

Notes

For a contrary view, see *Brown* v. *Stone*, 378 So.2d 218 (Miss. 1980), *cert. denied*, 449 U.S. 887 (1980), where a religious exemption was not allowed. This court declared that the exemption based on religious beliefs would discriminate against the great majority of children whose parents did not have those religious convictions. Exemption may not be provided for students receiving a note of medical exemption from a chiropractor. See *Heard v. Payne*, 665 S.W.2d 865 (Ark. 1984).

A school rule requiring a tetanus shot as a condition of playing on a baseball team was upheld. A Pennsylvania court held that a school district's compelling interest to immunize did not infringe on a boy's religious practice. See *Calendra v. State College Area School District*, 512 A.2d 809 (1986).

B. Distribution of Condoms

Some school authorities, primarily in urban areas, have attempted to deal with problems associated with high levels of student pregnancy and a student-wide AIDS epidemic by making condoms available. Such school districts contend that condom distribution is not only a valuable component of the sex-education and/or health-education curriculum but also invaluable in preventing the spread of sexually transmitted diseases such as AIDS. Parents who oppose such a scheme generally argue that such distribution is tantamount to condoning promiscuity and sexual permissiveness, and encourages sexual relations at an earlier age and/or with more frequency. When litigated, condom distribution programs have been upheld by the courts.

In *Curtis v. School Committee of Falmouth*, 652 N.E.2d 580 (Mass. 1995), a condom-availability program for grades seven through twelve was upheld. Under this program junior high school students could request free condoms from the school nurse, who would counsel the students and provide them with pamphlets on AIDS/HIV and other sexually transmitted diseases. At the high school, students could request free condoms from the school nurse or purchase them from the condom vending machines located in the girls' and boys' restrooms. Counseling was provided if requested. This program did not provide for an "opt-out" under which parents had the option of excluding their student from the availability of condoms, nor a parental notification provision whereby parents would be notified of their children's requests for condoms. The court ruled that this program did not violate parental liberties or privacy rights. Additionally, the court stated that although the program may offend the religious sensibilities of parents, mere exposure to offensive programs does not amount to a violation of free exercise. Parents have no right to tailor public school programs to meet their individual religious or moral preference.

A condom distribution program, including an "opt-out" provision, was challenged by parents who argued that their Fourteenth Amendment right to bring up their children without unnecessary governmental interference was violated. The court in, *Parents United for Better Schools, Inc. v. School District of Philadelphia*, 148 F.3d 260 (3rd Cir. 1998), upheld the consensual program and argued that because the program did not demand student participation and gave parents the option to exclude their children from receiving condoms, it did not violate the parents' rights. The condom distribution program was a result of the school board's concern about an epidemic in adolescent pregnancy, sexually transmitted diseases, and HIV infection. It was a part of a larger program to educate students about health and hygiene. Given the program's goals, the court agreed that the program was within the implied definition of health services.

CHAPTER THREE

Students and the Law

Countless interactions between students and school officials occur in the public schools, and inevitably, some students or their parents become displeased either with a school official's actions or with school policy. The vast majority of such disputes are not litigable, however, unless school authorities have violated a student's constitutional rights, not followed applicable federal or state statutes, or not had appropriate policies or procedures.

Prior to the 1970s, courts usually upheld school authorities who demonstrated no more than that their actions were reasonable. Public schools were perceived as enjoying parental prerogatives, and it was uncertain whether constitutional rights extended to students. However, in a 1969 landmark decision, the United States Supreme Court declared that students do not "shed their constitutional rights to freedom of speech or expression at the schoolhouse gate." Subsequently, in 1975 the high court held that public school students possess liberty and property interests in their education, and therefore, that constitutional principles of due process apply to school officials' treatment of students. Several important federal statutes also emerged in the early 1970s, further expanding the scope of student rights. As a result of these changes in students' legal status, a period ensued during which students often were successful in challenging school policies and procedures and in which many school officials perceived an erosion of their authority.

In the mid-1980s, however, a shift became evident in the courts' tendency to uphold students. In particular, several Supreme Court decisions since then clearly increased the authority of public school officials regarding students' freedom of expression and several other areas of conflict.

In addition to discussing students' rights to free expression, this chapter addresses issues associated with suspension, expulsion, and involuntary disciplinary transfer from school; corporal punishment; search of students and their lockers; student appearance; pregnancy, parenthood, and marriage; participation in extracurricular activities; and school punishment for out-of-school offenses.

An examination of court decisions in these areas reveals that courts must often balance students' constitutional rights against the duty of public school officials to maintain an appropriate environment for learning and safety. A deceptively simple administrative practice emerges that reduces legal confrontations and also facilitates school operations; namely, school officials should ensure the adoption of policies that are legally and educationally sound, that are clearly written, that are adequately communicated to students and their parents, and that are enforced in a fair manner.

I. FREEDOM OF EXPRESSION

A. The *Tinker* Doctrine

Students were not recognized as having the First Amendment right of freedom of expression in 1969 when the United States Supreme Court addressed the question in *Tinker v. Des Moines Independent Community School District*. Although this seven-to-two decision did not address the question of "pure speech"—the issue before the Court involved the wearing of armbands by students—the Court's decision in *Tinker* provided the public school community with a clear message that a student has the right of political freedom of expression.

TINKER v. DES MOINES INDEPENDENT COMMUNITY SCHOOL DISTRICT
Supreme Court of the United States, 1969
393 U.S. 503

MR. JUSTICE FORTAS delivered the opinion of the Court.

Petitioner John F. Tinker, 15 years old, and petitioner Christopher Eckhardt, 16 years old, attended high schools in Des Moines, Iowa. Petitioner Mary Beth Tinker, John's sister, was a 13-year-old student in junior high school.

In December 1965, a group of adults and students in Des Moines held a meeting at the Eckhardt home. The group determined to publicize their objections to the hostilities in Vietnam and their support for a truce by wearing black armbands during the holiday season and by fasting on December 16 and New Year's Eve. Petitioners and their parents had previously engaged in similar activities, and they decided to participate in the program.

The principals of the Des Moines schools became aware of the plan to wear armbands. On December 14, 1965, they met and adopted a policy that any student wearing an armband to school would be asked to remove it, and if he refused he would be suspended until he returned without the armband. Petitioners were aware of the regulation that the school authorities adopted.

On December 16, Mary Beth and Christopher wore black armbands to their schools. John Tinker wore his armband the next day. They were all sent home and suspended from school until they would come back without their armbands. They did not return to school until after the planned period for wearing armbands had expired—that is, until after New Year's Day.

This complaint was filed in the United States District Court by petitioners, through their fathers, under § 1983 of Title 42 of the United States Code. It prayed for an injunction restraining the respondent school officials and the respondent members of the board of directors of the school district from disciplining the petitioners, and it sought nominal damages. After an evidentiary hearing the District Court dismissed the complaint. It upheld the constitutionality of the school authorities' action on the ground that it was reasonable in order to prevent disturbance of school discipline. * * * The court referred to but expressly declined to follow the Fifth Circuit's holding in a similar case that the wearing of symbols like the armbands cannot be prohibited unless it "materially and substantially interfere[s] with the requirements of appropriate discipline in the operation of the school." * * *

On appeal, the Court of Appeals for the Eighth Circuit considered the case *en banc*. The court was equally divided, and the District Court's decision was accordingly affirmed, without opinion. * * * We granted certiorari. * * *

The District Court recognized that the wearing of an armband for the purpose of expressing certain views is the type of symbolic act that is within the Free Speech Clause of the First Amendment. * * * As we shall discuss, the wearing of armbands in the circumstances of this case was entirely divorced from actually or potentially disruptive conduct by those participating in it. It was closely akin to "pure speech" which, we have repeatedly held, is entitled to comprehensive protection under the First Amendment. * * *

First Amendment rights, applied in light of the special characteristics of the school environment, are available to teachers and students. It can hardly be argued that either students or teachers shed their constitutional rights to freedom of speech or expression at the schoolhouse gate. This has been the unmistakable holding of this Court for almost 50 years. * * *

* * * On the other hand, the Court has repeatedly emphasized the need for affirming the comprehensive authority of the States and of school officials, consistent with fundamental constitutional safeguards, to prescribe and control conduct in the schools. * * * Our problem lies in the area where students in the exercise of First Amendment rights collide with the rules of the school authorities.

The problem posed by the present case does not relate to regulation of the length of skirts or the type of clothing, to hair style, or deportment. * * * It does not concern aggressive, disruptive action or even group demonstrations.

Our problem involves direct, primary First Amendment rights akin to "pure speech."

The school officials banned and sought to punish petitioners for a silent, passive expression of opinion, unaccompanied by any disorder or disturbance on the part of petitioners. There is no evidence whatever of petitioners' interference, actual or nascent, with the schools' work or of collision with the rights of other students to be secure and to be let alone. Accordingly, this case does not concern speech or action that intrudes upon the work of the schools or the rights of other students.

Only a few of the 18,000 students in the school system wore the black armbands. Only five students were suspended for wearing them. There is no indication that the work of the schools or any class was disrupted. Outside the classrooms, a few students made hostile remarks to the children wearing armbands, but there were no threats or acts of violence on school premises.

The District Court concluded that the action of the school authorities was reasonable because it was based upon their fear of a disturbance from the wearing of the armbands. But, in our system, undifferentiated fear or apprehension of disturbance is not enough to overcome the right of freedom of expression. Any departure from absolute regimentation may cause trouble. Any variation from the majority's opinion may inspire fear. Any word spoken, in class, in the lunchroom, or on the campus, that deviates from the views of another person may start an argument or cause a disturbance. But our Constitution says we must take this risk, * * * ; and our history says that it is this sort of hazardous freedom—this kind of openness—that is the basis of our national strength and of the independence and vigor of Americans who grow up and live in this relatively permissive, often disputatious, society.

In order for the State in the person of school officials to justify prohibition of a particular expression of opinion, it must be able to show that its action was caused by something more than a mere desire to avoid the discomfort and unpleasantness that always accompany an unpopular viewpoint. Certainly where there is no finding and no showing that engaging in the forbidden conduct would "materially and substantially interfere with the requirements of appropriate discipline in the operation of the school," the prohibition cannot be sustained. * * *

In the present case, the District Court made no such finding, and our independent examination of the record fails to yield evidence that the school authorities had reason to anticipate that the wearing of the armbands would substantially interfere with the work of the school or impinge upon the rights of other students. Even an official memorandum prepared after the suspension that listed the reasons for the ban on wearing the armbands made no reference to the anticipation of such disruption.

On the contrary, the action of the school authorities appears to have been based upon an urgent wish to avoid the controversy which might result from the expression, even by the silent symbol of armbands, of opposition to this Nation's part in the conflagration in Vietnam. It is revealing, in this respect, that the meeting at which the school principals decided to issue the contested regulation was called in response to a student's statement to the journalism teacher in one of the schools that he wanted to write an article on Vietnam and have it published in the school paper. (The student was dissuaded.)

It is also relevant that the school authorities did not purport to prohibit the wearing of all symbols of political or controversial significance. The record shows that students in some of the schools wore buttons relating to national political campaigns and some even wore the Iron Cross, traditionally a symbol of Nazism. The order prohibiting the wearing of armbands did not extend to these. Instead, a particular symbol—black armbands worn to exhibit opposition to this Nation's involvement in Vietnam—was singled out for prohibition. Clearly, the prohibition of expression of one particular opinion, at least without evidence that it is necessary to avoid material and substantial interference with schoolwork or discipline, is not constitutionally permissible.

In our system, state-operated schools may not be enclaves of totalitarianism. School officials do not possess absolute authority over their students. Students in school as well as out of school are "persons" under our Constitution. They are possessed of fundamental rights which the State must respect, just as they themselves must respect their obligations to the State. In our system, students may not be regarded as closed-circuit recipients of only that which the State chooses to communicate. They may not be confined to the expression of those sentiments that are officially approved. In the absence of a specific showing of constitutionally valid reasons to regulate their speech, students are entitled to freedom of expression of their views. * * *

* * *

* * * The principal use to which the schools are dedicated is to accommodate students during prescribed hours for the purpose of certain types of activities. Among those activities is personal intercommunication among the students. This is not only an inevitable part of the process of attending school; it is also an important part of the educational process. A student's rights, therefore, do not embrace merely the classroom hours. When he is in the cafeteria, or on the playing field, or on the campus during the authorized hours, he may express his opinions, even on controversial subjects like the conflict in Vietnam, if he does so without "materially and substantially interfer[ing] with the requirements of appropriate discipline in the operation of the school" and without colliding with the rights of others. * * * But conduct by the student, in class or out of it, which for any reason—whether it stems from time, place, or type of behavior—materially disrupts classwork or involves substantial disorder or invasion of the rights of others is, of course, not immunized by the constitutional guarantee of freedom of speech. * * *

Under our Constitution, free speech is not a right that is given only to be so circumscribed that it exists in principle but not in fact. Freedom of expression would not truly exist if the right could be exercised only in an area that a benevolent government has provided as a safe haven for crackpots. The Constitution says that Congress (and the States) may not abridge the right to free speech. This provision means what it says. We properly read it to permit reasonable regulation of speech-connected activities in carefully restricted circumstances. But we do not confine the permissible exercise of First Amendment rights to a telephone booth or the four corners of a pamphlet, or to supervised and ordained discussion in a school classroom.

If a regulation were adopted by school officials forbidding discussion of the Vietnam conflict, or the expression by any student of opposition to it anywhere on school property except as part of a prescribed classroom exercise, it would be obvious that the regulation would violate the constitutional rights of students, at least if it could not be justified by a showing that the students' activities would materially and substantially disrupt the work and discipline of the school. * * * In the circumstances of the present case, the prohibition of the silent passive "witness of the armbands," as one of the children called it, is no less offensive to the Constitution's guarantees.

As we have discussed, the record does not demonstrate any facts which might reasonably have led school authorities to forecast substantial disruption of or material interference with school activities, and no disturbances or disorders on the school premises in fact occurred. These petitioners merely went about their ordained rounds in school. Their deviation consisted only in wearing on their sleeve a band of black cloth, not more than two inches wide. They wore it to exhibit their disapproval of the Vietnam hostilities and their advocacy of a truce, to make their views known, and, by their example, to influence others to adopt them. They neither interrupted school activities nor sought to intrude in the school affairs or the lives of others. They caused discussion outside of the classrooms, but no interference with work and no disorder. In the circumstances, our Constitution does not permit officials of the State to deny their form of expression.

We express no opinion as to the form of relief which should be granted, this being a matter for the lower courts to determine. We reverse and remand for further proceedings consistent with this opinion.

Reversed and remanded.

* * *

MR. JUSTICE BLACK, dissenting.

The Court's holding in this case ushers in what I deem to be an entirely new era in which the power to control pupils by the elected "officials of state-supported public schools . . ." in the United States is in ultimate effect transferred to the Supreme Court. * * *

* * *

Assuming that the Court is correct in holding that the conduct of wearing armbands for the purpose of conveying political ideas is protected by the First Amendment * * * , the crucial remaining questions are whether students and teachers may use the schools at their whim as a platform for the exercise of free speech—"symbolic" or "pure"—and whether the courts will allocate to themselves the function of deciding how the pupils' school day will be spent. While I have always believed that under the First and Fourteenth Amendments neither the State nor the Federal Government has any authority to regulate or censor the content of speech, I have never believed that any person has a right to give speeches or engage in demonstrations where he pleases and when he pleases. * * *

While the record does not show that any of these armband students shouted, used profane language, or were violent in any manner, detailed testimony by some of them shows their armbands caused comments, warnings by other students, the poking of fun at them, and a warning by an older football player that other, nonprotesting students had better let them alone. There is also evidence that a teacher of mathematics had his lesson period practically "wrecked" chiefly by disputes with Mary Beth Tinker, who wore her armband for her "demonstration." Even a casual reading of the record shows that this armband did divert students' minds from their regular lessons, and that talk, comments, etc., made John Tinker "self-conscious" in attending school with his armband. While the absence of obscene remarks or boisterous and loud disorder perhaps justified the Court's statement that the few armband students did not actually "disrupt" the classwork, I think the record overwhelmingly shows that the armbands did exactly what the elected school officials and principals foresaw they would, that is, took the students' minds off their classwork and diverted them to thoughts about the highly emotional subject of the Vietnam war. And I repeat that if the time has come when pupils of state-supported schools, kindergartens, grammar schools, or high schools, can defy and flout orders of school officials to keep their minds on their own schoolwork, it is the beginning of a new revolutionary era of permissiveness in this country fostered by the judiciary. The next logical steps, it appears to me, would be to hold unconstitutional laws that bar pupils under 21 or 18 from voting or from being elected members of the boards of education.

* * *

* * * But even if the record were silent as to protests against the Vietnam war distracting students from their assigned class work, members of this Court, like all other citizens, know, without being told, that the disputes over the wisdom of the Vietnam war have disrupted and divided this country as few other issues ever have. Of course students, like other people, cannot concentrate on lesser issues when black armbands are being ostentatiously displayed in their presence to call attention to the wounded and dead of the war, some of the wounded and the dead being their friends and

neighbors. It was, of course, to distract the attention of other students that some students insisted up to the very point of their own suspension from school that they were determined to sit in school with their symbolic arm-bands.

Change has been said to be truly the law of life but sometimes the old and the tried and true are worth holding. The schools of this Nation have undoubtedly contributed to giving us tranquility and to making us a more law-abiding people. Uncontrolled and uncontrollable liberty is an enemy to domestic peace. We cannot close our eyes to the fact that some of the country's greatest problems are crimes committed by the youth, too many of school age. School discipline, like parental discipline, is an integral and important part of training our children to be good citizens—to be better citizens. Here a very small number of students have crisply and summarily refused to obey a school order designed to give pupils who want to learn the opportunity to do so. One does not need to be a prophet or the son of a prophet to know that after the Court's holding today some students in Iowa schools and indeed in all schools will be ready, able, and willing to defy their teachers on practically all orders. This is the more unfortunate for the schools since groups of students all over the land are already running loose, conducting break-ins, sit-ins, lie-ins, and smash-ins. Many of these student groups, as is all too familiar to all who read the newspapers and watch the television news programs, have already engaged in rioting, property seizures, and destruction. They have picketed schools to force students not to cross their picket lines and have too often violently attacked earnest but frightened students who wanted an education that the pickets did not want them to get. Students engaged in such activities are apparently confident that they know far more about how to operate public school systems than do their parents, teachers, and elected school officials. It is no answer to say that the particular students here have not yet reached such high points in their demands to attend classes in order to exercise their political pressures. Turned loose with lawsuits for damages and injunctions against their teachers as they are here, it is nothing but wishful thinking to imagine that young, immature students will not soon believe it is their right to control the schools rather than the right of the States that collect the taxes to hire the teachers for the benefit of the pupils. This case, therefore, wholly without constitutional reasons in my judgment, subjects all the public schools in the country to the whims and caprices of their loudest-mouthed, but maybe not their brightest, students. I, for one, am not fully persuaded that school pupils are wise enough, even with this Court's expert help from Washington, to run the 23,390 public school systems in our 50 States. I wish, therefore, wholly to disclaim any purpose on my part to hold that the Federal Constitution compels the teachers, parents, and elected school officials to surrender control of the American public school system to public school students. I dissent.

Notes

It should be kept in mind that the freedom of expression protected in *Tinker* pertains to the expression of social, political, and economic issues by high school and junior high school students. Not protected is such student conduct as insolence, disrespect, screaming, or cursing at staff members or fellow students.

Tinker was filed as a legal action under § 1983 of Title 42 of the United States Code. This section of the Civil Rights Act is often employed as a legal basis for bringing a suit involving students or teachers. See Chapter 8 for a brief discussion of this act.

According to *Tinker*, "undifferentiated fear or apprehension of disturbance is not enough to overcome the right of freedom of expression," and school authorities must accept "mere disturbance" when students exercise their First Amendment rights. Only when students engage in conduct that would "*materially and substantially* interfere with the requirements of appropriate discipline in the operation of the school" (emphasis added) may authorities prohibit the conduct. Unfortunately, the Court did not provide a test that school authorities could employ to determine whether actual disruption or merely a forecast of "substantial disruption" was necessary before they could prohibit conduct where freedom of expression was at issue. Further complicating the picture for school administrators was the failure by the Court to provide sufficient guidance concerning the meaning of a forecast of "substantial disruption."

There is little doubt that school officials may enforce reasonable rules to ensure the orderly operation of the school. However, *Tinker* proclaimed that when freedom of expression is involved, school officials may not restrict this freedom because the political viewpoint expressed displeases an official or has the potential to bring about a degree of disruption. Part of the desired political socialization of students is that they learn that a government official—a school authority in this instance—may not restrict certain types of freedom of expression merely because it may be annoying or somewhat disruptive. Although some school officials may feel uncomfortable with such a doctrine, its rationale is based on the notion that if students are to become full participants in a free and democratic society, they must thoroughly understand that they are free to express themselves on any social, political, or economic issue without undue restraint or reprisal from government. The Court's contention was that the school is the proper place for a student to come to this understanding through the observance of freedom of expression in the school environment rather than through lectures or through policies that imply that freedom of expression is conferred at a specific age or upon graduation from high school.

Do contemporary notions about being "politically correct" fly in the face of the above? Why, for instance, should students not be allowed to make negative comments related to another student's religion, race, ethnic background, gender, or group association merely because it may be offensive or disagreeable? Is it because a school has a duty to teach good manners and civility? Or is it because, in addition to impeding the orderly operation of the school, students are required by law to attend and that it would appear to be an endorsement by the school if such views were allowed to be uttered?

A middle school student's suspension for drawing a picture of a confederate flag on a piece of paper during a math class was upheld in *West v. Derby Unified School District*, 206 F. 3d 1358 110th cir. 2000), *cert. denied* 531 U.S. 104 (2000). In this instance, the school district had a "Racial Harassment or Intimidation" policy that prohibited "any written material, either printed or in their own handwriting, that is racially divisive or creates ill will or hatred" and specifically included confederate flags or articles. In its decision, the court held that given the past history of racial incidents between white and black students, the district had a reasonable basis to assume that this student's conduct would lead to a substantial disruption of school activities.

A student was suspended for having created an Internet home page on his personal computer containing vulgar language and that was critical of his school. In upholding the student, the court declared that his First Amendment Rights had been violated and that allowing provocative and challenging speech did not interfere with school discipline. See *Beussink v. Woodland R-IV School District*, 30 F. Supp.2d 1175 (Mo. 1998).

A school system's policy requiring students to engage in sixty hours of community service as a condition of graduation was challenged on the grounds that it compelled expression that was protected by the First Amendment. In rejecting this claim, a federal appellate court contended that participation in the program did not affirm a belief in the philosophy of altruism on the part of participating students. See *Steirer v. Bethlehem Area School District*, 987 F.2d 989 (3rd Cir. 1993), *cert. denied*, 510 U.S. 824 (1993). Other federal courts of appeals have upheld similar community service programs. See *Immediato v. Rye Neck School District*, 73 F.3d 454 (2nd Cir. 1996), *cert. denied*, 519 U.S. 813 (1996), and *Herndon v. Chapel Hill-Carrboro City Board of Education*, 89 F.3d 174 (4th Cir. 1996), *cert. denied*, 519 U.S. 1111 (1997).

Students attending private schools do not have the First Amendment protections provided by the *Tinker* decision, nor do such students necessarily have all of the civil rights guaranteed by other amendments through the Fourteenth Amendment. Such rights are available to public school students because the public school operates under the "color of the State." Because most private school activities are not considered "state action," a substantial linkage between a private school and the state or federal government would have to be present for a private school to be considered acting under the "color of the state." As a result, private school students do not have many of the rights afforded public school students discussed in the succeeding sections of this chapter. Disagreements over "student rights" in a private school setting are generally resolved by applying contract law to the agreement governing the student's attendance.

B. Limiting the *Tinker* Doctrine

Active and lively litigation after *Tinker* addressed such issues as the wearing of buttons or other symbols, the use of obscenity and "fighting words," censorship of student publications, and distribution of "underground" newspapers. Frequently, this litigation did little to dispel fears that the *Tinker* court had bestowed on students unbridled license to behave as they pleased. Several federal courts, relying on the *Tinker* decision, upheld forms of student expression that many parents and school authorities considered inappropriate. However, Supreme Court decisions, such as *Bethel School District No. 403 v. Fraser* and *Hazelwood School District v. Kuhlmeier*, in the late 1980s, have tended to limit what many observers heretofore thought the *Tinker* decision allowed.

1. Nonpolitical Speech

BETHEL SCHOOL DISTRICT NO. 403
v. FRASER
Supreme Court of the United States, 1986
478 U.S. 675

CHIEF JUSTICE BURGER delivered the opinion of the Court.

We granted certiorari to decide whether the First Amendment prevents a school district from disciplining a high school student for giving a lewd speech at a school assembly.

On April 26, 1983, respondent Matthew N. Fraser, a student at Bethel High School in Bethel, Washington, delivered a speech nominating a fellow student for student elective office. Approximately 600 high school students, many of whom were 14-year-olds, attended the assembly. Students were required to attend the assembly or to report to the study hall. The assembly was part of a school-sponsored educational program in self-government. Students who elected not to attend the assembly were required to report to study hall. During the entire speech, Fraser referred to his candidate in terms of an elaborate, graphic, and explicit sexual metaphor.

Two of Fraser's teachers, with whom he discussed the contents of his speech in advance, informed him that the speech was "inappropriate and that he probably should not deliver it," * * * and that his delivery of the speech might have "severe consequences." * * *

During Fraser's delivery of the speech, a school counselor observed the reaction of students to the speech. Some students hooted and yelled; some by gestures graphically simulated the sexual activities pointedly alluded to in the respondent's speech. Other students appeared to be bewildered and embarrassed by the speech. One teacher reported that on the day following the speech, she found it necessary to forgo a portion of the scheduled class lesson in order to discuss the speech with the class.

A Bethel High School disciplinary rule prohibiting the use of obscene language in the school provides:

> Conduct which materially and substantially interferes with the educational process is prohibited, including the use of obscene, profane language or gestures.

The morning after the assembly, the assistant principal called Fraser into her office and notified him that the school considered his speech to have been a violation of this rule. Fraser was presented with copies of five letters submitted by teachers, describing his conduct at the assembly; he was given a chance to explain his conduct, and he admitted to having given the speech described and that he deliberately used sexual innuendo in the speech. Fraser was then informed that he would be suspended for three days, and that his name would be removed from the list of candidates for graduation speaker at the school's commencement exercises.

Fraser sought review of this disciplinary action through the School District's grievance procedures. The hearing officer determined that the speech given by the respondent was "indecent, lewd, and offensive to the modesty and decency of many of the students and faculty in attendance at the assembly." The examiner determined that the speech fell within the ordinary meaning of "obscene," as used in the disruptive conduct rule, and affirmed the discipline in its entirety. Fraser served two days of his suspension, and was allowed to return to school on the third day.

Respondent, by his father as guardian *ad litem*, then brought this action in the United States District Court for the Western District of Washington. Respondent alleged a violation of his First Amendment right to freedom of speech and sought both injunctive relief and monetary damages under 42 U.S.C. § 1983. The District Court held that the school's sanctions violated respondent's right to freedom of speech under the First Amendment to the United States Constitution, that the school's disruptive conduct rule is unconstitutionally vague and overbroad, and that the removal of respondent's name from the graduation speaker's list violated the Due Process Clause of the Fourteenth Amendment because the disciplinary rule makes no mention of such removal as a possible sanction. The District Court awarded respondent $278 in damages, $12,750 in litigation costs and attorney's fees, and enjoined the School District from preventing respondent from speaking at the commencement ceremonies. Respondent, who had been elected graduation speaker by a write-in vote of his class-mates, delivered a speech at the commencement ceremonies on June 8, 1983.

The Court of Appeals for the Ninth Circuit affirmed the judgment of the District Court, ∗ ∗ ∗ holding that respondent's speech was indistinguish-able from the protest armband in *Tinker* v. *Des Moines Independent Com-munity School Dist.* The court explicitly rejected the School District's argument that the speech, unlike the passive conduct of wearing a black armband, had a disruptive effect on the educational process. The Court of Appeals also rejected the School District's argument that it had an interest in protecting an essentially captive audience of minors from lewd and in-decent language in a setting sponsored by the school, reasoning that the school board's "unbridled discretion" to determine what discourse is "de-cent" would "increase the risk of cementing white, middle-class standards for determining what is acceptable and proper speech and behavior in our public schools." ∗ ∗ ∗ Finally, the Court of Appeals rejected the School Dis-trict's argument that, incident to its responsibility for the school curriculum, it had the power to control the language used to express ideas during a school-sponsored activity.

We granted certiorari ∗ ∗ ∗ . *We reverse.*

This Court acknowledged in *Tinker* v. *Des Moines Independent Com-munity School Dist.* ∗ ∗ ∗ that students do not "shed their constitutional rights to freedom of speech or expression at the schoolhouse gate." ∗ ∗ ∗

The Court of Appeals read that case as precluding any discipline of Fraser for indecent speech and lewd conduct in the school assembly. That court appears to have proceeded on the theory that the use of lewd and ob-scene speech in order to make what the speaker considered to be a point in a nominating speech for a fellow student was essentially the same as the wearing of an armband in *Tinker* as a form of protest or the expression of a political position.

The marked distinction between the political "message" of the arm-bands in *Tinker* and the sexual content of respondent's speech in this case seems to have been given little weight by the Court of Appeals. In upholding the students' right to engage in a nondisruptive, passive expression of a po-litical viewpoint in *Tinker*, this Court was careful to note that the case did "not concern speech or action that intrudes upon the work of the schools or the rights of other students." ∗ ∗ ∗

It is against this background that we turn to consider the level of First Amendment protection accorded to Fraser's utterances and actions before an official high school assembly attended by 600 students.

The role and purpose of the American public school system was well described by two historians, saying "public education must prepare pupils for citizenship in the Republic. . . . It must inculcate the habits and manners of civility as values in themselves conducive to happiness and as indispensable to the practice of self-government in the community and the nation." * * *

These fundamental values of "habits and manners of civility" essential to a democratic society must, of course, include tolerance of divergent political and religious views, even when the views expressed may be unpopular. But these "fundamental values" must also take into account consideration of the sensibilities of others, and, in the case of a school, the sensibilities of fellow students. The undoubted freedom to advocate unpopular and controversial views in schools and classrooms must be balanced against the society's countervailing interest in teaching students the boundaries of socially appropriate behavior. Even the most heated political discourse in a democratic society requires consideration for the personal sensibilities of the other participants and audiences.

* * *

Surely it is a highly appropriate function of public school education to prohibit the use of vulgar and offensive terms in public discourse. Indeed, the "fundamental values necessary to the maintenance of a democratic political system" disfavor the use of terms of debate highly offensive or highly threatening to others. Nothing in the Constitution prohibits the states from insisting that certain modes of expression are inappropriate and subject to sanctions. The inculcation of these values is truly the "work of the schools." * * * The determination of what manner of speech in the classroom or in school assembly is inappropriate properly rests with the school board.

The process of educating our youth for citizenship in public schools is not confined to books, the curriculum, and the civics class; schools must teach by example the shared values of a civilized social order. Consciously or otherwise, teachers—and indeed the older students—demonstrate the appropriate form of civil discourse and political expression by their conduct and deportment in and out of class. Inescapably, like parents, they are role models. The schools, as instruments of the state, may determine that the essential lessons of civil, mature conduct cannot be conveyed in a school that tolerates lewd, indecent, or offensive speech and conduct such as that indulged in by this confused boy.

The pervasive sexual innuendo in Fraser's speech was plainly offensive to both teachers and students—indeed to any mature person. By glorifying male sexuality, and in its verbal content, the speech was acutely insulting to teenage girl students. * * * The speech could well be seriously damaging to its less mature audience, many of whom were only 14 years old and on the threshold of awareness of human sexuality. Some students were reported as bewildered by the speech and the reaction of mimicry it provoked.

* * *

We hold that petitioner School District acted entirely within its permissible authority in imposing sanctions upon Fraser in response to his offensively lewd and indecent speech. Unlike the sanctions imposed on the students wearing armbands in *Tinker*, the penalties imposed in this case were unrelated to any political viewpoint. The First Amendment does not prevent the school officials from determining that to permit a vulgar and lewd speech such as respondent's would undermine the school's basic educational mission. A high school assembly or classroom is no place for a sexually explicit monologue directed toward an unsuspecting audience of teenage students. Accordingly, it was perfectly appropriate for the school to disassociate itself to make the point to the pupils that vulgar speech and lewd conduct are wholly inconsistent with the "fundamental values" of public school education. * * *

* * *

Respondent contends that the circumstances of his suspension violated due process because he had no way of knowing that the delivery of the speech in question would subject him to disciplinary sanctions. * * * Two days' suspension from school does not rise to the level of a penal sanction calling for the full panoply of procedural due process protections applicable to a criminal prosecution. * * * The school disciplinary rule proscribing "obscene" language and the prespeech admonitions of teachers gave adequate warning to Fraser that his lewd speech could subject him to sanctions.

The judgment of the Court of Appeals for the Ninth Circuit is

Reversed.

JUSTICE BRENNAN, concurring in the judgment.

Respondent gave the following speech at a high school assembly in support of a candidate for student government office:

> I know a man who is firm—he's firm in his pants, he's firm in his shirt, his character is firm—but most . . . of all, his belief in you, the students of Bethel, is firm.
>
> Jeff Kuhlman is a man who takes his point and pounds it in. If necessary, he'll take an issue and nail it to the wall. He doesn't attack things in spurts—he drives hard, pushing and pushing until finally—he succeeds.
>
> Jeff is a man who will go to the very end—even the climax, for each and every one of you.
>
> So vote for Jeff for A. S. B. vice-president—he'll never come between you and the best our high school can be.

The Court, referring to these remarks as "obscene," "vulgar," "lewd," and "offensively lewd," concludes that school officials properly punished respondent for uttering the speech. Having read the full text of respondent's remarks, I find it difficult to believe that it is the same speech the Court describes. To my mind, the most that can be said about respondent's speech—and all that need be said—is that in light of the discretion school officials have to teach high school students how to conduct civil and effective public discourse, and to prevent disruption of school educational activities, it was not unconstitutional for school officials to conclude, under the circumstances of this case, that respondent's remarks exceeded permissible limits. Thus, while I concur in the Court's judgment, I write separately to express my understanding of the breadth of the Court's holding.

Notes

Chief Justice Warren E. Burger, who wrote the seven-to-two majority opinion in *Fraser*, was nominated by President Nixon in 1969. Prior to his nomination, he was a judge on the U.S. Court of Appeals for the District of Columbia Circuit since 1956. Chief Justice Burger retired from the Court in 1986.

In *Fraser* the Court made it clear that *Tinker* was not to be read as recognizing that student rights are coextensive with those of adults. It is important to note that Mr. Fraser's speech if made by an adult in public almost certainly would have enjoyed constitutional protection. *Fraser*, however, disclosed the Court's conviction that public schools have an important role in imparting respect for civility of public discourse. The holding also revealed the majority's view that judging the appropriateness of student speech ought to be left to school officials rather than to federal judges.

Several other courts have cited *Fraser* as they attempted to determine the extent to which students could express themselves. A court upheld the suspension, for the use of an obscenity by a white female student, for retorting that she was not a "white ass fucking bitch" to a black female student who had called her that. The exchange of words occurred as a result of the black female cutting in line at the school cafeteria. The court opined that using these words was clearly disruptive in addition to their being "fighting words." Both students received the same five-day suspension. The court found no equal protection violation, although the instigating student had an extensive disciplinary history while the other student had no prior record of disciplinary problems. See *Heller v. Hodgin*, 928 F. Supp. 789 (Ind. 1996). Again citing *Fraser*, a student candidate for student council president was disqualified for that position for making "discourteous" and "rude" remarks about an assistant principal during a speech at a school-sponsored assembly. See *Poling v. Murphy*, 872 F.2d 757 (6th Cir. 1989).

2. School-Sponsored Expressive Activities

Another widely litigated freedom-of-expression issue dealt with school authorities' control over school-sponsored expressive activities such as student publications. Although several federal appellate courts had addressed the issue prior to 1988, the United States Supreme Court had not. The result was a complex, confusing body of case law.

In many jurisdictions, school newspapers have been considered to be "public forums," immune from attempts to regulate the viewpoints expressed therein. Student writing that was sexually suggestive, that advocated drug use, or that was potentially libelous seemingly enjoyed constitutional protection. Thus many school authorities saw their only options as either allowing the publication of such material or ceasing altogether to publish student newspapers. Against this background the United States Supreme Court's five-to-three decision in *Hazelwood School District* v. *Kuhlmeier*, which addressed a school principal's censorship of student news articles, has enormous significance.

HAZELWOOD SCHOOL DISTRICT
v. KUHLMEIER
Supreme Court of the United States, 1988
484 U.S 260

JUSTICE WHITE delivered the opinion of the Court.

This case concerns the extent to which educators may exercise editorial control over the contents of a high school newspaper produced as part of the school's journalism curriculum.

* * *

Spectrum was written and edited by the Journalism II class at Hazelwood East. The newspaper was published every three weeks or so during the 1982–1983 school year. More than 4,500 copies of the newspaper were distributed during that year to students, school personnel, and members of the community.

The Board of Education allocated funds from its annual budget for the printing of *Spectrum*. These funds were supplemented by proceeds from sales of the newspaper. The printing expenses during the 1982–1983 school year totaled $4,668.50; revenue from sales was $1,166.84. The other costs associated with the newspaper—such as supplies, textbooks, and a portion of the journalism teacher's salary—were borne entirely by the Board.

* * *

We deal first with the question whether *Spectrum* may appropriately be characterized as a forum for public expression. The public schools do not possess all of the attributes of streets, parks, and other traditional public forums that "time out of mind, have been used for purposes of assembly, communicating thoughts between citizens, and discussing public questions." * * * Hence, school facilities may be deemed to be public forums only if school authorities have "by policy or by practice" opened those facilities "for indiscriminate use by the general public" * * * or by some segment of the public, such as student organizations. ∗ ∗ ∗ If the facilities have instead been reserved for other intended purposes, "communicative or otherwise," then no public forum has been created, and school officials may impose reasonable restrictions on the speech of students, teachers, and other members of the school community. ∗ ∗ ∗ "The government does not create a public forum by inaction or by permitting limited discourse, but only by intentionally opening a nontraditional forum for public discourse."

The policy of school officials toward *Spectrum* was reflected in Hazelwood School Board Policy 348.51 and the Hazelwood East Curriculum Guide. Board Policy 348.51 provided that "[s]chool sponsored publications are developed within the adopted curriculum and its educational implications in regular classroom activities." ∗ ∗ ∗ The Hazelwood East Curriculum Guide described the Journalism II course as a "laboratory situation in which the students publish the school newspaper applying skills they have learned in Journalism I." ∗ ∗ ∗ The lessons that were to be learned from the Journalism II course, according to the Curriculum Guide, included development of journalistic skills under deadline pressure, "the legal, moral, and ethical restrictions imposed upon journalists within the school community," and "responsibility and acceptance of criticism for articles of opinion." ∗ ∗ ∗ Journalism II was taught by a faculty member during regular class hours. Students received grades and academic credit for their performance in the course.

School officials did not deviate in practice from their policy that production of *Spectrum* was to be part of the educational curriculum and a "regular classroom activit[y]." The District Court found that Robert Stergos, the journalism teacher during most of the 1982–1983 school year, "both had the authority to exercise and in fact exercised a great deal of control over *Spectrum*." ∗ ∗ ∗ For example, Stergos selected the editors of the newspaper, scheduled publication dates, decided the number of pages for each issue, assigned story ideas to class members, advised students on the development of their stories, reviewed the use of quotations, edited stories, selected and edited the letters to the editor, and dealt with the printing company. Many of these decisions were made without consultation with the Journalism II students.

∗ ∗ ∗

∗ ∗ ∗ Board Policy 348.51, which stated in part that "[s]chool sponsored student publications will not restrict free expression or diverse viewpoints within the rules of responsible journalism," also stated that such publications were "developed within the adopted curriculum and its educational implications." One might reasonably infer from the full text of Policy 348.51 that school officials retained ultimate control over what constituted "responsible journalism" in a school-sponsored newspaper. Although the Statement of Policy published in the September 14, 1982, issue of *Spectrum* declared that "*Spectrum*, as a student-press publication, accepts all rights implied by the First Amendment," this statement, understood in the context of the paper's role in the school's curriculum, suggests at most that the administration will not interfere with the students' exercise of those First Amendment rights that attend the publication of a school-sponsored newspaper. It does not reflect an intent to expand those rights by converting a curricular newspaper into a public forum. Finally, that students were permitted to exercise some authority over the contents of *Spectrum* was fully consistent with the Curriculum Guide objective of teaching the Journalism II students "leadership responsibilities as issue and page editors." A decision to teach leadership skills in the context of a classroom activity hardly implies a decision to relinquish school control over that activity. * * * School officials did not evince either "by policy or by practice" * * * any intent to open the pages of *Spectrum* to "indiscriminate use" by its student reporters and editors, or by the student body generally. Instead, they "reserve[d] the forum for its intended purpos[e]" as a supervised learning experience for journalism students. Accordingly, school officials were entitled to regulate the contents of *Spectrum* in any reasonable manner. It is this standard, rather than our decision in *Tinker*, that governs this case.

The question whether the First Amendment requires a school to tolerate particular student speech—the question that we addressed in *Tinker*—is different from the question whether the First Amendment requires a school affirmatively to promote particular student speech. The former question addresses educators' ability to silence a student's personal expression that happens to occur on the school premises. The latter question concerns educators' authority over school-sponsored publications, theatrical productions, and other expressive activities that students, parents, and members of the public might reasonably perceive to bear the imprimatur of the school. These activities may fairly be characterized as part of the school curriculum, whether or not they occur in a traditional classroom setting, so long as they are supervised by faculty members and designed to impart particular knowledge or skills to student participants and audiences.

Educators are entitled to exercise greater control over this second form of student expression to assure that participants learn whatever lessons the activity is designed to teach, that readers or listeners are not exposed to material that may be inappropriate for their level of maturity, and that the views of the individual speaker are not erroneously attributed to the school. Hence, a school may in its capacity as publisher of a school newspaper or producer of a school play "disassociate itself" * * * not only from speech that would "substantially interfere with [its] work . . . or impinge upon the rights of other students" * * * but also from speech that is, for example, ungrammatical, poorly written, inadequately researched, biased or prejudiced, vulgar or profane, or unsuitable for immature audiences. A school must be able to set high standards for the student speech that is disseminated under its auspices—standards that may be higher than those demanded by some newspaper publishers or theatrical producers in the "real" world—and may refuse to disseminate student speech that does not meet those standards. In addition, a school must be able to take into account the emotional maturity of the intended audience in determining whether to disseminate student speech on potentially sensitive topics, which might range from the existence of Santa Claus in an elementary school setting to the particulars of teenage sexual activity in a high school setting. A school must also retain the authority to refuse to sponsor student speech that might reasonably be perceived to advocate drug or alcohol use, irresponsible sex, or conduct otherwise inconsistent with "the shared values of a civilized social order" * * * or to associate the school with any position other than neutrality on matters of political controversy. Otherwise, the schools would be unduly constrained from fulfilling their role as "a principal instrument in awakening the child to cultural values, in preparing him for later professional training, and in helping him to adjust normally to his environment." * * *

Accordingly, we conclude that the standard articulated in *Tinker* for determining when a school may punish student expression need not also be the standard for determining when a school may refuse to lend its name and resources to the dissemination of student expression. Instead, we hold that educators do not offend the First Amendment by exercising editorial control over the style and content of student speech in school-sponsored expressive activities so long as their actions are reasonably related to legitimate pedagogical concerns.

This standard is consistent with our oft-expressed view that the education of the Nation's youth is primarily the responsibility of parents, teachers, and state and local school officials, and not of federal judges. * * * It is only when the decision to censor a school-sponsored publication, theatrical production, or other vehicle of student expression has no valid educational purpose that the First Amendment is so "directly and sharply implicate[d]" as to require judicial intervention to protect students' constitutional rights.

* * *

In sum, we cannot reject as unreasonable Principal Reynolds' conclusion that neither the pregnancy article nor the divorce article was suitable for publication in *Spectrum*. Reynolds could reasonably have concluded that the students who had written and edited these articles had not sufficiently mastered those portions of the Journalism II curriculum that pertained to the treatment of controversial issues and personal attacks, the need to protect the privacy of individuals whose most intimate concerns are to be revealed in the newspaper, and "the legal, moral, and ethical restrictions imposed upon journalists within [a] school community" that includes adolescent subjects and readers. Finally, we conclude that the principal's decision to delete two pages of *Spectrum*, rather than to delete only the offending articles or to require that they be modified, was reasonable under the circumstances as he understood them. Accordingly, no violation of First Amendment rights occurred.

The judgment of the Court of Appeals for the Eighth Circuit is therefore *Reversed.*

Notes and Questions

Courts in the United States have looked especially skeptically at attempts to censor materials prior to their publication. Was the Supreme Court's upholding of Principal Reynolds significant in this regard?

Will the holding in *Kuhlmeier*, a five-to-three decision, coupled with the seven-to-two decision in *Fraser*, have a chilling effect on related suits being brought before the courts? For example, what effect will the decision have on other "school-sponsored expressive activities" such as plays, yearbooks, program notices, and debates?

It is clear that a majority on the Court perceived a major purpose of public schooling to be the inculcation of society's values as defined by society's elders. Does the Court's articulation of this viewpoint represent a retreat from the educational philosophy expressed in *Tinker*, that a school should be a marketplace of ideas and that the proper socialization for a free people is the early exercise of freedom?

As a consequence of *Fraser* and *Kuhlmeier*, it seems likely that school authorities will be less hesitant to prohibit student expression that they heretofore may have thought was protected under the *Tinker* doctrine. Nevertheless, authorities apparently may choose to establish public forums within their schools and, thus, to surrender their discretion to censor student expression. To preserve such discretion they should clearly distinguish curricular activities from activities intended for students' expression of their views. Hazelwood authorities prevailed partly because they retained, "by policy and practice," the curricular identity of *Spectrum*, and consequently they "retained ultimate control over what constituted responsible journalism." Written policies and curriculum coupled with consistent practices bolstered their position and may be considered a model for legally defensible behavior in school administration.

Prohibiting a marching band from performing the song "White Rabbit," which the school superintendent thought promoted the illegal use of drugs, did not violate students' freedom of speech. In its decision in *McCann v. Fort Zumwalt School District*, 50 F. Supp.2d 918 (Mo. 1999), the court contended that: band activity such as playing at football games constituted school-sponsored speech and bore the imprimatur of the school; the marching band was part of the curriculum for those enrolled in symphonic band; and participating in scheduled performances was part of a student's grade.

May a school refuse to publish a student's picture in the yearbook because the student was in violation of the grooming code? The Ohio

Supreme Court held that a picture of a student whose hairstyle was in violation of the code could not be excluded from the school yearbook, which was to be distributed after the school year ended. However, the school could refrain from publishing a yearbook. See *McClung v. Board of Education of City of Washington C.H.*, 346 N.E.2d 691 (Ohio 1976). Also see *Stanton v. Brunswick School Department*, 577 F. Supp. 1560 (Me. 1984), which addressed the appropriateness in a yearbook of a student-selected quotation vividly describing execution by electrocution. The court stated that the school had created a public forum by permitting students to include a quote under their pictures and that matters of taste may not be censored by vague, subjective, or nondiscrete standards.

A federal district court upheld a school board's decision not to produce *Runaways*, a play in which child abuse, rape, murder, and drug abuse were simulated. In its holding the court declared that seventh- through twelfth-grade students were not denied their First Amendment rights and that the school board was within its authority to protect the well-being of its students. See *Bell v. U-32 Board of Education*, 630 F. Supp. 939 (Vt. 1986).

School newspapers often accept, and in fact solicit, advertising to defray expenses and to provide students with valuable business experience relating to the operation of a newspaper. A federal appellate court did not uphold a school board's refusal to accept advertising from the San Diego Committee Against Registration and the Draft. The court in this instance reasoned that the school board had created a limited public forum by allowing some members of the public to use its newspapers to engage in speech that combined elements of political and commercial speech. See *San Diego Committee Against Registration and the Draft v. Governing Board of Grossmont Union High School District*, 790 F.2d 1471 (9th Cir. 1986). However, see *Planned Parenthood v. Clark County School District*, 941 F.2d 817 (9th Cir. 1991), in which the en banc court rejected Planned Parenthood advertisements in the high school papers, yearbooks, and athletic event programs. The advertisements referred to gynecological exams, birth control methods, pregnancy testing and verification, and pregnancy counseling and referral. In its decision, the court contended that all three publications constituted nonpublic forums rather than designated public forums and that these advertisements were reasonably rejected by school authorities because they would be controversial and would distract from the school's mission.

Student editors of a school newspaper and yearbook refused to accept an advertisement promoting sexual abstinence that was submitted as part of a condoms-versus-abstinence debate taking place in the school. The student editors' rejection was based on their policy of not accepting political or controversial advertising. In its en banc decision to uphold the student editors, in *Yeo v. Town of Lexington*, 131 F.3d 241 (1st Cir.1997), *cert. denied*, 524 U.S. 904 (1998), the court emphasized that the decision not to print the ad was solely a student decision and therefore did not constitute "state action." In discussing the state action issue, the court asserted that not only had the school officials granted the students editorial autonomy, but evidence revealed that their relationship with the students at times was close to adversarial.

Does your school system have policies pertaining to school-sponsored expressive activities?

C. Participation in Patriotic Exercises

Students have challenged local policies or state statutes requiring their participation in patriotic exercises. The most common challenge centers on participation in the pledge of allegiance. *Sherman* v. *Community School District 21* upheld a student's position not to participate in the pledge and follows the rationale of other courts that have addressed this issue.

SHERMAN v. COMMUNITY SCHOOL DISTRICT 21
United States Court of Appeals, 7th Circuit, 1992
980 F.2d 437
cert. denied, 508 U. S. 950 (1993)

EASTERBROOK, Circuit Judge.

"[N]o official, high or petty, can prescribe what shall be orthodox in politics, nationalism, religion, or other matters of opinion or force citizens to confess by word or act their faith therein." *West Virginia State Board of Education* v. *Barnette*. A state therefore may not compel any person to recite the Pledge of Allegiance to the flag. On similar grounds, *Wooley* v. *Maynard* adds that a state may not compel any person to display its slogan. Does it follow that a pupil who objects to the content of the Pledge may prevent teachers and other pupils from reciting it in his presence? We conclude that schools may lead the Pledge of Allegiance daily, so long as pupils are free not to participate.

In 1979 Illinois enacted this statute: "The Pledge of Allegiance shall be recited each school day by pupils in elementary institutions supported or maintained in whole or in part by public funds." Ill. Rev. Stat. ch 122 ¶ 27-3. ∗ ∗ ∗

∗ ∗ ∗

What the law requires of principals, teachers, and pupils depends on the language it contains rather than the penalties it omits. And what ¶ 27-3 says is that the pledge "shall be recited each school day by pupils" in public schools. Some pupils? Willing pupils? All pupils? It does not specify. If it means "all pupils" then it is blatantly unconstitutional; if it means "willing pupils" then the most severe constitutional problem dissolves. When resolving statutory ambiguities, the Supreme Court of Illinois adopts readings that save rather than destroy state laws. Given *Barnette*, which long predated enactment of this statute, it makes far more sense to interpolate "by willing pupils" than "by all pupils." School administrators and teachers satisfy the "shall" requirement by leading the Pledge and ensuring that at least some pupils recite. Leading the Pledge is not optional, but participating is. This makes sense of the statute without imputing a flagrantly unconstitutional act to the State of Illinois.

This understanding is consistent with the practice in the Wheeling schools. The superintendent of schools, the principal of Riley School, and his first grade teacher when this suit began, all filed affidavits stating that neither Richard nor any other pupil is compelled to recite the Pledge, to place his hand over his heart, to stand, or to leave the room while others recite. Marilyn Barden, Richard's teacher, averred that she brooks no hazing of those who decline to participate, and that she has never noticed any. * * *

* * *

A pupil who takes exception to the prescribed curriculum of the public schools—whether the textbooks or the class discussions or the civic ceremonies such as the pledge of Allegiance—is asserting a right to accommodation of his political or religious beliefs. Humane government often calls for accommodation; programs such as tuition vouchers serve this interest without offending other constitutional norms. Government nonetheless retains the right to set the curriculum in its own schools and insist that those who cannot accept the result exercise their right under *Pierce* v. *Society of Sisters*, and select private education at their own expense. The private market supports a profusion of schools, many tailored to religious or cultural minorities, making the majoritarian curriculum of the public schools less oppressive. * * * All that remains is *Barnette* itself, and so long as the school does not compel pupils to espouse the content of the Pledge as their own belief, it may carry on with patriotic exercises. Objection by the few does not reduce to silence the many who *want* to pledge allegiance to the flag "and to the Republic for which it stands."

* * *

Notes and Questions

In an earlier decision, a student's position was upheld in a refusal to stand at respectful attention during the salute to the flag. The student in this case contended that the words of the pledge were not true. See *Lipp* v. *Morris*, 579 F.2d 834, (3rd Cir. 1978). A student's position was also upheld in a refusal to stand during the pledge, because he believed "that there [isn't] liberty and justice for all in the United States." The court did not agree that the option of either leaving the room or standing quietly during the pledge ceremony was a viable option. See *Goetz v. Ansell*, 477 F.2d 636 (2nd Cir. 1973).

The United States Supreme Court upheld the rights of Jehovah's Witnesses not to participate in the pledging of the flag. See *West Virginia State Board of Education v. Barnette*, 319 U.S. 624 (1943). This opinion was rendered while the United States was engaged in World War II, and many observers contend that the decision is a dramatic espousal of the individual's right of freedom of expression. In often quoted sections, the Court stated:

> . . . One's right to life, liberty and property, to free speech, a free press, freedom to worship and assembly, and other fundamental rights may not be submitted to vote; they depend on the outcome of no elections. (p. 638)
>
> * * *
>
> If there is any fixed star in our constellation, it is that no official, high or petty, can prescribe what shall be orthodox in politics, nationalism, religion, or other matters of opinion or force citizens to confess by word or act their faith therein. If there are any circumstances which permit an exception, they do not now occur to us. (p. 642)

Georgia has a statutory provision that states:

> Each student in the public schools of the State of Georgia shall be afforded the opportunity to recite the Pledge of Allegiance to the flag of the United States of America during each school day. It shall be the duty of each local board of education to establish a policy setting the time and manner for recitation of the Pledge of Allegiance. Said policy shall be established in writing and shall be distributed to each teacher within the school. Ga. Code Ann. § 20-2-286 (1976).

Disrespect such as burning the American flag has been the subject of political, statutory, and judicial debate. Following the United States Supreme Court decision in *Texas v. Johnson*, 491 U.S. 397 (1989), which held a Texas law criminalizing desecration of the flag as unconstitutional, Congress enacted the Flag Protection Act of 1989, which made it a crime for anyone who "knowingly mutilates, defaces, physically defiles, burns, maintains on the floor or ground, or tramples upon" a United States flag. In a five-to-four decision invalidating this act, the Court stated: "While flag desecration—like virulent ethnic and religious epithets, vulgar repudiations of the draft, and scurrilous caricatures—is deeply offensive to many, the Government may not prohibit the expression of an idea simply because society finds the idea itself offensive or disagreeable." See *United States v. Eichman*, 496 U.S. 310 (1990).

Does your state have a provision addressing student participation in patriotic exercises? What is your local school system's policy on this issue?

II. SUSPENSION, EXPULSION, AND DISCIPLINARY TRANSFER

Students may be excluded from school for failure to conform to legitimate rules. Exclusion from school for ten days or less—the usual practice for minor violations of school rules—is considered to be a suspension. Expulsion is an exclusion from school for the remainder of a quarter, for a semester, for an academic year, or permanently and occurs on repeated or major infractions of school rules or criminal conviction. Court opinions have held that because students have a valuable property interest in attending school, they must be provided due process prior to their being excluded from school. Careful reading of these opinions reveals that the degree of due process that must be afforded a student varies in direct proportion to the length of the exclusion. Nondisabled students may also be transferred, for disciplinary reasons, to another school from the one they are attending. Consequently, courts have had to determine the degree of due process required, if any, prior to such a transfer.

A. Suspension

GOSS v. LOPEZ
Supreme Court of the United States, 1975
419 U.S. 565

MR. JUSTICE WHITE delivered the opinion of the Court.

This appeal by various administrators of the Columbus, Ohio, Public School System (CPSS) challenges the judgment of a three-judge federal court, declaring that appellees—various high school students in the CPSS—were denied due process of law contrary to the command of the Fourteenth Amendment in that they were temporarily suspended from their high schools without a hearing either prior to suspension or within a reasonable time thereafter, and enjoining the administrators to remove all references to such suspensions from the students' records.

Ohio law, Rev. Code Ann. § 3313.64 (1972), provides for free education to all children between the ages of six and 21. Section 3313.66 of the Code empowers the principal of an Ohio public school to suspend a pupil for misconduct for up to 10 days or to expel him. In either case, he must notify the student's parents within 24 hours and state the reasons for his action. A pupil who is expelled, or his parents, may appeal the decision to the Board of Education and in connection therewith shall be permitted to be heard at the board meeting. The Board may reinstate the pupil following the hearing. No similar procedure is provided in § 3313.66 or any other provision of state law for a suspended student. Aside from a regulation tracking the statute, at the time of the imposition of the suspensions in this case the CPSS itself had not issued any written procedure applicable to suspensions. Nor, so far as the record reflects, had any of the individual high schools involved in this case. Each, however, had formally or informally described the conduct for which suspension could be imposed.

The nine named appellees, each of whom alleged that he or she had been suspended from public high school in Columbus for up to 10 days without a hearing pursuant to § 3313.66, filed an action under 42 U.S.C. § 1983 against the Columbus Board of Education and various administrators of the CPSS. The complaint sought a declaration that § 3313.66 was unconstitutional in that it permitted public school administrators to deprive plaintiffs of their rights to an education without a hearing of any kind, in violation of the procedural due process component of the Fourteenth Amendment. It also sought to enjoin the public school officials from issuing future suspensions pursuant to § 3313.66 and to require them to remove references to the past suspensions from the records of the students in question.

The proof below established that the suspensions arose out of a period of widespread student unrest in the CPSS during February and March 1971. Six of the named plaintiffs, Rudolph Sutton, Tyrone Washington, Susan Cooper, Deborah Fox, Clarence Byars, and Bruce Harris, were students at the Marion-Franklin High School and were each suspended for 10 days on account of disruptive or disobedient conduct committed in the presence of the school administrator who ordered the suspension. One of these, Tyrone Washington, was among a group of students demonstrating in the school auditorium while a class was being conducted there. He was ordered by the school principal to leave, refused to do so, and was suspended. Rudolph Sutton, in the presence of the principal, physically attacked a police officer who was attempting to remove Tyrone Washington from the auditorium. He was immediately suspended. The other four Marion-Franklin students were suspended for similar conduct. None was given a hearing to determine the operative facts underlying the suspension, but each, together with his or her parents, was offered the opportunity to attend a conference, subsequent to the effective date of the suspension, to discuss the student's future.

Two named plaintiffs, Dwight Lopez and Betty Crome, were students at the Central High School and McGuffey Junior High School, respectively. The former was suspended in connection with a disturbance in the lunchroom which involved some physical damage to school property. Lopez testified that at least 75 other students were suspended from his school on the same day. He also testified below that he was not a party to the destructive conduct but was instead an innocent bystander. Because no one from the school testified with regard to this incident, there is no evidence in the record indicating the official basis for concluding otherwise. Lopez never had a hearing.

Betty Crome was present at a demonstration at a high school other than the one she was attending. There she was arrested together with others, taken to the police station, and released without being formally charged. Before she went to school on the following day, she was notified that she had been suspended for a 10-day period. Because no one from the school testified with respect to this incident, the record does not disclose how the McGuffey Junior High School principal went about making the decision to suspend Crome, nor does it disclose on what information the decision was based. It is clear from the record that no hearing was ever held.

* * *

On the basis of this evidence, the three-judge court declared that plaintiffs were denied due process of law because they were "suspended without hearing prior to suspension or within a reasonable time thereafter," and that Ohio Rev. Code Ann. § 3313.66 (1972) and regulations issued pursuant thereto were unconstitutional in permitting such suspensions. It was ordered that all references to plaintiffs' suspensions be removed from school files.

Although not imposing upon the Ohio school administrators any particular disciplinary procedures and leaving them "free to adopt regulations providing for fair suspension procedures which are consonant with the educational goals of their schools and reflective of the characteristics of their school and locality," the District Court declared that there were "minimum requirements of notice and a hearing prior to suspension, except in emergency situations." In explication, the court stated that relevant case authority would: (1) permit "[i]mmediate removal of a student whose conduct disrupts the academic atmosphere of the school, endangers fellow students, teachers or school officials, or damages property"; (2) require notice of suspension proceedings to be sent to the student's parents within 24 hours of the decision to conduct them; and (3) require a hearing to be held, with the student present, within 72 hours of his removal. Finally, the court stated that, with respect to the nature of the hearing, the relevant cases required that statements in support of the charge be produced, that the student and others be permitted to make statements in defense or mitigation, and that the school need not permit attendance by counsel.

* * *

Although Ohio may not be constitutionally obligated to establish and maintain a public school system, it has nevertheless done so and has required its children to attend. * * * The authority possessed by the State to prescribe and enforce standards of conduct in its schools although concededly very broad, must be exercised consistently with constitutional safeguards. Among other things, the State is constrained to recognize a student's legitimate entitlement to a public education as a property interest which is protected by the Due Process Clause and which may not be taken away for misconduct without adherence to the minimum procedures required by that Clause.

The Due Process Clause also forbids arbitrary deprivations of liberty. "Where a person's good name, reputation, honor, or integrity is at stake because of what the government is doing to him," the minimal requirements of the Clause must be satisfied. * * * School authorities here suspended appellees from school for periods of up to 10 days based on charges of misconduct. If sustained and recorded, those charges could seriously damage the students' standing with their fellow pupils and their teachers as well as interfere with later opportunities for higher education and employment. It is apparent that the claimed right of the State to determine unilaterally and without process whether that misconduct has occurred immediately collides with the requirements of the Constitution.

Appellants proceed to argue that even if there is a right to a public education protected by the Due Process Clause generally, the Clause comes into play only when the State subjects a student to a "severe detriment or grievous loss." The loss of 10 days, it is said, is neither severe nor grievous and the Due Process Clause is therefore of no relevance. * * * A 10-day suspension from school is not *de minimis* in our view and may not be imposed in complete disregard of the Due Process Clause.

A short suspension is, of course, a far milder deprivation than expulsion. But "education is perhaps the most important function of state and local governments," * * * and the total exclusion from the educational process for more than a trivial period, and certainly if the suspension is for 10 days, is a serious event in the life of the suspended child. Neither the property interest in educational benefits temporarily denied nor the liberty interest in reputation, which is also implicated, is so insubstantial that suspensions may constitutionally be imposed by any procedure the school chooses, no matter how arbitrary.

"Once it is determined that due process applies, the question remains what process is due." * * *

* * * At the very minimum, therefore, students facing suspension and the consequent interference with a protected property interest must be given *some* kind of notice and afforded *some* kind of hearing. "Parties whose rights are to be affected are entitled to be heard; and in order that they may enjoy that right they must first be notified." * * *

It also appears from our cases that the timing and content of the notice and the nature of the hearing will depend on appropriate accommodation of the competing interests involved. * * * The student's interest is to avoid unfair or mistaken exclusion from the educational process, with all of its unfortunate consequences. The Due Process Clause will not shield him from suspensions properly imposed, but it disserves both his interest and the interest of the State if his suspension is in fact unwarranted. The concern would be mostly academic if the disciplinary process were a totally accurate, unerring process, never mistaken and never unfair. Unfortunately, that is not the case, and no one suggests that it is. Disciplinarians, although proceeding in utmost good faith, frequently act on the reports and advice of others; and the controlling facts and the nature of the conduct under challenge are often disputed. The risk of error is not at all trivial, and it should be guarded against if that may be done without prohibitive cost or interference with the educational process.

The difficulty is that our schools are vast and complex. Some modicum of discipline and order is essential if the educational function is to be performed. Events calling for discipline are frequent occurrences and sometimes require immediate, effective action. Suspension is considered not only to be a necessary tool to maintain order but a valuable educational device. The prospect of imposing elaborate hearing requirements in every suspension case is viewed with great concern, and many school authorities may well prefer the untrammeled power to act unilaterally, unhampered by rules about notice and hearing. But it would be a strange disciplinary system in an educational institution if no communication was sought by the disciplinarian with the student in an effort to inform him of his dereliction and to let him tell his side of the story in order to make sure that an injustice is not done. * * *

We do not believe that school authorities must be totally free from notice and hearing requirements if their schools are to operate with acceptable efficiency. Students facing temporary suspension have interests qualifying for protection of the Due Process Clause, and due process requires, in connection with a suspension of 10 days or less, that the student be given oral or written notice of the charges against him and, if he denies them, an explanation of the evidence the authorities have and an opportunity to present his side of the story. The Clause requires at least these rudimentary precautions against unfair or mistaken findings of misconduct and arbitrary exclusion from school.

There need be no delay between the time "notice" is given and the time of the hearing. In the great majority of cases the disciplinarian may informally discuss the alleged misconduct with the student minutes after it has occurred. We hold only that, in being given an opportunity to explain his version of the facts at this discussion, the student first be told what he is accused of doing and what the basis of the accusation is. * * * Since the hearing may occur almost immediately following the misconduct, it follows that as a general rule notice and hearing should precede removal of the student from school. We agree with the District Court, however, that there are recurring situations in which prior notice and hearing cannot be insisted upon. Students whose presence poses a continuing danger to persons or property or an ongoing threat of disrupting the academic process may be immediately removed from school. In such cases, the necessary notice and rudimentary hearing should follow as soon as practicable, as the District Court indicated.

In holding as we do, we do not believe that we have imposed procedures on school disciplinarians which are inappropriate in a classroom setting. Instead we have imposed requirements which are, if anything, less than a fair-minded school principal would impose upon himself in order to avoid unfair suspensions. Indeed, according to the testimony of the principal of Marion-Franklin High School, that school had an informal procedure, remarkably similar to that which we now require, applicable to suspension generally but which was not followed in this case. * * *

We stop short of construing the Due Process Clause to require, countrywide, that hearings in connection with short suspensions must afford the student the opportunity to secure counsel, to confront and cross-examine witnesses supporting the charge, or to call his own witnesses to verify his version of the incident. Brief disciplinary suspensions are almost countless. To impose in each such case even truncated trial-type procedures might well overwhelm administrative facilities in many places and, by diverting resources, cost more than it would save in educational effectiveness. Moreover, further formalizing the suspension process and escalating its formality and adversary nature may not only make it too costly as a regular disciplinary tool but also destroy its effectiveness as part of the teaching process.

* * *

We should also make it clear that we have addressed ourselves solely to the short suspension, not exceeding 10 days. Longer suspensions or expulsions for the remainder of the school term, or permanently, may require more formal procedures. Nor do we put aside the possibility that in unusual situations, although involving only a short suspension, something more than the rudimentary procedures will be required.

The District Court found each of the suspensions involved here to have occurred without a hearing, either before or after the suspension, and that each suspension was therefore invalid and the statute unconstitutional insofar as it permits such suspensions without notice or hearing. Accordingly, the judgment is

Affirmed.

MR. JUSTICE POWELL, with whom THE CHIEF JUSTICE, MR. JUSTICE BLACKMUN, and MR. JUSTICE REHNQUIST join, dissenting.

The Court today invalidates an Ohio statute that permits student suspensions from school without a hearing "for not more than ten days." The decision unnecessarily opens avenues for judicial intervention in the operation of our public schools that may affect adversely the quality of education. The Court holds for the first time that the federal courts, rather than educational officials and state legislatures, have the authority to determine the rules applicable to routine classroom discipline of children and teenagers in the public schools. It justifies this unprecedented intrusion into the process of elementary and secondary education by identifying a new constitutional right: the right of a student not to be suspended for as much as a single day without notice and a due process hearing either before or promptly following the suspension.

The Court's decision rests on the premise that, under Ohio law, education is a property interest protected by the Fourteenth Amendment's Due Process Clause and therefore that any suspension requires notice and a hearing. In my view, a student's interest in education is not infringed by a suspension within the limited period prescribed by Ohio law. Moreover, to the extent that there may be some arguable infringement, it is too speculative, transitory, and insubstantial to justify imposition of a *constitutional* rule.

* * *

One of the more disturbing aspects of today's decision is its indiscriminate reliance upon the judiciary, and the adversary process, as the means of resolving many of the most routine problems arising in the classroom. * * *

The Ohio statute, providing as it does for due notice both to parents and the Board, is compatible with the teacher-pupil relationship and the informal resolution of mistaken disciplinary action. We have relied for generations upon the experience, good faith and dedication of those who staff our public schools, and the nonadversary means of airing grievances that always have been available to pupils and their parents. One would have thought before today's opinion that this informal method of resolving differences was more compatible with the interests of all concerned than resort to any constitutionalized procedure, however blandly it may be defined by the Court.

* * *

It hardly need be said that if a student, as a result of a day's suspension, suffers "a blow" to his "self-esteem," "feels powerless," views "teachers with resentment," or feels "stigmatized by his teachers," identical psychological harms will flow from many other routine and necessary school decisions. The student who is given a failing grade, who is not promoted, who is excluded from certain extracurricular activities, who is assigned to a school reserved for children of less than average ability, or who is placed in the "vocational" rather than the "college preparatory" track, is unlikely to suffer any less psychological injury than if he were suspended for a day for a relatively minor infraction.

* * *

Not so long ago, state deprivations of the most significant forms of state largesse were not thought to require due process protection on the ground that the deprivation resulted only in the loss of a state-provided "benefit." * * * In recent years the Court, wisely in my view, has rejected the "wooden distinction between 'rights' and 'privileges,' " * * * and looked instead to the significance of the state-created or state-enforced right and to the substantiality of the alleged deprivation. Today's opinion appears to abandon this reasonable approach by holding in effect that government infringement of any interest to which a person is entitled, no matter what the interest or how inconsequential the infringement, requires *constitutional* protection. As it is difficult to think of any less consequential infringement than suspension of a junior high school student for a single day, it is equally difficult to perceive any principled limit to the new reach of procedural due process.

Notes and Questions

Goss, a five-to-four decision, reveals a sharp division among the Court's justices. Does such a division make *Goss* any less the supreme law of the land? Is the due process requirement established in *Goss* educationally sound? Would seriatim ten-day suspensions for the same offense violate the rationale established in *Goss*?

Students were suspended five days for fighting at a football game and the next day in the principal's office. Although no notice or hearing was given prior to the suspension, a federal district court contended that this case fit within an exception to the predeprivation and notice hearing requirement of *Goss*. The court also concluded that their subsequent expulsion hearing was fair, even though the students were not provided with a copy of the Code of Conduct or a copy of the principal's written report before the hearing, nor were they allowed to cross-examine witnesses. See *Craig v. Selma City School Board*, 801 F. Supp. 585 (Ala. 1992).

A student challenged his principal's denial of readmission to school for one day following the student's arrest for allegedly raping another student. The court in *Durso v. Taylor*, 624 A.2d 449 (D.C. App. 1993) ruled that informal hearings with the principal and assistant principal, and a subsequent formal hearing, satisfied due process requirements.

A high school senior who admitted to drinking on a school outing was suspended for three days at the end of the academic year, and consequently he missed a final examination and failed to make the required grade point for graduation. His parents contended that the punishment amounted to more than a suspension. However, although seeming to sympathize with the student, a federal appellate court did not agree that he was entitled to the same degree of due process as that for an expulsion. A meeting with the principal and an opportunity for the parents to present a "mitigative argument" to the principal met the due process requirement. The court stated that "it is not the role of the federal courts to set aside the decisions of school administrators which the court may view as lacking a basis in wisdom or compassion." See *Lamb v. Panhandle Community Unit School District No. 2*, 826 F.2d 526 (7th Cir. 1987).

The use of a so-called timeout box, a device to temporarily isolate unruly students, has been upheld in *Dickens v. Johnson County Board of Education*, 661 F. Supp. 155 (Tenn. 1987). In this instance, the "box" had three sides enclosing a desk at which the student could see the teacher and hear the class but could not see other pupils. He was allowed to go to the rest room and to attend scheduled activities such as lunch, physical education, and specialty classes. It was alleged that he had spent as long as four and one-half hours on six consecutive days in the "box." In explaining that the student's due process property interest had not been violated, the court stated:

Of course, students are entitled to hearings before they are expelled or suspended since these actions totally excluded them from the educational process. But teachers should be free to impose minor forms of classroom discipline, such as admonishing students, requiring special assignments, restricting activities, and denying certain privileges, without being subjected to the strictures of due process scrutiny. (p. 157)

And the court further stated:

It appears that judicious use of behavioral modification techniques such as "timeout" should be favored over expulsion in disciplining disruptive students. This is not to say that educators may arbitrarily cage students in a corner of the classroom for an indeterminate length of time. Nevertheless, the Court finds the defendants' use of timeout in this case was not unduly harsh or grossly disproportionate. (p. 158)

Does your state have statutory provisions pertaining to suspension? What are your local school system's rules regarding suspension?

B. Expulsion

1. Public School Expulsion

GONZALES v. McEUEN
United States District Court, Central District of California, 1977
435 F. Supp. 460

TAKASUGI, District Judge.
Eleven high school students, by their next friends, have brought this action under the Civil Rights Act, 42 U.S.C. § 1983, and the Due Process Clause of the Fourteenth Amendment to the Constitution of the United States. The case stems from the suspension and expulsion of the named plaintiffs from Oxnard Union High School following a period of student unrest on campus during October 14–15, 1976. The plaintiffs were charged with having committed certain acts which, it was alleged, led to a riot at Oxnard High School.

* * *

Plaintiffs' strongest and most serious challenge is to the impartiality of the Board. They contend that they were denied their right to an impartial hearing before an independent fact-finder. The basis for this claim is, first, overfamiliarity of the Board with the case; second, the multiple role played by defendants' counsel; and third, the involvement of the Superintendent of the District, Mr. McEuen, with the Board of Trustees during the hearings.

No one doubts that a student charged with misconduct has a right to an impartial tribunal * * * . There is doubt, however, as to what this means. Various situations have been identified in which experience teaches that the probability of actual bias on the part of the judge or decisionmaker is too high to be constitutionally tolerable. Bias is presumed to exist, for example, in cases in which the adjudicator has a pecuniary interest in the outcome; * * * or in which he has been the target of personal attack or criticism from the person before him. * * * The decisionmaker may also have such prior involvement with the case as to acquire a disqualifying bias. * * * The question before the Court is not whether the Board was actually biased, but whether, under the circumstances, there existed probability that the decisionmaker would be tempted to decide the issues with partiality to one party or the other. It is with this view that the plaintiffs' claims must be considered.

Much has been made of "The Red Book" which, it is claimed, contained information about the academic and disciplinary records of plaintiffs. It is alleged that the Board had access to this material from twenty to thirty days before the expulsion hearings. Depositions submitted to the court show that the members of the Board met with school officials prior to the hearings. Plaintiffs contend that this prior involvement by the Board deprived plaintiffs of the opportunity for a fair hearing. The court rejects this contention. Exposure to evidence presented in a nonadversary investigative procedure is insufficient in itself to impugn the fairness of the Board members at a later adversary hearing. * * * Nor is a limited combination of investigatory and adjudicatory functions in an administrative body necessarily unfair, absent a showing of other circumstances such as malice or personal interest in the outcome. * * * A school board would be amiss in its duties if it did not make some inquiry to know what was going on in the district for which it is responsible. Some familiarity with the facts of the case gained by an agency in the performance of its statutory role does not disqualify a decisionmaker. * * *

Turning now to the issue of the multiple roles performed by defendants' counsel, the court notes that the board members are defendants in this pending related action and may thereby become subject to personal liability.

It is undisputed that attorneys for the District who prosecuted the charges against the plaintiffs in the expulsion proceedings, also represent the Board members in this action. Plaintiffs claim that the attorneys acted in dual roles at the expulsion hearing: as prosecutors for the Administration and as legal advisors to the Board. Counsel for defendants admit that they advised the Board prior to the hearings with respect to its obligations regarding these expulsions, but they deny that they advised the Board during the proceedings themselves.

A reading of the transcripts reveals how difficult it was to separate the two roles. Special mention should be made of the fact that the Board enjoys no legal expertise and must rely heavily upon its counsel. This places defendants' attorneys in a position of intolerable prominence and influence.

It is the opinion of this court that the confidential relationship between the attorneys for the District and the members of the Board, reinforced by the advisory role played by the attorneys for the Board, created an unacceptable risk of bias. Bearing in mind also that the Board members are subject to personal liability in this action, the court concludes that bias can be presumed to exist.

Superintendent McEuen sat with the Board members during the expulsion hearings; he acted as Secretary of the Board on at least one occasion. By statute, Mr. McEuen is the chief advisor to the Board. The fact remains, however, that he is also the chief of the "prosecution" team, to wit, the District.

It is clear from the record that at least on one occasion, at the joint hearing of plaintiffs, Flores, Chavez and Rodriguez, Superintendent McEuen was present with the Board for approximately forty-five minutes during its deliberations on the issue of expelling these plaintiffs. The plaintiffs contend that their due process rights were violated by the involvement of Mr. McEuen with the Board. This court agrees.

Defendants' counsel maintain that Mr. McEuen did not participate in the deliberations and did no more, perhaps, than serve cookies and coffee to the Board members. Whether he did or did not participate, his presence to some extent might operate as an inhibiting restraint upon the freedom of action and expression of the Board. Defendants argue that there is no evidence that Mr. McEuen influenced or biased the Board. Proof of subjective reasoning processes are incapable of corroboration or disproval. Plaintiffs should not be forced to rely upon the memory or sense of fairness of Superintendent McEuen or the Board as to what occurred there. Perhaps Mr. McEuen's physical presence in deliberation becomes more offensive because of the pre-hearing comments which showed something less than impartiality.

The court concludes that the process utilized by the Board was fundamentally unfair. This raises a presumption of bias. In view of the alternatives for the selection of an impartial hearing body under California Education Code Section 10608, it would have been more reasonable to provide procedures that insured not only that justice was done, but also that it appeared to have been done.

* * *

Plaintiffs Barrington and Munden were expelled at a meeting of the Board on November 10, 1976. Neither Barrington nor Munden was present; neither was represented by either parent or counsel.

On October 29, 1976, letters had been sent to the parents advising them that the principal was recommending expulsion of the students. The letters contained a specific statement of the charges: in the case of Barrington, that he was involved in a riot at school at which time he had threatened physical violence against a teacher; in the case of Munden, that he was involved in a fight with another student, Wayne Berry. The letters contained no notice to the student or parent of the student's right to be present at the hearing, to be represented by counsel, and to present evidence. This was a clear violation of § 10608 of the California Education Code. The letters to the parents stated, "If you feel that the school does not have just cause for this recommendation, you may want to attend this meeting to present your reasons why [the students] should not be expelled."

* * *

Goss clearly anticipates that where the student is faced with the severe penalty of expulsion he shall have the right to be represented by and through counsel, to present evidence on his own behalf, and to confront and cross-examine adverse witnesses.

* * *

Notice to be adequate must communicate to the recipient the nature of the proceeding. In an expulsion hearing, the notice given to the student must include a statement not only of the specific charge, but also the basic rights to be afforded the student: to be represented by counsel, to present evidence, and to confront and cross-examine adverse witnesses. Section 10608 of the California Education Code provides, *inter alia*, for notice to the student and the parent of the specific charge, of the right to be represented by counsel, and of the right to present evidence. Federal due process requires no less.

Defendants next argue that even if the notice was defective, the court must still determine whether the plaintiffs were given a fair and impartial hearing. Defendants misapprehend the meaning of notice. It is not "fair" if the student does not know, and is not told, that he has certain rights which he may exercise at the hearing.

* * *

The court holds that the notice given to plaintiffs Barrington and Munden was defective in that it did not adequately inform them of their constitutional rights. It follows that their expulsions were improper.

* * *

Notes and Questions

According to *Gonzales*, a notice of expulsion hearing, to be adequate, must communicate the nature of the proceedings to the recipient. Such a notice must also include a statement of the specific charges and basic rights available to the student, such as the right to be represented by counsel, to present evidence, and to confront and cross-examine adverse witnesses. Several decisions prior to *Gonzales* did not require notice of the right to be represented by counsel.

May a school superintendent participate, merely by being present at the expulsion deliberations, according to *Gonzales*?

The question of whether the same attorney may advise the school board and present the superintendent's case at a hearing is discussed in *Breitling* v. *Solenberger*, 585 F. Supp. 289 (Va. 1984). The federal district court in this instance held that this dual role did not violate due process requirements.

A school district's policy of expelling students for possession of marijuana on school grounds was upheld. The court stated that "[t]he policy of the Board as clearly set forth in its Code of Conduct is not arbitrary or capricious, but is a commendable effort in dealing with a serious, destructive problem." See *Rucker* v. *Colonial School District*, 517 A.2d 703 (Del. Super. Ct. 1986). However, an expulsion was not upheld in a case dealing with possession of marijuana off the school grounds. In this instance, the authority to expel was limited by statute to possession of marijuana on school grounds or on school buses. See *Labrosse* v. *Saint Bernard Parish School Board*, 483 So.2d 1253 (La. Ct. App. 1986).

A student was expelled after being arrested for possession of marijuana after school hours and off campus. Under the state's expulsion statute, a student's conduct had to be "seriously disruptive of the educational process." The school claimed that his arrest violated school policy and thereby seriously disrupted the educational environment. In upholding the student, the Connecticut Supreme Court held that "In order to subject a student to expulsion, conduct off school grounds must not only violate school policy, it must also be 'seriously disruptive of the educational process' for reasons other than the fact that it violated school policy." Additionally, the court concluded that the student was not provided constitutionally adequate notice that such an incident would subject him to expulsion from school. See *Packer* v. *Board of Education*, 717 A.2d 117 (Conn. 1998).

Permanent expulsion was upheld for a student who violated a school district's code for student conduct by being in possession of a knife and stabbing another student. The court in, *D.B.* v. *Clarke County Board of Education*, 469 S.E.2d 438 (Ga. App. 1996), held that the student's constitutional right to a free public education and the state's compulsory school attendance statute had not been violated.

A federal statute entitled the "Gun-Free Schools Act of 1994" mandates expulsion for students who bring weapons to school. The law provides, in part, that:

> . . . each state receiving Federal funds . . . shall have in effect a State law requiring local educational agencies to expel from school for a period of not less than one year a student who is determined to have brought a weapon to a school under the jurisdiction of local educational agencies in that State, except that such State law shall allow the chief administering officer of such local educational agency to modify such expulsion requirement for a student on a case-by-case basis.
>
> Nothing in this subchapter shall be construed to prevent a State from allowing a local educational agency that has expelled a student from such a student's regular school setting from providing educational services to such student in an alternative setting. 20 U.S.C.A. § 8921 (1994).

A perception of increased school violence since passage of the Gun-Free Schools Act of 1994 has resulted in the growth of zero tolerance policies by many school systems. These well-intentioned policies were originally designed as a type of "one-strike-you're-out" antidote for such serious offenses as student on campus drug trafficking or possession of dangerous weapons. Unfortunately, what many observers thought was a relatively tough-minded and simple panacea for school violence has become embroiled in controversy. Enforcing zero tolerance policies has often ensnared students in activities that parents view as relatively innocuous. The policies have been attacked for attempting to exclude students for the following types of alleged infractions: bringing a nail file to school that school officials viewed as a knife, a student's writing a story about a murderous rampage at his school in addition to promising he would "mess" with the class, a student using her thumb and index finger to simulate a gun and saying "bang" to fellow students, and bringing a ceremonial sword to a history class. There is little doubt that school systems would decrease antagonism toward zero tolerance policies if they adopt policies that are clearly written, adequately communicated to both students and parents, fairly enforced, and, perhaps most importantly, show that there is a need for such a policy by demonstrating the serious threat which exists to the school environment.

In a case involving a zero tolerance policy, a seventh-grade student was expelled for filing his nails with a miniature Swiss army knife he had found in a school hallway. The student and his parents had a meeting with his principal and participated in a hearing before he was expelled for possession of a knife under the district's zero tolerance policy. In holding for the student, the court in *Lyons v. Penn Hills School District*, 723 A.2d 1073 (Pa. Commw. Ct. 1999), held that the school district's failure to develop a written policy regarding expulsion for weapon possession and to provide the school superintendent with discretionary review of the expulsion on a case-by-case basis, violated the state statute governing school weapons policies.

Does your state have statutory provisions pertaining to expulsion? What are your local school system's rules or policies regarding expulsion? If a student moved, would an expulsion in one school district automatically carry over to the new district?

2. Private School Expulsion

Contract law, not the law of due process, generally governs the issue of expulsion from a private school. As was discussed earlier, unless a substantial linkage exists between a private school and the state or federal government, the notion of due process does not apply because the private school does not operate under the "color of the state," and, therefore, no process is due.

ALLEN v. *CASPER*
Court of Appeals of Ohio, 1993
622 N.E.2d 367

PER CURIAM.

* * *

Prior to enrolling their children at Bethlehem Christian, the Allens filled out an application for enrollment. As part of the application process, the Allens were provided with a copy of the school's admission policies, which applied to parents as well as students.

Paragraph 3 of the Policies and Procedures states:

"The school reserves the right to refuse admittance, suspend, or expel any student who does not cooperate with policies established in this book. The high standard and Biblical principles that our school holds apply to after school hours as well. *If any parent or student* refuses to follow those standards, then they place their privilege of attending B.C.S. in jeopardy."

Paragraph 7 states:

"Parents of students (as set forth on the application) must have received Jesus Christ as Savior and Lord. They must also be in agreement with our doctrinal statement, demonstrate a spirit of cooperation, and uphold the student handbook."

After their application was accepted, the Allens signed a parents' agreement and were sent a copy of the school handbook, which related to disciplinary procedures and parental involvement. As part of their parents' agreement, the Allens agreed as follows:

"We recognize that confidence in our child's teachers and school administration is essential. Therefore, we will encourage our child to respect and obey school policies and school officials. We agree that, if our child should become involved in any difficulty at school, we will not complain to other parents, but, with a prayerful Christian spirit, will register only necessary complaints with the appropriate teacher and/or administrator."

The school handbook, which relates to disciplinary procedures and parental involvement, provides in relevant part as follows:

"If a parent has a question or concern related to a classroom situation, he should first meet with the particular classroom teacher. If the matter is not resolved, the administrator is the proper person to contact. Thereafter, a conference with the parents, the teacher, and the administrator may be in order.

"If a parent feels that he cannot accept the decision or explanation given by the administrator, his final recourse is to take the matter before the school board, with the administrator and teacher present, by submitting a written request for such a meeting to the administrator."

A series of events involving Kristen Allen led to a dispute between the Allens and the school administrator as to how the matters should have been handled. As a result of the failure of the Allens and the school to come to any agreement, the school requested by letter dated November 27, 1990 that the Allens voluntarily withdraw their children. * * *

Sometime in September 1990, Kristen informed her mother that two male kindergarten children chased her on the playground and that one child pulled her hands behind her back while the other pulled her dress up and ran his hand across her panties. The following day, Mrs. Allen telephoned Michael Staub, the school administrator, and informed him of the incident. * * *

* * * After speaking with the boys, Staub was certain that the children, then age six, did not realize that they had done anything wrong. Staub told them that they should not touch children in the manner that they had touched Kristen and told them that if any such incident occurred in the future, he would paddle them.

In October, Kristen told her mother that one of the boys involved in the first incident touched her again in a similar way. * * *

Staub spoke with the young boy, who admitted that he had touched Kristen. Staub telephoned the boy's parents and arranged a meeting with them. He described the parents as very concerned and cooperative. With their consent, Staub paddled the boy.

According to Staub, Mrs. Allen became angry and demanded to know what he had done to the young boy. Staub assured her that he was taking care of the matter, but that it was the school's policy to discuss disciplinary matters only with the parents of the child involved. Unsatisfied with this response, the Allens met with Rev. Hlad, who had no responsibility for the day-to-day running of the school, to discuss the matter. At no time did the Allens seek a meeting with the school board as required by the school handbook.

* * *

In November, * * * Kristen told her mother that a different young boy had spit upon her as the children were leaving school. Mrs. Allen * * * confronted the teacher Kristen had informed of the incident on the playground. The teacher * * * explained to Mrs. Allen that the boy had a dental malformation * * * and that the boy did not intentionally spit on Kristen. * * * According to Staub, Mrs. Allen was upset and angry at the teacher's handling of the incident and wanted to know what he was going to do about it. Staub told her he would speak with the child's parents. * * *

At this point, Staub contacted Rev. Hlad, explained that he could reach no agreement with the Allens as to how matters involving Kristen should be handled, and felt that perhaps the withdrawal of the Allen children would be in the best interests of all parties involved. * * * After further discussion, it seemed that the parties could develop no working relationship with the school administrator regarding matters involving their children, and Rev. Hlad asked the Allens to withdraw their children prior to December 3, 1990. The Allens were given a week to locate a new school and were told that their tuition would be refunded.

* * *

On November 27, 1991, the Allens filed suit against Bethlehem Baptist Church, Michael Staub and Rev. Hlad for unlawfully dismissing their children from Bethlehem Baptist Christian School.

* * *

There is no question that the relationship between the parties here is a contractual one, that the terms of that relationship may be expressed in school policies and handbooks, and that those expressed terms may govern the circumstances under which a student may be expelled. Because contracts for private education have unique qualities, they are to be construed in a manner which leaves the school board broad discretion to meet its educational and doctrinal responsibilities. Absent a clear abuse of discretion by the school in the enforcement of its policies and regulations, courts will not interfere in these matters.

* * *

* * * The Allens have failed to adduce any evidence of a violated contractual right. They have also failed to present any facts to show a clear abuse of discretion on the part of Bethlehem Christian School, Michael Staub or Rev. Hlad.

On the contrary, the evidence suggests that the appellees acted within their proper discretion in removing the Allen children. The record demonstrates that Michael Staub, who was responsible for the day-to-day running of the school, responded promptly to the complaints by Mrs. Allen in a manner that he believed would yield fairness to all parties involved. The Allens refused to agree to his disposition of the matters, bypassed the grievance procedures, engaged in confrontational tactics and failed to abide by the school handbook. After Mrs. Allen called Staub unchristian and accused him of working with the devil, Staub felt that he could not work together with the Allens and that the best interest of all parties would be served by the removal of the children from the school. That the Allens understood that their children could be removed from Bethlehem Christian School based upon their failure to comply with the admission policies and the terms of the school handbook is not disputed.

* * *

Judgment affirmed.

Note

A private Catholic high school student alleged that his constitutional rights to due process had been violated when he was expelled for violating his disciplinary probation. Some of the alleged infractions leading to his expulsion included: an argument with a fellow student on the school bus, "trashing" a teacher's house, slashing the teacher's automobile tires, and making prank calls to the teacher, using and distributing steroids, and urinating in students' lockers. In upholding the private school, a New Jersey court in *Hernandez* v. *Don Bosco Preparatory High*, 730 A. 2d 365 (N.J. Super. Ct. App. Div. 1999), declared that the expulsion was not "state action" within the meaning of the Fourteenth Amendment's Due Process clause. The court stated that "Private schools are only bound to the constitutional requirements of due process if the private school has substantial involvement with the state." Additionally, the court noted that the school followed its procedures by notifying the student of all charges against him and allowing him an opportunity to appeal and present a defense. The court emphasized that it would only interfere when a private organization failed to follow its own procedures.

C. Disciplinary Transfer

Transfer to a so-called alternative school, designed to meet the needs of nondisabled disruptive students, is not considered to be the equivalent of an expulsion. Appropriate due process in such an instance includes: (1) written notice to both the student and his or her parents; (2) an opportunity for a meeting among school authorities, parents, and the student, at which the situation may be discussed; and (3) a meeting at which evidence may be presented and witnesses examined. See *Jordan* v. *School District of City of Erie*, 583 F.2d 91 (3d Cir. 1978), and *Zamora* v. *Pomeroy*, 639 F.2d 662 (10th Cir. 1981). A lawyer need not be present at such a conference. See *Madera* v. *Board of Education of the City of New York*, 386 F.2d 778 (2d Cir. 1967).

    Would courts uphold more stringent rules pertaining to conduct, dress, search, overall discipline, and freedom of expression at such alternative schools?

III. CORPORAL PUNISHMENT

Corporal punishment may be defined as the use of such physical contact as striking, paddling, or spanking of a student by an educator. Although once widely used, it is a controversial practice that has received much debate. Proponents view it as a necessary and educationally sound disciplinary measure. Those opposed view the practice as archaic, cruel, and inhumane, and an unjustifiable act on the part of the state.

    The issue had been litigated repeatedly until the United States Supreme Court upheld the practice in *Ingraham* v. *Wright*. In its opinion, the Court addressed two major issues: whether or not the administration of corporal punishment represented cruel and unusual punishment in violation of the Eighth Amendment; and whether or not prior notice and an opportunity to be heard were required.

INGRAHAM v. WRIGHT
Supreme Court of the United States, 1977
430 U.S. 651

MR. JUSTICE POWELL delivered the opinion of the Court.

This case presents questions concerning the use of corporal punishment in public schools: First, whether the paddling of students as a means of maintaining school discipline constitutes cruel and unusual punishment in violation of the Eighth Amendment; and, second, to the extent that paddling is constitutionally permissible, whether the Due Process Clause of the Fourteenth Amendment requires prior notice and an opportunity to be heard.

* * *

Petitioners' evidence may be summarized briefly. In the 1970–1971 school year, many of the 237 schools in Dade County used corporal punishment as a means of maintaining discipline pursuant to Florida legislation and a local school board regulation. The statute then in effect authorized limited corporal punishment by negative inference, proscribing punishment which was "degrading or unduly severe" or which was inflicted without prior consultation with the principal or the teacher in charge of the school. * * * The regulation * * * contained explicit directions and limitations. The authorized punishment consisted of paddling the recalcitrant student on the buttocks with a flat wooden paddle measuring less than two feet long, three to four inches wide, and about one-half inch thick. The normal punishment was limited to one to five "licks" or blows with the paddle and resulted in no apparent physical injury to the student. School authorities viewed corporal punishment as a less drastic means of discipline than suspension or expulsion. Contrary to the procedural requirements of the statute and regulation, teachers often paddled students on their own authority without first consulting the principal.

* * * Because he was slow to respond to his teacher's instructions, Ingraham was subjected to more than 20 licks with a paddle while being held over a table in the principal's office. The paddling was so severe that he suffered a hematoma requiring medical attention and keeping him out of school for several days. Andrews was paddled several times for minor infractions. On two occasions he was struck on his arms, once depriving him of the full use of his arm for a week.

* * *

The use of corporal punishment in this country as a means of disciplining schoolchildren dates back to the colonial period. It has survived the transformation of primary and secondary education from the colonials' reliance on optional private arrangements to our present system of compulsory education and dependence on public schools. Despite the general abandonment of corporal punishment as a means of punishing criminal offenders, the practice continues to play a role in the public education of schoolchildren in most parts of the country. Professional and public opinion is sharply divided on the practice, and has been for more than a century. Yet we can discern no trend toward its elimination.

At common law a single principle has governed the use of corporal punishment since before the American Revolution: Teachers may impose reasonable but not excessive force to discipline a child. * * * The basic doctrine has not changed. The prevalent rule in this country today privileges such force as a teacher or administrator "reasonably believes to be necessary for [the child's] proper control, training, or education." * * * To the extent that the force is excessive or unreasonable, the educator in virtually all States is subject to possible civil and criminal liability.

Although the early cases viewed the authority of the teacher as deriving from the parents, the concept of parental delegation has been replaced by the view—more consonant with compulsory education laws—that the State itself may impose such corporal punishment as is reasonably necessary "for the proper education of the child and for the maintenance of group discipline." * * * All of the circumstances are to be taken into account in determining whether the punishment is reasonable in a particular case. Among the most important considerations are the seriousness of the offense, the attitude and past behavior of the child, the nature and severity of the punishment, the age and strength of the child, and the availability of less severe but equally effective means of discipline. * * *

Of the 23 States that have addressed the problem through legislation, 21 have authorized the moderate use of corporal punishment in public schools. Of these States only a few have elaborated on the common-law test of reasonableness, typically providing for approval or notification of the child's parents, or for infliction of punishment only by the principal or in the presence of an adult witness. Only two States, Massachusetts and New Jersey, have prohibited all corporal punishment in their public schools. Where the legislatures have not acted, the state courts have uniformly preserved the common-law rule permitting teachers to use reasonable force in disciplining children in their charge.

Against this background of historical and contemporary approval of reasonable corporal punishment, we turn to the constitutional questions before us.

The Eighth Amendment provides: "Excessive bail shall not be required, nor excessive fines imposed, nor cruel and unusual punishments inflicted." Bail, fines, and punishment traditionally have been associated with the criminal process, and by subjecting the three to parallel limitations the text of the Amendment suggests an intention to limit the power of those entrusted with the criminal-law function of government. An examination of the history of the Amendment and the decisions of this Court construing the proscription against cruel and unusual punishment confirms that it was designed to protect those convicted of crimes. We adhere to this long-standing limitation and hold that the Eighth Amendment does not apply to the paddling of children as a means of maintaining discipline in public schools.

* * *

"[T]he question remains what process is due." * * * Were it not for the common-law privilege permitting teachers to inflict reasonable corporal punishment on children in their care, and the availability of the traditional remedies for abuse, the case for requiring advance procedural safeguards would be strong indeed. But here we deal with a punishment—paddling—within that tradition, and the question is whether the common-law remedies are adequate to afford due process. * * * Whether in this case the common-law remedies for excessive corporal punishment constitute due process of law must turn on an analysis of the competing interests at stake, viewed against the background of "history, reason, [and] the past course of decisions." The analysis requires consideration of three distinct factors: "First, the private interest that will be affected. . . . ; second, the risk of an erroneous deprivation of such interest . . . and the probable value, if any, of additional or substitute procedural safeguards; and finally, the [state] interest, including the function involved and the fiscal and administrative burdens that the additional or substitute procedural requirement would entail." * * *

* * *

Florida has continued to recognize, and indeed has strengthened by statute, the common-law right of a child not to be subjected to excessive corporal punishment in school. Under Florida law the teacher and principal of the school decide in the first instance whether corporal punishment is reasonably necessary under the circumstances in order to discipline a child who has misbehaved. But they must exercise prudence and restraint. For Florida has preserved the traditional judicial proceedings for determining whether the punishment was justified. If the punishment inflicted is later found to have been excessive—not reasonably believed at the time to be necessary for the child's discipline or training—the school authorities inflicting it may be held liable in damages to the child and, if malice is shown, they may be subject to criminal penalties.

* * *

It still may be argued, of course, that the child's liberty interest would be better protected if the common-law remedies were supplemented by the administrative safeguards of prior notice and a hearing. We have found frequently that some kind of prior hearing is necessary to guard against arbitrary impositions on interests protected by the Fourteenth Amendment. * * * But where the State has preserved what "has always been the law of the land," * * * the case for administrative safeguards is significantly less compelling.

* * *

But even if the need for advance procedural safeguards were clear, the question would remain whether the incremental benefit could justify the cost. Acceptance of petitioners' claims would work a transformation in the law governing corporal punishment in Florida and most other States. Given the impracticability of formulating a rule of procedural due process that varies with the severity of the particular imposition, the prior hearing petitioners seek would have to precede *any* paddling, however moderate or trivial.

Such a universal constitutional requirement would significantly burden the use of corporal punishment as a disciplinary measure. Hearings—even informal hearings—require time, personnel, and a diversion of attention from normal school pursuits. School authorities may well choose to abandon corporal punishment rather than incur the burdens of complying with the procedural requirements. Teachers, properly concerned with maintaining authority in the classroom, may well prefer to rely on other disciplinary measures—which they may view as less effective—rather than confront the possible disruption that prior notice and a hearing may entail. Paradoxically, such an alteration of disciplinary policy is most likely to occur in the ordinary case where the contemplated punishment is well within the common-law privilege.

Elimination or curtailment of corporal punishment would be welcomed by many as a societal advance. But when such a policy choice may result from this Court's determination of an asserted right to due process, rather than from the normal processes of community debate and legislative action, the societal costs cannot be dismissed as insubstantial. We are reviewing here a legislative judgment, rooted in history and reaffirmed in the laws of many States, that corporal punishment serves important educational interests. This judgment must be viewed in light of the disciplinary problems commonplace in the schools. * * *

* * * In view of the low incidence of abuse, the openness of our schools, and the common-law safeguards that already exist, the risk of error that may result in violation of a schoolchild's substantive rights can only be regarded as minimal. Imposing additional administrative safeguards as a constitutional requirement might reduce that risk marginally, but would also entail an intrusion into an area of primary educational responsibility. We conclude that the Due Process Clause does not require notice and a hearing prior to the imposition of corporal punishment in the public schools, as that practice is authorized and limited by the common law.

Petitioners cannot prevail on either of the theories before us in this case. The Eighth Amendment's prohibition against cruel and unusual punishment is inapplicable to school paddlings, and the Fourteenth Amendment's requirement of procedural due process is satisfied by Florida's preservation of common-law constraints and remedies. We therefore agree with the Court of Appeals that petitioners' evidence affords no basis for injunctive relief, and that petitioners cannot recover damages on the basis of any Eighth Amendment or procedural due process violation.

Affirmed.

Notes and Questions

Ingraham was a five-to-four decision. Justice Powell, who wrote the *Ingraham* decision, brought a background of public school experience to the Court. He was chairman of the Richmond, Virginia, School Board during the time public schools were being desegregated in the 1950s, and he headed the Virginia State Board of Education. Although a Democrat, he was nominated to the Court by President Nixon and took office in 1972. He retired in 1987 and was replaced by Justice Anthony Kennedy in 1988.

According to *Ingraham,* in the absence of legislation to the contrary, teachers may inflict corporal punishment. More than half of the states do not allow the practice of corporal punishment. Legislation or state regulation have prohibited the practice in Alaska, California, Connecticut, Hawaii, Illinois, Iowa, Maine, Maryland, Massachusetts, Michigan, Minnesota, Montana, Nebraska, Nevada, New Hampshire, New Jersey, New York, North Dakota, Oregon, Utah, Vermont, Virginia, Washington, and Wisconsin. All local school boards in Rhode Island have done likewise. In some instances, local school boards in states that allow corporal punishment, have banned or curtailed the practice.

Is it possible to reconcile the majority opinion in *Ingraham* with the majority opinion in *Goss?*

Should the *Ingraham* decision have cited empirical data that establish the effectiveness of corporal punishment? Are such data necessary to support the Court's ruling?

A decision discussing the doctrine of *in loco parentis* concluded that the application of corporal punishment to public school children by means of a paddle, whip, stick, or other mechanical devices could not be permitted under this doctrine; however, the doctrine did not prohibit spanking by hand, physically seizing and removing unruly students from a classroom, or using physical force to restrain students from fighting or engaging in destructive or illegal acts. See *Smith* v. *West Virginia State Board of Education,* 295 S.E.2d 680 (W.Va. 1982).

The Court's decision in *Ingraham* did not put the issue to rest. A federal appellate court, in *Garcia* v. *Miera,* 817 F.2d 650 (10th Cir. 1987), *cert. denied,* 485 U.S. 959 (1988), has held that excessive force used for corporal punishment is a violation of substantive due process. The court stated:

> Although *Ingraham* makes clear that ordinary corporal punishment violates no substantive due process rights of school children, by acknowledging that

corporal punishment implicates a fundamental liberty interest protected by the due process clause, we believe that, at some degree of excessiveness or cruelty, the meting out of such punishment violates the substantive due process rights of the pupil. (p. 654)

Additionally, the court revealed that three categories of corporal punishment exist:

Punishments that do not exceed the traditional common law standard of reasonableness are not actionable; punishments that exceed the common law standard without adequate state remedies violate procedural due process rights; and finally, punishments that are so grossly excessive as to be shocking to the conscience violate substantive due process rights, without regard to the adequacy of state remedies. (p. 656)

Tying a child to a chair for a full day and part of the next, which was alleged to be an instructional technique, was also held to be a violation of substantive due process. See *Jefferson* v. *Ysleta Independent School District,* 817 F.2d 303 (5th Cir. 1987). In both *Garcia* and *Jefferson,* the courts ruled that a claim for damages had arisen under 42 U.S.C. § 1983.

As mentioned in *Ingraham,* a remedy for what is perceived as excessive corporal punishment is a civil or criminal lawsuit. In one such criminal case, a private school principal was sentenced to twelve months probation, 150 hours of community service and a $500 fine for having inflicted "extreme pain" during the administration of corporal punishment consisting of fifty to sixty swats. In that state, to sustain a simple assault conviction, it was necessary to prove that a teacher, principal, parent, or person otherwise entrusted with the care or supervision of a minor for a special purpose, inflicted not merely substantial pain, but rather extreme pain as a result of administering corporal punishment. Such a higher standard of proof is designed to shield this group of individuals from simple assault liability in instances where the degree and manner of force used and the attendant justifications are neither excessive nor unreasonable under the circumstances. See *Commonwealth* v. *Douglass,* 588 A.2d 53 (Pa. Super. Ct. 1991).

Are you familiar with the statutory provisions, if any, in your state pertaining to corporal punishment? Are practices in your school system regarding the administration of corporal punishment in conformance with state and local provisions? Are there statutory provisions designed to protect teachers and administrators from suits resulting from their administration of corporal punishment?

IV. SEARCH OF STUDENTS AND LOCKERS

The desire to have the Fourth Amendment included in the Bill of Rights grew out of British practices prior to the Revolutionary War. Early Americans wanted assurance that their homes would not be invaded without just cause. Many held that without this protection, government authorities could intimidate the citizenry by pursuing "fishing expeditions" such as conducting searches of homes of politically nonconforming citizens until something incriminating was found. With this fear in mind, the Fourth Amendment was included in the Bill of Rights, to protect the individual from possible harassment by an unresponsive government. Originally, the protection of the Fourth Amendment applied only to the federal government, as was the case with the other first eight amendments of the Constitution; however, as a result of decisions involving the Fourteenth Amendment, this protection for the individual is now also available against the state.

Public school officials may be placed in the position of searching a student because of a suspicion that the student has stolen an article or money or has something illegal in his or her possession, such as drugs or weapons. Over the years, several important Fourth Amendment issues have emerged as courts attempted to grapple with cases involving student search. Foremost among these issues was establishing the proper balance between an individual student's right to Fourth Amendment protection from unreasonable search and the duty of school officials to provide all students with a safe and secure school environment. Other more specific legal questions have also been addressed by the courts. These included whether or not students in the school setting had the protection of the Fourth Amendment, and if so, whether their protection equalled that of adults or did students have a lesser protection; determining if school officials were to be considered government officials, because the Fourth Amendment applies only when a government official acting under the color of the state conducts the search; the degree of suspicion a school official must have to conduct an individualized search (police, for instance, must have probable cause to search someone, a considerably higher standard than reasonable suspicion); and whether a search warrant is required in the school setting. Courts adjudicated these difficult legal questions (although not always similarly) as they increasingly dealt with such search-related issues as the constitutionality of searching a student suspected of having drugs on his or her person, the use of drug-detecting dogs, mass search of the entire student body, random drug testing of high school athletes, random searches with handheld metal-detector wands, and strip searches. In 1985 the United States Supreme Court addressed one of these issues in *New Jersey* v. *T.L.O.*, and in its decision provided public school educators with guidance regarding the search of individual students.

A. Student Search

NEW JERSEY v. T.L.O.

Supreme Court of the United States, 1985
469 U.S. 325

JUSTICE WHITE delivered the opinion of the Court.

We granted certiorari in this case to examine the appropriateness of the exclusionary rule as a remedy for searches carried out in violation of the Fourth Amendment by public school authorities. Our consideration of the proper application of the Fourth Amendment to the public schools, however, has led us to conclude that the search that gave rise to the case now before us did not violate the Fourth Amendment. Accordingly, we here address only the questions of the proper standard for assessing the legality of searches conducted by public school officials and the application of that standard to the facts of this case.

On March 7, 1980, a teacher at Piscataway High School in Middlesex County, N.J., discovered two girls smoking in a lavatory. One of the two girls was the respondent T.L.O., who at that time was a 14-year-old high school freshman. Because smoking in the lavatory was a violation of a school rule, the teacher took the two girls to the Principal's office, where they met with Assistant Vice Principal Theodore Choplick. In response to questioning by Mr. Choplick, T.L.O.'s companion admitted that she had violated the rule. T.L.O., however, denied that she had been smoking in the lavatory and claimed that she did not smoke at all.

Mr. Choplick asked T.L.O. to come into his private office and demanded to see her purse. Opening the purse, he found a pack of cigarettes, which he removed from the purse and held before T.L.O. as he accused her of having lied to him. As he reached into the purse for the cigarettes, Mr. Choplick also noticed a package of cigarette rolling papers. In his experience, possession of rolling papers by high school students was closely associated with the use of marijuana. Suspecting that a closer examination of the purse might yield further evidence of drug use, Mr. Choplick proceeded to search the purse thoroughly. The search revealed a small amount of marijuana, a pipe, a number of empty plastic bags, a substantial quantity of money in one dollar bills, an index card that appeared to be a list of students who owed T.L.O. money, and two letters that implicated T.L.O. in marijuana dealing.

Mr. Choplick notified T.L.O.'s mother and the police, and turned the evidence of drug dealing over to the police. At the request of the police, T.L.O.'s mother took her daughter to police headquarters, where T.L.O. confessed that she had been selling marijuana at the high school. On the basis of the confession and the evidence seized by Mr. Choplick, the State brought delinquency charges against T.L.O. in the Juvenile and Domestic Relations Court of Middlesex County. Contending that Mr. Choplick's search of her purse violated the Fourth Amendment, T.L.O. moved to suppress the evidence found in her purse as well as her confession, which, she argued, was tainted by the allegedly unlawful search.

* * *

In determining whether the search at issue in this case violated the Fourth Amendment, we are faced initially with the question whether that Amendment's prohibition on unreasonable searches and seizures applies to searches conducted by public school officials. We hold that it does.

It is now beyond dispute that "the Federal Constitution, by virtue of the Fourteenth Amendment, prohibits unreasonable searches and seizures by state officers." * * * Equally indisputable is the proposition that the Fourteenth Amendment protects the rights of students against encroachment by public school officials:

> "The Fourteenth Amendment, as now applied to the States, protects the citizen against the State itself and all of its creatures—Boards of Education not excepted. These have, of course, delicate, and highly discretionary functions, but none that they may not perform within the limits of the Bill of Rights. That they are educating the young for citizenship is reason for scrupulous protection of Constitutional freedoms of the individual, if we are not to strangle the free mind at its source and teach youth to discount important principles of our government as mere platitudes." *West Virginia State Board of Education* v. *Barnette* 319 U.S. 624, 637 (1943).

These two propositions—that the Fourth Amendment applies to the States through the Fourteenth Amendment, and that the actions of public school officials are subject to the limits placed on state action by the Fourteenth Amendment—might appear sufficient to answer the suggestion that the Fourth Amendment does not proscribe unreasonable searches by school officials. On reargument, however, the State of New Jersey has argued that the history of the Fourth Amendment indicates that the Amendment was intended to regulate only searches and seizures carried out by law enforcement officers; accordingly, although public school officials are concededly state agents for purposes of the Fourteenth Amendment, the Fourth Amendment creates no rights enforceable against them.

It may well be true that the evil toward which the Fourth Amendment was primarily directed was the resurrection of the pre-Revolutionary practice of using general warrants or "writs of assistance" to authorize searches for contraband by officers of the Crown. * * * But this Court has never limited the Amendment's prohibition on unreasonable searches and seizures to operations conducted by the police. Rather, the Court has long spoken of the Fourth Amendment's strictures as restraints imposed upon "governmental action"—that is, "upon the activities of sovereign authority." * * * Accordingly, we have held the Fourth Amendment applicable to the activities of civil as well as criminal authorities: building inspectors, * * * and even firemen entering privately owned premises to battle a fire * * * are all subject to the restraints imposed by the Fourth Amendment. As we observed * * * [t]he basic purpose of this Amendment, as recognized in countless decisions of this Court, is to safeguard the privacy and security of Individuals against arbitrary invasions by governmental officials."

* * *

Notwithstanding the general applicability of the Fourth Amendment to the activities of civil authorities, a few courts have concluded that school officials are exempt from the dictates of the Fourth Amendment by virtue of the special nature of their authority over schoolchildren. * * * Teachers and school administrators, it is said, act *in loco parentis* in their dealings with students: Their authority is that of the parent, not the State, and is therefore not subject to the limits of the Fourth Amendment.

Such reasoning is in tension with contemporary reality and the teachings of this Court. * * * Today's public school officials do not merely exercise authority voluntarily conferred on them by individual parents; rather, they act in furtherance of publicly mandated educational and disciplinary policies. * * * In carrying out searches and other disciplinary functions pursuant to such policies, school officials act as representatives of the State, not merely as surrogates for the parents, and they cannot claim the parents' immunity from the strictures of the Fourth Amendment.

* * *

Although this Court may take notice of the difficulty of maintaining discipline in the public schools today, the situation is not so dire that students in the schools may claim no legitimate expectations of privacy. * * *

Nor does the State's suggestion that children have no legitimate need to bring personal property into the schools seem well anchored in reality. Students at a minimum must bring to school not only the supplies needed for their studies, but also keys, money, and the necessaries of personal hygiene and grooming. In addition, students may carry on their persons or in purses or wallets such nondisruptive yet highly personal items as photographs, letters, and diaries. Finally, students may have perfectly legitimate reasons to carry with them articles of property needed in connection with extracurricular or recreational activities. In short, schoolchildren may find it necessary to carry with them a variety of legitimate, noncontraband items, and there is no reason to conclude that they have necessarily waived all rights to privacy in such items merely by bringing them onto school grounds.

Against the child's interest in privacy must be set the substantial interest of teachers and administrators in maintaining discipline in the classroom and on school grounds. Maintaining order in the classroom has never been easy, but in recent years, school disorder has often taken particularly ugly forms: drug use and violent crime in the schools have become major social problems. * * *

* * *

How, then, should we strike the balance between the schoolchild's legitimate expectations of privacy and the school's equally legitimate need to maintain an environment in which learning can take place? It is evident that the school setting requires some easing of the restrictions to which searches by public authorities are ordinarily subject. The warrant requirement, in particular, is unsuited to the school environment: Requiring a teacher to obtain a warrant before searching a child suspected of an infraction of school rules (or of the criminal law) would unduly interfere with the maintenance of the swift and informal disciplinary procedures needed in the schools. Just as we have in other cases dispensed with the warrant requirement when "the burden of obtaining a warrant is likely to frustrate the governmental purpose behind the search," * * * we hold today that school officials need not obtain a warrant before searching a student who is under their authority.

The school setting also requires some modification of the level of suspicion of illicit activity needed to justify a search. Ordinarily, a search—even one that may permissibly be carried out without a warrant—must be based upon "probable cause" to believe that a violation of the law has occurred. * * * However, "probable cause" is not an irreducible requirement of a valid search. The fundamental command of the Fourth Amendment is that searches and seizures be reasonable, and although "both the concept of probable cause and the requirement of a warrant bear on the reasonableness of a search, . . . in certain limited circumstances neither is required." * * * Thus, we have in a number of cases recognized the legality of searches and seizures based on suspicions that, although "reasonable," do not rise to the level of probable cause. * * * Where a careful balancing of governmental and private interests suggests that the public interest is best served by a Fourth Amendment standard of reasonableness that stops short of probable cause, we have not hesitated to adopt such a standard.

We join the majority of courts that have examined this issue in concluding that the accommodation of the privacy interests of schoolchildren with the substantial need of teachers and administrators for freedom to maintain order in the schools does not require strict adherence to the requirement that searches be based on probable cause to believe that the subject of the search has violated or is violating the law. Rather, the legality of a search of a student should depend simply on the reasonableness, under all the circumstances, of the search. Determining the reasonableness of any search involves a twofold inquiry: first, one must consider "whether the . . . action was justified at its inception," * * * second, one must determine whether the search as actually conducted "was reasonably related in scope to the circumstances which justified the interference in the first place." Under ordinary circumstances, a search of a student by a teacher or other school official will be "justified at its inception" when there are reasonable grounds for suspecting that the search will turn up evidence that the student has violated or is violating either the law or the rules of the school. Such a search will be permissible in its scope when the measures adopted are reasonably related to the objectives of the search and not excessively intrusive in light of the age and sex of the student and the nature of the infraction.

This standard will, we trust, neither unduly burden the efforts of school authorities to maintain order in their schools nor authorize unrestrained intrusions upon the privacy of schoolchildren. By focusing attention on the question of reasonableness, the standard will spare teachers and school administrators the necessity of schooling themselves in the niceties of probable cause and permit them to regulate their conduct according to the dictates of reason and common sense. At the same time, the reasonableness standard should ensure that the interests of students will be invaded no more than is necessary to achieve the legitimate end of preserving order in the schools.

There remains the question of the legality of the search in this case.

* * *

* * * It cannot be said that Mr. Choplick acted unreasonably when he examined T.L.O.'s purse to see if it contained cigarettes.

Our conclusions that Mr. Choplick's decisions to open T.L.O.'s purse was reasonable brings us to the question of the further search for marijuana once the pack of cigarettes was located. The suspicion upon which the search for marijuana was founded was provided when Mr. Choplick observed a package of rolling papers in the purse as he removed the pack of cigarettes. Although T.L.O. does not dispute the reasonableness of Mr. Choplick's belief that the rolling papers indicated the presence of marijuana, she does contend that the scope of the search Mr. Choplick conducted exceeded permissible bounds when he seized and read certain letters that implicated T.L.O. in drug dealing. This argument, too, is unpersuasive. The discovery of the rolling papers concededly gave rise to a reasonable suspicion that T.L.O. was carrying marijuana as well as cigarettes in her purse. This suspicion justified further exploration of T.L.O.'s purse, which turned up more evidence of drug-related activities: a pipe, a number of plastic bags of the type commonly used to store marijuana, a small quantity of marijuana, and a fairly substantial amount of money. Under these circumstances, it was not unreasonable to extend the search to a separate zippered compartment of the purse; and when a search of that compartment revealed an index card containing a list of "people who owe me money" as well as two letters, the inference that T.L.O. was involved in marijuana trafficking was substantial enough to justify Mr. Choplick in examining the letters to determine whether they contained any further evidence. In short, we cannot conclude that the search for marijuana was unreasonable in any respect.

Because the search resulting in the discovery of the evidence of marijuana dealing by T.L.O. was reasonable, the New Jersey Supreme Court's decision to exclude that evidence from T.L.O.'s juvenile delinquency proceedings on Fourth Amendment grounds was erroneous. Accordingly, the judgment of the Supreme Court of New Jersey is

Reversed.

Notes and Questions

In its decision, the *T.L.O.* Court established a two-prong test to determine the reasonableness of a search. First, a court must determine whether the search was "justified at its inception." Second, whether the search, "as actually conducted, was reasonably related in scope to the circumstances which justified the interference in the first place." In striking the balance between a student's legitimate expectations of privacy and the school's equally legitimate need to maintain an appropriate learning environment, this decision clearly demonstrates the Court's resolve to foster a drug-free school. There is little doubt that this decision has reduced the fear many school authorities had about possibly violating a student's Fourth Amendment rights.

Having high school students blow in the face of a dance monitor so he could smell their breath was held to be a reasonable search, especially because the students had been in the company of another student who had been under the influence of alcohol. See *Martinez v. School District No. 60,* 852 P.2d 1275 (Colo. Ct. App. 1992).

A federal appellate court addressed the issue of a school official's search of a student's hotel room during a spring break trip, 5,000 miles from home. Citing *T.L.O.,* the court held that the search required extraordinary justification, owing to the fact that the student had paid for the room and that the incident occurred in less than a fully educational context. Nevertheless, the court found such a justification because school officials were charged with supervisory duties in an environment requiring unusual vigilance. Relying also on the doctrine of *in loco parentis,* the court stated that many parents would be reluctant to allow their children on such trips if school officials did not have sufficient authority to supervise. See *Webb v. McCullough,* 828 F.2d 1151 (6th Cir. 1987).

B. Search for Drugs and Weapons

The prevalence of drugs and weapons in the public schools has resulted in school administrators often employing extraordinary means to control this problem. In addition to increased search of suspected students, administrators have resorted to patting down students, drug-detecting dogs, drug testing as a condition for attending school or participating in extracurricular activities, use of metal-detector wands, and not allowing pagers in the schools in order to combat drug use and selling.

Requiring random urinalysis drug tests as a condition for participation in interscholastic athletics was upheld in a six-to-three decision by the United States Supreme Court in *Vernonia School District 47J v. Acton*, 515 U.S. 646 (1995). Evidence in this case revealed that the drug testing was instituted because the school had experienced a sharp increase in disciplinary problems and drug use, rudeness during class increased, outbursts of profane language became common, and students boasted that the school could do nothing about their attraction to the drug culture; not only were student athletes drug users but they were the leaders of the drug culture; and coaches reported an increase in the number and severity of sports-related injuries. In its decision, the Court held that "students within the school environment have a lesser expectation of privacy than members of the population generally" (citing *T.L.O.*) and that student athletes have even less legitimate privacy expectations than nonathletes. The Court noted that under the drug detection program, the collection of urine, its testing, disclosure of results, and request for medical information regarding medication information were relatively unobtrusive and well-thought-out. Lastly, the Court contended that the program served an important government interest by deterring drug use by students. The Court concluded that the search was reasonable, and hence constitutional, in the light of "the decreased expectation of privacy, the relative unobtrusiveness of the search, and the severity of the need met by the search." Dissenters in the decision argued forcefully that the majority decision, unfortunately, overlooks history and precedent, which requires individualized suspicion in Fourth Amendment cases.

Two decisions of the Court of Appeals for the Seventh Circuit reveal interesting post-*Acton* issues. In *Todd v. Rush County Schools*, 133 F.3d 984 (7th Cir. 1998). *cert. denied*, 525 U.S. 824 (1998), the court wrestled with the issue of random and suspicionless drug testing, with parental consent, of all students wishing to participate in extracurricular activities or driving a car to and from school. The list of extracurricular activities included athletic teams, Student Council, foreign language clubs, Fellowship of Christian Athletes, Future Farmers of America Officers, and the Library Club. In upholding the drug testing program, the court held that evidence that some students used drugs, tobacco, or alcohol was sufficient justification and outweighed any diminished expectations of public school students' privacy. In the other decision, *Willis v. Anderson Community School Corporation*, 158 F.3d 415 (7th Cir. 1998), *cert. denied*, 526 U.S. 1019 (1999), the court addressed the issue of a student's refusal to take a drug test after his return to school after being suspended for fighting. In this instance, drug testing was required for students possessing or using tobacco products, suspended for three days or more for fighting, being habitually truant, or violating any rule that requires at least a three-day suspension. In holding the policy unconstitutional, the court declared that the causal nexus between illegal substances and violent behavior was not strong enough to create a reasonable suspicion warranting a search such as drug testing. The *Willis* court distinguished its decision from *Acton* both on the basis of the voluntary participation of the athletes in *Acton* and that athletes in general have less expectation of privacy.

Again citing *Acton*, a federal court of appeals upheld a generalized search in which all male students from grades six to twelve were searched for dangerous weapons by emptying their pockets and being patted down if a metal detector sounded. In this case, there was a concern on the part of school officials that a knife or other cutting weapon was on the school grounds because there were fresh knife cuts on the seats of a school bus. The appellate court reasoned that although there was no basis for suspecting any particular student, the possibility of a dangerous weapon at school was a risk to student safety and school discipline that no "reasonable guardian and tutor" (citing *Acton*) could ignore. See *Thompson* v. *Carthage School District*, 87 F.3d 979 (8th Cir. 1996).

Because private schools do not have the same Fourth Amendment restrictions as public schools, some have begun testing hair to detect illicit drug use. Such testing is based on the premise that drugs ingested in the body are deposited in hair follicles roughly in the proportion to the amount taken. Because traces remain in the hair, such tests also reveal how long the drugs have been used. To date, standards for such tests have not been established by the federal government, and some studies have shown that drug traces remain in black hair up to 50 times longer than in blond hair.

Several states have prohibited students from carrying telephone pagers in public schools because of their relationship to illegal drug sales. See, for instance, *Rowell* v. *State*, 666 So.2d 830 (Ala. 1995).

C. Intrusive Search

In their zeal to locate stolen money, drugs, or weapons, educators occasionally engage in intrusive searches commonly referred to as strip searches. Historically, this type of search has most often been used with younger children; however, with the advent of drugs and weapons in the school it has increasingly been used with older students. In this type of search, students may be asked to strip down to their underpants, partially disrobe, remove all their clothes, or be patted down. Courts take several factors into consideration when determining reasonableness in intrusive search cases. These include the student's age, the student's record and disciplinary history, the seriousness and prevalence of the problem, and the exigency requiring an immediate warrantless search. In recent years, courts have increasingly upheld teachers who had engaged in strip searches, especially if it involved younger students. Generally, however, individualized suspicion is required to conduct an intrusive search; therefore, teachers should refrain from conducting blanket intrusive searches when money or articles of value are involved.

A strip search of two eight-year-old female second graders for allegedly stealing $7.00 was upheld in *Jenkins* v. *Talladega City Board of Education*, 115 F.3d 821 (11th Cir. 1997), *cert. denied* 522 U.S. 966 (1997). In this case, based on a student's accusation of the theft, a series of searches took place that did not produce the money. These included initially searching Jenkins's backpack, asking Jenkins and another accused student to remove their shoes and socks, taking the girls to the girls' restroom and ordering them to enter the bathroom stalls and "come back with their underpants down to their ankles," and subsequently taking them to the restroom a second time and asking them to remove their dresses (which left one girl in a slip and the other in only her underpants) in a final attempt to retrieve the money. In its holding, the court relying extensively on *T.L.O.*, asserted that these searches were reasonably related to the objective of recovering the stolen $7.00 and not "excessively intrusive in light of the age and sex of the students and the nature of the infraction." The court contended that school officials should consider the stealing of $7.00 in an elementary school a serious concern, female students were searched by female teachers, the eight-year-old students were prepubescent, and teachers frequently assist students of that age in the bathroom.

A search of a sixteen-year-old male student in a behavioral disorder program who was suspected of "crotching" drugs was held to be reasonable. The court contended that there were several factors influencing its decision, in addition to the unusual bulge in the student's crotch area. These included allegations of several recent prior incidents such as dealing in drugs, testing positive for marijuana, possession of drugs, having "crotched" drugs during a police raid at his mother's house, failing a urinalysis for cocaine, unsuccessful completion of a drug rehabilitation program, and a report by a bus driver that there was a smell of marijuana where the student had sat on the bus. See *Cornfield* v. *Consolidated High School District No. 230*, 991 F.2d 1316 (7th Cir. 1993).

Another strip search was upheld in *Williams* v. *Ellington*, 936 F.2d 881 (6th Cir. 1991). In this instance, a female student suspected of possessing a drug was asked by a female assistant principal, and witnessed by a female secretary, to empty her pockets, remove her T-shirt, and lower her blue jeans to her knees. The student alleged that the assistant principal pulled on the elastic of her undergarments to see if anything would fall out. No evidence of drugs was found. In its decision, the court emphasized that school officials need discretionary authority to function with efficiency and speed in certain situations, and their decisions should not be questioned with the benefit of hindsight as that would undermine the authority necessary to ensure the safety and order of our schools.

May school officials conduct a schoolwide search for drugs by using drug-detecting dogs and then engage in a strip search of suspected students? A federal appellate court has held that sniffing by a dog was not a search and therefore not protected by the Fourth Amendment; requesting students to empty their pockets and purses did not violate the Fourth Amendment; but conducting a nude search of a student as a result of the dog's alert was unreasonable. In entitling the student to damages, the court contended that a nude search was not only unconstitutional but also contrary to common decency. See *Doe* v. *Renfrow*, 635 F.2d 582 (7th Cir. 1980), *cert. denied*, 451 U.S. 1022 (1981).

Parents often allege a Fourth Amendment violation in suspected child-abuse cases, claiming that school personnel should not have questioned or examined a student's person to determine possible child abuse. The court in *Picarella* v. *Terrizzi*, 893 F. Supp. 1292 (Pa. 1995), concluded that the Fourth Amendment had not been violated as a result of school personnel questioning a student about suspected abuse. The court reasoned that under Pennsylvania's Child Protective Services Law, enumerated persons such as teachers and administrators were required to determine if there was "reason to believe" that a student had been abused.

In another case involving suspected child abuse, school officials were given qualified immunity from civil rights claims by parents for removing a student from her classroom and questioning and physically examining her to determine whether she had been physically abused. The court reasoned that minor schoolchildren suspected of being victims of child abuse did not have a clearly established right to be free from visual examination of unexposed parts of their bodies to determine such suspected abuse. See *Landstrom* v. *Illinois Department of Children and Family Services*, 892 F.2d 670 (7th Cir. 1990). In this case, the first grader removed her dress and her underpants and her buttocks were examined by the school nurse in the presence of the child's teacher, a school psychologist, a social worker, and the principal. Several states have enacted laws that grant a limited immunity to those officials who have been made legally responsible for investigating and reporting child abuse. Educators should be aware of their state's statutes dealing with reporting child abuse.

D. Locker Search

Courts have tended to allow school officials to search a student's locker without a warrant and without the student's permission, reasoning that schools retain ultimate control over lockers and act *in loco parentis*. This issue was addressed three decades ago in *Kansas* v. *Stein*, 203 Kan. 638, 456 P.2d 1 (1969), *cert. denied*, 397 U.S. 947 (1970), which discussed the public nature of student lockers. The court held that school authorities must protect both the school's educational functions and the students' welfare and may, therefore, inspect lockers to prevent their illicit use.

Courts have continued to uphold locker searches by school authorities, usually applying a standard that declares students to have legitimate expectations of privacy in their lockers. However, the expectation is not absolute and must be balanced against the school's need to maintain order and discipline. In a case involving a gun and cocaine, a random search of a school locker was upheld. In its decision, the court stressed that there was an environment of fear and tension at the school due to gun-related activities and a written policy under which the school retained ownership and control of school lockers. Having such a policy in place, the court reasoned, resulted in the student having no reasonable expectation of privacy in his locker. See *Isiah B.* v. *State*, 500 N.W.2d 637 (Wis. 1993), *cert. denied*, 510 U.S. 884 (1993). Also see *Commonwealth* v. *Cass*, 709 A.2d 350 (Pa. 1998), *cert. denied*, 525 U.S. 833 (1998), where the reasonableness of using drug-detecting dogs for the search of students' lockers was upheld.

V. STUDENT APPEARANCE

There have been many challenges to dress and grooming regulations over the years. In the earliest cases, essentially beginning in the 1960s, students and their parents often questioned rules, particularly those pertaining to grooming, which they believed to be unfair or anachronistic. In their suits, parents commonly alleged that they, not schools, were responsible for the appearance of their children and that the contested rules violated their privacy rights. They contended that school authorities were warranted in imposing only those standards necessary for health, safety, or an educationally sound program. School authorities, on the other hand, contended that they possessed the discretion to determine which policies aided in maintaining order and discipline.

There has been a markedly reduced number of dress and grooming suits in recent times, perhaps not only due to a dissipation of the environment that drove them in the 1960s, but also because adequate school policies were crafted and school officials learned to deal appropriately with these issues when they arose. Additionally, many school officials discovered that attempting to enforce dress and grooming codes was a losing battle, because students often found ways, subtle or otherwise, to assert their individual identities through their hairstyles and what they wore.

In recent cases, school officials often contend that dress and grooming violations are gang related and, therefore, pose a serious threat to safety in the school. In addition to the privacy issue, allegations in these recent cases may include violations of the First Amendment, gender discrimination, and racial discrimination. Despite the continuing controversy over the years surrounding the issue and the judiciary's frequent involve-ment, the Supreme Court has not ruled substantively in a dress and grooming case.

A. Dress

The prevalence of gangs, hate groups, and those opposed to "political cor-rectness" in public schools poses serious problems for school officials, be-cause the presence of such groups on a campus may contribute to substantial disruption and threats to safety. Members of such groups often wear clothing or symbols signifying their group membership. Because such dress may be in violation of dress and grooming codes, when litigated, given all the circumstances surrounding the school's environment, courts must balance the First Amendment rights of students to express themselves against the legitimate right of school authorities to maintain a safe and disruption-free environment. Examples of controversial student expres-sion that may involve First Amendment protection include T-shirts de-picting violence, drugs (e.g., marijuana leafs), racial epithets, or characters such as Bart Simpson; ripped, baggy, or saggy pants or jeans; sneakers with lights; colored bandannas, baseball or other hats; words shaved into scalps, brightly colored hair, distinctive haircuts or hairstyles, or ponytails for males; exposed underwear; Malcolm X symbols; Walkmans, cellular phones, or beepers; backpacks; tattoos, unusual-colored lipsticks, pierced noses, or earrings; and decorative dental caps. Courts generally contend that such "expression" does not have protection under the First Amend-ment when there is violence in the community or school such as intimida-tion of students and faculty, shootings or knifings, rampant drug use, or racial turmoil that is related to gang or hate-group activity.

A dress code prohibiting the wearing of clothing with writing, pic-tures, or any insignia that identified any professional or college sports team was challenged on the basis of its violating students' free speech rights. A court agreed that the code violated the rights of elementary and middle school students but not those of high school students. Evidence revealed that there was gang presence and intimidation of students and faculty at the high school, associated with the sports-oriented clothing, that could lead to disruption and disturbance of school activities. The court declared that the justification for curtailing the students' rights did not "demand a certainty that disruption will occur, but only the existence of facts which might reasonably lead school officials to forecast substantial disruption." See *Jeglin v. San Jacinto Unified School District*, 827 F. Supp. 1459 (Cal. 1993). Revealing the lengths students will go to make a statement, school author-ities at a Massachusetts high school noticed that white students wore Notre Dame caps and black students wore University of Nevada at Las Vegas caps. In time, the authorities learned that the ND caps worn by some white students were meant to send the message Niggers Die. Some black students retaliated by wearing the UNLV caps, which were meant to signify Us Niggers Love Violence.

Not being allowed to wear a Confederate flag jacket to school was upheld as not violating of a student's freedom of expression in *Phillips* v. *Anderson County School District*, 987 F. Supp. 488 (S.C. 1997). The court based its decision on prior incidents of racial tension and unrest and reasoned that the wearing of such a jacket would likely result in substantial disruption of the school's environment. Additionally, the court asserted, the student and his parents had notice of the policy as he had been asked not to wear the jacket on previous occasions.

A policy prohibiting the wearing or display of any gang symbol, any act or speech showing gang affiliation, and any conduct in furtherance of gang activity was also upheld by a federal district court. The court related that in this instance the wearing of earrings by males generally connoted gang membership and did not have First Amendment protection. An equal protection argument was rejected by the court's stating that "while girls may be gang members they symbolize their affiliation in other ways—ways that are prohibited by school policy." See *Olesen* v. *Board of Education*, 676 F. Supp. 820 (Ill. 1987). Although not involving the issue of gang membership, prohibiting a fourth-grade male from wearing an earring was upheld in *Hines* v. *Caston School Corporation*, 651 N.E.2d 330 (Ind. App. 1995). The court held that enforcing community standards of dress to instill discipline is a legitimate educational function and prohibiting males from wearing earrings did not violate their equal protection.

In response to a gang problem, a dress code was adopted that prohibited the wearing of "sagging" pants. A black student who was suspended for wearing such pants alleged that his First Amendment rights of speech, expression, and association were violated because this attire was part of a style known as "hip hop," whose roots were African American. In rejecting the student's contention, the court asserted that a two-part test must be met for nonverbal conduct to be protected under the First Amendment. First, there must be an intent to convey a particularized message, and, second, there must be a great likelihood that the message would be understood by those who observe the conduct. In this case, the court declared that the second part of the test had not been met. See *Bivens* v. *Albuquerque Public Schools*, 899 F. Supp. 556 (N. M. 1995).

Another decision, *Pyle* v. *South Hadley School Committee*, 861 F. Supp. 157 (Mass. 1994) upheld the provision of a school's dress code prohibiting vulgar apparel by not allowing students to wear T-shirts on school premises with slogans such as "Co-ed Naked Band; Do It to the Rhythm" and "See Dick Drive. See Dick Die. Don't Be a Dick." However, the provision which prohibited clothing that "harasses, threatens, intimidates, or demeans" individuals or groups, which was neither vulgar nor disruptive, was found to violate students' First Amendment rights.

A "no hats" policy was upheld in *Isaacs ex. rel. Isaacs* v. *Board of Education of Howard County*, 40 F. Supp.2d 335 (Md. 1999). In this case, the school had refused to permit a high school student from wearing a head-wrap in celebration of her African American and Jamaican cultural heritage. School rules did make exceptions for religious headgear such as yarmulkes and Muslim hijab, including head scarves. The court stated that the policy did not violate the student's free speech rights, which were not absolute, and that the "no hats" rule furthered an important government interest in providing a safe, respectful school environment.

Not being permitted to attend a high school prom because they were wearing clothing of the opposite sex was held not to be violative of the students' First Amendment rights in *Harper* v. *Edgewood Board of Education*, 655 F. Supp. 1353 (Ohio 1987). The court contended that the dress regulations were reasonably related to the valid educational purposes of teaching community values and maintaining school discipline.

A dress regulation requiring proper attire to participate in a graduation ceremony was upheld. The court maintained that receiving a diploma at a commencement program was not a property right under state law, and the student was entitled to receive his diploma separately after the program. See *Fowler* v. *Williamson*, 251 S.E.2d 889 (N.C. Ct. App. 1979).

Some observers suggest that at one time in our history, schools, especially when serving a homogeneous community, were accepted as a socializing agency that was the arbiter of "proper" dress. If this is an accurate assessment, what factors have contributed to the demise of such a role for the school?

Does your state or school system have dress regulations?

B. Uniforms

Requiring the wearing of uniforms, as many private and parochial schools have done over the years, has increasingly been adopted by public school systems across the country. Presently, school districts in half the states have school uniform requirements, and estimates suggest that over the next several years, one in four public school students may be wearing uniforms. Typically, when school uniform dress codes are adopted, they apply to students in kindergarten through eighth grade and may be either voluntary or mandatory with opt-out provisions for claims of conscience.

California passed dress code and school uniform legislation in 1994. It provides, in part:

(a) The legislature finds and declares each of the following:

(1) The children of this state have the right to an effective public school education. Both students and staff of the primary, elementary, junior and senior high school campuses have the constitutional right to be safe and secure in their persons at school. However, children in many of our public schools are

forced to focus on the threat of violence and the messages of violence contained in many aspects our society, particularly reflected in gang regalia that disrupts the learning environment.

(2) "Gang-related apparel" is hazardous to the health and safety of the school environment.

(3) Instructing teachers and administrators on the subtleties of identifying constantly changing gang regalia and gang affiliation takes an increasing amount of time away from educating our children.

(4) Weapons including firearms and knives, have become commonplace upon even our elementary school campuses. Students often conceal weapons by wearing clothing, such as jumpsuits and overcoats, and by carrying large bags.

(5) The adoption of a schoolwide uniform policy is a reasonable way to provide some protection for students. A required uniform may protect students from being associated with any particular gang. Moreover, by requiring schoolwide uniforms teachers and administrators may not need to occupy as much of their time learning the subtleties of gang regalia.

(6) To control the environment in public schools to facilitate and maintain an effective learning environment and to keep the focus of the classroom on learning and not personal safety, schools need the authorization to implement uniform clothing requirements for our public school children.

(7) Many educators believe that school dress significantly influences pupil behavior. This influence is evident on school dressup days and color days. Schools that have adopted school uniforms experience a "coming together feeling," greater school pride, and better behavior in and out of the classroom.

(b) The governing board of any school district may adopt or rescind a reasonable dress code policy that requires pupils to wear a schoolwide uniform or prohibits pupils from wearing "gang-related apparel" if the governing board of the school district approves a plan that may be initiated by an individual school's principal, staff, and parents and determines that the policy is necessary for the health and safety of the school environment. . . .

(c) . . . If a schoolwide uniform is required, the specific uniform selected shall be determined by the principal, staff, and parents of the individual school.

(d) A dress code policy that requires pupils to wear a schoolwide uniform shall not be implemented with less than six months notice to parents and the availability of resources to assist economically disadvantaged pupils.

(e) The governing board shall provide a method whereby parents may choose not to have their children comply with an adopted school uniform policy.

(f) If a governing board chooses to adopt a policy pursuant to this section, the policy shall include a provision that no pupil shall be penalized academically or otherwise discriminated against nor denied attendance to school if the pupil's parents chose not to have the pupil comply with the school uniform policy. The governing board shall continue to have responsibility for the appropriate education of those pupils.

(g) A policy adopted pursuant to this section shall not preclude pupils that participate in a nationally recognized youth organization from wearing organization uniforms on days that the organization has a scheduled meeting. Cal. Educ. Code § 35183 (West 1994).

Courts have upheld mandatory school uniform policies. The New York City Board of Education adopted a mandatory citywide uniform policy for all students in grades pre-K through 8 except in schools designated as middle schools, intermediate schools, junior high schools, and high schools. The policy's stated intentions were to: "promote a more effective learning climate; foster school unity and pride; improve student performance; foster self-esteem; eliminate label competition; simplify dressing and minimize costs to parents; teach children appropriate dress and decorum in the 'workplace'; and help to improve student conduct and discipline." Under the policy, parents could seek an exemption for their children. A parent who challenged the policy alleged that his constitutional right to raise his child in the manner in which he deemed appropriate was violated and that the opt-out provision would merely make his daughter "stick out." In its unreported decision in *Lipsman v. New York City Board of Education*, No.98 Civ.2008(SHS), 1999 WL 498230 (N.Y.), the court held that the policy was rationally related to the board's legitimate interest in educating children and that the father's constitutional rights had not been violated. In another decision, an Arizona appellate court upheld a school uniform policy in *Phoenix Elementary School District No. 1 v. Green*, 943 P.2d 836 (Ariz. Ct. App.1997). The judge reasoned that the school was a nonpublic forum and therefore could limit expression that was not deemed to further safety or the school's educational mission.

Does your state have a dress code or school uniform legislation?

C. Grooming

Court decisions dealing with grooming issues have not been consistent. Judicial views range from upholding the right of males to wear "long" hair, on the basis that this right is protected by the federal Constitution, to declaring the question an unworthy one for federal court attention. Federal appellate courts in the Fifth, Sixth, Ninth, and Tenth Circuits either upheld grooming regulations or contended that grooming regulations were unworthy of their attention. See *Ferrell v. Dallas Independent School District*, 392 F.2d 697 (5th Cir. 1968), cert. denied, 393 U.S. 856 (1968); *Jackson v. Dorrier*, 424 F.2d 213 (6th Cir. 1970), cert. denied, 400 U.S. 850 (1970); *King v. Saddleback Junior College District*, 445 F.2d 932 (9th Cir. 1971); and *Freeman v. Flake*, 448 F.2d 258 (10th Cir. 1971). In contrast the First, Fourth, Seventh, and Eighth Circuits found regulations limiting the length of hair invalid. See *Richards v. Thurston*, 424 F.2d 1281 (1st Cir. 1970); *Massie v.*

Henry, 455 F.2d 779 (4th Cir. 1972); *Breen* v. *Kahl*, 419 F.2d 1034 (7th Cir. 1969), *cert. denied*, 398 U.S. 937 (1970); and *Bishop* v. *Colaw*, 450 F.2d 1069 (8th Cir. 1971). To date, the United States Supreme Court has not rendered a substantive decision in school grooming cases, denying certiorari in cases dealing with male students' hair length.

State courts in Oklahoma, Oregon, and Alaska have held that schools do not have the authority to regulate hairstyles. See *Independent School District No. 8 of Seiling* v. *Swanson*, 553 P.2d 496 (Okla. 1976); *Neuhaus* v. *Federico*, 505 P.2d 939 (Or. Ct. App. 1973); and *Breese* v. *Smith*, 501 P.2d 159 (Alaska, 1972). However, Supreme Courts in Texas, Missouri, and Kansas have not held similarly. See *Barber* v. *Colorado Independent School District*, 901 S.W.2d 447 (Tex. 1995); *Kraus* v. *Board of Education of the City of Jennings*, 492 S.W.2d 783 (Mo. 1973); and *Blaine* v. *Board of Education, Haysville Unified School District No. 261*, 502 P.2d 693 (Kan. 1972).

The Supreme Court of Texas, in *Barber* v. *Colorado Independent School District*, 901 S.W.2d 447 (Tex. 1995), upheld a code that included the following:

> The district's dress code is established to teach grooming and hygiene, instill discipline, prevent disruption, avoid safety hazards, and teach respect for authority.
>
> Boys may wear hair to the bottom of the collar, the bottom of the ear, and combed out of the eyes. Boys may not wear earrings of any kind. Caps and hats not a part of women's formal attire may not be worn in the building. Sudden, unbecoming fashions or anything designed to attract undue attention to the individual or activities are not acceptable. These guidelines are subject to administrative discretion. Extra-curricular organizations may impose a more stringent dress code. (p. 448)

The dress code was challenged on the basis of the student's being eighteen years old (age of majority) and that the restrictions for males regarding hair length and earrings violated his fundamental constitutional rights because the policy did not apply to female students. In its holding, the court ruled that the student's constitutional rights had not been violated and that it was "a matter of common sense that the state judiciary is less competent to deal with students' hair length than a parent, school board, administrator, principal, or teacher." One dissenting justice accused the majority of dismissing the student's claims without the benefit of legal analysis and declared that the "Court turns its back on an indisputable finding of sex discrimination, and unashamedly proclaims that such matters are not worthy of this Court's consideration." This decision, another dissenter argued, immunizes local Texas school boards from claims of gender discrimination.

How does your school deal with students who wear hair "spiked," brightly colored, or unusually styled? Are your school's policies adequate to deal with this issue?

VI. PREGNANCY, PARENTHOOD, AND MARRIAGE

Years ago, public school policies often excluded students who were married or pregnant or who were parents. The rationale for such policies was that exclusion would serve as a deterrent and thereby discourage students from becoming pregnant or getting married. Such policies, which in practice applied disproportionately to females, were successfully attacked in the courts. Enactment of Title IX of the Education Amendments of 1972 addressed the issue on the basis of prohibiting gender discrimination in any educational programs receiving federal funds.* The section Marital or Parental Status of the implementing regulations for Title IX states:

Marital or parental status.

(a) Status generally. A recipient shall not apply any rule concerning a student's actual or potential parental, family, or marital status which treats students differently on the basis of sex.

(b) Pregnancy and related conditions. (1) A recipient shall not discriminate against any student, or exclude any student from its education program or activity, including any class or extracurricular activity, on the basis of such student's pregnancy, childbirth, false pregnancy, termination of pregnancy or recovery therefrom, unless the student requests voluntarily to participate in a separate portion of the program or activity of the recipient.

(2) A recipient may require such a student to obtain the certification of a physician that the student is physically and emotionally able to continue participation in the normal education program or activity so long as such a certification is required of all students for other physical or emotional conditions requiring the attention of a physician.

(3) A recipient which operates a portion of its education program or activity separately for pregnant students, admittance to which is completely voluntary on the part of the student as provided in paragraph (b)(1) of this section shall ensure that the instructional program in the separate program is comparable to that offered to non-pregnant students.

(4) A recipient shall treat pregnancy, childbirth, false pregnancy, termination of pregnancy and recovery therefrom in the same manner and under the same policies as any other temporary disability with respect to any medical or hospital benefit, service, plan or policy which such recipient administers, operates, offers, or participates in with respect to students admitted to the recipient's educational program or activity.

(5) In the case of a recipient which does not maintain a leave policy for its students, or in the case of a student who does not otherwise qualify for leave under such a policy, a recipient shall treat pregnancy, childbirth, false pregnancy, termination of pregnancy and recovery therefrom as a justification for a leave of absence for so long a period of time as is deemed medically neces-

*See Appendix D for Title IX of the Education Amendments of 1972.

sary by the student's physician, at the conclusion of which the student shall be reinstated to the status which she held when the leave began. 45 C.F.R. § 86.40 (1972).

In an alleged Title IX violation, a federal court of appeals addressed a female student's dismissal from a chapter of the National Honor Society because of her pregnancy. In its decision, the court stated that premarital sex, rather than gender, and pregnancy or failure to marry could be reasons taken into account for the student's dismissal. Faculty members had stated that failure to uphold standards of leadership and character, not the pregnancy, were the basis for dismissal. The court also concluded that not dismissing from the society a male member who had engaged in premarital sex was relevant in determining whether members of the faculty had a double standard and, therefore, intentionally discriminated against the pregnant student. See *Pfeiffer* v. *Marion Center Area School District*, 917 F.2d 779 (3rd Cir. 1990). However, see *Chipman* v. *Grant County School District*, 30 F. Supp.2d 975 (Ky. 1998), which granted an injunction compelling a school to admit to an honor society two unmarried female students who became pregnant and had children. The court in this case applied the Pregnancy Discrimination Act* and contended that they had been discriminated against under both a disparate impact (the policy had caused a significant adverse effect on, in this case, women who have become pregnant from premarital sex and have become visibly pregnant) and disparate treatment (member of a protected class who has been treated differently, in this case, because of pregnancy) theory and that they would likely prevail in a subsequent discrimination suit.

Should pregnant cheerleaders be allowed to continue their cheering? Should a cheerleader who has had an abortion be allowed back on the squad? Do school systems generally attempt to regulate male athletes who are fathers or responsible for pregnancies? Does a double standard continue to exist that brands sexually active girls but not their male partners?

Does your local school system or state have policies regarding students who are married or pregnant or who are parents?

VII. PARTICIPATION IN EXTRACURRICULAR ACTIVITIES

Extracurricular activities are usually thought of as being conducted outside the classroom before or after regular school hours, usually noncredit, generally supervised by school officials, academically nonremedial and of a voluntary nature on the part of the students. They may include activities such as athletics, drama, clubs, band, cheerleading, and debate.

---

*See Appendix D for the Pregnancy Discrimination Act of 1978, P.L. 95-555.

Two basic legal issues have surfaced when policies excluding a student from extracurricular activities are attacked. One of the issues raises the question of the status of extracurricular activities as a protected property interest and the requisite process due, if any. The other issue deals with the equal protection claim that an excluded student is the victim of a school's arbitrary classification scheme.

A. LEGAL STATUS OF EXTRACURRICULAR ACTIVITIES

In following *Goss*, courts have generally held that students have a property interest in the entire educational process. However, courts have not agreed whether or not participation in one aspect of the process, such as extracurricular activities, is a constitutionally protected property interest. If it is held that such a property interest does exist, courts must then decide the extent of due process that must be provided. These issues were examined in *Palmer* v. *Merluzzi*.

PALMER v. MERLUZZI
United States Court of Appeals, Third Circuit, 1989
868 F.2d 90

STAPLETON, Circuit Judge.
This is an appeal from a summary judgment in favor of the defendants, Peter Merluzzi, Superintendent of Schools for the Hunterdon Central High School District, and the Hunterdon Central Board of Education, Plaintiff Dan Palmer, a student and football player at Hunterdon, claims that his Constitutional rights to due process and equal protection were violated when Superintendent Merluzzi suspended him from playing interscholastic football for sixty days. We will affirm.

In September of 1986, Dan Palmer was a senior at Hunterdon Central High School and a starting wide receiver on the high school's football team. He was also enrolled in a high school course called "Careers in Broadcasting Technology." On the evening of September 28, 1986, in order to fill a course requirement, Palmer and three other students were assigned, without faculty supervision, to the school radio station which is located on the school premises. The next morning, beer stains and a marijuana pipe were discovered at the radio station. Later that day, Palmer, school disciplinarian Dr. Grimm, and Mr. Buckley, Palmer's former football coach, met in Mr. Buckley's office and Palmer was questioned about this discovery. During that meeting, Palmer admitted that the evening before he had smoked marijuana and consumed beer at the radio station.

On September 30, 1986, Dr. Grimm sent Mr. and Mrs. Palmer a letter advising them that their son had been assigned a ten-day out-of-school suspension effective from September 30, 1986 to October 13, 1986. The letter asked the Palmers to call Dr. Grimm if they had additional questions and suggested that they and their son consider counseling. The Palmers took no action to contest the ten-day suspension.

* * *

On October 13, the eve of the expiration of the ten-day suspension, the Board of Education met. Palmer's father, James Palmer, hearing "rumors" concerning the possible imposition of additional sanctions on his son, attended the meeting and spoke with Merluzzi shortly before it started. Merluzzi confirmed that he was inclined to impose a sixty-day extracurricular suspension, but told James Palmer that he could raise the issue with the Board. James Palmer was accorded half an hour in closed session to present his views; he argued that the additional suspension would adversely affect his son's chances of playing football in college and would also reduce his chances of being awarded college scholarships. The Board declined to intervene and, after the meeting, Merluzzi informed all concerned parents that he was definitely going to impose the sixty-day extracurricular suspension.

* * *

The threshold issue is whether the interests that could be adversely affected in the proceeding against Palmer were such that the due process clause was implicated. The answer seems clear. In *Goss* vs. *Lopez,* * * * the Supreme Court concluded that due process was required when a student faced a ten-day scholastic suspension. A *fortiori,* due process is required when a student faces a ten-day academic suspension *and* a sixty-day athletic suspension.

Having concluded that "some process" was due, we turn to the issue of how much was due. We know from *Goss* what process would have been due if only a ten-day academic suspension had been at stake. After balancing the competing interests involved, the Court decided that the student must be given "oral or written notice of the charges against him and, if he denies them, an explanation of the evidence the authorities have and an opportunity to present his side of the story." The Court continued, stating that "[t]here need be no delay between the time 'notice' is given and the time of the hearing. . . . We hold only that . . . the student first be told what he is accused of doing and what the basis of the accusation is." * * * The Court also stopped short of requiring that the student be given "the opportunity to secure counsel, to confront and cross-examine witnesses supporting the charge, or to call his own witnesses to verify his version of the incident." As long as the student "at least ha[s] the opportunity to characterize his conduct and put it in what he deems the proper context," due process has been satisfied.

Palmer received the process required by *Goss.* The day after the incident at the radio station, in an informal hearing with Dr. Grimm and

Mr. Buckley, he was advised of what had been found in the radio station and thus of the character of the offense being investigated. He then admitted his participation in the smoking of marijuana and the drinking of beer at the station. Palmer's involvement in the activities of that evening has never been disputed. During the conference, Palmer had the opportunity to put the events of the prior evening into what he perceived to be their proper context and could have argued for leniency had he so chosen.

* * *

In this case, Palmer was advised at the outset that he was suspected of consuming alcohol and a drug on school property. The Student Handbook, which was applicable to all students, specified that "alcohol and/or drug use" would, if a first offense, result in "10 days suspension" from school. The Interscholastic Athletic Program policy statement, which was applicable to Palmer and other students participating in that program, warned that "no student may participate who has not demonstrated good citizenship and responsibility." Based on these provisions, the nature of the offense, and common sense, we, like the New Jersey Commissioner of Education, are confident that Palmer must have realized from the outset that his football eligibility, as well as his status as a student, was at stake. Accordingly, we hold that Palmer's interview with Dr. Grimm and Mr. Buckley provided just as meaningful an opportunity to argue against the athletic suspension as against the scholastic suspension.

* * *

Due process is a flexible concept and the process due in any situation is to be determined by weighing (1) the private interests at stake, (2) the governmental interests at stake, and (3) the fairness and reliability of the existing procedures and the probable value, if any, of additional procedural safeguards.

* * *

We accept for present purposes Palmer's contention that, while called an extracurricular activity, the school's football program is an integral part of its educational program. Nevertheless, it is but one part of that program and in terms of lost educational benefit, the loss occasioned by a football suspension is far less than that occasioned by a suspension from school for a comparable period of time. In terms of the student's standing with teachers and peers, we believe the potential loss is likely to be a function of the nature of the offense rather than the penalty; it is therefore unlikely to be affected by the fact that the sanction includes an athletic as well as a school suspension. As a general proposition, we believe the same can be said for the potential for interference with later opportunities for higher education and employment. Indeed, Palmer does not argue otherwise. The loss that he emphasizes is the possible loss of the opportunity to play college football. Although we acknowledge that the loss of the opportunity to impress college scouts with one's senior year play can have a significant adverse effect on one's chances for a college football career, we believe it would be unduly disruptive of a school's educational process to require one disciplinary process for football players and similarly situated athletes and another disciplinary process for other students.

* * *

Palmer also contends that his suspension violated his right to equal protection under the Fourteenth Amendment. Since participation in extracurricular activities is not a fundamental right under the Constitution and since Palmer's suspension was not based on a suspect classification, * * * we must examine Palmer's argument under the "rational relationship test." * * * We conclude that the disciplinary actions taken by the school were rationally related to a valid state interest. The State has very strong interests in preserving a drug-free environment in its schools and in discouraging drug use by its students. We are unwilling to say that the sanctions imposed on Palmer were not reasonably designed to serve those legitimate interests.

Since Palmer's suspensions from school and participation in interscholastic football did not violate any right secured by the Constitution, we will affirm the judgment of the district court.

Notes and Questions

Many courts have addressed this issue over the years. In one instance, students who had allegedly violated a school's alcohol policy were suspended from such extracurricular activities as sports, clubs, and the National Honor Society. In denying the students' request for a preliminary injunction, the court in *Farver* v. *Board of Education*, 40 F. Supp2d 323 (Md. 1999), held that there was no constitutionally protected right to participate in extracurricular activities. The court recognized that although the harshness of the penalty could be questioned, it was a matter for state law to address and not a federal court.

In an earlier decision, *Dallam* v. *Cumberland Valley School District*, 391 F. Supp. 358 (Pa. 1975) the court stated:

> . . . [T]he property interest in education created by the state is participation in the entire process. The myriad activities which combine to form that educational process cannot be dissected to create hundreds of separate property rights, each cognizable under the Constitution. Otherwise, removal from an athletic team, a club or any extracurricular activity, would each require ultimate satisfaction of procedural due process. (p. 361)

In *Pegram* v. *Nelson*, 469 F. Supp.1134 (N.C. 1979), the court declared:

> Since there is not a property interest in each separate component of the "educational process," denial of the opportunity to participate in merely one of several extracurricular activities would not give rise to a right to due process. However, *total exclusion* from participation in that part of the educational process designated as extracurricular activities for a *lengthy period* of time could, depending upon the particular circumstances, be a sufficient deprivation to implicate due process. (p. 1140)

And in *Albach v. Olde*, 531 F.2d 983 (10th Cir. 1976), the court maintained that:

> . . . The educational process is a broad and comprehensive concept with a variable and indefinite meaning. It is not limited to classroom attendance but includes innumerable separate components, such as participation in athletic activity and membership in school clubs and social groups, which combine to provide an atmosphere of intellectual and moral advancement. We do not read Goss to establish a property interest subject to constitutional protection in each of these separate components. (p. 985)

Similar views were expressed in *Mazevski v. Horseheads Central School District*, 950 F. Supp. 69 (N.Y. 1997), which upheld the dismissal of a student from the marching band for missing a competition performance without permission, to participate in a Macedonian music festival in Canada. The court held that although the student had a protectible property interest in the entire educational process, exclusion from a particular course, event, or activity was of no constitutional import.

School authorities were upheld in declaring a champion high school wrestler ineligible for the state wrestling championship. The school board's decision resulted from the wrestler's participation with three other students in having multiple acts of sexual intercourse with a sixteen-year-old female student. In responding to the issue of the loss of a scholarship, the court stated:

> When scholarships are awarded at the discretion of a college coach, and such discretion has not yet been exercised, no property interest in the receipt of a scholarship can exist, and the plaintiff cannot invoke his expectation that he would earn a scholarship at the state tournament in order to claim a property interest in wrestling there. (p. 631)

See *Brands v. Sheldon Community School*, 671 F. Supp. 627 (Iowa 1987).

Courts have addressed the issue of academic requirements for participation in extracurricular activities. These requirements, often referred to as "no pass, no play" rules, generally require that a student maintain a passing grade ("C" or 70%) in all academic classes in order to be eligible to participate in extracurricular activities. Courts have not upheld contentions that such rules violate the Equal Protection Clause of the Fourteenth Amendment. See *Montana v. Board of Trustees of School District No. 1*, 726 P.2d 801 (Mont. 1986); *Spring Branch Independent School District v. Stamos*, 695 S.W.2d 556 (Tex. 1985); and *Bailey v. Truby*, 321 S.E.2d 302 (W. Va. 1984).

What is your school system's policy regarding the restriction of students from participating in extracurricular activities?

B. Athletics

Exclusion or suspension from participation in athletics makes up the vast majority of court cases dealing with extracurricular activities. Rules barring married students, females, and students with disabilities from participating in athletics are frequently challenged. Those barred generally allege that they have not received equal protection guaranteed under the Fourteenth Amendment or that the school conduct violates a federal statute.

1. Married Students

Cases dealing with married students barred from participating in athletics have often involved "star" athletes who claim they will be deprived of an opportunity to be considered for athletic scholarships. Those barred have also alleged that such rules infringe on the fundamental right of marriage. Historically, courts had upheld rules barring married students from participating in athletics. However, beginning in the early 1970s, courts have uniformly and consistently invalidated such rules.

BEESON v. KIOWA COUNTY SCHOOL DISTRICT RE-1
Colorado Court of Appeals, 1977
567 P.2d 801

RULAND, Judge

* * *

Plaintiff was a senior in high school, married, and the mother of a child at the time she initiated this action seeking to enjoin the school board from enforcing its policy so that she could participate on the girl's varsity basketball team. * * *

* * *

The facts pertinent to this review are not disputed. Plaintiff was a "star player" on the girl's varsity basketball team during her freshman year in high school. However, she married the following summer and a child was born to the married couple during her sophomore year. Plaintiff was aware of the policy at the time she married.

Plaintiff did not seek to participate on the varsity team during either her sophomore or junior years. Plaintiff sought, however, to rejoin the team for her senior year, but was precluded by the school policy from doing so. While she was allowed to practice with the team, she was not allowed to participate in interscholastic competition.

Plaintiff testified that by reason of her inability to compete on the varsity team during her senior year, she lost any opportunity for a college athletic scholarship. She expressed the belief that she would have been offered an athletic scholarship based on her previously demonstrated ability and on the fact that her sister had been offered such a scholarship at some time in the past.

* * *

We first emphasize that the issue on appeal is whether the school board's policy is valid in the context of plaintiff being a married student. Therefore, we do not consider the validity of a policy which would preclude plaintiff from participating in extracurricular activities because she was the mother of a young child, or whether a policy would be valid if it required married women to meet certain requirements in order to assure the board that no injuries would result from an undetected pregnancy. The additional considerations inherent in such policies are irrelevant here because the policy at issue excluded plaintiff from participating in extracurricular activities based solely on the fact that she was married.

According to § 14-12-101, C.R.S. 1973, "[i]t is the declared public policy of this state . . . to promote and foster the marriage relationship. . . . We are therefore compelled to hold that the creation of a "marriage relationship" is a fundamental right in this jurisdiction. * * *

Nor is this fundamental right vitiated by the fact that plaintiff needed parental consent to enter her marriage. Plaintiff's marriage was entered into in compliance with § 14-2-106, C.R.S. 1973, of the Uniform Marriage Act. That Act has as one of its purposes "to strengthen and preserve the integrity of marriage and to safeguard meaningful family relationships." * * * [T]he General Assembly has obviously determined that this purpose is fulfilled, if as here, parental consent for plaintiff's marriage is first obtained. Hence, it is clear that a board policy which discriminates against those who exercise that _marriage_ right violates the Equal Protection Clause of the Fourteenth Amendment, unless there exists a compelling interest which justifies that discrimination. * * *

* * *

Looking then to the reasons offered by the school board, we conclude that the acknowledged intent to discourage eligible persons from marrying obviously contravenes the declared public policy of this State "to promote and foster the marriage relationship." * * * Illustrative of the inhibiting effect of the policy is evidence in the record indicating that another star basketball player in the same school district who had fathered a child during his senior year remained eligible for interscholastic competition because he did not marry the mother until after his graduation.

This impact of the policy upon the marriage relationship requires us to consider whether the discrimination created by the board's policy is justified by the need to require married students to focus on their basic education and their family responsibilities by excluding them from extracurricular activities. We find no support for the discrimination here. The focus on basic education can be supplied by a board policy which establishes academic requirements for both married and unmarried students to be eligible for extracurricular activities. On the other hand, the fulfillment of family responsibilities may, in many cases, depend upon further education at the college level, and depriving students of the opportunity to earn a college athletic scholarship, or to participate in extracurricular activities to broaden their general background, could close the door to any opportunity to obtain that education. * * *

Finally, we must evaluate the board's contention that married students who participate in extracurricular activities may tend to promote a lack of discipline among the other students and may not be dependable because of their family responsibility. Since the policy has been in effect for approximately 20 years, we understand why no incidents were cited by the board where these problems have arisen. On the other hand, we are unable to perceive why the same policies which govern the discipline and dependability of unmarried students who participate in extracurricular activities would not serve to resolve any such problems. At least we cannot characterize this potential problem, standing alone, as sufficient justification for discrimination against the fundamental right to marry. * * *

Accordingly, the judgment of the district court is reversed and the cause remanded with directions to enter judgment declaring the board's policy invalid as a denial of equal protection under the Fourteenth Amendment.

Notes and Questions

May a divorced student be barred from engaging in extracurricular activities? See *Romans* v. *Crenshaw*, 354 F. Supp. 868 (Tex. 1972), which upheld a divorced student's right to engage in such activities.

Does your state have a statutory provision pertaining to married students participating in extracurricular activities? What are your local school system's rules or policies regarding married students engaging in such activities?

2. Gender Equity

Historically, there has been both *de facto* and *de jure* segregation of male and female public school students. In some school systems, entire schools have been segregated on the basis of sex. More common, however, has been the separation of the sexes in certain classes and in interscholastic athletic participation. A flagrant example has been the routine assignment of girls to home economics classes and boys to "shop" courses. Opportunities for females in athletic competition were limited, and the stereotypic role for a female was often that of cheerleader, flag girl, or pom-pom girl.

Many female students and their parents considered such treatment, especially in the limited opportunity for athletic competition, to be in violation of the equal protection provision of the Fourteenth Amendment and a form of sex discrimination. Many courts have agreed with this contention, and although Title IX addresses this issue, litigation pertaining to female participation in athletic programs has not abated. Although Title IX has been primarily associated with increasing female participation in heretofore male-dominated activities, it provides gender equity for both males and females.

Section 86.41, Athletics, of the implementing regulations for Title IX stipulates:

Athletics.

(a) General. No person shall, on the basis of sex, be excluded from participation in, be denied the benefits of, be treated differently from one another or otherwise be discriminated against in any interscholastic, intercollegiate, club or intermural athletics offered by a recipient, and no recipient shall provide any such athletics separately on such basis.

(b) Separate teams. Notwithstanding the requirements of paragraph (a) of this section, a recipient may operate or sponsor separate teams for members of each sex where selection for such teams is based upon competitive skill or the activity involved is a contact sport. However, where a recipient operates or sponsors a team in a particular sport for members of one sex but operates or sponsors no such team for members of the other sex, and athletic opportunities for members of that sex have previously been limited, members of the excluded sex must be allowed to try out for the team offered unless the sport involved is a contact sport. For the purposes of this part, contact sports include boxing, wrestling, rugby, ice hockey, football, basketball, and other sports the purpose or major activity of which involves bodily contact.

(c) Equal opportunity. A recipient which operates or sponsors interscholastic, intercollegiate, club or intermural athletics shall provide equal athletic opportunity for members of both sexes. In determining whether equal opportunities are available the Director will consider, among other factors:

(1) Whether the selection of sports and levels of competition effectively accommodate the interests and abilities of members of both sexes;
(2) The provision of equipment and supplies;
(3) Scheduling of games and practice time;
(4) Travel and per diem allowance;
(5) Opportunity to receive coaching and academic tutoring;
(6) Assignment and compensation of coaches and tutors;
(7) Provision of locker rooms, practice and competitive facilities;
(8) Provision of medical and training facilities and services;
(9) Provision of housing and dining facilities and services;
(10) Publicity.

Unequal aggregate expenditures for members of each sex or unequal expenditures for male and female teams if a recipient operates or sponsors separate teams will not constitute noncompliance with this section, but the Director may consider the failure to provide necessary funds for teams for one sex in assessing equality of opportunity for members of each sex. 45 C.F.R. § 86.41 (1972).*

---

*See Appendix D for Title IX of the Education Amendments of 1972.

Title IX's passage has greatly enhanced opportunities for female athletes at both the public school and collegiate levels, although it has had a particularly dramatic effect at the collegiate level. This may be seen by increased emphasis, at the collegiate level, in such sports as gymnastics, volleyball, basketball, swimming, soccer, track, golf, tennis, and softball.

VIII. SCHOOL PUNISHMENT FOR OUT-OF-SCHOOL OFFENSES

Out-of-school conduct of students may have an impact on the overall well-being of the school. When there is a problem with out-of-school conduct, school authorities must reconcile their control of student conduct necessary for the orderly operation of the school with their obligation to comply with the standards of constitutionality and reasonableness required by the judiciary to ensure that students receive just treatment.

Several court decisions have addressed issues dealing with noncriminal, off-campus student activity. In one case, it was alleged that two students were assaulted by a group of others while they were all walking home after school. Although the court agreed that school authorities may punish students for out-of-school physical abuse directed at other students, punishment such as expulsion may not be based on unsigned and unidentified statements by student witnesses. See *Tibbs* v. *Board of Education of the Township of Franklin*, 276 A.2d 165 (N.J. Super. Ct. 1971).

Parking an automobile off campus contrary to school rules was an issue in *McLean Independent School District* v. *Andrews*, 333 S.W.2d 886 (Tex. Civ. App. 1960). A student's suspension for breaking the school rules was upheld, primarily on the basis of promoting the safety of student pedestrians on the streets adjacent to the school during noon recess. The court noted, however, that the rule in question might provide future complications as students parked at more remote distances from the campus.

An Ohio appellate court, in *McNaughton* v. *Circleville Board of Education*, 345 N.E.2d 649 (Ohio Comm. Pleas 1974), upheld the suspension from school and from participation in athletic activities of students who held an out-of-school initiation and hazing of new members of an officially recognized high school club. The club's advisor had not been notified nor was he present at the initiation, which occurred at the home of one of the offending students. Initiates were struck with belts, forced to eat onions, and required to rub tabasco sauce on the faces of fellow initiates.

Cases have addressed the dismissal of students' school chapters of the National Honor Society owing to their violation of a rule against the use of alcohol. In two such cases, *Warren* v. *National Association of Secondary School Principals*, 375 F. Supp. 1043 (Tex. 1974), and *Ector County Independent School District* v. *Hopkins*, 518 S.W.2d 576 (Tex. Civ. App. 1975), the violative drinking took place off campus. These courts stressed that students facing dismissal from an honor society as a result of their drinking had to be afforded appropriate due process.

Courts have held that public school students' out-of-school criminal conduct may be subject to school disciplinary hearings, although as a practical matter the particular kind of school response will be influenced by the nature and seriousness of the criminal charges. A non-school-related speeding charge, for instance, might be ignored by authorities, while a murder or rape charge would not be.

R.R. v. *Board of Education of the Shore Regional High School District,* 263 A.2d 180 (N.J. Sup. Ct. Ch. Div. 1970), addressed the question of whether public school officials can deprive a student of his or her right to attend school because of criminal acts committed off school grounds. In this instance, a fifteen-year-old boy stabbed a girl during an altercation in a neighbor's house after the boy had returned home at the end of a school day. This court concluded that officials do have the right to expel or suspend students for out-of-school activities when it is reasonably necessary either for the transgressing student's physical or emotional safety and well-being or for the safety and well-being of other students, teachers, or public school property. Despite this conclusion, the court ordered the school to readmit the student because of due process violations.

A California court upheld the suspension of students involved in such offenses as kidnapping, rape, assault with a bumper jack, assault resulting in the death of a boy whose head struck a sidewalk curb, carrying a concealed weapon, and disturbing the peace. The California court made no attempt to distinguish between offenses that occurred on campus and those that occurred off campus. See *S.* v. *Board of Education, San Francisco Unified School District,* 97 Cal. Rptr. 422 (Cal. Ct. App. 1971).

A federal district court in *Caldwell* v. *Cannady,* 340 F. Supp. 835 (Tex. 1972), upheld the reasonableness of a local school board policy mandating the expulsion of any student possessing, using, or selling dangerous or narcotic drugs. In this instance students were disciplined after they were arrested when marijuana was found in their automobile in a series of incidents at night and away from school.

Authority of school officials to discipline a student acquitted of out-of-school reckless driving charges was addressed by the Supreme Court of Wyoming in *Clements* v. *Board of Trustees of the Sheridan County School District No. 2,* 585 P.2d 197 (Wyo. 1978). The student had been charged with reckless driving for purposely impeding the progress of a school bus. The court held that school authorities may discipline pupils for out-of-school conduct having a direct and immediate effect on the discipline or general welfare of the school.

Constitutional questions regarding double jeopardy and self-incrimination have been raised in the cases ruling on the legality of actions taken by public school officials in response to charges of out-of-school criminal violations against students. Courts have consistently held that both school sanctions and judicial sanctions are permitted without violating the Fifth Amendment prohibition against double jeopardy. They maintain that school hearings and criminal proceedings have different purposes, with school responses being civil or remedial whereas judicial responses are punitive. Although acknowledging that school discipline has punitive effects, the courts contend that its underlying purpose is the protection of the school environment.

Courts have also held that public school students' out-of-school criminal conduct properly may be the subject of school disciplinary hearings without violating Fifth Amendment rights against compulsory self-incrimination. Students may not be required to testify in these proceedings, and if students' rights are infringed upon in the hearings, courts reason, the students may then ask for a judicial review of the proceedings.

Analysis reveals that the judiciary supports the rationale that students may be subject to school discipline, including suspension or expulsion, if their out-of-school conduct threatens the efficient operation of the school. Generally, the courts recognize that the authority to make and enforce policies designed to protect the safety and welfare of students is a reasonable and necessary exercise of the power invested in local school boards. Nevertheless, courts will support the use of that authority over out-of-school criminal conduct only when they perceive the conduct as having a direct and substantial impact on the school and its programs.

When the out-of-school conduct has involved physical violence or otherwise threatened the safety or well-being of students, the judiciary has not been concerned with whether the conduct occurred out of school or in school. Decisions indicate that the test of the public school's authority to control student conduct is not the time or place of the conduct, but rather its effect on the morale and efficiency of the school. It may be concluded that the nature and seriousness of the conduct and its potential impact on the public school and its programs are more important than where the conduct occurred.

CHAPTER FOUR

Teachers and the Law

Teachers have often employed the courts to remedy treatment by school authorities with whom they disagreed. In many instances, personnel practices that had become institutionalized through custom have been challenged as being discriminatory, violative of statutory or constitutional provisions, or unfair. Although teachers have not always been successful in actions brought before the judiciary, their willingness to employ the courts for a redress of grievances has produced a climate in which public school administrators have become more sensitive to the necessity of treating teachers in a legally defensible manner.

This chapter focuses on law relating to nonrenewal and dismissal of teachers; teachers' freedom of expression; academic freedom; drug testing; standards of dress; the teacher as exemplar; employment discrimination; collective bargaining; and the political rights of teachers.

I. NONRENEWAL AND DISMISSAL

Over the years, the development of state statutory provisions and the existence of a sizable body of case law have provided teachers with safeguards against arbitrary dismissal. Although school administrators have the primary task of evaluating teachers and determining their fitness, this task must be done in accordance with state statutory provisions and in the light of constitutional protections.

According to a United States Supreme Court decision, *Board of Regents of State Colleges* v. *Roth*, a nontenured teacher need not be given reasons for nonrenewal unless the nonrenewal deprived the teacher of a "liberty" interest or if there was a "property" interest in continued employment. Any statement regarding the reason for the nonrenewal could result in the teacher's requesting a due process hearing.

Depending on a state's statutory provisions, dismissal of a tenured teacher or one under a continuing contract must be in conformance with the state law. State provisions usually contain grounds for dismissal such as nonperformance of duty, incompetency, insubordination, conviction of crimes involving moral turpitude, failure to comply with reasonable orders, violation of contract provisions or local rules or regulations, persistent failure or refusal to maintain orderly discipline of students, and revocation of the teaching certificate. Additionally, all of the procedural aspects of the hearing process provided by state statute must be afforded the teacher. These often include the following requirements: proper notice, containing charges and the names and nature of the testimony of witnesses and stating the time and place of the hearing; compulsory process or subpoena requiring the attendance of witnesses and the production of relevant papers and documents; a fair hearing; and an opportunity for appeal.

This relationship between public school teachers and their employers is significantly different from that which operates in the private sector. Although workers in the private sector may have protection under contract law, union agreements, or governmental antidiscrimination provisions against arbitrary dismissal, when a private sector employee is not covered by these protections, specific grounds for dismissal do not have to be given. Nor do private sector employees, because their employment relationship is not with a government entity, have the protection of constitutional guarantees such as due process and equal protection.

BOARD OF REGENTS OF STATE COLLEGES v. *ROTH*
Supreme Court of the United States, 1972
408 U.S. 564

MR. JUSTICE STEWART delivered the opinion of the Court.

In 1968 the respondent, David Roth, was hired for his first teaching job as assistant professor of political science at Wisconsin State University-Oshkosh. He was hired for a fixed term of one academic year. The notice of his faculty appointment specified that his employment would begin on September 1, 1968, and would end on June 30, 1969. The respondent completed that term. But he was informed that he would not be rehired for the next academic year.

The respondent had no tenure rights to continued employment. Under Wisconsin statutory law a state university teacher can acquire tenure as a "permanent" employee only after four years of year-to-year employment. Having acquired tenure, a teacher is entitled to continued employment "during efficiency and good behavior." A relatively new teacher without tenure, however, is under Wisconsin law entitled to nothing beyond his one-year appointment. There are no statutory or administrative standards defining eligibility for re-employment. State law thus clearly leaves the decision whether to rehire a nontenured teacher for another year to the unfettered discretion of university officials.

The procedural protection afforded a Wisconsin State University teacher before he is separated from the University corresponds to his job security. As a matter of statutory law, a tenured teacher cannot be "discharged except for cause upon written charges" and pursuant to certain procedures. A nontenured teacher, similarly, is protected to some extent *during* his one-year term. Rules promulgated by the Board of Regents provide that a nontenured teacher "dismissed" before the end of the year may have some opportunity for review of the "dismissal." But the Rules provide no real protection for a nontenured teacher who simply is not re-employed for the next year. He must be informed by February 1 "concerning retention or nonretention for the ensuing year." But "no reason for non-retention need be given. No review or appeal is provided in such case."

In conformance with these Rules, the President of Wisconsin State University-Oshkosh informed the respondent before February 1, 1969, that he would not be rehired for the 1969–1970 academic year. He gave the respondent no reason for the decision and no opportunity to challenge it at any sort of hearing.

The respondent then brought this action in Federal District Court alleging that the decision not to rehire him for the next year infringed his Fourteenth Amendment rights. He attacked the decision both in substance and procedure. First, he alleged that the true reason for the decision was to punish him for certain statements critical of the University administration, and that it therefore violated his right to freedom of speech. Second, he alleged that the failure of University officials to give him notice of any reason for nonretention and an opportunity for a hearing violated his right to procedural due process of law.

The District Court granted summary judgment for the respondent on the procedural issue, ordering the University officials to provide him with reasons and a hearing. * * * The Court of Appeals, with one judge dissenting, affirmed this partial summary judgment. * * * We granted certiorari. * * * The only question presented to us at this stage in the case is whether the respondent had a constitutional right to a statement of reasons and a hearing on the University's decision not to rehire him for another year. We hold that he did not.

The requirements of procedural due process apply only to the deprivation of interests encompassed by the Fourteenth Amendment's protection of liberty and property. When protected interests are implicated, the right to some kind of prior hearing is paramount. But the range of interests protected by procedural due process is not infinite.

The District Court decided that procedural due process guarantees apply in this case by assessing and balancing the weights of the particular interests involved. It concluded that the respondent's interest in re-employment at Wisconsin State University-Oshkosh outweighed the University's interest in denying him re-employment summarily. * * * Undeniably, the respondent's re-employment prospects were of major concern to him—concern that we surely cannot say was insignificant. And a weighing process has long been a part of any determination of the *form* of hearing required in particular situations by procedural due process. But, to determine whether due process requirements apply in the first place, we must look not to the "weight" but to the *nature* of the interest at stake. * * * We must look to see if the interest is within the Fourteenth Amendment's protection of liberty and property.

"Liberty" and "property" are broad and majestic terms. They are among the "[g]reat [constitutional] concepts . . . purposely left to gather meaning from experience . . . [T]hey relate to the whole domain of social and economic fact, and the statesmen who founded this Nation knew too well that only a stagnant society remains unchanged." * * * For that reason, the Court has fully and finally rejected the wooden distinction between "rights" and "privileges" that once seemed to govern the applicability of procedural due process rights. The Court has also made clear that the property interests protected by procedural due process extend well beyond actual ownership of real estate, chattels, or money. By the same token, the Court has required due process protection for deprivations of liberty beyond the sort of formal constraints imposed by the criminal process.

Yet, while the Court has eschewed rigid or formalistic limitations on the protection of procedural due process, it has at the same time observed certain boundaries. For the words "liberty" and "property" in the Due Process Clause of the Fourteenth Amendment must be given some meaning.

"While this Court has not attempted to define with exactness the liberty . . . guaranteed [by the Fourteenth Amendment], the term has received much consideration and some of the included things have been definitely stated. Without doubt, it denotes not merely freedom from bodily restraint but also the right of the individual to contract, to engage in any of the common occupations of life, to acquire useful knowledge, to marry, establish a home and bring up children, to worship God according to the dictates of his own conscience, and generally to enjoy those privileges long recognized . . . as essential to the orderly pursuit of happiness by free men." * * * In a Constitution for a free people, there can be no doubt that the meaning of "liberty" must be broad indeed. * * *

There might be cases in which a State refused to reemploy a person under such circumstances that interests in liberty would be implicated. But this is not such a case.

The State, in declining to rehire the respondent, did not make any charge against him that might seriously damage his standing and associations in his community. It did not base the nonrenewal of his contract on a charge, for example, that he had been guilty of dishonesty, or immorality. Had it done so, this would be a different case. For "[w]here a person's good name, reputation, honor, or integrity is at stake because of what the government is doing to him, notice and an opportunity to be heard are essential." * * * In such a case, due process would accord an opportunity to refute the charge before University officials. In the present case, however, there is no suggestion whatever that the respondent's "good name, reputation, honor, or integrity" is at stake.

Similarly, there is no suggestion that the State, in declining to reemploy the respondent, imposed on him a stigma or other disability that foreclosed his freedom to take advantage of other employment opportunities. The State, for example, did not invoke any regulations to bar the respondent from all other public employment in state universities. Had it done so, this, again, would be a different case. * * *

To be sure, the respondent has alleged that the nonrenewal of his contract was based on his exercise of his right to freedom of speech. But this allegation is not now before us. The District Court stayed proceedings on this issue, and the respondent has yet to prove that the decision not to rehire him was, in fact, based on his free speech activities.

Hence, on the record before us, all that clearly appears is that the respondent was not rehired for one year at one university. It stretches the concept too far to suggest that a person is deprived of "liberty" when he simply is not rehired in one job but remains as free as before to seek another. * * *

The Fourteenth Amendment's procedural protection of property is a safeguard of the security of interests that a person has already acquired in specific benefits. These interests—property interests—may take many forms.

Certain attributes of "property" interests protected by procedural due process emerge from these decisions. To have a property interest in a benefit, a person clearly must have more than an abstract need or desire for it. He must have more than a unilateral expectation of it. He must, instead, have a legitimate claim of entitlement to it. It is a purpose of the ancient institution of property to protect those claims upon which people rely in their daily lives, reliance that must not be arbitrarily undermined. It is a purpose of the constitutional right to a hearing to provide an opportunity for a person to vindicate those claims.

Property interests, of course, are not created by the Constitution. Rather, they are created and their dimensions are defined by existing rules or understandings that stem from an independent source such as state law—rules or understandings that secure certain benefits and that support claims of entitlement to those benefits. Thus, the welfare recipients * * * had a claim of entitlement to welfare payments that was grounded in the statute defining eligibility for them. The recipients had not yet shown that they were, in fact, within the statutory terms of eligibility. But we held that they had a right to a hearing at which they might attempt to do so.

Just as the welfare recipients' "property" interest in welfare payments was created and defined by statutory terms, so the respondent's "property" interest in employment at Wisconsin State University-Oshkosh was created and defined by the terms of his appointment. Those terms secured his interest in employment up to June 30, 1969. But the important fact in this case is that they specifically provided that the respondent's employment was to terminate on June 30. They did not provide for contract renewal absent "sufficient cause." Indeed, they made no provision for renewal whatsoever.

Thus, the terms of the respondent's appointment secured absolutely no interest in re-employment for the next year. They supported absolutely no possible claim of entitlement to re-employment. Nor, significantly, was there any state statute or University rule or policy that secured his interest in re-employment or that created any legitimate claim to it. In these circumstances, the respondent surely had an abstract concern in being rehired, but he did not have a *property* interest sufficient to require the University authorities to give him a hearing when they declined to renew his contract of employment.

Our analysis of the respondent's constitutional rights in this case in no way indicates a view that an opportunity for a hearing or a statement of reasons for nonretention would, or would not, be appropriate or wise in public colleges and universities. For it is a written Constitution that we apply. Our role is confined to interpretation of that Constitution.

We must conclude that the summary judgment for the respondent should not have been granted, since the respondent has not shown that he was deprived of liberty or property protected by the Fourteenth Amendment. The judgment of the Court of Appeals, accordingly, is reversed and the case is remanded for further proceedings consistent with this opinion.

It is so ordered.

Notes and Questions

Roth was a five-to-three decision. In his dissent, Justice Douglas argued that:

> . . . Nonrenewal of a teacher's contract is tantamount in effect to a dismissal and the consequences may be enormous. Nonrenewal can be a blemish that turns into a permanent scar and effectively limits any chance the teacher has of being rehired as a teacher, at least in his State.

Do you agree with his assessment? Why?

Another United States Supreme Court decision dealt with an issue that may have significance in states without tenure statutes. In that decision, the Court held that if a teacher had *de facto* tenure—an expectation of continued employment after many years of satisfactory service although a formal tenure system did not exist—a hearing could be requested to challenge grounds for nonretention. See *Perry* v. *Sindermann*, 408 U.S 593 (1972).

The United States Supreme Court upheld the dismissal of a tenured teacher who refused to comply with a continuing education policy requiring teachers who held only a bachelor's degree to earn at least five semester hours of college credit every three years. See *Harrah Independent School District* v. *Martin*, 440 U.S. 194 (1979).

A nontenured teacher's nonrenewal was not upheld in *Stoddard* v. *School District No. 1*, 590 F.2d 829 (10th Cir. 1979). The teacher in this case was advised in a letter from her principal that her contract would not be renewed because of failure to maintain order in the classroom and lack of dynamics in motivating students. The teacher alleged that in a private conversation the principal informed her that the "real" reasons for nonrenewal were (1) rumors regarding an affair with another resident of her trailer park, (2) her propensity for playing cards and not attending church regularly, and (3) her obesity, which was the "lack of dynamics" referred to in the letter.

A school district's refusal to renew a teacher's contract for violating a policy against outside employment was not upheld because the policy was not uniformly applied. See *Gosney* v. *Sonora Independent School District*, 603 F.2d 522 (5th Cir. 1979). The court declared that the district's no-outside-employment policy was not itself unconstitutional.

The United States Supreme Court has upheld a New York statute forbidding permanent certification as a public school teacher of any person who is not a United States citizen unless that person has manifested an intention to apply for citizenship. See *Ambach* v. *Norwick*, 441 U.S. 68 (1979).

State statutes often contain a catchall phrase such as "for other due and sufficient cause" as a ground for dismissal. The question of overbreadth and vagueness of such a phrase was discussed in *diLeo* v. *Greenfield*, 541 F.2d 949 (2d Cir. 1976), and the court agreed that the phrase was too general.

A probationary teacher may not be dismissed at midyear except for the same reasons that a tenured teacher may be dismissed, such as lack of funding. Dismissal must be according to the procedures applicable to midyear discharge of tenured teachers. See *Taborn* v. *Hammonds*, 350 S.E.2d 880 (N.C. Ct. App. 1986).

In the private sector, federal statutes protect union members from arbitrary dismissal and all private sector employees from discrimination based on race, color, religion, sex, age, national origin, or disability. Nonunion employees in the private sector generally fall under the common-law "at-will employment" legal doctrine, which allows for dismissal without cause when the aforementioned discrimination is not involved. The doctrine is followed in many states; yet, court actions in approximately forty states overall, especially in Alaska, California, Montana, and Wyoming, appear to be modifying the doctrine. Those examining this area of law have coined the phrase "corporate due process" to describe it. Successful private-sector court challenges dealing with dismissal have involved an employee's refusal to break a law, failure to discharge a long-service worker "fairly" or "in good faith," improper notice of dissatisfaction, a broken promise of job security, the false advertisement of a "permanent position," and jury service. In an at-will case before the United States Supreme Court, *Haddle* v. *Garrison*, 525 U.S. 824 (1998), the Court stated a claim for damages could be brought for an alleged wrongful firing. Haddle alleged that his employer conspired to have him fired from his job in retaliation for obeying a federal grand jury subpoena and deter him from testifying at a federal criminal crime in which his employer was charged with Medicare fraud. In this instance, applicable federal law stated that if injury were incurred to one's "person or property," damages could be recovered. In reversing a lower court, which had held that there had to be injury to a "constitutionally protected property interest," the Court held that although at-will employment is not "property" for purposes of the Due Process Clause, harm to one's "person" may be a compensable injury.

Does your state have statutory provisions dealing with nonrenewal and dismissal of teachers? What are your local school system's policies regarding nonrenewal and dismissal?

II. FREEDOM OF EXPRESSION

Public school teachers' status regarding their rights of freedom of expression has received considerable court attention. Prior to this attention, several historic forces had contributed to the commonly held view that public employees, which included teachers, had a limited right of freedom of expression. The strongest force contributing to this view was that public employment was considered a privilege rather than a right. Although this distinction has been modified, the belief that public employment was a privilege had received considerable credibility, especially since 1892, as the result of Justice Holmes' often-quoted statement, "The petitioner may have a constitutional right to talk politics, but he has no constitutional right to be a policeman." This judicial view, coupled with the notion that the quid pro quo for government employees' increased job security (a result of the ravages of the spoils system), had the effect of allowing the forfeiture of certain constitutional rights. Formal restrictions of government employees' political activities were embodied in the Hatch Act at the federal level. Several states have enacted "little Hatch Acts," and other states have statutory provisions restricting certain activities of state employees and/or teachers. Such legislation, combined with a judicial view that public employment was a privilege and not a right, tended to solidify the long-held contention that government employees, which included teachers, had a limited right of freedom of expression.

A heightened concern with individual rights during the 1960s, combined with a seemingly receptive federal judiciary, resulted in some teachers challenging the position that teachers had a limited right of freedom of expression. Several Supreme Court and lower court decisions have upheld the teachers' contention.

Pickering v. *Board of Education of Township High School District 205*, a Supreme Court decision, established the principle that public school teachers have the First Amendment right of freedom of expression. Pickering was dismissed from his teaching position for writing a letter, published in a newspaper, critical of several of the school board's actions. These included allocation of school funds between educational and athletic programs and the board's and superintendent's methods of informing, or neglecting to inform, the school district's taxpayers of the real reasons why additional tax revenues were being sought for the schools. In attempting to balance the teacher's interest as a citizen in making public comments, against the state's interest in promoting the efficiency of its employees' public services, the court struck the balance on the side of the teacher.

Another Supreme Court decision, *Mt. Healthy City School District Board of Education* v. *Doyle*, involved an untenured teacher who had been in an altercation with a colleague, argued with school cafeteria employees, swore at students, and made obscene gestures to female pupils. He also called a radio station and provided them with a memorandum from the principal relating to teacher dress and appearance. Doyle alleged that his not being rehired was due to his exercising his First Amendment rights in calling the radio station. The Court, in vacating the lower court's decision, reasoned that the proper test in such a case is whether or not the school board would have rehired the teacher even in "the absence of the protected conduct."

A. Tenured Teacher's Public Expression

PICKERING v. BOARD OF EDUCATION OF TOWNSHIP HIGH SCHOOL DISTRICT 205
Supreme Court of the United States, 1968
391 U.S. 563

MR. JUSTICE MARSHALL delivered the opinion of the Court.

Appellant Marvin L. Pickering, a teacher in Township High School District 205, Will County, Illinois, was dismissed from his position by the appellee Board of Education for sending a letter to a local newspaper in connection with a recently proposed tax increase that was critical of the way in which the Board and the district superintendent of schools had handled past proposals to raise new revenue for the schools. Appellant's dismissal resulted from a determination by the Board, after a full hearing, that the publication of the letter was "detrimental to the efficient operation and administration of the schools of the district" and hence, under the relevant Illinois statute, * * * that "interests of the school require[d] [his dismissal]."

* * *

In February of 1961 the appellee Board of Education asked the voters of the school district to approve a bond issue to raise $4,875,000 to erect two new schools. The proposal was defeated. Then, in December of 1961, the Board submitted another bond proposal to the voters which called for the raising of $5,500,000 to build two new schools. This second proposal passed and the schools were built with the money raised by the bond sales. In May of 1964 a proposed increase in the tax rate to be used for educational purposes was submitted to the voters by the Board and was defeated. Finally, on September 19, 1964, a second proposal to increase the tax rate was submitted by the Board and was likewise defeated. It was in connection with this last proposal of the School Board that appellant wrote the letter to the editor * * * that resulted in his dismissal.

Prior to the vote on the second tax increase proposal a variety of articles attributed to the District 205 Teachers' Organization appeared in the local paper. These articles urged passage of the tax increase and stated that failure to pass the increase would result in a decline in the quality of education afforded children in the district's schools. A letter from the superintendent of schools making the same point was published in the paper two days before the election and submitted to the voters in mimeographed form the following day. It was in response to the foregoing material, together with the failure of the tax increase to pass, that appellant submitted the letter in question to the editor of the local paper.

The letter constituted, basically, an attack on the School Board's handling of the 1961 bond issue proposals and its subsequent allocation of financial resources between the schools' educational and athletic programs. It also charged the superintendent of schools with attempting to prevent teachers in the district from opposing or criticizing the proposed bond issue.

The Board dismissed Pickering for writing and publishing the letter. Pursuant to Illinois law, the Board was then required to hold a hearing on the dismissal. At the hearing the Board charged that numerous statements in the letter were false and that the publication of the statements unjustifiably impugned the "motives, honesty, integrity, truthfulness, responsibility and competence" of both the Board and the school administration. The Board also charged that the false statements damaged the professional reputations of its members and of the school administrators, would be disruptive of faculty discipline, and would tend to foment "controversy, conflict and dissension" among teachers, administrators, the Board of Education, and the residents of the district. * * *

* * *

To the extent that the Illinois Supreme Court's opinion may be read to suggest that teachers may constitutionally be compelled to relinquish the First Amendment rights they would otherwise enjoy as citizens to comment on matters of public interest in connection with the operation of the public schools in which they work, it proceeds on a premise that has been unequivocally rejected in numerous prior decisions of this Court. * * * At the same time it cannot be gainsaid that the State has interests as an employer in regulating the speech of its employees that differ significantly from those it possesses in connection with regulation of the speech of the citizenry in general. The problem in any case is to arrive at a balance between the interests of the teacher, as a citizen, in commenting upon matters of public concern and the interest of the state, as an employer, in promoting the efficiency of the public services it performs through its employees.

* * * Because of the enormous variety of fact situations in which critical statements by teachers and other public employees may be thought by their superiors, against whom the statements are directed, to furnish grounds for dismissal, we do not deem it either appropriate or feasible to attempt to lay down a general standard against which all such statements may be judged. However, in the course of evaluating the conflicting claims of First Amendment protection and the need for orderly school administration in the context of this case, we shall indicate some of the general lines along which an analysis of the controlling interests should run.

An examination of the statements in appellant's letter objected to by the Board reveals that they, like the letter as a whole, consist essentially of criticism of the Board's allocation of school funds between educational and athletic programs, and of both the Board's and the superintendent's methods of informing, or preventing the informing of, the district's taxpayers of the real reasons why additional tax revenues were being sought for the schools. The statements are in no way directed towards any person with whom appellant would normally be in contact in the course of his daily work as a teacher. Thus no question of maintaining either discipline by immediate superiors or harmony among coworkers is presented here. Appellant's employment relationships with the Board and, to a somewhat lesser extent, with the superintendent are not the kind of close working relationships for which it can persuasively be claimed that personal loyalty and confidence are necessary to their proper functioning. * * *

We next consider the statements in appellant's letter which we agree to be false. The Board's original charges included allegations that the publication of the letter damaged the professional reputations of the Board and the superintendent and would foment controversy and conflict among the Board, teachers, administrators, and the residents of the district. However, no evidence to support these allegations was introduced at the hearing. So far as the record reveals, Pickering's letter was greeted by everyone but its main target, the Board, with massive apathy and total disbelief. The Board must, therefore, have decided, perhaps by analogy with the law of libel, that the statements were *per se* harmful to the operation of the schools.

However, the only way in which the Board could conclude, absent any evidence of the actual effect of the letter, that the statements contained therein were *per se* detrimental to the interest of the schools was to equate the Board members' own interests with that of the schools. Certainly an accusation that too much money is being spent on athletics by the administrators of the school system * * * cannot reasonably be regarded as *per se* detrimental to the district's schools. Such an accusation reflects rather a difference of opinion between Pickering and the Board as to the preferable manner of operating the school system, a difference of opinion that clearly concerns an issue of general public interest.

In addition, the fact that particular illustrations of the Board's claimed undesirable emphasis on athletic programs are false would not normally have any necessary impact on the actual operation of the schools, beyond its tendency to anger the Board. For example, Pickering's letter was written after the defeat at the polls of the second proposed tax increase. It could, therefore, have had no effect on the ability of the school district to raise necessary revenue, since there was no showing that there was any proposal to increase taxes pending when the letter was written.

More importantly, the question whether a school system requires additional funds is a matter of legitimate public concern on which the judgment of the school administration, including the School Board, cannot, in a society that leaves such questions to popular vote, be taken as conclusive. On such a question free and open debate is vital to informed decision-making by the electorate. Teachers are, as a class, the members of a community most likely to have informed and definite opinions as to how funds allotted to the operation of the schools should be spent. Accordingly, it is essential that they be able to speak out freely on such questions without fear of retaliatory dismissal.

In addition, the amounts expended on athletics which Pickering reported erroneously were matters of public record on which his position as a teacher in the district did not qualify him to speak with any greater authority than any other taxpayer. The Board could easily have rebutted appellant's errors by publishing the accurate figures itself, either via a letter to the same newspaper or otherwise. We are thus not presented with a situation in which a teacher has carelessly made false statements about matters so closely related to the day-to-day operations of the schools that any harmful impact on the public would be difficult to counter because of the teacher's presumed greater access to the real facts. Accordingly, we have no occasion to consider at this time whether under such circumstances a school board could reasonably require that a teacher make substantial efforts to verify the accuracy of his charges before publishing them.

What we do have before us is a case in which a teacher has made erroneous public statements upon issues then currently the subject of public attention, which are critical of his ultimate employer but which are neither shown nor can be presumed to have in any way either impeded the teacher's proper performance of his daily duties in the classroom or to have interfered with the regular operation of the schools generally. In these circumstances we conclude that the interest of the school administration in limiting teachers' opportunities to contribute to public debate is not significantly greater than its interest in limiting a similar contribution by any member of the general public.

* * *

In sum, we hold that, in a case such as this, absent proof of false statements knowingly or recklessly made by him, a teacher's exercise of his right to speak on issues of public importance may not furnish the basis for his dismissal from public employment. * * *

Notes

Justice Thurgood Marshall, who wrote the *Pickering* opinion, became the first black to be named to the Supreme Court. He was appointed by President Johnson in 1967. He had been counsel for the National Association for the Advancement of Colored People and the NAACP Legal Defense and Educational Fund for twenty-five years. During that time, he argued many civil rights cases, including the 1954 landmark public school desegregation case, and he "won" twenty-nine out of the thirty-two cases in which he appeared before the Court. Justice Marshall resigned from the Court in 1991 and was replaced by Clarence Thomas in the same year.

Although the case did not involve educators, the United States Supreme Court, in *Connick* v. *Myers*, 461 U.S. 138 (1983), a five-to-four decision, did not extend the *Pickering* rationale to a questionnaire circulated within a district attorney's office. In this case, an assistant district attorney was transferred to different job responsibilities. In protest, she circulated among her coworkers a questionnaire related primarily to the transfer policy. In approving her termination, the Court contended that protecting the circulation of the questionnaire would "require a public office to be run as a roundtable for employee complaints over internal office affairs" and that normal office functioning would be endangered. Additionally, the Court asserted: "When employee expression cannot be fairly considered as relating to any matter of political, social, or other concern to the community, government officials should enjoy wide latitude in managing their offices, without intrusive oversight by the judiciary in the name of the First Amendment." However, the majority reiterated the following caveat from *Pickering:* "Because of the enormous variety of fact situations in which critical statements by . . . public employees may be thought by their superiors . . .

to furnish grounds for dismissal, we do not deem it either appropriate or feasible to lay down a general standard against which all such statements may be judged."

Subsequent decisions have discussed a two-step process to determine whether a teacher's speech enjoys First Amendment protection. First, the disputed speech must address a matter of "public concern." Second, the interests of the teacher must be balanced against the interests of the state as employer in rendering a public service through its employees. The second determination, known as the "*Pickering* balance," may be based on: (1) the need for harmony in the office or workplace; (2) the need for a close working relationship between the speaker and coworkers and whether the speech in question undermines that relationship; (3) the time, place, and manner of the speech; (4) the context in which a dispute arises; (5) the degree of public interest in the speech; and (6) whether the speech impedes the employee's ability to perform his or her duties. See *Roberts* v. *Van Buren Public Schools*, 773 F.2d 949 (8th Cir. 1985); *Cox* v. *Dardanelle Public School District*, 790 F.2d 668 (8th Cir. 1986); and *Day* v. *South Park Independent School District*, 768 F.2d 696 (5th Cir. 1985), *cert. denied*, 474 U.S. 1101 (1986).

A teacher's use of satirical language allegedly demeaning female students in a letter to a high school newspaper, for which he was disciplined, was viewed by a court as commenting on a matter of public concern. See *Seemuller* v. *Fairfax County School Board*, 878 F.2d 1578 (4th Cir. 1989). The suspension of a high school coach for referring to team members as cowards to a reporter did not violate his free speech because such expression did not rise to the level of "public concern," which is protected by the First Amendment. Conditions imposed for the soccer coach's reinstatement, which were also held not to violate the coach's First Amendment free speech or associational rights, included not communicating with coaches or players regarding soccer and not participating in or attending games, practices, award programs, or any other activities related to the soccer program. The coach's ultimate termination from his extracurricular position, which he had held for over twenty-five years, was also upheld because he had no protected property interest in his position as extracurricular coach. See *Brayton* v. *Monson Public Schools*, 950 F. Supp. 33 (Mass. 1997). In another instance, a school superintendent who, though unsuccessfully, actively supported a slate of school board members, contended that his subsequent suspension was in retaliation for exercising his First Amendment rights. In its decision, a court held that the superintendent's free speech and political association rights were not violated and he was not deprived of his constitutionally protected property interest, nor denied due process, because he was fully compensated. See *Kinsey* v. *Salado Independent School District*, 950 F.2d 988 (5th Cir. 1992).

A teacher's dismissal based on her privately expressed complaints and opinions to her principal was addressed in *Givhan* v. *Western Line*

Consolidated School District, 439 U.S. 410 (1979). Here, the Court announced that teachers do not forfeit their protection against governmental abridgement of freedom of speech if they decide to express their views privately rather than publicly.

Pickering would not apply to private school teachers because a private school does not operate under the "color of the state." Nor would private school teachers necessarily have the civil rights protections available to public school teachers. Rights of private school teachers would be governed by their individual contracts with their school and the degree to which a linkage existed between a private school and the state or federal government. A private school was upheld in its dismissal of a high school teacher who wore a beard in violation of the school's rules. The school's participation in a state-operated teacher pension fund did not sufficiently bring the school under the "color of the state." See *Johnson* v. *Pinkerton Academy*, 861 F.2d 335 (1st Cir. 1988).

B. Nontenured Teacher's Freedom of Expression

MT. HEALTHY CITY SCHOOL DISTRICT BOARD OF EDUCATION v. DOYLE
Supreme Court of the United States, 1977
429 U.S. 274

MR. JUSTICE REHNQUIST delivered the opinion of the Court.

Respondent Doyle sued petitioner Mt. Healthy Board of Education in the United States District Court for the Southern District of Ohio. Doyle claimed that the Board's refusal to renew his contract in 1971 violated his rights under the First and Fourteenth Amendments to the United States Constitution. After a bench trial the District Court held that Doyle was entitled to reinstatement with backpay. The Court of Appeals for the Sixth Circuit affirmed the judgment. * * *

* * *

Doyle was first employed by the Board in 1966. He worked under one-year contracts for the first three years, and under a two-year contract from 1969 to 1971. In 1969 he was elected president of the Teachers' Association, in which position he worked to expand the subjects of direct negotiation between the Association and the Board of Education. During Doyle's one-year term as president of the Association, and during the succeeding year when he served on its executive committee there was apparently some tension in relations between the Board and the Association.

Beginning early in 1970, Doyle was involved in several incidents not directly connected with his role in the Teachers' Association. In one instance, he engaged in an argument with another teacher which culminated in the other teacher's slapping him. Doyle subsequently refused to accept an apology and insisted upon some punishment for the other teacher. His persistence in the matter resulted in the suspension of both teachers for one day, which was followed by a walk-out by a number of other teachers, which in turn resulted in the lifting of the suspensions.

On other occasions, Doyle got into an argument with employees of the school cafeteria over the amount of spaghetti which had been served him; referred to students in connection with a disciplinary complaint, as "sons of bitches"; and made an obscene gesture to two girls in connection with their failure to obey commands made in his capacity as cafeteria supervisor. Chronologically the last in the series of incidents which respondent was involved in during his employment by the Board was a telephone call by him to a local radio station. It was the Board's consideration of this incident which the court below found to be a violation of the First and Fourteenth Amendments.

In February 1971, the principal circulated to various teachers a memorandum relating to teacher dress and appearance, which was apparently prompted by the view of some in the administration that there was a relationship between teacher appearance and public support for bond issues. Doyle's response to the receipt of the memorandum—on a subject which he apparently understood was to be settled by joint teacher-administration action—was to convey the substance of the memorandum to a disc jockey at WSAI, a Cincinnati radio station, who promptly announced the adoption of the dress code as a news item. Doyle subsequently apologized to the principal, conceding that he should have made some prior communication of his criticism to the school administration.

Approximately one month later the superintendent made his customary annual recommendations to the Board as to the rehiring of nontenured teachers. He recommended that Doyle not be rehired. The same recommendation was made with respect to nine other teachers in the district, and in all instances, including Doyle's, the recommendation was adopted by the Board. Shortly after being notified of this decision, respondent requested a statement of reasons for the Board's actions. He received a statement citing "a notable lack of tact in handling professional matters which leaves much doubt as to your sincerity in establishing good school relationships." That general statement was followed by references to the radio station incident and to the obscene-gesture incident.

The District Court found that all of these incidents had in fact occurred. It concluded that respondent Doyle's telephone call to the radio station was "clearly protected by the First Amendment," and that because it had played a "substantial part" in the decision of the Board not to renew Doyle's employment, he was entitled to reinstatement with backpay. * * * The District Court did not expressly state what test it was applying in determining that the incident in question involved conduct protected by the First Amendment, but simply held that the communication to the radio station was such conduct. The Court of Appeals affirmed in a brief *per curiam* opinion. * * *

Doyle's claims under the First and Fourteenth Amendments are not defeated by the fact that he did not have tenure. Even though he could have been discharged for no reason whatever, and had no constitutional right to a hearing prior to the decision not to rehire him, * * * he may nonetheless establish a claim to reinstatement if the decision not to rehire him was made by reason of his exercise of constitutionally protected First Amendment freedoms. * * *

That question of whether speech of a government employee is constitutionally protected expression necessarily entails striking "a balance between the interests of the teacher, as a citizen, in commenting upon matters of public concern and the interest of the State, as an employer, in promoting the efficiency of the public services it performs through its employees." *Pickering* v. *Board of Education*. There is no suggestion by the Board that Doyle violated any established policy, or that its reaction to his communication to the radio station was anything more than an ad hoc response to Doyle's action in making the memorandum public. We therefore accept the District Court's finding that the communication was protected by the First and Fourteenth Amendments. We are not, however, entirely in agreement with that court's manner of reasoning from this finding to the conclusion that Doyle is entitled to reinstatement with backpay.

The District Court made the following "conclusions" on this aspect of the case:

> "1) If a non-permissible reason, e.g., exercise of First Amendment rights, played a substantial part in the decision not to renew—even in the face of other permissible grounds—the decision may not stand (citations omitted).
> "2) A non-permissible reason did play a substantial part. That is clear from the letter of the Superintendent immediately following the Board's decision, which stated two reasons—the one, the conversation with the radio station clearly protected by the First Amendment. A court may not engage in any limitation of First Amendment rights based on 'tact'—that is not to say that the "tactfulness" is irrelevant to other issues in this case." * * *

At the same time, though, it stated that:

> "[i]n fact, as this Court sees it and finds, both the Board and the Superintendent were faced with a situation in which there did exist in fact reason . . . independent of any First Amendment rights or exercise thereof, to not extend tenure." * * *

Since respondent Doyle had no tenure, and there was therefore not even a state-law requirement of "cause" or "reason" before a decision could be made not to renew his employment, it is not clear what the District Court meant by this latter statement. Clearly the Board legally *could* have dismissed respondent had the radio station incident never come to its attention. One plausible meaning of the court's statement is that the Board and the

Superintendent not only could, but in fact *should* have reached that decision had not the constitutionally protected incident of the telephone call to the radio station occurred. We are thus brought to the issue whether, even if that were the case, the fact that the protected conduct played a "substantial part" in the actual decision not to renew would necessarily amount to a constitutional violation justifying remedial action. We think that it would not.

A rule of causation which focuses solely on whether protected conduct played a part, "substantial" or otherwise, in a decision not to rehire, could place an employee in a better position as a result of the exercise of constitutionally protected conduct than he would have occupied had he done nothing. The difficulty with the rule enunciated by the District Court is that it would require reinstatement in cases where a dramatic and perhaps abrasive incident is inevitably on the minds of those responsible for the decision to rehire, and does indeed play a part in that decision—even if the same decision would have been reached had the incident not occurred. The constitutional principle at stake is sufficiently vindicated if such an employee is placed in no worse a position than if he had not engaged in the conduct. A borderline or marginal candidate should not have the employment question resolved against him because of constitutionally protected conduct. But that same candidate ought not to be able, by engaging in such conduct, to prevent his employer from assessing his performance record and reaching a decision not to rehire on the basis of that record, simply because the protected conduct makes the employer more certain of the correctness of its decision.

This is especially true where, as the District Court observed was the case here, the current decision to rehire will accord "tenure." The long-term consequences of an award of tenure are of great moment both to the employee and to the employer. They are too significant for us to hold that the Board in this case would be precluded, because it considered constitutionally protected conduct in deciding not to rehire Doyle, from attempting to prove to a trier of fact that quite apart from such conduct Doyle's record was such that he would not have been rehired in any event.

* * *

Initially, in this case, the burden was properly placed upon respondent to show that his conduct was constitutionally protected, and that this conduct was a "substantial factor"—or, to put it in other words, that it was a "motivating factor" in the Board's decision not to rehire him. Respondent having carried that burden, however, the District Court should have gone on to determine whether the Board had shown by a preponderance of the evidence that it would have reached the same decision as to respondent's reemployment even in the absence of the protected conduct.

We cannot tell from the District Court opinion and conclusions, nor from the opinion of the Court of Appeals affirming the judgment of the District Court, what conclusions those courts would have reached had they applied this test.

The judgment of the Court of Appeals is therefore vacated, and the case remanded for further proceedings consistent with this opinion.

So ordered.

Notes

The Court's opinion in *Doyle* reaffirms the doctrine that nontenured teachers have First Amendment rights, and they may establish a claim to reinstatement if the reason for not being rehired was in violation of these rights. However, as the Court stresses, engaging in constitutionally protected conduct may not prevent an employer from dismissing a teacher on the basis of his or her total performance record. Later decisions have referred to using the total performance record in conjunction with constitutionally protected conduct as "mixed-motive" analysis. Prior to this decision, some administrators claimed that poorly performing employees would purposely engage in protected activities to claim that such action was the reason for their dismissal and not their alleged poor performance.

A probationary teacher may not be terminated solely for refusing to participate in a flag-salute ceremony. The teacher stood silently at attention during daily classroom recitation of the pledge of allegiance, in which school regulations required her to participate. See *Russo* v. *Central School District No. 1*, 469 F.2d 623 (2nd Cir. 1972), *cert. denied*, 411 U.S. 932 (1973). However, see *Palmer* v. *Board of Education of the City of Chicago*, 603 F.2d 1271 (7th Cir. 1979), *cert. denied*, 444 U.S. 1026 (1980), which upheld the discharge of a teacher who, based on her Jehovah's Witness faith, refused to lead her kindergarten students in patriotic exercises and failed to comply with certain aspects of the curriculum. In upholding the discharge, the court distinguished between the freedom to believe in certain religious tenets and following an appropriate curriculum.

III. ACADEMIC FREEDOM

Academic freedom is difficult to conceptualize definitively because its extent is influenced by such factors as grade level and the nature of certain courses. Litigation often occurs when a school system's views regarding academic freedom are not in congruence with a teacher's perception of autonomy in determining specific subject matter for a particular class, appropriate teaching methods, and the selection of appropriate materials. In this type of litigation, teachers generally allege that they have a constitutional right to present material to which students, parents, or school officials may object. Although courts have recognized that teachers have the right to academic freedom, as with other constitutional rights, it is not absolute and must be balanced against the competing interests of the larger society.

A. Appropriate Material

FOWLER v. BOARD OF EDUCATION OF LINCOLN COUNTY
United States Court of Appeals, Sixth Circuit, 1987
819 F.2d 657
cert. denied, 484 U.S. 986 (1987)

MILBURN, Circuit Judge.

Defendants, the Board of Education of Lincoln County, Kentucky, individual board members, and the Superintendent of the Lincoln County Schools, appeal from the judgment of the district court awarding reinstatement and damages to plaintiff Jacqueline Fowler on the ground that her employment was terminated in violation of her First Amendment rights. Plaintiff cross-appeals on the ground that K.R.S. § 161.-790(1), which proscribes conduct unbecoming a teacher, is unconstitutionally vague as applied to her conduct. For the reasons that follow, we vacate the judgment of the district court and dismiss plaintiff's action.

Plaintiff Jacqueline Fowler was a tenured teacher employed by the Lincoln County, Kentucky, school system for fourteen years. She was discharged in July, 1984 for insubordination and conduct unbecoming a teacher. The basis for this action was that she had an "R" rated movie, *Pink Floyd—The Wall*, shown to her high school students on the last day of the 1983–84 school year. The students in Fowler's classes were in grades nine through eleven and were of the ages fourteen through seventeen.

The day on which the movie was shown, May 31, 1984, was a non-instructional day used by teachers for completing grade cards. A group of students requested that Fowler allow the movie to be shown while she was completing the grade cards. Fowler was unfamiliar with the movie and asked the students whether it was appropriate for viewing at school. Charles Bailey, age fifteen, who had seen the movie on prior occasions, indicated that the movie had "one bad place in it." * * *

* * *

When Fowler had the movie shown on the morning of May 31, 1984, she instructed Charles Bailey, the fifteen-year-old student who had seen the movie, to edit out any parts that were unsuitable for viewing at school. He did so by attempting to cover the 25" screen with an 8½" by 11" letter-sized file folder.

There is conflicting testimony as to whether, or how much, nudity was seen by the students. At the administrative hearing, several students testified that they saw no nudity. One student testified that she saw "glimpses" of nudity, but "nothing really offending." * * * It is undisputed that the audio portion of the movie, which contained enough offensive language to mandate an automatic "R" rating under motion picture industry standards, was played through the entire movie.

There is also conflicting testimony regarding the amount of sexual innuendo existing in the "unedited" version of the film. Because some parts of the film are animated, they are susceptible to varying interpretations. One particularly controversial segment of scenes is animated in which flowers appear on the screen, are transformed into the shape of male and female sex organs and then engage in an act of intercourse. This segment of the film was shown in the morning session. Other segments involving a violent rape, nudity, a suggestion of oral sex, and a naked woman and naked man in bed engaging in foreplay and intercourse were also shown in the morning.

* * *

In addition to the sexual aspects of the movie, there is a great deal of violence. One scene involves a bloody battlefield. Another shows police brutality. Another shows the protagonist cutting his chest with a razor. Another scene shows children being fed into a giant sausage machine. * * *

* * *

On July 10, 1984, plaintiff Fowler appeared with counsel at the administrative hearing. She testified that, despite the fact that she had never seen the movie before having it shown to her students, and despite the fact that she was posting grades on report cards and left the room several times while the movie was being shown, she believed it had significant value. She believed the movie portrayed the dangers of alienation between people and of repressive educational systems. She testified that she would show an edited version of the movie again if given the opportunity to explain it. She stated that she did not at any time discuss the movie with her students because she did not have enough time.

The board viewed the movie once in its entirety and once as it had been edited in the classroom. The board then retired into executive session. Following this executive session, the board returned to open session and voted unanimously to terminate plaintiff's employment for insubordination and conduct unbecoming a teacher.

* * *

The district court concluded that Fowler's conduct was protected by the First Amendment, and that she was discharged for exercising her constitutionally protected rights. Consequently, it awarded her reinstatement, back pay with interest, reimbursement of funds necessary for her reinstatement with the Kentucky Teachers Retirement System, damages for emotional distress and damage to professional reputation, compensatory damages for costs incurred in seeking new employment, costs, and attorney's fees.

* * *

The Supreme Court has consistently recognized the importance of the exercise of First Amendment rights in the context of public schools:

> First Amendment rights, applied in light of the special characteristics of the school environment, are available to teachers and students. It can hardly be argued that either students or teachers shed their constitutional rights to freedom of speech or expression at the schoolhouse gate. This has been the unmistakable holding of this Court for almost 50 years. Tinker, * * *

* * *

* * * Many courts have recognized that a teacher's First Amendment rights encompass the notion of "academic freedom" to exercise professional judgment in selecting topics and materials for use in the course of the educational process. * * *

Among the "special circumstances" which must be considered in defining the *scope* of First Amendment protection inside the classroom is the "inculcat[ion of] fundamental values necessary to the maintenance of a democratic political system." * * *

> Indeed, the "fundamental values necessary to the maintenance of a democratic political system" disfavor the use of terms of debate highly offensive or highly threatening to others. Nothing in the Constitution prohibits the states from insisting that certain modes of expression are inappropriate and subject to sanctions. The inculcation of these values is truly the "work of the schools." *Fraser* * * *

The single most important element of this inculcative process is the teacher. *Consciously or otherwise, teachers . . . demonstrate the appropriate form of civil discourse and political expression by their conduct and deportment in and out of class. Inescapably, like parents, they are role models.* *Fraser* (emphasis supplied). * * *

The accommodation of these sometimes conflicting fundamental values has caused great tension, particularly when the conflict arises within the classroom. * * * In the final analysis:

> the ultimate goal of school officials is to insure that the discipline necessary to the proper functioning of the school is maintained among both teachers and students. Any limitation on the exercise of constitutional rights can be justified only by a conclusion, based upon reasonable inferences flowing from concrete facts and not abstractions, that the interests of discipline or sound education are materially and substantially justified. . . . "The problem in any case is to arrive at a balance between the interests of the teacher, as a citizen, in commenting upon matters of public concern and the interest of the State, as an employer, in promoting the efficiency of the public services it performs through its employees." *James*, 461 F.2d at 571–72 (quoting *Pickering v. Board of Education*)

* * *

I conclude that Fowler's conduct in having the movie shown under the circumstances present here did not constitute expression protected by the

First Amendment. It is undisputed that Fowler was discharged for the show-ing of the movie, *Pink Floyd—The Wall.* Such conduct, under the circum-stances involved, clearly is not "speech" in the traditional sense of the expression of ideas through use of the spoken or written word.

* * *

In the present case, plaintiff Fowler had a fifteen-year-old student show a controversial, highly suggestive and somewhat sexually explicit movie to a group of high school students aged fourteen to seventeen. She did not pre-view the movie, despite the fact that she had been warned that portions were unsuitable for viewing in this context. She made no attempt at any time to explain the meaning of the movie or to use it as an educational tool. Rather, she had it shown for the purpose of keeping her students occupied during a noninstructional day while she was involved in posting grades on report cards. We conclude that the statute proscribing "conduct unbecoming a teacher" gave her adequate notice that such conduct would subject her to discipline. Accordingly, we conclude that the statute is not unconstitution-ally vague as applied to Fowler's conduct.

We conclude that plaintiff's conduct, although not illegal, constituted serious misconduct. Moreover, there was a direct connection between this misconduct and Fowler's work as a teacher. She introduced a controversial and sexually explicit movie into a classroom of adolescents without preview, preparation or discussion. In the process, she abdicated her function as an ed-ucator. Her having the movie shown under the circumstances involved demonstrates a blatant lack of judgment. Having considered the entire record, including the viewing of the movie, which we describe as gross and bizarre and containing material completely unsuitable for viewing by a classroom of students aged fourteen to seventeen, we conclude that such conduct falls within the concept of conduct unbecoming a teacher under Kentucky law.

Accordingly, for the reasons stated, the judgment of the district court is *vacated,* and this cause is *dismissed.*

* * *

MERRITT, Circuit Judge, dissenting.

Federal judges and local school boards do not make good movie crit-ics or good censors of movie content. What one judge sees as "gross and bizarre," another may find, * * * mild and not very "sexually suggestive."

The movie here seems to me to present a message similar to that ex-pounded by Dr. Spock: abuse of sex and drugs as well as various forms of mental instability and antisocial conduct are associated with an overly au-thoritarian society. The message is that unloving, overly rigid and authoritar-ian parents, teachers, judges and officials create disturbed individuals and societies. This lack of love is the figurative "wall" shown in the movie.

* * *

* * * Mrs. Fowler was not discharged because she entertained her stu-dents: she was discharged because the school board did not like the content of the movie. Mrs. Fowler proved at trial * * * that she was discharged because the board members regarded the movie as "immoral, antieducation, antifamily, antijudiciary, and antipolice." There is no support for the proposition—or does the school board argue—that a teacher's academic freedom or a student's right to hear may be abridged simply because a school board dislikes the content of the protected speech. Furthermore, since this was a "free day" for the students, no departure from a board-mandated curriculum occurred. It is obvious, therefore, that Mrs. Fowler's discharge was prompted by the content of the movie.

Assuming that the school board could have properly discharged Mrs. Fowler for poor judgment and lack of remorse in showing an "R-rated" movie which had short scenes depicting nudity and sexual foreplay, but not for the other reasons given, this case must be decided under the "mixed-motive" analysis of *Mt. Healthy City School Dist. Bd. of Educ. v. Doyle*. * * * Where a plaintiff can show that her constitutionally-protected conduct was a "substantial" or "motivating" factor in the discharge decision, the employer must prove "by a preponderance of the evidence that it would have reached the same decision as to . . . . re-employment even in the absence of the protected conduct." *Mt. Healthy*, * * *

* * *

In *Cohen v. California* * * * the Supreme Court held constitutionally protected the act of wearing a jacket bearing the words "!?X! the Draft" into a courthouse corridor. Writing for the Court, Justice Harlan stated that "while the particular four-letter word being litigated here is perhaps more distasteful than most others of its genre, it is nevertheless often true that one man's vulgarity is another's lyric. Indeed, we think it is largely because governmental officials cannot make principled distinctions in this area that the Constitution leaves matters of taste and style so largely to the individual." * * *

Therefore, I disagree with the distinction between instruction and entertainment drawn by Judge Milburn and the conflation of vulgarity and antiestablishment ideas set forth by Judge Peck. As the District Court correctly found, the school board in this case had to negate the testimony of its own members that the determinative causative factor in Mrs. Fowler's discharge was her decision to allow "antieducation, antifamily, antijudiciary, and antipolice" views to be expressed in her classroom. The District Court held that the school board failed to carry this *Mt. Healthy* burden. I agree with both of these findings. Therefore, I would affirm the judgment of the District Court.

Notes and Questions

A review of modern case law dealing with academic freedom reveals that it is no longer as strong a defense as it once was for teachers. Recent decisions suggest that the concept of academic freedom provides more protection for a teacher for what is said outside the school as a private citizen than for what is said inside the classroom. For the academic freedom defense to prevail for classroom conduct, it must be shown that the teacher did not defy legitimate state and local curriculum directives, followed accepted professional norms for that grade level and subject matter, discussed matters that were of public concern, and acted professionally and in good faith when there was no precedent or policy.

The majority held that Fowler's conduct was not expressive or communicative and therefore was not protected by the First Amendment. Additionally, they declared that the statute proscribing "conduct unbecoming a teacher" was not unconstitutionally vague. On the other hand, the district court judge and the dissenting court of appeals judge contended that the case should have been decided under the "mixed-motive" analysis of *Mt. Healthy City School District Board of Education* v. *Doyle*. Under such analysis, the burden switches to the defendant to show that the same decision to dismiss an employee would have been made even in the absence of using constitutionally protected conduct. What is the distinction between these differing legal viewpoints?

A drama teacher's reassignment due to her choice of plays for a statewide competition was upheld in *Boring* v. *Buncombe County Board of Education*, 136 F.3d 364 (4th Cir. 1998), a seven-to-six decision, by an en banc court. The controversial play dealt with a single-parent family including a divorced mother, a lesbian daughter, and an unmarried pregnant daughter. The teacher claimed a First Amendment right to participate in the development of the school curriculum through the selection and production of the play; however, the majority opinion held that curriculum development should be left to the local school authorities rather than to teachers. In its decision, the court held that the play was a part of the curriculum and the choice of plays was not a matter of public concern, consequently, not protected speech, [citing *Connick* v. *Myers*, 461 U.S. 138 (1983)]; therefore, the school had a legitimate pedagogical interest in not allowing the play [citing *Hazelwood School District* v. *Kuhlmeier*, 484 U.S. 260 (1988)]. Another teacher's termination for allowing excessive profanity in her students' creative projects was upheld in *Lacks* v. *Ferguson Reorganized School District R-2*, 147 F.3d 718 (8th Cir. 1998), *cert. denied*, 526 U.S. 1012 (1999). Words such as "fuck," "shit," "ass," "bitch," and "nigger" were used 150 times in a forty-minute videotape, and a student read a poem aloud in the classroom that contained profanity and graphic descriptions of oral sex. Although the teacher thought the district policy of not allowing student profanity in the classroom did not apply to creative projects, the court held that the school board had a legitimate interest in prohibiting such profanity and that the teacher could not claim her free speech rights were violated when she knowingly violating the district policy. Race was introduced in this case, but there was insufficient evidence that her termination was race related. Lacks was white, and her supervisors and students were black.

School officials were sued for compelling students to attend a sexually explicit AIDS (acquired immunodeficiency syndrome) awareness assembly at their public school without following school policy and state law requiring that parents be given advance notice and opportunity to opt-out of sex-education programs. In upholding school officials, a federal court of appeals held that conscience-shocking acts were not alleged that would have given rise to a claim for violation of substantive due process rights, even though the school officials' failure to provide opt-out procedures displayed callousness towards the teenagers' sensibilities. Furthermore, the court declared that parents' right to direct the upbringing and education of their children does not encompass a broad-based right to restrict the flow of information in public schools. See *Brown* v. *Hot, Sexy and Safer Productions, Inc.*, 68 F.3d 525 (1st Cir. 1995).

In another instance, a school board was upheld in its banning of a classroom management technique called "Learnball." This technique included a sports format, peer approval, dividing a class into teams, student election of team leaders and assistant teacher, giving students responsibility for establishing class rules and grading exercises, and imposing a system of rewards such as radio playing and shooting baskets with a foam ball in the classroom. The court held that the teacher did not have a First Amendment right of academic freedom to employ the technique and that the board's ban was constitutional. See *Bradley* v. *Pittsburgh Board of Education*, 910 F.2d 1172 (3rd Cir. 1990). Also, see *Murray* v. *Pittsburgh Board of Public Education*, 919 F. Supp. 838 (Pa. 1996), in which school policy was upheld that prohibited using "Learnball" with at-risk students at an alternative high school.

A Jewish student in a choir class alleged her music teacher's choice of explicitly Christian religious music and Christian religious sites for performance of the high school a cappella choir violated her rights under the United States and Utah Constitutions. The court, in *Bauchman* v. *West High School*, 900 F. Supp. 254 (Utah 1995), held that these actions did not violate the student's Establishment Clause rights because the teacher's selection had the primary purpose of teaching music appreciation, and the effect of the curriculum was not to advance or promote religion or constitute excessive entanglement. The court concluded that the choice of religious music, which was offensive to the student, did not automatically render its inclusion in the choir's performance repertoire violative of the student's free exercise rights, since the student would receive an "A" for the course and was expressly permitted to avoid classroom practice and performance of religious songs to which she objected. Additionally, the court noted that a cappella, to describe a choir, means "in the chapel" and that choral music is often associated with religion and is not automatically unconstitutional as excessive entanglement or primarily religious; nor, the court reasoned, were songs with religious content ipso facto equivalent of "prayer," despite reference in some songs to "God" and the "Lord."

Dissatisfaction with public education by parents, especially those concerned about replacing the teaching of a Judeo-Christian heritage with secularism and positivism (teaching only what can be scientifically proven) and those parents having the perception that the schools emphasize the teaching of politically correct values, has resulted in direct political attacks on curriculum initiatives. Parents holding such views have focused their attacks on such initiatives as so-called Mastery Learning and Outcomes Based Education. These parents often claim that the traditional Three Rs have been replaced by a new notion of the Three Rs, namely, reproduction, recycling, and racism.

"Winning" a school law suit may, at times, be akin to the aphorism "winning a battle but losing the war." An excellent example of this may be seen in the ultimate discontinuance of a popular elementary school reading series entitled Impressions, although two federal courts of appeal decisions, *Fleischfresser* v. *Directors of School District 200*, 15 F.3d. 680 (7th Cir. 1994) and *Brown* v. *Woodland Joint Unified School District*, 27 F.3d 1373 (9th Cir. 1994), held that the reading series did not promote the Wiccan religion in violation of the Establishment Clause. It had been alleged in the suits that the reading series presented religious concepts found in paganism and branches of witchcraft and Satanism. Notwithstanding these unsuccessful legal challenges and the fact that the Impressions series had been used in over 1,500 schools in thirty-four states, opposition to its use in many school districts, removal of the series by school boards in several instances, and refusal by four state textbook committees to allow the series onto their approved lists apparently had an enormous effect because the series has been withdrawn by the publisher.

A badly divided Supreme Court, as evidenced by seven separate opinions, addressed the issue of a school board's authority to remove books from a school library. Although there was no majority opinion, the plurality opinion does offer some guidance. School authorities may not exercise their discretion in the removal of books for narrow partisan or political purposes or to deny students access to ideas with which school authorities disagree. Additionally, the justices suggested several constitutionally legitimate standards that could be applied in determining a book's candidacy for removal, such as the book's educational suitability. Specific suitability criteria could include relevance to the curriculum and appropriateness for an age level. A book considered obscene for minors, pervasively vulgar, or offensive in its language could also be legitimately excluded. See *Board of Education, Island Trees Union Free School District No. 26 v. Pico*, 457 U.S. 853 (1982).

Removal of *The Adventures of Huckleberry Finn* and *A Rose for Emily* from a school's curriculum because they contained the word "nigger" was held to violate students' First Amendment rights in *Monteiro v. Tempe Union High School District*, 158 F.3d 1022 (9th Cir. 1998). Although the court recognized a history of racial prejudice towards blacks in America, it contended that removing such literary works would take away a school board's discretion to establish an appropriate and educational curriculum and ". . . could have a chilling effect on a school district's willingness to assign books with themes, characters, snippets of dialogue, or words that might offend the sensibilities of any number of persons or groups." Citing specific examples of this, the court averred:

> White plaintiffs could seek to remove books by Toni Morrison, Maya Angelou, or other prominent black authors on the ground that they portray caucasians in a derogatory fashion; Jews might try to impose civil liability for the teachings of Shakespeare . . . where writing exhibits a similar anti-Semitic strain. Female students could attempt to make a case for damages for the assignment of some the works of Tennessee Williams, Hemingway, or Freud, and male students for the writings of Andrea Dworkin or Margaret Atwood. (p. 1030)

In an earlier decision, barring a textbook that contained *Lysistrata* by Artistophanes and the *Miller's Tale* by Chaucer from an elective humanities course in which the readings were optional has been upheld. The court reasoned, under the deferential standard established in **Hazelwood School District v. Kuhlmeier**, that the school board's actions were reasonably related to its legitimate pedagogical concerns regarding the appropriateness of such readings given their explicit sexuality and admittedly vulgar language. The court pointed out that the materials were still available in the library and that the materials could be assigned or discussed in class. See *Virgil v. School Board of Columbia County*, 862 F.2d 1517 (11th Cir. 1988).

Apparently, academic freedom may be bargained away. A teachers' association negotiated an agreement with a provision that the board shall have the right to "determine the processes, techniques, methods and means of teaching any and all subjects." Several English teachers challenged the school board's action in directing that certain books not be purchased or assigned. The court held for the school board but contended it would have held for the teachers if the negotiated agreement had not existed. See *Cary v. Board of Education of Adams–Arapahoe School District 28-J*, 598 F.2d 535 (10th Cir. 1979).

B. Political Speakers

WILSON v. CHANCELLOR

United States District Court, District of Oregon, 1976
418 F. Supp. 1358

BURNS, District Judge.

Plaintiffs Wilson and Logue seek declaratory and injunctive relief from a school board order banning "all political speakers" from Molalla Union High School (MHS). They contend that the order violates the First Amendment and the equal protection clause of the Fourteenth Amendment, and is unconstitutionally vague and overbroad. * * *

Wilson teaches the political science class at MHS in which Logue was a student. This dispute arose when Wilson invited a Communist, Anton Kchmareck, to speak to that class. Wilson already and without objection had presented a Democrat, a Republican, and a member of the John Birch Society. The Communist was to be the last of this quadrumvirate through which Wilson hoped to present, in the words of the adherent, each of four points of view.

Wilson followed customary procedure and reported this invitation to the principal. The principal approved. Defendant school board discussed the invitation at its November 1975 meeting and also approved. This procedure was neither unprecedented nor customary.

The board's approval inspired mixed reviews. Two severe critics called a community meeting on December 4 where they circulated a petition asking the board to reverse the decision; approximately 800 persons eventually signed it. Several townsfolk, in letters to the newspaper, mentioned the possibility of voting down all school budgets and voting out the members of the board.

Faced with this petition and many outraged residents, the board on December 11 reversed its decision and issued orally an order banning "all political speakers" from the high school.

* * *

Miss Logue contends the order violates her First Amendment right to hear the speech of others.

The right to hear customarily is invoked by prisoners denied access to periodicals, * * * members of a potential audience for a speaker prohibited from speaking, * * * or persons asserting either the public's "right to know," * * * or the emerging right of privacy * * * .

Of these cases, only the potential audience cases are applicable here. * * * These cases and my recognition that the First Amendment exists to protect a broad range of interests persuade me that Logue suffered an infringement of her First Amendment rights. * * *

Few courts have considered whether and to what extent the First Amendment protects academic freedom. Honored in Germanic tradition and prominent in academic debates, the theory rarely surfaces in legal opinions. Moreover, even its most enthusiastic advocates usually distinguish between the freedom to be accorded university professors and that to be accorded elementary and secondary school teachers. It seems to be assumed that the former engage in the search for knowledge and therefore should have far greater freedom than the latter who merely disseminate knowledge.

The Supreme Court of the United States has discussed academic freedom in "eloquent and isolated statements." * * * Lower courts have spoken more frequently, but none has clearly defined the theory's legal contours. Nor will I. This case can be decided by using purely conventional freedom of expression analysis.

A teacher's teaching is expression to which the First Amendment applies. The right to freedom of expression is not absolute; it may be restricted, and restrictions on a teacher's expression should be judged in light of the "special characteristics of the school environment." * * *

In imposing restrictions and making other decisions, school boards should be allowed great discretion. No court should intervene merely because a board's decision seems unwise. But if school boards, in exercising their discretion, act so as to interfere impermissibly with the constitutional rights of students or teachers, or both, courts must and will intervene if their jurisdiction is properly invoked.

These considerations in mind, I address two pivotal questions: First, is a teaching method or vehicle a form of expression protected by the First Amendment? Second, if so, is the restriction at issue here reasonable?

Three cases have treated teaching methods as protected forms of expression: *Keefe* v. *Geanakos*, 418 F.2d 359 (1st Cir. 1969), *Parducci* v. *Rutland*, 316 F. Supp. 352 (M.D. Ala. 1970), and *Sterzing* v. *Fort Bend Independent School District*, 376 F. Supp. 657 (S.D. Tex. 1972).

The teacher in *Keefe* assigned his class an *Atlantic Monthly* article containing a word which "admittedly highly offensive, is a vulgar term for an incestuous son."

A school committee summoned Keefe to defend his conduct. When he was asked to agree not to use the word again, he declined. He subsequently was suspended, and sought a temporary injunction against the committee's dismissal hearing.

The district court denied an interlocutory injunction pending a decision on the merits. The court of appeals reversed, holding that plaintiff had demonstrated he probably would succeed on his lack of notice and academic freedom claims.

In *Parducci*, the teacher assigned her eleventh grade English class a Kurt Vonnegut, Jr. short story, "Welcome to the Monkey House." Several parents complained. School officials admonished the teacher not to use the story in any of her classes, and threatened to dismiss her if she refused. The teacher resigned. In her suit for injunctive relief she contended that the school's action violated her First Amendment rights.

The court recognized such a right, but concluded that it must be balanced against competing societal interests, most prominently the "state's vital interest in protecting its young people from any form of extreme propagandism in the classroom." * * * The court also recognized that *Tinker* * * * requires the state to demonstrate that:

> "[T]he forbidden conduct would 'materially and substantially interfere with the requirements of appropriate discipline in the operation of the school.' " * * *

The court then held that because the assignment was appropriate and presented no threat of disruption, the teacher's dismissal for assigning the short story violated her First Amendment rights.

In *Sterzing* a teacher disclosed to his civics class his lack of opposition to interracial marriage. After several parents complained, school officials urged Sterzing to confine his teaching to the assigned textbook. He ignored this request and several times departed from the text during the ensuing five months. Shortly after Sterzing administered an allegedly propagandistic test on race relations, the school board voted to discharge him for insubordination.

The district court ordered that Sterzing be reinstated. It held that a teacher has a substantive right to choose teaching methods which serve a demonstrated educational purpose. "A responsible teacher," wrote the court, "must have freedom to use the tools of his profession as he sees fit." * * *

* * *

These cases also recognize the validity of a popular maxim, "the medium is the message." The expresser's medium can affect the persuasiveness of his message, the duration of its influence, and the size and type of audience which it reaches. The act of teaching is a form of expression, and the methods used in teaching are media. Wilson's use of political speakers was his medium for teaching; similarly, the short story was Parducci's medium, the pamphlets were Sterzing's media, and the article containing the controversial words was Keefe's medium. The various school boards which restricted the media employed by Wilson here, and by Keefe, Parducci, and Sterzing in the cases cited, suppressed expression which the First Amendment protects.

But the school boards may restrict teachers' expression if the restrictions are reasonable in light of the special circumstances of the school environment. Thus, question two: was this order reasonable?

I conclude that the order was not reasonable and therefore violated the First Amendment.

The order barred political speakers absolutely, yet no disruptions had occurred in Wilson's classes, or at other school gatherings where political subjects were discussed. Further, none were expected in the future.

The defendants have not shown that outside speakers impair high school education. If they did, the board still would lack justification for banning only outside *political* speakers. Moreover, the evidence demonstrated that the use of outside speakers is widely recommended, widely practiced, and professionally accepted.

The boards cannot justify the ban by contending that political subjects are inappropriate in a high school curriculum. Political subjects frequently are discussed at Molalla High School and other schools throughout the country, as required by law. Nor does the board have a valid interest in suppressing, as it did, political expression occurring in the course of recognized extracurricular activities.

The board cannot contend it was acting within its discretionary power to exclude incompetent speakers. It acted under pressure from those who feared, rather than doubted, the speaker's competence by banning all speakers without regard to competence.

The board's only apparent reason for issuing the order which suppressed protected speech was to placate angry residents and taxpayers. The First Amendment forbids this; neither fear of voter reaction nor personal disagreement with views to be expressed justifies a suppression of free expression, at least in the absence of any reasonable fear of material and substantial interference with the educational process.

The order, by granting school officials discretion to bar political speakers before those persons speak, creates a system of prior restraint.

Prior restraints are not unconstitutional per se, but their invalidity is heavily presumed. * * * They are valid only if they include criteria to be followed by school authorities in determining whether to allow or forbid the expression and procedural safeguards in the form of an expeditious review procedure. * * *

The Molalla board order was completely bare; it failed to include either criteria by which to define "political speakers" or procedural safeguards in any form.

The order therefore constitutes an invalid prior restraint. Although our language contains many words and phrases which require no further definition, the phrase "political speakers" is not among them. * * *

* * *

Classifications which restrain conduct protected by the First Amendment are unconstitutional unless they suitably further an appropriate governmental interest. * * * Appropriate governmental interests include the desire to promote effective education by preventing material disruptions of classroom work, substantial disorders, or invasions of the rights of others, * * * or by averting a clear and present danger * * *.

Because I already have concluded that the order did not further any appropriate governmental interests, and therefore violated the First Amendment, I must also conclude that it violated the equal protection clause. The order exists to silence absolutely the expression of an unpopular political view, solely out of fear that some will listen. This the government, acting through the school board, cannot do.

The board discriminated in a third way. It allowed Wilson to invite a Republican, a Democrat, and a member of the John Birch Society to speak to his class, but it forbade him from inviting a Communist.

The effect was discriminatory. Persons with palatable views could speak; those with less readily digestible views could not.

An order prohibiting Wilson from inviting a Republican to class after a Democrat had spoken there clearly would be discriminatory. That Wilson invited a Communist rather than a champion of the current political orthodoxy has no constitutional significance.

* * *

I do not imply that members of a community now may sue to compel schools to open their doors to particular outside speakers. Such compulsion would restrict a teacher's freedom rather than protect it, contrary to the important policies that I have outlined.

Nor do I suggest that Federal courts stand ready to regulate the regimen and to control the curricula of our public schools. A teacher is not required to have outside speakers contribute to class. I hold only that this regulation, as it applied in this particular set of facts, does not withstand constitutional scrutiny.

And I do not malign the defendant board members. Their position is sensitive, at once both a challenge and an opportunity. They serve a community in which many persons equate Communism with violence, deception, and imperialism. Yet violence, deception, and imperialism have occurred under many flags and in the name of many creeds. School boards could eliminate much of the high schools' curricula by restricting them to theories, philosophies, and practices of resolutely pacifistic, honest, non-expansionist societies.

It seems these same residents fear that young Molallans will become young Marxists and Maoists, virtually overnight. Because Oregon law * * * requires the schools to specially emphasize our form of government, respect for the flag, and obedience to our laws, this fear seems ill-founded. Moreover, today's high school students are surprisingly sophisticated, intelligent, and discerning. They are far from easy prey to even the most forcefully expressed, cogent, and persuasive words.

Finally, I am firmly convinced that a course designed to teach students that a free and democratic society is superior to those in which freedoms are sharply curtailed will fail entirely if it fails to teach one important lesson: that the power of the state is never so great that it can silence a man or woman simply because there are those who disagree. Perhaps that carries with it a second lesson: that those who enjoy the blessings of a free society must occasionally bear the burden of listening to others with whom they disagree, even to the point of outrage.

* * *

Questions

Who has the ultimate authority to decide what will or will not take place in a classroom? a teacher? building-level administrators? central office administrators? the local school board? state department of education? state legislature? the Department of Education? courts? What factors would influence your decision? Does the grade level and/or nature of the subject matter being taught affect the decision?

IV. DRUG TESTING

In their reaction to the prevalence of drugs in American society, some school systems have attempted to screen teachers for drug use. When such screening policies are contested as a violation of a teacher's rights under the Fourth Amendment, courts must balance the privacy interests of teachers with the government's interest in having a drug-free environment. Courts take several factors into consideration when attempting to balance these competing interests, including: the intrusiveness of the search, the extent of an alleged drug problem; the degree of suspicion that triggered the search; and whether a "special needs" exception exists in a particular situation that would overcome the need for individualized suspicion. The court in *Knox County Education Association* v. *Knox County Board of Education*, 158 F.3d 361 (6th Cir. 1998), *cert. denied* 528 U.S. 812 (1999), determined the Fourth Amendment was not violated by a two-pronged policy that required (1) suspicionless drug testing for all individuals who apply for, transfer to, or are promoted to, "safety sensitive" positions within the school system, (safety sensitive positions include principals, assistant principals, teachers, traveling teachers, teacher aides, substitute teachers, school secretaries and bus drivers) and (2) "reasonable suspicion" drug and/or alcohol testing of all school employees. In upholding supicionless drug testing, the court emphasized: the unique role teachers play in the lives of their students and in the *in loco parentis* obligations imposed on them; the "safety sensitive" aspect of providing a safe and secure environment for students; and that teachers' privacy interests are diminished by their working in a highly regulated profession. The court also noted that the suspicionless drug testing policy did not include a random testing component and only tested those people who were candidates for, and attempting to transfer to, a select group of positions. Once the initial test was passed, there was no ongoing testing. The court found the "reasonable suspicion" feature of the second prong of the school's policy dealing with drugs, within the reasonableness requirement of the Fourth Amendment, because a search under this policy was clearly based upon a finding of individualized suspicion.

In *United Teachers of New Orleans* v. *Orleans Parish School Board*, 142 F.3d 853 (5th Cir. 1998), a rule was challenged that required teachers and other school employees injured in the course of employment to submit to drug testing. In holding the rule violative of the Fourth Amendment, the court held that there had not been any identified problem of drug use by teachers, their aides, or clerical workers. Additionally, the court stated, "there is an insufficient nexus between suffering an injury at work and drug impairment."

Termination of a teacher for insubordination, who refused to take a drug test within two hours after a partially burned marijuana cigarette was found in her car in the school's parking lot, was upheld in *Hearn* v. *Savannah Board of Education*, 191 F.3d 1329 (11th Cir.1999). The marijuana was discovered by a drug-sniffing dog during a campus-wide "drug lock down." The car was unlocked and the passenger side window open. Under the district's "Drug-Free Workplace Policy" and "zero tolerance" approach to drugs, the teacher was required to take the test within a two-hour limit of an incident that generated "reasonable suspicion." The policy also provided for immediate discharge for failing to cooperate by refusing to submit to testing.

Three United States Supreme Court decisions, although not dealing with school personnel, shed light on the drug testing issue. A Georgia statute requiring candidates for certain state offices to submit and pass a drug test within 30 days prior to qualifying for office was held to be unconstitutional in *Chandler* v. *Miller*, 520 U.S. 305 (1997). In its decision, the Court held that suspicionless testing did not meet the Fourth Amendment's "special needs" exception to overcome the need for individualized suspicion of wrongdoing because there was no evidence of a drug problem among state officeholders. In *Skinner* v. *Railway Executives' Association*, 489 U.S. 602 (1989), the Court upheld blood and urine tests for train crews, in cases of train accidents involving fatalities or release of hazardous material, without the necessity of showing individualized grounds for suspicion. Additionally, the Court opined that individual suspicion may be dispensed with when the individual's privacy interests are minimal and when an important governmental interest furthered by the intrusion would be placed in jeopardy by requiring individual suspicion. The Court, in *National Treasury Employees' Union* v. *Von Raab*, 489 U.S. 656 (1989), has also upheld mandatory drug testing for all applicants for employment with the Customs Service for positions in which the duties involve drug interdiction, enforcement of related laws, and the carrying of firearms. Additionally, courts have upheld the testing of employees who work on natural gas and hazardous liquid pipelines, *IBEW Local 1245* v. *Skinner*, 913 F.2d 1454 (9th Cir. 1990), and random urinalysis testing of airline personnel with safety responsibilities, *Bluestein* v. *Skinner*, 908 F.2d 451 (9th Cir. 1990), *cert. denied* 498 U.S. 1083 (1991).

V. PERSONAL APPEARANCE

Personal appearance of teachers in respect to dress and grooming has received considerable attention in the courts. School authorities generally contend that proper dress and grooming establish a professional image for teachers, promote good grooming among students, and aid in the maintenance of respect and decorum in the classroom. Teachers, in contrast, generally allege that local regulations governing their personal appearance invade their rights of privacy and liberty. Issues raised in these conflicts have included the wearing of "long" hair, sideburns, or a beard for males; wearing of a tie and/or jacket for males; and improper skirt length or immodest attire for females.

EAST HARTFORD EDUCATION ASSOCIATION v. BOARD OF EDUCATION OF TOWN OF EAST HARTFORD

United States Court of Appeals, Second Circuit, 1977

562 F.2d 838

Before KAUFMAN, Chief Judge, and SMITH, FEINBERG, MANSFIELD, MULLIGAN, OAKES, TIMBERS, GURFEIN, VAN GRAAFEILAND and MESKILL, Circuit Judges.

On petition for Rehearing En Banc

MESKILL, Circuit Judge:

Although this case may at first appear too trivial to command the attention of a busy court, it raises important issues concerning the proper scope of judicial oversight of local affairs. The appellant here, Richard Brimley, is a public school teacher reprimanded for failing to wear a necktie while teaching his English class. Joined by the teachers union, he sued the East Hartford Board of Education, claiming that the reprimand for violating the dress code deprived him of his rights of free speech and privacy. Chief Judge Clarie granted summary judgment for the defendants. * * * A divided panel of this Court reversed and remanded for trial. At the request of a member of the Court, a poll of the judges in regular active service was taken to determine if the case should be reheard *en banc*. A majority voted for rehearing. We now vacate the judgment of the panel majority and affirm the judgment of the district court.

The facts are not in dispute. In February, 1972, the East Hartford Board of Education adopted "Regulations for Teacher Dress." At that time, Mr. Brimley, a teacher of high school English and filmmaking, customarily wore a jacket and sport-shirt, without a tie. His failure to wear a tie constituted a violation of the regulation and he was reprimanded for his delict. Mr. Brimley appealed to the school principal and was told that he was to wear a tie while teaching English, but that his informal attire was proper during filmmaking classes. He then appealed to the superintendent and the board without success, after which he began formal arbitration proceedings, which ended in a decision that the dispute was not arbitrable. This lawsuit followed. Although Mr. Brimley initially complied with the code while pursuing his remedies, he has apparently returned to his former mode of dress. * * *

In the vast majority of communities, the control of public schools is vested in locally-elected bodies. This commitment to local political bodies requires significant public control over what is said and done in school. * * * It is not the federal courts, but local democratic processes, that are primarily responsible for the many routine decisions that are made in public school systems. Accordingly, it is settled that "[c]ourts do not and cannot intervene in the resolution of conflicts which arise in the daily operation of school systems and which do not directly and sharply implicate basic constitutional values." * * *

* * *

Because the appellant's clash with his employer has failed to "directly and sharply implicate basic constitutional values," we refuse to upset the policies established by the school board.

Mr. Brimley claims that by refusing to wear a necktie he makes a statement on current affairs which assists him in his teaching. In his brief, he argues that the following benefits flow from his tielessness:

(a) He wishes to present himself to his students as a person who is not tied to "establishment conformity."
(b) He wishes to symbolically indicate to his students his association with the ideas of the generation to which those students belong, including the rejection of many of the customs and values, and of the social outlook, of the older generation.
(c) He feels that dress of this type enables him to achieve closer rapport with his students, and thus enhances his ability to teach.

Appellant's claim, therefore, is that his refusal to wear a tie is "symbolic speech," and, as such, "is protected against governmental interference by the First Amendment."

We are required here to balance the alleged interest in free expression against the goals of the school board in requiring its teachers to dress somewhat more formally than they might like. * * * When this test is applied, the school board's position must prevail.

Obviously, a great range of conduct has the symbolic, "speech-like" aspect claimed by Mr. Brimley. To state that activity is "symbolic" is only the beginning, and not the end, of constitutional inquiry. * * * Even though intended as expression, symbolic speech remains conduct, subject to regulation by the state. * * *

As conduct becomes less and less like "pure speech" the showing of governmental interest required for its regulation is progressively lessened. * * * In those cases where governmental regulation of expressive conduct has been struck down, the communicative intent of the actor was clear and "closely akin to 'pure speech.' " * * * Thus, the First Amendment has been held to protect wearing a black armband to protest the Vietnam War, * * * burning an American Flag to highlight a speech denouncing the government's failure to protect a civil rights leader, * * * or quietly refusing to recite the Pledge of Allegiance. * * *

In contrast, the claims of symbolic speech made here are vague and unfocused. Through the simple refusal to wear a tie, Mr. Brimley claims that he communicates a comprehensive view of life and society. It may well be, in an age increasingly conscious of fashion, that a significant portion of the population seeks to make a statement of some kind through its clothes. * * * However, Mr. Brimley's message is sufficiently vague to place it close to the "conduct" end of the "speech-conduct" continuum described above. * * * While the regulation of the school board must still pass constitutional muster, the showing required to uphold it is significantly less than if Mr. Brimley had been punished, for example, for publicly speaking out on an issue concerning school administration. * * *

At the outset, Mr. Brimley had other, more effective means of communicating his social views to his students. He could, for example, simply have told them his views on contemporary America; if he had done this in a temperate way, without interfering with his teaching duties, we would be confronted with a very different First Amendment case. * * * The existence of alternative, effective means of communication, while not conclusive, is a factor to be considered in assessing the validity of a regulation of expressive conduct. * * *

Balanced against appellant's claim of free expression is the school board's interest in promoting respect for authority and traditional values, as well as discipline in the classroom, by requiring teachers to dress in a professional manner. A dress code is a rational means of promoting these goals. * * *

This balancing test is primarily a matter for the school board. Were we local officials, and not appellate judges, we might find Mr. Brimley's arguments persuasive. However, our role is not to choose the better educational policy. We may intervene in the decisions of school authorities only when it has been shown that they have strayed outside the area committed to their discretion. If Mr. Brimley's argument were to prevail, this policy would be completely eroded. Because teaching is by definition an expressive activity, virtually every decision made by school authorities would raise First Amendment issues calling for federal court intervention.

The very notion of public education implies substantial public control. Educational decisions must be made by someone; there is no reason to create a constitutional preference for the views of individual teachers over those of their employers. * * * The First Amendment claim made here is so insubstantial as to border on the frivolous. We are unwilling to expand First Amendment protection to include a teacher's sartorial choice.

Mr. Brimley also claims that the "liberty" interest grounded in the due process clause of the Fourteenth Amendment protects his choice of attire. * * * This claim will not withstand analysis.

* * *

* * * If Mr. Brimley has any protected interest in his neckwear, it does not weigh very heavily on the constitutional scales. As with most legislative choices, the board's dress code is presumptively constitutional. It is justified by the same constitutional concerns for respect, discipline and traditional values described in our discussion of the First Amendment claim.

The rights of privacy and liberty in which appellant seeks refuge are important and evolving constitutional doctrines. To date, however, the Supreme Court has extended their protection only to the most basic personal decisions. * * * Nor has the Supreme Court been quick to expand these rights to new fields. * * * As with any other constitutional provision, we are not given a "roving commission" to right wrongs and impose our notions of sound policy upon society. There is substantial danger in expanding the reach of due process to cover cases such as this. By bringing trivial activities under the constitutional umbrella, we trivialize the constitutional provision itself. If we are to maintain the vitality of this new doctrine, we must be careful not to "cry wolf" at every minor restraint on a citizen's liberty. * * *

The two other Courts of Appeals which have considered this issue have reached similar conclusions. In *Miller* v. *School District*, 495 F.2d 658 (7th Cir. 1974), the Seventh Circuit upheld a grooming regulation for teachers. * * * The First Circuit reached the same result in *Tardif* v. *Quinn*, 545 F.2d 761 (1st Cir. 1976), where a school teacher was dismissed for wearing short skirts. * * *

Both *Miller* and *Tardif* are stronger cases for the plaintiff's position than the instant case. Both involved dismissals rather than, as here, a reprimand. Moreover, *Miller* involved a regulation of hair and beards, as well as dress. Thus, Miller was forced to appear as his employers wished both on and off the job. In contrast, Mr. Brimley can remove his tie as soon as the school day ends. If the plaintiffs in *Miller* and *Tardif* could not prevail, neither can Mr. Brimley.

Each claim of substantive liberty must be judged in the light of that case's special circumstances. In view of the uniquely influential role of the public school teacher in the classroom, the board is justified in imposing this regulation. As public servants in a special position of trust, teachers may properly be subjected to many restrictions in their professional lives which would be invalid if generally applied. * * * We join the sound views of the First and Seventh Circuits, and follow *Kelley* [425 U.S. 238 (1976), a challenge to a police department's hair grooming regulations], by holding that a school board may, if it wishes, impose reasonable regulations governing the appearance of the teachers it employs. There being no material factual issue to be decided, the grant of summary judgment is affirmed.

Notes and Questions

Other federal courts of appeals have held similarly to the *East Hartford* decision. Some observers find it incongruous that school authorities have more control over teachers' dress than they do over students' dress. How would you explain this seeming incongruity? As a practical matter, although authorities have been successful in the courts, teacher dress is no longer the contentious issue it once was and a "rule of reason" appears to prevail.

VI. TEACHER AS EXEMPLAR

Not too many years ago, a teacher's lifestyle was determined to a large extent by a school system's formal or informal, often rigid, rules. An example is Rules of Conduct for Teachers, which was published by a local West Virginia Board of Education in 1915:

Rules of Conduct for Teachers

1. You will not marry during the term of your contract.
2. You are not to keep company with men.
3. You must be home between the hours of 8:00 P.M. and 6:00 A.M. unless attending a school function.
4. You may not loiter downtown in ice cream stores.
5. You may not travel beyond the city limits unless you have the permission of the chairman of the board.
6. You may not ride in a carriage or automobile with any man unless he is your father or brother.
7. You may not smoke cigarettes.
8. You may not dress in bright colors.
9. You may under no circumstances dye your hair.
10. You must wear at least two petticoats.
11. Your dresses must not be any shorter than two inches above the ankle.
12. To keep the schoolroom neat and clean, you must sweep the floor at least once daily; scrub the floor at least once a week with hot, soapy water; clean the blackboards at least once a day, and start the fire at 7:00 A.M. so the room will be warm by 8:00 A.M.

Not all schoolteachers worked under such restrictive rules. However, a belief had developed over the years that teachers should act as examples to their charges and that they should be exemplars to their students in such areas as dress, grooming, the social amenities, and morals.

Although it may at times have been difficult for a teacher to uphold the community's view of exemplary conduct, this expectation was generally well known to the teacher. In those days, a teacher knew that improper dress or grooming, being seen drunk in public, and, for females, divorce would result not only in school authorities' disapproval but possibly in dismissal. The same rules applied to extramarital affairs, "improper" or "immoral" conduct on the part of single teachers, and homosexuality.

In the contemporary world, changing life-styles and frequent lack of agreement regarding not necessarily exemplary but merely "proper" conduct may make it difficult for a teacher to know when a norm is transgressed or exceeds school authorities' or a community's zone of acceptance. This problem is further heightened by the fact that teacher conduct that may be tolerated in a metropolitan area may not be condoned in a small town with a homogeneous population that considers itself conservative.

In examining controversial life-styles, courts have taken several factors into consideration including whether the conduct was criminal or immoral under a state statute, hampered teacher effectiveness, was based on unsubstantiated rumors, or infringed on the teacher's freedom of expression. Courts have demonstrated a reluctance to enforce or bar conduct solely on the basis of conformity, historical precedent, or "expert" opinion. However, in today's environment, dismissal of adulterous teachers, unmarried and pregnant teachers, or an unmarried teacher living with a person of the opposite sex is rarely brought before the courts.

A male tenured elementary school teacher who underwent sex-reassignment surgery to change his external anatomy to that of a female was dismissed because there was a fear that retention would have an adverse effect on the students. The legal issue the court had to address was whether the "incapacity" of the teacher, a term used in the state statute as grounds for dismissal, can be established by a teacher's allegedly having an adverse effect on the students. In its decision, the court in *In re Grossman*, 316 A.2d 39 (N.J. Super. Ct. App. Div. 1974), determined that a transsexual teacher who had been sexually reassigned could create anxieties among younger children and have a negative effect on their mental health. However, the court stressed that the decision applied only to this school system and expressed no opinion with respect to her fitness to teach elsewhere and under different circumstances than revealed in this case.

A. Homosexual Teacher

In the earliest cases dealing with claims by homosexual teachers of their denial of a teaching position, dismissal, or certificate revocation, court decisions generally upheld the school authorities. However, several recent decisions have tended to uphold the rights of homosexual teachers. And, in several states, state legislation and/or local ordinances protect homosexuals' employment rights.

GAYLORD v. TACOMA SCHOOL DISTRICT NO. 10

Supreme Court of Washington, 1977
559 P.2d 1340, *cert. denied*,
434 U.S. 879 (1977)

HOROWITZ, Associate Justice.

Plaintiff-appellant, James Gaylord, appeals a judgment of the trial court upholding Gaylord's discharge from employment as a high school teacher by defendant school district. * * *

* * *

We need consider only the assignments of error which raise two basic issues: (1) whether substantial evidence supports the trial court's conclusion plaintiff-appellant Gaylord was guilty of immorality; (2) whether substantial evidence supports the findings, that as a known homosexual, Gaylord's fitness as a teacher was impaired to the injury of the Wilson High School, justifying his discharge by the defendant school district's board of directors. The relevant findings of the trial court may be summarized as follows.

Gaylord knew of his homosexuality for 20 years prior to his trial, actively sought homosexual company for the past several years, and participated in homosexual acts. He knew his status as a homosexual, if known, would jeopardize his employment, damage his reputation and hurt his parents.

Gaylord's school superior first became aware of his sexual status on October 24, 1972, when a former Wilson High student told the school's vice-principal he thought Gaylord was a homosexual. The vice-principal confronted Gaylord at his home that same day with a written copy of the student's statement. Gaylord admitted he was a homosexual and attempted unsuccessfully to have the vice-principal drop the matter.

On November 21, 1972, Gaylord was notified the board of directors of the Tacoma School Board had found probable cause for his discharge due to his status as a publicly known homosexual. This status was contrary to school district policy No. 4119(5), which provides for discharge of school employees for "immorality." After hearing, the defendant board of directors discharged Gaylord effective December 21, 1972.

The court found an admission of homosexuality connotes illegal as well as immoral acts, because "sexual gratification with a member of one's own sex is implicit in the term 'homosexual.' " These acts were proscribed by RCW 9.79.120 (lewdness) and RCW 9.79.100 (sodomy).

After Gaylord's homosexual status became publicly known, it would and did impair his teaching efficiency. A teacher's efficiency is determined by his relationship with his students, their parents, the school administration and fellow teachers. If Gaylord had not been discharged after he became known as a homosexual, the result would be fear, confusion, suspicion, parental concern and pressure on the administration by students, parents and other teachers.

The court concluded "appellant was properly discharged by respondent upon a charge of immorality upon his admission and disclosure that he was a homosexual" and that relief sought should be denied.

Was Gaylord guilty of immorality?

Our concern here is with the meaning of immorality in the sense intended by school board policy No. 4119(5). School boards have broad management powers. * * * Under RCW 28A.58.100(1) the school board may discharge teachers for "sufficient cause." Policy No. 4119(5) adopted by the school board and in effect during the term of Gaylord's teaching contract with defendant school district permits the Tacoma School Board of Directors to treat "immorality" as sufficient cause for discharge.

"Immorality" as used in policy No. 4119(5) does not stand alone. RCW 28A.67.110 makes it the duty of all teachers to "endeavor to impress on the minds of their pupils the principles of morality, truth, justice, temperance, humanity, and patriotism. . . ." RCW 28A.70.140 requires an applicant for a teacher's certificate be "a person of good moral character." RCW 28A.70.160 makes "immorality" a ground for revoking a teacher's certificate. Other grounds include the commission of "crimes against the laws of the state." The moral conduct of a teacher is relevant to a consideration of that person's fitness or ability to function adequately as a teacher of the students he is expected to teach—in this case high school students. * * *

"Immorality" as a ground of teacher discharge would be unconstitutionally vague if not coupled with resulting actual or prospective adverse performance as a teacher. * * * The basic statute permitting discharge for "sufficient cause" (RCW 38A.58.100(1)) has been construed to require the cause must adversely affect the teacher's performance before it can be invoked as a ground for discharge. * * *

* * *

When, as in the case here, the term "immorality" has not been defined in policy No. 4119(5), it would seem reasonable to give the term its ordinary, common, everyday meaning as we would when construing an undefined term in a statute. * * *

* * *

The medical and psychological and psychiatric literature on the subject of homosexuality distinguishes between the overt homosexual and the passive or latent homosexual. An overt homosexual has homosexual inclinations consciously experienced and expressed in actual homosexual behavior as opposed to latent. A latent homosexual is one who has "an erotic inclination toward members of the same sex, not consciously experienced or expressed in overt action; opposite of overt." * * *

* * *

In the instant case Gaylord "admitted his status as a homosexual" * * * [a]nd "from appellant's own testimony it is unquestioned that homosexual acts were participated in by him, although there was no evidence of any overt act having been committed." * * *

This rule of construction concerning his admission of homosexuality is supported by evidence that Gaylord was and had been a homosexual for 20 years. He also testified that in the 2-year period before his discharge, he actively sought out the company of other male homosexuals and participated actively as a member of the Dorian Society (a society of homosexuals). He responded to a blind advertisement in the society's paper for homosexual company. He concealed his homosexuality from his parents until compelled to reveal it by the present dispute.

If Gaylord meant something other than homosexual in the usual sense, he failed to explain what he meant by his admission of homosexuality or being a homosexual so as to avoid any adverse inference, although he had adequate opportunity at trial to do so. He clearly had a right to explain that he was not an overt homosexual and did not engage in the conduct the court ascribed to him which the court found immoral and illegal. Evidence that explains the admission or qualifies it is clearly admissible. * * * There was uncontroverted evidence plaintiff was a competent and intelligent teacher so the court could reasonably assume Gaylord knew what homosexuality could mean. It was not a word to be thoughtlessly or lightly used. Gaylord's precaution for 20 years to keep his status of being a homosexual secret from his parents is eloquent evidence of his knowledge of the serious consequences attendant upon an undefined admission of homosexuality.

He testified that in June 1970 he realized that if he was "ever going to have [homosexual] friends . . . that I needed, that I was going to have to make more efforts of my own to find these people because I wasn't going to stumble across them by accident as I expected." It was about that time he joined the Dorian Society. He testified he "felt very comfortable with the people there." Eventually he began to attend a good many of their functions. On one occasion a high school boy conferred with the plaintiff about homosexuality and learned that plaintiff was "deeply involved" for a period of a month with a person whose advertisement he had answered. It would have been a simple matter for Gaylord to have explained the physical side, if any, of his relationship but he did not do so.

Our next inquiry is whether homosexuality as commonly understood is considered immoral. Homosexuality is widely condemned as immoral and was so condemned as immoral during biblical times. * * *

A sociologist testified in the instant case: "A majority of people and adults in this country react negatively to homosexuality." A psychiatrist testified "I would say in our present culture and certainly, in the last few hundred years in Western Europe and in America this [homosexuality] has been a frightening idea. . . ."

The court found "sexual gratification with a member of one's own sex is implicit in the term 'homosexual.' " * * * This finding would not necessarily apply to latent homosexuals, however, the court in effect found from the evidence and reasonable inferences therefrom, it applied to Gaylord. These acts—sodomy and lewdness—were crimes during the period of Gaylord's employment and at the time of his discharge. * * *

Volitional choice is an essential element of morality. One who has a disease, for example, cannot be held morally responsible for his condition: Homosexuality is not a disease, however. Gaylord's witness, a psychiatrist, testified on cross-examination that homosexuality except in a case of hormonal or congenital defect (not shown to be present here) is not inborn. Most homosexuals have a "psychological or acquired orientation." Only recently the Board of the American Psychiatric Association has stated: "homosexuality . . . by itself does not necessarily constitute a psychiatric disorder." * * *

Nevertheless it is a disorder for those who wish to change their homosexuality which is acquired after birth. In the instant case plaintiff desired no change and has sought no psychiatric help because he feels comfortable with his homosexuality. He has made a voluntary choice for which he must be held morally responsible. * * *

The remaining question on this point is whether the repeal of the sodomy statute (RCW 9.79.100), while this case was pending, deprives sodomy of its immoral character. In the first place the repeal did not go into effect until July 1, 1976, sometime after Gaylord's discharge. Sodomy between consenting adults is no longer a crime. * * * Generally the fact that sodomy is not a crime no more relieves the conduct of its immoral status than would consent to the crime of incest.

The next question is whether the plaintiff's performance as a teacher was sufficiently impaired by his known homosexuality to be the basis for discharge. The court found that Gaylord, prior to his discharge on December 21, 1972, had been a teacher at the Wilson High School in the Tacoma School District No. 10 for over 12 years, and had received favorable evaluations of his teaching throughout this time. * * *

First, he argues his homosexuality became known at the school only after the school made it known and that he should not be responsible therefore so as to justify his discharge as a homosexual. The difficulty with this argument is twofold. First, by seeking out homosexual company he took the risk his homosexuality would be discovered. It was he who granted an interview to the boy who talked to him about his homosexual problems. The boy had been referred to Gaylord for that purpose by the homosexual friend to whom Gaylord had responded favorably in answering his advertisement in the paper of the Dorian Society. As a result of that interview the boy came away with the impression plaintiff was a homosexual and later told the assistant high school principal about the matter. The latter in turn conferred with plaintiff for the purpose of verifying the charge that had been made. It was the vice-principal's duty to report the information to his superiors because it involved the performance capabilities of Gaylord. The school cannot be charged with making plaintiff's condition known so as to defeat the school board's duty to protect the school and the students against the impairment of the learning process in all aspects involved.

Second, there is evidence that at least one student expressly objected to Gaylord teaching at the high school because of his homosexuality. Three fellow teachers testified against Gaylord remaining on the teaching staff, testifying it was objectionable to them both as teachers and parents. The vice-principal and the principal, as well as the retired superintendent of instruction, testified his presence on the faculty would create problems. There is conflicting evidence on the issue of impairment but the court had the power to accept the testimony it did on which to base complained of findings. * * * The testimony of the school teachers and administrative personnel constituted substantial evidence sufficient to support the findings as to the impairment of the teacher's efficiency.

It is important to remember that Gaylord's homosexual conduct must be considered in the context of his position of teaching high school students. Such students could treat the retention of the high school teacher by the school board as indicating adult approval of his homosexuality. It would be unreasonable to assume as a matter of law a teacher's ability to perform as a teacher required to teach principles of morality * * * is not impaired and creates no danger of encouraging expression of approval and of imitation. Likewise to say that school directors must wait for prior specific overt expression of homosexual conduct before they act to prevent harm from one who chooses to remain "erotically attracted to a notable degree towards persons of his own sex and is psychologically, if not actually disposed to engage in sexual activity prompted by this attraction" is to ask the school directors to take an unacceptable risk in discharging their fiduciary responsibility of managing the affairs of the school district.

* * * It must be shown that "the conduct of the individual may reasonably be expected to interfere with the ability of the person's fitness in the job or against the ability to discharge its responsibility." * * * These principles are similar to those applicable here. The challenged findings and conclusions are supported by substantial evidence.

Affirmed.

DOLLIVER, Associate Justice (dissenting).

The appellant, Mr. Gaylord, had been a teacher at Wilson High School for over 12 years at the time of his discharge. In college, he had been an outstanding scholar: he graduated Phi Beta Kappa from the University of Washington and was selected "Outstanding Senior" in the political science department. He later received a masters degree in librarianship. As a teacher, the evaluations made of Mr. Gaylord were consistently favorable. The most recent evaluation of this teaching performance stated that "Mr. Gaylord continues his high standards and thorough teaching performance. He is both a teacher and student in his field."

Despite this outstanding record, the trial court found that Mr. Gaylord should be discharged for "immorality." To uphold this dismissal, we must find substantial evidence supporting the finding that Mr. Gaylord was discharged for "sufficient cause."

* * *

There is not a shred of evidence in the record that Mr. Gaylord participated in any of the acts stated above. While we have held in the past that "sufficient cause" requires certain *conduct* * * * , we are presented here with a record showing no illegal or immoral conduct; we have only an admission of a homosexual status and Gaylord's testimony that he sought male companionship. * * *

Undoubtedly there are individuals with a homosexual identity as there are individuals with a heterosexual identity, who are not sexually active. Mr. Gaylord, for all we know, may be one of these individuals. Certainly in this country we should be beyond drawing severe and far-reaching inferences from the admission of a status—a status which may be no more than a state of mind. Furthermore, there are homosexual activities involving a physical relationship which are not prohibited by statute. * * *

The trial court made a most puzzling finding that, "From appellant's own testimony it is unquestioned that homosexual acts were participated in by him, although there was no evidence of any overt acts having been committed." The trial court essentially found that, as an admitted homosexual, unless Mr. Gaylord denied doing a particular immoral or illegal act, he can be assumed to have done the act. The court has placed upon the appellant the burden to negate what it asserts are the implications that may be drawn from his testimony although he never was accused of participating in acts of sodomy or lewdness.

We must require here, as we have done in the past, proof of conduct to justify a dismissal. The only conceivable testimony on conduct was the comment of the student that Gaylord and another male were "deeply involved" for about a month. This hardly qualifies as testimony either as to "immorality," sodomy or lewdness. Finding no conduct, I am unwilling to take the leap in logic accepted by the majority that admission of a status or identity implies the commission of certain illegal or immoral acts.

Surely the majority has adopted a novel approach. Mr. Gaylord was never at any time accused of performing any "homosexual acts." Yet because of his declared status, he must assume the burden of proving he did not commit certain illegal or immoral acts which have at no time been referred to or mentioned, much less described, by the school board. Presumably under this reasoning, an unmarried male who declares himself to be heterosexual will be held to have engaged in "illegal or immoral acts." The opportunities for industrious school districts seem unlimited.

The majority goes to great lengths to differentiate between an overt and a latent homosexual. Authority is cited that overt homosexuality is "consciously experienced and expressed in actual homosexual behavior." Yet there is no evidence in the record of any actual behavior of acts, and the findings of the trial court specifically state "there was no evidence of any overt act having been committed." The real problem faced by the majority is that the term "homosexual" is not mentioned once in the Revised Code of Washington. There is no law in this state against being a homosexual. All that is banned (prior to July 1, 1976) are certain acts, none of which Mr. Gaylord was alleged to have committed and none of which can it be either assumed or inferred he committed simply because of his status as a homosexual.

The second glaring error in this proceeding is the respondent's failure to establish that Mr. Gaylord's performance as a teacher was impaired by his homosexuality. As pointed out by the trial court in its findings, the evidence is quite clear that, having been a homosexual for the entire time he taught at Wilson High School, the fact of Mr. Gaylord's homosexuality did not impair his performance as a teacher. In other words, homosexuality per se does not preclude competence. * * *

The evidence before the court is uncontroverted—Mr. Gaylord carefully kept his private life quite separate from the school. * * * He made no sexual advances toward his professional contemporaries or his students. There is absolutely no evidence that Mr. Gaylord failed in any way to perform the duties listed in RCW 28A.67.110. In over 12 years of teaching at the same school, his best friends on the teaching staff were unaware of his homosexuality until the time of his discharge. Gaylord did not use his classroom as a forum for discussing homosexuality. Given the discretion with which Gaylord conducted his private life, it appears that public knowledge of Gaylord's homosexuality occurred, as the trial court found, at the time of his dismissal. * * *

At the trial, a variety of witnesses speculated on the effect that Gaylord's homosexuality might have on his effectiveness in the classroom. The speculation varied considerably. Certainly there were witnesses who testified that Gaylord's effectiveness would be damaged. There were also those who testified to the contrary. As a result, the trial court found that "the continued employment of appellant after he became known as a homosexual would result, had he not been discharged, in confusion, suspicion, fear, expressed parental concern and pressure upon the administration." The question this court must ask is whether a finding of detrimental effect can be made on the basis of conjecture alone.

* * *

Historically, the private lives of teachers have been controlled by the school districts in many ways. There was a time when a teacher could be fired for a marriage, a divorce, or for the use of liquor or tobacco. * * * Although the practice of firing teachers for these reasons has ceased, there are undoubtedly those who could speculate that any of these practices would have a detrimental effect on a teacher's classroom efficiency as well as cause adverse community reaction. I find such speculation to be an unacceptable method for justifying the dismissal of a teacher who has a flawless record of excellence in his classroom performance. * * *

What if Mr. Gaylord's status was as a black, a Roman Catholic, or a young heterosexual single person, instead of a male homosexual? Would his dismissal be handled in such a manner? Mere speculation coupled with status alone is not enough. * * * In this finding, substitute the words "black" or "female" for "homosexual" and the defect of the majority approach is brought into sharp focus.

* * *

Notes and Questions

Gaylord turned on the issues of unfitness and immorality. Other issues in the earliest cases addressed whether or not knowledge of a teacher's homosexuality brought about such a high degree of notoriety and undue attention to the teacher and the school that it rendered him or her unfit to teach. The early decisions based on these issues were uniformly unfavorable to homosexuals who were denied positions, dismissed, or had certificates revoked. See *Jantz v. Muci*, 976 F.2d 623 (10th Cir. 1992), *cert. denied*, 508 U.S. 952 (1993), *Gish v. Board of Education of the Borough of Paramus*, 366 A.2d 1337 (1977), *cert. denied*, 434 U.S. 879 (1977); *Board of Education of Long Beach Unified School District v. Jack M.*, 566 P.2d 602 (Cal. 1977); *Burton v. Cascade School District Union High School No. 5*, 512 F.2d 850 (9th Cir. 1975); *Acanfora v. Board of Education of Montgomery County*, 491 F.2d 498 (4th Cir. 1974), *cert. denied*, 419 U.S. 836 (1974), *McConnell v. Anderson*, 451 F.2d 193 (8th Cir. 1971); and *Morrison v. State Board of Education*, 461 P.2d 375 (Cal. 1969). Recent decisions, however, have increasingly turned on freedom-of-expression issues; namely, whether teachers may publicly express their sexual preferences or advocate homosexuality.

A nontenured vocational guidance counselor informed several colleagues that she was bisexual and had a female lover. In upholding her nonrenewal, a federal appellate court held that her First Amendment rights had not been violated. In citing *Connick v. Myers*, 461 U.S. 138 (1983), the court stated, "If a public employee's statement cannot be fairly characterized as constituting speech on a matter of public concern, it is unnecessary to scrutinize the reasons for the discharge." The court opined that the teacher was speaking in her personal interest and that there was no evidence of any public concern in the high school or community with the issue of bisexuality among school personnel. See *Rowland v. Mad River School District*, 730 F.2d 444 (6th Cir. 1984), *cert. denied*, 470 U.S. 1009 (1985).

The U.S. Court of Appeals for the Tenth Circuit upheld a portion of an Oklahoma statute proscribing homosexual activity, but it declared unconstitutional the portion prohibiting the advocacy of such activity. Specifically, the court found fault with a section that barred "advocating, soliciting, imposing, encouraging or promoting public or private homosexual activity in a manner that creates a substantial risk that such conduct will come to the attention of school children or school employees. . . ." The court stated that this provision purported to regulate "pure speech" and that the First Amendment protects advocacy of legal as well as illegal conduct as long as such advocacy does not incite imminent lawlessness. See *National Gay Task Force v. Board of Education of Oklahoma City*, 729 F.2d 1270 (10th Cir. 1984), *aff'd by an equally divided Court*, 470 U.S. 903 (1985).

Homosexual teachers have prevailed in two decisions decided in the late 1990s. In *Glover v. Williamsburg Local School District Board of Education*, 20 F.Supp.2d 1160 (Ohio 1998), a gay teacher claimed his nonrenewal was based on discrimination because of his sexual orientation. The court found that administrators and board members had acted on the basis of false rumors that he had held hands at school with his partner during a holiday party. In its decision, the court criticized the defendants for accepting the rumor as fact, not confronting Glover with the rumors, lowering evaluations of Glover due in large part to the defendants' reliance on false rumors, and board members' testimony that was contradictory and not entirely credible. The court held that he was discriminated against by the board's action and stated that: "Homosexuals, while not a 'suspect class' for equal protection analysis, are entitled to at least the same protection as any other identifiable group which is subject to disparate treatment by the state." Glover received $46,492 for lost salary for two years, $25,000 for anguish and humiliation, in addition to attorneys fees and costs. In *Weaver v. Nebo School District*, 29 F.Supp.2d 1279 (Utah 1998) a school district sought to restrict a lesbian teacher's right to express her sexual orientation outside the classroom in addition to not rehiring her as volleyball coach. In its decision, the court found that the a community's perception about Weaver based on nothing more than unsupported assumptions, outdated stereotypes, and animosity did not furnish a rational basis for not rehiring her as volleyball coach. Regarding her free speech restriction, the court held: "As impermissible as it is to restrict a state employee's right to speak on a matter of public concern, it is equally impermissible to retaliate against that employee when he or she does indeed speak on a matter of public concern." The court ordered that Weaver be offered the volleyball coaching position and that letters requesting her not to discuss her homosexuality be removed from her personnel file.

Nationwide, the issue of gay rights continues to be increasingly controversial. An examination of governmental action reveals endeavors that may be described as being both pro- and anti-gay. Anti-gay actions include federal and state legislation that does not recognize gay marriage and court approval of the military policy requiring separation from service of homosexuals. In 1996, the Defense of Marriage Act was passed, which stated that the federal government would not recognize gay marriages and allowed states to refuse to recognize such marriages licensed in other states. Presently, more than 30 states have passed laws denying recognition of same-sex marriages. The military's policy of "Don't Ask, Don't Tell" for homosexuals, which if violated, provides for discharge from the military, has been upheld by several federal appellate courts. See, for instance, *Thomasson* v. *Perry*, 80 F.3d 915 (4th Cir. 1996), *cert. denied*, 519 U.S. 948 (1996) and *Able* v. *United States*, 155 F.3d 628 (2nd Cir. 1998). In these cases, the courts have upheld separation from the service if a person has stated that he or she is a homosexual.

There has also been governmental action that may be perceived as being pro-gay, resulting in homosexuals receiving protections and rights that they heretofore did not have. Presently, ten states (California, Connecticut, Hawaii, Massachusetts, Minnesota, New Hampshire, New Jersey, Rhode Island, Vermont, and Wisconsin) and the District of Columbia have passed laws prohibiting discrimination on the basis of sexual orientation in such areas as employment, housing, public accommodations, education, and credit. Several cities have passed antidiscrimination ordinances aimed at broadening employment protection for homosexuals by focusing on "job relatedness" as a basis for dismissal. In 2000, Vermont's legislature authorized "civil unions," which extended spousal rights for gay couples to areas covered by state law. Antisodomy statutes, which existed in all 50 states as recently as the 1960s, are coming under increased legal and legislative pressure. Presently, sodomy statutes that prohibit consensual sodomy among same-sex couples remain in only a handful of states. Teachers were often dismissed on the basis of their violating such statutes. *Romer* v. *Evans*, 517 U.S. 620 (1996) was instrumental in the drive to repeal antisodomy laws. In that case, the Court held that an amendment to Colorado's constitution, prohibiting any legislation or judicial action designed to protect the status of a person based on sexual orientation, violated the Fourteenth Amendment. The Court noted that the "inevitable inference" that arises from laws of this sort is that it is "born of animosity toward the class of persons affected."

Governmental actions that are designed to protect the rights of homosexuals in the larger population have special significance for the legal status of homosexuals employed in education. Striking down sodomy statutes, allowing "civil unions," and passing laws or ordinances that prohibit discrimination based on sexual orientation make it difficult, if not impossible, in states having taken these measures, to uphold the denial of employment or the discharge of homosexuals.

In retrospect, have the public schools had an unofficial "Don't Ask, Don't Tell" policy over the years? A reading of several early decisions reveals that some courts held that teaching effectiveness was impaired if homosexual teachers brought undue attention to themselves by acknowledging their sexual orientation. Did this suggest that homosexuality among teachers was acceptable if it was not admitted or overt? Would *Gaylord* be decided the same way today? Would geography be a major factor?

B. Adulterous Teacher

ERB v. *IOWA STATE BOARD OF PUBLIC INSTRUCTION*
Supreme Court of Iowa, 1974
216 N.W.2d 339

McCORMICK, Justice.

In this appeal plaintiff Richard Arlan Erb challenges the revocation of his teaching certificate. The certificate was revoked by defendant Board of Educational Examiners after a hearing on July 16, 1971. Erb brought an action in certiorari alleging the board's action was illegal. After the trial the writ of certiorari was annulled. Erb appealed. We reverse.

* * *

Erb, a native Iowan, military veteran, and holder of a master's degree in fine arts, received his Iowa teaching certificate in 1963. Since then he has taught art in the Nishna Valley Community School which serves an area including the towns of Strahn, Emerson, Hastings, and Stanton. He resides in Emerson, is married and has two young sons. In addition to teaching he has coached wrestling, assisted with football, and acted as senior class sponsor.

The complaint against Erb was made by Robert M. Johnson, a farmer whose wife Margaret taught home economics in the Nishna Valley School. Johnson told the board his goal was removal of Erb from the school and not revocation of his teaching certificate. He read an extensive statement in which he detailed his observations relating to an adulterous liaison between Erb and Johnson's wife which began and ended in spring 1970.

Margaret planned to quit teaching and open a boutique in Red Oak. Her association with Erb began in early spring when he agreed to assist her with design of the store. They saw each other often. By May, Johnson became suspicious of Margaret's frequent late-night absences from home. He suspected Margaret and Erb were meeting secretly and engaging in illicit activity in the Johnson automobile. One night in May he hid in the trunk of the car. Margaret drove the car to school, worked there for some time, and later drove to a secluded area in the country where she met Erb. Margaret and Erb had sexual intercourse in the back seat of the car while Johnson remained hidden in the trunk. Johnson did not disclose his presence or his knowledge of the incident.

Instead he consulted a lawyer with a view toward divorcing Margaret. He told the board he was advised his interests in a divorce action would be better served if he had other witnesses to his wife's misconduct. After several days of fruitless effort to catch Margaret and Erb in a compromising situation, he and his "raiding party" eventually located them one night in June parked in a remote area. Johnson and the others surrounded the car and took photographs of Margaret and Erb who were partially disrobed in the back seat. Johnson told Margaret not to come home and that further communication would be through lawyers. He told Erb to disclose the affair to his wife.

Erb did so. He and Margaret terminated their affair. Erb offered to resign his teaching position, but the local school board unanimously decided not to accept his resignation. The board president testified Erb's teaching was highly rated by his principal and superintendent, he had been forgiven by his wife and the student body, and he had maintained the respect of the community. Erb was retained for the ensuing school year and continued to teach in the Nishna Valley school.

Witnesses before the board included Erb's past and present high school principals, his minister, a parent of children in the school, and a substitute teacher. All vouched for his character and fitness to teach. His superintendent gave essentially the same testimony in district court. The board refused to allow Erb's attorney to cross-examine Johnson or two witnesses in support of Erb's character and fitness to teach. Trial court ruled in its pretrial order that under the admitted record Erb's teacher-student relationship had not been impaired by his conduct.

The board voted five to four to revoke Erb's teaching certificate and, without making any findings of fact or conclusions of law, ordered it revoked. Revocation was stayed by trial court and then by this court pending outcome of the certiorari action and appeal. Trial court held Erb's admitted adulterous conduct was sufficient basis for revocation of his certificate and annulled the writ.

* * * In this appeal Erb contends the board acted illegally (1) in denying his right to cross-examine witnesses against him and limiting the number of his witnesses, (2) in failing to make findings, and (3) in revoking his teaching certificate without substantial evidence that he is not morally fit to teach.

Limitations at the hearing. Erb did not object before the board to the board's denial of his right of cross-examination and limitation on the number of his witnesses. These questions cannot be presented for the first time here. Erb was obliged to raise them before the board and the trial court. ∗ ∗ ∗ Since he did not do so he failed to preserve error in these respects for review here.

Failure of the board to make findings. A different situation exists concerning the board's failure to make findings of fact. Erb's first opportunity to complain of the absence of board findings was in his certiorari action, and he did raise the issue there. We hold the board acted illegally in failing to make findings of fact.

Although Iowa does not have an administrative procedure act to guide administrative boards, we have held such boards are required, even without statutory mandate, to make findings of fact on issues presented in any adjudicatory proceeding. Such findings must be sufficiently certain to enable a reviewing court to ascertain with reasonable certainty the factual basis and legal principle upon which the administrative body acted. ∗ ∗ ∗

The board violated this precept in the present case. No findings were made. This would be sufficient basis to hold trial court should have sustained the writ of certiorari. However, reversing the case on that basis would return the case to the board which could make its findings on the present record and would not answer the remaining issue whether there is substantial evidence in the record which would permit the board to find Erb is not morally fit to teach. If that issue is resolved favorably to Erb, the case will be ended now in his favor rather than sent back to the board for findings.

Sufficiency of the evidence. Since the board made no findings there is no intelligible way to determine what interpretation the board gave to its statutory authorization to revoke the certificate of one not "morally fit to teach." But nothing prevents us from determining whether there is substantial evidence in the record which would have supported revocation if the proper standard had been applied. Erb contends there is not. We agree. We will first examine the standard and then the sufficiency of the evidence.

This court has not previously been called upon to decide what constitutes moral unfitness to teach. The legislature provided no definition in code chapter 260.

∗ ∗ ∗

The board contends the fact Erb admitted adultery is sufficient in itself to establish his unfitness to teach. This assumes such conduct automatically and invariably makes a person unfit to teach. We are unwilling to make that assumption. It would vest the board with unfettered power to revoke the certificate of any teacher whose personal, private conduct incurred its disapproval regardless of its likely or actual effect upon his teaching. The legislature did not give the board that kind of power in Code § 260.23. The label applied to the teacher's conduct is only a lingual abstraction until given content by its likely or actual effect on his fitness to teach. *Morrison* v. *State Board of Education*, 461 P.2d 375, 394 (Cal. 1969); ∗ ∗ ∗ 68 Am Jur. 2d

Schools § 134 at 465 ("Where the courts have been presented with the question whether or not specific conduct of a teacher constitutes moral unfitness which would justify revocation, they have apparently required that the conduct must adversely affect the teacher–student relationship before revocation will be approved.").

As observed by the Morrison court, "Surely incidents of extramarital heterosexual conduct against a background of years of satisfactory teaching would not constitute 'immoral conduct' sufficient to justify revocation of a life diploma without any showing of an adverse effect on fitness to teach." * * *

We emphasize the board's power to revoke teaching certificates is neither punitive nor intended to permit exercise of personal moral judgment by members of the board. Punishment is left to the criminal law, and the personal moral views of board members cannot be relevant. A subjective standard is impermissible and contrary to obvious legislative intent. The sole purpose of the board's power under § 260.23 is to provide a means of protecting the school community from harm. Its exercise is unlawful to the extent it is exercised for any other purpose. In Morrison the California court discussed factors relevant to application of the standard:

> "In determining whether the teacher's conduct thus indicates unfitness to teach the board may consider such matters as the likelihood that the conduct may have adversely affected students or fellow teachers, the degree of such adversity anticipated, the proximity or remoteness in time of the conduct, the type of teaching certificate held by the party involved, the extenuating or aggravating circumstances, if any, surrounding the conduct, the praiseworthiness or blameworthiness of the motives resulting in the conduct, the likelihood of the recurrence of the questioned conduct, and the extent to which disciplinary action may inflict an adverse impact or chilling effect upon the constitutional rights of the teacher involved or other teachers." * * *

These factors have relevance in deciding whether a teacher is morally fit to teach under Code § 260.2. Since the same standard is applicable in determining whether a certificate should be revoked under Code § 260.23, a certificate can be revoked only upon a showing before the board of a reasonable likelihood that the teacher's retention in the profession will adversely affect the school community.

There was no evidence of such adverse effect in the present case. No one even asserted such an effect. The complainant himself acknowledged his purpose was to remove Erb from the school rather than from teaching. The evidence showed Erb to be a teacher of exceptional merit. He is dedicated, hardworking and effective. There was no evidence to show his affair with Margaret Johnson had or is likely to have an adverse effect upon his relationship with the school administration, fellow teachers, the student body, or the community. Overwhelming and uncontroverted evidence of local regard and support for Erb is a remarkable testament to the ability of a community to understand, forgive and reconcile.

There was no evidence other than that Erb's misconduct was an isolated occurrence in an otherwise unblemished past and is not likely to recur. The conduct itself was not an open or public affront to community mores; it became public only because it was discovered with considerable effort and made public by others. * * * Erb made no effort to justify it; instead he sought to show he regretted it, it did not reflect his true character, and it would not be repeated.

* * * [W]e are persuaded the evidence adduced before the board would not support a finding that Erb is morally unfit to teach in Iowa.

The board acted illegally in revoking his certificate. Trial court erred in annulling the writ of certiorari.

Reversed.

Note

Changing American mores and a lack of agreed upon societal standards regarding "proper" conduct in American life would make it an unwarranted invasion of privacy for local school boards, other than in some insular communities, to attempt to monitor the private lives, especially living arrangements, of its teachers. However, such reasoning would not necessarily apply to private school employment. A female Catholic school teacher's contract was not renewed because she had an adulterous affair with a married father of three children enrolled in the same school. In upholding the nonrenewal, the court in *Gosche v. Calvert High School*, 997 F.Supp. 867 (Ohio 1998), *aff'd*, 181.F.3d 101 (6th Cir. 1999) held that Gosche was not meeting her employer's contractual expectations under which she agreed "by word and example . . . to reflect the values of the Catholic Church."

C. Criminal Activities

GILLETT v. *UNIFIED SCHOOL DISTRICT NO. 276*
Supreme Court of Kansas, 1980
605 P.2d 105

PRAGER, Justice:
This case involves a controversy between a schoolteacher and school board over the nonrenewal of her teaching contract. Unified school district No. 276 appeals from a judgment of the district court reversing the school

board's decision not to renew the teacher's employment contract. The trial court ordered the teacher to be reinstated with back pay.

The facts in the case are not greatly in dispute and essentially are as follows: Unified school district No. 276 is located in Jewell County. Jessie Mae Gillett is a tenured teacher who had been continuously employed by the school district for a period of seven years. Her last term of employment covered the 1976–77 school year. On March 11, 1977, the school board delivered to Mrs. Gillett a notice of nonrenewal of her teaching contract for the following year pursuant to K.S.A. 1977 Supp. 72–5437. The notice, which was contained in a letter from the president and clerk of the school board, was in the form required by statute. The reason given for nonrenewal was the existence of criminal charges of shoplifting pending against Mrs. Gillett in Hastings, Nebraska. Mrs. Gillett promptly filed a request for a due process hearing on the matter. On May 5, 1977, the board served on the teacher a notice which contained a supplemental list of reasons for nonrenewal including the following:

1. Inability to properly handle school funds;
2. Excessive absences from teaching school duties for allegedly being ill;
3. Improper use of sick leave;
4. Physical and mental instability; and
5. Loss of community, student, and school board respect for this teacher.

Mrs. Gillett, through her counsel, objected to the consideration of the supplemental reasons contending they were not timely served. The hearing committee overruled the objection, stating that it would consider the supplementary reasons.

* * *

The recommendation of the hearing committee was delivered to the school board, which considered all of the evidence presented in the case together with arguments and briefs of counsel. The board unanimously decided to follow its previous decision of nonrenewal of Mrs. Gillett's contract. The board made no findings of fact and gave no specific reason in writing for rejecting the committee's recommendation. Mrs. Gillett then appealed the school board's decision to the district court, using K.S.A. 60–2101(d) as required by K.S.A. 1977 Supp. 72–5443. The district court reviewed the transcript of the evidence presented at the due process hearing and heard arguments of counsel. The district court entered judgment in favor of Mrs. Gillett, ordering her reinstated with back pay. * * *

* * *

The primary issue raised on this appeal is whether the district court erred in holding that the school board had failed to present substantial evidence to support its reason for nonrenewal. From the evidentiary record in the case, we have concluded that there was substantial competent evidence showing good cause which justified the school board in its decision not to renew the teaching contract of Mrs. Gillett. In the original notice of nonrenewal served on the teacher on March 11, 1977, the reason given for nonrenewal was the criminal charges pending against Mrs. Gillett in Hastings, Nebraska. The evidence of the pendency of these two criminal cases was undisputed. Although Mrs. Gillett did not take the stand herself, the evidence presented on her behalf showed without question that she had taken articles at two stores in Hastings, Nebraska, on October 16, and November 17, 1976. The teacher did not deny that she took the articles of property. Her defense to the accusation was that, because of her mental condition at the time, she was not criminally responsible for her actions. Dr. Dale W. Peters, a practicing psychiatrist, testified that he was a consultant to the Sunflower Guidance Center in Concordia. Mrs. Gillett was referred to that center for psychiatric evaluation in March of 1977. Dr. Peters examined her to determine her mental capacity and state of health, primarily for determining her mental state in relationship to the shoplifting incidents in Hastings, Nebraska. From these examinations, he concluded that, although she was not mentally ill, she was subject to altered states of consciousness resulting from sensitive reactions to a wide variety of foods. Various tests showed her sensitive to numerous foods which at times interfered with the functioning of her brain cells. During these attacks, she would become mentally disturbed and her judgment adversely affected.

At the time of her arrests in Hastings, Nebraska, it appeared that Mrs. Gillett was acting strangely and out of touch with reality. The thrust of Dr. Peters testimony was that, at the time of the shoplifting incidents in Hastings, Nebraska, Mrs. Gillett, being in an altered state of consciousness, was not responsible for her actions. The evidence showed that she had been involved in another shoplifting incident in 1973. Apparently on a number of occasions, she had become confused and lost while driving her motor vehicle. Each of these situations involved an altered state of consciousness which came on gradually. Dr. Peters testified that acute episodes can be dramatic. Such episodes could last up to one hour and could occur at any time, including during classroom hours. Dr. Peters conceded that Mrs. Gillett could again be involved in shoplifting incidents in the future and that she was still under treatment at the time of the hearing. Although Dr. Peters was of the opinion that there was no danger to the students in the classroom, he indicated an attack during class could be disruptive. Similar attacks could occur either from the consumption of certain foods or from a withdrawal from such foods. At the time of the hearing Mrs. Gillett was in the course of an elimination diet which, hopefully, might eliminate her problem. If it did not work, then additional testing and treatment would be required. Dr. Peters mentioned over 80 foods which could cause Mrs. Gillett to go into an altered state of consciousness. He further stated that this list was inconclusive and that there might be other foods which could affect her in the same way.

A teacher testified that at one time she had observed Mrs. Gillett in an altered state of consciousness while seated in her automobile. After the arrests at Hastings, she heard a student discussing the fact that Mrs. Gillett had been arrested. Another teacher testified that she had also heard students mention the fact that Mrs. Gillett had been arrested. This was the first time the teacher had known about it. There was no evidence presented at the hearing as to the ultimate outcome of the criminal actions. There was testimony tending to show that Mrs. Gillett had been careless in keeping candy sale proceeds in her desk drawer and in failing to make daily deposits at the bank as directed by the school superintendent. However, there was no proof of any misappropriation or loss of any money as the result of Mrs. Gillett's handling of the school funds. In regard to excessive absences from teaching duties for allegedly being ill, the record is devoid of any misconduct on the part of the teacher in this regard. In regard to loss of community, student, and school respect for the teacher, the president of the school board testified that in his opinion the school board had community support in the nonrenewal of Mrs. Gillett's contract. A substitute teacher testified about a classroom incident where students were caught copying. When she told them copying wasn't allowed, the students responded: "The teacher can get away with it."

Mr. Ralph Hooten, who was president of the school board at the time the letter of nonrenewal was delivered to Mrs. Gillett, testified that the school board had unanimously decided that Mrs. Gillett's teaching contract should not be renewed because of the criminal charges of shoplifting pending in Nebraska. This conclusion was reached only after substantial discussion by the board over a period of hours. The board had concluded that these shoplifting charges reduced her efficiency as a teacher. It appeared to him that, with the charges pending, the learning atmosphere would be improved if her contract was not renewed. Mr. Hooten stated that the board was aware of a similar charge of shoplifting in the year 1973 which was subsequently dismissed. At the time the board decided not to pursue the matter further. When the charges came up again in 1976, the board felt that they could not ignore those charges, having knowledge of the prior incident in 1973. It is fair to conclude, from Mr. Hooten's testimony, that the school board was very much concerned about the criminal charges against Mrs. Gillett, that the board spent hours discussing the situation, and that they decided to nonrenew her contract rather than to terminate her in midyear.

The issue to be determined here is whether there is substantial evidence in the record sufficient to establish good cause, justifying the school board's decision of nonrenewal of the teaching contract. The district court found that there was not. We have concluded there was. The problem presented in this case was obviously one of great difficulty for the school board. The trial court specifically found that the school board had not arbitrarily and fraudulently refused to accept the findings of the hearing committee. The district court was correct in that finding. It is difficult to reconcile that finding with the additional finding that there was no substantial evidence to support the board's reason for nonrenewal. Here the evidence was undisputed that, for a period of at least three years, the teacher had been subject to altered states of consciousness, during which she did not know what she was doing and her judgment and her conduct were adversely affected. At the time of the hearing, a testing and treatment program for Mrs. Gillett had been undertaken but not completed. She was attempting to get to the cause of her problem and was taking appropriate action to do something about it. However, we do not believe that, at that time, the school board acted unreasonably in concluding that it would be for the best interests of the school system to nonrenew Mrs. Gillett's teaching contract for the following school year.

We think it significant that in this case the teacher did not personally take the witness stand to give her own explanation as to her physical and mental condition or to deny that she, knowingly with larcenous intent, took property from the stores in Hastings, Nebraska. She did not testify that the treatment then being administered was effective or was beginning to solve her problem. She did not testify as to her relationship with the students, or with other teachers, or with the school administrators. Not a single witness testified as to any contributions she was making to the educational program of the school district.

We cannot in good conscience find from the evidence that the board's action was not taken in good faith, or that it was arbitrary, irrational, unreasonable, or irrelevant to the school board's objective of maintaining an efficient school system for the students in the school district. It follows that the judgment of the district court must be reversed and the case remanded to the district court with directions to enter judgment in favor of the school board.

It is so ordered.

Notes

In a similar case, a permanent teacher's indefinite contract was terminated because of three instances of alleged immoral conduct: stealing a teapot that was a prop in a school play, stealing twenty dollars from a basketball game's receipts, and stealing a set of the school's books. See *Kimble* v. *Worth County R-III Board of Education*, 669 S.W.2d 949 (Mo. Ct. App. 1984).

A teacher who had pled guilty to possession of marijuana and cocaine in a criminal proceeding was not reinstated to his teaching position after his criminal record had been expunged. The court, in *Dubuclet* v. *Home Insurance Company*, 660 So.2d 67 (La. Ct. App. 1995), contended that expungement did not erase the fact that he had committed the act, nor did it erase the moral turpitude of the teacher's conduct.

Failure to take appropriate measures in response to her husband's use of the family home for growing and selling marijuana was not held to be a "neglect of duty" on a teacher's part, and her reinstatement by the Oregon Fair Dismissal Appeal Board was upheld. See *Kari v. Jefferson County School District*, 852 P.2d 235 (Or. Ct. App. 1993).

D. Impropriety with Students

BARCHESKI v. BOARD OF EDUCATION OF GRAND RAPIDS PUBLIC SCHOOLS
Court of Appeals of Michigan, 1987
412 N.W.2d 296

PER CURIAM.

* * *

On October 18, 1976, the Board of Education of the Grand Rapids Public Schools voted to proceed on three charges brought against petitioner. * * * Those charges were as follows:

"1. That on or about August 10, 1976, Mr. Barcheski invited two female members of his driver education class to a party to be held on Friday night, August 13, 1976, the night before the raft race.
"2. The two female students attended the party and drank beer and smoked pot during the evening in the presence of Mr. Barcheski.
"3. Mr. Barcheski took one of the female students, Mary . . . , home in his automobile after leaving the party. Mary . . . was 15 years of age at the time in question. On the way to the residence of Mary . . . , Mr. Barcheski parked his automobile and had sexual intercourse with [her] in his automobile.

* * *

Our review of the record discloses that the tenure commission's findings are supported by substantial, material and competent evidence, and we therefore affirm.

Regarding the first finding, i.e., that petitioner invited two female members of his driver's education class to a party, Commissioner Gibson's majority opinion relied heavily on the credibility of one of petitioner's students, "Mary." Mary admitted to the board of education that she had originally misled board investigators in her account of the party and petitioner's invitation, but stated that shortly thereafter she told them the truth. Mary testified before the board of education that on about August 10, 1976, she discussed an upcoming raft race with petitioner and that petitioner told her that he was going to a party on Friday, August 13, 1976, the night before the raft race. She stated that petitioner invited her and Wendy to attend the party and that the three of them talked about the party "every day" that week. At the tenure commission hearing, Mary's testimony concerning petitioner's alleged invitation was substantially the same as that offered before the board of education.

* * *

Petitioner testified before the board of education that he had never invited the two students to the party. He said that when they asked him one day at the driving range whether he was going to attend the upcoming raft race he told them "no," but explained to them that he went to an annual pre-raft-race party at the Michigan Wheel Test Basin. When they asked where Michigan Wheel was located, he simply gave them directions. Moreover, although he did not specifically remember having written down a telephone number on Wendy's book, he said he often provided his number to students in case they needed a ride home from driver's training classes. Petitioner conceded that, out of fear, he had originally lied to board of education investigators about the girls' presence at the party.

In the tenure commission's decision, Commissioner Gibson gave little weight to the testimony of Wendy and petitioner, finding that the former's midstream change in story which had apparently been precipitated by prior meetings with petitioner and the latter's attempts to persuade Wendy to falsify her testimony seriously jeopardized the credibility of these witnesses. On the other hand, Commissioner Gibson saw no reason not to credit Mary's testimony, even though Mary herself had experienced many personal problems, such as drug and alcohol use and unwed motherhood.

* * *

We believe that the tenure commission majority's finding that petitioner invited at least one female student to the party was supported by competent, material and substantial evidence on the record when viewed as a whole.

* * *

The tenure commission's second finding, i.e., that the two female students drank beer and smoked marijuana in petitioner's presence at the party, is also supported by competent, material and substantial evidence.

Petitioner stated that he arrived at the party at about 7:30 p.m. with two male friends and that about one-half hour later the students arrived. Two friends of petitioner who were at the party said petitioner looked surprised to see the students. There was conflicting testimony as to what occurred when the two students first came in contact with petitioner at the party. Petitioner testified that the students said they were "out partying" and that they looked somewhat "loose," like they had been drinking. Petitioner said that he introduced the students to his friends and chatted with them for about ten minutes, after which they disappeared. Petitioner said he never told the students to leave because he thought they had left on their own. He acknowledged that fifteen minutes after he initially saw the two students he saw Wendy standing down near the cement foundation of a metal derrick constructed on the riverbank, but that thereafter he saw neither of the students until preparing to leave the party several hours later. He testified that he spent most of the party in an out-of-the-way spot behind a wrecker parked next to the Michigan Wheel building, some seventy feet from the derrick where the students allegedly spent most of their evening. It was undisputed that many of those attending the party were drinking alcoholic beverages and smoking marijuana.

Mary admitted to the board of education that she and Wendy had smoked two "bowls" (two pipes full) of marijuana and had drunk several beers before having arrived at the party. She also testified that when they arrived, petitioner gave them some beer and that, during the course of the evening, they smoked marijuana in petitioner's presence. Before the tenure commission, Mary altered her testimony somewhat and testified that petitioner had not handed them their first beer but had, instead, directed them to a refrigerator where they could get their own. Petitioner and several of his friends denied that petitioner had ever given the students beer at the party.

* * *

Both before the board of education and the tenure commission Mary testified that she had smoked marijuana and had drunk beer in petitioner's presence at the party. At the board of education hearing, Wendy also affirmed that Mary had smoked marijuana and had drunk beer in front of petitioner. She noted, however, that she intentionally hid her own marijuana smoking from petitioner out of embarrassment.

Before the tenure commission, Wendy recanted part of her board of education testimony. She testified that neither she nor Mary smoked marijuana or drank beer in petitioner's presence during the party. Six of petitioner's friends testified that although each had seen the students smoke marijuana and drink beer at the party, this had never taken place in petitioner's presence.

Some of Wendy's unrecanted testimony weakened petitioner's blanket denial that he had lost sight of the two students through most of the middle portion of the party. Wendy testified before the tenure commission that during the party petitioner and Wendy would sometimes see each other and acknowledge each other's presence with a smile. Wendy also reluctantly testified before the tenure commission that she had seen a blonde-haired woman next to petitioner and later at the party, or at some later time, had asked petitioner if the woman was his wife. Petitioner's wife testified before the board of education that she arrived at the party at about 8:30 p.m. and that she and her husband spent most of their time in the cement area down by the river, an area very near the derrick where the two students spent most of their evening.

Wendy also gave unrecanted testimony before the board of education that just before leaving the party, Mary was sitting in a police car with her arm around petitioner and at one point reached over and kissed him. Wendy said that both she and Mary drank beer during this time by the police car. Petitioner conceded before the tenure commission that just as he was leaving the party he saw the two students standing next to a police car drinking beer. Observing that the students were intoxicated, petitioner convinced a friend to drive the students home. Petitioner, two of his male friends, Mary and Wendy then left the party together in a car.

Thus, besides the direct testimony of Mary, who flatly asserted that she had smoked marijuana and had drunk beer in petitioner's presence at the party, there was also testimony suggesting that petitioner maintained some visual contact with the students during the party and had spent at least some of his time near where the students were smoking and drinking. Under these circumstances, we cannot conclude that the tenure commission's finding that the students drank beer and smoked marijuana in petitioner's presence is not supported by substantial evidence.

* * *

Next, petitioner argues that the tenure commission improperly made its third finding regarding petitioner's having driven Mary home alone after the party because he was never put on notice that taking the student home by itself constituted a basis for a charge of wrongful conduct.

* * *

Based on petitioner's own testimony, however, we believe that petitioner was, or should have been, well aware that taking Mary, a young, intoxicated female student home alone in his car constituted, by itself, grounds for discipline. Petitioner stated that the students appeared intoxicated when they arrived at the party and were in even worse shape when he found them several hours later as he was leaving the party. Moreover, petitioner testified that on previous occasions, he had asked another driver's training instructor to give Mary a ride home because he thought she had a "crush" on him. Petitioner also explained that on one occasion Mary had placed her head on his shoulder while his class was watching a movie. As noted previously, Wendy testified that at the end of the party Mary put her arm around petitioner and kissed him. Wendy gave unrecanted testimony that when petitioner's friend, Michael Maxim, gave the two students and petitioner a ride to the social hall where petitioner had left his car, Mary kept her hand near the zipper of petitioner's pants and that petitioner made no effort to remove it. Mary herself said that she and petitioner kissed passionately while riding in the back seat of Maxim's car.

Given this factual scenario and the earlier findings of the board of education on this issue, petitioner was adequately put on notice that driving Mary home alone constituted by itself conduct supporting a charge of improper or wrongful conduct which could properly be considered in deciding whether a penalty would be appropriate.

* * *

For the foregoing reasons, the circuit court's affirmance of the tenure commission's ruling that petitioner's discharge was based on reasonable and just cause is affirmed.

Affirmed.

Notes

Dismissal was upheld of a tenured middle school teacher accused of "inappropriate conduct." The teacher had made repeated offensive sexual statements toward female students and placed his hand on a student's back and snapped her bra strap. See *Knowles* v. *Board of Education*, 857 P.2d 553 (Colo. Ct. App. 1993).

Termination of a teacher who was tried by his school for sexual misconduct occurring twenty-four years earlier was upheld. The teacher objected to the school publicizing his disciplinary conviction; however, the court in *De Michele* v. *Greenburgh Central School District. No. 7*, 167 F.3d 784 (2d Cir. 1999) held that the public had a strong interest in protecting school children from a sexual predator and the public's interest outweighed those of the teacher.

A teacher's dismissal, based on a grand jury's indictment for sexual misconduct with teenage pupils, was upheld. Although the teacher was not provided a hearing before the school board to refute the allegations of misconduct, the court ruled that the dismissal did not violate his right of due process. In the event that the school board brought the charges, the court held, the teacher would have been entitled to a hearing before the board. The court stated:

> After the grand jury had acted, the issue for the board was not whether Moore had committed the acts charged by the girls or whether he was guilty or innocent under the indictments but whether the existence and pendency of the indictments justified his suspension and the refusal to act upon the matter of his contract renewal. (p. 1073)

See *Moore* v. *Knowles*, 482 F.2d 1069 (5th Cir. 1973).

Revocation of the teaching certificate of a junior high school teacher, accused of immorality because of her sexual misconduct with school-age children, especially a fifteen-year-old male student, was upheld in *Howard* v. *Missouri State Board of Education*, 913 S.W.2d 887 (Mo. Ct. App. 1996). In her defense, the teacher alleged that she was acting under the influence of either mental illness or medications associated with that illness and lacked the intent to commit any immoral act. In rejecting this defense, the court declared that it was not necessary to prove intent in order to revoke a teaching license for immorality.

VII. EMPLOYMENT DISCRIMINATION

Certain personnel practices that have an impact on racial minorities, women, pregnant women, religious groups, older persons, and people with disabilities have been challenged as being discriminatory. Although it has been argued that some of these practices may have reflected custom and did not have an overt discriminatory intent when instituted, those directly affected by them have alleged that they were in fact discriminatory.

In addition to constitutional protections under the Fourteenth Amendment's Equal Protection and Due Process Clauses, several federal statutes protect public school personnel against employment discrimination. These statutes include Sections 1981 through 1983 of Title 42, United States Code; Title IX of the Education Amendments of 1972; the Americans with Disabilities Act of 1990 as amended and Section 504 of the Rehabilitation Act of 1973; the Pregnancy Discrimination Act of 1978; and Title VII of the Civil Rights Act of 1964.* The Civil Rights Act of 1964 was the seminal legislative enactment of the movement to eradicate discrimination in the United States. Title VII, the section dealing with discrimination in both the public and private workplaces, provides in part:

SECTION 703

(a)   It shall be an unlawful employment practice for an employer

   (1) to . . . discriminate against any individual with respect to his compensation, terms, conditions, or privileges of employment, because of such individual's race, color, religion, sex, or national origin; or

   (2) to limit, segregate, or classify his employees or applicants for employment in any way which would deprive or tend to deprive any individual of employment opportunities or otherwise adversely affect his status as an employee, because of such individual's race, color, religion, sex, or national origin.

(e) (1) it shall not be an unlawful employment practice . . . to hire and employ employees . . . on the basis of . . . religion, sex, or national origin in those certain instances where religion, sex, or national origin is a bona fide occupational qualification reasonably necessary to the normal operation of that particular business or enterprise.

(h)   It shall not be an unlawful employment practice . . . to use a bona fide seniority or merit system . . . provided that such differences are not the result of an intention to discriminate. . . . Nor shall it be an unlawful employment practice . . . to give and to act upon the results of any professionally developed ability test, provided that such test, its administration, or action upon the results is not designed, intended, or used to discriminate.

(j)   Nothing contained in this Title shall be interpreted to require any employer . . . to grant preferential treatment to an individual or to any group because of the race, color, religion, sex, or national origin of such individual or group on account of an imbalance which may exist between the percentage employed by any employer and the percentage . . . in any community, State, section, or other area.

SECTION 706

(g)   If the court finds that the [employer] has intentionally engaged in . . . an unlawful employment practice . . . the court . . . may order such affirmative action as may be appropriate.

*See Appendix D for these statutes.

A. Racial Discrimination

Racial discrimination against teachers has been a much-litigated issue since the Supreme Court's decision in *Brown* v. *Board of Education of Topeka*, 347 U.S. 483 (1954), in which *de jure* segregation was declared to be a violation of the Equal Protection Clause of the Fourteenth Amendment. Court-ordered desegregation plans subsequent to *Brown* often contain provisions effectively regulating the hiring, promotion, and dismissal of minority school personnel. Courts also may impose affirmative action plans on school districts that have violated Title VII.

Involuntary termination of black teachers in school systems that have been under court order to desegregate has resulted in severe action against offending school systems. Court action in such cases has included awarding monetary damages, back pay, and attorneys' fees to minority plaintiffs; assessing court costs against defendant school districts; reinstating personnel; freezing the hiring of white teachers; and requiring districts to report all personnel actions to the court for a specified time. Such severe judicial enforcement of desegregation remedies, coupled with the vigorous application of Title VII, has been effective in reducing discriminatory employment practices against black teachers.

Several Supreme Court decisions have addressed the limits of affirmative action plans. Although not a decision dealing with educators, a six-to-three Supreme Court decision upheld the "last-hired–first-fired" principle as applied to Memphis firefighters. The Court asserted that seniority systems, as long as they are unbiased, may not be disrupted to save the jobs of newly hired minority workers. The decision states: "It is inappropriate to deny an innocent employee the benefits of his seniority in order to provide a remedy in a pattern or practice suit such as this." *Firefighters Local Union No. 1784* v. *Stotts*, 467 U.S. 561 (1984).

Additionally, the Supreme Court did not uphold a layoff plan that was part of a school district's collective bargaining agreement. Although the plan called for retaining teachers by seniority, it also stipulated that minorities were not to be dismissed in proportions greater than their representation in the district. When, in accordance with the racially sensitive stipulation, white teachers were terminated instead of less-senior black teachers, the displaced white teachers claimed reverse discrimination. In its five-to-four decision, the Court agreed, holding that the policy was a violation of the nonminority teachers' constitutional equal protection. Racial classifications such as that imposed by the policy were justified only when narrowly tailored to accomplish a compelling state purpose. However, the Court found that other, less intrusive, means were available to the district to accomplish its purpose—for example, the adoption of hiring goals. Although the policy would have been allowable to remedy past *de jure* discrimination, no such finding had been made in court. See *Wygant* v. *Jackson Board of Education*, 476 U.S. 267 (1986).

A federal court rejected an affirmative action plan preferring minority teachers over nonminority teachers when candidates to be laid off appeared to be equally qualified. Under this plan, a white female business education teacher was laid off instead of a black female teacher with the same seniority, solely on the basis of race. The court held that the board's plan violated Title VII, was not adopted to remedy discrimination or the effects of past discrimination, was designed to promote racial diversity for the sake of educational purposes, unnecessarily trammelled nonminority interests, was devoid of goals and governed by the board's whim, and imposed job loss on tenured nonminority employees. See *Taxman* v. *Board of Education of the Township of Piscataway*, 91 F.3d 1547 (3rd Cir. 1996), *cert. dismissed*, 522 U.S. 1010 (1997). Prior to the Supreme Court making its decision, a settlement of $433,500 by the school board, 70 percent of which was paid by the Black Leadership Forum, preempted further Court review. Since the case dealt with the loss of a job, based solely on race, opponents of affirmative action claim that the settlement was effected to prevent a possible Supreme Court assault on both private and public affirmative action programs. Title VII of the Civil Rights Act of 1964 applies to both private and public employment.

A teacher's union challenge to a teacher transfer policy designed to ensure that faculty reflected a systemwide racial balance was not upheld. In its decision, a federal appellate court contended that although the policy was "race conscious," it was "specific race neutral" and had no disparate impact. The court agreed that in "some instances, it will benefit or harm white teachers; in others, it will benefit or harm black teachers." See *Jacobson* v. *Cincinnati Board of Education*, 961 F.2d 100 (6th Cir. 1992).

A Supreme Court decision involving cannery workers in Alaska, *Wards Cove Packing Company* v. *Atonio*, 490 U. S. 642 (1989), had a dramatic, if not chilling, effect on civil rights litigation. Prior to this decision, statistics revealing a racial imbalance between unskilled and more highly skilled positions were, in many instances, sufficient to make out a case of "disparate impact" under Title VII of the Civil Rights Act of 1964. Courts often ruled that disparate impact occurred when an identical standard was equally applied to all applicants or employees, but its application negatively affected some groups such as African Americans. This view was originally established in *Griggs* v. *Duke Power Company*, 401 U.S. 424 (1971), when the Court held that a facially neutral employment practice may be deemed to be violative of Title VII without evidence of an employer's subjective intent to discriminate. The decision in *Wards Cove* significantly altered these notions by holding that statistics alone were not enough to prove discrimination, rather causation must be shown between an employment practice and the alleged disparity in hiring; although minorities may be disproportionately concentrated in unskilled positions, the relevant question is the size of the pool of minority candidates for the higher skilled positions; and the burden of proof is on the plaintiffs to show that employers engage in practices that disproportionately exclude minorities and women.

The Civil Rights Act of 1991 nullified or modified Supreme Court decisions such as *Wards Cove* and several others rendered in the late 1980s that had made it more difficult for workers to win antidiscrimination suits. Under this law, victims of employment bias based on race, sex, disability, religion, or national origin may collect limited compensatory and punitive damages. Damages had heretofore only been available to victims of discrimination based on race. Employment practices, under the Civil Rights Act of 1991, must be "job-related for the position in question and consistent with business necessity." Another major purpose of the law was to return to the standard set by the Supreme Court prior to the *Wards Cove* decision, which required employers to prove that an employment standard that results in adverse impact is necessary for successful job performance.

Although accepting evidence that the school district's overlooking a minority candidate's teaching application was a mistake, a federal court of appeals held that evidence of nepotism and the practice of word-of-mouth hiring had a disparate impact on minorities and were violative of Title VII. See *Thomas* v. *Washington County School Board*, 915 F.2d 922 (4th Cir. 1990).

Title VII was employed by a black assistant principal who had been denied the position of director of vocational education in favor of a white applicant. In upholding the white applicant's selection, a court recognized that superior qualifications were a valid, nondiscriminatory reason. See *Clark* v. *Huntsville City Board of Education*, 717 F.2d 525 (11th Cir. 1983). In another case involving Title VII, a white and more-senior social worker was not retained for her position as part of a reduction in force. In its holding, a court declared that she had not been retained for the position solely because of her race and the school district's desire to fill the position with its only black administrator. Additionally, the court averred that there had been no past discriminatory conduct by the school district in its hiring practices that would justify remedial, race-conscious affirmative action. See *Cunico* v. *Pueblo School District*, 917 F.2d 431 (10th Cir. 1990).

A high school band teacher who failed to have his contract renewed claimed that his discharge was racially discriminatory. Reasons for the nonrenewal included parental concern over disorder and inconsistency in the band program; failure to care for the band's equipment and facilities; the program's being loosely structured; failure to provide leadership or to command respect; and deficiency of organizational skills. The federal appellate court held that "the reasons asserted by the school district may have been based partly on subjective considerations, but they were premised on objective factual observations that clearly constitute legitimate reasons for not renewing the plaintiff's contract." See *Tyler v. Hot Springs School District No. 6*, 827 F.2d 1227 (8th Cir. 1987).

In some instances, teachers and other public school employees are urged not to enroll their children in private schools. A decision, in which a public school secretary was punished for sending her daughter to an all-white private school, stated that such action on the part of the school district violated her civil rights. See *Fyfe v. Curlee*, 902 F.2d 401 (5th Cir. 1990), *cert. denied*, 498 U.S. 940 (1990).

Concern over excellence in the public schools has brought increased attention to the quality of teachers and to the adequacy of teacher-training programs. One result of this concern has been the increased use of competency testing of both prospective and practicing teachers, prior to their certification, hiring, promotion, or retention. Such tests have raised racial discrimination issues because these tests have often had an impact disproportionate on racial minorities. It should be noted that Title VII specifically condones professionally developed employment tests when such tests are not used to discriminate.

To date, teacher competency tests have been challenged, primarily in southern states, on a variety of constitutional and statutory grounds, including alleged racially biased content and alleged failure sufficiently to validate the tests' job relatedness. Courts have found that such testing fulfills a legitimate state function, and they have upheld tests and cutoff scores that objective validation has shown to be indicative of actual job qualifications. The decision in *United States v. South Carolina*, 445 F. Supp. 1094 (S.C. 1977), upheld the use of the National Teacher Examination as a requirement for state certification, despite the fact that its use disproportionately disqualified African Americans. And in *United States v. LULAC*, 793 F.2d 636 (5th Cir. 1986), the Texas Pre-Professional Skills Test, which college students were required to pass before scheduling more than six hours of professional education courses at any state college or university, was upheld. The testing of veteran teachers was upheld in *Texas v. Project Principle*, 724 S.W.2d 387 (Tex. 1987).

B. Sex Discrimination

Although not challenged on the basis of Title VII, *Marshall v. Kirkland* addresses the issue of sex-based discrimination in not hiring females for administrative and specialty positions. The decision depicts a once prevalent attitude about hiring females for other than classroom duties.

MARSHALL v. *KIRKLAND*

United States Court of Appeals, Eighth Circuit, 1979
602 F.2d 1282

HANSON, Senior District Judge.

* * *

Appellants' complaint alleges gender-based discrimination. Women have predominated as teachers in Barton-Lexa School District by a ratio of between three and four to one. Evidence was presented to the district court which indicated that the assignment to "specialty" positions (a position with extra duties for which an increment in compensation was provided), and promotion to one of the three administrative positions in the district (principal of the elementary school, principal of the high school, and superintendent of the district) was influenced by the sex of the employee and statistically favored males with a concomitant differential in pay as between men and women.

The district court concluded:

the plaintiffs have failed in their burden of presenting any testimony to the effect that discrimination due to sex existed within a period of 3 years from the commencement of this litigation.

* * * Plaintiffs appeal from this determination that they failed to prove a prima facie case of sex discrimination.

* * *

* * * The district court held that a prima facie case of unconstitutional sex discrimination had not been made and that no rebuttable presumption arose. We conclude that the district court's finding in this regard is clearly erroneous and contrary to recently articulated constitutional principles with respect to the assignment of specialty personnel and promotion of teachers to administrative positions.

Appellants do not distinguish the elements involved in a constitutional as opposed to a Title VII statutory claim of sex discrimination. The two actions are different, however, as the Supreme Court has recently made clear. The evidence raises the question of whether defendants violated the right of female teachers, administrators, and applicants to equal protection of the law, a claim cognizable under 42 U.S.C. § 1983. Title VII is not involved.

As a general proposition, the equal protection clause of the Fourteenth Amendment, substantively inherent in the Fifth Amendment, grants to public employees "a federal constitutional right to be free from gender discrimination" unless a gender classification serves important governmental objectives and is substantially related to the achievement of those objectives. * * *

In *Feeney* the Supreme Court elaborated on what constitutes "discriminatory purpose": "It implies that the decisionmaker . . . selected or reaffirmed a particular course of action at least in part 'because of,' not merely 'in spite of,' its adverse effects upon an identifiable group." If employment decisions or policies in the public employment area are made in part "because it would accomplish the collateral goal of keeping women in a stereotypic and predefined place," the Constitution is violated. * * *

* * *

The record indicates that during the relevant years there were ten or eleven administrative and specialty positions. As noted, the administrative positions were the superintendent and the elementary and high school principals. The seven or eight specialty positions, which carried an increment in pay because of extra duties involved, consisted of various jobs—coaching, physical education, counselor, agriculture and home economics teachers. The practice of the school district was that the three administrators usually came from the ranks of teachers, and the specialists were of course teachers compensated for extra duties.

With regard to the specialty positions, the home economics and girls' physical education teacher positions were occupied by women during the relevant years, while the other specialty positions were filled by men. Women teachers outnumbered men by a ratio of three or four to one with the net result that all or nearly all male teachers in the district had specialty positions while the great majority of women did not. With regard to pay, the women specialty teachers received less than the males, though this evidence was poorly developed. School board president W. F. Burney testified that "[i]t has . . . been the policy of the school to hire men" for coaching positions, * * * and he agreed "that the men always get specialty jobs and the women almost never get specialty jobs." * * * School superintendent Kirkland, prior to 1973 the principal at the high school and like Burney, a decisionmaker, agreed that the football, basketball, and track coaches had traditionally been men and that, with the exception of the girls' basketball coach (a special pay job established relatively recently), should continue to be men. * * * Kirkland candidly testified:

> [T]here is no evidence, to indicate that only men could perform those jobs, but again, this is something that has been traditionally done in this Country and I concur with it.

* * * He also testified that men had previously taught girls' physical education and that men would be capable of coaching girls' basketball. In contrast, women were not qualified to coach male athletic teams because "I just feel that a man could do [a] better job of handling a group of young men like that, than a woman." * * *

With respect to administrators, the evidence suggests that at the time of trial women were virtually disqualified from holding the position of high school principal and, as a consequence, superintendent. Mrs. Todd, the elementary principal during the relevant years, was the lowest paid of the three administrators. In 1973 David Bagley, a high school teacher, was promoted to high school principal to replace Mr. Kirkland who assumed the duties of

superintendent. Mrs. Todd was concededly better qualified than Bagley, * * *
but was not considered for the job. Mrs. Todd testified and did not indicate
any interest in the high school principal or superintendent positions. However, Superintendent Kirkland did not indicate in his testimony that Todd's
lack of interest was a factor in failing to consider her for the position. Instead,
he testified that Todd was not considered "[b]ecause with the situation we
had, and the students we had, I felt that we needed a man for the job." * * *
Thereupon occurred the following colloquy between appellants' counsel
and Mr. Kirkland:

> Q Now, fully explain that please. The situation you had and the students you
>   had . . .
> A Because with high school students I feel that men are stronger disciplinari-
>   ans than women are, and this particular instance I felt we needed a man in
>   this position because part of the job was to be at athletic events, this sort of
>   thing . . . to see that things . . . everything goes off as it should and I felt that
>   a man could do a better job than a woman.
> Q Well, what is the objective evidence that you have for arriving at the con-
>   clusion that a woman can't do those things?
> A I don't have any, Mr. Walker.
> Q Is that just a natural bias?
> A I suppose it is. * * *

Coupled with objective evidence showing a clear pattern of disproportionate gender representation in administrative and specialty positions, the
testimony of school board president Burney and former principal and superintendent Kirkland strongly indicates that the sex of a teacher was an important
part of assignment and promotion decisions in this area of the school district's
employment. At the very least, appellants made a prima facie showing that de-
cisionmakers in the school district sought to maintain women teachers in a
"stereotypic and predefined place" in the school district and the district court
clearly erred in finding otherwise. * * * Indeed, the testimony of Burney and
Kirkland would support a factual finding that the school district had a discernible policy or practice of hiring only men (or women) for certain specific
administrative or specialty jobs. Such a finding would raise the question of
whether the non-neutral gender classification could be justified as bearing a
close and substantial relationship to important governmental objectives. * * *

* * *

The district court observed that the school district "presented substantial
testimony that no sex discrimination existed in the operation of the school
system," but the court did not elaborate in view of its finding on the prima
facie issue. Accordingly, on remand the district court should, on the basis of
the present record, determine (1) by appropriate order whether the named
plaintiffs may sue as representative parties on behalf of the class of all female
teachers and applicants; (2) if the cause may be maintained as a class action,

whether the evidence of no sex discrimination referred to by the district court rebuts the presumption in favor of class-wide equitable relief ∗ ∗ ∗ ; and (3) whether the presumption in favor of individual relief has been rebutted with respect to those women who testified. Judgment may then be entered on the district court's supplemental findings and conclusions.

∗ ∗ ∗

∗ ∗ ∗ We reverse the district court's dismissal of the class and individual claims for relief predicated on alleged unconstitutional sex discrimination to the extent it relates to the assignment of female teachers to specialty positions and promotion to administrative positions. We remand the cause to the district court for further proceedings consistent with this opinion.

Though the results here are mixed, because on this appeal appellants' counsel has successfully established a prima face case of sex discrimination, we award costs on appeal to appellants including $500 in attorney fees. 42 U.S.C. § 1988.

∗ ∗ ∗

Notes

Does Kirkland's attitude about hiring females still prevail today?

See *Jepsen* v. *Florida Board of Regents*, 610 F.2d 1379 (5th Cir. 1980) for an action brought under Title VII.

Title IX regulations were vague on the question of whether the amendment covered employment practices of schools and colleges. A six-to-three decision by the United States Supreme Court reasoned that Congress had intended Title IX to cover employment. See *North Haven Board of Education* v. *Bell*, 456 U.S. 512 (1982).

In *Grove City College* v. *Bell*, 465 U.S. 555 (1984), the Supreme Court, referring to private institutions, declared that Title IX did not apply to schools and colleges as a whole but only to those parts of an institution that received federal aid directly. However, provisions of the Civil Rights Restoration Act of 1988 were designed to overturn the *Grove City College* decision. The act made it clear that if one part of an entity receives federal funds, then the entire entity is covered.

Title VII prohibits unequal treatment with respect to "conditions of employment." Courts have construed "conditions" to include insulting and degrading treatment; therefore, Title VII applies to sexual harassment on the job.

In a decision involving a male teacher's request for a one-year's, child-rearing leave without pay under a collective bargaining agreement, a court held such a provision to contravene Title VII because it allowed such leave only for female teachers. However, the court held void that portion of the provision granting leave beyond the period of actual physical disability due to the pregnancy, childbirth, or related medical conditions. See *Schafer* v. *Board of Education of Pittsburgh*, 903 F.2d 243 (1990).

C. Pregnancy

A challenge to local school board policies that provided for mandatory leave at a particular time in a pregnancy and rules pertaining to reemployment after delivery has been heard by the United States Supreme Court. In its decision in *Cleveland Board of Education* v. *La Fleur*, 414 U.S. 632 (1974), the Court held that mandatory maternity termination provisions stating the number of months before anticipated childbirth violated the Due Process Clause of the Fourteenth Amendment. The court reasoned that arbitrary cutoff dates have no valid relationship to the state's interest in preserving continuity of instruction, as long as the teacher is required to give substantial advance notice that she is pregnant. And the Court stated that the challenged provisions created a conclusive presumption that every teacher is physically incapable of continuing her duties at a specified time in her pregnancy. Additionally, the Court struck down the provision that a mother could not return to work until the next regular semester after her child was three months old.

Shortly after this decision, many court challenges were brought against policies pertaining to disability benefits, sick leave, and health insurance involving pregnancy. The issue was addressed by the United States Supreme Court in a noneducator-related case, *General Electric Company* v. *Gilbert*, 429 U.S. 125 (1976). Largely as a result of the *Gilbert* decision, which upheld the exclusion of pregnancy-related disabilities from General Electric's comprehensive disability plan, Congress passed the Pregnancy Discrimination Act, which went into effect in 1979.

This act is an amendment to Title VII. The Pregnancy Discrimination Act stipulates that employment discrimination "because of sex" or "on the basis of sex," as prohibited by Title VII, includes discrimination "because of or on the basis of pregnancy, childbirth or related medical conditions." Women so situated must be treated as other applicants or employees are: on the basis of their ability to work. Women may not be fired, be denied promotions, or be refused employment as a consequence of their being pregnant or having an abortion. They may not be forced to take leave while they still can work. They may not be required to exhaust their vacation benefits prior to receiving sick leave or disability benefits, unless the same policy applies to other disabled employees. If other employees are entitled to resume their jobs after disability leave, so too are women who have been absent because of pregnancy. Usually, however, they have no guarantee of returning to their former positions or schools.

In the area of fringe benefits, such as disability benefits, sick leave, and health insurance, the same principle applies. A woman unable to work for pregnancy-related reasons is entitled to disability benefits or sick leave on the same basis as employees unable to work for other temporary medical reasons. Also, any health insurance provided must cover expenses for pregnancy-related conditions on the same basis as coverage given for other medical conditions. However, health insurance for expenses resulting from abortion is not required, except where the life of the mother would be endangered if the fetus were carried to term or where medical complications have arisen from such an abortion.

ECKMANN v. *BOARD OF EDUCATION OF HAWTHORN SCHOOL DISTRICT*
United States District Court, Northern District of Illinois, 1986
636 F. Supp. 1214

ROSZKOWSKI, District Judge.
* * *

On June 6, 1982, plaintiff Jeanne Eckmann instituted this civil rights action against the Board of Education of Hawthorn School District No. 17 (the "School Board") and various School Board members. Plaintiff sought compensatory and punitive damages for her allegedly unconstitutional discharge. * * *
* * *

The burden of proof instruction tendered to the jury in this case was drafted according to the dictates of *Mount Healthy City Board of Education* v. *Doyle.* * * *
* * *

Based on *Mount Healthy*, there are three burdens in a case of this sort. The teacher must first show some constitutionally protected conduct. Once this is established, the teacher carries the burden of showing that the protected conduct was a "substantial" or "motivating" factor behind the school board's conduct. Once the teacher carries these two burdens the school board must then show by a preponderance of the evidence that it would have taken its action even if the teacher had not engaged in the constitutionally protected conduct. * * *

The constitutionally protected conduct plaintiff alleges motivated the School Board to fire her in this case was her out-of-wedlock pregnancy coupled with her decision to raise her child as a single parent. While plaintiff's conduct is not protected by a specifically enumerated constitutional right, this court considered it to be covered by "substantive due process."

In *Loving* v. *Virginia*, * * * the Supreme Court held that the freedom to decide whom "to marry, or not marry . . . resides with the individual and cannot be infringed by the state." In other words, it is improper for the state to interfere with a person's decision to marry, or as it relates to this case, *not* to marry. The Supreme Court later stated that:

> If the right of privacy means anything, it is the right of the *individual*, married or single, to be free from unwarranted governmental intrusion into matters so fundamentally affecting a person as the decision whether to bear or beget a child.

Eisenstadt v. *Baird* (1972). The next year, in *Roe* v. *Wade* (1973), the Court held that the constitutional right to privacy "is broad enough to encompass a woman's decision whether or not to terminate her pregnancy." Supreme Court precedent thus clearly shows that the individual's decisions regarding marriage and child bearing are constitutionally protected from improper state infringement. * * * Under the overwhelming weight of this authority, it is beyond question that plaintiff had a substantive due process right to conceive and raise her child out of wedlock without unwarranted state (School Board) intrusion.

In its motion for a JNOV (judgment notwithstanding the verdict), the School Board does not contest that plaintiff's out-of-wedlock pregnancy and her decision to raise her son as a single mother are protected by substantive due process. Rather, the School Board focuses its attack on whether plaintiff showed that her conduct in fact motivated the Board when discharging her. In a nutshell, the School Board's position is that:

> In this case a review of all of the evidence taken as a whole, in the light most favorable to the plaintiff *without speculation or drawing unreasonable inferences* which conflict with undisputed facts clearly shows that beyond any doubt the Defendant School Board would have taken the same action against the Plaintiff if the language referencing immorality had never been included in the documentation. * * *

To support its position, the School Board states that "[e]very witness called by the Plaintiff or the Defendant testified that the Board would have taken the same action even without the immorality language." * * *

This court agrees with the School Board that each Board member specifically testified that plaintiff would have been terminated even if she had not been pregnant. This court also agrees that each Board member testified that the *only* reason charges of "immorality" were included in plaintiff's "Notice to Remedy," "Letter of Dismissal" and the accompanying Bill of Particulars, was on advice of the Board's lawyer. The Board's lawyer confirmed this testimony. This court also recalls the numerous defense witnesses that testified as to "the cruelty, abuse, disregard and other difficulties that they had with [plaintiff] from 1979 until the time of dismissal." * * *

What the School Board overlooks however ∗ ∗ ∗ is that plaintiff did present evidence that her supposed "immorality" was the motivating factor for her discharge.

For example, plaintiff submitted the "Notice to Remedy" given her by the School Board. The Notice listed numerous charges of deficiencies in plaintiff's teaching abilities and stated that there were 11 matters that could be remedied. One such charge was:

> Your conduct in becoming pregnant outside the state of marriage has diminished your ability to teach and the ability of your students to learn their lessons from you.

The Notice then cautioned plaintiff "not to engage in such conduct in the future."

Plaintiff also presented Administrative Law Judge Sidney Mogul's written report ordering her reinstatement with full back pay. The issue in front of ALJ Mogul was whether the School Board could prove by a preponderance of the evidence that plaintiff was guilty of "negligence, insubordination, cruelty and immorality" as charged in the "Letter of Dismissal." Following a lengthy hearing, ALJ Mogul issued a twenty-five page decision in which he found that:

(1) "In support of the charge that the Teacher is an unfit role model, the Board has failed to show that the Teacher proselytized pupils or that the fact of childbirth out of wedlock had any substantial effect upon the Teacher's students."

(2) "The Board has shown no evidence of significant harm to students, faculty or school, resulting from the Teacher's unwed motherhood." and,

(3) "There is no evidence in the record that the Teacher was an immoral person. On the contrary, the record indicates that she was an eminently moral person, a religious person and staunch in her beliefs."

ALJ Mogul went on to note that "were it not for her pregnancy and childbirth out of wedlock, this dismissal would probably not have taken place," and that "the charges of negligence, insubordination or incompetency were purely embellishments to soften the effect of the Board's reliance upon its charge of immorality." ∗ ∗ ∗

∗ ∗ ∗

Also submitted was evidence to the effect that following the Notice to Remedy in July of 1981, the School Board voted to cut plaintiff's pay and instructed the superintendent to tell her that she could no longer manage the student council, coach the cheerleaders, organize school fund raisers or trips, or participate in graduation exercises. All of these restrictions were imposed because she was a mother.

Plaintiff also submitted an evaluation written by Board member Ed O'Brien to the effect that she was doing fine at school and that the quality of the teaching in her classroom was excellent. Plaintiff never received this evaluation. Mr. O'Brien mailed it to Board Attorney Weiler for approval. Attorney Weiler simply filed the letter away.

The School Board makes much of the fact that the immorality language was only used at the suggestion of Attorney Weiler. While this may have relevance with regard to the good faith of the Board members, the School Board as an entity enjoys no such immunity. * * *

Juries are not required to determine cases merely by weighing the number of witnesses and volume of testimony presented by each side. Were this so, the School Board would clearly have carried the day. Juries are allowed—indeed it is their task—to judge the credibility of witnesses and they are free to believe or disbelieve testimony as they see fit. The fact that the jury in this case chose to discredit the Board member's self-serving testimony and credit plaintiff's admittedly less-voluminous evidence does not require that its verdict be set aside.

* * *

Since the verdict in this case depended in large part upon the credibility of the Board member's testimony and since plaintiff presented sufficient evidence to support a jury verdict contrary to this testimony, the School Board's motion for a JNOV must be denied.

* * *

* * * While the exact dollar amount of compensatory damages requested by plaintiff's counsel is somewhat confusing, he never asked for an amount even approaching $2,000,000. This court is fully aware that plaintiff is not limited to the amount of damages requested in argument. The amount awarded however must bear at least some relationship to the evidence presented at trial. In this court's opinion, $750,000 will more than adequately serve to compensate plaintiff for the injuries she suffered in this case. The damage award against the School Board is remitted accordingly.

* * *

Notes and Questions

Several other courts have ruled similarly to **Eckmann**. See *Ponton* v. *Newport News School Board*, 632 F. Supp. 1056 (Va. 1986); *Avery* v. *Homewood City Board of Education*, 674 F.2d 337 (5th Cir. 1982); *Cochran* v. *Chidester School District*, 456 F. Supp. 390 (Ark. 1978); *Brown* v. *Bathke*, 566 F.2d 588 (8th Cir. 1977); *New Mexico State Board of Education* v. *Stoudt*, 571 P.2d 1186 (N.M. 1977); *Andrews* v. *Drew Municipal Separate School District*, 507 F.2d 611 (5th Cir. 1975); and *Drake* v. *Covington County Board of Education*, 371 F. Supp. 974 (Ala. 1974).

In a seven-to-two decision, the Court established that an insurance plan violated the 1964 Civil Rights Act and the Pregnancy Discrimination

Act because it offered full hospitalization benefits to husbands of female workers but excluded pregnancy from the full coverage offered to the wives of male workers. The decision stated that under the plan "husbands of female employees receive a specified level of hospitalization coverage for all conditions; the wives of male employees receive such coverage except for pregnancy-related conditions. . . . The 1978 act makes clear that it is discriminatory to treat pregnancy-related conditions less favorably than other medical conditions." Therefore, the plan "unlawfully gives married male employees a benefit package for their dependents that is less inclusive than the dependency coverage provided to married female employees." See *Newport News Shipbuilding and Dry Dock Company* v. *Equal Employment Opportunity Commission*, 462 U.S. 669 (1983).

A U.S. Court of Appeals for the Fifth Circuit recognized that a Florida teacher's decision to breast-feed her baby had some constitutional dimensions. In its decision, the court contended that the teacher's right to breast-feed her baby could be limited if this practice interfered with important educational interests that were furthered by the rules that prohibited teachers from bringing their children to work with them for any reason. See *Dike* v. *School Board of Orange County*, 650 F.2d 783 (5th Cir. 1981). In 1993, Florida became the first state in the nation to pass legislation guaranteeing a woman's right to breast-feed her baby in public. The law forbids the arrest of a breast-feeding mother for obscenity, lewdness, or public nudity.

Two other Court decisions addressed issues related to pregnancy. In *California Federal Savings and Loan Association* v. *Guerra*, 479 U.S. 272 (1987), a six-to-three decision, the Court upheld a California law granting four months of unpaid maternity leave to pregnant workers and guaranteeing that they could return to their former jobs. However, a unanimous Supreme Court decision upheld a Missouri law that did not provide either reinstatement or unemployment benefits to a woman who left her job because of pregnancy. Under the law, benefits were available only to those who left work for job-related reasons. Layoffs or illnesses caused by a job were considered job-related; pregnancy was not. See *Wimberly* v. *Labor and Industrial Relations Commission of Missouri*, 479 U.S. 511 (1987).

A federal district court held that a single teacher had a constitutional right to become pregnant by artificial insemination. Denying her this right, the court reasoned, would be sex discrimination under Title VII. See *Cameron* v. *Board of Education of Hillsboro, Ohio City School District*, 795 F.Supp. 228 (Ohio 1992).

A private school's dismissal of a teacher for engaging in nonmarital sex was upheld in *Boyd* v. *Harding Academy of Memphis, Inc.*, 88 F.3d 410 (6th Cir. 1996). Although the teacher alleged she was dismissed because she was pregnant, which would have been a violation of Title VII, the school maintained her dismissal was based on violation of the extramarital sex policy for which both men and women had been dismissed over the years.

D. Religious Discrimination

Title VII of the Civil Rights Act of 1964 provides in part that an employer must "reasonably accommodate to an employee's . . . religious observances or practice without undue hardship on the conduct of the employer's business." In *Ansonia Board of Education* v. *Philbrook*, 479 U.S. 60 (1986), the Court considered a teacher's request to use, for religious purposes, his allotment of "necessary personal business" leave. The teacher's collective-bargaining agreement allowed three days of paid religious leave and three days of paid personal business leave; religious observances were not included among the enumerated reasons for taking a leave of absence for personal business. The school board required the teacher to take unpaid leave for all religious observances exceeding three days. Upholding the board, the Court declared the policy to be a "reasonable accommodation" under Title VII.

Most states have laws that, like Title VII, require employers to accommodate employees' religious practices. However, a point exists at which such accommodation may violate the Establishment Clause of the United States Constitution's First Amendment. The Supreme Court struck down a Connecticut statute that allowed employees to absent themselves from work on any day that they claimed as their Sabbath. The Court found that the statute imposed on employers the absolute duty to conform their business practices to the religious practices of their employees. The statute allowed no exceptions, for example, in the event of a teacher's claiming a Friday Sabbath. The Court concluded that the law's primary effect was the advancement of a particular religious practice. See *Estate of Thornton* v. *Caldor, Inc.*, 472 U.S. 703 (1985).

Pennsylvania's "Garb Statute" was challenged under Title VII by a Muslim teacher who had the conviction that Muslim women should, when in public, cover their entire body except for the hands and face. A federal appellate court upheld the school district's refusal to allow her to wear such dress. The court ruled that the preservation of an atmosphere of religious neutrality in the public schools is a compelling state interest justifying statutes prohibiting teachers from wearing religious garb while teaching. The court concluded that it would have imposed an "undue hardship" on the school system to accommodate the teacher. See *United States* v. *Board of Education for the School District of Philadelphia*, 911 F.2d 882 (3rd Cir. 1990). However, a lower court held that a person who was not given a job because she wore head coverings, in keeping with her religious faith, during the interview was religious discrimination. The sought-after position was for a third-grade counselor with a private corporation providing services to nonpublic school students under a contract with a public school district. The court reasoned that Pennsylvania's religious garb statute was inapplicable because third-grade students would not recognize the head coverings as indicating the applicant's Muslim faith. The fact that the head coverings would offend the religious sensibilities of persons affiliated with parochial schools was also insufficient in bringing this issue under the statute. See *EEOC v. READS, Inc.*, 759 F. Supp. 1150 (Pa. 1991). Oregon laws that disallowed the wearing of religious dress while teaching and that provided for suspension and teaching certificate revocation have also been upheld. In this instance, the teacher wore the white clothes and turban of a Sikh Hindu. See *Cooper v. Eugene School District No. 4J*, 301 Or. 358, (1986), *appeal dismissed*, 480 U.S. 942 (1987). "Garb" in such statutes is often defined as any dress, mark, emblem, or insignia indicating a teacher's membership in or adherence to a religious order, sect, or denomination. Would such a definition include a cross, crucifix, Star of David, hairstyle, or yarmulke?

A federal appellate court struck down a requirement that teachers at the private Kamehameha School be Protestant. The court reasoned that except for the school's religious education teachers (who had a "bona fide occupational qualification" under Title VII), other teachers at the school provided instruction in the traditional secular way and there was nothing to suggest that adherence to the Protestant faith was essential to the performance of that job. The interpreted section of Title VII stated:

> . . . it shall not be an unlawful employment practice for an employer to hire and employ employees . . . on the basis of his religion . . . in those certain instances where religion . . . is a bona fide occupational qualification reasonably necessary to the normal operation of that particular business or enterprise. (p. 465)

See *EEOC v. Kamehameha Schools/Bishop Estate*, 990 F.2d 458 (9th Cir. 1993), *cert. denied*, 510 U.S. 963 (1993).

Teachers' use of school facilities for religious meetings has also come under judicial purview. An Indiana school-district policy that banned religious meetings of teachers on school property, before the teachers were to report for duty, was upheld. See *May v. Evansville-Vanderburgh School Corporation*, 787 F.2d 1105 (7th Cir. 1986).

E. Age Discrimination

Under the Age Discrimination in Employment Act (ADEA) of 1967 and its amendments,* it is unlawful for an employer to discriminate against any employee or potential employee on the basis of age except "where age is a

---

*See Appendix D for material pertaining to this legislation.

bona fide occupational qualification reasonably necessary to the normal operation of the particular business, or where the differentiation is based on reasonable factors other than age." As originally passed in 1967, the act did not apply to the federal government, to the states and their political subdivisions, or to private employers with fewer than twenty-five employees. In 1974, however, Congress extended the act's substantive prohibitions to employers having at least twenty workers and to the federal and state governments and, thus, to public school employees.

Coverage of the act is limited to employees within a specified range of ages. An important effect of the range's upper limit is to define the minimum age for mandatory retirement. Coverage in 1967 was limited to workers between the ages of forty and sixty-five. Amendments of 1978 raised the upper limit to age seventy and removed the cap entirely for federal workers. Amendments of 1986 removed the cap for tenured faculty in higher education in 1994.

However, in *Kimel* v. *Florida Board of Regents*, 528 U.S. 62 (2000), the United States Supreme Court declared the ADEA unconstitutional as applied to the states, including state public educational institutions. In *Kimel*, university employees filed suit against the Florida Board of Regents, claiming age discrimination in violation of the ADEA. In defending against these claims, the State asserted immunity from suit under the Eleventh Amendment. Because of the complex interaction of the Eleventh and Fourteenth Amendments in the Court's analysis in *Kimel*, this decision resulted in some initial misunderstandings regarding the current status of age discrimination laws. But a careful reading of *Kimel* clearly establishes that absent a voluntary state waiver of immunity, employees of state agencies, including public school employees, can no longer sue under the ADEA. State employees in most states are still protected by state statutes prohibiting age discrimination. However, coverage under some states' statutes may be less comprehensive than under the ADEA. Because the Court's decision in *Kimel* was based on Eleventh Amendment state immunity, the ADEA still applies to federal agencies, as well as private businesses with 20 or more employees, including private schools. Does your state have legislation prohibiting age discrimination in employment? If so, does coverage under your state statute differ from coverage under the ADEA?

Courts have generally held that those teaching beyond a specified retirement age do so on a year-to-year basis. In addressing this issue, the South Dakota Supreme Court in *Monnier* v. *Todd County Independent School District*, 245 N.W. 2d 503 (S.D. 1976) has contended that:

> after a school district has adopted a mandatory retirement policy, teachers within that district who attain the age of retirement specified in the policy

are no longer entitled to the benefits of the continuing contract law. By its very terms the concept of mandatory retirement is inconsistent with the concept of continuing contract rights. . . . (p. 505)

VIII. TEACHER BARGAINING

A wide range of practices exists among the fifty states pertaining to school employment relations. These practices vary from states that either have no statutory provisions or prohibit collective bargaining to those that mandate bargaining and allow teachers to strike. Although the majority of states have statutory provisions addressing issues surrounding school employment relations, several states rely on the authority of case law, and a handful of states rely on attorney general opinions.

In those states having statutes pertaining to school employment relations, provisions vary considerably. Some leave teacher negotiation or bargaining rights to the discretion of local school boards, whereas others provide bargaining rights that compare favorably with those held by employees in the private sector. The range of issues addressed in the various statutes include whether or not there are exclusive bargaining rights for one teacher group, which groups may be included in the bargaining unit, dues checkoff, the establishment of agency shops, service fees, the scope of bargaining, impasse procedures, and strike provisions.

According to National Education Association data, approximately 70 percent of the states have statutes providing for good-faith bargaining between local school boards and bargaining groups. Alabama and Maryland have statutes requiring that a school board "meet and confer" with representatives of employee organizations. In contrast, North Carolina and Texas prohibit bargaining by statute, and Georgia and Virginia prohibit the practice by court order.

Virtually all of the states with collective bargaining legislation require supervisory personnel—individuals above the assistant principal level—to be in separate bargaining units. In some of these states, statutory provisions or local policies exclude supervisory personnel from the collective bargaining process entirely.

The right of public school teachers to strike is a highly controversial subject. Not all statutory school employment provisions address the issue of strikes. According to National Education Association statistics, several states (Alaska, Hawaii, Illinois, Minnesota, Ohio, Oregon, Pennsylvania, and Wisconsin) have statutory provisions that allow teachers to strike under certain conditions. Statutes in approximately half of the states specifically prohibit strikes by teachers, and in some instances penalties for striking are specified.

An important and often litigated issue for teachers who do not wish to join a union has to do with the collection of and uses of compulsory union dues. This issue is addressed in *Lehnert v. Ferris Faculty Association.*

LEHNERT v. FERRIS FACULTY ASSOCIATION
Supreme Court of the United States, 1991
500 U. S. 507

JUSTICE BLACKMUN announced the judgment of the Court and delivered the opinion of the Court * * *

This case presents issues concerning the constitutional limitations, if any, upon the payment, required as a condition of employment, of dues by a nonmember to a union in the public sector.

Michigan's Public Employment Relations Act (Act), Mich. Comp. Laws §§ 423.201 *et seq.* (1978), provides that a duly selected union shall serve as the exclusive collective-bargaining representative of public employees in a particular bargaining unit. The Act, which applies to faculty members of a public educational institution in Michigan, permits a union and a government employer to enter into an "agency shop" arrangement under which employees within the bargaining unit who decline to become members of the union are compelled to pay a "service fee" to the union.

Respondent Ferris Faculty Association (FFA), an affiliate of the Michigan Education Association (MEA) and the National Education Association (NEA), serves, pursuant to this provision, as the exclusive bargaining representative of the faculty of Ferris State College in Big Rapids, Mich. Ferris is a public institution established under the Michigan Constitution and is funded by the State. * * * Since 1975, the FFA and Ferris have entered into successive collective-bargaining agreements containing agency shop provisions. Those agreements were the fruit of negotiations between the FFA and respondent Board of Control, the governing body of Ferris. * * *

Subsequent to this Court's decision in *Abood* v. *Detroit Board of Education,* in which the Court upheld the constitutionality of the Michigan agency-shop provision and outlined permissible uses of the compelled fee by public-employee unions, Ferris proposed, and the FFA agreed to, the agency-shop arrangement at issue here. That agreement forced all employees in the bargaining unit who did not belong to the FFA to pay a service fee equivalent to the amount of dues required of a union member. Of the $284.00 service fee for 1981–1982, the period at issue, $24.80 went to the FFA, $211.20 to the MEA, and $48.00 to the NEA.

* * *

Following a partial settlement, petitioners took an appeal limited to the claim that the District Court erred in holding that the costs of certain disputed union activities were constitutionally chargeable to the plaintiff faculty members. Specifically, petitioners objected to the District Court's conclusion that the union constitutionally could charge them for the costs of (1) lobbying and electoral politics; (2) bargaining, litigation, and other activities on behalf of persons not in petitioners' bargaining unit; (3) public relations efforts; (4) miscellaneous professional activities; (5) meetings and conventions of the parent unions; and (6) preparation for a strike which, had it materialized, would have violated Michigan law.

* * *

It was not until the decision in *Abood* that this Court addressed the constitutionality of union-security provisions in the public-employment context. There, the Court upheld the same Michigan statute which is before us today against a facial First Amendment challenge. At the same time, it determined that the claim that a union has utilized an individual agency-shop agreement to force dissenting employees to subsidize ideological activities could establish, upon a proper showing, a First Amendment violation. In so doing, the Court set out several important propositions:

First, it recognized that "[t]o compel employees financially to support their collective-bargaining representative has an impact upon their First Amendment interests." * * * Unions traditionally have aligned themselves with a wide range of social, political, and ideological viewpoints, any number of which might bring vigorous disapproval from individual employees. To force employees to contribute, albeit indirectly, to the promotion of such positions implicates core First Amendment concerns. * * *

Second, the Court in *Abood* determined that, as in the private sector, compulsory affiliation with, or monetary support of, a public-employment union does not, without more, violate the First Amendment rights of public employees. Similarly, an employee's free speech rights are not unconstitutionally burdened because the employee opposes positions taken by a union in its capacity as collective-bargaining representative. * * *

In this connection, the Court indicated that the considerations that justify the union shop in the private context—the desirability of labor peace and eliminating "free riders"—are equally important in the public-sector workplace. Consequently, the use of dissenters' assessments "for the purposes of collective bargaining, contract administration, and grievance adjustment," * * * approved under the Railway Labor Act (RLA) is equally permissible when authorized by a State vis-á-vis its own workers.

Third, the Court established that the constitutional principles that prevent a State from conditioning public employment upon association with a political party, see *Elrod* v. *Burns*, * * * or upon professed religious allegiance, see *Torcaso* v. *Watkins*, * * * similarly prohibit a public employer "from requiring [an employee] to contribute to the support of an ideological cause he may oppose as a condition of holding a job" as a public educator. * * *

* * *

Thus, although the Court's decisions in this area prescribe a case-by-case analysis in determining which activities a union constitutionally may charge to dissenting employees, they also set forth several guidelines to be followed in making such determinations. *Hanson* and *Street* and their progeny teach that chargeable activities must (1) be "germane" to collective-bargaining activity; (2) be justified by the government's vital policy interest in labor peace and avoiding "free riders"; and (3) not significantly add to the burdening of free speech that is inherent in the allowance of an agency or union shop.

* * *

The Court of Appeals determined that unions constitutionally may subsidize lobbying and other political activities with dissenters' fees so long as those activities are "pertinent to the duties of the union as a bargaining representative." * * * In reaching this conclusion, the court relied upon the inherently political nature of salary and other workplace decisions in public employment. "To represent their members effectively," the court concluded, "public sector unions must necessarily concern themselves not only with negotiations at the bargaining table but also with advancing their members' interests in legislative and other 'political' arenas." * * *

This observation is clearly correct. Public-sector unions often expend considerable resources in securing ratification of negotiated agreements by the proper state or local legislative body. * * * Similarly, union efforts to acquire appropriations for approved collective-bargaining agreements often serve as an indispensable pre-requisite to their implementation. * * * It was in reference to these characteristics of public employment that the Court in *Abood* discussed the "somewhat hazier" line between bargaining-related and purely ideological activities in the public sector. * * * The dual roles of government as employer and policymaker in such cases make the analogy between lobbying and collective bargaining in the public sector a close one.

This, however, is not such a case. Where, as here, the challenged lobbying activities relate not to the ratification or implementation of a dissenter's collective bargaining agreement, but to financial support of the employee's profession or of public employees generally, the connection to the union's function as bargaining representative is too attenuated to justify compelled support by objecting employees.

* * *

Labor peace is not especially served by allowing such charges because, unlike collective-bargaining negotiations between union and management, our national and state legislatures, the media, and the platform of public discourse are public fora open to all. Individual employees are free to petition their neighbors and government in opposition to the union which represents them in the workplace. Because worker and union cannot be said to speak with one voice, it would not further the cause of harmonious industrial relations to compel objecting employees to finance union political activities as well as their own.

Similarly, while we have endorsed the notion that nonunion workers ought not be allowed to benefit from the terms of employment secured by union efforts without paying for those services, the so-called "free-rider" concern is inapplicable where lobbying extends beyond the effectuation of a collective-bargaining agreement. The balancing of monetary and other policy choices performed by legislatures is not limited to the workplace but typically has ramifications that extend into diverse aspects of an employee's life.

* * *

Accordingly, we hold that the State constitutionally may not compel its employees to subsidize legislative lobbying or other political union activities outside the limited context of contract ratification or implementation.

* * *

The essence of the affiliation relationship is the notion that the parent will bring to bear its often considerable economic, political, and informational resources when the local is in need of them. Consequently, that part of a local's affiliation fee which contributes to the pool of resources potentially available to the local is assessed for the bargaining unit's protection, even if it is not actually expended on that unit in any particular membership year.

* * *

We therefore conclude that a local bargaining representative may charge objecting employees for their pro rata share of the costs associated with otherwise chargeable activities of its state and national affiliates, even if those activities were not performed for the direct benefit of the objecting employees' bargaining unit. This conclusion, however, does not serve to grant a local union carte blanche to expend dissenters' dollars for bargaining activities wholly unrelated to the employees in their unit. The union surely may not, for example, charge objecting employees for a direct donation or interest-free loan to an unrelated bargaining unit for the purpose of promoting employee rights or unionism generally. Further, a contribution by a local union to its parent that is not part of the local's responsibilities as an affiliate but is in the nature of a charitable donation would not be chargeable to dissenters. There must be some indication that the payment is for services that may ultimately enure to the benefit of the members of the local union by virtue of their membership in the parent organization. And, as always, the union bears the burden of proving the proportion of chargeable expenses to total expenses. * * * We conclude merely that the union need not demonstrate a direct and tangible impact upon the dissenting employee's unit.

* * *

The Court of Appeals found that the union could constitutionally charge petitioners for the costs of a Preserve Public Education (PPE) program designed to secure funds for public education in Michigan, and that portion of the MEA publication, the Teacher's Voice, which reported these activities. Petitioners argue that, contrary to the findings of the courts below, the PPE program went beyond lobbying activity and sought to affect the outcome of ballot issues and "millages" or local taxes for the support of public schools. Given our conclusion as to lobbying and electoral politics generally, this factual dispute is of little consequence. None of these activities was shown to be oriented toward the ratification or implementation of petitioner's collective-bargaining agreement. We hold that none may be supported through the funds of objecting employees.

Petitioners next challenge the Court of Appeals' allowance of several activities that the union did not undertake directly on behalf of persons within petitioners' bargaining unit. This objection principally concerns NEA "program expenditures" destined for States other than Michigan, and the expenses of the Teacher's Voice listed as "Collective Bargaining" and "Litigation." Our conclusion that unions may bill dissenting employees for their share of general collective-bargaining costs of the state or national parent union is dispositive as to the bulk of the NEA expenditures. The District Court found these costs to be germane to collective bargaining and similar support services and we decline to disturb that finding. No greater relationship is necessary in the collective-bargaining context.

This rationale does not extend, however, to the expenses of litigation that do not concern the dissenting employees' bargaining unit or, by extension, to union literature reporting on such activities. * * *

The Court of Appeals determined that the union constitutionally could charge petitioners for certain public-relations expenditures. In this connection, the court said: "Public relations expenditures designed to enhance the reputation of the teaching profession . . . are, in our opinion, sufficiently related to the unions' duty to represent bargaining unit employees effectively so as to be chargeable to dissenters." * * * We disagree. * * *

* * *

The District Court and the Court of Appeals allowed charges for those portions of the Teachers' Voice that concern teaching and education generally, professional development, unemployment, job opportunities, award programs of the MEA, and other miscellaneous matters. Informational support services such as these are neither political nor public in nature. Although they do not directly concern the members of petitioners' bargaining unit, these expenditures are for the benefit of all and we discern no additional infringement of First Amendment rights that they might occasion. In short, we agree with the Court of Appeals that these expenses are comparable to the *de minimis* social activity charges approved in *Ellis.* * * *

The Court of Appeals ruled that the union could use the fees of objecting employees to send FFA delegates to the MEA and the NEA conventions and to participate in the 13E Coordinating Council, another union structure.

Petitioners challenge that determination and argue that, unlike the national convention expenses found to be chargeable to dissenters in *Ellis*, the meetings at issue here were those of affiliated parent unions rather than the local, and therefore do not relate exclusively to petitioners' unit.

We need not determine whether petitioners could be commanded to support all the expenses of these conventions. The question before the Court is simply whether the unions may constitutionally require petitioners to subsidize the participation in these events of delegates from the local. We hold that they may. That the conventions were not solely devoted to the activities of the FFA does not prevent the unions from requiring petitioners' support. We conclude above that the First Amendment does not require so close a connection. Moreover, participation by members of the local in the formal activities of the parent is likely to be an important benefit of affiliation. * * *

The chargeability of expenses incident to preparation for a strike which all concede would have been illegal under Michigan law, * * * is a provocative question. At the beginning of the 1981–1982 fiscal year, the FFA and Ferris were engaged in negotiating a new collective-bargaining agreement. The union perceived these efforts to be ineffective, and began to prepare a "job action" or, in more familiar terms, to go out on strike. These preparations entailed the creation by the FFA and the MEA of a "crisis center' or "strike headquarters." * * *

* * *

Petitioners can identify no determination by the State of Michigan that mere preparation for an illegal strike is itself illegal or against public policy, and we are aware of none. Further, we accept the rationale provided by the Court of Appeals in upholding these charges that such expenditures fall "within the range of reasonable bargaining tools available to a public sector union during contract negotiations." * * *

In sum, these expenses are substantively indistinguishable from those appurtenant to collective-bargaining negotiations. The District Court and the Court of Appeals concluded, and we agree, that they aid in those negotiations and enure to the direct benefit of members of the dissenters' unit. Further, they impose no additional burden upon First Amendment rights. The union may properly charge petitioners for those costs.

It is so ordered.

* * *

Notes

As seen in this decision, Michigan employs an agency shop arrangement under which union membership is not mandatory; however, nonunion members must pay a "service fee" to the union. Although under state law there may be differences between the public and private sectors, generally under a "closed shop," union membership is a condition of employment, and under an "open shop" union membership and related activities may be restricted or not allowed.

In addition to *Abood* v. *Detroit Board of Education*, 431 U.S. 209 (1977) mentioned in *Lehnert*, another Court decision, *Chicago Teachers Union Local No. 1* v. *Hudson*, 475 U.S. 292 (1986), addressed fair procedures governing a union's collection of agency fees from nonmembers. In its decision, the Court held that the Constitution requires (1) an adequate explanation of the basis for the fee; (2) a reasonably prompt opportunity to challenge, before an impartial decision maker, the amount of the fee; and (3) an escrow for the amounts reasonably in dispute while such a challenge is pending.

Educators in states without collective bargaining, negotiation, or even "meet and confer" legislation usually find the *Lehnert* decision startling in its description of union activity. For instance, such educators often have no notion of the "free-rider" problem discussed in the decision.

IX. POLITICAL ACTIVITIES

Not many states have addressed the issue of whether restrictions should be placed on the political activities of public school teachers. Although several states have statutes covering the political candidacy of public school employees, most of the statutory provisions are far from comprehensive.

Four significant legal issues are involved when a public school employee becomes a candidate for public office or campaigns for other political candidates and issues. These issues are (1) the school employee's First Amendment rights of freedom of expression and association, (2) incompatibility of office provisions, (3) conflict-of-interest provisions, and (4) nepotism provisions.

Although a public school employee has the First Amendment right to run for public office, a distinction must be made between the employee's right to run for public office and the right to continue school employment while holding public office. Well-settled case law has established that a public school employee may not simultaneously hold a public office and his or her school employment if this is against (1) incompatibility-of-office provisions, (2) conflict-of-interest provisions, and (3) provisions providing for the tripartite separation of the divisions of government. Courts have consistently held that these provisions represent a compelling state need that justifies infringements on the school employee's political rights.

Under state incompatibility-of-office and conflict-of-interest provisions, courts have established that public school employees may not maintain their employment while holding office on (1) their employing board of education or (2) any governmental body, or while holding an office that has supervisory powers over their employing school district. However, in the absence of statutory prohibitions, public school employees may serve on a board of education that is not their employing board.

Whether public school employees may maintain their employment and serve in the state legislature depends on the conflict-of-interest statute covering the state's legislators. In those states that prohibit legislators from having a direct or indirect interest in any contract dependent upon funds appropriated while they serve in the legislature, school employees may not be able to continue school employment. However, in states that do not have this type of statutory provision, courts have held that the school employee may serve in the legislature but that it is reasonable for the board of education to require the employee to take an unpaid leave of absence while so serving. Under incompatibility-of-office provisions, courts have held that there is no incompatibility between local school employment and serving in the state legislature. However, some courts have held that it is incompatible for employees of the state university system to serve simultaneously in the legislature and hold their university jobs.

Under state nepotism provisions, a school employee's continued employment may be in jeopardy when a relative is elected to his or her employing board of education. Or the board member's continuation in office may be in jeopardy if he or she has relatives who are employed by the school board. Some state courts, under general nepotism statutes, do not strictly apply nepotism provisions to certificated school personnel. These courts have applied the rationale that state certification requirements and teacher tenure acts prevent nepotism practices in the hiring of school employees. On the other hand, where an education statute addresses nepotism issues on the part of members of a board of education, the courts strictly apply the language of such a statute.

A public vocational school district's antinepotism policy that prevented a married couple from working together at the same school was challenged in *Montgomery* v. *Carr*, 101 F.3d 117 (6th Cir. 1996). In its decision, the court held that the policy did not violate the teachers' First Amendment associational rights. The court declared that the policy was rationally related to legitimate goals, including avoiding friction if the marriage broke down, promoting collegiality among teachers, minimizing the friction caused by married teachers who have a "you and I against the world" mentality, and easing the task of managers. Interestingly enough, the antinepotism policy did not apply to couples who were simply living together.

Public school employees have the First Amendment right to campaign for other political candidates and issues; however, this right is not absolute. Courts have held that these types of activities (1) may not take place during working hours, (2) may not take place in the classroom,

(3) may not interfere with the school employee's job performance, and (4) are not permissible if the employee uses his or her position of employment to influence the outcome of a political election. Further, courts have held that these activities can be restricted if they result in material disruption of the normal administrative operations of the school system.

A school district policy that prohibited teachers from engaging in political activities on district property at any time, thereby preventing off-duty employees from soliciting votes at official polling places located on school property, was held to violate the teachers' First Amendment rights. The court, in *Castle* v. *Colonial School District*, 939 F. Supp. 458 (Pa. 1996), held that the views of the employees on the merits of candidates for the school board involved matters of "public concern." The court asserted that the school district's alleged interests, such as disruption of the educational process, protecting voters from undue influence, and avoiding the appearance of official endorsement of candidates, did not outweigh the teachers' freedom-of-speech interests.

Although school employees become actively involved in school board elections in some states, the Kentucky Supreme Court upheld legislation that prohibited employees of local school districts from taking part in the management of any political campaign for school board and that forbade school board candidates from soliciting or accepting any political assessment, contribution, or service of any employee of the school district. The legislation had been enacted to cleanse public education of political patronage and influence. See *State Board for Elementary and Secondary Education* v. *Howard*, 834 S.W. 2d 657 (Ky. 1992).

CHAPTER FIVE

School Desegregation

A Supreme Court decision in 1896 established the "separate but equal" doctrine regarding public facilities and services used by Negroes. This decision, *Plessy v. Ferguson,* established a legal basis for segregated public facilities and services, thereby ushering in the era of *de jure* segregation in America. Where there were no state statutory or constitutional provisions pertaining to segregation, *Plessy* enabled custom to be affirmed by also providing a legal basis for dual school systems in which black and white students were segregated. Although generally associated with the Southern states, dual school systems were operated in several non-Southern states. Under the dual school system, black students in a community attended segregated schools, which were staffed solely by black teachers, and white students attended schools exclusively for whites. Little or no interaction of any kind took place between the schools serving black students and those attended by white students. Such *de jure* segregation, which had its most rigid codification and practice in the Southern public schools, had the force of the law behind it because it was mandated by state constitutional and/or statutory provisions and official local school policies.

A 1954 United States Supreme Court decision, *Brown v. Board of Education,* reversed the *Plessy* doctrine as it pertained to public schools by declaring that in the field of education the doctrine of "separate but equal" had no place. This landmark reversal by the Supreme Court held *de jure* public school segregation to be unconstitutional. Since this decision, courts have had a veritable stream of cases brought before them in which they have had to determine whether alleged segregative policies in Southern schools, non-Southern schools, and private schools were unconstitutional.

This chapter's primary objective is to provide a historical perspective to public school desegregation. Paramount to gaining such a perspective is an understanding of the concept of *de jure* segregation, which provided the courts with a legal mechanism to attack racial segregation in the public schools. Employing this stratagem resulted in the earliest desegregation efforts focusing almost entirely in the Southern public schools. Additionally, this analysis includes revealing the progress of the dramatic influence of the federal courts, particularly the United States Supreme Court, for two decades in attempting to effect desegregation to more recent times when the Court no longer provides a consistent sympathetic ear for further desegregation efforts.

Plessy v. *Ferguson* poignantly describes the then prevalent state view of inferiority in which black Americans were held. The decision clearly reveals the official stamp of *de jure* separation placed between the races a century ago, a view that prevailed for nearly six decades until overturned by the dramatic *Brown* decisions.

I. HISTORICAL PERSPECTIVE

A. Separate but Equal Doctrine

PLESSY v. *FERGUSON*
Supreme Court of the United States, 1896
163 U.S. 537

MR. JUSTICE BROWN, after stating the case, delivered the opinion of the court.

This case turns upon the constitutionality of an act of the General Assembly of the State of Louisiana, passed in 1890, providing for separate railway carriages for the white and colored races. * * *

The first section of the statute enacts "that all railway companies carrying passengers in their coaches in this State, shall provide equal but separate accommodations for the white, and colored races, by providing two or more passenger coaches for each passenger train, or by dividing the passenger coaches by a partition so as to secure separate accommodations: *Provided,* That this section shall not be construed to apply to street railroads. No person or persons shall be admitted to occupy seats in coaches other than the ones assigned to them on account of the race they belong to."

By the second section it was enacted "that the officers of such passenger trains shall have the power and are hereby required to assign each passenger to the coach or compartment used for the race to which such passenger belongs; any passenger insisting on going into a coach or compartment to which by race he does not belong, shall be liable to a fine of twenty-five dollars, or in lieu thereof to imprisonment for a period of not more than twenty days in the parish prison, and any officer of any railroad insisting on assigning a passenger to a coach or compartment other than the one set aside for the race to which said passenger belongs, shall be liable to a fine of twenty-five dollars, or in lieu thereof to imprisonment for a period of not more than twenty days in the parish prison; and should any passenger refuse to occupy the coach or compartment to which he or she is assigned by the officer of such railway, said officer shall have power to refuse to carry such passenger on his train, and for such refusal neither he nor the railway company which he represents shall be liable for damages in any of the courts of this State."

The third section provides penalties for the refusal or neglect of the officers, directors, conductors and employees of railway companies to comply with the act, with a proviso that "nothing in this act shall be construed as applying to nurses attending children of the other race." The fourth section is immaterial.

The information filed in the criminal District Court charged in substance that Plessy, being a passenger between two stations within the State of Louisiana, was assigned by officers of the company to the coach used for the race to which he belonged, but he insisted upon going into a coach used by the race to which he did not belong. Neither in the information nor the plea was his particular race or color averred.

The petition for the writ of prohibition averred that petitioner was seven-eighths Caucasian and one-eighth African blood; that the mixture of colored blood was not discernible in him, and that he was entitled to every right, privilege and immunity secured to citizens of the United States of the white race; and that, upon such theory, he took possession of a vacant seat in a coach where passengers of the white race were accommodated, and was ordered by the conductor to vacate said coach and take a seat in another assigned to persons of the colored race, and having refused to comply with such demand he was forcibly ejected with the aid of a police officer, and imprisoned in the parish jail to answer a charge of having violated the above act.

The constitutionality of this act is attacked upon the ground that it conflicts both with the Thirteenth Amendment of the Constitution, abolishing slavery, and the Fourteenth Amendment, which prohibits certain restrictive legislation on the part of the States.

1. That it does not conflict with the Thirteenth Amendment, which abolished slavery and involuntary servitude, except as a punishment for crime, is too clear for argument. Slavery implies involuntary servitude—a state of bondage; the ownership of mankind as a chattel, or at least the control of the labor and services of one man for the benefit of another, and the absence of a legal right to the disposal of his own person, property and services. * * *

* * *

A statute which implies merely a legal distinction between white and colored races—a distinction which is founded in the color of the two races, and which must always exist so long as white men are distinguished from the other race by color—has no tendency to destroy the legal quality of the two races, or reestablish a state of involuntary servitude. Indeed, we do not understand that the Thirteenth Amendment is strenuously relied upon by the plaintiff in error in this connection.

2. By the Fourteenth Amendment, all persons born or naturalized in the United States, and subject to the jurisdiction thereof, are made citizens of the United States and of the State wherein they reside; and the States are forbidden from making or enforcing any law which shall abridge the privileges or immunities of citizens of the United States, or shall deprive any person of life, liberty or property without due process of law, or deny to any person within their jurisdiction the equal protection of the laws.

The proper construction of this amendment was first called to the attention of this court in the *Slaughter-house cases*, 16 Wall. 36, which involved, however, not a question of race, but one of exclusive privileges. The case did not call for any expression of opinion as to the exact rights it was intended to secure to the colored race, but it was said generally that its main purpose was to establish the citizenship of the negro; to give definitions of citizenship of the United States and of the States, and to protect from the hostile legislation of the States the privileges and immunities of citizens of the United States, as distinguished from those of citizens of the States.

The object of the amendment was undoubtedly to enforce the absolute equality of the two races before the law, but in the nature of things it could not have been intended to abolish distinctions based upon color, or to enforce social, as distinguished from political equality, or a commingling of the two races upon terms unsatisfactory to either. Laws permitting, and even requiring, their separation in places where they are liable to be brought into contact do not necessarily imply the inferiority of either race to the other, and have been generally, if not universally, recognized as within the competency of the state legislatures in the exercise of their police power. The most common instance of this is connected with the establishment of separate schools for white and colored children, which has been held to be a valid exercise of the legislative power even by courts of States where the political rights of the colored race have been longest and most earnestly enforced.

One of the earliest of these cases is that of *Roberts v. City of Boston*, 5 Cush. 198, in which the Supreme Judicial Court of Massachusetts held that the general school committee of Boston had power to make provision for the instruction of colored children in separate schools established exclusively for them, and to prohibit their attendance from the other schools. * * * It was held that the powers of the committee extended to the establishment of separate schools for children of different ages, sexes and colors, and that they might also establish special schools for poor and neglected children, who have become too old to attend the primary school, and yet have not acquired the rudiments of learning, to enable them to enter the ordinary schools. Similar laws have been enacted by Congress under its general power of legislation over the District of Columbia, * * * as well as by the legislatures of many of the States, and have been generally, if not uniformly, sustained by the courts. * * *

Laws forbidding the intermarriage of the two races may be said in a technical sense to interfere with the freedom of contract, and yet have been universally recognized as within the police power of the State. * * *

The distinction between laws interfering with the political equality of the negro and those requiring the separation of the two races in schools, theatres and railway carriages has been frequently drawn by this court. Thus in *Strauder* v. *West Virginia*, it was held that a law of West Virginia limiting white male persons, 21 years of age and citizens of the State, the right to sit upon juries, was a discrimination which implied a legal inferiority in civil society, which lessened the security of the right of the colored race, and was a step toward reducing them to a condition of servility. Indeed, the right of the colored man that, in the selection of jurors to pass upon his life, liberty and property, there shall be no exclusion of his race, and no discrimination against them because of color, has been asserted in a number of cases. * * *

* * *

So far, then, as a conflict with the Fourteenth Amendment is concerned, the case reduces itself to the question of whether the statute of Louisiana is a reasonable regulation, and with respect to this there must necessarily be a large discretion on the part of the legislature. In determining the question of reasonableness it is at liberty to act with reference to the established usages, customs and traditions of the people, and with a view to the promotion of their comfort, and the preservation of the public peace and good order. Gauged by this standard, we cannot say that a law which authorized or even requires the separation of the two races in public conveyances is unreasonable, or more obnoxious to the Fourteenth Amendment than the acts of Congress requiring separate schools for colored children in the District of Columbia, the constitutionality of which does not seem to have been questioned, or the corresponding acts of state legislatures.

We consider the underlying fallacy of the plaintiff's argument to consist in the assumption that the enforced separation of the two races stamps the colored race with a badge of inferiority. If this be so, it is not by reason of anything found in the act, but solely because the colored race chooses to put that construction upon it. The argument necessarily assumes that if, as had been more than once the case, and is not unlikely to be so again, the colored race should become the dominant power in the state legislature, and should enact a law in precisely similar terms, it would thereby relegate the white race to an inferior position. We imagine that the white race, at least, would not acquiesce in this assumption. The argument also assumes that social prejudices may be overcome by legislation, and that equal rights cannot be secured to the negro except by an enforced commingling of the two races.

We cannot accept this proposition. If the two races are to meet upon terms of social equity, it must be the result of natural affinities, a mutual appreciation of each other's merits and a voluntary consent of individuals. * * * Legislation is powerless to eradicate racial instincts or to abolish distinctions based upon physical differences, and the attempt to do so can only result in accentuating the difficulties of the present situation. If the civil and political rights of both races be equal one cannot be inferior to the other civilly or politically. If one race be inferior to the other socially, the Constitution of the United States cannot put them upon the same plane.

It is true that the question of the proportion of colored blood necessary to constitute a colored person, as distinguished from a white person, is one upon which there is a difference of opinion in the different States, some holding that any visible admixture of black blood stamps the person as belonging to the colored race, * * * others that it depends upon the preponderance of blood, * * * and still others that the predominance of white blood must only be in the proportion of three-fourths. * * * But these are questions to be determined under the laws of each State and are not properly put in issue in this case. Under the allegations of his petition it may undoubtedly become a question of importance whether, under the laws of Louisiana, the petitioner belongs to the white or colored race.

The judgment of the court below is, therefore,

Affirmed.

MR. JUSTICE HARLAN dissenting.

* * *

* * * [W]e have before us a state enactment that compels, under penalties, the separation of the two races in railroad passenger coaches, and makes it a crime for a citizen of either race to enter a coach that has been assigned to citizens of the other race.

* * *

However apparent the injustice of such legislation may be, we have only to consider whether it is consistent with the Constitution of the United States.

* * *

In respect of civil rights, common to all citizens, the Constitution of the United States does not, I think, permit any public authority to know the race of those entitled to be protected in the enjoyment of such rights. Every true man has pride of race, and under appropriate circumstances when the rights of others, his equals before the law, are not to be affected, it is his privilege to express such pride and to take such action based upon it as to him seems proper. But I deny that any legislative body or judicial tribunal may have regard to the race of citizens when the civil rights of those citizens are involved. Indeed, such legislation, as that here in question, is inconsistent not only with that equality of rights which pertains to citizenship,

National and State, but with the personal liberty enjoyed by every one within the United States.

The Thirteenth Amendment does not permit the withholding or the deprivation of any right necessarily inhering in freedom. It not only struck down the institution of slavery as previously existing in the United States, but it prevents the imposition of any burdens or disabilities that constitute badges of slavery or servitude. It decreed universal civil freedom in this country. This court has so adjudged. But that amendment having been found inadequate to the protection of the rights of those who had been in slavery, it was followed by the Fourteenth Amendment, which added greatly to the dignity and glory of American citizenship, and to the security of personal liberty, by declaring that "all persons born or naturalized in the United States, and subject to the jurisdiction thereof, are citizens of the United States and of the State wherein they reside," and that "no State shall make or enforce any law which shall abridge the privileges or immunities of citizens of the United States; nor shall any State deprive any person of life, liberty or property without due process of law, nor deny to any person within its jurisdiction the equal protection of the laws." These two amendments, if enforced according to their true intent and meaning, will protect all the civil rights that pertain to freedom and citizenship. Finally, and to the end that no citizen should be denied, on account of his race, the privilege of participating in the political control of his country, it was declared by the Fifteenth Amendment that "the right of the citizens of the United States to vote shall not be denied or abridged by the United States or by any State on account of race, color or previous condition of servitude."

These notable additions to the fundamental law were welcomed by the friends of liberty throughout the world. They removed the race line from our governmental systems. They had, as this court has said, a common purpose, namely, to secure "to a race recently emancipated, a race that through many generations has been held in slavery, all the civil rights that the superior race enjoys." They declared, in legal effect, this court has further said, "that the law in the States shall be the same for the black as for the white; that all persons, whether colored or white, shall stand equal before the laws of the States, and, in regard to the colored race, for whose protection the amendment was primarily designed, that no discrimination shall be made against them by law because of their color." We also said: "The words of the amendment, it is true, are prohibitory, but they contain a necessary implication of a positive immunity, or right, most valuable to the colored race—the right to exemption from unfriendly legislation against them distinctively as colored—exemption from legal discriminations, implying inferiority in civil society, lessening the security of their enjoyment of the rights which others enjoy, and discriminations which are steps towards reducing them to the condition of a subject race." It was, consequently, adjudged that a state law that excluded citizens of the colored race from juries, because of their race and however well qualified in other respects to discharge the duties of jurymen, was repugnant to the Fourteenth Amendment. * * *

* * *

It was said in argument that the statute of Louisiana does not discriminate against either race, but prescribes a rule applicable alike to white and colored citizens. But this argument does not meet the difficulty. Every one knows that the statute in question had its origins in the purpose, not so much to exclude white persons from railroad cars occupied by blacks, as to exclude colored people from coaches occupied by or assigned to white persons. Railroad corporations of Louisiana did not make discrimination among whites in the matter of accommodation for travellers. The thing to accomplish was, under the guise of giving equal accommodation for whites and blacks, to compel the latter to keep to themselves while travelling in railroad passenger coaches. No one would be so wanting in candor as to assert the contrary. The fundamental objection, therefore, to the statute is that it interferes with the personal freedom of citizens. * * * If a white man and a black man choose to occupy the same public conveyance on a public highway, it is their right to do so, and no government proceeding alone on grounds of race can prevent it without infringing the personal liberty of each.

* * *

The white race deems itself to be the dominant race in this country. And so it is, in prestige, in achievements, in education, in wealth and power. So, I doubt not, it will continue to be for all time, if it remains true to its great heritage and holds fast to the principles of constitutional liberty. But in view of the Constitution, in the eye of the law, there is in this country no superior, dominant, ruling class of citizens. There is no caste here. Our Constitution is color-blind, and neither knows nor tolerates classes among citizens. In respect of civil rights, all citizens are equal before the law. The humblest is the peer of the most powerful. The law regards man as man, and takes no account of his surroundings or of his color when his civil rights as guaranteed by the supreme law of the land are involved. It is, therefore, to be regretted that this high tribunal, the final expositor of the fundamental law of the land, has reached the conclusion that it is competent for a State to regulate the enjoyment by citizens of their civil rights solely upon the basis of race.

In my opinion, the judgment this day rendered will, in time, prove to be quite as pernicious as the decision made by this tribunal in the *Dred Scott case*. It was adjudged in that case that the descendants of Africans who were imported into this country and sold as slaves were not included nor intended to be included under the word "citizens" in the Constitution, and could not claim any of the rights and privileges which that instrument provided for and ensured to citizens of the United States; that at the time of the adoption of the Constitution they were "considered as a subordinate and inferior class of beings, who had been subjugated by the dominant race, and, whether emancipated or not, yet remained subject to their authority, and had no rights or privileges but such as those who held the power and the government might choose to grant them." * * * The recent amendments of the Constitution, it was supposed, had eradicated these principles from our institutions. But it seems that we have yet, in some of the States, a dominant race—a superior class of citizens, which assumes to regulate the enjoyment of civil rights, common to all citizens, upon the basis of race. The present decision, it may well be apprehended, will not only stimulate aggressions, more or less brutal and irritating, upon the admitted rights of colored citizens, but will encourage the belief that it is possible, by means of state enactments, to defeat the beneficent purposes which the people of the United States had in view when they adopted the recent amendments of the Constitution, by one of which the blacks of this country were made citizens of the United States and of the States in which they respectively reside, and whose privileges and immunities, as citizens, the States are forbidden to abridge. Sixty millions of whites are in no danger from the presence here of eight millions of blacks. The destinies of the two races, in this country, are indissolubly linked together, and the interests of both require that the common government of all shall not permit the seeds of race hate to be planted under the sanction of law. What can more certainly arouse race hate, what more certainly create and perpetuate a feeling of distrust between these races, than state enactments, which, in fact, proceed on the ground that colored citizens are so inferior and degraded that they cannot be allowed to sit in public coaches occupied by white citizens? That, as all will admit, is the real meaning of such legislation as was enacted in Louisiana.

* * *

There is a race so different from our own that we do not permit those belonging to it to become citizens of the United States. Persons belonging to it are, with few exceptions, absolutely excluded from our country. I allude to the Chinese race. But by the statute in question, a Chinaman can ride in the same passenger coach with white citizens of the United States, while citizens of the black race in Louisiana, many of whom, perhaps, risked their lives for the preservation of the Union, who are entitled, by law, to participate in the political control of the State and nation, who are not excluded, by law or by reason of their race, from public stations of any kind, and who have all the legal rights that belong to white citizens, are yet declared to be criminals, liable to imprisonment, if they ride in a public coach occupied by citizens of the white race. * * *

* * *

I do not deem it necessary to review the decisions of state courts to which reference was made in argument. Some, and the most important, of them are wholly inapplicable, because rendered prior to the adoption of the last amendment of the Constitution, when colored people had very few rights which the dominant race felt obliged to respect. Others were made at a time when public opinion, in many localities, was dominated by the institution of slavery; when it would not have been safe to do justice to the black man; and when, so far as the rights of blacks were concerned, race prejudice was, practically, the supreme law of the land. Those decisions cannot be guides in the era introduced by the recent amendments of the supreme law, which established universal civil freedom, gave citizenship to all born or naturalized in the United States and residing here, obliterated the race line from our systems of governments, National and State, and placed our free institutions upon the broad and sure foundation of the equality of all men before the law.

* * *

For the reasons stated, I am constrained to withhold my assent from the opinion and judgment of the majority.

Notes and Questions

It was during the Reconstruction period that Southern states adopted so-called Jim Crow laws under which white and black Americans were required to use such separate public facilities as toilets, water fountains, and recreational facilities. In some instances, these laws required using separate telephone booths, gambling tables, Bibles for swearing in witnesses, cemeteries, theaters, and restaurants. The segregative intent of these laws was to prevent contact between white and black Americans.

Justice Harlan's dissenting opinion has proven to be prophetic. As we shall see, it is an example of how a dissent's rationale, in time, may be adopted as a majority view. Justice Harlan, a Kentuckian, was considered a strong defender of civil liberties and is remembered as the "great dissenter."

As used in the *Plessy* decision, what did the term *equal* in "separate but equal" mean? Did it mean that facilities and services would be equal to those provided white Americans, or did it mean services and facilities afforded black Americans should be equal? Could "equal" have had any other meaning than the latter one because at the time of the decision whites dominated political, economic, and social life?

Given the racial attitudes of that day, some argue that a contrary decision in *Plessy* would have been widely flouted, thereby weakening the status of the Court as an institution. Do you think it possible that the Court would take such a factor into consideration in rendering a decision?

The Court drew a distinction between "social" and "political" equality. Is the key to this distinction the involvement of state action? Do you agree that the Constitution should protect only "political" equality?

It was not until 1927 that the Court specifically extended the *Plessy* doctrine to public education. See *Gong Lum* v. *Rice*, 275 U.S. 78 (1927).

B. *De Jure* Public School Segregation Unconstitutional (*Brown I*)

Several United States Supreme Court decisions dealing with higher education segregative practices successfully eroded the *Plessy* doctrine before it received a mortal blow from *Brown* v. *Board of Education.* In one of these cases, a black law school applicant challenged a policy under which he had to attend an out-of-state law school because his home state did not have a "separate" law school for black students. The Court held that such an arrangement did not meet the "separate but equal" doctrine. See *Missouri ex rel. Gaines* v. *Canada*, 305 U.S. 337 (1938). In another decision, *Sweatt* v. *Painter*, 339 U.S. 629 (1950), the Court contended that "separate" law schools in Texas were not "equal" to those attended by white law students. In its decision, the Court not only compared tangible factors between racially segregated law schools but also compared such intangible factors as prestige, faculty reputation, and experience of the administration.

Decisions such as *Gaines, Sweatt*, and others set the stage for a challenge to the *de jure* segregative practices in the primary and secondary public schools. This challenge was presented in *Brown*, and the Court declared that segregation in public education was a denial of the Fourteenth Amendment's guarantee of the equal protection of the laws.

BROWN v. *BOARD OF EDUCATION OF TOPEKA*
Supreme Court of the United States, 1954
347 U.S. 483

MR. CHIEF JUSTICE WARREN delivered the opinion of the Court.

These cases come to us from the States of Kansas, South Carolina, Virginia, and Delaware. They are premised on different facts and different local conditions, but a common legal question justifies their consideration together in this consolidated opinion.

In each of the cases, minors of the Negro race, through their legal representatives, seek the aid of the courts in obtaining admission to the public schools of their community on a nonsegregated basis. In each instance, they had been denied admission to schools attended by white children under laws requiring or permitting segregation according to race. This segregation was alleged to deprive the plaintiffs of the equal protection of the laws under the Fourteenth Amendment. In each of the cases other than the Delaware case, a three-judge federal district court denied relief to the plaintiffs on the so-called "separate but equal" doctrine announced by this Court in *Plessy* v. *Ferguson.* Under that doctrine, equality of treatment is accorded when the races are provided substantially equal facilities, even though these facilities be separate. In the Delaware case, the Supreme Court of Delaware adhered to that doctrine, but ordered that the plaintiffs be admitted to the white schools because of their superiority to the Negro schools.

The plaintiffs contend that segregated public schools are not "equal" and cannot be made "equal," and that hence they are deprived of the equal protection of the laws. Because of the obvious importance of the question presented, the Court took jurisdiction. Argument was heard in the 1952 Term, and reargument was heard this Term on certain questions propounded by the Court.

Reargument was largely devoted to the circumstances surrounding the adoption of the Fourteenth Amendment in 1868. It covered exhaustively consideration of the Amendment in Congress, ratification by the states, then existing practices in racial segregation, and the views of proponents and opponents of the Amendment. This discussion and our own investigation convince us that, although the sources cast some light, it is not enough to resolve the problem with which we are faced. At best, they are inconclusive. The most avid proponents of the post-War Amendments undoubtedly intended them to remove all legal distinctions among "all persons born or naturalized in the United States." Their opponents, just as certainly, were antagonistic to both the letter and the spirit of the Amendments and wished them to have the most limited effect. What others in Congress and the state legislatures had in mind cannot be determined with any degree of certainty.

An additional reason for the inconclusive nature of the Amendment's history, with respect to segregated schools, is the status of public education at that time. In the South, the movement toward free common schools, supported by general taxation, had not yet taken hold. Education of white children was largely in the hands of private groups. Education of Negroes was almost nonexistent, and practically all of the race were illiterate. In fact, any education of Negroes was forbidden by law in some states. Today, in contrast, many Negroes have achieved outstanding success in the arts and sciences as well as in the business and professional world. It is true that public school education at the time of the Amendment had advanced further in the North, but the effect of the Amendment on Northern States was generally ignored in the congressional debates. Even in the North, the conditions of public education did not approximate those existing today. The curriculum was usually rudimentary; ungraded schools were common in rural areas; the school term was but three months a year in many states; and compulsory school attendance was virtually unknown. As a consequence, it is not surprising that there should be so little in the history of the Fourteenth Amendment relating to its intended effect on public education.

In the first cases in this Court construing the Fourteenth Amendment, decided shortly after its adoption, the Court interpreted it as proscribing all state-imposed discriminations against the Negro race. The doctrine of "separate but equal" did not make its appearance in this Court until 1896 in the case of *Plessy* v. *Ferguson, supra,* involving not education but transportation. American courts have since labored with the doctrine for over half a century. In this Court, there have been six cases involving the "separate but equal" doctrine in the field of public education. In *Cumming* v. *County Board of Education,* 175 U.S. 528, and *Gong Lum* v. *Rice,* 275 U.S. 78, the validity of the doctrine itself was not challenged. In more recent cases, all on the graduate school level, inequality was found in that specific benefits enjoyed by white students were denied to Negro students of the same educational qualifications. *Missouri ex rel. Gaines* v. *Canada,* 305 U.S. 337; *Sipuel* v. *Oklahoma,* 332 U.S. 631; *Sweatt* v. *Painter,* 339 U.S. 629; *McLaurin* v. *Oklahoma State Regents,* 339 U.S. 637. In none of these cases was it necessary to reexamine the doctrine to grant relief to the Negro plaintiff. And in *Sweatt* v. *Painter, supra,* the Court expressly reserved decision on the question whether *Plessy* v. *Ferguson* should be held inapplicable to public education.

In the instant cases, that question is directly presented. Here, unlike *Sweatt* v. *Painter,* there are findings below that the Negro and white schools involved have been equalized, or are being equalized, with respect to buildings, curricula, qualifications and salaries of teachers, and other "tangible" factors. Our decision, therefore, cannot turn on merely a comparison of these tangible factors in the Negro and white schools involved in each of the cases. We must look instead to the effect of segregation itself on public education.

In approaching this problem, we cannot turn the clock back to 1868 when the Amendment was adopted, or even to 1896 when *Plessy* v. *Ferguson* was written. We must consider public education in the light of its full development and its present place in American life throughout the Nation. Only in this way can it be determined if segregation in public schools deprives these plaintiffs of the equal protection of the laws.

Today, education is perhaps the most important function of state and local governments. Compulsory school attendance laws and the great expenditures for education both demonstrate our recognition of the importance of education to our democratic society. It is required in the performance of our most basic public responsibilities, even service in the armed forces. It is the very foundation of good citizenship. Today it is a principal instrument in awakening the child to cultural values, in preparing him for later professional training, and in helping him to adjust normally to his environment. In these days, it is doubtful that any child may reasonably be expected to succeed in life if he is denied the opportunity of an education. Such an opportunity, where the state has undertaken to provide it, is a right which must be made available to all on equal terms.

We come then to the question presented: Does segregation of children in public schools solely on the basis of race, even though the physical facilities and other "tangible" factors may be equal, deprive the children of the minority group of equal educational opportunities? We believe that it does.

In *Sweatt* v. *Painter, supra,* in finding that a segregated law school for Negroes could not provide them equal educational opportunities, this Court relied in large part on "those qualities which are incapable of objective measurement but which make for greatness in a law school." In *McLaurin* v. *Oklahoma State Regents, supra,* the Court, in requiring that a Negro admitted to a white graduate school be treated like all other students, again resorted to intangible considerations: ". . . his ability to study, to engage in discussions and exchange views with other students, and, in general, to learn his profession." Such considerations apply with added force to children in grade school and high schools. To separate them from others of similar age qualifications solely because of their race generates a feeling of inferiority as to their status in the community that may affect their hearts and minds in a way unlikely ever to be undone. The effect of this separation on their educational opportunities was well stated by a finding in the Kansas case by a court which nevertheless felt compelled to rule against the Negro plaintiffs:

> "Segregation of white and colored children in public schools has a detrimental effect upon the colored children. The impact is greater when it has the sanction of the law: for the policy of separating the races is usually interpreted as denoting the inferiority of the negro group. A sense of inferiority affects the motivation of a child to learn. Segregation with the sanction of law, therefore, has a tendency to retard the educational and mental development of negro children and to deprive them of some of the benefits they would receive in a racially integrated school system."

Whatever may have been the extent of psychological knowledge at the time of *Plessy* v. *Ferguson,* this finding is amply supported by modern authority. Any language in *Plessy* v. *Ferguson* contrary to this finding is rejected.

We conclude that in the field of public education the doctrine of "separate but equal" has no place. Separate educational facilities are inherently unequal. Therefore, we hold that the plaintiffs and others similarly situated for whom the actions have been brought are, by reason of the segregation complained of, deprived of the equal protection of the laws guaranteed by the Fourteenth Amendment. This disposition makes unnecessary any discussion whether such segregation also violates the Due Process Clause of the Fourteenth Amendment.

Because these are class actions, because of the wide applicability of this decision, and because of the great variety of local conditions, the formulation of decrees in these cases presents problems of considerable complexity. On reargument, the consideration of appropriate relief was necessarily subordinated to the primary question—the constitutionality of segregation in public education. We have now announced that such segregation is a denial of the equal protection of the laws. * * *

Notes and Questions

Brown may be one of the most significant decisions rendered by the United States Supreme Court. By declaring *de jure* segregation in the public schools unconstitutional, the decision had reverberations far beyond schools. It was a catalyst that forced Americans to examine many forms of government-condoned separation of the races.

It should be emphasized that the consolidated opinion in *Brown* addressed *de jure* segregation in the public schools. Constitutional and statutory provisions in South Carolina, Virginia, and Delaware and statutory provisions in Kansas required the segregation of black and white students. Consequently, *Brown* applied only to those states having government-imposed segregation at the time of the decision. It did not have applicability to *de facto* segregated public schools outside the South.

The decision was widely criticized by those opposed to desegregation and applauded by those who were for it. Criticism on legalistic grounds focused on the fact that the Court relied on sociological evidence to establish the negative effect of segregation on black students rather than relying on precedent. In this regard, the Court was influenced by the work of Gunnar Myrdal, a Swedish sociologist and economist, who had written *An American Dilemma: The Negro Problem and Modern Democracy*, which was published in 1944. The Court's employing such data raises the question of precisely which factors should be taken into consideration when attempting to determine whether or not persons have received the "equal protection of the laws" guaranteed by the Fourteenth Amendment to the Constitution.

Proponents of "judicial activism" argued that because the executive and legislative branches were apparently unwilling to address this issue, it was the duty of the judiciary to ensure that all persons, in this instance black Americans, receive their constitutional rights. Opponents of the decision contended that nine appointed judges, as opposed to elected officials, should not have the power to institute such fundamental social change. Which view do you hold?

C. Implementation (*Brown II*)

Brown discussed the broad issue of public school segregation and declared *de jure* segregation to be unconstitutional. However, the decision did not provide a remedy for those whom it affected. As the Court stated:

> Because these are class actions, because of the wide applicability of this decision, and because of the great variety of local conditions, the formulation of decrees in these cases presents problems of considerable complexity. (p. 495)

Therefore, the Court addressed this question in a separate opinion in *Brown II*.

BROWN v. BOARD OF EDUCATION OF TOPEKA
Supreme Court of the United States, 1955
349 U.S. 294

MR. CHIEF JUSTICE WARREN delivered the opinion of the Court.

These cases were decided on May 17, 1954. The opinions of that date, declaring the fundamental principle that racial discrimination in public education is unconstitutional, are incorporated herein by reference. All provisions of federal, state, or local law requiring or permitting such discrimination must yield to this principle. There remains for consideration the manner in which relief is to be accorded.

Because these cases arose under different local conditions and their disposition will involve a variety of local problems, we requested further argument on the question of relief. * * *

These presentations were informative and helpful to the Court in its consideration of the complexities arising from the transition to a system of public education freed of racial discrimination. The presentations also demonstrated that substantial steps to eliminate racial discrimination in public schools have already been taken, not only in some of the communities in which these cases arose, but in some of the states appearing as *amici curiae,* and in other states as well. Substantial progress has been made in the District of Columbia and in the communities in Kansas and Delaware involved in this litigation. The defendants in the cases coming to us from South Carolina and Virginia are awaiting the decision of this Court concerning relief.

Full implementation of these constitutional principles may require solution of varied local school problems. School authorities have the primary responsibility for elucidating, assessing, and solving these problems; courts will have to consider whether the action of school authorities constitutes good faith implementation of the governing constitutional principles. Because of their proximity to local conditions and the possible need for further hearings, the courts which originally heard these cases can best perform this judicial appraisal. Accordingly, we believe it appropriate to remand the cases to those courts.

In fashioning and effectuating the decrees, the courts will be guided by equitable principles. Traditionally, equity has been characterized by a practical flexibility in shaping its remedies and by a facility for adjusting and reconciling public and private needs. These cases call for the exercise of these traditional attributes of equity power. At stake is the personal interest of the plaintiffs in admission to public schools as soon as practicable on a nondiscriminatory basis. To effectuate this interest may call for elimination of a variety of obstacles in making the transition to school systems operated in accordance with the constitutional principles set forth in our May 17, 1954, decision. Courts of equity may properly take into account the public interest in the elimination of such obstacles in a systematic and effective manner. But it should go without saying that the vitality of these constitutional principles cannot be allowed to yield simply because of disagreement with them.

While giving weight to these public and private considerations, the courts will require that the defendants make a prompt and reasonable start toward full compliance with our May 17, 1954, ruling. Once such a start has been made, the courts may find that additional time is necessary to carry out the ruling in an effective manner. The burden rests upon the defendants to establish that such time is necessary in the public interest and is consistent with good faith compliance at the earliest practicable date. To that end, the courts may consider problems related to administration, arising from the physical condition of the school plant, the school transportation system, personnel, revision of school districts and attendance areas into compact units to achieve a system of determining admission to the public schools on a nonracial basis, and revision of local laws and regulations which may be necessary in solving the foregoing problems. They will also consider the adequacy of any plans the defendants may propose to meet these problems and to effectuate a transition to a racially nondiscriminatory school system. During this period of transition, the courts will retain jurisdiction of these cases.

The judgments below, except that in the Delaware case, are accordingly reversed and the cases are remanded to the District Courts to take such proceedings and enter such orders and decrees consistent with this opinion as are necessary and proper to admit to public schools on a racially nondiscriminatory basis with all deliberate speed the parties to these cases. The judgment in the Delaware case—ordering the immediate admission of plaintiffs to schools previously attended only by white children—is affirmed on the basis of the principles stated in our May 17, 1954, opinion, but the case is remanded to the Supreme Court of Delaware for such further proceedings as that Court may deem necessary in light of this opinion.

It is so ordered.

Notes and Questions

Did *Brown II* temper the original decision by employing such an imprecise standard as "all deliberate speed"? In this regard, Justice Frankfurter suggested: "Nothing could be worse from my point of view than for this court to make an abstract declaration that segregation is bad and then to have it evaded by tricks." Would the establishment of a specific time frame, for instance, have been enforceable?

In addition to not setting a time frame, why do you believe the Court did not offer specific desegregation guidelines to the lower courts that were effecting desegregation? Do *Brown I* and *Brown II* provide sufficient instructions and guidance from the Supreme Court to the lower federal courts for the latter to have effected desegregation adequately? Because the Court did not provide a test for compliance with the desegregation ruling, what criteria would one use to determine if a school system was in compliance with *Brown I*?

II. EARLY DESEGREGATION IN THE SOUTH

Under the *Brown II* formula, local school authorities were given the primary responsibilities for fashioning desegregation plans. Lower-level federal courts were to determine whether such plans constituted good-faith implementation of the principles enunciated in *Brown I*. However, the Court's abstract doctrine, lack of clear guidance, and imprecise time frame, especially in those areas of the South where there was considerable animosity to the decision, all contributed to attempts at delay if not outright noncompliance with *Brown I*.

Consequently, lower federal courts in the South were inundated with school desegregation cases. Some of these cases represented resistance in complying with *Brown I* on the part of local school systems, yet in other instances local authorities were thwarted in their attempt to desegregate by state-level action. An example of this latter problem, which gained nationwide notoriety at the time, is the events in Little Rock, Arkansas. Here, the local school system had made good-faith efforts to desegregate; however, the governor ordered the national guard to prevent black students from entering the school to which they had been assigned. Under the circumstances, the local authorities sought a postponement of the desegregation plan by citing preservation of the public peace. In addressing this issue, the Supreme Court, in *Cooper* v. *Aaron*, 358 U.S. 1 (1958), declared that although the Court was sympathetic to the authorities' good-faith efforts that had been hindered by state action, desegregation of the schools could not be postponed.

In Virginia, that state's compulsory-education laws were repealed, and school attendance was made a matter of local option. Prince Edward County closed its schools, and private schools for whites-only were operated in their place with state and county assistance. The Supreme Court rejected such a course in *Griffin* v. *County School Board of Prince Edward County*, 377 U.S. 218 (1964), by instructing the local district court to require the authorities to levy taxes, thereby raising funds to reopen and operate a nondiscriminatory public school system such as those in other Virginia counties.

A so-called freedom-of-choice plan was another method school systems employed to comply with the necessity to desegregate. Under such a plan, parents had the choice of determining which school their children would attend, with the result that there was often little or no actual desegregation within a school system. This issue was addressed in *Green* v.

County School Board of New Kent County, 391 U.S. 430 (1968) by the United States Supreme Court. In not ruling freedom-of-choice out as a desegregation tool, the court stated:

> Although the general experience under "Freedom of Choice" to date has been such as to indicate its ineffectiveness as a tool of desegregation, there may well be instances in which it can serve as an effective device. Where it offers real promise of aiding a desegregation program to effectuate conversion of a state-imposed dual system to a unitary, nonracial system there might be no objection to allowing such a device to prove itself in operation. On the other hand, if there are reasonable available other ways, such for illustration as zoning, promising speedier and effective conversion to a unitary, nonracial school system, "freedom of choice" must be held unacceptable. (p. 440–441)

In a per curiam opinion one year after *Green*, the Court declared that with respect to continued operation of racially segregated schools, the standard of "all deliberate speed" was no longer constitutionally permissible and that school districts must immediately terminate dual school systems based on race or color. See *Alexander* v. *Holmes County Board of Education*, 396 U.S. 19 (1969).

In its next major desegregation decision, the Court in *Swann* v. *Charlotte-Mecklenburg Board of Education*, 402 U.S. 1 (1971), defined the scope of the duty to eliminate the dual school system. The decision represented another example of the Supreme Court's continued effort to render decisions that unequivocally reflected its desire to eliminate the dual school system. The unanimous decision ruled that the dismantling of the dual school system could be accomplished by: assigning teachers to achieve a particular degree of faculty desegregation; ensuring that future school construction and abandonment would not perpetuate or reestablish a dual system; scrutinizing one-race schools to ensure that the racial composition did not result from present or past discriminatory action; altering attendance zones and employing pairing and grouping of noncontiguous zones to counteract past segregation; and although not requiring it, employing bus transportation as a constitutionally permissible method of dismantling the dual system. Would the path to eliminating *de jure* segregation have been smoother if **Brown I** had contained such guidelines?

III. DESEGREGATION IN THE NON-SOUTH

Continued and successful desegregation efforts in the Southern states clearly revealed the lack of similar efforts in many non-Southern states where public school racial segregation existed. The legitimate question was often raised, of why one section of the country was required to desegregate its schools, yet obviously segregated school systems continued to operate in the northern and western portions of the United States. From a legal standpoint, a partial answer to this question was the Supreme Court's reliance on the distinction between *de jure* and *de facto* segregation.

As has been noted, the presence of constitutional and/or statutory provisions and local policies mandating segregated schools in the Southern states made it possible to address this form of state-sanctioned *de jure* segregation. Segregated school systems existed outside the South, and although such segregation was not always based on officially stated state or local policy, in some areas it had been. Several non-Southern states had statutes authorizing separate but equal public schools, and although eventually repealed, such statutes remained on the books in New York until 1938, in Wyoming until 1954, and in Indiana until 1959. The presence of such statutes established persistent patterns of segregated schools that were not always easily changed.

Segregation outside the South existed for other reasons. In some instances, long-standing "customs" were present at the local level, which also contributed to racial attitudes and resultant segregated schools. Perhaps the most significant force, however, contributing to segregated schools outside the South resulted from housing patterns, which in some areas found black Americans living in neighborhoods and attending schools populated solely by blacks. Such *de facto* segregation was often based on housing patterns that allegedly were not the result of direct state action. Because the Supreme Court had not considered *de facto* segregation a violation of the *Brown I* edict, non-Southern public schools that were segregated on that basis were not immediately challenged in the courts. However, in time, segregative practices of non-Southern school systems were examined by the judiciary. One of the contentions made against segregated non-Southern school systems was that they had engaged in a form of *de jure* segregation, perhaps not as blatant as in the South, but nevertheless resulting in impermissible racial discrimination.

Although United States Supreme Court decisions dealing with Southern school segregation had a certain consistency and unanimity in attempting to eradicate *de jure* segregation, the same may not be said for the Court's decisions regarding non-Southern school segregation. These differences may be seen by examining the often split Court decisions dealing with such issues as intentional segregation and interdistrict integration.

A. Intentional Segregative Action

Desegregation litigation in the two decades after *Brown I* focused primarily on dismantling dual-school systems, for the most part, in the rural South. During the mid-1970s, however, school desegregation entered its "second generation," and the locus of school desegregation efforts shifted outside the South and to the nation's large urban centers. In decisions involving Dayton and Columbus, Ohio, the United States Supreme Court revealed a continued reliance on the *de jure/de facto* distinction. The Court maintained that if racially segregated dual school systems were operated at the time of *Brown I* in 1954, boards of education had an "affirmative duty" not to engage in actions that would have impeded the desegregation process. See for instance, *Columbus Board of Education* v. *Penick*, 443 U.S. 449 (1979).

In a decision involving Denver, Colorado, the Court held that

> a finding of intentionally segregative school board actions in a meaningful portion of a school system, as in this case, creates a presumption that other segregated schooling within the system is not adventitious. It establishes, in other words, a prima facie case of unlawful segregative design on the part of school authorities, and shifts to those authorities the burden of proving that other segregated schools within the system are not also the result of intentionally segregative actions. *Keyes* v. *School District No. 1*, 413 U.S. 189, 208 (1973).

Keyes was the first case of a school system without a history of state-mandated racial assignment before the Supreme Court.

B. Interdistrict Integration

As a result of increasing white flight from urban areas to the suburbs, it became increasingly difficult to keep urban schools desegregated because there simply were not enough white students. As a result, many urban school districts became virtually all black and/or Hispanic. In response to such a situation in Detroit, a federal district court ordered a metropolitan integration remedy that, in effect, would have required the consolidation with the Detroit school system of 53 independent school districts surrounding the city that had historically been administered as separate units into a vast new super-school district. At the time, many parents who had moved from Detroit to the often more affluent suburbs, with school systems that they considered to be considerably better than inner-city schools, faced the prospect of their children being bused long distances to perceived inferior and often dangerous schools. Many of these parents vowed to fight this court order. When the issue came before the United States Supreme Court in *Milliken* v. *Bradley*, 418 U.S. 717 (1974) (*Milliken I*), a five-to-four decision, the Court declared

> The record before us, voluminous as it is, contains evidence of *de jure* segregated conditions only in the Detroit schools; indeed, that was the theory on which the litigation was initially based and on which the District Court took evidence. * * * With no showing of significant violations by the 53 outlying school districts and no evidence of any Interdistrict violation or effect, the court went beyond the original theory of the case as framed by the pleading and mandated a metropolitan area remedy. To approve the remedy ordered by the court would impose on the outlying districts, not shown to have committed any constitutional violation, a wholly impermissible remedy based on a standard not hinted at in *Brown I* and *Brown II* or any holding of this Court. (p. 745)

On remand, the district court approved a desegregation plan that included educational components in the areas of reading, in-service teacher training, testing, and counseling. Costs were to be borne by both the Detroit School Board and the state. The Supreme Court upheld the lower court's action and stated that such a remedy was reasonable in the light of past acts of *de jure* segregation. See *Milliken* v. *Bradley*, 433 U.S. 267 (1977) (*Milliken II*).

Many observers consider *Milliken I* as marking an end to the United States Supreme Court's unwavering support of desegregation efforts. Subsequent to this decision, the Court has been viewed decreasingly as a friendly and receptive forum for achieving school desegregation.

The plight of an urban school system similar to the one described in *Milliken* was addressed by Connecticut's supreme court in *Sheff* v. *O'Neill*, 678 A.2d 1267 (Conn. 1996). In that decision, the court found that there was an extreme concentration of poor children in Hartford's schools, that Hartford students scored last on the state's standardized tests, and that although statewide there were 26 percent minority students, Hartford schools had 95 percent minority students; the court held the state's school districting and attendance statutes unconstitutional. The court found that Hartford students suffered from unconstitutional segregation and that disparities in racial and ethnic composition of the city's schools in comparison with surrounding school districts violated their constitutional right for equal educational opportunity. The court noted that the state had ample notice of ongoing trends toward racial and ethnic isolation in the public schools, and whether or not the legislature created or intended to create the conditions that led to racial and ethnic isolation did not relieve state officials of their responsibility to provide effective remedies. The court announced that the legislature was required to take affirmative responsibility to remedy segregation in the public schools regardless of whether the segregation occurred *de jure* or *de facto*.

In *Sheff* v. *O'Neill*, the Connecticut Supreme Court describes in detail the state's speedy and thorough attempt to remedy the conditions described in the earlier *Sheff* decision.

SHEFF V. O'NEILL
Supreme Court of Connecticut, 1999
733 A.2d 925

AURIGEMMA, J.

On July 9, 1996, the Connecticut Supreme Court issued its decision in this case, Sheff v. O'Neill, 238 Conn. 1, 678 A.2d 1267 (1996), in which it held that students in the Hartford public schools were racially, ethnically and economically isolated and that, as a result, Hartford public school students had not been provided a substantially equal educational opportunity under the state constitution, * * *

The court clearly recognized that the state had not intentionally segregated racial and ethnic minorities in the Hartford public school system. But it also recognized that the state had created local school districts, which it identified as the most important factor contributing to the concentration of racial and ethnic minorities in Hartford. * * *

Although the court noted that "according to the findings of the trial court, poverty, and not race or ethnicity, is the principal causal factor in lower educational achievement of Hartford students"; its holding implicitly recognized a strong causal relationship between racial and ethnic isolation and lower educational achievement.

* * *

The court did not order judicial intervention to remedy the racial, ethnic and economic isolation existing in the Hartford public schools. Instead, the court directed the trail court to issue a declaratory judgment and to retain jurisdiction in order to give the legislature the opportunity to act. Specifically, the court directed "the legislature and the executive branch to put the search for appropriate remedial measures at the top of their respective agendas." * * *

The state's response to the Supreme Court's decision was swift. On July 25, 1996, Governor John Rowland issued Executive Order No. 10, creating the education improvement panel (the panel), which was charged to "explore, identify and report on a broad range of options for reducing racial isolation in our state's public schools, improving teaching and learning, enhancing a sense of community and encouraging parental involvement." * * *

* * *

Within five months of receiving the final report of the panel, the Connecticut legislature had passed Public Acts 1997, No. 97-290, entitled "An Act Enhancing Educational Choices and Opportunities." This legislation was aimed at reducing racial, ethnic and economic isolation, as well as improving the quality of education throughout the state—with an emphasis on improving urban education.

The first section of * * * the statute which defines the "educational interests of the state," to include the reduction of "racial, ethnic and economic isolation," to impose a duty on each school district to "provide educational opportunities for its students to interact with students and teachers from other racial, ethnic and economic backgrounds. . . ." * * *

Section 2 of Public Act 97-290 provided that school boards could reduce racial, ethnic and economic isolation by using programs or methods such as: "(1) Interdistrict magnet school programs; (2) charter schools; (3) interdistrict after-school, Saturday and summer programs and sister-school projects; (4) intradistrict and interdistrict public school choice programs; (5) interdistrict school building projects; (6) interdistrict program collaboratives for students and staff; (7) minority staff recruitment; (8) distance learning through the use of technology; and (9) any other experience that increases awareness of the diversity of individuals and cultures."

Interdistrict cooperative programs are school sponsored programs in which students from different school districts participate together in a diverse array of educational experiences. These programs, funded largely by the state, bring urban and suburban students together in the context of quality educational experiences. * * *

In order to receive state funding, interdistrict programs must promote diversity as well as academic improvement. The state department of education operates a competitive process in which local school districts or Regional Educational Service Centers submit written proposals for such programs. * * *

* * *

Interdistrict magnet schools are created by two or more districts combining their ideas, skills and resources to create a new school centered around a unique or unusual theme, specifically designed to foster both excellence in academics and the reduction of racial, ethnic or economic isolation. Interdistrict magnet schools existed prior to the Supreme Court's decision. Since, by definition, a magnet school is made up of students from different districts, however, both the state and the plaintiffs have recognized the magnet school as an excellent method of reducing racial, ethnic and economic isolation.

Overall, state spending on magnet schools will be $17.5 million dollars for fiscal year 1998–99, representing an increase in excess of $7 million over the spending level for fiscal year 1997–98. * * *

* * *

If a magnet school is housed in a new building, the state provides 100 percent funding for the construction of the building. In order to receive the state construction money, the districts must commit to the new school for at least twenty years. * * *

The state department of education has a division which includes employees who meet regularly with those planning new interdistrict magnet schools. They provide guidance and assistance in the development process, including supplying a "nuts and bolts" set of guidelines for the process. The founders of a proposed magnet school must submit a detailed "operations plan" which is carefully scrutinized. * * *

The structure for the operational funding of interdistrict magnet schools is designed to encourage racial and ethnic diversity. Magnet schools are rewarded through financial incentives for accomplishing the greatest diversity in the racial and ethnic makeup of their student bodies. * * * If the districts participating in the magnet school send no more than 30 percent of the students to the school, then the magnet school receives 90 percent of the foundation level for each pupil from each such district.As the percentage from the sending district rises above the 30 percent threshold, the operational reimbursement decreases correspondingly. This funding formula provides a strong financial incentive to the founders of magnet schools to seek to have three or more districts involved in the magnet school, with each contributing less than 30 percent of the students. Since the school must show it will reduce racial and/or ethnic isolation, this funding formula ensures participation of both urban and suburban districts in appropriate proportions while avoiding the pitfalls and possible legal challenges of having raced based quotas. As with the interdistrict cooperative grants, by July, 2000, the law will prohibit more than 80 percent of the students in a magnet school from coming from any one district.

The state has provided a further financial incentive for local districts to participate in magnet schools. The sending districts are permitted to count the students they are sending to the magnet school in their student counts for education cost sharing purposes. For example, if West Hartford sent seven children to the Montessori magnet school in Hartford in 1998, it would receive the same amount in education cost sharing monies from the state as it would if the students remained in West Hartford schools. Obviously, under this formula, the sending district could secure substantial state funds in excess of those normally received for education. Transportation funding is also available for students who do not live in the district in which the school is located at the level of $1200 per student.

* * *

Like magnet schools, charter schools are conceived and implemented by local educators and parents. Charter schools arise from an entrepreneurial approach to providing education and use a unique, autonomous governance structure. They can be created quickly, but if they fail to meet their educational mission, they can also be dismantled quickly through the state's revocation or nonrenewal of their charters. Typically, they are small in size, with smaller class sizes, and the stakeholders and founder of the school take on full accountability and responsibility for the school. * * * Charter schools generally center around a particular theme and adopt innovative approaches to education. * * *

The establishment of a charter school is a competitive process. Prospective founders of such a school must respond to a state request for proposals, which requires spelling out in detail the parameters of the proposed school. Legislation concerning charter schools predated Public Act 97-290. Public Act 97-290, however, amended the law governing the establishment and operation of charter schools to require the consideration of the reduction of racial, ethnic and economic isolation as a factor in approving new state or local charter schools or in renewing the charters of existing schools. * * *

* * *

In addition to changing the substantive requirements of charter school approval to reduce racial and ethnic isolation, the state has increased charter school funding significantly. Six million dollars has been allocated for 1997–98 and nine million for 1998–99, with the concomitant increase in the number of authorized seats.

Section 2 of Public Act 97-290 also listed minority staff recruitment as one method whereby schools could attempt to alleviate racial, ethnic and economic isolation. There is no dispute that increasing the diversity of school staff and administrators, including minority representation in teacher preparation programs, can play a role in the reduction of racial and ethnic isolation. * * * each local or regional board of education must now develop and implement a written plan for minority staff recruitment, along with reporting requirements. In addition, legislation in 1998 added additional funds to the Connecticut state universities and the University of Connecticut for scholarships for future minority educators. * * *

* * *

Under the new Choice Program, beginning first in the Hartford, New Haven and Bridgeport areas, and then later throughout the state, districts must report to their respective Regional Educational Service Centers seats available for students from other districts to allow interdistrict attendance. Project Concern, which operated in the Hartford area until this school year, has been folded into this program. Three million dollars has been allocated for the Choice Program from the 1998–99 school year alone, as compared to just $900,000 for Project Concern in the year before the Supreme Court's decision in this case. * * *

. . . Under the Choice Program, all students are free to apply, and unlike Project Concern, special education students and students with limited English proficiency are not turned away. The Latino participation rate in the Choice Program has already exceeded the "best" years of Project Concern.

If a Choice Program student needs special education, the receiving district must provide the services and if the cost of the services exceeds the $2000 per student the district receives from the state, the sending district picks up that extra cost. The student is also the responsibility of the receiving district for all disciplinary purposes.

* * *

The state is providing several incentives to encourage local districts to offer seats in the Choice Program. Any school district that builds a school facility that includes extra room for the interdistrict transfer of students will receive funds from the state in an amount that is 10 percent higher than the district's normal reimbursement rate. * * *

. . . The concept of the lighthouse school came about as a result of a number of legislators describing the need to enable educators to improve the quality of a school in a district to the degree that it would attract students from across the district, and, eventually, from other school districts. A lighthouse school can be the predecessor of an interdistrict magnet school.

* * *

The executive and legislative branches of this state both acted very expeditiously to comply with the Supreme Court's order. Governor Rowland issued Executive Order No. 10, which created the education improvement panel, just sixteen days after the Supreme Court's decision issued. In the following six month period, Governor Rowland and the legislative leadership appointed twenty-one citizens to the panel. Those citizens devoted many days in discussion, deliberations and information gathering and issued the final report of the panel on January 22, 1997. Within five months after it received that report, the Connecticut legislature passed Public Act 97-290. Notwithstanding the speed with which the legislature acted to pass that legislation, the legislation was not cursory, but rather, was a comprehensive, carefully drafted, and well funded plan.

* * *

In order to determine the efficacy as well as the timeliness of the state's response to the Supreme Court's decision, it is necessary to consider the alternative remedies available to the state in its attempts to reduce racial, ethnic and economic isolation in Hartford schools. The remedies fall into two basic categories: voluntary and mandatory.

The measures mandated by Public Act 97-290 and the other legislation referred to above are voluntary. * * *

* * *

The second type of desegregation remedy is mandatory. * * * The term "mandatory reassignment" is, essentially, a synonym for "forced busing."

Christine Rossell, Ph.D., an expert witness called by the defendants, presented convincing testimony that mandatory reassignment would not have the effect sought by the plaintiffs, and would in fact, be counterproductive. Unlike Orfield, whose testimony was not based on any statistical research, Rossell has conducted extensive empirical studies of the effects of various types of desegregation plans. Stating that she previously had been a proponent of mandatory reassignment, she testified that her views changed when her empirical studies began to indicate that mandatory reassignment of white students to minority schools did, in fact, produce significant white enrollment loss or "white flight" from those schools.

Rossell testified that mandatory reassignment plans are only mandatory for the poorest people in a school district: "Everybody else has a choice. Poor people have to go where they're reassigned by some court or government agency who says you must go there. The rest of us can put our kids in private schools. We can move to another school district and we do. So even though these plans were implemented with the best of intentions and you have to understand that I supported them in the early years. Even though they were implemented with the best of intentions, the problem is they're mandatory for only the poorest people in the school district."

Rossell testified that the state's approach is to implement a state-wide remedy that is based on the premise that voluntary integration is more likely to produce a lasting integration and will have more positive social effects and that this will be enhanced by their equal emphasis on improving educational quality for all children. Her research shows that a voluntary approach to school desegregation is the most effective approach and it will produce the most lasting integration. In other words, according to Rossell, in the area of school desegregation, slow and steady wins the race.

. . . Rossell predicted that if white suburban students were manditorily assigned to Hartford, Hartford public schools would experience a white enrollment loss of approximately 45 to 50 percent.

* * *

The rapid rate of desegregation that the plaintiffs seek can only be accomplished through a mandatory reassignment plan. Based on the evidence presented at the hearing, this court finds that voluntary plans are generally superior to mandatory ones because they promote integration of more lasting duration with a minimum of opposition and disruption. * * *

Voluntary integration plans make particular sense in situations where, as here, the past segregation was de facto and not de jure. * * *

* * *

The plaintiffs have sought court intervention before the state has had an opportunity to take even a "second step" in the remedial process. The state has acted expeditiously and in good faith to respond to the decision of the Supreme Court in this case. It has devised a comprehensive, interrelated, well funded set of programs and legislation designed to improve education for all children, with a special emphasis on urban children, while promoting diverse educational environments. The legislative and executive branches should have a realistic opportunity to implement their remedial programs before further court intervention. This will not only satisfy the Supreme Court's desire to be sensitive to the "constitutional authority of coordinate branches of government"; but will also allow any educational reform plan to gain grassroots popular support which is crucial to the success of any plan. The best way to achieve popular support is not to impose a judicially mandated remedial plan, but to encourage Connecticut's populace as a whole, both directly and through their elected representatives, to solve the problems facing the state's schools.

For the reasons set forth above, this court finds that the state has complied with the decision of the Supreme Court.

IV. CURRENT DESEGREGATION ISSUES

A. Release from Court Order

Many school systems across the United States were placed under federal court supervision in order to remedy past discrimination. In fact, by the mid-1990s there were approximately four hundred formerly segregated local school systems under some form of federal court jurisdiction. The issue of when such supervision should end, in addition to being extensively litigated over the years, has increasingly become highly charged emotionally and politically. Consequently, two United States Supreme Court decisions in the early 1990s provided educators with useful guidance. The four-to-three decision in *Board of Education of Oklahoma City Public Schools* v. *Dowell*, 498 U.S. 237 (1991), addresses an injunction's termination. It reveals the Court's views regarding the use of the term "unitary," the importance of local control, and that court supervision was intended to be a temporary measure. *Freeman* v. *Pitts*, 503 U.S. 467 (1992), an eight-to-zero decision, held that federal district courts have the discretion to withdraw their supervision over formerly segregated school systems incrementally and are not responsible for segregation based on demographic changes in student population. *Freeman* required the following test to determine whether a school system had attained unitary status:

> [W]hether there has been full and satisfactory compliance with the decree in those aspects of the system where supervision is to be withdrawn; whether retention of judicial control is necessary or practicable to achieve compliance with the decree in other facets of the school system; and whether the school district has demonstrated, to the public and to the parents and students of the once disfavored race, its good-faith commitment to the whole of the court's decree and to those provisions of the law and the Constitution that were the predicate for judicial intervention in the first instance. (p. 491)

Kansas City has had a long history of school desegregation litigation beginning in 1985. At issue, in what was to become extensive litigation, was an extremely controversial plan that has been considered to be the most ambitious desegregation program in the country. The program consisted of a capital improvements plan to rectify the decay in the schools' physical facilities, numerous quality education programs, and a far-reaching magnet school plan. The goals of the remedial programs were to compensate the former victims of segregation by improving the education given them; to enhance the programs so as to reverse the white-flight pattern, winning back white students from private and suburban schools and thus ending the racial isolation of the former victims; and to use the magnet schools as a way of bringing about voluntary redistribution of students within the Kansas City schools. A federal appellate court originally held that the state of Missouri had to provide funding for the Kansas City desegregation program in *Jenkins* v. *Missouri*, 807 F.2d 657 (8th Cir. 1986) (*Jenkins I*), *cert. denied*, 484 U.S. 816 (1987), and in *Missouri* v. *Jenkins*, 495 U.S. 33 (1990), the Court held that the school system could be ordered to levy taxes in excess of statutory limitations to pay for desegregation remedies. In *Missouri* v. *Jenkins*, 515 U.S. 70 (1995) (*Jenkins III*), the Court challenged the notion that the state should indefinitely be required to fund remedial "quality education" programs until national norms were met. In instructing the lower court, the Supreme Court articulated a standard for unitary status that required a showing of "compliance in good faith with the desegregation decree since it was entered" and that the "vestiges of past discrimination have been eliminated to the extent possible." The Court reminded the lower court that on remand, an important end purpose, in addition to remedying violations, was the restoration of control of the school system to state and local authorities.

After *Jenkins III,* the state of Missouri and the Kansas City School Board entered into an agreement under which the state would pay the school district $320 million over three years and be released from any further obligation in the desegregation litigation in 1999. This agreement was upheld in *Jenkins* v. *Missouri,* 959 F. Supp. 1151 (Mo. 1997) (*Jenkins VIII*), *aff'd,* 122 F.3d 588 (8th Cir. 1997) (*Jenkins XIV*). The *Jenkins XIV* decision also declared that the school district still had not remedied the "achievement gap vestige" and had not remedied four of the *Green* factors: student assignment, faculty and staff assignments, transportation, and facilities.

A lengthy decision in *Brown* v. *Board of Education of Topeka,* 892 F. 2d 851 (10th Cir. 1989) (*Brown III*), a progeny of the landmark school desegregation case, had pronounced the Topeka schools not to be a racially unitary system because the school district had exercised a form of benign neglect by insufficiently attending to desegregation efforts. However, in 1992, the United States Supreme Court vacated and remanded this decision for further consideration in the light of *Dowell* and *Freeman.* On reflection, the federal appellate court reinstated its original opinion in full and entered an additional opinion. The court argued that the facts underlying *Brown III* were far different from those before the Supreme Court in *Dowell* and *Freeman* because the Topeka school board had not fulfilled its affirmative duty in the areas of student and faculty/staff assignments. See *Brown* v. *Board of Education of Topeka,* 978 F.2d 585 (10th Cir. 1992)(*Brown IV*), *denied sub nom. Unified School District No. 501* v. *Smith,* 509 U.S. 903 (1993). Finally, in *Brown* v. *Unified School District No. 501,* 56 F.Supp.2d 1212 (Kan. 1999), the court declared:

> After careful consideration, the court has no reservation in finding that: defendant has complied in good faith with the mandates of the court over a reasonable period of time; the vestiges of past discrimination in the school district have been eliminated to the extent practicable; and defendant has demonstrated a good faith commitment to the law and the Constitution which presages no future need for judicial intervention. (p. 1214)

Cleveland schools were released from further remedial obligations in *Reed* v. *Rhodes,* 1 F. Supp2d 705 (Ohio 1998). In its decision, the court declared that socioeconomic factors were the primary cause of disparities in achievement on reading tests between blacks and other students. The court also declared that it was "not convinced the voluminous remedial orders issued in this case benefitted the students . . . to the degree that all Parties and the Court had hoped."

B. Race-Related Placement

Many school systems, which may or may not have been under court order, attempt to have their community's diversity reflected in classes, schools, and/or enrichment programs. In their attempt to accomplish such diversity, school systems have employed admissions schemes to ensure that members of minority groups are properly represented. These schemes have included magnet schools, preferences, set-asides, underrepresentation racial balancing, racial quota, controlled choice, and weighted lottery. In recent years, these schemes have been legally challenged by white students who are denied access to a neighborhood school or an enrichment program, although they have higher scores than minority students who have been accepted.

In many of the cases, courts use the strict scrutiny standard in their constitutional analysis. Under this standard, a disputed racial policy must further a compelling government interest and be narrowly tailored to serve that interest. Courts have had great difficulty in defining a concept such as diversity and exactly what constitutes a compelling state interest; therefore, courts often assume, without deciding, that diversity may be a compelling state interest. Once that threshold is crossed, decisions are based on whether a disputed admissions policy is sufficiently narrowly tailored to pass constitutional muster. If racial balancing is a factor in an admissions policy, courts find the policy unconstitutional. These cases are quite fascinating. For many years, school desegregation cases were concerned with ensuring that blacks were not discriminated against, in these cases, whites are alleging discrimination. To date, the Supreme Court has not resolved the question of whether diversity is a compelling state interest.

1. Magnet Schools

Magnet schools have an accelerated, enriched, or specialized curriculum. Acceptance is often extremely competitive and is determined by meeting established criteria. They are only feasible in relatively larger school systems, and they were not originally designed to effect desegregation efforts. When used as a desegregation scheme, however, their emphasis has been to entice white suburban students to remain in the school system or be willing to attend magnet schools located in the inner city. Controversy and attendant legal problems have arisen when white students with higher scores are denied access and students, because of their race or ethnicity, with lower scores are accepted.

A policy under which a white first grader was denied entry into a magnet school because of "impact on diversity"—his neighborhood school was already losing whites—was not upheld. In its decision, the court in *Eisenberg v. Montgomery County Public Schools*, 197 F.3d 123 (4th Cir. 1999), *denied* 529 U.S. 1019 (2000), contended that had he been African

American, Asian American, or Hispanic he would have been able to attend the magnet school. The court held that the school system was engaging in unconstitutional racial balancing, which is not a narrowly tailored remedy; therefore, race could not be considered in granting or denying transfer to the magnet school. Although race-based classifications have been tolerated to correct past constitutional violations, the court explained, this did not apply here. The school system had never been under court order to desegregate and had voluntarily dismantled its formerly segregated system after *Brown*.

A race-based admission policy used by the Boston Latin School, a prestigious public school, was challenged in *Wessmann* v. *Gittens*, 160 F.3d 790 (1st Cir.1998). An original admissions policy required that at least 35 percent of an entering class be composed of African American and Hispanic students. Although a 1987 court decision had declared that the quota was no longer necessary because unitariness had been achieved in student assignment, the 35 percent quota continued to be implemented until 1996. Under a subsequent admissions plan, a standardized test was given and applicants had to score in the top 50 percent of the overall qualified applicant pool. Half of the available slots were given to those applicants who ranked highest, and the other half were given to the remaining pool of qualified applicants in rank order based on the overall proportion of blacks, whites, Hispanic, Asian, and Native American of all the qualified applicants. This suit came about when white applicants were denied admission who had a higher composite score than the minority students who were accepted. In its decision, the court stated "any program which induces schools to grant preferences based on race and ethnicity is constitutionally suspect," and examined the policy using the strict scrutiny standard. In its decision, the court held that the race conscious admission policy failed the strict scrutiny test and was therefore invalid under the Equal Protection Clause. In its analysis, the court acknowledged that there was no clear legal definition regarding what exactly constituted a legitimate government interest when a classification is based on race. The court agreed that the schools had achieved unitary status years ago and that no "causal connection" between past discriminatory conduct and present effects were shown.

In San Francisco, after years of contentious litigation, the San Francisco schools, the National Association for the Advancement of Colored People, and Chinese American students (the parties) put their differences aside and submitted a stipulated settlement for court approval. The parties thought it best to work out an agreement among themselves rather than continue litigation. A suit by Chinese American students had been contemplated that sought to end the use of racial quotas such as the 40 percent ceiling that had been set for any ethnic group at such prestigious institutions as Lowell High School. In this instance, Chinese American students were being discriminated against because of their overrepresentation. The settlement was approved in *San Francisco NAACP v. San Francisco Unified School District*, 59 F.Supp.2d 1021 (Cal. 1999). In addressing student assignment, the court stated:

> In fact, the settlement expressly acknowledges that, in assigning students to the schools of the SFUSD, "state and federal law provide that district officials may consider many factors, including the desire to promote residential geographic, economic, racial and ethnic diversity in all SFUSD schools." The settlement merely precludes the SFUSD from using race or ethnicity as the primary or predominant consideration in determining student admissions. . . ." (p. 1034)

The terms of the settlement provided that it will terminate no later than December 31, 2002, subject to court approval.

A school system may continue to use a policy of considering race, however, in assigning students to magnet schools when a school system is still under court order. Although the Charlotte-Mecklenburg school system had achieved integration in its faculty and staff, extracurricular activities, and student discipline practices, the court held, in *Belk v. Charlotte-Mecklenburg Board of Education*, 233 F.3d 232 (4th Cir. 2000), that segregation continued to exist in student assignments, school locations, transportation policies, and student achievement levels. Therefore, the court concluded, employing a magnet school program that considered race in student assignment was not unconstitutional. The race-sensitive method of student selection that was employed, the court reasoned, "was undertaken both to remedy the effects of past desegregation and to comply with governing court orders," and therefore, "did not and could not violate the Constitution."

2. Weighted Lottery

Tuttle v. Arlington County School Board, 195 F.3d 698 (4th Cir. 1999) held that using a weighted lottery, under which each applicant's lottery number was weighted, so that applicants from underrepresented groups had a better chance of being selected, was unconstitutional. The school system's goals for using this scheme were (1) to prepare and educate students to live in a diverse, global society by reflecting the diversity of the community and (2) to help the school board serve the diverse groups of students in the district, including those from backgrounds that suggest they may come to school with educational needs that are different from or greater than others. Diversity was defined by using three equally weighted factors: (1) whether the applicant was from a low-income or special family background, (2) whether English was the applicant's first or second language, and (3) the racial or ethnic groups to which the applicant belonged. Because the case dealt with racial classification, the court applied the strict scrutiny standard under which the admissions policy must serve a compelling governmental interest and be narrowly tailored to achieve that interest. In its holding the court declared, "Until the Supreme Court provides decisive guidance, we will assume, without so holding, that diversity may be a compelling governmental interest and proceed to examine whether the Policy is narrowly tailored to achieve diversity." In holding the admissions policy unconstitutional because it was not narrowly tailored, the court determined that the policy had no logical ending period, granted special treatment to certain minority groups, and unduly burdened people outside of specific minority groups. The court declared, "We find it ironic that a Policy that seeks to teach young children to view people as individuals rather than members of certain racial and ethnic groups classified those same children as members of certain racial and ethnic groups."

V. EPILOGUE

As public education enters the twenty-first century, a cross-current of forces appears to be operating on the desegregation landscape. The federal judiciary can no longer be relied on to assist in furthering historic desegregation measures. Large-scale, costly desegregation efforts in inner-city school systems have not brought about desired results. There is little public support for traditional public school desegregation efforts, especially busing, which is now often viewed as a major reason for bringing about white flight. Observers argue that large urban school systems, after years of desegregation efforts, appear to be undergoing resegregation rather than further desegregation. And, these days, black students have been replaced by white students who claim discrimination because they are excluded from prestigious public schools that have quotas to ensure diversity.

The *Brown I* decision set off an avalanche of civil-rights decisions and legislation that gave black Americans equality before the law, not only in education but also in such areas as public accommodation, housing, and voting. However, almost fifty years after the decision, the educational racial scene is not all that its proponents had hoped it would be. Such court-ordered efforts as numerical quotas and forced busing of students, in too many instances, have not had the desired effect, and, unfortunately, in many instances, increased racial tension.

Although the South went from being completely segregated to being the least segregated area in the United States, this accomplishment is diminishing. According to a 1997 report for the Harvard Project on School Desegregation, Southern states, which have had an enviable record in desegregating their school systems, are resegregating and following a national trend of blacks attending poor and inferior schools while their white counterparts attend affluent and superior schools. Inner-city schools increasingly have become totally "minority" because of the flight of whites and middle-class blacks. The report further states that schools in the Midwest and Northeast remain the most segregated between black and white students, and in the West segregation between white and Hispanic students is growing.

Efforts such as magnet schools, which have been widely touted, have had spotty success in desegregation efforts. The ambitious court-ordered program of heavily funded magnet schools in Kansas City did not achieve its original goal of drawing significant numbers of white students from the suburbs. After the full program had been in place for two years, a 1994 Harvard study revealed relatively small academic and racial gains. Elementary students made "modest" gains in academic achievement, yet half the students entering high school did not graduate. The percent of minority students in the district climbed slightly from 73.5 percent to 74.8 percent between 1986 and 1993. In 2000, Kansas City schools were characterized by the director of the Council of the Great City Schools as being "an island of incompetence in a sea of indifference." As a result of the district's dismal scholastic record, the state of Missouri has revoked its accreditation, and the district has been placed in danger of being broken up or taken over by the state if there is no improvement. Total expenses for the two-decade court-ordered desegregation program, which after 1999 no longer received state funding, reached nearly two billion dollars.

Several mid- and late-1990s legal events may have an important impact on the future of public school desegregation. In one instance, a federal appellate court, in *Hopwood* v. *Texas*, 78 F.3d 932 (5th Cir. 1996), *cert. denied*, 518 U.S. 1033 (1996), held that a state university law school could no longer consider race or ethnicity when admitting students. Although dealing specifically with law school admission, the decision has the potential to affect other higher education affirmative action admissions policies. The *Hopwood* decision has direct applicability only in Texas, Louisiana, and Mississippi, but it has spawned similar suits in other states. In another desegregation setback, California voters passed Proposition 209 in 1996, a measure providing that the "state shall not discriminate against, or grant preferential treatment to any individual or group on the basis of race, sex, color, ethnicity, or national origin in the operation of public employment, public education, or public contracting." Proposition 209 effectively ended affirmative action in California's public sector, and the Supreme Court's refusal to review a lower court's upholding of the measure provides a positive signal to other states contemplating a similar measure. See *Coalition for Economic Equity* v. *Wilson*, 122 F.3d 692 (9th Cir. 1997), *cert. denied*, 522 U.S. 963 (1997). In 1998, Washington State voted for a similar measure to eliminate state-sponsored affirmative action.

The fostering of the notion of "diversity" is increasingly being attacked. Proponents who foster the diversity notion argue that an institution should attempt to reflect the racial and/or ethnic makeup of the community. Opponents argue that by emphasizing diversity over merit too often results in academic programs being watered down. Race-based admission programs designed to further diversity, when challenged by white students, are consistently struck down by the courts.

A half-century after *Brown I*, two views on opposite ends of the desegregation continuum may be illuminating in describing the desegregation landscape as the twenty-first century begins. Dinesh D'Souza, author of *The End of Racism*, argues that attempting to effect desegregation through judicial involvement and antidiscriminatory legislation "has failed." He further contends that the major problem facing blacks today is no longer racism but "destructive and pathological cultural patterns of behavior" within the subculture of the black underclass. He contends that while discrimination still exists, it is "rational discrimination"; namely, whites rationally choose to steer clear of that pathological subculture. Gary Orfield, director of the Harvard Project on School Desegregation, disagrees with D'Souza's assessment. He cites the profound transformation of Southern society due to the full implementation of desegregation efforts. Orfield believes that the lack of judicial support in the non-South in implementing desegregation remedies has essentially stopped the desegregation process nationwide. He thinks that desegregation gains made since *Brown* will increasingly be lost.

Given this climate surrounding desegregation efforts, especially in the inner cities, do you agree that there is a possibility of public school desegregation efforts returning full circle to "separate but equal" again?

CHAPTER SIX*

Individuals with Disabilities and the Law

As the United States Congress recognized in its 1997 reauthorization of the Individuals with Disabilities Education Act (IDEA), disabilities are a natural part of the human experience, and should in no way diminish the right of individuals to participate in or contribute to society. With appropriate educational services, children with disabilities, like all other children, can be prepared to lead productive, independent, adult lives to the maximum extent possible. But prior to the passage of laws protecting children with disabilities, many of these children were excluded from public schools or were not receiving appropriate educational services. The prevailing educational philosophy held that children with disabilities that prevented them from conforming to ordinary cognitive, physical, or hygiene standards did not belong in regular public schools. The burden of educating these children remained primarily with their families, who often lacked sufficient resources to provide appropriate educational services. Educational services that were available to these children were often provided in segregated facilities, preventing these children from interacting with their nondisabled peers. Congress found that before the enactment of the landmark Education for All Handicapped Children Act of 1975 (Public Law 94-142), a million children with disabilities were entirely excluded from public schools, and more than half of the children with disabilities in the United States were not receiving appropriate educational services.

Following the United States Supreme Court's mandate to racially desegregate schools in *Brown v. Board of Education*, advocates for individuals with disabilities championed desegregated education for children with disabilities. Based on legal theories rooted in *Brown*, dozens of cases

*This chapter was written by John Dayton, J.D., Ed.D., an associate professor in the Department of Educational Leadership, College of Education, the University of Georgia.

were filed nationwide alleging that children with disabilities were being excluded from public schools and denied equal protection and due process rights. Two of these cases, *Pennsylvania Association for Retarded Children* (PARC) v. *Pennsylvania*, 343 F. Supp. 279 (E.D. Pa. 1972), and *Mills* v. *Board of Education of the District of Columbia*, 348 F. Supp. 866 (D.C. 1972) resulted in landmark decisions recognizing educational rights for children with disabilities. In *PARC*, a federal district court held that mentally retarded students ages six through twenty-one should be provided with access to a free public education, and that children with disabilities should be placed in regular classrooms when possible or in special classes when necessary. In *Mills*, another federal district court extended this doctrine to all school-age children with disabilities, holding that they must be provided with a free and adequate public education.

Legislation protecting the rights of individuals with disabilities was also passed by the United States Congress. Some of the earliest federal legislation included the Elementary and Secondary Education Act of 1965, and Title VI, which was a 1966 amendment to that Act. In 1970, Title VI was repealed and replaced by the Education of the Handicapped Act. This Act created a Bureau of Education for the Handicapped and brought increased national attention to the concerns of students with disabilities. This early legislation did not provide for "mainstreaming" or a "free appropriate public education," but it established the groundwork for future legislation concerning these issues. In 1973, Congress passed Section 504 of the Rehabilitation Act, prohibiting discrimination against handicapped persons in programs receiving federal funds. In 1975, Congress passed Public Law 94-142, the Education for All Handicapped Children Act, providing significant new substantive legal rights and procedural protections for handicapped children. This Act was renamed the Individuals with Disabilities Education Act (IDEA) in 1990, with the addition of some important substantive changes such as provisions for "transition services" and changes in terminology, including a change from "handicapped children" to "children with disabilities." In that same year, Congress also passed the Americans with Disabilities Act (ADA). The ADA extended antidiscrimination protections similar to Section 504 protections in public institutions to many private sector areas, including employment, public accommodations, transportation, and telecommunications. These three laws, Section 504, the IDEA, and the ADA, provide the primary legal protections available for individuals with disabilities.

Of these three laws, the IDEA has had the most significant impact on public schools. Legislation, regulations, and judicial opinions concerning the IDEA form a complex system of legal rights and responsibilities, and schools are frequently involved in litigation concerning the IDEA. Accordingly, this chapter focuses greater attention on the IDEA, including significant provisions from the 1997 amendments and the 1999 regulations. But because the law concerning individuals with disabilities continues to develop rapidly, educators responsible for compliance with the IDEA, Section 504, and the ADA should closely monitor new legislation, regulations, and judicial decisions concerning these laws.

I. THE INDIVIDUALS WITH DISABILITIES EDUCATION ACT

Congress reauthorized the IDEA in 1997, adding some significant new amendments and extending federal funding for special education services. The purpose of the 1997 IDEA is to assure that all children with disabilities are provided with a "free appropriate public education" (FAPE) that emphasizes special education and related services designed to meet their unique needs, and to prepare them for employment and independent living. The IDEA is also intended to assure that the rights of children with disabilities are protected, and to assist states in providing appropriate services.

A. Eligibility

To be eligible for IDEA services, a child must be declared a "child with a disability" as defined in the IDEA, requiring a two-part test. First, the child's disability must fit within one of the categories of eligibility. Under section 1401 of the IDEA these categories include:

> [M]ental retardation, hearing impairments (including deafness), speech or language impairments, visual impairments (including blindness), serious emotional disturbance . . . , orthopedic impairments, autism, traumatic brain injury, other health impairments, or specific learning disabilities. 20 U.S.C. § 1401 (1997).

Second, the child must need special education and related services because of the disability. The IDEA defines special education as special instruction designed to meet the unique needs of a child with a disability. Related services are services required to assist a child with a disability to benefit from special education services. A 1997 amendment to the IDEA also allows states to classify children ages three through nine that are "experiencing developmental delays" and in need of special education and related services as "children with disabilities."

Not all children with physical or mental impairments will satisfy the IDEA's two-part eligibility test, and these children will not be eligible for IDEA services. Some children will not fit within an IDEA-eligible category. For example, there is no specific category for children with Attention Deficit Disorder (ADD), diabetes, cancer, or many other chronic health problems. Further, these children would only be eligible as "other health impaired" if their illnesses sufficiently limit their strength, vitality, or alertness and adversely affect their educational performance, requiring special education and related services. Some children may fit in an IDEA-eligible category, but not need special education and related services. For example, although "orthopedic impairment" is a proper category for IDEA eligibility, some orthopedically impaired children do not need special education and related services. These children may qualify under Section 504, and may require reasonable accommodations in facilities and transportation, but they are not eligible for IDEA services if they do not need special education and related services because of their disability.

B. Identification and Evaluation of Students

The IDEA creates an affirmative duty for states to identify children with disabilities through the "child find" provisions, which mandate that "All children with disabilities residing in the State, including children with disabilities attending private schools, regardless of the severity of their disabilities, and who are in need of special education and related services, are identified." 20 U.S.C. § 1412 (1997). Some of these children are identified through mass screening tests including vision tests, hearing tests, and other basic tests administered to all schoolchildren. Also, parents, school personnel, or other persons that suspect a child needs IDEA services may refer the child for an evaluation to determine whether the child is eligible for these services. But before any individual evaluations for IDEA eligibility may be conducted, schools must obtain parental consent for the evaluation.

If parents refuse consent, school officials may use counseling or mediation to encourage parental cooperation. In more difficult cases, school officials may initiate due process proceedings to obtain permission for an evaluation from a hearing officer. Parental refusal does not absolve the school district of its duty to provide a FAPE for children with disabilities. In cases where parents refuse consent and the school suspects the child may be a child with a disability, a hearing officer's determination concerning whether there is an adequate basis for suspecting a disability may help assure that children with disabilities receive needed services, and help to protect the school from future liability for failure to provide the student with a FAPE.

According to the IDEA, an evaluation for eligibility should include a variety of assessment tools and strategies, using technically sound instruments to assess the role of physical, cognitive, behavioral, and developmental factors in the child's disability. To avoid inaccurate conclusions, no single procedure should determine whether a child has a disability. For example, children should not be improperly labeled as mentally retarded based on a single test result, or because of vision, hearing, or language problems in the testing process. Tests should be validated for the intended purpose, administered by qualified personnel, not racially or culturally discriminatory, and administered in the child's native language if feasible. Based on evaluation data, including information from parents and classroom assessments, a determination is made concerning whether the child has an IDEA eligible disability, and whether the child needs special education and related services.

C. Substantive Educational Rights

Children eligible for IDEA services have a right to a "free appropriate public education" (FAPE). According to the IDEA, the right to a FAPE includes special education and related services that are free and without cost to parents or students, and provided through an appropriate educational program that is under public supervision and direction, and in conformity with the child's individualized education program (IEP). Although the meanings of the terms "free," "public," and "education" are relatively clear, "appropriate" is a highly subjective term. Further, the IDEA does not define "appropriate." Because the provision of a FAPE is essential to compliance with the IDEA, it is not surprising that the first United States Supreme Court case to address this law concerned defining the parameters of "appropriate" under the Act. It seemed to many observers that the Act obligated schools to provide, on demand and regardless of cost, optimal education services to meet any demonstrated educational need. Then, in 1982, the United States Supreme Court delivered a six-to-three decision in *Rowley* that addressed the limitations of the Act's substantive guarantees.

BOARD OF EDUCATION OF THE HENDRICK HUDSON CENTRAL SCHOOL DISTRICT v. ROWLEY

Supreme Court of the United States, 1982

458 U.S. 176

JUSTICE REHNQUIST delivered the opinion of the court.

This case represents a question of statutory interpretation. Petitioners contend that the Court of Appeals and the District Court misconstrued the requirements imposed by Congress upon States which receive federal funds under the Education of the Handicapped Act. We agree and reverse the judgment of the Court of Appeals.

The Education of the Handicapped Act (Act), 84 Stat. 175, as amended, 20 U.S.C. § 1401 *et seq.* (1976 ed. and Supp. IV), provides federal money to assist state and local agencies in educating handicapped children, and conditions such funding upon a State's compliance with extensive goals and procedures. The Act represents an ambitious federal effort to promote the education of handicapped children, and was passed in response to Congress' perception that a majority of handicapped children in the United States "were either totally excluded from schools or [were] sitting idly in regular classrooms awaiting the time when they were old enough to 'drop out.'" * * *

* * *

In order to qualify for federal assistance under the Act, a State must demonstrate that it "has in effect a policy that assures all handicapped children the right to a free appropriate public education." * * * That policy must be reflected in a state plan submitted to and approved by the Secretary of Education * * * which describes in detail the goals, programs, and timetables under which the State intends to educate handicapped children within its borders. * * * States receiving money under the Act must provide education to the handicapped by priority, first "to handicapped children who are not receiving an education" and second "to handicapped children . . . with the most severe handicaps who are receiving an inadequate education," * * * and "to the maximum extent appropriate" must educate handicapped children "with children who are not handicapped." * * * The Act broadly defines "handicapped children" to include "mentally retarded, hard of hearing, deaf, speech impaired, visually handicapped, seriously emotionally disturbed, orthopedically impaired, [and] other health impaired children. . . . [and] children with specific learning disabilities." * * *

* * *

Thus, although the Act leaves to the States the primary responsibility for developing and executing educational programs for handicapped children, it imposes significant requirements to be followed in the discharge of that responsibility. Compliance is assured by provisions permitting the withholding of federal funds upon determination that a participating state or local agency has failed to satisfy the requirements of the Act, * * * and by the provision for judicial review. At present, all States except New Mexico receive federal funds under the portions of the Act at issue today. * * *

This case arose in connection with the education of Amy Rowley, a deaf student at the Furnace Woods School in the Hendrick Hudson Central School District, Peekskill, N.Y. Amy has minimal residual hearing and is an excellent lipreader. During the year before she began attending Furnace Woods, a meeting between her parents and school administrators resulted in a decision to place her in a regular kindergarten class in order to determine what supplemental services would be necessary to her education. Several members of the school administration prepared for Amy's arrival by attending a course in sign-language interpretation, and a teletype machine was installed in the principal's office to facilitate communication with her parents who are also deaf. At the end of the trial period it was determined that Amy should remain in the kindergarten class, but that she should be provided with an FM hearing aid which would amplify words spoken into a wireless receiver by the teacher or fellow students during certain classroom activities. Amy successfully completed her kindergarten year.

As required by the Act, an IEP was prepared for Amy during the fall of her first-grade year. The IEP provided that Amy should be educated in a regular classroom at Furnace Woods, should continue to use the FM hearing aid, and should receive instruction from a tutor for the deaf for one hour each day and from a speech therapist for three hours each week. The Rowleys agreed with parts of the IEP but insisted that Amy also be provided a qualified sign-language interpreter in all her academic classes in lieu of the assistance proposed in other parts of the IEP. Such an interpreter had been placed in Amy's kindergarten class for a 2-week experimental period, but the interpreter had reported that Amy did not need his services at that time. The school administrators likewise concluded that Amy did not need such an interpreter in her first-grade classroom. They reached this conclusion after consulting the school district's Committee on the Handicapped, which had received expert evidence from Amy's parents on the importance of a sign-language interpreter, received testimony from Amy's teacher and other persons familiar with her academic and social progress, and visited a class for the deaf.

When their request for an interpreter was denied, the Rowleys demanded and received a hearing before an independent examiner. After receiving evidence from both sides, the examiner agreed with the administrators' determination that an interpreter was not necessary because "Amy was achieving educationally, academically, and socially" without such assistance. * * *

* * *

The District Court found that Amy "is a remarkably well-adjusted child" who interacts and communicates well with her classmates and has "developed an extraordinary rapport" with her teachers * * * It also found that "she performs better than the average child in her class and is advancing easily from grade to grade," * * * but "that she understands considerably less of what goes on in class than she could if she were not deaf" and thus "is not learning as much, or performing as well academically, as she would without her handicap," * * * This disparity between Amy's achievement and her potential led the court to decide that she was not receiving a "free appropriate public education," which the court defined as "an opportunity to achieve [her] full potential commensurate with the opportunity provided to other children." * * * According to the District Court, such a standard requires that the potential of the handicapped child be measured and compared to his or her performance, and that the resulting differential or 'shortfall' be compared to the shortfall experienced by non-handicapped children. * * * District Court's definition arose

from its assumption that the responsibility for "giv[ing] content to the requirement of an 'appropriate education'" had "been left entirely to the [federal]
courts and the hearing officers." * * *

* * *

This is the first case in which this Court has been called upon to interpret any provision of the Act. * * *

* * *

According to the definitions contained in the Act, a "free appropriate
public education" consists of educational instruction specially designed to
meet the unique needs of the handicapped child, supported by such services
as are necessary to permit the child "to benefit" from the instruction. Almost
as a checklist for adequacy under the Act, the definition also requires that
such instruction and services be provided at public expense and under public supervision, meet the State's educational standards, approximate the
grade levels used in the State's regular education, and comport with the
child's IEP. Thus, if personalized instruction is being provided with sufficient
supportive services to permit the child to benefit from the instruction, and
the other items on the definitional checklist are satisfied, the child is receiving a "free appropriate public education" as defined by the Act.

Other portions of the statute also shed light upon congressional intent.
Congress found that of the roughly eight million handicapped children in the
United States at the time of enactment, one million were "excluded entirely
from the public school system" and more than half were receiving an inappropriate education. * * * In addition, as mentioned in Part I, the Act requires
States to extend educational services first to those children who are receiving no education and second to those children who are receiving an "inadequate education." * * * When these express statutory findings and priorities
are read together with the Act's extensive procedural requirements and its
definition of "free appropriate public education," the face of the statute
evinces a congressional intent to bring previously excluded handicapped
children into the public education systems of the States and to require the
States to adopt *procedures* which would result in individualized consideration of and instruction for each child.

Noticeably absent from the language of the statute is any substantive
standard prescribing the level of education to be accorded handicapped
children. Certainly the language of the statute contains no requirement like
the one imposed by the lower courts—that States maximize the potential of
handicapped children "commensurate with the opportunity provided to
other children." * * * That standard was expounded by the District Court
without reference to the statutory definitions or even to the legislative history
of the Act. Although we find the statutory definition of "free appropriate public education" to be helpful in our interpretation of the Act, there remains the
question of whether the legislative history indicates a congressional intent
that such education meet some additional substantive standard. * * *

* * *

The educational opportunities provided by our public school systems undoubtedly differ from student to student, depending upon a myriad of factors that might affect a particular student's ability to assimilate information presented in the classroom. The requirement that States provide "equal" educational opportunities would thus seem to present an entirely unworkable standard requiring impossible measurements and comparisons. Similarly, furnishing handicapped children with only such services as are available to nonhandicapped children would in all probability fall short of the statutory requirement of "free appropriate public education"; to require, on the other hand, the furnishing of every special service necessary to maximize each handicapped child's potential is, we think, further than Congress intended to go. Thus to speak in terms of "equal" services in one instance gives less than what is required by the Act and in another instance more. The theme of the Act is "free appropriate public education," a phrase which is too complex to be captured by the word "equal" whether one is speaking of opportunities or services.

* * *

The District Court and the Court of Appeals thus erred when they held that the Act requires New York to maximize the potential of each handicapped child commensurate with the opportunity provided nonhandicapped children. Desirable though that goal may be, it is not the standard that Congress imposed upon States which receive funding under the Act. Rather, Congress sought primarily to identify and evaluate handicapped children, and to provide them with access to a free public education.

* * *

The determination of when handicapped children are receiving sufficient educational benefits to satisfy the requirements of the Act presents a more difficult problem. The Act requires participating States to educate a wide spectrum of handicapped children, from the marginally hearing-impaired to the profoundly retarded and palsied. It is clear that the benefits obtainable by children at one end of the spectrum will differ dramatically from those obtainable by children at the other end, with infinite variations in between. One child may have little difficulty competing successfully in an academic setting with nonhandicapped children while another child may encounter great difficulty in acquiring even the most basic of self-maintenance skills. We do not attempt today to establish any one test for determing the adequacy of educational benefits conferred upon all children covered by the Act. Because in this case we are presented with a handicapped child who is receiving substantial specialized instruction and related services and who is performing above average in the regular classrooms of a public school system, we confine our analysis to that situation.

The Act requires participating States to educate handicapped children with nonhandicapped children whenever possible. When that "mainstreaming" preference of the Act has been met and a child is being educated in the regular classrooms of a public school system, the system itself monitors the educational progress of the child. Regular examinations are administered, grades are awarded, and yearly advancement to higher grade levels is permitted for those children who attain an adequate knowledge of the course material. The grading and advancement system thus constitutes an important factor in determining educational benefit. Children who graduate from our public school systems are considered by our society to have been "educated" at least to the grade level they have completed, and access to an "education" for handicapped children is precisely what Congress sought to provide in the Act.

When the language of the Act and its legislative history are considered together, the requirements imposed by Congress become tolerably clear. Insofar as a State is required to provide a handicapped child with a "free appropriate public education," we hold that it satisfies this requirement by providing personalized instruction with sufficient support services to permit the child to benefit educationally from that instruction. Such instruction and services must be provided at public expense, must meet the State's educational standards, must approximate the grade levels used in the State's regular education, and must comport with the child's IEP. In addition, the IEP, and therefore the personalized instruction, should be formulated in accordance with the requirements of the Act and, if the child is being educated in the regular classrooms of the public education system, should be reasonably calculated to enable the child to achieve passing marks and advance from grade to grade.

* * *

Applying these principles to the facts of this case, we conclude that the Court of Appeals erred in affirming the decision of the District Court. Neither the District Court nor the Court of Appeals found that petitioners had failed to comply with the procedures of the Act, and the findings of neither court would support a conclusion that Amy's educational program failed to comply with substantive requirements of the Act. On the contrary, the District Court found that the "evidence firmly establishes that Amy is receiving an 'adequate' education, since she performs better than the average child in her class and is advancing easily from grade to grade." * * * In light of this finding, and of the fact that Amy was receiving personalized instruction and related services calculated by the Furnace Woods school administrators to meet her educational needs, the lower courts should not have concluded that the Act requires the provision of a sign-language interpreter. Accordingly, the decision of the Court of Appeals is reversed, and the case is remanded for further proceedings consistent with this opinion.

So ordered.

Notes and Questions

Because the term "appropriate" was not defined in the statute, a broad range of interpretations was possible concerning the Act's substantive guarantees of an "appropriate" education. The Court could have found that Congress intended schools to maximize the potential of each handicapped child or to eliminate the effects of the handicap as much as possible. In applying a less stringent standard, the Court held that schools need only provide sufficient services to "permit the child to benefit educationally." Dissenting Justices in *Rowley* criticized the majority's decision by stating: "It would apparently satisfy the Court's standard of 'access to specialized instruction and related services which are individually designed to provide educational benefit to the handicapped child' for a deaf child such as Amy to be given a teacher with a loud voice, for she would benefit from that service." Is this a fair criticism of the Court's decision in *Rowley*? What would happen to IDEA costs if the Court had determined that the IDEA required schools to maximize the potential of each disabled child or eliminate the effects of the disability as much as possible?

Courts have also addressed the issue of whether a child with disabilities is eligible for special education if no benefit can be shown from that education. In a case involving a child suffering from severe spasticity, cerebral palsy, brain damage, joint contractures, cortical blindness, not being ambulatory, and being a quadriplegic, the court held that such a child was a "handicapped child" within the meaning of the Act. The court concluded that the Act did not require a demonstration of benefiting from special education for a child to be eligible for that education. See *Timothy* v. *Rochester School District*, 875 F.2d 954 (1st Cir. 1989), *cert. denied*, 493 U.S. 983 (1989).

In a case concerning whether schools could be required to provide educational services when public schools are not generally in session, the Court of Appeals for the Eleventh Circuit held that the Georgia policy of refusing to provide more than 180 days of schooling to children with disabilities violated P.L. 94-142 and Section 504 of the Rehabilitation Act. The court concluded that the law requires an "appropriate education" suited to the individual needs of the students, and for some students the 180-day limit was not sufficient to provide a free appropriate public education. See *Georgia Association of Retarded Citizens* v. *McDaniel*, 716 F.2d 1565 (11th Cir. 1983). The general test for determining when extended school year services are required is an assessment of whether the child will experience a significant regression in the absence of services, and whether sufficient educational recoupment will occur in a reasonable time when services are resumed. Based on the United States Supreme Court's decision in *Rowley*, that schools are not required to maximize the potential of each child with a disability, extended school-year services are not required merely because a child may benefit from these services. The Court of Appeals for the Sixth Circuit held that extended school year services were not required merely because a child with a disability would benefit more from a twelve-month program than a nine-month program. See *Cordrey* v. *Euckert*, 917 F.2d 1460 (6th Cir. 1990).

D. Individualized Education Programs

The "individualized education program" (IEP) is the basic plan for providing special education and related services. The IDEA describes an IEP as a written statement for each child with a disability that is developed, reviewed, and revised in accordance with IDEA requirements. The IEP is designed by an IEP Team. The IEP Team's membership varies but must generally include the child's parents, a representative of the educational agency, a special education teacher, a regular education teacher when the child is or may be participating in regular education, other persons having special knowledge about the child, and when appropriate the child with the disability. There must also be someone on the IEP Team capable of determining the instructional implications of evaluation results.

The IEP drafted by the IEP Team includes statements concerning the child's present levels of educational performance, measurable goals, what special education and related services are to be provided, and an explanation of the extent, if any, to which the child will not participate with nondisabled children in the regular classroom. The IEP is developed based on considerations of the strengths of the child, the parents' concerns, and the results of evaluations. An IEP should also address any serious behavior problems. The IDEA states that the IEP Team must "in the case of a child whose behavior impedes his or her learning or that of others, consider, when appropriate, strategies, including positive behavioral interventions, strategies, and supports to address that behavior." See 20 U.S.C. § 1414 (1997). The child's IEP is reviewed periodically, but not less than annually, to determine whether annual goals are being achieved.

E. Appropriate Placements

In developing an IEP, a decision must be made concerning an appropriate placement for the child. According to Section 1412 of the IDEA, children with disabilities must be placed in the "least restrictive environment" (LRE). To comply with LRE requirements, the IDEA mandates that

> To the maximum extent appropriate, children with disabilities, including children in public or private institutions or other care facilities, are educated with children who are not disabled, and special classes, separate schooling,

or other removal of children with disabilities from the regular educational environment occurs only when the nature or severity of the disability of a child is such that education in regular classes with the use of supplementary aids and services cannot be achieved satisfactorily. 20 U.S.C. § 1412 (1997).

In accordance with the IDEA, placement decisions should be based on information from a variety of sources, these sources should be documented and carefully considered, and placement decisions should conform to LRE requirements. The IDEA mandates parental participation in placement decisions, but no single factor, including parental preferences, should be determinative in a placement decision. Children should be placed in the LRE, preferring regular classroom placements and education with nonhandicapped students to the maximum extent appropriate. Further, unless the IEP requires other arrangements in order to provide a FAPE, children should be placed in the schools they would attend if nondisabled, or as close as possible to their homes.

However, the IDEA does not require "full inclusion" of all children in the regular classroom. The term "full inclusion" does not appear anywhere in the IDEA, and universal "full inclusion" of all children with disabilities would violate the mandates of the IDEA. The IDEA prohibits any "one-size-fits-all" approach to placements and instead requires an individualized placement decision for each child with a disability. Further, Section 1401 of the IDEA defines "special education" as "instruction conducted in the classroom, in the home, in hospitals and institutions, and in other settings," and the IDEA requires schools to offer a "continuum of alternative placements" in recognition that some children cannot receive a FAPE in the regular classroom.

Although children with disabilities must be educated in the LRE and in regular classrooms with nondisabled children to the maximum extent appropriate, in order to provide a FAPE for some children, placement in more restrictive settings may be necessary. Placement in more restrictive settings is appropriate when education in regular classes cannot be achieved satisfactorily, even with the use of supplementary aids and services. Further, more restrictive placements are appropriate when a less restrictive placement threatens the safety of the disabled child or other students, or when a disabled child is so disruptive in a regular classroom that the education of other students is significantly impaired. As the Court of Appeals for the Ninth Circuit recognized in *Clyde K. v. Puyallup School District*, 35 F.3d 1396 (9th Cir. 1994), "[w]hile school officials have a statutory duty to ensure that disabled students receive an appropriate education, they are not required to sit on their hands when a disabled student's behavioral problems prevent both him and those around him from learning." Further, the U.S. Department of Education's notice of interpretation concerning the 1999 IDEA regulations states that: "If the child's behavior in the regular classroom, even with the provision of appropriate behavioral supports, strategies or interventions, would significantly impair the learning of others, that placement would not meet his or her needs and would not be appropriate for that child." 34 C.F.R.§ 300 app. A at 39 (1999).

Children with disabilities are generally placed in public schools, but some children may be placed in private schools by school officials or their parents. Through the IEP process, a school district may place a child with disabilities in a private school to provide special education and related services needed by the child. Parents may also place their children in a private school, but they cannot receive financial reimbursement from schools for a unilateral placement unless the parents can establish that the public school failed to make a FAPE available to the child. Section 1412 of the IDEA provides some additional limitations on reimbursement, including requirements that parents notify school officials of their objections and their intent to enroll the child in private school, make the child available for evaluation, and otherwise act reasonably in the opinion of a reviewing judge.

The provision of IDEA services in private religious schools raises some additional legal concerns. However, a 1997 amendment to the IDEA states that IDEA services "may be provided to children with disabilities on the premises of private, including parochial, schools, to the extent consistent with law." See 20 U.S.C. § 1412 (1997). In recent decisions, courts have held that the provision of IDEA services in religious schools did not violate the Establishment Clause. In a five-to-four decision dealing with the refusal of a school district to provide a sign-language interpreter to accompany a deaf child to classes at a Roman Catholic high school, the United States Supreme Court held that this service was not barred by the Establishment Clause. The Court found that such a service was part of a general government program that distributes benefits neutrally to any child qualifying as disabled under the IDEA, without regard to the sectarian–nonsectarian, or public–nonpublic nature of the school the child attends. Regarding the interpreter, the Court determined that, unlike a teacher or counselor, the interpreter neither added to nor subtracted from the sectarian school's message but merely translated whatever material was presented, and the Establishment Clause required no absolute bar to placing a public employee in a sectarian school. See *Zobrest* v. *Catalina Foothills School District*, 509 U.S. 1 (1993). Similarly, providing a disabled student with publicly funded transportation from a public sidewalk in front of her parochial school to her special education classes at a public school was upheld under the Missouri Constitution. A federal district court stressed that the transportation was a related service to her educational program under the IDEA and that the service benefitted the student, not the parochial school. See *Felter* v. *Cape Girardeau School District*, 810 F. Supp. 1062 (Mo. 1993).

F. Related Services

Under the IDEA, "related services" may include the following:

> [T]ransportation, and such developmental, corrective, and other supportive services (including speech-language pathology and audiology services, psychological services, physical and occupational therapy, recreation, including therapeutic recreation, social work services, counseling services, including rehabilitation counseling, orientation and mobility services, and medical services, except that such medical services shall be for diagnostic and evaluation purposes only) as may be required to assist a child with a disability to benefit from special education, and includes the early identification and assessment of disabling conditions in children. 20 U.S.C. § 1401 (1997).

This list of related services is illustrative, not exhaustive, and other supportive, corrective, or developmental services may be required to assist a child with a disability to benefit from special education.

Because of the high costs associated with providing health related services for children with disabilities, there is often controversy over whether school districts must pay for particular health services as related services. The line between health services required as related services and medical services that are not required is not always clear. The United States Supreme Court first addressed this issue in *Irving Independent School District* v. *Tatro*, 468 U.S. 883 (1984). In this case, the parents of an eight-year-old girl born with spina bifida requested that clean intermittent catheterization (CIC) be performed by school personnel as a related service. The child needed CIC services every three to four hours, including during school, to avoid injury to her kidneys. Performing CIC takes only a few minutes, does not require medical expertise, and can be learned by a layperson with less than an hour's training. The Court held that CIC was not a medical service that the school need only provide for purposes of diagnosis or evaluation but was a required related service necessary for the child to benefit from special education. However, the Court did recognize that required related services included "only those services necessary to aid a handicapped child to benefit from special education . . . regardless how easily a school nurse or lay-person could furnish them. For example, if a particular medication or treatment may appropriately be administered to a handicapped child other than during the school day, a school is not required to provide nursing services to administer it." Further, the Court noted that "school nursing services must be provided only if they can be performed by a nurse or other qualified person, not if they must be performed by a physician."

The United States Supreme Court addressed the issue of school nursing services again in 1999. In *Cedar Rapids* v. *Garret F.*, 526 U.S. 66 (1999), the Court applied the two-part test established in *Tatro* to determine whether a school district must provide requested health services as related services. Under the *Tatro* test, requested health services must be provided as related services if (1) the requested "supportive services" are necessary for the child to benefit from special education; and (2) the services are not excluded as "medical services" that would require the services of a physician for other than diagnostic or evaluation purposes. In *Garret F.*, parents requested one-on-one nursing care for a wheelchair-bound and ventilator-dependent student. In a seven-to-two decision, the Court held that the school district must provide the requested services as related services under the IDEA. Under the *Tatro* test, the services were necessary for the student to benefit from special education, and although very expensive, need not be performed by a physician.

G. Procedural Protections

In order to protect the rights of children with disabilities, the IDEA provides significant procedural due process protections. Notice and hearing rights are provided throughout the special education process, from initial identification and consideration of eligibility through completion of the special education program or a determination of ineligibility. The procedural safeguards in the IDEA include:

(1) an opportunity for the parents of a child with a disability to examine all records relating to such child and to participate in meetings with respect to the identification, evaluation, and educational placement of the child, and the provision of a free appropriate public education to such child, and to obtain an independent educational evaluation of the child;

(2) procedures to protect the rights of the child whenever the parents of the child are not known . . . ;

(3) written prior notice to the parents of the child whenever such agency—

A. proposes to initiate or change; or

B. refuses to initiate or change;

the identification, evaluation, or educational placement of the child . . . or the provision of a free appropriate public education to the child.

(4) procedures designed to ensure that the notice required . . . is in the native language of the parents, unless it clearly is not feasible to do so;

(5) an opportunity for mediation . . . ;

(6) an opportunity to present complaints with respect to any matter relating to the identification, evaluation, or educational placement of
the child, or the provision of a free appropriate public education to
such child. 20 U.S.C. § 1415 (1997).

The written prior notice referred to in Section 1415 of the IDEA must
include:

(1) a description of the action proposed or refused by the agency;

(2) an explanation of why the agency proposes or refuses to take the action;

(3) a description of any other options that the agency considered and the
reasons why those options were rejected;

(4) a description of each evaluation procedure, test, record, or report the
agency used as a basis for the proposed or refused action;

(5) a description of any other factors that are relevant to the agency's
proposal or refusal;

(6) a statement that the parents of a child with a disability have protection under the procedural safeguards of this part and, if this is not an
initial referral for evaluation, the means by which a copy of a description of the procedural safeguards can be obtained; and

(7) sources for parents to contact to obtain assistance in understanding
the provisions of this part. 20 U.S.C. § 1415 (1997).

A document describing these procedural safeguards must be given
to parents on initial referral of the child for evaluation, on notification of
an IEP meeting and reevaluation of the child, and on registration of a complaint by a parent. The school must also have a model form available to assist parents in filing an IDEA complaint. The document describing these
procedural safeguards must be written in the native language of the parents, unless it is clearly not feasible, and written in an easily understandable manner. The IDEA requires that this document must contain a full
explanation of rights related to

(A) independent educational evaluation;

(B) prior written notice;

(C) parental consent;

(D) access to educational records;

(E) opportunity to present complaints;

(F) the child's placement during the pendency of due process proceedings;

(G) procedures for students who are subject to placement in an interim
alternative educational setting;

(H) requirements for unilateral placement by parents of children in private schools at public expense;

(I) mediation;
(J) due process hearings, including requirements for disclosure of evaluation results and recommendations;
(K) State-level appeals (if applicable in that State);
(L) civil actions; and
(M) attorneys' fees. 20 U.S.C. § 1415 (1997).

One of the most important procedural protections in the IDEA is the right to an impartial due process hearing. Under the IDEA, any party to a hearing shall be accorded:

1. the right to be accompanied and advised by counsel and by individuals with special knowledge or training with respect to the problems of children with disabilities;
2. the right to present evidence and confront, cross-examine, and compel the attendance of witnesses;
3. the right to a written, or, at the option of the parents, electronic verbatim record of such hearing; and
4. the right to written, or, at the option of the parents, electronic findings of fact and decisions. 20 U.S.C. § 1415 (1997).

The IDEA also includes a "stay-put" provision that states:

[D]uring the pendency of any proceedings conducted pursuant to this section, unless the State or local educational agency and the parents otherwise agree, the child shall remain in the then-current educational placement of such child, or, if applying for initial admission to a public school shall, with the consent of the parents, be placed in the public school program until all such proceedings have been completed. 20 U.S.C. § 1415 (1997).

However, there are exceptions to this "stay-put" provision, such as when the special education student poses a serious threat to safety or engages in certain other types of misconduct.

H. Discipline

Although all students are guaranteed due process of law, including notice and hearing prior to significant impingements on liberty or property rights, special concerns exist in disciplining children with disabilities. When school officials seek to suspend or expel children with disabilities, the IDEA imposes significant additional legal protections for these children, including a "stay-put" provision to protect them from unilateral removal from their current placements. These special protections are rooted in concerns over historical prejudices against individuals with disabilities, misunderstandings about physical and mental conditions that may cause problem behaviors, and fears that school officials may suspend or expel children with disabilities based on prejudice, misunderstanding, financial concerns, or other improper motives. The United States Supreme Court addressed the issue of disciplinary removals of children with disabilities and the effect of the "stay-put" provision in *Honig v. Doe*, 484 U.S. 305 (1988).

In *Honig*, California school officials were attempting to expel two emotionally disturbed children from school indefinitely for violent and disruptive conduct related to their disabilities. In determining whether the "stay-put" provision prohibited unilateral removal of these students, the Court stated:

> The language of the [stay-put provision] is unequivocal. It states plainly that during the pendency of any proceedings initiated under the Act, unless the state or local educational agency and the parents or guardian of a disabled child otherwise agree, "the child shall remain in the then current educational placement" . . . Faced with this clear directive, [school officials ask] us to read a "dangerousness" exception into the stay-put provision . . . [school officials'] arguments proceed . . . from a simple, common-sense proposition: Congress could not have intended the stay-put provision to be read literally, for such a construction leads to the clearly unintended, and untenable, result that school districts must return violent or dangerous students to school while the often lengthy [due process] proceedings run their course. We think it clear, however, that Congress very much meant to strip schools of the unilateral authority they had traditionally employed to exclude disabled students . . . from school. In so doing, Congress did not leave school administrators powerless to deal with dangerous students; it did, however, deny school officials their former right to "self-help," and directed that in the future the removal of disabled students could be accomplished only with the permission of the parents or, as a last resort, the courts . . . Congress passed the [Act] after finding that school systems across the country had excluded one out of every eight disabled students from classes. In drafting the law, Congress was largely guided by the recent decisions in [*PARC v. Pennsylvania* and *Mills v. Board of Education*], both of which involved the exclusion of hard-to-handle disabled students . . . Our conclusion that [the stay-put provision] means what it says does not leave educators hamstrung. The Department of Education has observed that, "[w]hile the [child's] placement may not be changed [during any complaint proceeding], this does not preclude the agency from using its normal procedures for dealing with children who are endangering themselves or others." * * *
>
> Such procedures may include the use of study carrels, timeouts, detention, or the restriction of privileges. More drastically, where a student poses an immediate threat to the safety of others, officials may temporarily suspend him or her for up to 10 schooldays. This authority, which respondent in no way disputes, not only ensures that school administrators can protect the safety of others by promptly removing the most dangerous of students, it also provides a "cooling down" period during which officials can initiate IEP review and seek to persuade the child's parents to agree to an interim placement. And in those cases in which the parents of a truly dangerous child adamantly refuse to permit any change in placement, the 10-day respite gives school officials an opportunity to invoke the aid of the courts. (pp. 323–326)

In a case occurring after *Honig*, a federal district court allowed school officials to change the placement of an overly aggressive student classified as emotionally disturbed, learning-disabled, and speech-disabled, and diagnosed as exhibiting psychotic disorder. He had been involved in thirty assaults on teachers, staff, and other students; had run into other classrooms; attempted to jump out of a second-story window on two occasions; had virtually destroyed a time-out room, used profanity extensively; and on one occasion tried to run in front of a moving car. See *Texas City Independent School District* v. *Jorstad*, 752 F. Supp. 231 (S.D. Tex. 1990).

In response to heightened concerns over school violence and drug use, the 1997 amendments to the IDEA provided school officials with additional authority to change the placement of special education students that carry weapons, are involved with drugs, or are dangerous to themselves or others. The amendments state:

> School personnel under this section may order a change in the placement of a child with a disability—
>
> (i) to an appropriate interim alternative educational setting, another setting, or suspension, for not more than 10 school days (to the extent such alternatives would be applied to children without disabilities); and
>
> (ii) to an appropriate interim alternative educational setting for the same amount of time that a child without a disability would be subject to discipline, but for not more than 45 days if—
>
> (I) the child carries a weapon to school or to a school function . . .
>
> (II) the child knowingly possesses or uses illegal drugs or sells or solicits the sale of a controlled substance while at school or a school function. 20 U.S.C. § 1415 (1997).

If children with disabilities present a serious danger to themselves or others, school officials may ask a hearing officer to place a dangerous child in an alternative setting. The 1997 amendments to the IDEA provide that:

> A hearing officer . . . may order a change in the placement of a child with a disability to an appropriate interim alternative educational setting for not more than 45 days if the hearing officer—
>
> (a) determines that the public agency has demonstrated by substantial evidence that maintaining the current placement of such child is substantially likely to result in injury to the child or to others;
>
> (b) considers the appropriateness of the child's current placement;
>
> (c) considers whether the public agency has made reasonable efforts to minimize the risk of harm in the child's current placement, including the use of supplementary aids and services; and
>
> (d) determines that the interim alternative education setting meets [other requirements of the IDEA]. 20 U.S.C. § 1415 (1997).

The statute requires school officials to establish by "substantial evidence" that maintaining the current placement of the child is likely to result in injury. The 1997 IDEA amendments did not define the term "substantial evidence." But the 1999 IDEA regulations state that "substantial evidence" means "beyond a preponderance of the evidence." See 34 C.F.R. § 300.521(e) (1999). The IDEA also requires that the interim alternative educational setting must enable the child to continue to participate in the general curriculum, to receive services described in the IEP, to meet IEP goals, and receive services and modifications designed to avoid recurrences of the problem behavior. The 1999 IDEA regulations clarify that while this alternative placement may not exceed 45 days, additional 45-day extensions may be repeated as necessary to avoid a dangerous placement. 34 C.F.R. § 300.526(c)(4) (1999).

Another important consideration in disciplining children with disabilities is determining whether the problem behavior is a manifestation of the student's disability. If a child's behavior is a manifestation of a disability, it would be unfair to punish that child for behavior that was caused by the disability. For example, children suffering from Tourette's syndrome exhibit symptoms including lack of muscle coordination, involuntary movements, tics, incoherent grunts and barks, and the use of vulgar, obscene, or sacrilegious language, resulting in behaviors that would merit punishment in most children, but may be uncontrollable for a child suffering from Tourette's syndrome. Accordingly, the IDEA requires the IEP Team and other qualified personnel to conduct a review to determine whether a child with a disability's problem behavior is a manifestation of the child's disability, if disciplinary actions constitute a change in placement.

Manifestation determinations are only required when a child is subjected to a disciplinary change of placement. 34 C.F.R. § 300.523(a) (1999). A change in placement occurs when a student is removed for more than 10 consecutive days or when: "The child is subjected to a series of removals that constitute a pattern because they cumulate to more than 10 school days in a school year, and because of factors such as the length of each removal, the total amount of time the child is removed, and the proximity of the removals to one another." 34 C.F.R. § 300.519(b) (1999).

To find that the problem behavior is not a manifestation of the child's disability, it must be determined that

(i)　In relationship to the behavior subject to disciplinary action, the child's IEP and placement were appropriate and the special education services, supplementary aids and services, and behavior intervention strategies were provided consistent with the child's IEP and placement;

(ii)　The child's disability did not impair the ability of the child to understand the impact and consequences of the behavior subject to disciplinary action; and

(iii)　The child's disability did not impair the ability of the child to control the behavior subject to disciplinary action. 34 C.F.R. § 300.523(2) (1999).

If the result of the review is a determination that the student's behavior was not a manifestation of the disability, school officials may discipline the student in the same manner that other students would be disciplined, including suspension for up to 10 days. No special services are required during this initial 10-day suspension. However, an exclusion for more than 10 days triggers the procedural protections of the IDEA. When a student's behavior is not a manifestation of the student's disability, school officials may lawfully long-term suspend for more than 10 days or expel the student, subject to the IDEA procedural protections. However, schools cannot terminate special education services for these students. Section 1412 of the IDEA requires the continuation of FAPE services for children with disabilities who have been suspended or expelled from school for more than 10 days. The 1999 IDEA regulations clarify that although schools do not have to provide IDEA services during the first 10 days a child is removed during the school year, for subsequent removals schools must provide services "to the extent necessary" to allow the child to make appropriate progress toward IEP goals. For subsequent removals of 10 days or less, school personnel make this service determination in consultation with the child's special education teacher. For any longer removals the child's IEP team makes this determination. 34 C.F.R. § 300.121 (1999). The 1999 IDEA regulations clarify that there is no absolute limit on the number of days that a child may be removed during the school year, but school officials may not engage in a pattern of removals that would constitute a denial of a FAPE. As noted previously, factors considered in determining whether there is a pattern of removals include the length of each removal, the total amount of time the child is removed, and the proximity of the removals to one another.

If the student's behavior is a manifestation of the student's disability, the student generally cannot be punished for that behavior. Nonetheless, there are still many behavior management options available to school officials. As the Court noted in *Honig* v. *Doe*, school officials may use in-school methods such as study carrels, time-out, detention, or the restriction of privileges that are used with other students. Because these procedures are in-school, courts have held that they are not considered a change in placement and do not trigger the IDEA due process protections, unless they are used so extensively that they deny the student a FAPE. As noted previously, the 1997 amendments to the IDEA also allow school officials to establish a 45-day interim educational placement for students with weapons or drugs, or by convincing a hearing officer that the student is dangerous. Further, there is legal support for removing a student from the regular classroom when the student's disability-related behavior results in excessive disruption of the regular classroom. See *Clyde K.* v. *Puyallup School District*, 35 F.3d 1396 (9th Cir. 1994). School officials may also obtain a court order for a removal or change of placement of a student that presents a serious danger to either the student or others. Permanent changes in the student's placement should be accomplished through the IEP process by establishing that the current placement is not appropriate for the student. Finally, it should be remembered that the IDEA limitations on disciplinary changes in placements only apply to situations in which schools have failed to obtain parental consent to proposed actions. The above limitations do not apply to situations in which school officials can successfully negotiate a mutually agreeable resolution with the student's parents.

It should also be noted that according to the Office for Civil Rights (OCR), exclusions from bus transportation are subject to the same procedural safeguards as other disciplinary exclusions, regardless of whether transportation is a required related service for that student. Nonetheless, if a student's behavior on the bus presents a serious problem, school officials may offer appropriate alternative transportation services to parents, or seek a change in the student's transportation services through a change in the IEP when appropriate.

The 1997 amendments to the IDEA also establish that students not currently eligible for IDEA services and facing disciplinary action may assert any of the protections under the IDEA if school officials "had knowledge" that the student had a disability before the occurrence of the behavior that precipitated the disciplinary action. The IDEA states that school officials shall be deemed to have knowledge that a student had a disability if:

(i) the parent of the child has expressed concern in writing (unless the parent is illiterate or has a disability that prevents compliance with the requirements contained in this clause) to personnel of the appropriate educational agency that the child is in need of special education and related services;

(ii) the behavior or performance of the child demonstrates the need for such services;

(iii) the parent of the child has requested an evaluation of the child . . . ; or

(iv) the teacher of the child, or other personnel of the local educational agency, has expressed concern about the behavior or performance of the child to the director of special education of such agency or to other personnel of the agency. 20 U.S.C. § 1415 (1997).

School officials may also choose to refer students to law enforcement agents when students are suspected of committing criminal acts. The IDEA states:

Nothing in this part shall be construed to prohibit an agency from reporting a crime committed by a child with a disability to appropriate authorities or to prevent State law enforcement and judicial authorities from exercising their responsibilities with regard to the application of Federal and State law to crimes committed by a child with a disability. 20 U.S.C. § 1415 (1997).

School officials that report a crime must also transmit copies of the student's special education and disciplinary records to the appropriate authorities. However, law enforcement agents and judicial authorities have a duty to protect the public by enforcing criminal laws and are not bound by the mandates of the IDEA. Students with disabilities that are convicted of crimes may be subjected to the same penalties imposed on others convicted of those crimes, including incarceration.

Summary
Discipline procedures under the IDEA may be both the most significant and the most confusing provisions for many educators. Accordingly, the following summary of incrementally severe disciplinary options is provided:

Behavior Management Strategies—To attempt to modify problem behavior, school officials may utilize a variety of behavior and conflict management strategies, including student carrels, time-outs, detention, restrictions in privileges, etc. As long as IEP services are provided, and there is no change in placement, school officials may unilaterally implement these behavior management strategies.

Obtaining Parental Consent—If more serious measures are necessary, school officials may first obtain parental consent for needed changes in placement or for other appropriate behavior management strategies. If parental consent is obtained, the IDEA limitations on disciplinary actions are generally not triggered.

Unilateral 10-Day Removal—Provided their actions are not discriminatory, school officials may unilaterally remove a student for up to 10 days for misconduct. No services are required, and no manifestation determination is necessary.

Subsequent 10-Day Removals—The 1999 IDEA regulations clarify that there is no absolute limit on the total number of days per year that a student may be removed for separate incidents of misconduct, so long as no single removal exceeds 10 days and there is no pattern of removals. Factors considered in determining whether there is a pattern of removals include the length of each removal, the total amount of time the child is removed, and the proximity of the removals to one another. However, schools must provide services to the extent necessary to allow the child to make appropriate progress toward IEP goals. School personnel make this service determination in consultation with the child's special education teacher. Manifestation determinations are only required when a child is subjected to a disciplinary change of placement.

Long-Term Suspensions and Expulsions—Students may be long-term suspended or expelled for misconduct that is not a manifestation of the student's disability. However, any removal beyond 10 days constitutes a change in placement, triggering IDEA due process protections. Further, schools must continue to provide a FAPE to these students. For removals beyond 10 days, the child's IEP team determines what services are necessary to provide a FAPE.

45-Day Removals for Weapons or Drugs—School officials may unilaterally remove a student to an alternative educational placement for up to 45 days for possession of weapons or drugs.

45-Day Removals for Dangerousness—School officials may ask a hearing officer to remove a potentially dangerous student to an alternative educational placement for up to 45 days by presenting "substantial evidence that maintaining the current placement of such child is substantially likely to result in injury to the child or to others." The 1999 IDEA regulations state that "substantial evidence" means "beyond a preponderance of the evidence." Additional 45-day extensions may be repeated as necessary to prevent a dangerous placement.

Obtaining a Court Order—If the above options fail, school officials may obtain a court order for a removal or change of placement of a student that presents a serious danger to either the student or others.

Reporting Crimes—School officials may report students suspected of committing crimes to law enforcement agents, who have a duty to enforce criminal laws, and are not bound by IDEA limitations.

I. Transition Services

The transition from school to work, independent living, or further education is difficult for many young adults. Special education students may have unique difficulties in making this transition. In 1990, Congress amended the IDEA to require the provision of "transition services" for children with disabilities. Transition services are a coordinated set of activities designed to facilitate movement from school to postschool activities. Transition services may include instruction, related services, community experiences, and the development of employment and adult living skills.

A 1997 amendment to the IDEA requires that a "statement of the transition service needs" must be included in the IEP beginning at age fourteen, and updated annually. This new amendment focuses earlier attention on educational programming designed to transition the child from school to postschool activities. It is intended to augment, not replace, the transition services requirement that begins at age sixteen, or sooner if deemed appropriate by the IEP Team. A determination of what transition services are appropriate should be based on the individual student's needs and should take into account the student's preferences and interests.

330   CHAPTER SIX

J. Graduation and Competency Exams

Special education services terminate on graduation or age ineligibility. Generally, to be eligible for graduation, a child with a disability must have completed an appropriate IEP. Graduation is a change in placement, and parents must receive notification that the student is scheduled for graduation. However, some students will reach the maximum age for IDEA eligibility before completing their IEP goals and objectives. If a child with a disability has not graduated, the IDEA provides federal funds for special education services through age twenty-one. But if state law does not provide for public education for nondisabled children from ages eighteen through twenty-one, states are not required by the IDEA to provide special education for children with disabilities in that age group.

Further, all students, including special education students, may be required to pass competency exams before obtaining a high school diploma. Because of the severity of their disabilities, some children with disabilities will be unable to pass these exams and obtain a high school diploma. Courts have upheld competency exam requirements, even for children with disabilities, provided that students were given notice of the general contents of the exam, and an opportunity to learn the required academic content. See *Brookhart* v. *Illinois State Board of Education,* 697 F.2d 179 (7th Cir. 1983).

K. Cost Issues

When facing parental requests for excessively expensive services, schools may find some potential relief in the United States Supreme Court's decision in *Board of Education* v. *Rowley.* In *Rowley,* the Court held that schools are not required to maximize a child's educational potential by providing superior special education and related services regardless of expense. Instead, the Court found that the requirements of the IDEA are satisfied when children with disabilities are provided with appropriate "personalized instruction with sufficient support services to permit the child to benefit educationally from that instruction."

According to *Rowley,* special education services need only be appropriate for the child and sufficient to provide educational benefits. The services offered do not have to be the best services available regardless of cost. As long as the school's decision concerning the provision of special education services is appropriate, the choice of which educational methodology and service to provide is left to the school. Parents may express their wishes, but if the school's choice is also appropriate, the school may choose between appropriate options and need not choose the most expensive option, regardless of parental wishes. See *Springdale School District* v. *Grace,* 693 F.2d 41 (8th Cir. 1982).

However, for some children, the only appropriate option may still be very expensive. Before the school may raise cost alone as a defense under the IDEA, the school must establish that it has provided a proper continuum of placements, that the child in question would not experience a total denial of education because of the failure to provide the expensive service, and that other special education students may be denied a FAPE because of excessive expenditures on one child. See *Roncker* v. *Walter*, 700 F.2d 1058 (6th Cir. 1983).

Notes and Questions

Significant progress has occurred in providing educational services for children with disabilities. Prior to the passage of P.L. 94-142, Congress heard the following testimony:

> Some years ago, during the course of a visit to the State Institution for the mentally retarded, I encountered a little girl who was lying in a crib. Wondering why she was so confined while the other children were not, I began to play with her. I found that even though I could make eye contact with her, she was unable to follow me with her eyes for more than about 12 inches. I began to try to teach her. In about 15 minutes she could follow me about a quarter of the way around the bed. I was convinced then, and still am, that with a little work the child could have been taught some useful behavior and could have been gotten out of the crib. It seems safe to say that no one with any authority was concerned about the education of that little girl . . . It seems antithetical to American philosophy, as I see it, that whether or not a handicapped child gets proper care and proper educational treatment depends on the fatness of that child's father's wallet.

Appropriate educational services can have tremendous benefits for children with disabilities, helping them to live more independent and productive adult lives. Although this education is expensive, what are the economic costs of failing to educate children with disabilities? In addition to the economic costs of failing to educate disabled children, how should the incalculable personal costs of denying education to disabled children be weighed, including the diminished quality of life for the girl discussed previously, and the possibility that she might spend the rest of her life lying in a bed staring at the ceiling, absent appropriate educational assistance?

Since the passage of P.L. 94-142 in 1975, providing special education and related services for children with disabilities has required a constantly increasing allocation of resources to special education programs. Many school districts now spend 20 percent of their total budgets on special education programs. Although funding per student in United States schools leveled off in the 1990s, spending on special education programs continued to increase. How have escalating expenditures for special education programs affected regular education programs? How should

Congress, the states, and schools balance the educational needs of children with disabilities and the fiscal realities of limited resources? Are the costs of current special education programs justified by the benefits? Are there more efficient ways of achieving similar benefits? Like all laws, current special education laws are the product of a complex governmental process. In examining the results of this process, do current special education laws seem predominant to reflect a rational balancing of competing interests, or the power of special interest politics?

Limitations on disciplining special education students and the placement of disruptive special education students in regular classrooms continue to generate controversy. Are different disciplinary policies for special education and regular education students justified? Will students, parents, and others in your community accept this justification? Regular education students and their parents have no legal standing under the IDEA to challenge the placement of disruptive or potentially dangerous students in their classroom. Should they? If current provisions in the IDEA are problematic, what alternatives would you suggest?

II. SECTION 504 OF THE REHABILITATION ACT

Section 504 of the Rehabilitation Act of 1973 protects both handicapped children and adults from discrimination in institutions receiving federal funds, unlike the IDEA, which applies only to eligible children with disabilities.* As recipients of federal funds, public schools must comply with the mandates of Section 504. Section 504 protections may also apply to private schools, if they receive federal funds. Further, religious schools are not exempt from Section 504 protections if they receive federal funds. The Department of Education Regulations for Section 504 state:

> No otherwise qualified handicapped person shall, on the basis of handicap, be excluded from the participation in, be denied the benefits of, or otherwise be subjected to discrimination under any program or activity which receives or benefits from Federal financial assistance. 34 C.F.R. § 104.4 (1997).

To qualify for protection under Section 504, an individual must be a "handicapped person," which is defined as follows:

> [A]ny person who (i) has a physical or mental impairment which substantially limits one or more major life activities, (ii) has a record of such an impairment, or (iii) is regarded as having such an impairment. 34 C.F.R. § 104.3 (1997).

---

*Although amended sections of the Rehabilitation Act use the term "individual with a disability," current Department of Education Regulations retain the term "handicapped person," and this term is used consistently throughout this section to avoid confusion.

Other relevant terms are defined as follows:

(i) "Physical or mental impairment" means (A) any physiological disorder or condition, cosmetic disfigurement, or anatomical loss affecting one or more of the following body systems: neurological; musculoskeletal; special sense organs; respiratory, including speech organs; cardiovascular; reproductive; digestive; genito-urinary; hemic and lymphatic; skin; and endocrine; or (B) any mental or psychological disorder, such as mental retardation, organic brain syndrome, emotional or mental illness, and specific learning disabilities.

(ii) "Major life activities" means functions such as caring for one's self, performing manual tasks, walking, seeing, hearing, speaking, breathing, learning, and working.

(iii) "Has a record of such an impairment" means has a history of, or has been misclassified as having, a mental or physical impairment that substantially limits one or more major life activities.

(iv) "Is regarded as having an impairment" means (A) has a physical or mental impairment that does not substantially limit major life activities but that is treated by a recipient as constituting such a limitation; (B) has a physical or mental impairment that substantially limits major life activities only as a result of the attitudes of others toward such impairment; or (C) has none of the impairments defined in . . . this section but is treated by a recipient as having such an impairment. 34 C.F.R. § 104.3 (1997).

If otherwise qualified handicapped persons fall within the protections of Section 504, they may not be discriminated against in programs receiving federal assistance, and are entitled to "reasonable accommodations" to facilitate their participation. Reasonable accommodations often include making facilities accessible and usable by handicapped persons, and making reasonable modifications in academic requirements or working conditions. An accommodation is not reasonable, and therefore not required, if it would result in unreasonable safety risks, health risks, or costs. Further, an institution is not required to provide a specific accommodation requested by an individual. Instead, an institution is only required to provide a reasonable accommodation, and when more than one reasonable accommodation exists, the institution may choose which reasonable accommodation to provide.

A. Students and Section 504

Section 504 protects handicapped students from discrimination in all programs receiving federal funds. As recipients of federal funds, schools may not discriminate against or exclude handicapped students from participation in any school program or activity solely because they are handicapped. However, handicapped students must be otherwise qualified for participation in particular school programs or activities. Schools are not required to accommodate participation of a handicapped student when no reasonable accommodation is possible, or when the student is not otherwise qualified for participation in a program or activity. For example, a school's exclusion of a blind student from driving in a driver's education program would not violate the mandates of Section 504 because the student could not be safely accommodated in this activity. Further, a handicapped student that failed to qualify for the school basketball team because of inadequate preparation and skills could not demand inclusion on the team simply because the student was handicapped.

Section 504 does not require unreasonable accommodations or preferential treatment of handicapped students. Instead, Section 504 requires reasonable accommodations and nondiscrimination, to assure fair treatment of handicapped students. Accordingly, tests and other assessments of handicapped students should be designed to measure relevant essential qualifications, and not the effects of a student's handicap. If tests or other assessments have a disproportionate impact on handicapped students, and are not related to essential qualifications, a waiver may be required to accommodate handicapped students. Further, testing conditions may need to be modified to accommodate handicapped students, including alternative locations for exams, extended time limits, oral examinations, and other reasonable accommodations to assure that tests are measuring relevant skills and not the effects of a student's handicap.

Handicapped students may not be suspended, expelled, or otherwise punished for manifestations of their disability. See *Jonathan G. v. Caddo Parish School Board*, 875 F. Supp. 352 (W.D. La. 1994), holding that a school district could not suspend a learning disabled student for conduct related to his disability. The Office for Civil Rights (OCR) generally applies the same standards to the suspension or expulsion of 504-eligible students as are applied to IDEA-eligible students.

Schools may sometimes want to exclude a student not for disciplinary reasons, but because the student carries a contagious disease. Although schools may lawfully exclude students that pose a serious risk of infection to others, controversy continues in many communities concerning whether to allow children infected with human immunodeficiency virus (HIV) or acquired immunodeficiency syndrome (AIDS) to attend regular public school classes. Many parents fear that their children could contract HIV or AIDS through contact with infected children by being bitten, by having body fluids enter an open wound, or even by being breathed on. Media portrayals of the disease's ravages and the absence of a cure heighten parents' concern. Statements from such authorities as the Surgeon General of the United States and officials of the Center for Disease Control often fail to persuade parents that their fears are unfounded.

Suits have been brought both by parents whose infected children were banned from regular school programs and by parents who objected to the admission of these students to regular classes. To date, courts have revealed a high degree of sensitivity to students with HIV or AIDS and to their being included in the public school mainstream. This view is presented in *Thomas v. Atascadero Unified School District.*

THOMAS v. ATASCADERO UNIFIED SCHOOL DISTRICT

United States District Court, Central District of California, 1987
662 F.Supp. 376

STOTLER, District Judge

* * *

Plaintiffs Robin and Judy Thomas are the parents and guardians of Ryan Thomas and bring this action on his behalf. Ryan Thomas is a five-year-old boy eligible under California law to attend kindergarten in the Atascadero Unified School District.

Defendant Atascadero Unified School District ("School District") is a public entity organized under the laws of the State of California. The School District is a recipient of "federal financial assistance" within the meaning of 29 U.S.C. § 794.

* * *

Acquired Immune Deficiency Syndrome (AIDS) is the clinical manifestation of a dysfunction of the human immune system caused by a recently discovered virus. The AIDS virus has received several names: Human T-Lymphotropic Virus Type III (HTLV-III); Lymphadenopathy Associated Virus (LAV); AIDS-Associated Retrovirus (ARV); and, most recently, *Human Immunodeficiency Virus* (HIV).

To date, there is no vaccine against or cure for AIDS. A range of symptoms may result from infection with the AIDS virus which have been classified by the Centers for Disease Control ("CDC") into four groups of symptoms: (I) early acute, though transient, signs of the disease; (II) asymptotic infection; (III) persistent swollen lymph nodes; and (IV) presence of opportunistic disease and/or rare types of cancer, including one known as Kaposi's Sarcoma.

* * *

Ryan Thomas is infected with the AIDS virus. He became infected with the AIDS virus as an infant as the result of a contaminated blood transfusion received at Oakland's Children's Hospital where he was being treated for complications arising out of his premature birth. He suffers from significant impairment of his major life activities.

Ryan was diagnosed as being infected with the AIDS virus in early 1985. During the first four years of his life, Ryan Thomas had frequent pulmonary and middle ear problems as well as chronic lymphadenopathy. These difficulties are attributable to his infection with the AIDS virus.

For over a year, since the diagnosis that he was infected with the AIDS virus, and since his treatment for this condition began, Ryan's medical condition has improved. * * * At this point it is unclear what course his medical condition will take. Both of Ryan's treating physicians, Dr. Fields and Dr. Church, have written to the School District indicating that there is no medical reason why Ryan cannot attend regular kindergarten classes.

The best available medical evidence shows that the AIDS virus is not spread in the air by infected droplets as are the common cold, influenza and tuberculosis. The virus is fragile and is killed by most household disinfectants. The virus is transmitted from one person to another only by infected blood, semen or vaginal fluids (and, possibly, mother's milk). Transmission by either semen or blood accounts for virtually all reported cases.

There are no reported cases of the transmission of the AIDS virus in a school setting. The CDC has stated that "[n]one of the identified cases of HTLV-III/LAV infection in the United States are known to have been transmitted in the school, daycare, or foster-care setting or through casual person-to-person contact."

The overwhelming weight of medical evidence is that the AIDS virus is not transmitted by human bites, even bites that break the skin. Based upon the abundant medical and scientific evidence before the Court, Ryan poses no risk of harm to his classmates and teachers. Any theoretical risk of transmission of the AIDS virus by Ryan in connection with his attendance in regular kindergarten class is so remote that it cannot form the basis for any exculsionary action by the School District.

In May 1986, the School District adopted a policy concerning the admission of students infected with "communicable diseases" including the "HTLV-III (AIDS)" virus. Pursuant to this policy a Placement Committee was created, including health professionals, parents, school officials and San Luis Obispo County's Public Health Officer, to advise the School Board on the placement of children covered by the Policy.

On August 28, 1986, the Placement Committee met to make a recommendation concerning Ryan's placement. At this meeting the Committee recommended Ryan's admission to kindergarten. This recommendation was accepted by the School Board on September 2, 1986. No other kindergarten student had his placement considered in this manner. The standard procedure in the District is for a child's parents to decide whether a child of kindergarten age will attend regular kindergarten classes.

Ryan attended kindergarten without incident from September 3 to 5, 1986. On September 8, 1986, Ryan was involved in an incident in which another child and Ryan got into a skirmish and Ryan bit the other child's pants leg. No skin was broken.

Defendant Avina instructed Plaintiffs to keep Ryan at home after the incident so that the Placement Committee could reconsider its August 28th recommendation in light of this incident and determine "whether or not Ryan's potential for again biting another student poses any danger to the health of others in the class." On September 12, 1986, the Placement Committee recommended that Ryan be evaluated by a psychologist. This recommendation was accepted by the School Board. No similar action was taken concerning the other child involved in this incident.

In late September, Dr. Marcus Shira, a psychologist employed by the San Luis Obispo County Board of Education, conducted a "psychoeducational study" of Ryan. Dr. Shira prepared a report dated September 30, 1986, in which he concluded that Ryan would behave "aggressively" in a kindergarten setting because his level of social and language skills and maturity was below those of his classmates. Dr. Shira could not predict what form such "aggressive" behavior might take. Specifically, he did not predict that Ryan would "bite again."

Based upon Dr. Shira's study, on October 2, 1986, the Placement Committee recommended that Ryan be kept out of class and in "home tutoring" for the rest of the academic year. The County Public Health Officer, Dr. Rowland, abstained from this decision. On October 6, 1986, the School Board voted to exclude Ryan from his class until January 1987, and to have Ryan evaluated before the decision to exclude him would be reconsidered.

Ryan suffered injury because of his exclusion from his kindergarten class after September 8, 1986, even though his injuries were not as great as they would have been if he was an older child.

In taking the actions outlined above, the School District acted cautiously and reasonably in attempting to balance all of the interests involved and to address the fear of AIDS which exists within the Atascadero community.

In August of 1985, the Centers for Disease Control for the United States Government (CDC) published information and recommendations concerning the education of children infected with the AIDS virus. Among the CDC's recommendations are the following:

"Decisions regarding this type of educational and care setting for HTLV-III/LAV-infected children should be based on the behavior, neurologic development, and physical condition of the child and the expected type of interaction with others in that setting. These decisions are best made using the team approach including the child's physician, public health personnel, the child's parent or guardian, and personnel associated with the proposed care or educational setting. In each case, risks and benefits to both the infected child and to others in the setting should be weighed."

"For the infected preschool-aged child and for some neurologically handicapped children who lack control of their body secretions or who display behavior, such as biting, and those children who have uncoverable, oozing lesions, a more restricted environment is advisable until more is known about transmission in these settings. Children infected with HTLV-III/LAV should be cared for and educated in settings that minimize exposure of other children to blood or body fluids."

Substantially similar guidelines and recommendations were issued by the American Academy of Pediatrics (AAP) in March of 1986 and the California State Department of Education (SDE) in May of 1986.

The placement Committee took the recommendations of the CDC into account in its determinations and recommendations regarding Ryan Thomas following the biting incident on September 5, 1986.

Aside from its citation to the recommendations of the CDC, AAP, and SDE, the School District has presented no medical evidence to prove that the AIDS virus can be transmitted by human bites. The information and recommendations published by the CDC, AAP, and SDE cite no such medical evidence and do not, of themselves, prove that transmission by biting is possible.

The Defendant School District is a recipient of federal funds within the meaning of 29 U.S.C. § 794, § 504 of the Federal Rehabilitation Act of 1973.

Ryan Thomas is a "handicapped person" within the meaning of § 504 of the Rehabilitation Act of 1973. * * *

Ryan Thomas is "otherwise qualified" to attend a regular kindergarten class within the meaning of § 504 of the Rehabilitation Act of 1973. Defendants have failed to meet their burden of demonstrating that Ryan is not "otherwise qualified" to attend kindergarten. * * * There is no evidence that Ryan Thomas poses a significant risk of harm to his kindergarten classmates or teachers.

Ryan Thomas has been subjected to different treatment from the treatment received by other kindergarten students in the District and excluded from his kindergarten class because of his "handicap."

Defendants have not complied with the requirements of 45 C.F.R. § 88.4(b). In particular, Defendants have not complied with the requirement that "[a] recipient shall place a handicapped person in the regular educational environment created by the recipient unless it is demonstrated by the recipient that the education of the person in the regular environment with the use of supplementary aids and services cannot be achieved satisfactorily."

Based on the foregoing, Plaintiffs are likely to succeed on the merits. Ryan Thomas has suffered irreparable injury because of his exclusion from class. There are serious questions presented by Plaintiff's Motion and the balance of hardships tips in Plaintiff's favor. Plaintiffs are entitled to the issuance of a preliminary injunction. * * *

* * *

Plaintiffs are awarded the amount of $40,000.00 in attorneys fees and $2,387.50 in costs.

* * *

Notes

A decision similar to *Thomas*, was rendered in *District 27 Community School Board* v. *Board of Education of the City of New York*, 502 N.Y.S.2d 325 (N.Y. Sup. Ct. 1986). Here, the court held that excluding students with AIDS violated not only Section 504 of the Rehabilitation Act but also the Equal Protection Clause of the Fourteenth Amendment. Additionally, the opinion provides a detailed description of AIDS' epidemiology. See also *Martinez* v. *School Board of Hillsborough County*, 711 F. Supp. 1066 (M.D. Fla. 1990), where a student classified as trainable mentally handicapped (TMH) was diagnosed as suffering from AIDS-related complex, was able to control a condition of continuously sucking on her fingers, and "is well on her way to being fully toilet trained" was found to be "otherwise qualified" to attend a TMH classroom. The court in this instance was persuaded by several factors. These included findings that (1) the American Academy of Pediatrics' Redbook had been revised, eliminating its earlier recommendations that "children who cannot control their bodily secretions should be placed in a more restricted environment"; (2) the student's physician considered the risk to other students so low statistically that he did not think it required the precaution of separation from other students; and (3) there had been responsible conduct on the part of the student and her family through the accomplishment of substantial compliance with personal hygiene requirements as a prerequisite to interaction with other children.

Attempting to exclude children from regular school classes due to infectious diseases is not a new issue. Whether the exclusion is lawful is determined by weighing the legitimate interests of the infected child against the risk of infection. A decision to exclude a child must be based on sound medical data and not mere speculation or phobia. For example, a federal appellate court held that, under the Rehabilitation Act, mentally retarded students thought to be carriers of hepatitis could not be excluded without sufficient cause. In this instance, school authorities could not demonstrate that the health hazard posed by the children was anything more than a remote possibility, and the court agreed that isolating the carrier children would have detrimental effects. See *New York State Association for Retarded Children* v. *Carey*, 612 F.2d 644 (2nd Cir. 1979).

Schools may also seek to exclude a handicapped student from certain athletic activities to protect the student or to protect others. A decision on whether to exclude a handicapped student from participation in athletics requires balancing the student's legitimate interests and the school system's legitimate concerns. For example, the student may wish to have the most well-rounded school experience possible, or the opportunity for a collegiate athletic scholarship, but the school has a responsibility to protect the physical well-being of the student and others if the handicapped student is allowed to participate in interscholastic athletics.

GRUBE v. BETHLEHEM AREA
SCHOOL DISTRICT

United States District Court, Eastern District of
Pennsylvania, 1982
550 F.Supp. 418

HUYETT, District Judge

* * *

Before me is plaintiffs' request for a preliminary injunction. In order to prevail, the plaintiffs must show a strong likelihood of success on the merits, that immediate, irreparable harm will result if the preliminary injunction does not issue, that the grant of the injunction will not substantially harm other parties, and that the public interest favors granting the injunction. * * *

The plaintiffs' complaint presents two legal theories. First, they assert that Richard has been discriminated against in violation of the Rehabilitation Act of 1973 (Act) § 504. Secondly, they assert that he has been deprived of his Fourteenth Amendment right to equal protection giving rise to an action under 42 U.S.C. § 1983. At the preliminary injunction hearing, plaintiffs acknowledged that they rely primarily upon the Rehabilitation Act. I turn to the law applicable to a claim of discrimination under the Act and consider whether plaintiffs have shown a likelihood of success on the merits of this claim.

Section 504 of the Act as amended provides: "No otherwise qualified handicapped individual in the United States . . . shall, solely by reason of his handicap, be excluded from the participation in, be denied the benefits of, or be subjected to discrimination under any program or activity receiving Federal financial assistance. . . ." In interpreting this section, the Supreme Court has held that an "otherwise qualified" person "is one who is able to meet all of a program's requirements in spite of his handicap." * * * The Court interpreted § 504 as follows:

> Section 504 by its terms does not compel educational institutions to disregard the disabilities of handicapped individuals or to make substantial modifications in their programs to allow disabled persons to participate. Instead, it requires only that an "otherwise qualified handicapped individual" not be excluded from participation in a federally funded program "solely by reason of his handicap," indicating only that mere possession of a handicap is not a permissible ground for assuming an inability to function in a particular context.

Three lower courts have addressed the import of § 504 in contexts similar to the present case. In *Kampmeier v. Nyquist*, the Court of Appeals for the Second Circuit considered an appeal from the denial of a preliminary injunction sought on behalf of children with one eye who were barred from participation in their school's contact sports program. The school's decision to bar the children was based upon the opinion of the school physician. The medical evidence the children introduced to refute the school physician's opinion was equivocal. Referring to the school's reliance on the opinion of the school physician, the court stated: "The plaintiffs have presented little evidence—medical, statistical or otherwise—which would cast doubt on the substantiality of this rationale." Noting that the equities in the case were very close, the court concluded that this absence of evidence was fatal to plaintiffs' claim. On the evidence presented, it could not be said that the school district lacked "substantial justification" for its action.

In *Poole* v. *South Plainfield Board of Education*, the plaintiff was a high school student with one kidney who was barred from his school's wrestling team. Before the court were the defendant's motions to dismiss for lack of subject matter jurisdiction and in the alternative, for judgment on the pleadings. The court denied both motions because on the facts as assumed in the opinion, the plaintiff had demonstrated a right to recovery. The school system's medical director advised the system that it was inadvisable to permit a student with one kidney to participate in contact sports. The student refuted this opinion with medical opinions by his own experts. It was apparent to the court that both the school system physician and the Board itself were making a philosophical and not a medical judgment. The court stated:

> [T]he Board of Education decided that it was part of its function to protect its students against rational judgments reached by themselves and their parents. In effect, the Board's decisions stands the doctrine of *in loco parentis* on its head. Traditionally, this doctrine has meant that a school system must act "in place of the parent" when the parent are absent. Finally, the court observed: It is undoubtedly true that injury to Richard's kidney would have grave consequences, but so might other injuries that might befall him or any other member of the wrestling team. Hardly a year goes by that there is not at least one instance of the tragic death of a healthy youth as a result of competitive sports activity. Life has risks. The purpose of § 504, however, is to permit handicapped individuals to live life as fully as they are able, without paternalistic authorities deciding that certain activities are too risky for them.

Turning to the present case, I begin with reluctance an analysis which compels me to disturb a well-intended decision of local school authorities. The administration of our public schools is a matter almost always better left in the hands of members of the community which the schools serve. Had the plaintiffs relied solely on a conclusory equal protection challenge to the school district's decision, the result I now reach may very well have been different. However, in this case, I am bound to uphold an act of Congress which is specifically designed to protect Richard and the right he is asserting.

The school district has advanced two reasons as "substantial justification" for its action. First, according to Dr. LaFrankin was his concern for the liability that might be imposed upon the school district if Richard loses the use of his kidney. This concern may be answered by the releases which the parents and son have offered to execute. However, the real issue is whether the risk of injury is significant enough to make this concern any justification for the district's decision. Since the existence of a risk is also an issue under the district's second justification, I will resolve these issues together. The district's second justification for precluding Richard from participating in football is concern for his health, safety, and welfare. This concern is based on a risk perceived by the district that Richard could lose his one functioning kidney.

This case began when Dr. Delp decided that it would be helpful to get an opinion from Richard's kidney physician with regard to his ability to play. From this I conclude that Dr. Delp did not consider himself qualified to make the determination. At least, he did not hold an opinion concerning Richard's playing. The letters that were produced from Dr. Lennart were equivocal. His letter of August 16, 1982 is the most enlightening. He recognized in that letter that the decision whether or not Richard should play is not properly the subject of a medical opinion. The evidence is clear that neither Dr. Lennart, Dr. Delp, nor Dr. Hemmerlie had any facts which would permit them to make a rational medical evaluation of the existence of a risk. In an understandable abundance of caution, all three eventually concluded that the safest course was to say that Richard could not play. I conclude that the opinion of these three doctors cannot serve as substantial justification for the district's actions where their decision lacks a medical basis.

Even if the letter signed by Dr. Delp and Dr. Hemmerlie could be considered as substantial justification at the time it was received, it is not justification for the continued refusal of the district to permit Richard to play in light of Dr. Moyer's opinion. Dr. Moyer has the clinical experience and has performed the research required to come to a medical evaluation of the risk to Richard. His conclusion was that the risk of injury to the kidney is so slim that there is no medical reason why Richard cannot play football. Essentially, his testimony is consistent with that portion of Dr. Lennart's correspondence which concluded that whether Richard should engage in contact sports is not a medical issue.

Richard's selection for the team established that he is otherwise qualified to play football. For the reasons stated above, the defendant's decision to preclude him from playing lacks substantial justification. Accordingly, I conclude that the plaintiffs have made a strong showing of likelihood of success on the merits.

* * *

On the facts similar to ours, the courts in *Kampmeier* and *Wright* believed irreparable harm existed. * * * In the case before me, the plaintiff is being deprived of an important right guaranteed by federal legislation. Even assuming that the denial alone might be compensated for by money damages, other injury flowing from the denial could not. Richard is a collegiate caliber football player who hopes that this talent will be his entree to college. Neither his grades, which are average, nor his family's financial status offer as good an opportunity for him to attend college as does his athletic ability in this sport. Whether such an opportunity will materialize depends upon his having a chance to play his senior year. Even then, much will depend on his performance and other intangibles. It would be nealry impossible for him if he is denied the opportunity to play, to prove later, with the degree of certainty required for an award of money damages, the existence of a loss and its value.

Finally, I conclude that no injury is likely to result to the defendant or the public interest by granting this relief. The plaintiffs are willing to take responsibility for the decision that they have reached. The only credible medical opinion, Dr. Moyer's, shows that the likelihood of the type of injury that concerns the defendant is almost nil. Finally, the public interest is served when plaintiffs such as these vindicate important federal rights.

For the reasons stated above, the motion for preliminary injunction will be granted.

* * *

Note

A federal district court held that a state athletic association's age-limit rule, as applied to a student with Down's syndrome, violated Section 504 and the student was entitled to a waiver. The nineteen-year-old student, who always placed last in the swimming meets, would otherwise be excluded from participation. The court rejected the argument that granting the waiver in this case would lead to a flood of new waiver applications. See *Dennin v. Connecticut Interscholastic Athletic Conference*, 913 F. Supp. 663 (D. Conn. 1996).

B. Employees and Section 504

Section 504 mandates that employers in institutions receiving federal funds must make "reasonable accommodations" to the limitations of handicapped employees who are otherwise qualified. Providing reasonable accommodations may mean restructuring physical access in work areas, redistributing tasks among jobs so that handicapped employees can function in their positions, eliminating unnecessary job qualifications, and other reasonable modifications. It does not mean that employers must tolerate substandard job performance or hire persons whose employment would threaten the safety of others.

The United States Supreme Court addressed the issue of whether having a contagious disease, tuberculosis in this instance, is a handicapping condition under Section 504. In its decision in *School Board of Nassau County v. Arline*, 480 U.S. 273 (1987), the Court stated:

> Allowing discrimination based on the contagious effects of a physical impairment would be inconsistent with the basic purpose of § 504, which is to ensure that handicapped individuals are not denied jobs or other benefits because of the prejudiced attitudes or the ignorance of others. By amending the definition of "handicapped individual" to include not only those who are actually physically impaired, but also those who are regarded as impaired and who, as a result, are substantially limited in a major life activity, Congress

acknowledged that society's accumulated myths and fears about disability and disease are as handicapping as are the physical limitations that flow from actual impairment. Few aspects of a handicap give rise to the same level of public fear and misapprehension as contagiousness. Even those who suffer or have recovered from such noninfectious diseases as epilepsy or cancer have faced discrimination based on the irrational fear that they might be contagious. The Act is carefully structured to replace such reflexive reactions to actual or perceived handicaps with actions based on reasoned and medically sound judgments: the definition of "handicapped individual" is broad, but only those individuals who are both handicapped and otherwise qualified are eligible for relief. The fact that some persons who have contagious diseases may pose a serious health threat to others under certain circumstances does not justify excluding from the coverage of the Act all persons with actual or perceived contagious diseases. Such exclusion would mean that those accused of being contagious would never have the opportunity to have their condition evaluated in light of medical evidence and a determination made as to whether they were "otherwise qualified." Rather, they would be vulnerable to discrimination on the basis of mythology—precisely the type of injury Congress sought to prevent. (pp. 284–285)

The Court cited several "well-established" criteria to be used to determine whether a "handicapped" person is an "otherwise qualified" employee: whether, given "reasonable accommodation," the person can meet all of a program's requirements or can perform "the essential functions" of the job. Accommodation is not reasonable if it imposes "undue financial and administrative burdens" on the employer or requires a fundamental alteration in the "nature of the program."

A teacher diagnosed as having the AIDS virus alleged that his reassignment to an administrative position violated Section 504. In a decision filled with references to Arline, a federal court of appeals upheld the teacher's motion for a preliminary injunction reinstating him to classroom duties. The court noted the overwhelming consensus of medical testimony, which revealed that the teacher posed no significant risk of spreading the disease. Additionally, the court found that the reassignment to an administrative position, although involving no monetary deprivation, failed to utilize the teacher's skills and, thus, injured him emotionally and psychologically. See *Chalk* v. *United States District Court*, 840 F.2d 701 (9th Cir. 1988).

A visually disabled and hearing-impaired teacher's discharge was upheld by a state supreme court after substantial evidence showed that the disability affected his performance. The teacher experienced problems with student discipline, exhibited deficient professional preparation, failed to establish appropriate educational objectives, and generally jeopardized the welfare and safety of the students in his charge. See *Clark* v. *Shoreline School District No. 412*, 720 P.2d 793 (Wash. 1986). According to the court in *Gonzalez* v. *California State Personnel Board*, 39 Cal. Rptr.2d 282 (Cal. App. 3d Dist. 1995), handicapped persons are not entitled to any special protections in employment and may be disciplined or fired for misconduct that is not solely a result of their disability.

III. THE AMERICANS WITH DISABILITIES ACT

The Americans with Disabilities Act (ADA) of 1990 is considered by many to be the most sweeping antidiscrimination law since the Civil Rights Act of 1964. Although Section 504 protected handicapped persons from discrimination in institutions receiving federal funds, individuals with disabilities remained unprotected in many other important areas of life. Congress passed the ADA to provide protections for individuals with disabilities in employment, public accommodations, telecommunications, and other areas. Many provisions in the ADA are similar to Section 504 provisions, but provide broader coverage. Because passage of the ADA was based on Congress's power to enforce the Fourteenth Amendment and to regulate interstate commerce, the ADA prohibits discrimination against individuals with disabilities in both the public and private sectors, regardless of whether any federal funds are received.

Title II of the ADA prohibits discrimination against individuals with disabilities in all state and local government programs, including public schools. Similar to Section 504, Title II of the ADA declares that:

> [N]o qualified individual with a disability shall, by reason of such disability, be excluded from participation in or be denied the benefits of the services, programs, or activities of a public entity, or be subjected to discrimination by any such entity. 42 U.S.C. § 12132 (1997).

The ADA prohibits discrimination based on a disability, and requires modifications for accessibility and other reasonable accommodations for individuals with disabilities. Although the ADA provided significant new protections for individuals with disabilities, especially in the private sector, the impact of the ADA in public schools was less dramatic. Discrimination against handicapped persons in schools receiving federal funds was already prohibited by Section 504.

Nonetheless, there are some situations in which the ADA impacts the operation of schools. For example, schools are required to make public accommodations such as athletic stadiums, auditoriums, and other facilities barrier-free for individuals with disabilities attending school events. Further, all new school construction must comply with barrier-free design requirements mandated by the ADA.

CHAPTER SEVEN

School Finance and School Choice Issues

This chapter focuses on two finance-related issues. The first section provides an historical perspective to the legal attacks on the constitutionality of the financing and adequacy of state school finance plans. These legal attacks began in the early 1970s and continue to be litigated in many states. The second section examines the legal issues surrounding various states' responses to the notion of providing increasing parental choice in selecting appropriate educational opportunities for their children.

I. SCHOOL FINANCE REFORM

A. Background

Successful court decisions involving racial segregation in the public schools revealed that the judiciary would deal with issues that other branches of government were unwilling to be concerned with or were reluctant to recognize. Consequently, many persons who perceived that they were being denied rights owing to governmental action or inaction increasingly employed the courts in an attempt to redress alleged grievances. One such group of persons brought the issue of equality of educational opportunity before the courts. Their contention in the earliest cases was that many state methods of financing public education were unconstitutional because they violated the Equal Protection Clause for certain classes of people.

Reliance on local revenue to support a large portion of the total public school budget, it was alleged, was unfair because of the disparity in taxable wealth among local school systems.* Because the property tax is the most commonly used local school tax, many school finance experts have defined school system wealth as the ratio of taxable property divided by the number of students. Consequently, a "wealthy" school system would achieve such status by having much valuable taxable property, such as factories, utilities, or natural resources, and few children to educate. Conversely, a "poor" school system would have little valuable property and many children to educate. A school system composed largely of trailer parks, where each trailer contained several school-age children, would be an example of a poor system. School-district wealth is based on property wealth and not on income wealth; consequently, there may or may not be a relationship in property-poor or wealthy school systems with the income wealth of its inhabitants.

Those who contend that a state's method of financing the public schools is unfair often argue that wealthy school systems can raise large amounts of money with lower tax rates than can poor systems. It is alleged that allowing this situation under a state-authorized method of financing public education is unfair to both taxpayers and the recipients of school services in poor systems. For example, assume that the wealthiest school system in a state has a taxable assessed valuation per student (usually expressed on the basis of average daily attendance, membership, or full-time equivalent) of $800,000, and the poorest school system has a taxable assessed valuation per student of $50,000. A levy of one mill (one-tenth of one percent, also expressed as a tax rate of $1 per $1,000 of property value) would raise $800 per student in the wealthiest system and only $50 per student in the poorest school system. Because education is a responsibility of the state, school finance reformers allege that a state's allowing a school financing system in which such disparities operate in favor of wealthy school systems denies equality of educational opportunity to those students in poorer school systems.

Many school finance issues have been raised since the earliest court cases. Those that have received the greatest sustained court attention addressed the alleged inequality of educational opportunity resulting from statewide school finance systems that make educational funding a function of district property wealth; whether or not a disputed finance scheme provides each child with at least a basic or adequate education; the importance of local control; and the extent, if any, of courts' involvement

---

*Nationally, local revenue has made up approximately 45 percent of the total revenue for elementary and secondary schools, whereas state revenue made up approximately 48 percent and federal revenue nearly 7 percent. Across the country, local support for public elementary and secondary education has ranged from a high of approximately 90 percent to a low of approximately 10 percent. Hawaii is the only state having no official local support for education.

in providing remediation. Widely diverse collateral issues have included the effects of municipal overburden and allowing recapture, that is, excess revenue raised in "wealthy" districts to be distributed by the state to "poor" districts. Court attention to these issues will be the subject of the remainder of this section on school finance reform.

B. Early Decisions

In one of the earliest decisions, *McInnis* v. *Shapiro*, 293 F. Supp. 327 (Ill. 1968), *aff'd sub nom. McInnis* v. *Ogilvie*, 394 U.S. 322 (1969), the Illinois method of financing public education was described by plaintiffs as being particularly inequitable because it permitted wide variations in expenditures per student and did not apportion funds according to the educational needs of students. In rejecting this contention, the court declared that the controversy was essentially nonjusticiable because of a lack of judicially manageable standards. The court contended that equal expenditures per student were inappropriate as a standard and that courts were ill equipped to devise an equitable financing plan for the public schools. A virtually indistinguishable case, *Burruss* v. *Wilkerson*, 310 F. Supp. 572 (Va. 1969), *aff'd mem.*, 397 U.S. 44 (1970), essentially reached the same conclusion as *McInnis*.

Questions raised in these early cases revealed the lack of empirical data necessary to have a clear and accurate understanding of the effects of a state's finance system. Additionally, these cases revealed other methodological shortcomings, such as the lack of consensus over the goals of schooling and especially what constituted a "basic" education, an absence of meaningful cost-effectiveness analysis, a clear definition of educational need, and the inexactitude of measurement technology. Courts, it soon became evident, had great difficulty in dealing with broad generalizations or abstractions concerning education, requiring instead quantifiable evidence.

C. Fiscal Neutrality

Lack of success in *McInnis* and *Burruss* did not dissuade others interested in school finance reform from continuing a legal assault on interdistrict resource inequality. A California case, *Serrano* v. *Priest*, 487 P.2d 1241 (Cal. 1971) (*Serrano I*), provided the court with a judicially manageable standard, which had been missing in *McInnis* and *Burruss*. In this case, the plaintiffs attempted to demonstrate that the California method of financing public education allowed substantial disparities among the various school districts in the amount of revenue available for education, thereby denying students equal protection of the laws under both the United States and California constitutions.

Furthermore, plaintiffs alleged that under this system, parents were required to pay taxes at a higher rate than taxpayers in many other districts to provide the same or lesser educational opportunities for their children. In its decision, the California Supreme Court established that education was a constitutionally protected fundamental interest and that "wealth" was a "suspect classification." When a fundamental interest or suspect classification is involved, the court contended, the state must establish not only that it has a compelling interest that justifies the law, but that the distinctions drawn by the law are necessary to further its purpose. Employing this line of reasoning places the so-called burden of proof on the state. Perhaps most important in this decision was the standard established by the court to determine whether or not a school finance plan was constitutional. Under this standard, which the court called "fiscal neutrality," the quality of a child's education could not be based on the wealth of a child's local school district but rather had to be based on the wealth of the state as a whole. This provided the court with a judicially manageable standard, in contrast to the "needs" standard in *McInnis,* as the court merely had to reject the present financing plan as unconstitutional, thereby placing the burden of adopting a constitutionally acceptable finance plan with the state.*

Serrano advanced the notion that the state had the responsibility for financing education. This issue, whether the state or local school districts have ultimate financial control over public schooling, has become central in most school finance decisions.

D. *Rodriguez*

Suits were filed in both state and federal courts in more than three dozen states after the California *Serrano I* decision in this first "wave" of initial attacks on existing school financing schemes. In many of these suits, plaintiffs were successful in the lower courts in their request that the court endorse the fiscal neutrality standard adopted in *Serrano I* to remedy wealth disparity. One of these cases, **San Antonio Independent School District v. Rodriguez,** provided the United States Supreme Court with an opportunity to address this issue.

---

*A subsequent decision by a California Supreme Court in *Serrano II,* 557 P.2d 929 (Cal. 1976), *cert. denied,* 432 U.S. 907 (1977), again affirmed the trial court's finding that the California school finance system was unconstitutional under the equal protection provision of the state constitution. *Serrano III,* 226 Cal. Rptr. 584 (1986) held that there had been full compliance with the original *Serrano* mandate to improve equity.

SAN ANTONIO INDEPENDENT SCHOOL DISTRICT v. RODRIGUEZ
Supreme Court of the United States, 1973
411 U.S. 1

MR. JUSTICE POWELL delivered the opinion of the Court.

This suit attacking the Texas system of financing public education was initiated by Mexican-American parents whose children attend the elementary and secondary schools in the Edgewood Independent School District, an urban school district in San Antonio, Texas. They brought a class action on behalf of schoolchildren throughout the State who are members of minority groups or who are poor and reside in school districts having a low property tax base. * * * The complaint was filed in the summer of 1968 and a three-judge court was impaneled in January 1969. In December 1971 the panel rendered its judgment in a per curiam opinion holding the Texas school finance system unconstitutional under the Equal Protection Clause of the Fourteenth Amendment. The State appealed, and we noted probable jurisdiction to consider the far-reaching constitutional questions presented. * * * For the reasons stated in this opinion, we reverse the decision of the District Court.

The first Texas State Constitution, promulgated upon Texas' entry into the Union in 1845, provided for the establishment of a system of free schools. Early in its history, Texas adopted a dual approach to the financing of its schools, relying on mutual participation by the local school districts and the State. * * *

Until recent times, Texas was a predominantly rural State and its population and property wealth were spread relatively evenly across the State. Sizable differences in the value of assessable property between local school districts became increasingly evident as the State became more industrialized and as rural-to-urban population shifts became more pronounced. The location of commercial and industrial property began to play a significant role in determining the amount of tax resources available to each school district. These growing disparities in population and taxable property between districts were responsible in part for increasingly notable differences in levels of local expenditure for education.

* * *

Recognizing the need for increased state funding to help offset disparities in local spending and to meet Texas' changing educational requirements, the state legislature in the late 1940s undertook a thorough evaluation of public education with an eye toward major reform. * * * [It established] the Texas Minimum Foundation School Program. Today, this Program accounts for approximately half of the total educational expenditures in Texas.

The Program calls for state and local contributions to a fund earmarked specifically for teacher salaries, operating expenses, and transportation costs. The State, supplying funds from its general revenues, finances approximately

80% of the Program, and the school districts are responsible—as a unit—for providing the remaining 20%. The districts' share, known as the Local Fund Assignment, is apportioned among the school districts under a formula designed to reflect each district's relative taxpaying ability. ∗ ∗ ∗

∗ ∗ ∗

The school district in which appellees reside, the Edgewood Independent School District, has been compared throughout this litigation with the Alamo Heights Independent School District. This comparison between the least and most affluent districts in the San Antonio area serves to illustrate the manner in which the dual system of finance operates and to indicate the extent to which substantial disparities exist despite the State's impressive progress in recent years. Edgewood is one of seven public school districts in the metropolitan area. Approximately 22,000 students are enrolled in its 25 elementary and secondary schools. The district is situated in the core-city sector of San Antonio in a residential neighborhood that has little commercial or industrial property. The residents are predominantly of Mexican-American descent: approximately 90% of the student population is Mexican-American and over 6% is Negro. The average assessed property value per pupil is $5,960—the lowest in the metropolitan area—and the median family income ($4,686) is also the lowest. At an equalized tax rate of $1.05 per $100 of assessed property—the highest in the metropolitan area—the district contributed $26 to the education of each child for the 1967–1968 school year above its Local Fund Assignment for the Minimum Foundation Program. The Foundation Program contributed $222 per pupil for a state–local total of $248. Federal funds added another $108 for a total of $356 per pupil.

Alamo Heights is the most affluent school district in San Antonio. Its six schools, housing approximately 5,000 students, are situated in a residential community quite unlike the Edgewood District. The school population is predominantly "Anglo," having only 18% Mexican-Americans and less than 1% Negroes. The assessed property value per pupil exceeds $49,000, and the median family income is $8,001. In 1967–1968 the local tax rate of $.85 per $100 of valuation yielded $333 per pupil over and above its contribution to the Foundation Program. Coupled with the $225 provided from that Program, the district was able to supply $558 per student. Supplemented by a $36 per-pupil grant from federal sources, Alamo Heights spent $594 per pupil.

Although the 1967–1968 school year figures provide the only complete statistical breakdown for each category of aid, more recent partial statistics indicate that the previously noted trend of increasing state aid has been significant. For the 1970–1971 school year, the Foundation School Program allotment of Edgewood was $356 per pupil. ∗ ∗ ∗ Alamo Heights enjoyed a similar increase under the Foundation Program, netting $491 per pupil in 1970–1971. These recent figures also reveal the extent to which these two districts' allotments were funded from their own required contributions to the

Local Fund Assignment. Alamo Heights, because of its relative wealth, was required to contribute out of its local property tax collections approximately $100 per pupil, or about 20% of its Foundation grant. Edgewood, on the other hand, paid only $8.46 per pupil, which is about 2.4% of its grant. It appears then that, at least as to these two districts, the Local Fund Assignment does reflect a rough approximation of the relative taxpaying potential of each.

Despite these recent increases, substantial interdistrict disparities in school expenditures found by the District Court to prevail in San Antonio and in varying degrees throughout the State still exist. And it was these disparities, largely attributable to differences in the amounts of money collected through local property taxation, that led the District Court to conclude that Texas' dual system of public school financing violated the Equal Protection Clause. * * *

* * *

* * * We must decide, first, whether the Texas system of financing public education operates to the disadvantage of some suspect class or impinges upon a fundamental right explicitly or implicitly protected by the Constitution, thereby requiring strict judicial scrutiny. If so, the judgment of the District Court should be affirmed. If not, the Texas scheme must still be examined to determine whether it rationally furthers some legitimate, articulated state purpose and therefore does not constitute an invidious discrimination in violation of the Equal Protection Clause of the Fourteenth Amendment.

* * *

The wealth discrimination discovered by the District Court in this case, and by several other courts that have recently struck down school financing laws in other states, is quite unlike any of the forms of wealth discrimination heretofore reviewed by this Court. * * *

The case comes to us with no definitive description of the classifying facts or delineation of the disfavored class. Examination of the District Court's opinion and of appellees' complaint, briefs, and contentions at oral arguments suggests, however, at least three ways in which the discrimination claimed here might be described. The Texas system of school financing might be regarded as discriminating (1) against "poor" persons whose incomes fall below some identifiable level of poverty or who might be characterized as functionally "indigent," (2) against those who are relatively poorer than others, or (3) against all those who, irrespective of their personal incomes, happen to reside in relatively poorer school districts. Our task must be to ascertain whether, in fact, the Texas system has been shown to discriminate on any of these possible bases and, if so, whether the resulting classification may be regarded as suspect.

The precedents of this Court provide the proper starting point. The individuals, or groups of individuals, who constituted the class discriminated against in our prior cases shared two distinguishing characteristics: because of their impecunity they were completely unable to pay for some desired benefit, and as a consequence, they sustained an absolute deprivation of a meaningful opportunity to enjoy that benefit. * * *

* * *

Only appellees' first possible basis for describing the class disadvantaged by the Texas school financing system—discrimination against a class of definably "poor" persons—might arguably meet the criteria established in these prior cases. Even a cursory examination, however, demonstrates that neither of the two distinguishing characteristics of wealth classifications can be found here. First, in support of their charge that the system discriminates against the 'poor,' appellees have made no effort to demonstrate that it operates to the peculiar disadvantage of any class fairly defined as indigent, or as composed of persons whose incomes are beneath any designated poverty level. Indeed, there is reason to believe that the poorest families are not necessarily clustered in the poorest property districts. A recent and exhaustive study of school districts in Connecticut concluded that "[i]t is clearly incorrect . . . to contend that the 'poor' live in 'poor' districts. . . . Thus, the major factual assumption of *Serrano*—that the educational financing system discriminates against the 'poor'—is simply false in Connecticut." Defining "poor" families as those below the Bureau of the Census "poverty level," the Connecticut study found, not surprisingly, that the poor were clustered around commercial and industrial areas—those same areas that provide the most attractive sources of property tax income for school districts. Whether a similar pattern would be discovered in Texas is not known, but there is no basis on the record in this case for assuming that the poorest people—defined by reference to any level of absolute impecunity—are concentrated in the poorest districts.

Second, neither appellees nor the District Court addressed the fact that, unlike each of the foregoing cases, lack of personal resources had not occasioned an absolute deprivation of the desired benefit. The argument here is not that the children in districts having relatively low assessable property values are receiving no public education; rather, it is that they are receiving a poorer-quality education than that available to children in districts having more assessable wealth. Apart from the unsettled and disputed question whether the quality of education may be determined by the amount of money expended for it, a sufficient answer to appellees' argument is that, at least where wealth is involved, the Equal Protection Clause does not require absolute equality or precisely equal advantages. * * *

For these two reasons—the absence of any evidence that the financing system discriminates against any definable category of "poor" people or that it results in the absolute deprivation of education—the disadvantaged class is not susceptible of identification in traditional terms.

As suggested above, appellees and the District Court may have embraced a second or third approach, the second of which might be characterized as a theory of relative comparative discrimination based on family income. Appellees sought to prove that a direct correlation exists between the wealth of families within each district and the expenditures therein for education. That is, along a continuum, the poorer the family, the lower the dollar amount of education received by the family's children.

* * *

This brings us, then, to the third way in which the classification scheme might be defined—*district* wealth discrimination. Since the only correlation indicated by the evidence is between district property wealth and expenditures, it may be argued that discrimination might be found without regard to the individual income characteristics of district residents. * * *

However described, it is clear that appellees' suit asks this Court to extend its most exacting scrutiny to review a system that allegedly discriminates against a large, diverse, and amorphous class, unified only by the common factor of residence in its districts that happen to have less taxable wealth than other districts. The system of alleged discrimination and the class it defines have none of the traditional indicia of suspectness: The class is not saddled with such disabilities, subjected to such a history of purposeful unequal treatment, or relegated to such a position of political powerlessness as to command extraordinary protection from the majoritarian political process.

We thus conclude that the Texas system does not operate to the peculiar disadvantage of any suspect class. But in recognition of the fact that this Court has never heretofore held that wealth discrimination alone provides an adequate basis for invoking strict scrutiny, appellees have not relied solely on this contention. They also assert that the State's system impermissibly interferes with the exercise of a "fundamental" right and that accordingly the prior decisions of this Court require the application of the strict standard of judicial review. * * * It is this question—whether education is a fundamental right, in the sense that it is among the rights and liberties protected by the Constitution—which has so consumed the attention of courts and commentators in recent years.

* * *

Nothing this Court holds today in any way detracts from our historic dedication to public education. We are in complete agreement with the conclusion of the three-judge panel below that "the grave significance of education both to the individual and to our society" cannot be doubted. But the importance of a service performed by the State does not determine whether it must be regarded as fundamental for purposes of examination under the Equal Protection Clause. * * *

* * *

* * * It is not the province of this Court to create substantive constitutional rights in the name of guaranteeing equal protection of the laws. Thus, the key to discovering whether education is "fundamental" is not to be found in comparisons of the relative societal significance of education as opposed to subsistence or housing. Nor is it to be found by weighing whether education is as important as the right to travel. Rather, the answer lies in assessing whether there is a right to education explicitly or implicitly guaranteed by the Constitution. * * *

Education, of course, is not among the rights afforded explicit protection under our Federal Constitution. Nor do we find any basis for saying it is implicitly so protected. As we have said, the undisputed importance of education will not alone cause this Court to depart from the usual standard for reviewing a State's social and economic legislation. It is appellees' contention, however, that education is distinguishable from other services and benefits provided by the State because it bears a peculiarly close relationship to other rights and liberties accorded protection under the Constitution. Specifically, they insist that education is itself a fundamental personal right because it is essential to the effective exercise of First Amendment freedoms and to intelligent utilization of the right to vote. In asserting a nexus between speech and education, appellees urge that the right to speak is meaningless unless the speaker is capable of articulating his thoughts intelligently and persuasively. The "marketplace of ideas" is an empty forum for those lacking basic communicative tools. Likewise, they argue that the corollary right to receive information becomes little more than a hollow privilege when the recipient has not been taught to read, assimilate, and utilize available knowledge.

* * *

Even if it were conceded that some identifiable quantum of education is a constitutionally protected prerequisite to the meaningful exercise of either right, we have no indication that the present levels of educational expenditures in Texas provides an education that falls short. Whatever merit appellees' argument might have if a State's financing system occasioned an absolute denial of educational opportunities to any of its children, that argument provides no basis for finding an interference with fundamental rights where only relative differences in spending levels are involved and where— as is true in the present case—no charge fairly could be made that the system fails to provide each child with an opportunity to acquire the basic minimal skills necessary for the enjoyment of the rights of speech and of full participation in the political process.

Furthermore, the logical limitations on appellees' nexus theory are difficult to perceive. How, for instance, is education to be distinguished from the significant personal interests in the basics of decent food and shelter? Empirical examination might well buttress an assumption that the ill-fed, ill-clothed, and ill-housed are among the most ineffective participants in the political process, and that they derive the least enjoyment from the benefits of the First Amendment. * * *

* * *

Thus, we stand on familiar ground when we continue to acknowledge that the Justices of this Court lack both the expertise and the familiarity with local problems so necessary to the making of wise decisions with respect to the raising and disposition of public revenues. Yet, we are urged to direct the States either to alter drastically the present system or to throw out the property tax altogether in favor of some other form of taxation. No scheme of taxation, whether the tax is imposed on property, income, or purchases of goods and services, has yet been devised which is free of all discriminatory impact. In such a complex arena in which no perfect alternatives exist, the Court does well not to impose too rigorous a standard of scrutiny lest all local fiscal schemes become subjects of criticism under the Equal Protection Clause.

In addition to matters of fiscal policy, this case also involves the most persistent and difficult questions of educational policy, another area in which this Court's lack of specialized knowledge and experience counsels against premature interference with the informed judgments made at the state and local levels. Education, perhaps even more than welfare assistance, presents a myriad of "intractable economic, social, and even philosophical problems." * * * The very complexity of the problems of financing and managing a statewide public school system suggests that "there will be more than one constitutionally permissible method of solving them," and that, within the limits of rationality, "the legislature's efforts to tackle the problems" should be entitled to respect. * * * On even the most basic questions in this area the scholars and educational experts are divided. Indeed, one of the major sources of controversy concerns the extent to which there is a demonstrable correlation between educational expenditures and the quality of education—an assumed correlation underlying virtually every legal conclusion drawn by the District Court in this case. Related to the questioned relationship between cost and quality is the equally unsettled controversy as to the proper goals of a system of public education. And the question regarding the most effective relationship between state boards of education and local school boards, in terms of their respective responsibilities and degrees of control, is now undergoing searching re-examination. The ultimate wisdom as to these and related problems of education is not likely to be divined for all time even by the scholars who now so earnestly debate the issues. In such circumstances, the judiciary is well advised to refrain from imposing on the States inflexible constitutional restraints that could circumscribe or handicap the continued research and experimentation so vital to finding even partial solutions to educational problems and to keeping abreast of ever-changing conditions.

* * *

The foregoing considerations buttress our conclusion that Texas' system of public school finance is an inappropriate candidate for strict judicial scrutiny. * * *

* * *

Appellees further urge that the Texas system is unconstitutionally arbitrary because it allows the availability of local taxable resources to turn on "happenstance." They see no justification for a system that allows, as they contend, the quality of education to fluctuate on the basis of the fortuitous positioning of the boundary lines of political subdivisions and the location of valuable commercial and industrial property. But any scheme of local taxation—indeed the very existence of identifiable local governmental units—requires the establishment of jurisdictional boundaries that are inevitably arbitrary. It is equally inevitable that some localities are going to be blessed with more taxable assets than others. Nor is local wealth a static quantity. Changes in the level of taxable wealth within any district may result from any number of events, some of which local residents can and do influence. For instance, commercial and industrial enterprises may be encouraged to locate within a district by various actions—public and private.

Moreover, if local taxation for local expenditures were an unconstitutional method of providing for education, then it might be an equally impermissible means of providing for other necessary services customarily financed largely from local property taxes, including local police and fire protection, public health and hospitals, and public utility facilities of various kinds. We perceive no justification for such a severe denigration of local property taxation and control as would follow from appellees' contentions. It has simply never been within the constitutional prerogative of this Court to nullify statewide measures for financing public services merely because the burdens or benefits thereof fall unevenly depending upon the relative wealth of the political subdivisions in which citizens live.

∗ ∗ ∗ One also must remember that the system here challenged is not peculiar to Texas or to any other State. In its essential characteristics, the Texas plan for financing public education reflects what many educators for a half century have thought was an enlightened approach to a problem for which there is no perfect solution. We are unwilling to assume for ourselves a level of wisdom superior to that of legislators, scholars, and educational authorities in 50 States, especially where the alternatives proposed are only recently conceived and nowhere yet tested. ∗ ∗ ∗

∗ ∗ ∗

∗ ∗ ∗ The consideration and initiation of fundamental reforms with respect to state taxation and education are matters reserved for the legislative processes of the various States, and we do no violence to the values of federalism and separation of powers by staying our hand. We hardly need add that this Court's action today is not to be viewed as placing its judicial imprimatur on the status quo. The need is apparent for reform in tax systems which may well have relied too long and too heavily on the local property tax. And certainly innovative thinking as to public education, its methods, and its funding is necessary to assure both a higher level of quality and greater uniformity of opportunity. These matters merit the continued attention of the scholars who already have contributed much by their challenges. But the ultimate solutions must come from the lawmakers and from the democratic pressures of those who elect them.

Reversed.

* * *

MR. JUSTICE WHITE, with whom MR. JUSTICE DOUGLAS and MR. JUSTICE BRENNAN join, dissenting.

* * *

I cannot disagree with the proposition that local control and local decisionmaking play an important part in our democratic system of government. * * * Much may be left to local option, and this case would be quite different if it were true that the Texas system, while insuring minimum educational expenditures in every district through state funding, extended a meaningful option to all local districts to increase their per-pupil expenditures and so to improve their children's education to the extent that increased funding would achieve that goal. The system would then arguably provide a rational and sensible method of achieving the stated aim of preserving an area for local initiative and decision.

The difficulty with the Texas system, however, is that it provides a meaningful option to Alamo Heights and like school districts but almost none to Edgewood and those other districts with a low per-pupil real estate tax base. In these latter districts, no matter how desirous parents are of supporting their schools with greater revenues, it is impossible to do so through the use of the real estate property tax. In these districts, the Texas system utterly fails to extend a realistic choice to parents because the property tax, which is the only revenue-raising mechanism extended to school districts, is practically and legally unavailable. * * *

* * *

* * * If the State aims at maximizing local initiative and local choice, by permitting school districts to resort to the real property tax if they choose to do so, it utterly fails in achieving its purpose in districts with property tax bases so low that there is little if any opportunity for interested parents, rich or poor, to augment school district revenues. Requiring the State to establish only that unequal treatment is in furtherance of a permissible goal, without also requiring the State to show that the means chosen to effectuate that goal are rationally related to its achievement, makes equal protection analysis no more than an empty gesture. In my view, the parents and children in Edgewood, and in like districts, suffer from an invidious discrimination violative of the Equal Protection Clause.

This does not, of course, mean that local control may not be a legitimate goal of a school financing system. Nor does it mean that the State must guarantee each district an equal per-pupil revenue from the state school financing system. Nor does it mean, as the majority appears to believe, that, by affirming the decision below, this Court would be "imposing on the States inflexible constitutional restraints that could circumscribe or handicap the continued research and experimentation so vital to finding even partial solutions to educational problems and to keeping abreast of ever-changing conditions." On the contrary, it would merely mean that the State must fashion a financing scheme which provides a rational basis for the maximization of local control, if local control is to remain a goal of the system, and not a scheme with "different treatment be[ing] accorded to persons placed by a statute into different classes on the basis of criteria wholly unrelated to the objective of that statute." * * *

* * *

Notes and Questions

Rodriguez was a five-to-four decision. Joining Justice Powell in the majority opinion were Chief Justice Burger and Justices Stewart, Blackmun, and Rehnquist. In addition to upholding the constitutionality of the Texas method of financing public schools, the Court held that education was not a fundamental interest requiring strict scrutiny under the Equal Protection Clause. The Court also concluded that school finance reform should flow from state legislative processes.

Some observers have contended that, if the Court had mandated equality of educational opportunity for public school students, floodgates would have opened resulting in judicial attacks on statewide inequality in other governmental services, such as police and fire protections, recreational facilities, and health care. Do you agree with this contention? Does the fact that most state constitutions contain language committing the state to a responsibility for providing education negate this contention?

Despite the *Rodriguez* outcome, plaintiffs in Louisiana attempted to distinguish between practices in Louisiana and Texas in a suit alleging that the Equal Protection Clause of the Fourteenth Amendment was violated by the Louisiana school finance system. Nevertheless, a federal district court found the issues indistinguishable from *Rodriguez* and dismissed the case. See *Scarnato* v. *Parker*, 415 F. Supp. 272 (La. 1976), *aff'd*, 430 U.S. 960 (1977).

E. Post-*Rodriguez* Litigation

Proponents of the school finance reform movement viewed the *Rodriguez* decision as essentially eliminating the federal courts as a viable battleground. Consequently, their attention turned to the state courts. In addition to relying on state equal protection grounds, litigation was brought under state constitutional provisions requiring public education to be "uniform," "adequate," or "thorough and efficient." However, largely because of the differences among states in the constitutional language or the specific statutory provisions that were challenged, state court holdings have not been uniform. To date, there has been litigation in nearly 80 percent of states, and the states are virtually even in court decisions upholding challenged state school finance schemes and those that hold them unconstitutional. The judicial cauldron has continued to boil unabated since *Rodriguez.*

1. Decisions Upholding State Finance Provisions

The highest courts in Alaska, Colorado, Georgia, Idaho, Illinois, Maine, Maryland, Michigan, Minnesota, Nebraska, New York, North Carolina, Oklahoma, Oregon, Pennsylvania, Rhode Island, South Carolina, Virginia, and Wisconsin have concluded that state methods of financing public education are not constitutionally deficient.[*] A federal appellate court in 1987 upheld the Louisiana finance plan. Many of the decisions upholding states' plans espoused the legal rationale enunciated by the Supreme Court in *Rodriguez.* In their decisions, the courts agreed that education was unquestionably high on the list of priorities of governmental concern and responsibility; however, this did not automatically entitle public education to a classification as a fundamental right that would trigger a higher standard of judicial review for purposes of equal protection analysis. Public education in many of these cases was viewed as merely another public service battling for scarce resources in the political arena. The proper arena, these courts contended, was the legislature and not the courtroom. Additionally, decisions upholding existing state finance plans strongly favored the preservation of local control of education. Although courts, in many instances, found that disparity in local wealth and expenditures existed, they contended that this was not unconstitutional. In several cases, courts, recognizing that there were inequities, asserted that the state should ensure that every child had a basic or adequate education. The highest court in New York declared that even if gross wealth disparities were present among school systems, plaintiffs had not shown that these disparities resulted in students from poorer districts receiving "less than a sound basic education." A few courts complained that there were no judicially manageable standards on which to base a decision. However, it was emphasized in decisions upholding state finance plans that if reform was needed, it was not the province of the judiciary to effect it; rather, it should be instituted by the legislative branch.

---

[*]See list of selected school finance-related cases and citations on pages 379–382.

To varying degrees, the earlier court decisions upholding school finance systems primarily involved suits that were based on allegations of unconstitutional wealth and per-pupil expenditure disparities. However, novel issues were addressed in several states. In New York state, New York City intervened on behalf of plaintiffs and added a "municipal overburden" issue to the case. Municipal overburden refers to the contention that city school systems have higher costs than nonmunicipal districts, and intervenors alleged that this overburden represented a disequalizing force. Several new issues were raised in the earlier Ohio decision. These included (1) the contention that voter control over tax levies should not have been permissible in a state that required a thorough and efficient educational program and (2) the argument that property-poor school districts tended to be income poor in that state and therefore constituted a more clearly identifiable suspect classification. Ohio plaintiffs also claimed that fiscal capacity should not be represented solely by property value per student. In Maryland, plaintiffs also attempted to base their case, in part, on a correlation between income and property wealth. Additionally, they sought to convince the court that a constitutional requirement of a "thorough and efficient" education should be construed as disallowing wide expenditure variations, even those resulting from factors other than local wealth disparity.

2. Decisions Effecting Reform

Decisions by the highest courts in a number of states have ordered school finance reform. In these decisions, the courts generally held that statutes governing state and local financing of public education were unconstitutional, that delivery of educational opportunity was not adequate, or that local control was not a rational basis for justifying disparate educational opportunities. In several instances, courts revisited earlier decisions or examined legislative reform based on a previous decision. These so-called reform states include Alabama, Arizona, Arkansas, California, Connecticut, Kansas, Kentucky, Massachusetts, Montana, New Hampshire, New Jersey, North Dakota, Ohio, Tennessee, Texas, Vermont, Washington, West Virginia, and Wyoming.

Several legal rationales are woven through the decisions invalidating school finance schemes. Courts often held that either district wealth or per-pupil expenditure disparities, or both, were unconstitutional, based either on equal protection grounds or on the wording pertaining to education in their state constitutions. Although these courts usually imposed "strict scrutiny" for equal protection analysis, they commonly declared that contested schemes failed to satisfy even the less stringent "rational basis" standard. In assessing the local control issue, these decisions usually reasoned that finance schemes, rather than preserving local control, thwarted it by requiring poor school systems merely to administer state-financed educational programs. However, the most pervasive theme threading through these decisions was the courts' recognition of the irrationality of the contested finance schemes. Several decisions ordered legislative restructuring of the basic formula for the distribution of state funds or the receipt of local revenues in order to eliminate or reduce local wealth disparity as a factor influencing expenditure variation among school districts or their ability to provide an adequate education. Largely beginning in the late 1980s, emphasis on the issue of wealth and spending disparity (equality of educational opportunity) was replaced by one of adequacy (ensuring quality of education for all children).

Litigation continues in some states, generally as a consequence of dissatisfaction on the part of original plaintiffs or new parties with the quantity or quality of reforms enacted by legislatures in response to court orders. To date, no court has retreated from its initial requirement that inequities be corrected. Standards for alleviating disparities, after being promulgated by courts, have not been relaxed in subsequent orders. In New Jersey, Texas, and Connecticut, multigeneration decisions have addressed plaintiffs' claims of inadequate legislative response. Decisions rendered in the early 1970s in Arizona and Texas, and in Ohio in 1980, which upheld those states' methods for financing public education, have been replaced two decades later by decisions holding those systems unconstitutional. In several states, school finance reform was effected by lower court decisions that were not appealed. In Georgia, significant school finance reform legislation was enacted, although that state's supreme court did not hold the funding system unconstitutional.

In Kentucky, the state's supreme court ordered the dramatic restructuring of the entire education system. The court's order in ***Rose v. Council for Better Education*** has been the most radical judicial response of any school finance suit to date.

ROSE v. COUNCIL FOR BETTER EDUCATION
Supreme Court of Kentucky, 1989
790 S.W. 2d 186

CHIEF JUSTICE STEPHENS delivered the opinion of the court.

The issue we decide on this appeal is whether the Kentucky General Assembly has complied with its constitutional mandate to "provide an efficient system of common schools throughout the state."

In deciding that it has not, we intend no criticism of the substantial efforts made by the present General Assembly and by its predecessors, nor do we intend to substitute our judicial authority for the authority and discretion of the General Assembly. We are, rather, exercising our constitutional duty in declaring that, when we consider the evidence in the record, and when we apply the constitutional requirement of Section 183 to that evidence, it is crystal clear that the General Assembly has fallen short of its duty to enact legislation to provide for an efficient system of common schools throughout the state. In a word, the present system of common schools in Kentucky is not an "efficient" one in our view of the clear mandate of Section 183. The common school system in Kentucky is constitutionally deficient.

In reaching this decision, we are ever mindful of the immeasurable worth of education to our state and its citizens, especially to its young people. The framers of our constitution intended that each and every child in this state should receive a proper and an adequate education, *to be provided for by the General Assembly.* This opinion dutifully applies the constitutional test of Section 183 to the existing system of common schools. We do no more, nor may we do any less.

* * *

The complaint included allegations that the system of school financing provided for by the General Assembly is inadequate; places too much emphasis on local school board resources; and results in inadequacies, inequities and inequalities throughout the state so as to result in an inefficient system of common school education in violation of Kentucky Constitution, Sections 1, 3 and 183 and the equal protection clause and the due process of law clause of the 14th Amendment to the United States Constitution. Additionally the complaint maintains the entire system is not efficient under the mandate of Section 183.

The relief sought by the plaintiffs was a declaration of rights to the effect that the system be declared unconstitutional; that the funding of schools also be determined to be unconstitutional and inadequate; that the defendant, Superintendent of Public Instruction, be enjoined from further implementing said school statutes; that a mandamus be issued, directing the Governor to recommend to the General Assembly the enactment of appropriate legislation which would be in compliance with the aforementioned constitutional provisions; that a mandamus be issued, directing the President *Pro Tempore* of the Senate and the Speaker of the House of Representatives to place before the General Assembly appropriate legislation which is constitutionally valid; and that a mandamus be issued, directing the General Assembly to provide for an "equitable and adequate funding program for all school children so as to establish an 'efficient system of common schools.' "

* * *

The trial judge identified four issues before him: (1) The necessity for defining the phrase "an efficient system of common schools" as contained in Section 183 of the Kentucky Constitution; (2) Whether education is a "fundamental right" under our Constitution; (3) Whether Kentucky's current method of financing its common schools violates Section 183, and (4) whether students in the so-called "poor" school districts are denied equal protection of the laws.

"Efficient," in the Kentucky constitutional sense, was defined as a system which required "substantial uniformity, substantial equality of financial resources and substantial equal educational opportunity for all students." Efficient was also interpreted to require that the educational system must be adequate, uniform and unitary.

Because of the language of Section 183, the trial court ruled that education, indeed, is a fundamental right in Kentucky.

In ruling on the issue of whether Kentucky's method of school financing violates Section 183 and underpinning the point with extensive findings of fact, the trial court declared that students in property-poor school districts are offered a minimal level of educational opportunities, which is inferior to those offered to students in more affluent districts. Such "invidious" discrimination, based on the place of a student's residence, was determined to be unconstitutional. The trial court ruled that the school finance system violates the equal protection guarantees of Section 1 and 3 of the Kentucky Constitution.

In its judgment, the trial court ruled: (1) The Kentucky finance "system" of its common schools is unconstitutional and discriminatory; and (2) The system of common schools is not efficient within the purview of Section 183 of the Kentucky Constitution. The Court indicated it would appoint a "small select committee," the purpose of which was to review all relevant data, provide additional analysis, consult with financial experts and propose remedies to "correct the deficiencies in the present common school financing system." * * *

* * *

If one were to summarize the history of school funding in Kentucky, one might well say that every forward step taken to provide funds to local districts and to equalize money spent for the poor districts has been countered by one backward step.

It is certainly true that the General Assembly, over the years, has made substantial efforts to infuse money into the system to improve and equalize the educational efforts in the common schools of Kentucky. What we must decide, based solely on the evidence in the record as tested by the Kentucky Constitution, Section 183, is whether the trial court was correct in declaring that those efforts have failed to create an efficient system of common schools in this Commonwealth.

* * *

The evidence in this case consists of numerous depositions, volumes of oral evidence heard by the trial court, and a seemingly endless amount of statistical data, reports, etc. We will not unduly lengthen this opinion with an extensive discussion of that evidence. As a matter of fact, such is really not necessary. The overall effect of appellants' evidence is a virtual concession that Kentucky's system of common schools is underfunded and inadequate; is fraught with inequalities and inequities throughout the 177 local school districts; is ranked nationally in the lower 20–25% in virtually every category that is used to evaluate educational performance; and is not uniform among the districts in educational opportunities. When one considers the evidence presented by the appellants, there is little or no evidence to even begin to negate that of the appellees. The tidal wave of the appellees' evidence literally engulfs that of the appellants.

In spite of the Minimum Foundation Program and the Power Equalization Program, there are wide variations in financial resources and dispositions thereof which result in unequal educational opportunities throughout Kentucky. The local districts have large variances in taxable property per student. Even a total elimination of all mismanagement and waste in local school districts would not correct the situation as it now exists. A substantial difference in the curricula offered in the poorer districts contrasts with that of the richer districts, particularly in the areas of foreign language, science, mathematics, music and art.

The achievement test scores in the poorer districts are lower than those in the richer districts, and expert opinion clearly established that there is a correlation between those scores and the wealth of the district. Student-teacher ratios are higher in the poorer districts. Moreover, although Kentucky's per capita income is low, it makes an even lower per capita effort to support the common schools.

Students in property-poor districts receive inadequate and inferior educational opportunities as compared to those offered to those students in the more affluent districts.

That Kentucky's overall effort and resulting achievement in the area of primary and secondary education are comparatively low, nationally, is not in dispute. Thirty-five percent of our adult population are high school dropouts. Eighty percent of Kentucky's local school districts are identified as being "poor," in terms of taxable property. The other twenty percent remain under the national average. Thirty percent of our local school districts are "functionally bankrupt."

Evidence relative to educational performance was introduced by appellees to make a comparison of Kentucky with its neighbors—Ohio, Indiana, Illinois, Missouri, Tennessee, Virginia, and West Virginia. It also ranked Kentucky, nationally in the same areas.

In the area of per pupil expenditures, Kentucky ranks 6th among the 8 states and ranks 40th, nationally. With respect to the average annual salary of instructional staff, Kentucky again ranks 6th among its neighbors and 37th nationally. In the area of classroom teacher compensation, Kentucky is 7th and 37th. Our classroom teacher average salary is 84.68% of the national average and our per pupil expenditure is 78.20% of the national average.

When one considers the use of property taxes as a percent of sources of school revenue, Kentucky is 7th among our neighboring states and 43rd nationally. The national average is 30.1% while Kentucky's rate is 18.2%. If any more evidence is needed to show the inadequacy of our overall effort, consider that only 68.2% of ninth grade students eventually graduate from high school in Kentucky. That ranks us 7th among our eight adjacent sister states. Among the 6 of our neighboring states that use the ACT scholastic achievement test, our high school graduates' average score is 18.1, which ranks us 4th. Kentucky's ratio of pupil to teacher is 19 to 2 which ranks us 7th in this region. In spite of the appellants' claim, at both the trial level and on appeal, that appellees' statistics are not current, all the above figures are based on a 1986 study, which was published in 1987.

* * *

The numerous witnesses that testified before the trial court are recognized experts in the field of primary and secondary education. * * * Without exception, they testified that there is great disparity in the poor and the more affluent school districts with regard to classroom teachers' pay; provision of basic educational materials; student-teacher ratio; curriculum; quality of basic management; size, adequacy and condition of school physical plants; and per year expenditure per student. Kentucky's children, simply because of their place of residence, are offered a virtual hodgepodge of educational opportunities. The quality of education in the poorer local school districts is substantially less in most, if not all, of the above categories.

Can anyone seriously argue that these disparities do not affect the basic educational opportunities of those children in the poorer districts? To ask the question is to answer it. Children in 80% of local school districts in this Commonwealth are not as well-educated as those in the other 20%.

Moreover, most of the witnesses before the trial court testified that not only were the state's educational opportunities unequal and lacking in uniformity, but that *all* were inadequate. Testimony indicated that not only do the so-called poorer districts provide inadequate education to fulfill the needs of the students but the more affluent districts' efforts are inadequate as well, as judged by accepted national standards.

As stated, when one reads the record, and when one considers the argument of counsel for the appellants, one can find no proof, no statement that contradicts the evidence about the existing inequalities and lack of uniformity in the overall performance of Kentucky's system of common schools.

* * *

Uniform testimony of the expert witnesses at trial, corroborated by data, showed a definite correlation between the money spent per child on education and the quality of the education received. As we have previously stated in our discussion of the history of Kentucky's school finances, our system does not *require* a minimum local effort. The MFP, being based on average daily attendance, certainly infuses more money into each local district, but is not designed to correct problems of inequality and lack of uniformity between local school districts. The experts stated that the PEP, although a good idea, was and is underfunded.

The disparity in per pupil expenditure by the local school boards runs in the thousands of dollars per year. Moreover, between the extreme high allocation and the extreme low allocation lies a wide range of annual per pupil expenditures. * * * The financing effort of local school districts is, figuratively speaking, a jigsaw puzzle.

It is argued by the appellants that the so-called permissive taxes are at least part of the solution to equalizing local financial efforts. There are two easy answers that dispose of this argument. First, the taxes are permissive. Responding to obvious voter resistance to the imposition of taxes, 89 districts have enacted the tax on gross utility receipts; 5 districts have enacted the occupational tax; 82 districts have also enacted a special building tax, normally for a specific project for one time only, and not affecting teacher pay, instructional equipment, or any of the specific needs of educational opportunity. * * *

Secondly, according to the testimony of the expert witnesses, even if all permissive taxes were enacted, the financial effort would still be inadequate, and because the population of the districts is in direct proportion to the amount of money that could and is raised by these taxes, the overall problem of an unequal local effort would be exacerbated by such action. Clearly, the permissive taxes are not the solution to the problems. Rather, they contribute to the disparity of per pupil expenditures.

Additionally, because the assessable and taxable real and personal property in the 177 districts is so varied, and because of a lack of uniformity in tax rates, the local school boards' tax effort is not only lacking in uniformity but is also lacking in adequate effort. The history of school financing in Kentucky certainly corroborates the trial court's finding as to the lack of uniformity and the lack of adequacy of local and state funding of education in the state. Based on the record before us, it is beyond cavil that the trial court's finding was correct.

* * *

We find no authority that would justify the appointment of the "special committee" which was to advise the trial court. While the purpose of the committee was undoubtedly an admirable one, and while the members of the committee did an excellent job, their work product essentially is not a proper tool in the formulation of a judicial decision. A judge must make his or her own decision, and must use only the evidence in the record, and the available legal precedents. A judge may not delegate part of his or her authority to non-judicial persons or institutions. We therefore hold the appointment of the committee was improper, and, obviously the assessment of the committee expenses against the Board of Education was improper as well.

We have decided this case solely on the basis of our Kentucky Constitution, Section 183. We find it unnecessary to inject any issues raised under the United States Constitution or the United States Bill of Rights in this matter.

We decline to issue any injunctions, restraining orders, writs of prohibition or writs of mandamus.

We have decided one legal issue—and one legal issue only—viz., that the General Assembly of the Commonwealth has failed to establish an efficient system of common schools throughout the Commonwealth.

Lest there be any doubt, the result of our decision is that Kentucky's *entire system* of common schools is unconstitutional. There is no allegation that only part of the common school system is invalid, and we find no such circumstance. This decision applies to the entire sweep of the system—all its parts and parcels. This decision applies to the statutes creating, implementing and financing the *system* and to all regulations, etc., pertaining thereto. This decision covers the creation of local school districts, school boards, and the Kentucky Department of Education to the Minimum Foundation Program and Power Equalization Program. It covers school construction and maintenance, teacher certification—the whole gamut of the common school system in Kentucky.

While individual statutes are not herein addressed specifically or considered and declared to be facially unconstitutional, the statutory system as a whole and the interrelationship of the parts therein are hereby declared to be in violation of Section 183 of the Kentucky Constitution. Just as the bricks and mortar used in the construction of a schoolhouse, while contributing to the building's facade, do not ensure the overall structural adequacy of the schoolhouse, particular statutes drafted by the legislature in crafting and designing the current school system are not unconstitutional in and of themselves. Like the crumbling schoolhouse which must be redesigned and revitalized for more efficient use, with some component parts found to be adequate, some found to be less than adequate, statutes relating to education may be reenacted as components of a constitutional system if they combine with other component statutes to form an efficient and thereby constitutional system.

Since we have, by this decision, declared the system of common schools in Kentucky to be unconstitutional, Section 183 places an absolute duty on the General Assembly to re-create, re-establish a new system of common schools in the Commonwealth. As we have said, the premise of this opinion is that education is a basic, fundamental constitutional right that is available to all children within this Commonwealth. The General Assembly should begin with the same premise as it goes about its duty. The system, as we have said, must be efficient, and the criteria we have set out are binding on the General Assembly as it develops Kentucky's new system of common schools.

As we have previously emphasized, the *sole responsibility* for providing the system of common schools lies with the General Assembly. If they choose to delegate any of this duty to institutions such as the local boards of education, the General Assembly must provide a mechanism to assure that the ultimate control remains with the General Assembly, and assure that those local school districts also exercise the delegated duties in an efficient manner.

The General Assembly must provide adequate funding for the system. How they do this is their decision. However, if ad valorem taxes on real and personal property are used by the General Assembly as part of the financing of the redesigned state system of common schools, the General Assembly has the obligation to see that *all such property* is assessed at 100% of its market value. Moreover, because of the great disparities of local tax efforts in the present system of common schools, the General Assembly must establish a uniform tax rate for such property. In this way, all owners of real and personal property throughout the state will make a comparable effort in the financing of the state system of common schools.

* * *

Because of the enormity of the task before the General Assembly to recreate a new statutory system of common schools in the Commonwealth, and because we realize that the educational process must continue, we withhold the finality of this decision until 90 days after the adjournment of the General Assembly, *sine die*, at its regular session in 1990.

Notes

The **Rose** decision departed significantly from previous school finance decisions. It not only broadened the scope of court examination of related school finance issues but also ordered an unprecedented restructuring of the state's entire educational system.

Significant reforms were incorporated by the legislature in the Kentucky Education Reform Act, which emerged as a result of the **Rose** decision. These reforms included equity provisions whereby wealthy and poor districts receive the same financing, a 60 percent increase in statewide funding, councils of parents and teachers who have budgetary and hiring authority, placing all children ages six to eight in the same classroom, and a comprehensive testing program. Test scores are the basis for rating schools, and teachers can earn bonuses if there is improvement. Bonuses end if scores decline. Results of output measures, to date, have been mixed. On state-created tests, fourth graders have scored higher than set targets. Fourth and eighth graders have improved on national math tests. National college admissions scores remain flat, and dropout rates have not changed. Interestingly enough, poor districts now perform as well on most tests as wealthier ones.

II. CHOICE

This section deals with the legal issues surrounding states' responses to the notion of providing increasing parental choice in selecting appropriate educational opportunities for their children. The section is not intended to be a definitive treatise on the various schemes labeled "educational choice" or a recitation of their positive and negative aspects. Rather, it is intended to be (1) a brief description of several of the plans, which in the largest sense of the term may be considered to be a form of choice, that have been proposed to date; (2) an exploration of the newly emerging case law and a discussion of the possible legal implications springing from the adoption of choice plans, such as federal and state constitutionality and compliance with state and federal statutory and regulatory provisions; and (3) a basis for class discussion of the concept and its legal implications because choice plans continue to be a viable school reform measure.

A. Choice Plans

Given the unrelenting harsh criticism of the public schools by some political leaders, members of the general public, educators, and educational policymakers have attempted to provide government officials with reforms that are both educationally sound and politically attractive. One of the highly touted reforms—choice—provides for increased consumer selection of educational services at public expense. Variations of choice policies have been enacted by many state legislatures. Unfortunately, the notion of choice does not describe a single, well-defined plan but is an umbrella term for a host of programs. Opponents see choice plans as a direct challenge to the egalitarian notion that the bright, not-so-bright, disabled, persons of color, white, and economically advantaged and disadvantaged all attend the same public school; that is, the "melting pot" idea. Its proponents argue that bringing a concept—consumer choice—to education will break the monopolistic stranglehold of the educational bureaucracy by introducing much-needed competition to the public schools. A brief description of various proposed and enacted plans follows.

1. Public School Inter- and Intradistrict Open Enrollment

Under these concepts, students would be allowed to attend the school of their choice in their own school district or any district in the state, provided there was room at that school and that their attendance did not create segregation along racial lines. Generally, federal and state monies would follow the student. Minnesota has been the acknowledged leader in this form of choice, passing a law that allows families to send their children outside their district so long as the receiving school district has room and desegregation efforts are not jeopardized. Several other states have passed similar legislation.

2. Interdistrict Specialized Schools and Plans

Larger school districts have experimented with plans that provide students with a choice of attending a school other than the one in their attendance zone. These plans, which may incorporate magnet schools, are often put into place to effect desegregation efforts, retain students who are contemplating dropping out of school, or offer specialized programs for academically advantaged students.

Magnet schools may emphasize particular educational features such as mathematics, science, arts, or "basics." In addition to parental application, acceptance at these schools is determined by potential students meeting established criteria. Magnet schools have been considered a valuable tool in those school systems attempting to effect desegregation. Unfortunately, their feasibility is limited to relatively large school districts. To date, only an infinitesimal number of students nationwide attend magnet-type schools. Although not originally designed to effect desegregation, special schools for the academically advantaged in several large cities have had success. Examples of such schools, which have attained considerable national attention, include Boston's Latin School, New York City's Bronx High School of Science, and San Francisco's Lowell High School.

Minischools, or schools within schools, are variants of the magnet school and attempt to provide educational alternatives within a particular school site. Such schools often have a particular curriculum designed for students who are disabled, pregnant, unruly, or have other special needs and interests.

Majority to minority plans seek to assist desegregation efforts by allowing students who come from a school where their race is in the majority to transfer to a school in the district where their race is in the minority. Providing the necessary transportation is essential for these plans.

Second-chance or continuation schools are primarily designed for students who are likely to drop out or have dropped out of high school. These programs are often conducted in nontraditional settings and not during normal school hours.

3. Voucher Plan

Providing parents with school vouchers, thereby giving them an alternative to sending their children to their assigned public schools, was first proposed by the Nobel Laureate economist Milton Friedman decades ago. He saw vouchers as a solution to what he perceived to be an unresponsive public school monopoly. It was designed to give parents greater control of their children's schooling and to provide poor parents an opportunity for private education. Although variants of this plan have become exceedingly complex over the years, the original idea called for parents to receive a voucher redeemable for a specified maximum sum per child per year if spent on approved "educational services." The role of government would be confined to ensuring that schools met minimum standards. Later variants called for the voucher to have the value of the cost of a public school education. The voucher could be redeemed at any approved school, public or private, thereby providing parents with a measure of choice. Voters in Minnesota (1978), California (1980 and 2000), and Michigan (2000) had opportunities to approve voucher-type plans, but the measures were unsuccessful. In 1999, Florida became the first state to offer a statewide voucher program to help parents of students in failing schools offset the cost of private education. The plan has been challenged in Florida's courts. Despite vocal and mostly conservative support, voucher plans to date have not received significant popular support. The operation of several forces appears to be the reason for vouchers not gaining wider acceptance. These include: anxiety that public schools would become "dumping grounds" for the difficult to educate; concern on the part of private schools that vouchers would bring about increasing elements of government control; separation of church and state issues; issues surrounding desegregation and the eligibility of disabled students; and fear of government support for the establishment of an elitist educational system when vouchers act as a tuition subsidy for wealthy children but are insufficient to grant poorer children access to elite schools. Several cities are experimenting with variants of the voucher plan. A minivoucher plan allows students, usually advanced secondary students, to purchase specific and limited services outside the resident school system.

Courts, in the late 1990s, have addressed several issues regarding vouchers, tuition reimbursement programs, and tax credits for tuition payments. Many of the decisions, however, turned on separation of church and state issues. Voucher plans addressed by the courts, to date, have been state attempts to provide vouchers for mostly low-income students in low-achieving schools in Milwaukee, Cleveland, and various Florida cities.

In the first school-choice ruling by a state's highest court, *Jackson* v. *Benson*, 578 N.W.2d 602 (Wis. 1998), *cert. denied* 525 U.S. 997 (1998), the Milwaukee Parental Choice Program for low-income children was upheld. Under the program, eligible students were required to reside in Milwaukee, attend public schools or private schools in grades K–3, and meet certain income requirements; there was an "opt-out" provision under which private schools could not require participation in religious activities provided at that school; and parents had a choice of sending their children to a neighborhood public school, a different public school within the district, a specialized public school, a private nonsectarian school, or a private sectarian school (Wisconsin has a system of per-pupil financing under which public funds follow each child). A major issue in this case was whether the program violated the Establishment Clause of the First Amendment because state aid could be given to parents of qualified students for attendance at either sectarian or nonsectarian private schools and there were no restrictions on the uses to which the private schools could use the state aid. In its decision, the court stated that it reluctantly applied the *Lemon* test because five current United States Supreme Court justices have questioned its continued use; yet, the court in its four-to-two decision went to great lengths in stressing that the Milwaukee program had a secular legislative purpose, its principal or primary effect neither advanced nor inhibited religion, and it did not create excessive entanglement between government and religion. In addressing the issue that the program would violate the Equal Protection Clauses of the Fourteenth Amendment, the court stated that was not the case as the statute was not enacted with a purpose or intent to discriminate. The court held that the program, on its face, was race-neutral. It allowed students to be chosen without regard to race to attend schools of their choice and schools had to comply with antidiscrimination statutes.

Ohio's Supreme Court addressed its 1995 School Voucher Program, designed for low-income students in the failing Cleveland City Schools, in *Simmons-Harris* v. *Goff*, 711 N.E.2d 203 (Ohio 1999). In its decision, the court essentially followed the reasoning in *Jackson* by holding that the voucher program did not violate the First Amendment's Establishment Clause. However, the program was stricken by the court because it violated Ohio's "one-subject" rule. Under the rule, major legislation must be in a separate bill, and the court concluded "creation of a substantive program in a general appropriations bill violates the one-subject rule."

A 1999 re-enacted Ohio voucher program that had virtually all the elements of the stricken law was challenged in *Simmons-Harris* v. *Zelman*, 234 F3d 945 (6th Cir. 2000). In applying the *Lemon* test, the court held that the voucher program had the effect of advancing religion through government-sponsored religious indoctrination. The court found that over 82 percent of participating Cleveland schools were church-affiliated and over 96 percent of the students were enrolled in sectarian schools. The court contended that no attempt had been made in the Ohio program to guarantee that state aid only supported secular, as opposed to religious, educational functions. The court also noted that public school per pupil expenditures were $7,097, and because vouchers only provided a maximum of $2,250 per pupil, there was a financial disincentive for public schools outside the school district to take on students under the voucher program. Consequently, the court concluded that:

> The effect of the voucher program is in direct contravention to these Supreme Court cases which mandate that the state aid be neutrally available to all students who qualify, that the parents receiving the state aid have the

option of applying the funds to secular organizations or causes as well as to religious institutions, and that the state aid does not provide an incentive to choose a religious institution over a secular institution. Accordingly, we hold that no genuine issue of material fact remains for trial that the voucher program has the primary effect of advancing religion, and that is constitutes an endorsement of religion and sectarian education in violation of the Establishment Clause. (p. 961)

Florida's first-in-the-nation statewide voucher program was challenged (*Bush* v. *Holmes*) in 2000 as being in violation of that state's constitution. Under Florida's Opportunity Scholarship Program, students who attended a school that had been assigned a performance grade category "F" were eligible for state vouchers. The final appeal in this case will be by Florida's highest court rather than the United States Supreme Court, because the original ruling was on state constitutional grounds.

Maine had a statute under which tuition grants were made available if a student's community did not have public school facilities due to insufficient student density. Under the statute, direct grants were made to private nonsectarian schools but not to sectarian schools. Parents who sent their children to private Roman Catholic high schools challenged the constitutionality of the tuition program in *Strout* v. *Albanese*, 178 F.3d 57 (Me. 1999), *cert. denied*, 528 U.S. 931 (1999) and *Bagley* v. *Raymond School Department*, 728 A.2d 127 (Me. 1999), *cert. denied*, 528 U.S. 947 (1999). Both federal and state courts denied the parents' relief and upheld the statute's constitutionality by holding that the statute did not violate the Establishment Clause, Equal Protection Clause, and the Free Exercise Clause.

The Vermont Supreme Court in *Chittenden Town School District* v. *Department of Education*, 738 A.2d 539 (Vt. 1999) *cert. denied*, 528 U.S. 1066 (1999), held that a school district's secondary-education tuition reimbursement policy allowing tuition to be paid to sectarian schools was unconstitutional. Vermont's tuition reimbursement program, dating back 130 years, provided opportunities for students, whose local school district did not operate a public high school, to attend a public or private high school. The court reasoned that the policy was violative of the state Constitution's "compelled support" clause, which did not allow the state to interfere with or control an individual's free exercise of religious worship or compel attendance or support religious worship against that person's conscience.

A review of school voucher decisions reveals that state and lower federal courts are not entirely comfortable in using the *Lemon* test when making their decisions. Judges often cite the lack of agreement on the part of Supreme Court justices regarding that test. Unfortunately, such an uncertain environment makes it difficult for educational policy makers to provide their constituents with legally sound policies. Given this state of affairs, it would be useful if the Supreme Court entered the fray and provided judicial guidance.

4. Charter Schools

Charter schools, called "opt-out" schools in England, allow entities other than school boards to establish publicly funded schools. Founders may be teachers, parents, public bodies such as museums and universities, or in some instances, for-profit private organizations. A charter is typically issued by the local school board or state agency, for a period of five years or less, in return for a promise to achieve certain results. The theory behind such schools is to allow individuals or groups with innovative educational ideas to put them into practice without being unduly hampered by local or state bureaucracy. Charter schools may offer unconventional hours, experiment with curricula, specialize in certain types of teaching, or design programs tailored to a particular audience or community. Success of such schools depends on achieving promised results and parental satisfaction and on the public money, which follows each child. By 1999, various forms of charter school legislation have been passed in third-six states and the District of Columbia since Minnesota first passed such a law in 1991. Charters may be revoked if there is financial mismanagement, discrimination toward students, violation of state or federal laws, or nonfulfillment of the goals specified in the charter. To date, the charter movement has not drawn the political controversy associated with vouchers. There were approximately 100 charter schools in 1994, 1700 in 1999, and 3000 are expected by 2002.

Denial of a charter school application by a county school board was addressed by the South Carolina Supreme Court in *Beaufort County Board of Education* v. *Lighthouse Charter School Committee*, 516 S.E.2d 656 (S.C. 1999). In upholding the denial, the court discussed the failure to meet requirements in such areas as health and safety, civil rights, and racial composition. Specific requirements included: adherence to the same health, safety, civil rights, and disability rights requirements that applied to the district's public schools; approval for new school facilities from the U.S. Department of Education Office of Civil Rights and compliance with the reporting requirements under the district's voluntary desegregation plan; and ensuring that charter school enrollment did not differ by more than 10 percent from the racial composition of the school district.

New Jersey's Charter School Program Act was held not to be unconstitutional in *Grant of Charter School Application of Englewood on the Palisades Charter School*, 753 A.2d 687 (N.J. 2000). In its holding, the court stated that the choice to include charter schools among the array of public entities providing educational services is a choice appropriately made by the legislature so long as the constitutional mandate to provide a thorough and efficient system of education is satisfied. During the charter approval process, the court asserted, consideration must be given to the racial impact that the movement of pupils to a charter school would have on the district of residence, and there must be strong provisions for nondiscrimination and random selection of students to assure equal access to charter schools. The local school boards bringing the suit challenged the economic impact of charter schools on their districts. They maintained that having to pay charter schools 90 percent of the local levy budget per pupil would cause dire consequences for the respective school districts (under the statute, the state commissioner could set the amount higher or lower than 90 percent but not to exceed 100 percent). In rejecting this argument, the court maintained that allowing charter schools to operate would not jeopardize the districts' providing a thorough and efficient education to their remaining students.

5. Private Contractors

This option allows school systems to contract with private firms for specific educational services, ranging from providing foreign language instruction to broader services such as running an entire school. Attaining specific performance levels is generally a part of the contract between the school system and the private firm. Some observers wonder what the effects will be on the philosophical mission and operation of schools when they are profit-driven enterprises. Experiments with private management in large urban areas have not been successful to date. Both Hartford, the largest experiment in privatization, and Baltimore terminated their contracts before their expiration. Dade County, Florida, did not renew its contract with a private contractor.

A teacher's union sued its school board for contracting with a private company to operate and manage a school. Twenty-four teachers were to be furloughed as a result of the contract. The Pennsylvania Supreme Court held that it was constitutional under that state's Public School Code for a local board to enter into such a contract. See *School District of Wilkinsburg* v. *Wilkinsburg Education Association*, 667 A.2d 5 (Pa. 1995).

6. Tuition Tax Credits

Although not always labeled as a choice plan, providing tuition tax credits for parents of school-age children is designed to ease the financial burden of nonpublic school attendance. Under such plans, parents are allowed to claim a state income tax deduction from gross income on their state income tax returns or a tax credit for tuition or certain educational expenses incurred at either public or private schools. Courts had not upheld such plans, primarily because of separation of church and state problems, prior to the Supreme Court's decision upholding a Minnesota tax credit plan in *Mueller* v. *Allen*, 463 U.S. 388 (1983). See page 85 for a discussion of *Mueller*.

Arizona's Supreme Court upheld a state law that allowed taxpayers to contribute up to $500 to private schools and $200 to public schools every year, and then claim the amount as a credit against state taxes. In its holding, the court ruled that the tax credit did not violate the Establishment Clause of the Federal Constitution, it was not an "appropriation" of "public money" to establish religion or aid sectarian schools under the state constitution, and it did not violate the antigift clause of the state constitution. See *Kotterman* v. *Killian*, 972 P.2d 606 (Ariz. 1999), *cert. denied*, 528 U.S. 92 (1999).

B. Legal Implications

Legal issues associated with choice plans have only recently begun to be adjudicated. To date, there has been no United States Supreme Court decision pertaining to choice plans, and there have only been a handful of state and lower federal court decisions. Several legal issues have been raised in the cases to date, such as separation of church and state and racial discrimination; however, additional legal issues are bound to surface. The following is a brief exploration of potential legal issues surrounding various choice plans. It is presented to stimulate discussion, and its placement at this point in the text allows the student an opportunity to apply legal principles presented throughout the text.

An overall constitutional concern with such choice plans as magnet schools, for instance, includes their being challenged on equal protection grounds under the federal and state constitutions. The question of whether or not there was a rational basis—or a legitimate State purpose—for classifications of selectees made under such a choice plan will be central to many of the cases. Plans that by design or circumstances are not equally available to all students similarly situated, thereby resulting in seemingly unequal treatment for those not eligible or selected under the plan, may be particularly vulnerable. As we have seen in Chapter 5, for instance, a state cannot engage in unconstitutional racial balancing. Although their existence may be justified pedagogically, one-race or one-gender classes or schools would be carefully scrutinized, as would restricting the eligibility of disabled students.

Separation of church and state issues have been a major concern in several of the choice decisions because publicly disbursed funds have benefitted sectarian schools. As shown in Chapter 2, the Supreme Court has shown considerable interest in this issue over the years. The presently employed *Lemon* test establishes that a challenged statute must first, have a secular legislative purpose; second, its principal or primary effect must be one that neither advances nor inhibits religion; and, third, it must not foster an excessive government entanglement with religion. Until a new test is devised, courts will have to determine whether a challenged plan violates any or all of these three prongs or the coercion test enunciated in *Lee* v. *Weisman*. Complicating the issue further would be the matter of a sectarian school's acceptance of voucher students if the school had rigid policies tied to enrollment of white students and hiring of white faculty only, both of whom were required to have strongly held religious beliefs. The long-standing issue of providing transportation to students not attending public schools, would undoubtedly surface, particularly if transportation were tied to vouchers used for sectarian education.

Choice plans that had a racial segregative impact would be most vulnerable to challenge. This would certainly be the case if the operation of a choice plan allowed resegregation to take place. Choice plans insensitive to desegregation efforts would also be challenged in those districts that have voluntary diversity plans or remain under court order to strictly comply with desegregation mandates.

Legal difficulties conceivably might come into play if public schools, and perhaps entire public school districts, could be shown to have become "dumping grounds" if more teachable students were to withdraw because of the availability of a choice plan. In such an instance, it would have to be shown that the remaining students constituted an identifiable population that was illegally disadvantaged by the choice plan, such as students who were difficult to educate, disturbed, unruly, disabled, minority, disruptive, unwilling to do their homework, or suffering from learning disorders.

Many school finance issues, which have a potential for legal challenge, would also surface. A central issue would undoubtedly be which funds follow a student in interdistrict choice plans. Although a challenge to federal, state, and categorical funds following a student appears unlikely, controversy might arise concerning local funds (especially from a high-spending district) and state equalization funds following a student. Additional problems could center on which funds follow a student who wishes to attend a lower-spending neighboring district and who would be responsible for supplying the additional funds if the transfer is to a higher-spending district. Another issue may be whether or not all federal, state, and local monies accompany students who attend charter schools. Transportation issues must be considered as well. For instance, would the sending system be responsible for transporting a student to the school district's border (closest to the student's home?) and then have the receiving system continue the transportation? Whether charter schools receive funds for capital outlay could also become a legal issue.

Implementation of choice plans would require a re-examination of state athletic association rules and regulations. Some early evidence suggests that parental "choice" decisions are not necessarily made on the basis of a child's going to a better academic school or district but for such reasons as being closer to child care, better extracurricular activities, "easier grades," or just "more convenient." Consequently, allowing for the exercise of choice in school attendance has the potential to create athletic "powerhouses." This and allied issues could spur considerable litigation in those states where high school athletics are taken seriously.

Because private contractors and private schools that accept vouchers would make affirmative promises regarding their educational offerings and student performance, failure to deliver on such promises could bring lawsuits alleging false advertising and breach of contract. Also, significant legal issues could be raised upon a private contractor or school filing for bankruptcy.

*Listing of Selected School Finance–Related Cases**

Alabama

> *Opinion of the Justices*, 624 So.2d 107 (Ala. 1993).

Alaska

> *Matanuska-Sustina Borough School District* v. *State*, 931 P.2d 391 (Alaska 1997).

Arizona

> *Roosevelt Elementary School District No. 66* v. *Bishop*, 877 P.2d 806 (Ariz. 1994).
> *Shofstall* v. *Hollins*, 515 P.2d 590 (Ariz.1973).

Arkansas

> *Dupree* v. *Alma School District No. 30*, 651 S.W.2d 90 (Ark. 1983).

California

> *Serrano* v. *Priest*, 226 Cal. Rptr. 584 (1986) (*Serrano III*); 557 P.2d 929 (Cal. 1976), *cert. denied*, 432 U.S. 907 (1977) (*Serrano II*); 487 P.2d 1241 (Cal. 1971) (*Serrano I*).

Colorado

> *Lujan* v. *Colorado State Board of Education*, 649 P.2d 1005 (Colo.1982).

Connecticut

> *Horton* v. *Meskill*, 486 A.2d 1099 (Conn. 1985) (*Horton III*); 445 A.2d 579 (Conn. 1982) (*Horton II*); 376 A.2d 359 (Conn. 1977) (*Horton I*).

Florida

> *Coalition for Adequacy and Fairness in School Funding, Inc.* v. *Chiles*, 680 So.2d 400 (Fla. 1996).

Georgia

> *McDaniel* v. *Thomas*, 285 S.E.2d 156 (Ga. 1981).

Idaho

> *Idaho Schools for Equal Educational Opportunity* v. *Evans*, 850 P.2d 724 (Idaho 1993).
> *Thompson* v. *Engelking*, 537 P.2d 635 (Idaho 1975).

Illinois

> *Committee for Educational Rights* v. *Edgar*, 672 N.E.2d 1178 (Ill. 1996)
> *Blase* v. *Illinois*, 302 N.E.2d 46 (Ill. 1973).

---

*These cases primarily address the constitutionality of the financing and adequacy of state school finance plans.

McInnis v. *Shapiro*, 293 F. Supp. 327 (1968), *aff'd sub nom. McInnis* v. *Ogilvie*, 394 U.S. 322 (1969).

Kansas

Unified School District No. 229 v. *State*, 885 P.2d 1170 (Kan. 1994), cert. denied, 515 U.S. 1144 (1995).

Kentucky

Rose v. *Council for Better Education*, 790 S.W.2d 186 (Ky.1989).

Louisiana

Livingston School Board v. *Louisiana State Board of Education*, 830 F.2d 563 (5th Cir. 1987).

Scarnato v. *Parker*, 415 F. Supp. 272 (1976), aff'd, 430 U.S. 961 (1977).

Maine

School Administrative District No. 1 v. *Commissioner, Department of Education*, 659 A.2d 854 (Me. 1995)

Maryland

Hornbeck v. *Somerset County Board of Education*, 458 A.2d 758 (Md. 1983).

Massachusetts

McDuffy v. *Secretary of the Executive Office of Education*, 615 N.E.2d 516 (Mass. 1993).

Michigan

East Jackson Public Schools v. *Michigan*, 348 N.W.2d 303 (Mich. App. 1984).

Milliken v. *Green*, 212 N.W.2d 711 (Mich. 1973) (*Governor II*); 203 N.W.2d 457 (Mich. 1972) (*Governor I*).

Minnesota

Skeen v. *State*, 505 N.W.2d 299 (Minn. 1993).

Van Dusartz v. *Hatfield*, 334 F. Supp. 870 (1971).

Montana

Helena Elementary School District No. 1 v. *Montana*, 769 P.2d 684 (Mont. 1989).

State ex rel. Woodahl v. *Straub*, 520 P.2d 776 (Mont. 1974).

Nebraska

Gould v. *Orr*, 506 N.W.2d 349 (Neb. 1993).

New Hampshire

Claremont School District v. *Governor*, 703 A.2d 1353 (N.H. 1997)

Claremont School District v. *Governor*, 635 A.2d 1375 (N.H. 1993).

New Jersey

Abbott v. *Burke*, 710 A.2d 450 (N.J. 1998) (*Abbott V*); *Abbott* v. *Burke*, 693 A2d 417 (N.J. 1997) (*Abbott IV*); *Abbott* v. *Burke*, 643 A.2d 575 (N.J. 1994) (*Abbott III*); *Abbott* v. *Burke*, 575 A. 2d 359 (N.J. 1990) (*Abbott II*); 495 A.2d 376 (N.J. 1985) (*Abbott I*).

Robinson v. *Cahill*, 360 A.2d 400 (N.J. 1976) (*Robinson VII*); *Robinson* v. *Cahill*, 358 A.2d 457 (N.J. 1976) (*Robinson VI*); *Robinson*

v. *Cahill*, 355 A.2d 129 (N.J. 1976) (*Robinson V*); 351 A.2d 713 (N.J. 1975) (*Robinson IV*); 335 A.2d 6 (*N.J. 1975*) (*Robinson III*); 306 A.2d 65 (N.J. 1973), *cert. denied sub nom. Dickey* v. *Robinson*, 414 U.S. 976 (1973) (*Robinson II*); 303 A.2d 273 (N.J. 1973) (*Robinson I*).

New York

Reform Educational Financing Inequities Today v. *Cuomo*, 655 N.E.2d 647 (N.Y. 1995).

Board of Education, Levittown Union Free School District v. *Nyquist*, 439 N.E.2d 359 (N.Y. 1982), *appeal dismissed*, 459 U.S. 1139 (1983).

North Carolina

Leandro v. *State*, 488 S.E.2d 249 (N.C. 1997).

Britt v. *North Carolina State Board of Education*, 357 S.E.2d 432 (N.C. App.), *appeal dismissed*, 361 S.E.2d 71 (N.C. 1987).

North Dakota

Bismarck Public School District No. 1 v. *State*, 511 N.W.2d 247 (N.D. 1994).

Ohio

DeRolph v. *State*, 728 N.E.2d 993 (Ohio 2000)(*DeRolph II*).

DeRolph v. *State*, 677 N.E.2d 733 (Ohio 1997)(*DeRolph I*).

Board of Education of City School District of Cincinnati v. *Walter*, 390 N.E.2d 813 (Ohio 1979), *cert. denied*, 444 U.S. 1015 (1980).

Oklahoma

Fair School Finance Council of Oklahoma v. *Oklahoma*, 746 P.2d 1135 (Okla. 1987).

Oregon

Withers v. *State*, 891 P.2d 675 (Or. App. 1995), *rev. denied*, 896 P.2d 1213 (Or. 1995).

Coalition for Equitable School Funding, Inc. v. *State*, 811 P.2d 116 (Or. 1991).

Olsen v. *Oregon*, 554 P.2d 139 (Or. 1976).

Pennsylvania

Bensalem School District v. *Pennsylvania*, 524 A.2d 1027 (Pa. Commw. 1987).

Danson v. *Casey*, 399 A.2d 360 (Pa. 1979).

Rhode Island

City of Pawtucket v. *Sundlun*, 662 A.2d 40 (R.I. 1995).

South Carolina

South Carolina Richland County v. *Campbell*, 364 S.E.2d 470 (S.C. 1988).

Tennessee

Tennessee Small School Systems v. *McWherter*, 894 S.W.2d 734 (Tenn. 1995).

Tennessee Small School Systems v. *McWherter*, 851 S.W.2d 139 (Tenn. 1993).

Texas

Edgewood Independent School District v. *Meno*, 917 S.W.2d 717 (Tex. 1995) (*Edgewood V*); *Edgewood Independent School District* v. *Meno*, 893 S.W.2d 450 (1995) (*Edgewood IV*); *Carrollton-Farmers Branch Independent School District* v. *Edgewood Independent School District*, 826 S.W.2d 489 (Tex. 1992) (*Edgewood III*); *Edgewood Independent School District* v. *Kirby*, 804 S.W.2d 491 (Tex. 1991) (*Edgewood II*); 777 S.W.2d 391 (Tex. 1989) (*Edgewood I*).

San Antonio Independent School District v. Rodriguez, 411 U.S. 1 (1973).

Vermont

Brigham v. *State*, 692 A.2d 384 (Vt. 1997).

Virginia

Scott v. *Commonwealth*, 443 S.E.2d 138 (Va. 1994).

Burruss v. *Wilkerson*, 310 F. Supp. 572 (1969), aff'd, 397 U.S. 44 (1970).

Washington

Seattle School District No. 1 of King County v. *Washington*, 585 P.2d 71 (Wash. 1978).

Northshore School District No. 417 v. *Kinnear*, 530 P.2d 178 (Wash. 1974).

West Virginia

State v. *Chafin*, 376 S.E.2d 113 (W.Va. 1988).

Pauley v. *Bailey*, 324 S.E.2d 128 (W.Va. 1984).

Pauley v. *Kelly*, 255 S.E.2d 859 (W.Va 1979).

Wisconsin

Vincent v. *Voight*, 614 N.W.2d 388 (Wis. 2000).

Kukor v. *Grover*, 436 N.W.2d 568 (Wis. 1989).

Buse v. *Smith*, 247 N.W.2d 141 (Wis. 1976).

Wyoming

Campbell County School District v. *State*, 907 P.2d 1238 (Wyo. 1995).

Washakie County School District No. 1 v. *Herschler*, 606 P.2d 310 (Wyo. 1980), *reh'g denied*, 606 P.2d 340 (1980), *cert. denied sub. nom. Hot Springs County School District No. 1* v. *Washakie County School District No. 1*, 449 U.S. 824 (1980).

CHAPTER EIGHT

Educator and School District Liability

Educators are often concerned about the extent, if any, of their liability for damages as a result of their official action or inaction. The many types of concerns educators have in this area include possible liability on the part of the school district, individual board members, administrative personnel, and teachers for the injury or death of a child at school or while under school supervision; liability, if any, of a teacher or administrator for injuring a child while administering corporal punishment; school district, administrator, or teacher liability, if any, for depriving someone of his or her constitutional rights; and liability for malpractice.

The area of law that addresses these concerns is known as tort law. A tort is a civil wrong in which one suffers loss as a result of the improper conduct of another. This branch of law is concerned with the compensation of losses suffered by an individual owing to an intentional or negligent act. Some torts may also be criminal, and if so, the person or persons charged may be prosecuted and punished by the state. Tort law is a specialized branch of law that laymen often perceive as being exceedingly complicated. Generalizing about tort law is difficult, if not bordering on the impossible, due to individual state's applicable case law and constitutional and statutory provisions. Therefore, it is imperative when examining a state's case law that it be done within the context of a state's constitutional and statutory provisions. Due to these restraints, the purpose of this chapter is primarily to provide students with a brief discussion of broad principles and major issues of general concern.

I. SCHOOL DISTRICT IMMUNITY

A. Liability under State Law

In approximately half of the states, school districts have governmental or sovereign immunity from liability for torts committed by the school district, school board members, or employees. Governmental immunity is grounded in the theory that the state and its agencies are sovereign and cannot be sued without consent. Such a view has its basis in the historic notion that "the king can do no wrong." Additionally, the doctrine seeks to protect the limited resources of government agencies. School districts in particular often have limited funds for other-than-educational purposes and frequently, therefore, are unable to pay high judgments rendered against them. Employment of the defense of sovereign immunity indicates that unless state courts or the legislature have modified or abrogated the doctrine, school districts cannot be sued for tort actions in a court of law. Many legal scholars, however, have been critical of the doctrine of sovereign immunity because it often leaves an injured party without any means to be compensated for losses. Consequently, governmental immunity has been substantially abrogated or modified in approximately thirty states, resulting in considerable variation regarding liability in those states.

Application of the doctrine of immunity differs from state to state: in most states in which sovereign immunity has been preserved, statutory law has been modified to allow limited liability, particularly for school-bus accidents. Although the majority of these states allow school districts to purchase liability insurance without waiving their immunity, some states have asserted that the purchase of insurance will constitute a waiver of immunity within the limits of insurance protection.

Individual liability also varies among the states. Generally, school board members or other officials may be held personally liable for the improper performance of so-called ministerial duties; they may not be liable, however, for the performance of discretionary responsibilities. Ministerial functions are defined as those having to do with the execution of policy as opposed to the formulation of policy represented by discretionary actions. If a school official is required to decide or act without established or readily ascertainable standards for guidance, that act is a discretionary function. Protection of discretionary activity follows from a desire to encourage governmental decision making; ministerial decisions, involving a lesser degree of discretion and judgment, require less protection or immunity. In school-related decisions, courts have recognized a vital public interest in securing the free and independent judgment of school officials.

Historically, the immunity of school districts did not protect individual school employees from liability in tort. Many states, however, have reconsidered this notion, arguing that the individual school employees are least able to defend themselves in court. In Georgia, for instance, immunity has been extended to school principals and to classroom teachers. See *Hennessy* v. *Webb*, 264 S.E.2d 878 (1980), and *Truelove* v. *Wilson*, 285 S.E.2d 556 (Ga. 1981).

B. Liability under Federal Law

1. Liability under 42 U.S.C. § 1983

A section of the Civil Rights Act of 1871 provides for liability if a "person" operating under the color of the state violates another person's civil rights. Specifically, the law states:

> Every person who, under the color of any statute, ordinance, regulation, custom, or usage, of any State or Territory or the District of Columbia, subjects, or causes to be subjected, any citizen of the United States or other person within the jurisdiction thereof to the deprivation of any rights, privileges, or immunities secured by the Constitution and laws, shall be liable to the party injured in an action at law, suit in equity, or other proper proceeding for redress . . . 42 U.S.C. § 1983.

Although this law had not received much judicial attention for nearly one hundred years, several recent Supreme Court decisions have addressed school district and school officials' liability and the extent, if any, of damages under it. *Wood* v. *Strickland* addresses the issue of school board member immunity from liability under § 1983, whereas *Carey* v. *Piphus* clarifies the elements and prerequisites for recovery of damages under this act.

WOOD v. STRICKLAND

Supreme Court of the United States, 1975
420 U.S. 308

MR. JUSTICE WHITE delivered the opinion of the Court.

Respondents Peggy Strickland and Virginia Crain brought this lawsuit against petitioners, who were members of the school board at the time in question, two school administrators, and the Special School District of Mena, Ark., purporting to assert a cause of action under 42 U.S.C. § 1983, and claiming that their federal constitutional rights to due process were infringed under color of state law by their expulsion from the Mena Public High School on the grounds of their violation of a school regulation prohibiting the use or possession of intoxicating beverages at school or school activities. The complaint as amended prayed for compensatory and punitive damages against all petitioners, injunctive relief allowing respondents to resume attendance, preventing petitioners from imposing any sanctions as a result of the expulsion, and restraining enforcement of the challenged regulation, declaratory relief as to the constitutional invalidity of the regulation, and expunction of any record of their expulsion. * * *

The violation of the school regulation prohibiting the use or possession of intoxicating beverages at school or school activities with which respondents were charged concerned their "spiking" of the punch served at a meeting of an extracurricular school organization attended by parents and students. At the time in question, respondents were 16 years old and were in the 10th grade. The relevant facts begin with their discovery that the punch had not been prepared for the meeting as previously planned. The girls then agreed to "spike" it. Since the county in which the school is located is "dry," respondents and a third girl drove across the state border into Oklahoma and purchased two 12-ounce bottles of "Right Time," a malt liquor. They then bought six 10-ounce bottles of a soft drink, and after having mixed the contents of the eight bottles in an empty milk carton, returned to school. Prior to the meeting, the girls experienced second thoughts about the wisdom of their prank, but by then they were caught up in the force of events and the intervention of other girls prevented them from disposing of the illicit punch. The punch was served at the meeting, without apparent effect.

Ten days later, the teacher in charge of the extracurricular group and meeting, Mrs. Curtis Powell, having heard something about the "spiking," questioned the girls about it. Although first denying any knowledge, the girls admitted their involvement after the teacher said that she would handle the punishment herself. The next day, however, she told the girls that the incident was becoming increasingly the subject of talk in the school and that the principal, P. T. Waller, would probably hear about it. She told them that her job was in jeopardy but that she would not force them to admit to Waller what they had done. If they did not go to him then, however, she would not be able to help them if the incident became "distorted." The three girls then went to Waller and admitted their role in the affair. He suspended them from school for a maximum two-week period, subject to the decision of the school board. Waller also told them that the board would meet that night, that the girls could tell their parents about the meeting, but that the parents should not contact any members of the board.

Neither the girls nor their parents attended the school board meeting that night. Both Mrs. Powell and Waller, after making their reports concerning the incident, recommended leniency. At this point, a telephone call was received by S. L. Inlow, then the superintendent of schools, from Mrs. Powell's husband, also a teacher at the high school, who reported that he had heard that the third girl involved had been in a fight that evening at a basketball game. Inlow informed the meeting of the news, although he did not mention the name of the girl involved. Mrs. Powell and Waller then withdrew their recommendations of leniency, and the board voted to expel the girls from school for the remainder of the semester, a period of approximately three months.

The board subsequently agreed to hold another meeting on the matter, and one was held approximately two weeks after the first meeting. The girls, their parents, and their counsel attended this session. The board began with a reading of a written statement of facts as it had found them. The girls admitted mixing the malt liquor into the punch with the intent of "spiking" it, but asked the board to forgo its rule punishing such violations by such substantial suspensions. Neither Mrs. Powell nor Waller was present at this meeting. The board voted not to change its policy and, as before, to expel the girls for the remainder of the semester.

* * *

Petitioners as members of the school board assert here, as they did below, an absolute immunity from liability under § 1983 and at the very least seek to reinstate the judgment of the District Court. If they are correct and the District Court's dismissal should be sustained, we need go no further in this case. Moreover, the immunity question involves the construction of a federal statute, and our practice is to deal with possibly dispositive statutory issues before reaching questions turning on the construction of the Constitution. * * * We essentially sustain the position of the Court of Appeals with respect to the immunity issue.

The nature of the immunity from awards of damages under § 1983 available to school administrators and school board members is not a question which the lower federal courts have answered with a single voice. There is general agreement on the existence of a "good faith" immunity, but the courts have either emphasized different factors as elements of good faith or have not given specific content to the good faith standard.

* * *

Common law tradition, recognized in our prior decisions, and strong public policy reasons also lead to a construction of § 1983 extending a qualified good faith immunity to school board members from liability for damages under that section. Although there have been different emphases and formulations of the common law immunity of public school officials in cases of student expulsion or suspension, state courts have generally recognized that such officers should be protected from tort liability under state law for all good faith, nonmalicious action taken to fulfill their official duties.

* * *

Liability for damages for every action which is found subsequently to have been violative of a student's constitutional rights and to have caused compensable injury would unfairly impose upon the school decision maker the burden of mistakes made in good faith in the course of exercising his discretion within the scope of his official duties. School board members, among other duties, must judge whether there have been violations of school regulations and, if so, the appropriate sanctions for the violations. Denying any measure of immunity in these circumstances "would contribute not to principled and fearless decisionmaking but to intimidation." * * * The imposition of monetary costs for mistakes which were not unreasonable in the light of all the circumstances would undoubtedly deter even the most conscientious school decisionmaker from exercising his judgment independently, forcefully, and in a manner best serving the long-term interest of the school and the students. The most capable candidates for school board positions might be deterred from seeking office if heavy burdens upon their private resources from monetary liability were a likely prospect during their tenure.

These considerations have undoubtedly played a prime role in the development by state courts of a qualified immunity protecting school officials from liability for damages in lawsuits claiming improper suspensions or expulsions. But at the same time, the judgment implicit in this common law development is that absolute immunity would not be justified since it would not sufficiently increase the ability of school officials to exercise their discretion in a forthright manner to warrant the absence of a remedy for students subjected to intentional or otherwise inexcusable deprivations.

* * *

The disagreement between the Court of Appeals and the District Court over the immunity standard in this case has been put in terms of an "objective" versus a "subjective" test of good faith. As we see it, the appropriate standard necessarily contains elements of both. The official himself must be acting sincerely and with a belief that he is doing right, but an act violating a student's constitutional rights can be no more justified by ignorance or disregard of settled, indisputable law on the part of one entrusted with supervision of students' daily lives than by the presence of actual malice. To be entitled to a special exemption from the categorical remedial language of § 1983 in a case in which his action violated a student's constitutional rights, a school board member, who has voluntarily undertaken the task of supervising the operation of the school and the activities of the students, must be held to a standard of conduct based not only on permissible intentions, but also on knowledge of the basic, unquestioned constitutional rights of his charges. Such a standard imposes neither an unfair burden upon a person assuming a responsible public office requiring a high degree of intelligence and judgment for the proper fulfillment of its duties, nor an unwarranted burden in light of the value which civil rights have in our legal system. Any lesser standard would deny much of the promise of § 1983. Therefore, in the specific context of school discipline, we hold that a school board member is not immune from liability for damages under § 1983 if he knew or reasonably should have known that the action he took within his sphere of official responsibility would violate the constitutional rights of the student affected, or if he took the action with the malicious intention to cause a deprivation of constitutional rights or other injury to the student. * * * A compensatory award will be appropriate only if the school board member has acted with such an impermissible motivation or with such disregard of the student's clearly established constitutional rights that his action cannot reasonably be characterized as being in good faith.

* * *

Given the fact that there *was* evidence supporting the charge against respondents, the contrary judgment of the Court of Appeals is improvident. It is not the role of the federal courts to set aside decisions of school administrators which the court may view as lacking a basis in wisdom or compassion. Public high school students do have substantive and procedural rights while at school. * * * But § 1983 does not extend the right to relitigate in federal court evidentiary questions arising in school disciplinary proceedings or the proper construction of school regulations. The system of public education that has evolved in this Nation relies necessarily upon the discretion and judgment of school administrators and school board members, and § 1983 was not intended to be a vehicle for federal court corrections of errors in the exercise of that discretion which do not rise to the level of violations of specific constitutional guarantees. * * *

* * *

The judgment of the Court of Appeals is vacated and the case remanded for further proceedings consistent with this opinion.

So ordered.

MR. JUSTICE POWELL, with whom THE CHIEF JUSTICE, MR. JUSTICE BLACKMUN, and MR. JUSTICE REHNQUIST join, concurring in part and dissenting in part.

I join in Parts I, III, and IV of the Court's opinion, and agree that the judgment of the Court of Appeals should be vacated and the case remanded. I dissent from Part II which appears to impose a higher standard of care upon public school officials, sued under § 1983, than that heretofore required of any other official.

* * * It would impose personal liability on a school official who acted sincerely and in the utmost good faith, but who was found—after the fact— to have acted in "ignorance . . . of settled, indisputable law." * * * Or, as the Court also puts it, the school official must be held to a standard of conduct based not only on good faith "but also on knowledge of the basic, unquestioned constitutional rights of his charges." * * * Moreover, ignorance of the law is explicitly equated with "actual malice." * * * This harsh standard, requiring knowledge of what is characterized as "settled, indisputable law," leaves little substance to the doctrine of qualified immunity. The Court's decision appears to rest on an unwarranted assumption as to what lay school officials know or can know about the law and constitutional rights. These officials will now act at the peril of some judge or jury subsequently finding that a good faith belief as to the applicable law was mistaken and hence actionable.

The Court states the standard of required knowledge in two cryptic phrases: "settled, indisputable law" and "unquestioned constitutional rights." Presumably these are intended to mean the same thing, although the meaning of neither phrase is likely to be self-evident to constitutional law scholars—much less the average school board member. One need only look to the decisions of this Court—to our reversals, our recognition of evolving concepts, and our five-to-four splits—to recognize the hazard of even informed prophecy as to what are "unquestioned constitutional rights." * * *

* * *

There are some 20,000 school boards, each with five or more members, and thousands of school superintendents and school principals. Most of the school board members are popularly elected, drawn from the citizenry at large, and possess no unique competency in divining the law. Few cities and counties provide any compensation for service on school boards, and often it is difficult to persuade qualified persons to assume the burdens of this important function in our society. Moreover, even if counsel's advice constitutes a defense, it may safely be assumed that few school boards and school officials have ready access to counsel or indeed have deemed it necessary to consult counsel on the countless decisions that necessarily must be made in the operation of our public schools.

In view of today's decision significantly enhancing the possibility of personal liability, one must wonder whether qualified persons will continue in the desired numbers to volunteer for service in public education.

Notes and Questions

Although **Wood** specifically addresses school board member liability, the decision has implications for other school employees. Would the reasoning of the Court also apply to such school officials as superintendents and building-level administrators?

The majority opinion in **Wood** declared that ignorance of constitutional law pertaining to school discipline is no excuse. Do you agree, as the dissenters suggest, that the **Wood** standard is a "harsh" one that will place a board member's actions "at the peril of some judge or jury subsequently finding that a good-faith belief as to the applicable law was mistaken . . ."?

Wood was cited in *Stewart v. Baldwin County Board of Education*, 908 F.2d 1499 (11th Cir. 1990), in which the court held that a school board did not have qualified immunity or quasi-judicial absolute immunity. This controversy arose from the alleged improper termination of a maintenance worker who left a called district school meeting to reveal his displeasure over a forthcoming tax referendum. The court held that leaving such a meeting, after work hours, was clearly a First Amendment right.

Subsequent Supreme Court decisions not dealing specifically with education issues have continued to address the issue of governmental immunity under § 1983. *Monell v. Department of Social Services of City of New York*, 436 U.S. 658 (1978), ruled that school districts are considered "persons" subject to suit under § 1983. Additionally, the Court held that:

. . . a local government may not be sued under § 1983 for an injury inflicted solely by its employees or agents. Instead, it is when execution of a government's policy or custom, whether made by its lawmakers or by those whose edicts or acts may fairly be said to represent official policy, inflicts the injury that the government as an entity is responsible under § 1983 (p. 694)

Monell reversed an earlier Court decision, *Monroe* v. *Pape*, 365 U.S. 167 (1961), which had held governmental bodies absolutely immune from liability under § 1983. Another decision, *Owen* v. *City of Independence*, 445 U.S. 622 (1980), which addressed the discharge of a police chief, held that:

. . . there is no tradition of immunity for municipal corporations, and neither history nor policy support a construction of § 1983 that would justify the qualified immunity. . . . [T]he municipality may not assert the good faith of its officers or agents as a defense to liability under § 1983. (p. 638)

In *Harlow* v. *Fitzgerald*, 457 U.S. 800 (1982), the Court expanded government officials' immunity by abolishing the so-called subjective test. Under the Court's ruling, government officials performing discretionary functions generally are shielded from liability for civil damages insofar as their conduct does not violate "clearly established" statutory or constitutional rights that a reasonable person would have known. Further expanding the doctrine of immunity in favor of government officials is the decision in *Anderson* v. *Creighton*, 483 U. S. 635 (1987).

Potential areas of liability were expanded by the Court when it ruled that violations of federal statutory law as well as violations of constitutional provisions could be addressed under § 1983. See *Maine* v. *Thiboutot*, 448 U.S. 1 (1980). Additionally, the Court has ruled that state administrative remedies do not have to be exhausted before § 1983 claims are addressed in federal courts. See *Patsy* v. *Board of Regents of Florida*, 457 U.S. 496 (1982).

CAREY v. PIPHUS
Supreme Court of the United States, 1978
435 U.S. 247

MR. JUSTICE POWELL delivered the opinion of the Court.

In this case, brought under 42 U.S.C. § 1983, we consider the elements and prerequisites for recovery of damages by students who were suspended from public elementary and secondary schools without procedural due process. The Court of Appeals for the Seventh Circuit held that the students are entitled to recover substantial nonpunitive damages even if their suspensions were justified, and even if they do not prove that any other actual injury was caused by the denial of procedural due process. We disagree, and hold that in the absence of proof of actual injury, the students are entitled to recover only nominal damages.

Respondent Jarius Piphus was a freshman at Chicago Vocational High School during the 1973–74 school year. On January 23, 1974, during school hours, the school principal saw Piphus and another student standing outdoors on school property passing back and forth what the principal described as an irregularly shaped cigarette. The principal approached the students unnoticed and smelled what he believed was the strong odor of burning marihuana. He also saw Piphus try to pass a packet of cigarette papers to the other student. When the students became aware of the principal's presence, they threw the cigarette into a nearby hedge.

The principal took the students to the school's disciplinary office and directed the assistant principal to impose the "usual" 20-day suspension for violation of the school rule against the use of drugs. The students protested that they had not been smoking marihuana, but to no avail. Piphus was allowed to remain at school, although not in class, for the remainder of the school day while the assistant principal tried, without success, to reach his mother.

A suspension notice was sent to Piphus' mother, and a few days later two meetings were arranged among Piphus, his mother, his sister, school officials, and representatives from a legal aid clinic. The purpose of the meetings was not to determine whether Piphus had been smoking marihuana, but rather to explain the reasons for the suspension. Following an unfruitful exchange of views, Piphus and his mother, as guardian *ad litem*, filed suit against petitioners in Federal District Court under 42 U.S.C. § 1983 * * * , charging that Piphus had been suspended without due process of law in violation of the Fourteenth Amendment. The complaint sought declaratory and injunctive relief, together with actual and punitive damages in the amount of $3,000. Piphus was readmitted to school under a temporary restraining order after eight days of his suspension.

Respondent Silas Brisco was in the sixth grade at Clara Barton Elementary School in Chicago during the 1973–74 school year. On September 11, 1973, Brisco came to school wearing one small earring. The previous school year the school principal had issued a rule against the wearing of earrings by male students because he believed that this practice denoted membership in certain street gangs and increased the likelihood that gang members would terrorize other students. Brisco was reminded of this rule, but he refused to remove the earring asserting that it was a symbol of black pride, not of gang membership.

The assistant principal talked to Brisco's mother, advising her that her son would be suspended for 20 days if he did not remove the earring. Brisco's mother supported her son's position, and a 20-day suspension was imposed. Brisco and his mother, as guardian *ad litem*, filed suit in Federal District Court under 42 U.S.C. § 1983 * * * , charging that Brisco had been suspended without due process of law in violation of the Fourteenth

Amendment. The complaint sought declaratory and injunctive relief, together with actual and punitive damages in the amount of $5,000. Brisco was readmitted to school during the pendency of proceedings for a preliminary injunction after 17 days of his suspension.

* * *

Title 42 U.S.C. § 1983, Rev. Stat. § 1979, derived from § 1 of the Civil Rights Act of 1871, 17 Stat. 13, provides:

> "Every person who, under color of any statute, ordinance, regulation, custom, or usage, of any State or Territory, subjects, or causes to be subjected, any citizen of the United States or other person within the jurisdiction thereof to the deprivation of any rights, privileges, or immunities secured by the Constitution and laws, shall be liable to the party injured in an action at law, suit in equity, or other proper proceeding for redress."

The legislative history of § 1983 * * * demonstrates that it was intended to "[create] a species of tort liability" in favor of persons who are deprived of "rights, privileges, or immunities secured" to them by the Constitution. * * *

* * *

Insofar as petitioners contend that the basic purpose of a § 1983 damages award should be to compensate persons for injuries caused by the deprivation of constitutional rights, they have the better of the argument. Rights, constitutional and otherwise, do not exist in a vacuum. Their purpose is to protect persons from injuries to particular interests, and their contours are shaped by the interests they protect.

Our legal system's concept of damages reflects this view of legal rights. "The cardinal principle of damages in Anglo-American law is that of *compensation* for the injury caused to plaintiff by defendant's breach of duty." * * * The Court implicitly has recognized the applicability of this principle to actions under § 1983 by stating that damages are available under that section for actions "found . . . to have been violative of . . . constitutional rights *and to have caused compensable injury* . . ." *Wood v. Strickland* * * *

The Members of the Congress that enacted § 1983 did not address directly the question of damages, but the principle that damages are designed to compensate persons for injuries caused by the deprivation of rights hardly could have been foreign to the many lawyers in Congress in 1871. Two other sections of the Civil Rights Act of 1871 appear to incorporate this principle, and no reason suggests itself for reading § 1983 differently. To the extent that Congress intended that awards under § 1983 should deter the deprivation of constitutional rights, there is no evidence that it meant to establish a deterrent more formidable than that inherent in the award of compensatory damages. * * *

It is less difficult to conclude that damages awards under § 1983 should be governed by the principle of compensation than it is to apply this principle to concrete cases. But over the centuries the common law of torts has developed a set of rules to implement the principle that a person should be compensated fairly for injuries caused by the violation of his legal rights. These rules, defining the elements of damages and the prerequisites for their recovery, provide the appropriate starting point for the inquiry under § 1983 as well.

It is not clear, however, that common law tort rules of damages will provide a complete solution to the damages issue in every § 1983 case. In some cases, the interests protected by a particular branch of the common law of torts may parallel closely the interests protected by a particular constitutional right. In such cases, it may be appropriate to apply the tort rules of damages directly to the § 1983 action. * * * In other cases, the interests protected by a particular constitutional right may not also be protected by an analogous branch of the common law of torts. * * * In those cases, the task will be the more difficult one of adapting common law rules of damages to provide fair compensation for injuries caused by the deprivation of a constitutional right.

Although this task of adaptation will be one of some delicacy—as this case demonstrates—it must be undertaken. The purpose of § 1983 would be defeated if injuries caused by the deprivation of constitutional rights went uncompensated simply because the common law does not recognize an analogous cause of action. * * * In order to further the purpose of § 1983, the rules governing compensation for injuries caused by the deprivation of constitutional rights should be tailored to the interests protected by the particular right in question—just as the common law rules of damages themselves were defined by the interests protected in the various branches of tort law. * * *

* * *

Even if respondents' suspensions were justified, and even if they did not suffer any other actual injury, the fact remains that they were deprived of their right to procedural due process. "It is enough to invoke the procedural safeguards of the Fourteenth Amendment that a significant property interest is at stake, whatever the ultimate outcome of a hearing. . . ." * * *

Common-law courts traditionally have vindicated deprivations of certain "absolute" rights that are not shown to have caused actual injury through the award of a nominal sum of money. By making the deprivation of such rights actionable for nominal damages without proof of actual injury, the law recognizes the importance to organized society that those rights be scrupulously observed; but at the same time, it remains true to the principle that substantial damages should be awarded only to compensate actual injury or, in the case of exemplary or punitive damages, to deter or punish malicious deprivations of rights.

Because the right to procedural due process is "absolute" in the sense that it does not depend upon the merits of a claimant's substantive assertions, and because of the importance to organized society that procedural due process be observed, * * * we believe that the denial of procedural due process should be actionable for nominal damages without proof of actual injury. We therefore hold that if, upon remand, the District Court determines that respondents' suspensions were justified, respondents nevertheless will be entitled to recover nominal damages not to exceed one dollar from petitioners.

The judgment of the Court of Appeals is reversed, and the case is remanded for further proceedings consistent with this opinion.

It is so ordered.

2. Damages under Title IX

A unanimous ruling by the Supreme Court in *Franklin* v. *Gwinnett County Schools*, 503 U.S. 60 (1992), upheld a claim for monetary damages under Title IX when intentional sexual harassment was shown. In this case, a teacher had repeatedly sexually abused a student, and although administrators knew about the harassment, they took no action to stop it. The decision established that a school district can be held liable in damages under Title IX in cases involving a teacher's sexual harassment of a student. Since *Franklin*, two Supreme Court decisions, *Gebser* v. *Lago Vista Independent School District*, 524 U.S. 274 (1998) and *Davis* v. *Monroe County Board of Education*, 526 U.S. 629 (1999) have more fully addressed school district liability when teacher-to-student and student-to-student harassment occurs.

a. Teacher-to-Student Harassment

In *Gebser*, a five-to-four decision, the Court ruled that if a teacher harasses a student, the school is not liable for damages unless an official who could address the alleged discrimination and institute corrective measures knew and then acted with "deliberate indifference" to the harassment.

GEBSER V. LAGO VISTA INDEPENDENT SCHOOL DISTRICT
Supreme Court of the United States, 1998
524 U.S. 274

JUSTICE O'CONNOR delivered the opinion of the Court.

The question in this case is when a school district may be held liable in damages in an implied right of action under Title XI of the Education Amendments of 1972, * * * for the sexual harassment of a student by one of the district's teachers. We conclude that damages may not be recovered in those circumstances unless an official of the school district who at a minimum has authority to institute corrective measures on the district's behalf has actual notice of, and is deliberately indifferent to, the teacher's misconduct.

In the spring of 1991, when petitioner Alida Star Gebser was an eighth-grade student at a middle school in respondent Lago Vista Independent

School District (Lago Vista), she joined a high school book discussion group led by Frank Waldrop, a teacher at Lago Vista's high school. Lago Vista received federal funds at all pertinent times. During the book discussion sessions, Waldrop often made sexually suggestive comments to the students. Gebser entered high school in the fall and was assigned to classes taught by Waldrop in both semesters. Waldrop continued to make inappropriate remarks to the students, and he began to direct more of his suggestive comments toward Gebser, including during the substantial amount of time that the two were alone in his classroom. He initiated sexual contact with Gebser in the spring, when, while visiting her home ostensibly to give her a book, he kissed and fondled her. The two had sexual intercourse on a number of occasions during the remainder of the school year. Their relationship continued through the summer and into the following school year, and they often had intercourse during class time, although never on school property.

Gebser did not report the relationship to school officials, testifying that while she realized Waldrop's conduct was improper, she was uncertain how to react and she wanted to continue having him as a teacher. In October 1992, the parents of two other students complained to the high school principal about Waldrop's comments in class. The principal arranged a meeting, at which, according to the principal, Waldrop indicated that he did not believe he had made offensive remarks but apologized to the parents and said it would not happen again. The principal also advised Waldrop to be careful about his classroom comments and told the school guidance counselor about the meeting, but he did not report the parents' complaint to Largo Vista's superintendent, who was the district's Title IX coordinator. A couple of months later, in January 1993, a police officer discovered Waldrop and Gebser engaging in sexual intercourse and arrested Waldrop. Largo Vista terminated his employment, and subsequently, the Texas Education Agency revoked his teaching license. During this time, the district had not promulgated or distributed an official grievance procedure for lodging sexual harassment complaints; nor had it issued a formal anti-harassment policy.

* * *

In *Franklin* [v. *Gwinnett County Public Schools,* 503 U.S. 60 (1992)] a high school student alleged that a teacher had sexually abused her on repeated occasions and that the teachers and school administrators knew about the harassment but took no action, even to the point of dissuading her from initiating charges. * * * The lower courts dismissed Franklin's complaint against the school district on the ground that the implied right of action under Title IX, as a categorical matter, does not encompass recovery in damages. We reversed the lower courts' blanket rule, concluding that Title IX supports a private action for damages, at least "in a case such as this, in which intentional discrimination is alleged." * * * *Franklin* thereby establishes that a school district can be held liable in damages in cases involving a teacher's sexual harassment of a student; the decision, however, does not purport to define the contours of that liability.

* * *

In this case, moreover, petitioners seek not just to establish a Title IX violation but to recover *damages* based on theories of *respondeat superior* and constructive notice. It is that aspect of their action, in our view, which is most critical to resolving the case. Unlike Title IX, Title VII contains an express cause of action, and specifically provides for relief in the form of monetary damages. Congress therefore has directly addressed the subject of damages relief under Title VII and has set out the particular situations in which damages are available as well as the maximum amounts recoverable. With respect to Title IX, however, the private right of action is judicially implied, * * * and there is thus no legislative expression of the scope of available remedies, including when it is appropriate to award monetary damages. In addition, although the general presumption that courts can award any appropriate relief in an established cause of action, coupled with Congress' abrogation of the States' Eleventh Amendment immunity under Title IX, led us to conclude in *Franklin* that Title IX recognizes a damages remedy, * * * we did so in response to lower court decisions holding that Title IX does not support damages relief at all. We made no effort in *Franklin* to delimit the circumstances in which a damages remedy should lie.

* * *

Congress enacted Title IX in 1972 with two principal objectives in mind: "to avoid the use of federal resources to support discriminatory practices" and "to provide individual citizens effective protection against those practices." * * * That statute was modeled after Title VI of the Civil Rights Act of 1964, * * * which is parallel to Title IX except that it prohibits race discrimination, not sex discrimination, and applies in all programs receiving federal funds, not only in education programs. * * * The two statues operate in the same manner, conditioning an offer of federal funding on a promise by the recipient not to discriminate, in what amounts essentially to a contract between the Government and the recipient of funds.

* * *

Title IX's contractual nature has implications for our construction of the scope of available remedies. When Congress attaches conditions to the award of federal funds under its spending power, * * * as it has in Title IX and Title VI, we examine closely the propriety of private actions holding the recipient liable in monetary damages for noncompliance with the condition. * * * Our central concern in that regard is with ensuring "that the receiving entity of federal funds [has] notice that it will be liable for a monetary award." * * * We confront similar concerns here. If a school district's liability for a teacher's sexual harassment rests on principles of constructive notice or *respondeat superior*, it will likewise be the case that the recipient of funds was unaware of the discrimination. It is sensible to assume that Congress did not envision a recipient's liability in damages in that situation. * * *

* * *

Presumably, a central purpose of requiring notice of the violation "to the appropriate person" and an opportunity for voluntary compliance before the administrative enforcement proceedings can commence is to avoid diverting education funding from beneficial uses where the recipient was unaware of discrimination in its programs and is willing to institute prompt corrective measures. The scope of private damages relief proposed by petitioners is at odds with that basic objective. When a teacher's sexual harassment is imputed to a school district or when a school district is deemed to have "constructively" known of the teacher's harassment, by assumption the district had no actual knowledge of the teacher's conduct. Nor, of course, did the district have an opportunity to take action to end the harassment or to limit further harassment.

* * * Where a statute's express enforcement scheme hinges its most severe sanction on notice and unsuccessful efforts to obtain compliance, we cannot attribute to Congress the intention to have implied an enforcement scheme that allows imposition of greater liability without comparable conditions.

Because the express remedial scheme under Title IX is predicated upon notice to an "appropriate person" and an opportunity to rectify any violation, we conclude, in the absence of further direction from Congress, that the implied damages remedy should be fashioned along the same lines. An "appropriate person" is, at a minimum, an official of the recipient entity with authority to take corrective action to end the discrimination. Consequently, in cases like this one that do not involve official policy of the recipient entity, we hold that a damages remedy will not lie under Title IX unless an official who at a minimum has authority to address the alleged discrimination and to institute corrective measures on the recipient's behalf has actual knowledge of discrimination in the recipient's programs and fails adequately to respond.

We think, moreover, that the response must amount to deliberate indifference to discrimination. The administration enforcement scheme presupposes that an official who is advised of a Title IX violation refuses to take action to bring the recipient into compliance. The premise, in other words, is an official decision by the recipient not to remedy the violation. That framework finds a rough parallel in the standard of deliberate indifference. Under a lower standard, there would be a risk that the recipient would be liable in damages not for its own official decision but instead for its employee's independent actions.

Applying the framework to this case is fairly straightforward, as petitioners do not contend they can prevail under an actual notice standard. The only official alleged to have had information about Waldrop's misconduct is the high school principal. That information, however, consisted of a complaint from parents of other students charging only that Waldrop had made inappropriate comments during class, which was plainly insufficient to alert the principal to the possibility that Waldrop was involved in a sexual relationship with a student. Lago Vista, moreover, terminated Waldrop's employment upon learning of his relationship with Gebser. * * *

Petitioners focus primarily on Lago Vista's asserted failure to promulgate and publicize an effective policy and grievance procedure for sexual harassment claims. They point to Department of Education regulations requiring each funding recipient to "adopt and publish grievance procedures providing for prompt and equitable resolution" of discrimination complaints, and to notify students and others, "that it does not discriminate on the basis of sex in the education programs or activities which it operates." Lago Vista's alleged failure to comply with the regulations, however, does not establish the requisite actual notice and deliberate indifference. And in any event, the failure to promulgate a grievance procedure does not itself constitute "discrimination" under Title IX. * * *

The number of reported cases involving sexual harassment of students in schools confirms that harassment unfortunately is an all too common aspect of the education experience. No one questions that a student suffers extraordinary harm when subjected to sexual harassment and abuse by a teacher, and that the teacher's conduct is reprehensible and undermines the basic purposes of the education system. The issue in this case, however, is whether the independent misconduct of a teacher is attributable to the district that employs him under a specific federal statute designed primarily to prevent recipients of federal financial assistance from using the funds in a discriminatory manner. Our decision does not affect any right of recovery that an individual may have against the school district as a matter of state law or against the teacher in his individual capacity under state law or under 42 U. S. C. §1983. Until Congress speaks directly on the subject, however, we will not hold a school district liable in damages under Title IX for a teacher's sexual harassment of a student absent actual notice and deliberate indifference. We therefore affirm the judgment of the Court of Appeals.

It is so ordered.

Notes

Based on this decision, one may wonder why a teacher seemingly has more protection against harassment by her principal than a student has against harassment from a teacher. The reason for this apparent contradiction is that employment discrimination is dealt with under Title VII, which has a different standard from Title IX, which bars sex discrimination in education.

A former student sued her Catholic high school for alleged sexual harassment by a priest who was her teacher. Her claim was denied in *Buckley v. Archdiocese of Rockville Center*, 922 F. Supp. 586 (N.Y. 1998). The court stated that Title IX established that no person shall be subject to sexual discrimination under any educational program or activity receiving federal financial assistance. In this instance, the Catholic school received school services from a publicly employed psychologist; however, the court ruled that was insufficient to establish that the school received public funds.

b. Student-to-Student Harassment

Davis v. Monroe County Board of Education, another five-to-four decision, addressed the controversial and complicated issue of when, what some would characterize as juvenile behavior, playground pranks, flirtation and the like, rise to constitute a claim for damages under Title IX. *Davis* reveals the type of conduct and behavior for which a claim for damages may be made if a school shows "deliberate indifference" to "severe, pervasive and objectively offensive" harassment of which the school has "actual knowledge."

DAVIS V. MONROE COUNTY BOARD OF EDUCATION

Supreme Court of the United States, 1999

526 U.S. 629

JUSTICE O'CONNOR delivered the opinion of the Court.

Petitioner brought suit against the Monroe County Board of Education and other defendants, alleging that her fifth-grade daughter had been the victim of sexual harassment by another student in her class. Among petitioner's claims was the claim for monetary and injunctive relief under Title IX of the Education Amendments of 1972. * * * The District Court dismissed petitioner's Title IX claim on the ground that "student-on-student," or peer, harassment provides no ground for a private cause of action under the statute. The Court of Appeals for the Eleventh Circuit, sitting en banc, affirmed. We consider here whether a private damages action may lie against the school board in cases of student-on-student harassment. We conclude that it may, but only where the funding recipient acts with deliberate indifference to known acts of harassment in its programs or activities. Moreover, we conclude that such an action will lie only for harassment that is so severe, pervasive, and objectively offensive that it effectively bars the victim's access to an educational opportunity or benefit.

* * *

Petitioner's minor daughter, LaShonda, was allegedly the victim of a prolonged pattern of sexual harassment by one of her fifth-grade classmates at Hubbard Elementary School, a public school in Monroe County, Georgia. According to petitioner's complaint, the harassment began in December 1992, when the classmate, G. F., attempted to touch LaShonda's breast and genital area and made vulgar statements such as " 'I want to get in bed with you' " and " 'I want to feel your boobs.' " Similar conduct allegedly occurred on or about January 4 and January 12, 1993. LaShonda reported each of these incidents to her mother and to her classroom teacher, Diane Fort. Petitioner, in turn, also contacted Fort, who allegedly assured petitioner that the school principal, Bill Querry, had been informed of the incidents. Petitioner contents that, notwithstanding these reports, no disciplinary action was taken against G. F.

G. F.'s conduct allegedly continued for many months. In early February, G. F. purportedly placed a door stop in his pants and proceeded to act in a sexually suggestive manner toward LaShonda during physical education class. LaShonda reported G. F.'s behavior to her physical education teacher, Whit Maples. Approximately one week later, G. F. again allegedly engaged in harassing behavior, this time while under the supervision of another classroom teacher, Joyce Pippin. Again, LaShonda allegedly reported the incident to the teacher, and again petitioner contacted the teacher to follow up.

Petitioner alleges that G. F. once more directed sexually harassing conduct toward LaShonda in physical education class in early March, and that LaShonda reported the incident to both Maples and Pippen. In mid-April 1993, G. F. allegedly rubbed his body against LaShonda in the school hallway in what LaShonda considered a sexually suggestive manner, and LaShonda again reported the matter to Fort.

The string of incidents finally ended in mid-May, when G. F. was charged with, and pleaded guilty to, sexual battery for his misconduct. The complaint alleges that LaShonda had suffered during the months of harassment, however; specifically, her previously high grades allegedly dropped as she became unable to concentrate on her studies, and, in April 1993, her father discovered that she had written a suicide note. The complaint further alleges that, at one point, LaShonda told petitioner that she " 'didn't know how much longer she could keep [G. F.] off her.' "

Nor was LaShonda G. F.'s only victim; it is alleged that other girls in the class fell prey to G. F.'s conduct. At one point, in fact, a group composed of LaShonda and other female students tried to speak with Principal Querry about G. F.'s behavior. According to the complaint, however, a teacher denied that student's request with the statement, " 'If [Querry] wants you, he'll call you.' "

Petitioner alleges that no disciplinary action was taken in response to G. F.'s behavior toward LaShonda. In addition to her conversations with Fort and Pippen, petitioner alleges that she spoke with Principal Querry in mid-

May 1993. When petitioner inquired as to what action the school intended to take against G. F., Querry simply stated, " 'I guess I'll have to threaten him a little bit harder.' " Yet, petitioner alleges, at no point during the many months of his reported misconduct was G. F. disciplined for harassment. Indeed, Querry allegedly asked the petitioner why LaShonda " 'was the only one complaining.' "

Nor, according to the complaint, was any effort made to separate G. F. and LaShonda. On the contrary, notwithstanding LeShonda's frequent complaints, only after more than three months of reported harassment was she even permitted to change her classroom seat so that she was no longer seated next to G. F. Moreover, petitioner alleges that, at the time of the events in question, the Monroe County Board of Education (Board) had not instructed its personnel on how to respond to peer sexual harassment and had not established a policy on the issue.

* * *

We consider here whether the misconduct identified in *Gebser*—deliberate indifference to known acts of harassment—amounts to an intentional violation of Title IX, capable of supporting a private damages action, when the harasser is a student rather than a teacher. We conclude that, in certain limited circumstances, it does. * * *

* * *

Where, as here, the misconduct occurs during school hours and on school grounds—the bulk of G. F.'S misconduct, in fact, took place in the classroom—the misconduct is taking place "under" an "operation" of the funding recipient. In these circumstances, the recipient retains substantial control over the context in which the harassment occurs. More importantly, however, in this setting the Board exercises significant control over the harasser. We have observed, for example, "that the nature of [the State's] power [over public schoolchildren] is custodial and tutelary, permitting a degree of supervision and control that could not be exercised over free adults."

* * *

We stress that our conclusion here—that recipients may be liable for their deliberate indifference to known acts of peer sexual harassment—does not mean that recipients can avoid liability only by purging their schools of actionable peer harassment or that administrators must engage in particular disciplinary action. We thus disagree with respondents' contention that, if Title IX provides a cause of action for student-on-student harassment, "nothing, short of expulsion of every student accused of misconduct involving sexual overtones would protect school systems from liability or damages." * * *

School administrators will continue to enjoy the flexibility they require so long as funding recipients are deemed "deliberately indifferent" to acts of student-on-student harassment only where the recipient's response to the harassment or lack thereof is clearly unreasonable in light of the known circumstances. * * *

* * *

While it remains to be seen whether petitioner can show that the Board's response to reports of G. F.'s misconduct was clearly unreasonable in light of the known circumstances, petitioner may be able to show that the Board "subject[ed]" LaShonda to discrimination by failing to respond in any way over a period of five months to complaints of G. F.'s in-school misconduct from LaShonda and other female students.

The most obvious example of student-on-student sexual harassment capable of triggering a damages claim would thus involve the overt, physical deprivation of access to school resources. Consider, for example, a case in which male students physically threaten their female peers every day, successfully preventing the female students from using a particular school resource—an athletic field or a computer lab, for instance. District administrators are well aware of the daily ritual, yet they deliberately ignore requests for aid from the female students wishing to use the resource. The district's knowing refusal to take any action in response to such behavior would fly in the face of Title IX's core principles, and such deliberate indifference may appropriately be subject to claims for monetary damages. It is not necessary, however, to show physical exclusion to demonstrate that students have been deprived by the actions of another student or students of an educational opportunity on the basis of sex. Rather, a plaintiff must establish sexual harassment of students that is so severe, pervasive, and objectively offensive, and that so undermines and detracts from the victims' educational experience, that the victim-students are effectively denied equal access to an institution's resources and opportunities. * * *

Whether gender-oriented conduct rises to the level of actionable "harassment" thus "depends on a constellation of surrounding circumstances, expectations, and relationships," . . . including, but not limited to, the ages of the harasser and the victim and the number of individuals involved. . . . Courts, moreover, must bear in mind that schools are unlike the adult workplace and that children may regularly interact in a manner that would be unacceptable among adults. . . . Indeed, at least early on, students are still learning how to interact appropriately with their peers. It is thus understandable that, in the school setting, students often engage in insults, banter, teasing, shoving, pushing, and gender-specific conduct that is upsetting to the students subjected to it. Damages are not available for simple acts of teasing and name-calling among school children, however, even where these comments target differences in gender. Rather, in the context of student-on-student harassment, damages are available only where the behavior is so severe, pervasive, and objectively offensive that it denies its victims the equal access to education that Title IX is designed to protect.

The dissent fails to appreciate these very real limitations on a funding recipient's liability under Title IX. It is not enough to show, as the dissent would read this opinion to provide, that a student has been "teased" or "called offensive names." Comparisons to an "overweight child who skips gym class because the other children tease her about her size," the student "who refuses to wear glasses to avoid the taunts of 'four-eyes,' " and "the child who refuses to go to school because the school bully calls him a 'scardy-cat' at recess," are inapposite and misleading. Nor do we contemplate, much less hold, that a mere "decline in grades is enough to survive" a motion to dismiss. The drop-off in LaShonda's grades provides necessary evidence of a potential link between her education and G.F.'s misconduct, but petitioner's ability to state a cognizable claim here depends equally on the alleged persistence and severity of G.F.'s actions, not to mention the Board's alleged knowledge and deliberate indifference. We trust that the dissent's characterization of our opinion will not mislead courts to impose more sweeping liability than we read Title IX to require.

Moreover, the provision that the discrimination occur "under any education program or activity" suggests that the behavior be serious enough to have the systemic effect of denying the victim equal access to an educational program or activity. Although, in theory, a single instance of sufficiently severe one-on-one peer harassment could be said to have such an effect, we think it unlikely that Congress would have thought such behavior sufficient to rise to this level in light of the inevitability of student misconduct and the amount of litigation that would be invited by entertaining claims of official indifference to a single instance of one-on-one peer harassment. By limiting private damages actions to cases having a systemic effect on educational program or activities, we reconcile the general principle that Title IX prohibits official indifference to known peer sexual harassment with the practical realities of responding to student behavior, realities that Congress could not have meant to be ignored. * * *

The fact that it was a teacher who engaged in harassment in *Franklin* and *Gebser* is relevant. The relationship between the harasser and the victim necessarily affects the extent to which the misconduct can be said to breach Title IX's guarantee of equal access to educational benefits and to have a systemic effect on a program or activity. Peer harassment, in particular, is less likely to satisfy these requirements than is teacher–student harassment.

Applying this standard to the facts at issue here, we conclude that the Eleventh Circuit erred in dismissing petitioner's complaint. Petitioner alleges that her daughter was the victim of repeated acts of sexual harassment by G. F. over a 5-month period, and there are allegations in support of the conclusion that G. F.'s misconduct was severe, pervasive, and objectively offensive. The harassment was not only verbal; it included numerous acts of objectively offensive touching, and, indeed, G. F. ultimately pleaded guilty to criminal sexual misconduct. Moreover, the complaint alleges that there were multiple victims who were sufficiently disturbed by G. F.'s misconduct to seek an audience with the school principal. Further, petitioner contends that the harassment had a concrete, negative effect on her daughter's ability to receive an education. The complaint also suggests that petitioner may be able to show both actual knowledge and deliberate indifference on the part of the Board, which made no effort whatsoever either to investigate or to put an end to the harassment.

On this complaint, we cannot say "beyond doubt that [petitioner] can prove no set of facts in support of [her] claim which would entitle [her] to relief." . . . Accordingly, the judgment of the United States Court of Appeals for the Eleventh Circuit is reversed, and the case is remanded for further proceedings consistent with this opinion.

It is so ordered.

Question

Both *Gebser* and *Davis* were five-to-four decisions. Some have observed that the decisions were inconsistent. Do you agree? Why?

Several states and local school systems have taken action to combat student-to-student harassment. Such sexual harassment has been made punishable by suspension or expulsion and some states have required local schools to have policies prohibiting student-to-student harassment. Has your school system defined sexual harassment and implemented appropriate policies?

II. EDUCATOR LIABILITY

A. Intentional Torts

The most common intentional torts with which educators become involved are assault and battery. Battery is the unpermitted and unprivileged contact with another's person, such as striking someone. Actual harm is not necessary in order to bring suit. However, ordinary contact allowed by social usage is not actionable. Assault is the placing of someone in apprehension of immediate harmful or offensive contact. Shaking a fist at someone or holding a weapon in a hostile manner are examples of an assault. Although courts have allowed wide latitude, a teacher may be charged with assault and battery as a result of disciplining a student. A teacher could be held liable if he or she administered punishment while angry or in a brutal, cruel, or excessive manner. Other factors taken into consideration to determine liability would be where on the body the child was struck, the child's age, the child's mental capacity, and the nature of the child's offense. A teacher may use only sufficient force for self-protection when in an altercation with a student or when attempting to restrain a student.

B. Negligence

An educator may be liable if an injury to a student, for instance, can be shown to have resulted from the educator's negligence. Liability for negligence may accrue if it can be shown that the alleged negligent party should have anticipated the possible harmful results of his or her actions or inactions. It differs from the intentional torts in the sense that there is no conscious desire to injure someone. A commonly employed test to determine negligence in a particular factual situation is whether a reasonable and prudent degree of care has been exercised. When this test is used, the question often asked is whether the person accused of negligence acted as a reasonable and prudent person would have acted in a similar situation under similar circumstances.

Several elements must be present to have a valid cause of action for negligence: (1) a legal duty to conform to a standard of conduct for the protection of others, (2) a failure to exercise an appropriate standard of care, (3) a causal connection often referred to as "proximate cause" between the conduct and the resultant injury, and (4) actual loss or damage as a result of the injury.

1. Duty of Care

There is a duty of care not to harm or injure another person with whom a common-law or statutory relationship exists. The common law, for instance, has established a teacher–student relationship that imposes a duty of care on the part of the teacher. The common law liability may be reduced by statutory provision, as has been done in several states in which liability is imposed only for willful or wanton misconduct. A state's "Good Samaritan" law may be applicable to educators, and if so, may reduce liability.

2. Standard of Care

For the most part, the standard of care a teacher must exercise to avoid liability is defined as that of the "reasonable and prudent" person. It is that degree of care a reasonable and prudent teacher, charged with like duties, would exercise under similar circumstances. This standard is not absolute, and many factors are taken into consideration when determining liability. The standard of care varies according to such factors as the age of the student, the child's mental capacity, and the environment and circumstances under which an injury took place. The amount of care due schoolchildren increases with the immaturity of the child; therefore, it is expected that greater care will be given while supervising extremely young children.

A higher degree of care should also be exercised in such potentially dangerous classroom situations as a "shop" class or a chemistry laboratory than in an English class or a library. Particular circumstances surrounding an injury must also be taken into consideration. If a teacher suffered a disability prior to a student's injury, for instance, the disability would have to be taken into consideration. A teacher is not necessarily liable for all injuries sustained by students, as it would be impossible for a teacher to foresee every possible situation where student injury could result. However, whenever a school-related injury occurs, the question of whether it could have been foreseen will be raised. Because many factors impinge on liability for alleged negligence, dissimilar court judgments are often rendered regarding seemingly similar factual situations.

3. Proximate Cause

A causal connection must exist between a teacher's conduct and the resultant injury for an action in negligence to prevail. The teacher's negligence must be a substantial cause of the injury to a student. Liability may be mitigated, however, if it can be shown that the cause of injury was the result of an intervening act or if responsibility can be legitimately shifted. Misconduct by a student, for instance, could be advanced as an intervening act. Alleging failure to maintain a safe playground could be an example of a legitimate shift of responsibility from a teacher to those responsible for properly maintaining the playground.

4. Actual Loss or Injury

Proof of damage is an essential element in a negligence action. Damages to assuage one's feelings generally cannot be recovered in a negligence action where there has been no actual loss. Damages may be apportioned if more than one person has been adjudged to have been negligent.

C. Defenses for Negligence

In seeking to avoid liability for an allegedly negligent act, a teacher may attempt to demonstrate that the elements necessary to establish negligence discussed previously were not present. However, other defenses may be applicable. The more common defenses include contributory negligence and assumption of risk.

Contributory negligence may be available as a defense if it can be demonstrated that the injured party failed to exercise the required degree of care necessary to ensure safety. This defense is not always available to teachers, as courts generally consider children unable to act with the same standard of care as adults. Because of their youth, students are often careless and do not act in a responsible manner; therefore, it may be difficult to convince a court that they were contributorily negligent.

Assumption of risk may be available as a defense when the injured party knew of the possible danger and either by agreement or actions voluntarily accepted the possibility of harm. Participants or spectators in athletic contests assume the normal risks associated with these activities by voluntarily placing themselves in a potentially harmful environment.

III. DUTIES OF SUPERVISION

Variations in the required common-law, statutory, or constitutional standard of duty and care among the states make it difficult to generalize about the extent of educators' tort liability in certain situations. Further compounding the difficulty in generalizing about tort liability is that seemingly similar factual situations giving rise to an alleged tort may contain sufficient nuance to produce different court holdings. The following brief descriptions of court decisions are offered as illustrations. Caution should be exercised in generalizing from them because only a partial description of the factual situation is provided and because the duty and standard of care varies among the jurisdictions.

A. Before and after School

In the absence of statutory requirements, courts generally do not find a duty on the part of schools to supervise students on their way to and from school except when they are on school buses. There is no duty, for instance, in the absence of legislation, to provide a school safety patrol. In a case where a seven-year-old child was killed while crossing a road in front of his school, a Louisiana appellate court, *Johnson* v. *Ouachita Parish Police Jury*, 377 So.2d 397 (La. Ct. App. 1979), held that the public school did not have a legal duty to provide safety patrols or adult school crossing guards. However, by participating in and accepting the benefits of a city-instituted school crossing guard program, a school board voluntarily assumed the duty of verifying that the crossing guard would be present at designated intersections during normal duty hours. In this instance, a six-year-old girl was killed by an automobile while attempting to cross an intersection. The guard was absent from his post because of illness. See *Barnes* v. *Bott*, 571 So. 2d 183 (La. Ct. App. 1990).

A duty of care on the part of the school may not be established if parents do not follow school rules that have been communicated to them. This issue was raised by a case in which a first-grade student, having missed his bus, rode his bicycle to school and was injured while riding home that afternoon. School rules stated that riding a bicycle was a privilege given to students in grades four through six and that students who did not plan to ride the bus on a particular day should bring notification from home to the school. Although the case was remanded on the question of the school district's duty of care, the Colorado Supreme Court held that, as a matter of law, the school did not have a duty to prevent the student from riding his bicycle home. See *Jefferson County School District R-1 v. Justus*, 725 P.2d 767 (Colo. 1986).

Adequate supervision must be afforded students for a reasonable time as they congregate and wait for school to begin in the morning. In a New Jersey decision, *Titus v. Lindberg*, 49 N.J. 66, 228 A.2d 65 (1967), a principal was held liable for an injury that happened to a student before school. In this instance, the injury resulted from a paper clip that was propelled by a student waiting for transportation to another school. It was customary for students to arrive at school about 8:00 A.M., although classrooms did not officially open until 8:15 A.M. This incident occurred at approximately 8:05 A.M. The court offered several reasons for its holding that the principal's negligent supervision was a proximate cause of the injury: his failure to announce rules concerning playground supervision before school, to assign teachers to supervision, and personally to provide adequate supervision.

In another Louisiana decision, *Richard v. St. Landry Parish School Board*, 344 So.2d 1116 (La. Ct. App. 1977), a teacher was not held liable for an injury that happened to a third-grade student while unsupervised students were cleaning the classroom after school. While engaged at this task, one of the students went through the teacher's desk and found a knife, which subsequently was used to inflict injury. In its opinion, the court emphasized that the students had been forbidden to go near the desk and, furthermore, the teacher had not placed the knife in the student's hand.

In a California decision, *Bartell v. Palos Verdes Peninsula School District*, 147 Cal. Rptr. 898 (Cal. Ct. App. 1978), the school district was not held liable for an injury occurring after school hours. In this instance a twelve-year-old boy was fatally injured while playing a skateboard version of crack-the-whip after school hours. The court maintained that school districts and their employees are placed under a general duty to supervise the conduct of children on school grounds during school sessions, school activities, recesses, and lunch periods. Furthermore, the court stated:

> To require virtual round-the-clock supervision or prison-tight security for school premises, as plaintiffs suggest, would impose a financial burden which manifestly would impinge on the very educational purpose for which school exists. While it is common knowledge that children often heedlessly engage in games or activities which are dangerous or harmful to their health, at some point the obligation of the public entity to answer for the malfeasance or misfeasance of others, whether children or parents, reaches its outer limits. Public entities labor under budgetary constraints which peculiarly affect their obligation of care. * * * (p. 500)

B. During School Hours

Generally, the standard of care owed to pupils by a teacher during school hours is that care which a reasonable and prudent teacher would observe in comparable circumstances.

A court in Louisiana ruled that a school board was not liable for injuries to a student by a rock thrown on school property. The court held that adequate supervision had been provided for the students and that reasonable supervision did not require constant supervision of every child on the playground. See *Hampton* v. *Orleans Parish School Board*, 422 So.2d 202 (La. Ct. App. 1982).

Although a state statute may require a teacher to "keep good order" in the classroom, this implies the use of reasonable force and does not authorize the teacher's use of excessive force. Additionally, state statutes may provide that a teacher or principal shall not be liable in a civil lawsuit for the use of reasonable force on a pupil for the purpose of maintaining discipline at school, except in cases of gross disregard for the health and safety of the pupil. A Michigan court, in *Willoughby* v. *Lehrbass*, 388 N.W.2d 688 (Mich. Ct. App. 1986), concluded that a teacher had used reasonable force when in an attempt to take the student to the principal's office, he grabbed the student in a "full nelson"—with his arms underneath the student's armpits and his palms on the back of the student's neck—and pulled the student into the hall and up a stairway.

Schools must provide proper supervision during times, such as recess, passing through the halls, or lunch hour, when students are out of class. The California Supreme Court, in *Dailey* v. *Los Angeles Unified School District*, 470 P.2d 360 (Cal. 1970), contended that school authorities were negligent in the supervision provided at a noon recess. In this case, two high school students engaged in "slap fighting," a form of boxing employing open hands, which resulted in the death of one of the students. The court maintained that because adolescent high school students are not adults, they should not be expected to exhibit the degree of discretion and judgment associated with mature adults. Therefore, the court contended it was negligent not to have a comprehensive schedule of supervision assignments and proper instructions for subordinates as to what was expected of them while they were supervising.

A physical education teacher was found to have a duty of properly instructing students before a vertical jumping exercise was attempted. After she failed to provide sufficient instruction, a child suffered injury when she ran into a wall while performing the exercise. Although the court felt that the fact of the case should be ascertained in a jury trial, it was noted that proper instruction could have prevented the injury. See *Dibortolo* v. *Metropolitan School District of Washington Township*, 440 N.E.2d 506 (Ind. Ct. App. 1982).

Schools may be liable for injury to a student who leaves school without school or parental permission. In one such case, *Hoyem* v. *Manhattan Beach City School District*, 585 P.2d 851 (Cal. 1978), the California Supreme Court held that the school district could be held liable for injuries suffered by a ten-year-old truant student who was hit by a motorcycle. The court contended that the school district would not be liable for injury sustained by a truant under all circumstances; however, the school district would be legally responsible if the district's supervisory procedures to thwart truancy fell below that degree of care which reasonably prudent persons would exercise.

A Florida appellate court upheld a jury verdict in favor of a high school student who was attacked and beaten by three other students while he waited in the school cafeteria for transportation to his home. The court ruled that the school had a duty to provide some form of security to prevent such incidents from occurring. The student misbehavior in this case could reasonably have been foreseen, especially because the school was entrusted with the care of students and had a legal duty to supervise them. See *Broward County School Board* v. *Ruiz*, 493 So.2d 474 (Fla. Dist. Ct. App. 1986).

C. Off-Campus Activities

Required participation in off-campus activities such as a field trip or excursion, or interscholastic activities such as athletics or debate, places the school in the same position of duty to use care to prevent injury as if students were on campus.

In Florida, for instance, a teacher and principal were found to be negligent in failing to supervise school club activities. When a student was injured during a hazing incident, the court ruled that the school had violated a duty of supervision that had been established by school board policy when the club advisor was appointed. The court felt that the incident would not have occurred if the advisor had been present. See *Rupp* v. *Bryant*, 417 So.2d 658 (Fla. 1982).

A school district was found negligent in failing to provide adequate supervision at a required attendance by students of a downtown showing of a controversial movie entitled *King*. Students were bused to the theater accompanied by chaperones. Obscene racial comments were made by both Caucasian and African American students during the showing. On leaving the balcony for the lobby, a student was pushed, her wrist slashed, and her purse taken. The Minnesota Supreme Court in *Raleigh* v. *Independent School District No. 625*, 275 N.W.2d 572 Minn. 1979), upheld the awarding of damages against the school for failure to provide sufficient precautions in the light of having knowledge about racial tensions.

IV. PARENTAL CONSENT

Written parental consent for participation in extracurricular activities, such as athletic competition or travel related to a school activity, is often required by school district policy. The importance of having parental consent for travel to an off-campus activity is obvious. One can only imagine the difficulty, and increased legal complications, in having to inform parents of an off-campus injury to their child when those parents had no knowledge of an away-from-school activity or had not given consent for their child to participate. Parental consent forms may contain language purporting to release the school from liability in the event of an injury. It is questionable whether such a signed form would offer those supervising the school activity any immunity from suit in the event of negligence. Parental consent not only would be a surrendering of the independent claim of the child but would also be considered by many courts to be counter to public policy because it was the intentional waiving of a suit to recover damages for subsequent negligent supervision. This issue was addressed by the Washington Supreme Court, which held invalid, as against public policy, the practice of requiring students and their parents to sign a release of all potential future claims as a condition to student participation in certain school-related activities such as interscholastic athletics. See *Wagenblast v. Odessa School District No. 105-157-166j*, 758 P.2d 968 (Wash. 1988).

V. MALPRACTICE

Suits alleging "educational malpractice" have been brought in several states. Plaintiffs in these suits generally allege that the school district has been negligent because it has issued a certificate or diploma, yet the student does not have the basic academic skills necessary for such tasks as understanding and completing a job application. In one of the first suits of this kind, *Peter W. v. San Francisco Unified School District*, 131 Cal. Rptr. 854 (Cal. Ct. App. 1976), plaintiff's position was not upheld. The California court contended that failure of educational achievement is not an injury within the meaning of tort law. Additionally, the court stated:

> . . . Few of our institutions, if any, have aroused the controversies or incurred the public dissatisfaction, which have attended the operation of the public schools during the last few decades. Rightly or wrongly, but widely, they are charged with outright failure in the achievement of their educational objectives; according to some critics, they bear responsibility for many of the social and moral problems of our society at large. Their public plight in these respects is attested in the daily media, in bitter governing board elections, in wholesale rejections of school bond proposals, and in survey upon survey. To hold them to an actionable "duty of care," in the discharge of their

academic functions, would expose them to the tort claims—real or imagined—of disaffected students and parents in countless numbers. They are already beset by social and financial problems which have gone to major litigation, but for which no permanent solution has yet appeared. . . . The ultimate consequences, in terms of public time and money, would burden them—and society—beyond calculation. (p. 825)

In another decision, *Donohue* v. *Copiague Union Free School District*, 391 N.E.2d 1352 (N.Y. 1979), New York's Court of Appeals also disallowed a cause of action against a school district that sought monetary damages for educational malpractice. The plaintiff alleged that, notwithstanding his receipt of a certificate of graduation, he lacked "the rudimentary ability to comprehend written English on a level sufficient to enable him to complete applications for employment." In its decision, the court held that:

. . . the Constitution places the obligation of *maintaining and supporting* a system of public schools upon the *Legislature*. To be sure, this general directive was never intended to impose a duty flowing directly from a local school district to individual pupils to ensure that each pupil receives a minimum level of education, the breach of which duty would entitle a pupil to compensatory damages. . . . (p. 443)

An Ohio court refused to find a cause of action for educational malpractice as a matter of public policy. In this instance, a high school student sued her teacher after failing his course, which prevented her from graduating. In its decision, the court ruled that the student had failed to show that the teacher acted with malicious purpose, in bad faith, or in a wanton or reckless manner by failing to follow curricular guidelines and school district requirements. See *Poe* v. *Hamilton*, 565 N.E.2d 887 (Ohio Ct. App. 1990).

Educational malpractice litigation has addressed claims for monetary damages resulting from misdiagnoses of learning abilities or of special educational needs. In 1982, the Maryland Supreme Court considered a claim based on a complaint that a school system had negligently evaluated a first-grade student and had consequently caused him to be taught first-grade materials for a second year while he was physically placed in second grade. Charges were also made that certain educators had furnished false information concerning the child's learning problems, had altered school records to cover their actions, and had demeaned the child. In reviewing earlier malpractice claims, the court concluded that an award of monetary damages represents an inappropriate remedy for errors in the educational process. It noted, however, that the parents could take later legal action against the educators who had demonstrated alleged outrageous conduct. See *Hunter* v. *Board of Education of Montgomery County*, 292 Md. 481, 439 A.2d 582 (1982).

A Michigan appellate court also considered monetary claims resulting from misdiagnosis of a language impairment. Although the child had been treated for a period of time based on the diagnosis, the court held the speech therapist and the school system to be immune from liability. Because the evaluation and treatment of speech problems were a part of the regular functions of a school system, the court ruled that school personnel should not be held liable in tort for honest mistakes. See *Brosnan* v. *Livonia Public Schools*, 333 N.W.2d 288 (Mich. Ct. App. 1983). A Montana decision, however, supported the monetary claims of foster parents of a child who had been improperly placed in a program for the educable mentally retarded. As the child had been placed in the program despite scores showing that the placement was inappropriate, the court ruled that this case was not like other educational malpractice claims. This situation involved misplacement despite accurate knowledge of ability scores, not misdiagnosis of a disability. See *B. M.* v. *Montana*, 649 P.2d 425 (Mont. 1982).

VI. INSURANCE

Although it is important for educators to be aware of their potential liability for failure to act in a reasonable and prudent manner in preventing injury, the fear of significant monetary loss has been lessened by the availability of liability insurance. Many educators have such coverage as a part of their membership in a professional organization. Individual liability insurance policies are also available. Although a strong case for liability may be made against them, impecunious and uninsured educators are often unlikely candidates for suit.

Questions

What is the status of school district immunity in your state? What are the advantages and disadvantages of school district immunity?

What is the common law or statutory duty and standard of care in your state for tortious liability of individual school board members? Administrators? Teachers?

APPENDIX A

Analyzing a Court Decision

Significant information may be extracted from court decisions by employing an orderly process such as case analysis, sometimes referred to as "briefing" a case. General categories of information included in a case analysis are the title and citation of the case, the level or type of court hearing the case, the relevant facts involved in the case, the disputed issue or issues in the case, the holding or holdings of the court, the legal doctrine(s) or legal principle(s) underlying the decision, and the significance of the decision regarding future actions of individuals or institutions.

TITLE AND CITATION

The title of the decision contains the name of the litigants. A judicial citation contains the volume number and page number of the reporter system(s) in which the decision appears as well as the year in which the decision was issued. A complete citation includes reference to all reporter systems, official or unofficial, in which the decision appears. These are referred to as parallel citations. See Appendix B for a fuller explanation of the citation process.

LEVEL OR TYPE OF COURT

Noting the level or type of court hearing the case is important because it indicates the federal or state jurisdiction immediately affected by the decision. For example, decisions by the United States Supreme Court or states' highest courts represent the final authority on issues within the courts' respective jurisdictions.

FACTS

Facts include the actual circumstances, events, or occurrences involved in the case. Disputed facts must be resolved at the trial level. Appellate courts do not decide questions of fact. Their decision is based on the facts given. If these are insufficient, the case may be remanded to the lower court for further proceedings to determine additional facts.

ISSUE

An issue is a disputed point or question of law upon which a legal action is based. One or more issues may be present in a single case. Issues are of two types, procedural and substantive. Procedural issues involve specific disputed questions of law, and these issues are the basis for an appeal to a higher court. They may include whether a particular legal motion should have been granted or denied, whether certain information was admissible, or whether injunctive relief should have been granted. Substantive issues, on the other hand, involve broader questions of legal rights and principles, such as liberty and property interests. Substantive issues are generally of greater importance to the nonlawyer/student of school law.

HOLDING

The court's decision consists of a holding or holdings in regard to the question or questions before it and usually includes an opinion stating the reasons for the particular holding(s). Written opinions normally include an analysis of the arguments and supporting legal precedent presented by each side and the court's examination of the arguments, precedents, statutes, and facts applicable to the decision.

Concurring or dissenting opinions written by individual judges are frequently included in court decisions. In these opinions, judges may discuss reasons for agreeing or disagreeing with the action of the court, elaborate on the issues considered by the court, or introduce additional principles or concepts not considered in the majority opinion. Concurring and dissenting opinions are often quite beneficial in analyzing the decision of the court.

In addition, decisions often include dicta, additional statements of opinion by the court or an individual judge concerning a question or point of law that arises during the hearing of a case. Because these comments may not be vital to the formulation of the holding, they are not binding as precedent. However, dicta may indicate the persuasion of a particular court or judge.

In some instances, if specific legal relief is required or if the appellate court wishes the trial court to reexamine the case in the light of the appellate court's legal reasoning, a case may be remanded to the trial court.

LEGAL DOCTRINE

Court decisions generally are based on a particular legal doctrine or principle. Analysis of a decision includes identifying the doctrine or principle and determining how it is affected by the decision. For example, a student should attempt to ascertain whether a decision may establish, distinguish, extend, affirm, modify, overturn, or reverse a legal doctrine.

SIGNIFICANCE

A concise statement of the implications of the decision with regard to future actions by individuals and institutions completes the analysis. Naturally, certain decisions possess greater significance for educational practices than do others.

A court decision's significance is determined to a large degree by its generalizability to a particular judicial jurisdiction. For example, courts in different jurisdictions may disagree on particular issues when no precedent has been established by a higher court. Consequently, an authoritative decision in one jurisdiction may not be applicable to actions within other jurisdictions. In fact, courts in other jurisdictions may reach opposite decisions.

APPENDIX B

An Introduction to Research in School Law

There are several sources with which an educator may begin legal research. These may be divided into three broad categories—primary sources, secondary sources, and finding aids. Primary sources of law represent some form of binding or highly persuasive authority. State and federal statutes and constitutional provisions, along with court decisions interpreting them, are the most important primary sources of law. Secondary source materials provide interpretive references regarding primary sources of law. Textbooks and casebooks, periodicals and law reviews, dissertations, legal encyclopedias, and legal dictionaries are examples of secondary materials. In addition, finding aids facilitate the location of primary sources of law related to a particular topic of interest. These include digests of the case law, citators, and various indexing materials.

Thorough legal research involves a systematic examination of an appropriate portion of the voluminous legal literature. This examination may be facilitated by the use of numerous research aids. Although the aids are quite effective in locating relevant materials, a word of caution may be appropriate. A limitation to most legal research aids is the perspective of an aid's publisher. Many publications in the legal field are prepared primarily for use by attorneys and may not necessarily address the needs of the educational researcher.

Legal issues may be divided into substantive and procedural ones. Procedural issues address the various rules of form in legal proceedings, whereas substantive issues are concerned with legal rights and principles. Procedural questions are generally of greater interest to attorneys than to educators; therefore, the location of substantive legal information is emphasized in this discussion of legal research.

ELEMENTS OF SCHOOL LAW RESEARCH

Primary Sources of Law

Statutes

Federal statutes are officially compiled according to topic in the *United States Code* (U.S.C.). Unofficial annotated editions of the federal statutes are available in the *United States Code Annotated* (U.S.C.A.) and *United States Code Service* (U.S.C.S.). Annotated versions include supplemental historical notes, editorial comments, and a digest of interpretive court decisions related to each provision. Statutes are popularly known by reference to their enactment rather than to their place in the *Code*. Congressional acts in their chronological order of passage are compiled in the *United States Statutes at Large* (Stat.) by public law number (P.L. 94-142, for instance, was the 142nd law passed during the 94th Congressional session). A citation to the *Statutes* does not reflect subsequent changes to the law; because the *Code* is continuously modified to reflect amendments and deletions, it should be cited when referring to current law. When applicable, rules and regulations designed to assist in the implementation of federal statutes are published in the *Federal Register* (Fed. Reg.), and the *Code of Federal Regulations* (C.F.R.).

Official state codes and unofficial annotated versions generally group related statutes into chapters, which are indexed to facilitate search within the volumes. Laws related to the schools are often included in chapters entitled "Education" or "Schools and School Districts." Both official codes and related annotated publications are kept up to date by the use of paperback pocket supplements. Unofficial annotated codes often provide faster and more convenient supplementation as well as additional analytical and interpretive material. Local ordinances are not generally compiled in a standardized code; however, some counties and larger cities may publish local ordinances.

Constitutions

Provisions of federal and state constitutions may be located in several sources. The *United States Code* contains the official text of the Constitution of the United States. Annotated versions appear in the *United States Code Annotated* and *United States Code Service*. Similarly, state constitutions are generally set forth in official state codes. Annotated state constitutions are available for many states.

Court Decisions

Disputes between parties and the interpretation of statutory and constitutional provisions are resolved in court decisions. Lawsuits are initiated in trial courts, which examine the formal written statements of the parties and hear the parties' oral arguments as well as the testimony of witnesses. Trial court decisions may be appealed to higher courts. These appellate courts do not repeat the trial proceedings; rather, the courts review the written record of lower courts' decisions. They may affirm, reverse, vacate, or modify the judgment of the lower courts or order that a case be tried again.

Most trial court decisions are not reported for general distribution. Therefore, copies of trial court decisions usually must be obtained from the court issuing the decision. However, decisions of most appellate courts and certain trial courts are available in official and unofficial reporters. Reporters are published in a series of numbered bound volumes. Preliminary paperback booklets containing the most recent decisions available, referred to as advance sheets, are issued periodically as supplements to the bound volumes. These advance sheets are compiled to form the subsequent bound volumes of the reporters. Unofficial reporters are useful because of greater speed of publication through more extensive use of advance sheets. In addition, they include special research aids as well as other supplementary materials.

United States Supreme Court   Decisions of the United States Supreme Court are officially reported in the *United States Reports* (U.S.). Supreme Court decisions also appear in two privately published unofficial reporters called the *Supreme Court Reporter* (S. Ct.) and the *United States Supreme Court Reports, Lawyers' Edition* (L.Ed.). Although unofficial reporters include features unique to their particular series, text of the Court's decisions is identical in these reporters.

Each decision of the Supreme Court is reported by the Court in a separate pamphlet shortly after the decision is announced. These slip opinions are the first official text of the Court's decisions. Slip opinions are later paginated and compiled into advance sheets.

Supreme Court decisions also appear in two unofficial loose-leaf publications. *United States Law Week* (U.S.L.W.) and the *Supreme Court Bulletin* (S. Ct. Bull.) report Supreme Court decisions immediately after they are issued by the Court. These publications provide the researcher timely access to reported decisions of the Supreme Court.

Lower Federal Courts   Decisions of the lower federal courts may be found in two publications. Decisions of the United States Courts of Appeals are published in the *Federal Reporter* (F.), now in its third series, *Federal Reporter, Third Series* (F.3d). Selected decisions of the United States District Courts are contained in the *Federal Supplement* (F. Supp.). *Federal Rules Decisions* (F.R.D.) includes various lower federal court decisions addressing procedural issues. In addition to these publications, a selection of annotated federal court decisions addressing particular areas of legal questions is offered in *American Law Reports—Federal* (A.L.R.).

State Courts Decisions of state courts are published in two main sources. In many states, official reporters are published by the courts. Where such reporters are available, they provide the authoritative texts of the reported decisions. Generally, only decisions of the state's highest court are officially reported; however, several states also report decisions of lower appellate courts. Slip opinions and advance sheets are not always incorporated within state courts' reporting systems.

The National Reporter System provides the most comprehensive system of unofficial reports of state court decisions. Within the National Reporter System, which also includes the *Supreme Court Reporter, Federal Reporter,* and *Federal Supplement,* the nation is divided into geographic regions for the purpose of reporting state court decisions. Reporters for each of the seven regions are published periodically containing state supreme court decisions and many state appellate court decisions within the region.* These regional reporters are supplemented by the *California Reporter* (Cal. Rptr.) and *New York Supplement* (N.Y.S.), including selected decisions of the lower courts in those two states. Some states have ceased official publication of court decisions and have adopted the appropriate regional reporter as the state's official reporter.

West's Education Law Reporter includes the full text of all reported cases dealing with education from the United States Supreme Court, the United States Courts of Appeals, the United States District Courts, and all state appellate courts. Additionally, the *Reporter* includes commentaries on court opinions and legislation that promise to have a significant impact on education, along with reports of empirical research on school law topics.

Selected significant state court decisions are also published in *American Law Reports* (A.L.R.). These unofficial reports include analytical annotations to each decision, which discuss the various points of law presented in the case.

Judicial Citation In order to locate reported court decisions contained in the diverse official and unofficial reporters, a shorthand method of reference is provided by a system of judicial citation. A citation of a reported court decision reveals specific information regarding where the decision is reported. For example, a researcher investigating the subject of academic freedom may determine that the decision in *Fowler* v. *Board of Education of Lincoln County,* 819 F.2d 657 (1987), *cert. denied,* 484 U.S. 986 is applicable. In this instance, the title of the case, *Fowler* v. *Board of Education of*

---

*The seven regions and their states are *Atlantic* (A. or A.2d—Conn., Del., Me., Md., N.H., N.J., Pa., R.I., Vt.; *Northeastern* (N.E. or N.E.2d)—Ill., Ind., Mass., N.Y., Ohio; *Southeastern* (S.E. or S.E.2d)—Ga., N.C., S.C., Va; *Southern* (So. or So.2d)—Ala., Fla., La., Miss.; *Southwestern* (S.W. or S.W.2d)—Ark., Ky., Mo., Tenn., Tex.; *Northwestern* (N.W. or N.W.2d)—Iowa, Mich., Minn., Neb., N.D., S.D., Wis.; *Pacific* (P. or P.2d)—Alaska, Ariz., Cal., Colo., Hawaii, Idaho, Kan., Mont., Nev., N.M., Okla., Or., Utah, Wash., Wyo.

Lincoln County, indicates that Fowler and the Board of Education of Lincoln County are the parties involved in the action. In case titles, *versus* is abbreviated by a lowercase v. When legal action is initiated in the court of original jurisdiction, the plaintiff's name is listed first. However, on appeal of the case, the names of the parties may switch positions or be altered should the parties to the action change. Following the case title is a reference to the volume number, the title of the reporter, and the page number at which the decision appears. *Fowler v. Board of Education of Lincoln County*, for instance, is reported in volume number 819 of the *Federal Reporter, Second Series*, (F.2d), beginning on page 657. This particular format is consistent throughout all case citations. The initial number designates the volume number of the reporter; then the title of the reporter and the series are indicated, followed by the page number on which the text of the decision begins. Within parentheses following the information regarding the reporter is the year in which the decision was issued and in some instances the court issuing the decision. In 1987, the United States Court of Appeals for the Sixth Circuit issued the decision in *Fowler v. Board of Education of Lincoln County*. Explanatory words or phrases often appear as citations in explanation of the prior or subsequent history of a decision. In this instance, the United States Supreme Court denied certiorari (declined to review the case). This action by the Court in 1987 is reported on page 986 of volume 484 of the *United States Reports*.

As a second example, consider *Ponton v. Newport News School Board*, 632 F. Supp. 1056 (E.D.Va. 1986). Here the decision in the case of *Ponton v. Newport News School Board* is reported in volume 632 of the *Federal Supplement* at page 1056. A federal district court for the eastern district of Virginia rendered the decision in 1986.

When decisions appear in more than one reporter, parallel, also known as dual, citations are often used to indicate other sources in which the decision is reported. When parallel citations are used, the official reporter, or authoritative text of the decision, is cited first. For example, the citation to the well-known Bible reading and prayer decision of the United States Supreme Court may appear as *School District of Abington Township v. Schempp*, 374 U.S. 203, 83 S.Ct. 1560, 10 L.Ed.2d 844 (1963). This parallel citation reveals that the decision is officially reported in volume 374 of the *United States Reports* at page 203, and also appears in volume 83 of the *Supreme Court Reporter* at page 1560, and in the second series of the *United States Supreme Court Reports, Lawyers' Edition*, at page 844 of volume 10. The decision was issued by the Court in 1963.

Consider a decision of the California Supreme Court, cited as *Hartzell v. Connell*, 35 Cal.3d 899, 679 P.2d 35, 201 Cal. Rptr. 601 (1984). In 1984, the California Supreme Court issued a decision in the case, which was officially reported by the court in volume 35 of the *California Reports, Third Se-*

ries, at page 899. Two unofficial reporters of the National Reporter System contain the decision as well: volume 679 of the *Pacific Reporter, Second Series* at page 35 and volume 201 of the *California Reporter* at page 601.

In addition to court decisions, many other sources of legal literature are subject to similar uniform rules of citation. However, a treatment of all of these areas is beyond the scope of this discussion. For a generally accepted reference to rules of citation for all forms of legal literature, the researcher is directed to *The Bluebook: A Uniform System of Citation*, published by the Harvard Law Review Association.

Board of Education Policies and Regulations

At the state and local levels, the educational system is subject to policies and procedures implemented by the appropriate boards of education. State board of education policies are generally arranged according to subject matter and available in a form providing convenient access and rapid updating. Although local board policies are most likely available in printed form, access to them may be somewhat less convenient for the researcher.

Attorney General Opinions

States' legal counsels are frequently requested to issue advisory opinions concerning proposed legislative or administrative action or questions related to present constitutional and statutory provisions. Although these opinions are only advisory, they are often helpful in the study of legal topics. Reports of attorneys general are published by many states.

Secondary Sources of Legal Literature

Textbooks and Casebooks

Available textbooks in the field of school law vary from general texts to brief monographs presenting discussion of a specific area of school law. Some textbooks offer in-depth analysis of legal issues; others contain no endeavors at such scholarly analysis but provide convenient manuals to introduce the reader to particular issues in school law. Many textbooks contain tables of cases, bibliographies, or other reference materials that may serve as useful research aids. Casebooks contain edited versions of decisions with particular significance. These works often provide supplementary, explanatory, and interpretive material. Although textbooks and casebooks provide valuable information, they are somewhat limited in that they may become dated as the law changes and interpretive court decisions are rendered.

Periodical and Law Review Articles

Expositive articles of interest may be found in the legal and educational literature. Law reviews and bar journals are indexed in the *Index to Legal Periodicals. Shepard's Law Review Citations*, a compilation of citations to articles in over one hundred law reviews and legal periodicals, enables the researcher to determine where articles appearing in these publications in recent decades have been cited in subsequent articles and in federal or state court decisions. *The Journal of Law and Education* and *West's Education Law Quarterly* are specialized journals containing articles related to school law issues. Educational periodical articles related to legal topics may be located by utilizing the *Education Index, Current Index to Journals in Education,* and *Educational Administration Abstracts*.

Dissertations

Unpublished doctoral research often provides comprehensive treatment of particular topics regarding education and the law. Pertinent dissertations may be identified by examining the computer-generated *Dissertation Abstracts International* at ProQuest.

Encyclopedias

Corpus Juris Secundum and *American Jurisprudence 2d*, the two major legal encyclopedias of national scope, include narrative discussion of a wide variety of legal topics. Each series of encyclopedias includes volumes providing a general index and topical indexes (such as Schools and School Districts) of the subject matter. In addition, several state encyclopedias are published following the same basic format as the national publications.

Because the copious extended footnotes contain numerous case references, these encyclopedias are often quite helpful in locating pertinent court decisions. However, the encyclopedias may not always be as helpful as they might first appear. Although periodic supplements are published, it is difficult for works of this nature to reflect accurately the rapidly changing law. Suffering from the same limitations as many other encyclopedic efforts, the works are often criticized for a lack of scholarly analysis and a tendency toward oversimplification and generalization regarding complex legal issues.

Legally significant words and phrases are listed alphabetically in an encyclopedic collection entitled *Words and Phrases*. Each word or phrase is followed by brief summaries of judicial decisions in which it has been interpreted or defined, as well as citations to the decisions. Annual supplements are issued to keep *Words and Phrases* up to date.

Other Secondary Materials

Additional aids may be helpful in employing the various research procedures. For example, *The Bluebook: A Uniform Code of Citation*, commonly referred to as the Bluebook, provides a generally accepted standard for the rules of citation and style. This reference enables the researcher to report research effectively and may answer questions related to the short-hand system of legal citation. Legal terms and abbreviations may be clarified by the use of a reputable legal dictionary, such as *Black's Law Dictionary, Revised Seventh Edition*.

Finding Aids

Various methods may be employed to locate pertinent court decisions. Each of the various sources possesses particular strengths and limitations, but may be used effectively in reviewing the existing case law. It is not likely that a particular method of case finding will prove most effective in all situations. Consideration of the individual research problem, the tools available, and the researcher's personal preference will probably determine which sources are employed in the search for applicable case law.

Case Digests

The *American Digest System* provides an exhaustive compilation of case references, appearing under alphabetically arranged topic headings (such as Schools and School Districts). The system is divided into decennial digests, each addressing a ten-year period. The *Tenth Decennial Digest* deals with the years 1986–1996. Cases reported since 1996 are included in the *General Digest, Ninth Series*. The system's current component is kept up to date by the use of paperback supplements issued monthly.

In addition to the *American Digest System*, digests devoted to the geographic regions covered by most of the regional reporters and many of the individual states are available. There are also digests dealing solely with federal court decisions, as well as a digest covering decisions of the United States Supreme Court.

Loose-Leaf Services

Several loose-leaf services are published that aid in locating pertinent court decisions. A monthly publication of the Education Law Association, the *ELA School Law Reporter*, contains brief summaries and citations to judicial decisions related to school law. Among the looseleaf services available, the *School Law Reporter* provides the most comprehensive source of school law cases. Decisions addressing school law issues are also cited and summarized in the *School Law Bulletin*. *United States Law Week* and the *Supreme Court Reporter* provide rapid access to recent United States Supreme Court decisions. Both of these publications also include information concerning Court proceedings, calendars, cases docketed, and general

Court news. In addition, *United States Law Week* includes a section entitled *General Law*, summarizing significant weekly developments in all legal areas, including judicial, legislative, and administrative actions at both the state and federal levels.

Annotated Codes and Reporters

Annotated constitutions and statutory codes are useful sources for ascertaining applicable case law. Citations and summaries of interpretive court decisions are usually included in the analytical annotations to the particular provisions.

American Law Reports and *American Law Reports—Federal* report a small selection of significant cases, each annotated by an editorial discussion of the point of law dealt with in the case. Appropriate tables of cases, word indexes, and digests are published in conjunction with these, facilitating the location of decisions and annotations. Related cases are cited within the analytical annotations.

Secondary Materials

Secondary materials previously discussed may be helpful as sources of case citations. Textbooks, periodical and law review articles, dissertations, and encyclopedias often include numerous references to court decisions within their text and footnotes. In addition, *West's Education Law Reporter* contains new case highlights, commentary on school law related issues, case digests, and the text of newly reported decisions. Summaries of recent school law cases are also published in issues of the *Journal of Law and Education*. The *Yearbook of Education Law*, published annually by the Education Law Association, also contains numerous references to decisions addressing a diverse selection of school law issues.

Shepard's Citations

A court decision's current status may be determined by using an appropriate volume of *Shepard's Citations*. It is possible to ascertain whether a decision has been affirmed, reversed, overruled, vacated, distinguished, or otherwise modified by subsequent court action through the use of this comprehensive system of case citators. A series of bound volumes, paperback supplements, and advance sheets covers state and federal decisions reported in an official or unofficial reporter. Volumes are devoted to United States Supreme Court decisions, United States Courts of Appeals decisions, United States District Court decisions, the various regional reporters in the National Reporter System, and the individual states. Every volume of *Shepard's Citations* follows a similar format utilizing a system of symbols, which is described in the preliminary pages of each volume.

Besides verifying the current status of court decisions, *Shepard's Citations* provides a method by which parallel citations may be determined, the judicial history of a case may be traced, and citations to all subsequent proceedings in a case located. In addition, the citators indicate all subsequent decisions in which a case in question is cited and reveal other research leads, such as periodical and law review articles, attorney general opinions, and annotated reports in which the case is cited.

A system of *Shepard's Citations*, similar to the case citators, is also available to verify the current status of constitutional and statutory provisions. Volumes are devoted to the federal Constitution and statutes and to similar provisions of the individual states, with limited reference to local ordinances contained in the various state volumes. Although use of these citators is considerably more complex than the case citators, similar information is revealed. Subsequent legislative action or court interpretation regarding particular provisions is cited. The legislative and judicial history of a provision may be ascertained to determine whether it has been altered or otherwise affected by such action or interpretation.

Computer-Assisted Services

There are several commercially available, computer-assisted systems for legal research. Presently, these services include Lexis and Westlaw. Primary advantages of using these services include eliminating the need for direct access to a law library, availability of a wider selection of law materials than most law libraries contain, availability of decisions from most reporter systems, up-to-date Shepardizing, access to major law reviews, capability of parallel citations, and specific topic or subject matter search.

There is also a wealth of legal information on the Internet. This storehouse of material is expanding rapidly, and the following is provided to reveal the type of information available. Law.com (http://www11.law.com/nav.asp?h=88) is a comprehensive web site that contains: founding documents such as the Declaration of Independence, U.S. Constitution, and the Bill of Rights; legislative material such as the U.S. Code and the Code of Federal Regulations; judicial information about the United States Supreme Court, Courts of Appeals, and the District Courts; and Executive Orders of the President and Attorney General Opinions. Searchable full-text United States Supreme Court decisions are provided by the Legal Information Institute at the Cornell Law School (http://supct.law.cornell.edu/supct/). The United States Supreme Court has an informative site at http://supremecourtus.gov. Government Agency Links (http://www.fjc.gov/WWWlinks/govlinks.html) provides access to all the federal courts of appeals.

A Final Note

A legal researcher may be confident of the fruits of his or her labors when a systematic use of research tools continues to reveal references that have previously been identified. Depending on the particular problem or issue being examined, it may not be necessary or practical to employ all of the available research procedures that have been discussed.

The Constitution of the United States of America— Edited

PREAMBLE

We the People of the United States, in Order to form a more perfect Union, establish Justice, insure domestic Tranquility, provide for the common defence, promote the general Welfare, and secure the Blessings of Liberty to ourselves and our Posterity, do ordain and establish this Constitution for the United States of America.

ARTICLE I

Section 1. All legislative Powers herein granted shall be vested in a Congress of the United States, which shall consist of a Senate and House of Representatives.

* * *

Section 8. The Congress shall have Power To lay and collect Taxes, Duties, Imposts and Excises, to pay the Debts and provide for the common Defence and general Welfare of the United States; * * *

To constitute Tribunals inferior to the supreme Court; * * *

* * *

Section 10. No State shall * * * pass any * * * Law impairing the Obligation of Contracts, * * *

* * *

ARTICLE II

Section 1. The executive Power shall be vested in a President of the United States of America. * * *

* * *

ARTICLE III

Section 1. The judicial Power of the United States, shall be vested in one supreme Court, and in such inferior Courts as the Congress may from time to time ordain and establish. The Judges, both of the supreme and inferior Courts, shall hold their Offices during good Behavior, and shall, at stated Times, receive for their Services a Compensation, which shall not be diminished during their Continuance in Office.

Section 2. The judicial Power shall extend to all Cases, in Law and Equity, arising under this Constitution, the Laws of the United States. * * *

In all Cases affecting Ambassadors, other public Ministers and Consuls, and those in which a State shall be a Party, the supreme Court shall have original Jurisdiction. In all the other Cases before mentioned, the supreme Court shall have appellate Jurisdiction, both as to Law and Fact, with such Exceptions, and under such Regulations as the Congress shall make.

* * *

ARTICLE IV

Section 1. Full Faith and Credit shall be given in each State to the public Acts, Records, and judicial Proceedings of every other State. And the Congress may by general Laws prescribe the Manner in which such Acts, Records and Proceedings shall be proved, and the Effect thereof.

Section 2. The Citizens of each State shall be entitled to all Privileges and Immunities of Citizens in the several States. * * *

* * *

ARTICLE V

The Congress, whenever two-thirds of both Houses shall deem it necessary, shall propose Amendments to this Constitution, or, on the Application of the Legislatures of two-thirds of the several States, shall call a Convention for proposing Amendments, which, in either Case, shall be valid to all Intents and Purposes, as part of this Constitution, when ratified by the Legislatures of three-fourths of the several States, or by Conventions in three-fourths thereof, as the one or the other Mode of Ratification may be proposed by Congress; Provided that no Amendment which may be made prior to the Year One thousand eight hundred and eight shall in any Manner affect the first and fourth Clauses in the Ninth Section of the first Article; and that no State, without its Consent, shall be deprived of its equal Suffrage in the Senate.

ARTICLE VI

* * *

This Constitution, and the Laws of the United States which shall be made in Pursuance thereof; and all Treaties made, or which shall be made, under the Authority of the United States, shall be the supreme Law of the Land; and the Judges in every State shall be bound thereby, any Thing in the Constitution or Laws of any State to the Contrary notwithstanding.

The Senators and Representatives before mentioned, and the Members of the several State Legislatures, and all executive and judicial Officers, both of the United States and of the several States, shall be bound by Oath or Affirmation, to support this Constitution, but no religious Test shall ever be required as a Qualification to any Office or public Trust under the United States.

* * *

AMENDMENT I [1791]

Congress shall make no law respecting an establishment of religion, or prohibiting the free exercise thereof; or abridging the freedom of speech, or of the press; or the right of the people peaceably to assemble, and to petition the Government for a redress of grievances.

* * *

AMENDMENT IV [1791]

The right of the people to be secure in their persons, houses, papers, and effects, against unreasonable searches and seizures, shall not be violated, and no Warrants shall issue, but upon probable cause, supported by Oath or affirmation, and particularly describing the place to be searched, and the persons or things to be seized.

AMENDMENT V [1791]

No person shall * * * be subject for the same offense to be twice put in jeopardy of life or limb; nor shall be compelled in any criminal case to be a witness against himself, nor be deprived of life, liberty, or property, without due process of law; nor shall private property be taken for public use without just compensation.

AMENDMENT VI [1791]

In all criminal prosecutions, the accused shall enjoy the right to a speedy and public trial, by an impartial jury of the State and district wherein the crime shall have been committed, which district shall have been previously ascertained by law, and to be informed of the nature and cause of the accusation: to be confronted with the witnesses against him; to have compulsory process for obtaining witnesses in his favor, and to have the Assistance of Counsel for his defence.

AMENDMENT VII [1791]

In Suits at common law, where the value in controversy shall exceed twenty dollars, the right of trial by jury shall be preserved, and no fact tried by a jury, shall be otherwise reexamined in any Court of the United States, than according to the rules of the common law.

AMENDMENT VIII [1791]

Excessive bail shall not be required, nor excessive fines imposed, nor cruel and unusual punishments inflicted.

AMENDMENT IX [1791]

The enumeration in the Constitution, of certain rights, shall not be construed to deny or disparage others retained by the people.

AMENDMENT X [1791]

The powers not delegated to the United States by the Constitution, nor prohibited by it to the States, are reserved to the States respectively, or to the people.

AMENDMENT XI [1798]

The Judicial power of the United States shall not be construed to extend to any suit in law or equity, commenced or prosecuted against one of the United States by Citizens of another State, or by Citizens or Subjects of any Foreign State.

* * *

AMENDMENT XIII [1865]

Section 1. Neither slavery nor involuntary servitude, except as a punishment for crime whereof the party shall have been duly convicted, shall exist within the United States, or any place subject to their jurisdiction.

Section 2. Congress shall have power to enforce this article by appropriate legislation.

AMENDMENT XIV [1868]

Section 1. All persons born or naturalized in the United States, and subject to the jurisdiction thereof, are citizens of the United States and of the State wherein they reside. No State shall make or enforce any law which shall abridge the privileges or immunities of citizens of the United States; nor shall any State deprive any person of life, liberty, or property, without due process of law; nor deny to any person within its jurisdiction the equal protection of the laws.

* * *

AMENDMENT XV [1870]

Section 1. The right of citizens of the United States to vote shall not be denied or abridged by the United States or by any State on account of race, color, or previous condition of servitude.

Section 2. The Congress shall have power to enforce this article by appropriate legislation.

AMENDMENT XVI [1913]

The Congress shall have power to lay and collect taxes on incomes, from whatever source derived, without apportionment among the several States, and without regard to any census or enumeration.

* * *

AMENDMENT XIX [1920]

Section 1. The right of citizens of the United States to vote shall not be denied or abridged by the United States or by any State on account of sex.

Section 2. Congress shall have power to enforce this article by appropriate legislation.

* * *

AMENDMENT XXIV [1964]

Section 1. The right of citizens of the United States to vote in any primary or other election for President or Vice President, for electors for President or Vice President, or for Senator or Representative in Congress, shall not be denied or abridged by the United States or any State by reason of failure to pay any poll tax or other tax.

Section 2. The Congress shall have power to enforce this article by appropriate legislation.

* * *

AMENDMENT XXVI [1971]

Section 1. The right of citizens of the United States, who are eighteen years of age or older, to vote shall not be denied or abridged by the United States or by any State on account of age.

Section 2. The Congress shall have power to enforce this article by appropriate legislation.

APPENDIX D

Statutory Material

TITLE VII OF THE CIVIL RIGHTS ACT OF 1964— P.L. 88-352

Discrimination Because of Race, Color, Religion, Sex, or National Origin

SEC. 703. (a) It shall be an unlawful employment practice for an employer—

(1) to fail or refuse to hire or to discharge any individual, or otherwise to discriminate against any individual with respect to his compensation, terms, conditions, or privileges of employment, because of such individual's race, color, religion, sex, or national origin; or

(2) to limit, segregate, or classify his employees in any way which would deprive or tend to deprive any individual of employment opportunities or otherwise adversely affect his status as an employee, because of such individual's race, color, religion, sex, or national origin.

* * *

(e) * * * (1) it shall not be an unlawful employment practice to hire and employ employees. * * * on the basis of his religion, sex, or national origin in those certain instances where religion, sex, or national origin is a bona fide occupational qualification reasonably necessary to the normal operation of that particular business or enterprise, and (2) it shall not be an unlawful employment practice for a school, college, university, or other educational institution or institution of learning to hire and employ em-

Statutory material appearing in this appendix is edited. Complete versions can be found in *United States Statutes at Large*. Students requiring the latest text of the law, as amended, are directed to the *United States Code*. Regulations pertaining to these statutes can be found in the *Code of Federal Regulations*.

ployees of a particular religion if such school, college, university, or other educational institution or institution of learning is, in whole or in substantial part, owned, supported, controlled, or managed by a particular religion or by a particular religious corporation, association, or society, or if the curriculum of such school, college, university, or other educational institution or institution of learning is directed toward the propagation of a particular religion.

* * *

(h) Notwithstanding any other provision of this time, it shall not be an unlawful employment practice for an employee to apply different standards of compensation, or different terms, conditions, or privileges of employment pursuant to a bona fide seniority or merit system, or a system which measures earnings by quantity or quality of production or to employees who work in different locations, provided that such differences are not the result of an intention to discriminate because of race, color, religion, sex, or national origin, nor shall it be an unlawful employment practice for an employer to give and to act upon the results of any professionally developed ability test provided that such test, its administration or action upon the results is not designed, intended or used to discriminate because of race, color, religion, sex or national origin.

(j) Nothing contained in this title shall be interpreted to require * * * preferential treatment to any individual or to any group because of the race, color, religion, sex, or national origin of such individual or group on account of an imbalance which may exist with respect to the total number or percentage of persons of any race, color, religion, sex, or national origin employed by any employer, referred or classified for employment * * * in comparison with the total number or percentage of persons of such race, color, religion, sex, or national origin in any community, State, section, or other area, or in the available work force in any community, State, section, or other area.

* * *

Prevention of Unlawful Employment Practices

SEC. 706.

* * *

(g) If the court finds that the respondent has intentionally engaged in or is intentionally engaging in an unlawful employment practice charged in the complaint, the court may enjoin the respondent from engaging in such unlawful employment practice, and order such affirmative action as may be appropriate, which may include reinstatement or hiring of employees, with or without back pay.

* * *

Effect on State Laws

SEC. 708. Nothing in this title shall be deemed to exempt or relieve any person from any liability, duty, penalty, or punishment provided by any present or future law of any State or political subdivision of a State, other than any such law which purports to require or permit the doing of any act which would be an unlawful employment practice under this title.

Notices to Be Posted

SEC. 711. (a) Every employer, * * * shall post and keep posted in conspicuous places upon its premises where notices to employees, applicants for employment, and members are customarily posted a notice to be prepared or approved by the Commission setting forth excerpts from or, summaries of, the pertinent provisions of this title and information pertinent to the filing of a complaint.

(b) A willful violation of this section shall be punishable by a fine of not more than $100 for each separate offense.

PREGNANCY DISCRIMINATION ACT OF 1978— P.L. 95-555

Be it enacted by the Senate and House of Representatives of the United States of America in Congress assembled, That section 701 of the Civil Rights Act of 1964 is amended by adding at the end thereof the following new subsection:

"(k) The Terms 'because of sex' or 'on the basis of sex' include, but are not limited to, because of or on the basis of pregnancy, childbirth, or related medical conditions; and women affected by pregnancy, childbirth, or related medical conditions shall be treated the same for all employment-related purposes, including the receipt of benefits under fringe benefit programs, as other persons not so affected but similar in their ability or inability to work, and nothing in section 703(h) of this title shall be interpreted to permit otherwise. This subsection shall not require an employer to pay for health insurance benefits for abortion, except where the life of the mother would be endangered if the fetus were carried to term, or except where medical complications have arisen from an abortion: *Provided,* That nothing herein shall preclude an employer from providing abortion benefits or otherwise affect bargaining agreements in regard to abortion."

* * *

AGE DISCRIMINATION IN EMPLOYMENT ACT OF 1967—P.L. 90-202

Statement of Findings and Purpose

SEC. 2. (a) The Congress hereby finds and declares that—

(1) in the face of rising productivity and affluence, older workers find themselves disadvantaged in their efforts to retain employment, and especially to regain employment when displaced from jobs;

(2) the setting of arbitrary age limits regardless of potential for job performance has become a common practice, and certain otherwise desirable practices may work to the disadvantage of older persons;

(3) the incidence of unemployment, especially long-term unemployment with resultant deterioration of skill, morale, and employer acceptability is, relative to the younger ages, high among older workers; their numbers are great and growing; and their employment problems grave;

* * *

(b) It is therefore the purpose of this Act to promote employment of older persons based on their ability rather than age; to prohibit arbitrary age discrimination in employment; to help employers and workers find ways of meeting problems arising from the impact of age on employment.

* * *

Prohibition of Age Discrimination

SEC. 4. (a) It shall be unlawful for an employer—

(1) to fail or refuse to hire or to discharge any individual or otherwise discriminate against any individual with respect to his compensation, terms, conditions, or privileges of employment, because of such individual's age;

(2) to limit, segregate, or classify his employees in any way which would deprive or tend to deprive any individual of employment opportunities or otherwise adversely affect his status as an employee, because of such individual's age; or

(3) to reduce the wage rate of any employee in order to comply with this Act.

* * *

(f) It shall not be unlawful for an employer, employment agency, or labor organization—

(1) to take any action otherwise prohibited * * * where age is a bona fide occupational qualification reasonably necessary to the normal operation of the particular business, or where the differentiation is based on reasonable factors other than age;

(2) to observe the terms of a bona fide seniority system or any bona fide employee benefit plan such as a retirement, pension, or insurance plan, which is not a subterfuge to evade the purposes of this Act, except that no such employee benefit plan shall excuse the failure to hire any individual; or

(3) to discharge or otherwise discipline an individual for good cause.

* * *

AGE DISCRIMINATION IN EMPLOYMENT ACT AMENDMENTS OF 1978—P.L. 95-256

Seniority Systems and Employee Benefit Plans

SEC. 2. (a) Section 4(f) (2) of the Age Discrimination in Employment Act of 1967 * * * is amended by inserting after "individual" a comma and the following: "and no such seniority system or employee benefit plan shall require or permit the involuntary retirement of any individual specified * * * because of the age of such individual."

* * *

SEC. 3. (a) Section 12 of the Age Discrimination in Employment Act of 1967 (29 U.S.C. 631) is amended to read as follows:

* * *

"SEC. 12. (a) The prohibitions in this Act shall be limited to individuals who are at least 40 years of age but less than 70 years of age.

* * *

"(d) Nothing in this Act shall be construed to prohibit compulsory retirement of any employee who has attained 65 years of age but not 70 years of age, and who is serving under a contract of unlimited tenure at an institution of higher education * * *."

* * *

AGE DISCRIMINATION IN EMPLOYMENT ACT AMENDMENTS OF 1986—P.L. 99-592

SEC. 6. Special Rule for Tenured Faculty

(a) SPECIAL RULE.—Section 12 of the Age Discrimination in Employment Act of 1967 (29 U.S.C. 631) is amended by adding at the end thereof the following new subsection:

"(d) Nothing in this Act shall be construed to prohibit compulsory retirement of any employee who has attained 70 years of age, and who is serving under a contract of unlimited tenure (or similar arrangement providing for unlimited tenure) at an institution of higher education (as defined by section 1201(a) of the Higher Education Act of 1965)."

(b) TERMINATION PROVISION.—The amendment made by subsection (a) of this section is repealed December 31, 1993.

* * *

TITLE IX OF THE EDUCATION AMENDMENTS OF 1972—P.L. 92-318

Sex Discrimination Prohibited

SEC. 901. (a) No person in the United States shall, on the basis of sex, be excluded from participation in, be denied the benefits of, or be subjected to discrimination under any education program or activity receiving Federal financial assistance, except that:

(1) in regard to admissions to educational institutions, this section shall apply only to institutions of vocational education, professional education, and graduate higher education, and to public institutions of undergraduate higher education;

* * *

(3) this section shall not apply to an educational institution which is controlled by a religious organization if the application of this subsection would not be consistent with the religious tenets of such organization;

(4) this section shall not apply to an educational institution whose primary purpose is the training of individuals for the military services of the United States, or the merchant marines; and

(5) in regard to admissions this section shall not apply to any public institution of undergraduate higher education which is an institution that traditionally and continually from its establishment has had a policy of admitting only students of one sex.

(b) Nothing contained in subsection (a) of this section shall be interpreted to require any educational institution to grant preferential or disparate treatment to the members of one sex on account of an imbalance which may exist with respect to the total number or percentage of persons of that sex participating in or receiving the benefits of any federally supported program or activity, in comparison with the total number or percentage of persons of that sex in any community, State, section, or other area: *Provided*, That this subsection shall not be construed to prevent the consideration in any hearing or proceeding under this title of statistical evidence tending to show that such an imbalance exists with respect to the participation in, or receipt of the benefits of, any such program or activity by the members of one sex.

(c) For purposes of this title an educational institution means any public or private preschool, elementary, or secondary school, or any institution of vocational, professional, or higher education, except that in the case of an educational institution composed of more than one school, college, or department which are administratively separate units, such term means each such school, college, or department.

* * *

SECTION 504 OF THE REHABILITATION ACT OF 1973—P.L. 93-112

Nondiscrimination under Federal Grants

SEC. 504. No otherwise qualified handicapped individual in the United States, as defined in section 7(6), shall, solely by reason of his handicap, be excluded from the participation in, be denied the benefits of, or be subjected to discrimination under any program or activity receiving Federal financial assistance.

FAMILY EDUCATIONAL RIGHTS AND PRIVACY ACT OF 1974—P.L. 93-380 [BUCKLEY AMENDMENT]

Protection of the Rights and Privacy of Parents and Students

SEC. 438. (a)(1) No funds shall be made available under any applicable program to any State or local educational agency, any institution of higher education, any community college, any school, agency offering a preschool program, or any other educational institution which has a policy of denying, or which effectively prevents, the parents of students attending any school of such agency, or attending such institution of higher education, community college, school, preschool, or other educational institution, the right to inspect and review any and all official records, files, and data directly related to their children, including all material that is incorporated into each student's cumulative record folder, and intended for school use or to be available to parties outside the school or school system, and specifically including, but not necessarily limited to, identifying data, academic work completed, level of achievement (grades, standardized achievement test scores), attendance data, scores on standardized intelligence, aptitude, and psychological tests, interest inventory results, health data, family background information, teacher or counselor ratings and observations, and verified reports of serious or recurrent behavior patterns. Where such records or data include information on more than one student, the parents of any student shall be entitled to receive, or be informed of, that part of such record or data as pertains to their child. Each recipient shall establish appropriate procedures for the granting of a request by parents for access to their child's school records within a reasonable period of time, but in no case more than forty-five days after the request has been made.

(2) Parents shall have an opportunity for a hearing to challenge the content of their child's school records, to insure that the records are not inaccurate, misleading, or otherwise in violation of the privacy or other rights of students, and to provide an opportunity for the correction or deletion of any such inaccurate, misleading, or otherwise inappropriate data contained therein.

(b)(1) No funds shall be made available under any applicable program to any State or local educational agency, any institution of higher education, any community college, any school, agency offering a preschool program, or any other educational institution which has a policy of permitting the release of personally identifiable records or files (or personal information contained therein) of students without the written consent of their parents to any individual, agency, or organization, other than to the following—

(A) other school officials, including teachers within the educational institution or local educational agency who have legitimate educational interests;

(B) officials of other schools or school systems in which the student intends to enroll, upon condition that the student's parents be notified of the transfer, receive a copy of the record if desired, and have an opportunity for a hearing to challenge the content of the record;

(C) authorized representatives of (i) the Comptroller General of the United States, (ii) the Secretary, (iii) an administrative head of an education agency (as defined in section 409 of this Act), or (iv) State educational authorities, under the conditions set forth in paragraph (3) of this subsection; and

(D) in connection with a student's application for, or receipt of, financial aid.

(2) No funds shall be made available under any applicable program to any State or local educational agency, any institution of higher education, any community college, any school, agency offering a preschool program, or any other educational institution which has a policy or practice of furnishing, in any form, any personally identifiable information contained in personal school records, to any persons other than those listed in subsection (b)(1) unless—

(A) there is written consent from the student's parents specifying records to be released, the reasons for such release, and to whom, and with a copy of the records to be released to the student's parents and the student if desired by the parents, or

(B) such information is furnished in compliance with judicial order, or pursuant to any lawfully issued subpoena, upon condition that parents and the students are notified of all such orders or subpoenas in advance of the compliance therewith by the educational institution or agency.

* * *

(4)(A) * * * all persons, agencies, or organizations desiring access to the records of a student shall be required to sign a written form which shall be kept permanently with the file of the student, but only for inspection by the parents or student, indicating specifically the legitimate educational or other interest that each person, agency, or organization has in seeking this information. Such form shall be available to parents and to the school official responsible for record maintenance as a means of auditing the operation of the system.

(B) * * * personal information shall only be transferred to a third party on the condition that such party will not permit any other party to have access to such information without the written consent of the parents of the student.

* * *

(d) For the purpose of this section, whenever a student has attained eighteen years of age, or is attending an institution of postsecondary education the permission or consent required of and the rights accorded to the parents of the student shall thereafter only be required of and accorded to the student.

(e) No funds shall be made available under any applicable program unless the recipient of such funds informs the parents of students, or the students, if they are eighteen years of age or older, or are attending an institution of postsecondary education, of the rights accorded them by this section.

* * *

Note: An Amendment (P.L. 93-568) defined "directory information" to include the following: student's name, address, telephone listing, date and place of birth, major field of study, participation in officially recognized activities and sports, weight and height of members of athletic teams, dates of attendance, degrees and awards of attendance, degrees and awards received, and the most recent previous educational agency or institution attended by the student.

EQUAL ACCESS ACT OF 1984—P.L. 98-377

Denial of Equal Access Prohibited

SEC. 802. (a) It shall be unlawful for any public secondary school which receives Federal financial assistance and which has a limited open forum to deny equal access or a fair opportunity to, or discriminate against, any students who wish to conduct a meeting within that limited open forum on the basis of the religious, political, philosophical, or other content of the speech at such meetings.

(b) A public secondary school has a limited open forum whenever such school grants an offering to or opportunity for one or more noncurriculum related students groups to meet on school premises during noninstructional time.

(c) Schools shall be deemed to offer a fair opportunity to students who wish to conduct a meeting within its limited open forum if such school uniformly provides that—

(1) the meeting is voluntary and student-initiated;

(2) there is no sponsorship of the meeting by the school, the government, or its agents or employees;

(3) employees or agents of the school or government are present at religious meetings only in a nonparticipatory capacity;

(4) the meeting does not materially and substantially interfere with the orderly conduct of educational activities within the school; and

(5) nonschool persons may not direct, conduct, control, or regularly attend activities of student groups.

(d) Nothing in this title shall be construed to authorize the United States or any State or political subdivision thereof—

(1) to influence the form or content of any prayer or other religious activity;

(2) to require any person to participate in prayer or other religious activity;

(3) to expend public funds beyond the incidental cost of providing the space for student-initiated meetings,

(4) to compel any school agent or employee to attend a school meeting if the content of the speech at the meeting is contrary to the beliefs of the agent or employee;

(5) to sanction meetings that are otherwise unlawful;

(6) to limit the rights of groups of students which are not of a specified numerical size; or

(7) to abridge the constitutional rights of any person.

(e) Notwithstanding the availability of any other remedy under the Constitution or the laws of the United States, nothing in this title shall be construed to authorize the United States to deny or withhold Federal financial assistance to any school.

(f) Nothing in this title shall be construed to limit the authority of the school, its agents or employees, to maintain order and discipline on school premises, to protect the well-being of students and faculty, and to assure that attendance of students at meetings is voluntary.

Definitions

SEC. 803. As used in this title—

(1) The term "secondary school" means a public school which provides secondary education as determined by State law.

(2) The term "sponsorship" includes the act of promoting, leading, or participating in a meeting. The assignment of a teacher, administrator, or other school employee to a meeting for custodial purposes does not constitute sponsorship of the meeting.

(3) The term "meeting" includes those activities of student groups which are permitted under a school's limited open forum and are not directly related to the school curriculum.

(4) The term "noninstructional time" means time set aside by the school before actual classroom instruction begins or after actual classroom instruction ends.

* * *

CIVIL RIGHTS—42 U.S.C. § 1981–1983*

§ 1981. Equal Rights under the Law

All persons within the jurisdiction of the United States shall have the right in every State and Territory to make and enforce contracts, to sue, be parties, give evidence, and to full and equal benefit of all laws and proceedings for the security of persons and property as is enjoyed by white citizens, and shall be subject to like punishment, pains, penalties, taxes, licenses, and exactions of every kind, and to no other.

§ 1982. Property Rights of Citizens

All citizens of the United States shall have the same right, in every State and Territory, as is enjoyed by white citizens thereof to inherit, purchase, lease, sell, hold, and convey real and personal property.

§ 1983. Civil Action for Deprivation of Rights

Every person who, under the color of any statute, ordinance, regulation, custom or usage, of any State or Territory or the District of Columbia, subjects, or causes to be subjected, any citizen of the United States or other

*Original versions of these statutes were enacted shortly after the Civil War.

person within the jurisdiction thereof to the deprivation of any rights, privileges, or immunities secured by the Constitution and laws, shall be liable to the party injured in an action at law, suit in equity, or other proper proceeding for redress. * * *

Glossary

Action A proceeding in a court of law, often referred to as a suit or lawsuit.

Ad litem A guardian ad litem is one appointed to prosecute or defend a suit on behalf of a party incapacitated by infancy or otherwise.

Advisory opinion An opinion rendered by a court when no actual case is before it. Although some state courts render advisory opinions, the United States Supreme Court and lower federal courts do not.

Affirm To approve or uphold a lower court's judgment.

A fortiori A term used in argumentation to indicate that if one fact exists, with even greater certainty a more probable included or related fact must also exist.

Amicus curiae A friend of the court. Generally, one who has an indirect interest in a case and offers or is requested to provide information to the court in order to clarify particular matters before the court.

Appeal An application to a higher court to amend a lower court's ruling.

Appellant One who takes an appeal to a higher court. The appellant may have been the plaintiff or defendant in the lower court proceeding.

Appellee The party in an action against whom an appeal has been sought. Sometimes also called the respondent.

Bill A formal written statement or complaint filed in a court.

Case law A body of law created by judicial decisions. By establishing precedents on which courts rely, the case law provides a primary source of legal authority.

Certiorari A judicial process whereby a case is removed from a lower court to a higher court for review. The record of the proceedings is transmitted to the higher court.

Civil action A court action brought to gain or to recover individual or civil rights or to obtain redress for an alleged noncriminal injustice.

Class action A court action brought by one or more individuals on behalf of themselves and all others who have a similar interest in a particular issue.

Code A systematic compilation of statutes, usually incorporating an indexing procedure to facilitate location of pertinent provisions.

Collateral attack An attempt to challenge the credibility or validity of a judicial proceeding based on related or incidental issues.

Common law A system of law in which authority is not derived expressly from statutes. Rather, traditional legal principles are derived from usage and custom as enunciated by court decisions.

Compensatory damages Damages awarded to reimburse the injured party only for the actual loss incurred. Punitive or exemplary damages are not considered compensatory.

Complaint A formal pleading to a court demanding relief as well as informing the defendant of the grounds of the suit.

Concurring opinion An opinion written by a judge expressing agreement with the majority's holding. However, the concurring judge may disagree with the majority's reasoning or discuss additional principles or points of law.

Conflict of laws An area of law dealing with the clarification of inconsistencies and differences in laws or jurisdictions as they apply to the rights of individuals in particular actions.

Consent decree An agreement by parties to a dispute, and although not properly a judicial sentence, it is in effect an admission by them that the decree is a just determination of their rights based upon the facts of the case.

Constitution The supreme fundamental law of a nation or state. Provisions are included to establish and organize the government and to distribute, limit, and prescribe the manner of the exercise of sovereign powers. In addition, basic principles and rights of the citizenry are enumerated.

Court of record A court whose actions are recorded, possessing the authority to levy sanctions.

Criminal action A court action, brought by the state, against one charged with an offense against the state. This type of action may result in a fine or incarceration of the defendant.

Damages The compensation or indemnity claimed by the plaintiff or allowed by the court for injuries sustained as a result of a wrongful act or negligence of another.

De facto In fact. A state of affairs that must be accepted for all practical purposes, but does not have the sanction of laws behind it. As distinguished from *de jure*.

De jure By right. A legitimate state of affairs that has the force of law behind it.

De minimis Trifling or insignificant matters, with which a court will not concern itself.

De novo A new, afresh, a second time. A second trial of a case that has been sent back from a higher court for a new trial.

Decision A conclusion or judgment of a court, as opposed to the reasoning or opinion of the court.

Declaratory judgment Without issuing an order for anything to be done, a court clarifies questions of law, recognizes the rights of the parties, or expresses an opinion.

Decree A court order issued in an equity suit.

Defendant The party against whom an action is brought.

Demurrer An allegation by a defendant admitting that although the facts are correct, a suit is not justified nor do they require an answer by the defendant.

Dictum (obiter dictum) An opinion expressed by a judge in a proceeding that is not necessary in formulating the court's decision. Therefore, it does not establish binding precedent. However, it may indicate the judge's persuasion.

Dismissal A final disposition of a suit by a court by sending it out of court without a trial of the issues.

Dissenting opinion An opinion written by a judge in disagreement with the rationale and/or decision of the majority of judges hearing the case.

Due process of law Implies that the powers of the government are exercised similarly in similar situations in order to protect individual's rights. Denial of this right is prohibited by the Fifth and Fourteenth Amendments when life, liberty, or property are involved.

En banc A proceeding in which all judges of a court participate in the decision.

Enjoin An individual or institution is required by a court of equity to cease or abstain from a particular action. See Injunction.

Equal protection of the law A guarantee that no person or class of persons shall be denied the same protection of the laws that is enjoyed by other persons or classes in similar circumstances. Denial of this right is prohibited by the Fourteenth Amendment.

Equity law A particular branch of law that differs from the common law. Primarily concerned with providing justice and fair treatment, equity law addresses issues the common law is unable to consider.

Et al. And others. Indicates that unnamed parties are involved in the proceedings.

Exclusionary rule A procedure in search-and-seizure cases seeking to suppress the use of evidence which has been improperly obtained.

Ex parte A proceeding for the benefit of one party only.

Ex post facto After the fact, often thought of in terms of a law making an act illegal after someone has committed the act.

Ex rel. Designates a private individual on whose behalf the state is acting in a legal proceeding.

Finding A conclusion of a court or jury regarding a question of fact.

Governmental immunity (See Sovereign immunity.)

Hearing Judicial examination of factual or legal issues.

In loco parentis In place of the parent. Possessing a portion of the parent's rights, duties, and responsibilities.

In re In the matter of. A method of entitling a judicial proceeding in which there are no adversaries.

Injunction An order issued by a court of equity prohibiting a person from committing a threatened act or continuing to do some act that is injurious to the plaintiff.

Inter alia Among other things.

Ipso facto By the fact itself. As a necessary consequence.

Judgment A decision rendered by a court.

Liability A legal responsibility.

Litigation The formal contesting of a dispute in a court, a lawsuit.

Majority opinion The statement expressing the views of the majority of judges in a court decision.

Malfeasance Commission of an unlawful act.

Mandamus A court order compelling a public official or institution to perform a particular nondiscretionary duty.

Mandate A judicial command, order, or direction.

Minority opinion A statement expressing the views of a judge or a minority of judges in a court decision. This may take the form of separate minority opinion.

Misfeasance Improper performance of a lawful act.

Negligence Failure to exercise ordinary prudence and foresight when such failure results in an injury to another.

Nolens volens Whether willing or unwilling.

Nonfeasance   Failure to perform a required duty.

Nuisance   Continuous private or public use of property that results in injury, inconvenience, or damage.

Original jurisdiction   The jurisdiction of a court to entertain a case at its inception, as contrasted with appellate jurisdiction.

Parens patriae   The state as a sovereign—referring to the sovereign power of guardianship over persons such as minors.

Per curiam   An opinion rendered by an entire court, as opposed to an opinion of any one of several justices.

Petition   A written application to a court for the redress of a wrong or the grant of a privilege or license.

Petitioner   One who presents a petition to a court.

Plaintiff   One who brings an action or files a complaint in a court.

Plea   A formal allegation filed by a defendant in an action in reply to the plaintiff's complaint or charges.

Pleadings   Formal documents filed in a court action. They include the plaintiff's complaint and the defendant's reply, indicating that which is alleged by one party and denied or conceded by the other party.

Plenary   Full, entire, complete.

Prayer   A request by the plaintiff that the court of equity grant a particular relief sought.

Precedent   Previously decided authoritative court decisions addressing identical or similar questions of law.

Prima facie   At first view, before investigation. A fact presumed to be true unless disproved by some evidence to the contrary.

Pro se   In person, in their own behalf.

Quasi   As if. Almost as it were, analogous to.

Quid pro quo   A consideration, giving one valuable thing for another.

Quo warranto   A suit brought to determine whether an officer has the right to exercise the duties of his or her office. An extraordinary proceeding intended to prevent exercise of unlawful power and to inquire "by what authority" one supports a claim to a position.

Relief   Legal redress or assistance sought in court by the complainant.

Remand   To send back. Following an appellate decision a case may be sent back to the court from which it came for further proceedings.

Remedy   A court's enforcement of a right or the prevention of the violation of a right.

Res ipsa loquitur   The thing speaks for itself.

Res judicata   A matter judicially decided.

Respondent   The party against whom an appeal is taken in a higher court.

Restrain   To enjoin or prohibit.

Sovereign immunity   A doctrine providing that a governmental body is immune to suit without the expressed permission of the body itself.

Standing   The right to raise an issue in a lawsuit.

Stare decisis   To stand by decided cases. The doctrine whereby precedent assumes the authority of established law.

Status quo   The existing state of affairs.

Statute   An act of the state or federal legislature, a law.

Sub nom.   A different case name in subsequent judicial history.

Sui generis   Of its own kind or class, unique.

Suit   A proceeding in a court of law brought by a plaintiff.

Summary judgment   A court's decision to settle a controversy or dispose of a case promptly without conducting full legal proceedings.

Tort   A private or civil wrong or injury.

Trial   The examination of a civil or criminal case by a competent tribunal. It may be made by a judge or judges, with or without a jury.

Ultra vires   Exceeding the power or authority.

Vacate   To cancel or rescind a court decision.

Void   Without force or binding effect. Absolutely null.

Waive   To forego, renounce, or abandon a legal right. By waiver, the right is lost.

Writ   A written court order requiring performance of a specific act, such as a writ of injunction or mandamus.

Index